D1603826

LOEB CLASSICAL LIBRARY
FOUNDED BY JAMES LOEB 1911

EDITED BY
JEFFREY HENDERSON

# MAXIMUS OF TYRE

## PHILOSOPHICAL ORATIONS

## I

LCL 553

# MAXIMUS OF TYRE

## PHILOSOPHICAL ORATIONS

VOLUME I

EDITED AND TRANSLATED BY

WILLIAM H. RACE

HARVARD UNIVERSITY PRESS
CAMBRIDGE, MASSACHUSETTS
LONDON, ENGLAND
2023

*First published 2023*



Library of Congress Control Number 2023002950
CIP data available from the Library of Congress

ISBN 978-0-674-99756-1

*Composed in ZephGreek and ZephText by
Technologies 'N Typography, Merrimac, Massachusetts.
Printed on acid-free paper and bound by
Maple Press, York, Pennsylvania*

# CONTENTS

CONTENTS

For Michael Trapp

# GENERAL INTRODUCTION

## THE AUTHOR

What exiguous information we have of Maximus comes from three sources.

1. The entry in the *Suda*:

   Μάξιμος Τύριος, φιλόσοφος· διέτριψε δὲ ἐν Ῥώμῃ ἐπὶ Κομμόδου. Περὶ Ὁμήρου καὶ τίς ἡ παρ' αὐτῷ ἀρχαία φιλοσοφία· Εἰ καλῶς Σωκράτης οὐκ ἀπελογήσατο· καὶ ἄλλα τινὰ φιλόσοφα ζητήματα.

   Maximus of Tyre, a philosopher. He spent time in Rome during the reign of Commodus (180–192 AD). [He wrote] "On Homer and what his ancient philosophy was"; "Whether Socrates was right not to defend himself"; and certain other philosophical inquiries.[1]

2. The heading of manuscript R:

   Μαξίμου Τυρίου Πλατωνικοῦ Φιλοσόφου τῶν ἐν Ῥώμῃ Διαλέξεων τῆς πρώτης Ἐπιδημίας.

[1] The two works cited correspond to *Orr*. 26 and 3.

> The Discourses of Maximus of Tyre the Platonic philosopher [delivered] in Rome during his first visit.[2]

3. Eusebius Chron. ad olymp. 232 (= 149–152 AD):

> Ἀρριανὸς φιλόσοφος Νικομηδεὺς ἐγνωρίζετο, Μάξιμος Τύριος, Ἀπολλώνιος Στωϊκὸς Χαλκηδόνιος, Βασιλείδης Σκυθοπολίτης. Οὗτοι καὶ διδάσκαλοι Οὐηρισίμου Καίσαρος γεγόνασιν.

> Arrian the philosopher from Nicomedia came into prominence, as did Maximus of Tyre, Apollonius the Stoic from Calcedon, and Basilides the Scythian. They were instructors of Verus Caesar (= Marcus Aurelius).[3]

There is nothing in the forty-one orations that contradicts the assumption that Maximus was active in the second half of the second century AD. Moreover, the other two authors originally included with Maximus' work in manuscript R, Alcinous and Albinus, were also active in the middle of the second century. The only "personal" asides in the *Orations* are the speaker's claim to have seen the Marsyas and Maeander rivers and the square stone worshipped by the Arabians (*Or.* 2.8), both of which would

[2] It is most likely that these discourses delivered in Rome refer to all forty-one orations. There is nothing known of any second visit, if there was one.

[3] This date is probably too early for Maximus to have gained recognition, if he was active in Rome during Commodus' reign.

not be unreasonable for someone from Tyre to visit,[4] but his claims to have actually seen Asclepius and Heracles (*Or.* 9.7) are hardly credible.

## THE ORATIONS

Maximus' only surviving work consists of forty-one short orations on a variety of topics of ethical, philosophical, and theological import. The *Suda* calls these works "philosophical inquiries" (φιλόσοφα ζητήματα), whereas manuscript R labels them "discourses" (διαλέξεις) in the main heading and "philosophical works" (φιλοσοφούμενα) as a subtitle and at the end of the manuscript. Maximus, however, never calls his orations διαλέξεις or φιλοσοφούμενα, but refers to individual ones as an "inquiry "or "investigation" (σκέμμα, σκέψις, ἐξέτασις, or ζητούμενον) (*Orr.* 3.2, 11.1, 31.3, 32.5), or more generally as "philosophical discourse" (φιλόσοφος λόγος, *Orr.* 1.2–3 and 25.6). Indeed, they could be called orations, discourses, speeches, lectures, talks, inquiries, essays, or even sermons. These differing titles indicate the hybrid nature of these short works and the difficulty of determining their precise genre.

The longest oration is *Or.* 1 (word count 2,629), and the shortest is *Or.* 28 (870). *Orr.* 11 (2,502) and 18 (2,248) are closest to *Or.* 1, whereas the bulk are around 1,500 to 2,000 words, which Trapp (1997b, 1954) estimates would last in recitation "on average something around fifteen

[4] A starting point such as Tyre could suit the hypothetical journeys to Babylon and Eleusis in *Or.* 39.3.

to twenty minutes each." While it may be extreme to argue that they merely give the appearance of orally delivered lectures, it cannot be ascertained on what occasions they would have been delivered, either individually or in groups, perhaps ones on the same or similar subjects.[5]

As far as the *Orations* are concerned, Greek history ended with the breakup of the Macedonian empire after the death of Alexander in 323 BC, the latest historical event mentioned (*Or*. 28.1). The most recent philosopher cited is Clitomachus of Carthage (d. 110/9 BC), head of the Middle Academy (*Or*. 4.3), and the latest poet quoted is Aratus, who died ca. 240 BC (*Or*. 24.2). There is not a single indication of anyone or anything Roman.[6] The *Orations* thus draw on a canon of Greek poets from Homer to Aratus, and on Classical and Hellenistic philosophers and historians, and are wholly detached from two centuries of Roman rule.

## THE ORDER OF THE ORATIONS

There are three separate orderings of the orations in the manuscripts, and this causes considerable confusion when they are cited in scholarship. The early editions of Stephanus (1557), Heinsius (1607), and Davies$^1$ (1703) followed the order in codex Laurentius Conventi Soppressi 4 (manuscript I). The editions of Davies$^2$ (1740) and Dübner (1840) followed one of the orders in manuscript R desig-

[5] For example, *Or*. 11.1 on Plato's conception of god appears to refer back to the discussion of *daimones* in *Orr*. 8 and 9.

[6] Even the words Italy and Italian refer only to Magna Graecia at *Orr*. 8.2, 20.9, and 27.5.

nated by lower-case letters. Hobein (1910) established the third order by following an alternate numbering in manuscript R designated by upper-case letters. This order has been adopted by all subsequent editors and translators.[7] Because references to the speeches can follow different orders (this is especially true of earlier scholarship and the lexicons of LSJ and Montanari, which follow the order of Davies$^2$), I have provided a concordance of the three orderings at the end of this General Introduction.

## FORMAL STRUCTURES WITHIN THE CORPUS

Whichever of the three orders of speeches is chosen, the corpus exhibits a secondary ordering of certain speeches. In one group, opposing arguments are presented in two successive orations, where the second proves the winner: *Orr.* 15 and 16 treat the superiority of the active or contemplative life, *Orr.* 23 and 24 debate the relative benefits of soldiers and farmers, and *Orr.* 39 and 40 debate whether one good is greater than another. In another grouping, successive speeches on the same topic progress toward a conclusion. Both of these sequences deal with aspects of Socrates' career: *Orr.* 8 and 9 treat the nature of Socrates' *daimonion* and place it in the wider context of

[7] Koniaris (1982, 88–102) lays out the grounds for the revised order in great detail. *Orr.* 1–6 in manuscript R (designated by lower-case letters) become *Orr.* 30–35, while *Or.* 7, long recognized as introductory, becomes *Or.* 1. Manuscript I, however, placed *Or.* 11 ("What god is according to Plato") first, perhaps because its theological content was deemed especially important.

*daimones* in general, while *Orr.* 18 to 21 explore the nature of Socrates' erotic art, culminating in the vision of Beauty as depicted in the *Phaedrus* and *Symposium*. Finally, there is a series of five orations, beginning with *Or.* 29 and ending with *Or.* 33, both bearing the title "What the ultimate end of philosophy is." Between them *Orr.* 30, 31, and 32 consider the value of pleasure and whether it is stable, ending with a spirited refutation of Epicurus' hedonistic philosophy.

## MAXIMUS' PERSONA

Maximus' persona is quite consistent throughout the *Orations*. He presents himself as a well-educated (πεπαιδευμένος), earnest spokesman for the philosophical life of virtue, especially as exemplified in the career of Socrates and in the writings of Plato. Drawing on examples from the Hellenic cultural tradition, he invites his audience, sometimes addressed as young men, to share in his knowledge, to appreciate his fresh presentation of philosophical topics, and perhaps even to join him in pursuing philosophy. He offers a sort of cultural compendium of the famous historical figures, events, ideas, successes, and failures, from Homer to the death of Alexander the Great, that constituted Greek *paideia* in the so-called Second Sophistic. The *Orations* are relentlessly backward-looking, indeed so much so that they inhabit a long-past realm with virtually no acknowledgment of contemporary events or people.[8]

[8] "(Still) today" in the *Orations* refers only vaguely to the contemporary state of affairs.

Maximus' mode of presentation is oratorical: it is meant to engage, impress, and educate his listeners. His project is articulated in *Or.* 1, essentially an advertisement for his brand of philosophical oratory.[9] It lays out the need for the orator/philosopher to adapt his discourse to all sorts of audiences, to speak in many voices and adopt many guises, in order to inspire and instruct his young listeners. He is proud of his oratorical skills, as displayed in his discourses, which will serve ambitious young men in their chosen careers.

> Here in your presence, young men, stands this resource for speaking: it is copious, multifaceted, and very productive; it suits all listeners, all temperaments, all pursuits of oratory, and all forms of instruction; it is lavish, free of charge, readily available, unstinting, and open to all who are able to receive it. If anyone is in love with rhetoric, here at hand for him is a copious flow of speech, sufficient for many needs, abundant, lofty, impressive, continuous, strong, and unfailing. And if anyone is in love with poetry, only let him obtain his meter elsewhere, but come here to acquire the rest of poetry's materials: magnificence, clarity, brilliance, creativity, inspiration, composition, theatricality, lavish diction, and impeccable harmony. Or have you come in need of the art of politics and resources for addressing the people and the council chamber? You have found what you seek: here before your eyes are

[9] See Lauwers (2009) for a study of Maximus' pedagogical self-promotion in *Or.* 1.

> the people, the council chamber, the speaker, the persuasion, and the power. (*Or.* 1.7)

And yet philosophy, to which he aspires, requires a discourse that eschews sophistry as it instructs and guides the souls of the young.

> Now anyone who thinks that philosophy consists merely of nouns and verbs, techniques of speaking, refutations, disputations, sophisms, and the waste of time spent on these, has no difficulty finding an instructor. The world around all of you is full of such sophists; their instruction is readily available and is quickly found . . . But the main part of philosophy and the road leading to it require a teacher who uplifts the souls of the young, guides their ambitions, and aims at nothing other than moderating their desires by means of pains and pleasures. (*Or.* 1.8)

In *Or.* 26.1, Maximus defines philosophy as "an accurate knowledge of divine and human matters, the source of virtue and noble powers of reason and a harmonious life and refined pursuits." Elsewhere he defines the "true orator" as one who combines philosophy and rhetoric in his chosen pursuit:

> What we need is discourse that stands up straight and tall and shouts out loud and clear, that raises our souls with it up above the earth and beyond all the earthly suffering that ensues from pleasure, desire, ambition, lust, anger, grief, and drunkenness. All these the true orator who allies himself with philosophical discourse must rise above. He must

> not be some lazy, feeble, meretricious practitioner of his art, whose only job is to provide indiscriminate aid in a courtroom. No, he must prove himself everywhere and on every occasion to be a judicious adviser in assemblies, a just contender in law courts, a decorous performer at panegyric festivals, and a knowledgeable teacher in the classroom. (*Or.* 25.6)

He accordingly presents himself as an amiable instructor committed to the ethical and psychological wellbeing of his audience. He does not indulge in subtle or rigorously logical arguments, or require them to master specialized philosophical terminology ("For just as I agree with Plato in other matters, I do so as well in his free use of terms," *Or.* 21.4), but tries to persuade them with exhortations, stories, arguments by analogy, and literary and historical examples, drawn from the Hellenic tradition from Homer to Alexander and applied to the topic under consideration. He often addresses his audience with first-person plural imperatives, such as "let us set aside" (*Or.* 8.6), "let us inquire" (*Or.* 24.6), and "let us examine" (*Or.* 40.3), but he rarely refers to them in the plural. The major exception is *Or.* 1, where he addresses them three times as a group (ὑμεῖς, *Or.* 1.6; ὑμῶν, *Or.* 1.7; and ὑμῖν, *Or.* 1.8), and once specifically as "young men" (ὦ νέοι, *Or.* 1.7).[10] Otherwise, he consistently addresses (unidentified) single members of the audience or imagined interlocutors, who offer objections that are easily countered, sometimes

[10] The only other examples of plural addresses are in *Orr.* 7.6 (ὑμῖν), 13.6 (φύλαττε), and 21.7 (ὑμῖν), in all of which he immediately switches to singular addresses.

with a polite dismissal of "my friend" (e.g., ὦ τάν at *Orr.* 8.4, 25.4, and 30.2).

## MAXIMUS WITHIN THE SECOND SOPHISTIC

Maximus' orations are products of the so-called Second Sophistic of the second century AD, when Greek orators enjoyed great prestige among the Greek and Roman elite. Many came from the eastern part of the empire, including Dio Chrysostom from Prusa, Aelius Aristides from Mysia, Lucian from Samosata (Syria), and Maximus from Tyre. This kind of public oratory played an important role in reaffirming Greek cultural identity in the midst of the Roman Empire, through its blend of Greek philosophy, rhetoric, history, literature, ethics, and politics. Maximus resembles other second-century "sophists" in his publicly accessible oratory, elegant style, lively presentation, treatment of philosophical, ethical, and religious themes, and in his general display of *paideia*, but is unique in his complete disregard of Roman culture and institutions.[11] Furthermore, because of his reluctance to propose any philosophical innovations, his indifference to contemporary affairs, and his refusal to provide any autobiographical information, he has proved to be of limited interest to historians of philosophy and to scholars of the Second Sophistic.[12]

[11] The narrow scope of the *Orations* is especially clear when compared with the range of Plutarch's works.

[12] For example, he is not even mentioned in Philostratus' *Lives of the Sophists*. Important exceptions are the studies of Trapp (1997a and 2007a) and Lauwers (2015).

## MAXIMUS' RELATIONSHIP TO PLATO

Maximus' philosophical orientation is broadly and quite consistently Platonic.[13] As with Middle Platonism in general,[14] his Platonism overlaps—or even harmonizes—with many specific Peripatetic and Stoic tenets, but there is no systematic syncretism on his part or any attempt to reconcile schools. Stoic doctrines are occasionally entertained,[15] but a Stoic hard-line tenet such as the indivisibility of the Good, argued in *Or*. 39, is refuted in *Or*. 40. Apart from Socrates, who is mentioned more often than any other individual, only two other philosophers are treated in some detail: Epicurus, whom Maximus consistently condemns (*Orr*. 4.9, 30.3, and 33.3), and Diogenes the Cynic, whom he wholeheartedly praises (*Orr*. 15.9, 32.9, and 36.5–6).

He makes no claim to proposing new doctrines, but positions himself as an interpreter and expounder of the Greek intellectual and cultural tradition, principally through the lens of Plato's writings. He brings to life this tradition by means of an engaging discourse full of some-

[13] He names Plato thirty-nine times and relies on main Platonic tenets and images such as the immortality of the soul, *anamnēsis*, a transcendent divinity, *daimones* as intermediate between divinity and humanity, the body as a prison for the soul, the soul's ascent to the realm of truth, and the soul as a charioteer of impulsive horses.

[14] Dillon (1996) remains a foundational study of Middle Platonism and its many philosophical strands.

[15] A few examples include "fate" (εἱμαρμένη) at *Orr*. 5.5 and 13.8, "joy" (χαρά) at *Or*. 32.7, and "smooth flow of life" (εὔροια βίου) at *Or*. 34.2, as well as the categories of indifferent (ἀδιάφορον) or preferred (προηγμένον) goods at *Or*. 40.6.

times novel arguments, analogies, stories, anecdotes, and images. Therein lies his originality. A charitable assessment is that of Trapp (1997b, 1953): "Maximus sets himself midway between the great philosophers and his own contemporary audience, presenting himself as one dedicated to making their thought available afresh to a new generation of enquirers." Less charitable is that of Dillon (1996, 399): "He is primarily concerned with the artistic embellishment of platitudes."[16]

In contrast to other second-century expositions of Platonic philosophy that present bare accounts of Platonic doctrines, such as Albinus' *Eisagōgē* and Alcinous' *Didascalicus* (the latter included in the same manuscript R), Maximus' *Orations* refashion Plato's works. His audience is expected to know Plato's entire oeuvre well and to appreciate the ways in which he alludes to, yet recasts, well-known Platonic passages.[17] Although his adaptations of Platonic images, examples, and doctrines are evident throughout the corpus, verbatim quotations are surprisingly rare.[18]

He views his role as an assayer of Plato's doctrinal gold

[16] Lauwers (2015) presents a very favorable view of Maximus' cultural importance. For Maximus and Apuleius as popularizers of Platonic philosophy, see Trapp (2007b).

[17] For the scores of oblique references to Platonic texts throughout the orations, see the study of Puiggali (1983) and the extensive notes of Trapp (1997a), López Cruces and Daroca (2005), and Brumana (2019). Noticeably absent in the *Orations* is any mention of Platonic Forms.

[18] Apart from one several-line quotation from *Leg.* 4.709b–c at *Or.* 13.7, exact quotations are few: "great Zeus in heaven" (*Phdr.* 246e) at *Or.* 26.7; "divinely inspired," of Phaedrus (*Phdr.* 234d) at *Or.* 18.4; "lovely Sappho" and "wise Anacreon" (*Phdr.*

for the purpose of making it useful for his audience. "In fact, I would compare one's first acquaintance with Plato's writings to mining for gold ore. What comes next requires a different expertise, one that uses reason, rather than fire, to examine and purify what has been extracted, and only then can the refined and assayed gold be put to use" (*Or.* 11.2).

On a broader scale, Maximus shares Plato's disparagement of the masses, his distrust of democracy, his suspicious view of drama, and his condemnation of Athens for prosecuting and executing Socrates. He also shares Plato's (and Xenophon's) idealization of Sparta as a stable, well-ordered state, which he lauds for its rigorous training and military heroism. Where he openly differs from Plato is in his high regard for Homer, whom he defends against Plato's criticisms and treats with great respect.

## TOPICS IN THE ORATIONS

Maximus addresses a range of philosophical topics, current in Middle Platonism,[19] that are mainly ethical, theological, and psychological. These include (among many others) the nature of divinity and *daimones*; the immortality of the soul; virtue, knowledge, love, the Good, friendship, justice, prayer and worship; free will and prophecy; freedom from distress; the sources of good and evil; the

235c) at *Or.* 18.7; "Greetings, Ion" (*Ion* 530a) at *Or.* 18.9; "for I am not a poet" (*Resp.* 3.393d) at *Or.* 35.1; "for Envy stands outside the divine chorus" (*Phdr.* 247a) at *Or.* 41.3: and "the responsibility is the chooser's; god is blameless" (*Resp.* 10.617e) at *Or.* 41.5.

19 Cf. Dillon (1996, 399–400).

injustice of vengeance; the active and contemplative life; the tyranny of pleasures and desires; the pursuit of happiness; the contribution of the liberal arts; and divine dispensation. All these are proposed and discussed with easily accessible arguments, and illustrated with analogies, anecdotes, and concrete examples.

## FEATURES OF MAXIMUS' COMPOSITION

Maximus is primarily an Atticist, but he exhibits rhetorical features associated with Asianism:

> In their Atticizing vocabulary and syntax and in their Asianist rhythms [the *Dialexeis*] follow well-worn trends in Greek literature of the Imperial period . . . In their lively informality of tone, syntax and structure, and in their lavish use of the decorative resources of imagery and quotation, they are perfect examples of λόγος ἀφελής—that register of cultivated diction proper to such forms as letters, novels, dialogues and informal addresses, which found its main stylistic exemplars in such figures as Plato, Xenophon and Dio, and which stood in contrast to the Demosthenic splendors of λόγος πολιτικός. (Trapp 1997b, 1970)

The *Orations* often open indirectly with quotations, anecdotes, fables, and historical situations that lead to the topic under discussion.[20] More demanding logical arguments are conducted in the middle (e.g., the properties of *daimones* and of physical elements, *Or*. 9.2–4), while they often conclude with named individuals or historical examples.

They are replete with images and analogies (εἰκόνες), often catchy ("a gift of fortune . . . much like the friendly embraces of drunkards," *Or.* 5.1), often expansive (e.g., the prison of human existence, *Or.* 36.4; the invention of medicine, *Or.* 4.2–3), and occasionally mere substitutes for more careful analytical arguments. Allegorical readings (αἰνίγματα) abound, especially when arguing for Homer's philosophical sophistication. Fulsome, sometimes repetitive lists are frequent, when just one or two examples would have sufficed.

Maximus employs a lively style of engagement with exclamations (μὰ Δία), rhetorical questions (τί ἄλλο ἤ, τί δήποτε), expressions of self-doubt ("I sense that my ability is lacking," *Or.* 18.6), and feigned spontaneity ("Now, since our argument has somehow seized upon a nautical analogy," *Or.* 30.3).[21] Rhetorical set-pieces abound. Some prominent examples are:

*Or.* 2.3: praise of the human form
*Or.* 3.3: Socrates' fictitious defense before the Athenian jury
*Or.* 11.9–11: the journey of the intellect to comprehend god

---

[20] Quotations open *Orr.* 7.1, 12.1, 21.1, and 30.1. Anecdotes open *Orr.* 17.1 (Mithaecus), 25.1 (Anacharsis), and 41.1 (Alexander the Great); fables open *Orr.* 32.1 (the doe, lion, shepherd, and fox) and 36.1 (the creation of humans); *Or.* 5.1 opens with the myth of Midas, and *Or.* 14.1 opens with Prodicus' myth of Heracles.

[21] Also: "I see now that the train of my argument has led me to a clearer illustration" (*Or.* 7.6); "But wait—for I am now truly coming to realize what sort of experience this kind of discourse would resemble" (*Or.* 11.2); "I sense that I am drawing a subtle distinction in this matter and need to offer an illustration" (*Or.*

*Or*. 14.6: the characteristics that distinguish a friend from a flatterer
*Or*. 15.1: humans' dissatisfaction with their various lives
*Or*. 16.2–3: the "apology" of Anaxagoras
*Or*. 16.6: the flight of the philosophical soul
*Or*. 19.4: the differences between a virtuous and a vicious lover
*Or*. 20.2: true love overcomes all obstacles
*Or*. 21.7–8: the descent of Beauty into the physical world
*Or*. 22.5: the transport of the soul through reading history
*Or*. 29.1–4: a catalog of men's misguided pursuits of the Good
*Or*. 30.3: the Epicurean pleasure barge
*Or*. 36.2: the history of human audacity
*Or*. 36.4: the life of imprisonment to pleasure
*Or*. 41.2: the doxology of Zeus' creation and maintenance of the universe
*Or*. 41.3: the ills of human life

## MAJOR FIGURES TREATED

### *Homer*

Throughout the orations, Maximus seeks to demonstrate the cultural continuity from Homer to Plato, as summed

21.5); "And yet, what do I mean by this?" (*Or*. 24.3); "So why is it that Chiron has entered our discussion?" (*Or*. 28.2); and "But just as I was saying this, I recalled" (*Or*. 28.4). Dürr (1899, 146–50) provides an exhaustive list of Maximus' rhetorical tropes.

up in the phrase at *Or.* 41.2: "I believe Homer and I trust Plato." He attempts to reconcile Homer's work with Plato's by regarding Homer as a philosopher *avant la lettre*, who cloaks his *sophia* in narratives that must be interpreted allegorically. In *Or.* 26 ("Whether there is a Homeric school of philosophy"), he argues that Homer was the original philosopher and claims that Plato is one of his offspring: "I would boldly assert that Plato bears a greater similarity to Homer than he does to Socrates" (*Or.* 26.3). He then concludes:

> I wish you to consider Homer's work . . . as having two aspects: in terms of poetry, being cast in the form of a story; in terms of philosophy, being composed toward an emulation of virtue and knowledge of truth. (*Or.* 26.5)[22]

Homer is quoted and discussed constantly and is often "saved" by allegorical interpretations. Either by reference or by direct quotation, Homer is present in twenty-eight of the forty-one orations and is the main subject of two (*Orr.* 17 and 26). Homeric quotations often serve as proof texts and springboards to discussions.

### *Socrates*

A major focus is on the figure of Socrates, who serves as a model of the philosophical life. He is named 119 times in the Greek text, two more times even than Homer. His depiction is based mainly on Plato's dialogues but also draws on Xenophon's *Apology*, *Symposium*, and *Memora-*

[22] He addresses the thorny problem of Plato's banishment of Homer from his ideal republic in *Or.* 17.3.

*bilia*. Seven orations are devoted to three controversial aspects of his life: (1) Did Socrates actually defend himself before the Athenians, or did he remain silent (*Or*. 3);[23] (2) what was the nature of his *daimonion* (*Orr*. 8 and 9); and (3) what was the nature of his erotic art and his love of boys and young men (*Orr*. 18–21).

### *Epicurus*

Epicurus regularly comes in for scorn with the conventional condemnation of hedonism, often through the examples of Sardanapallus and Persian kings. His tenet that the gods do not bother themselves in worldly affairs is completely incompatible with Plato's conception of divinity (*Or*. 4.9). Especially entertaining is the elaborate comparison of Epicurus' philosophy to a great pleasure barge that enjoys all the pleasures in calm seas but is completely unequipped to weather a storm (*Or*. 30.3). Hedonism is accorded its defense of pleasure in *Or*. 32 but is then refuted in *Or*. 33.

### *Diogenes*

In stark contrast to Epicurus, Diogenes the Cynic is consistently praised. *Or*. 36 is entirely devoted to praise of Diogenes' life of freedom from involvement in human affairs. Paradoxically, he is also praised even by the Epicurean spokesman in *Or*. 32.9, who argues that Diogenes was actually motivated by pleasure to lead his austere life free of anxiety.

23 Here Maximus argues a thesis, found nowhere else, that Socrates refused to say anything at his trial.

### *Historical Individuals*

Maximus draws heavily on conventional historical figures found in Herodotus, Thucydides, and Xenophon. Favorable examples from the earlier period include Cyrus the Great, Harmodius and Aristogeiton, Themistocles, and Leonidas; negative are Croesus, Polycrates, Pisistratus, Darius I, Cambyses, Xerxes, and Mardonius. The only entirely favorable Athenian examples are Pericles and Aristides; negative ones include Alcibiades, Cleon, Critias, and Socrates' accusers. Later positive examples include Agesilaus and Epaminondas; negative ones include Artoxerxes II, Dionysius II of Syracuse, Darius III, Philip II of Macedon, and even Alexander the Great. The semilegendary Sardanapallus is frequently cited as an extreme example of hedonism.

## AUTHORS QUOTED

Homer is far and away the most often quoted:[24] 221 lines or partial lines are taken from the *Iliad* and the *Odyssey*, consisting of 128 separate quotations and 15 repeated ones. In the notes I have indicated the Homeric context to show how each is being repurposed.[25] Of prose authors,

[24] Analysis in Kindstrand (1973).

[25] When quotations from Homer are cited more than once, they are regularly invoked to make different points. For example, the episode of Glaucus and Diomedes' exchange of arms is used for different purposes at *Orr.* 32.5, 35.3, and 39.1; the Homeric epithet δῖος (godlike) is used to introduce the topic of friendship at *Or.* 35.1, and divine dispensation at *Or.* 38.1; and Demodocus' claim to be self-taught supports the Platonic doctrine of recollection at *Or.* 10.5, and divine dispensation at *Or.* 38.1.

Plato is quoted 11 times, followed by Herodotus and Thucydides (each quoted twice from their first books), and Heraclitus. Poets quoted besides Homer are Pindar, Sappho, Anacreon, Stesichorus, Ariphron, and Aratus (the latter two not named).

Attic drama plays a small role. There is not a single reference to or quotation from Sophocles. There are two brief quotations from Aeschylus' (lost) *Philoctetes* (*Or.* 7.5), one adaptation of Euripides' *Phoenissae* (*Or.* 13.5), and one quotation from Euripides' *Hippolytus* (*Or.* 40.6), none attributed to its author.[26] Of comic playwrights, Eupolis is named but not quoted, while Aristophanes is frequently named as a critic of Socrates, but the only quotation comes from *Frogs* (*Or.* 25.3). Epicharmus is quoted, but not named, at *Or.* 11.10. Menander is named, but the text of the quotation is corrupt, and its provenance is unknown (*Or.* 5.7).

## TERMS FOR COGNITION

Maximus is quite consistent in his use of terms denoting cognitive activity. I have translated them in the following ways.

| | |
|---|---|
| *νοῦς* | intellect, mind; intelligible (*νοητός*); intellective (*ἔννους*) |
| *φρόνησις* | (practical) intelligence |
| *λόγος* | reason, reasoned argument; rational (*λογικός*) |

[26] There is also one oblique reference to [Aesch.] *PV* 250, at *Or.* 1.5.

| | |
|---|---|
| λογισμός | reasoning, use of reason; powers of reason (plural) |
| σύνεσις | comprehension |
| ἐπιστήμη | knowledge |
| γνώμη | (sound) judgment, intelligence, good sense, opinion |
| γνῶσις | knowledge (as opposed to ignorance, ἄγνοια) |
| αἴσθησις | perception, sensation |
| ἐμπειρία | experience |

## HISTORY OF THE TEXT

### *Manuscripts*

The principal manuscripts providing the basis of modern editions are:

R Parisinus graecus (Regius) 1962 (ca. 875)
U Vaticanus graecus 1390 (ca. 1250)
I Laurentianus conv. sopp. 4 (ca. 1350)[27]

Koniaris and Trapp have demonstrated that R is the archetype of all subsequent manuscripts, which number thirty-four. This manuscript originally contained the works of three authors, two of which are extant: Alcinous' *Didascalicus* ("Handbook of Platonism")[28] and Maximus' *Philosophical Orations*. The two works of Albinus listed in the table of contents (*pinax*) in manuscript R, "Outlines of

[27] In his edition, Trapp notes corrections of Zenobius Acciaiolus in manuscript I.

[28] See the editions of Whittaker (1990) and Dillon (1993).

Platonism, from the Lectures of Gaius" and "Platonic Doctrines," were lost, evidently when the manuscript was reordered. All four works were devoted to an exposition of (Middle) Platonic philosophy for a second-century AD audience.

## *Editions*

The *editio princeps* is that of Henri Estienne (Stephanus) (Geneva, 1557). It relied mainly on a copy of Conv. Sopp. 4 (manuscript I), which it used to order the speeches. It was followed by the edition of Daniel Heinsius (Leiden, 1607; 2nd ed., 1614), which included a Latin translation, and served as the basis of John Davies' first edition (Davies$^1$; Cambridge, 1703).

A new phase began with Davies' second edition (Davies$^2$; London, 1740), completed posthumously by John Ward. This edition relied on manuscript R and reordered the speeches according to their presentation in that manuscript. Of importance in this edition is the series of notes, comments, and emendations offered by Jeremiah Markland.[29] In addition, Davies divided each oration into numbered sections, which have been retained by all subsequent editors. The edition was followed by that of Friedrich Dübner (Paris, 1840) in the Didot series.

The modern phase begins with the Teubner edition of Hermann Hobein (Leipzig, 1910), which was based primarily on manuscript R. Its reordering of the speeches

[29] A third edition of Davies was published in two volumes (Leipzig, 1774 and 1775), edited by Jacob Reiske with footnotes instead of endnotes.

has been followed in all subsequent editions.[30] Michael Trapp's 1994 Teubner edition is now the standard edition. It is a judicious text with many improvements and admirable clarity. It is supplemented by the excellent translation and thorough notes in his *Maximus of Tyre* (Oxford, 1997), as well as in many articles. The detailed edition of G. L. Koniaris, *Maximus Tyrius Philosophumena*: ΔΙΑΛΕΞΕΙΣ (Berlin/New York, 1995), presents a much more conservative text with an exhaustive apparatus. The present Loeb edition largely concurs with Trapp's text and makes frequent reference to his scholarship, translation, and notes. The dedication acknowledges that debt.

## *Translations*

The first translation into Latin was published in Rome by C. De' Pazzi (Paccius) in 1517. Subsequent versions appear in D. Heinsius (Leiden, 1607, 1614), C. Lariot (Lyon, 1630), J. Davies[1,2] (Cambridge, 1703; London, 1740; and Leipzig, 1774–1775), and F. Dübner (Paris, 1840). There are complete translations into Italian by P. de Bardi (Venice, 1642); French translations by J. H. S. Formey (Leiden, 1764) and J. J. Combes-Dounous (Paris, 1802); a German translation by C. T. Damm (Berlin, 1764); and an English translation by T. Taylor (London, 1804). Modern translations are: English, M. Trapp (Oxford, 1997); German, O. and E. Schönberger (Würzburg, 2001); Spanish, J. L.

30 Hobein also introduced lower-case letters to divide up the numbered sections of orations, a practice followed in Koniaris' edition. I have not seen the need to follow it in this edition.

López Cruces and J. Campos Daroca (Madrid, 2005); and Italian, S. I. S. Brumana (Milan, 2019).

### *This Edition*

The Greek text seldom differs from Trapp's 1994 Teubner edition. In the English translation I note only significant supplements with angular brackets. The introductions to each oration sketch the main arguments, but the art of Maximus lies in the rich texture of examples, analogies, and metaphors that enliven his discussions. I use "Maximus" when referring to the author and his views, and, where appropriate, "speaker" of the persona in individual orations, consistent with the argument in *Or.* 1 that the philosopher must be allowed to use many "voices." I have consistently used lower-case "god," even when it refers to the one god Zeus, to distinguish it from the Judeo-Christian God.

## CONCORDANCE TO THE THREE ORDERINGS OF THE ORATIONS[31]

| Hobein<br>Trapp<br>Koniaris | manuscript R<br>Davies$^2$<br>Dübner | manuscript I<br>Heinsius<br>Davies$^1$ |
|---|---|---|
| 1 | 7 | 37 |
| 2 | 8 | 38 |
| 3 | 9 | 39 |
| 4 | 10 | 29 |

31 Both LSJ and Montanari use the numbering of Davies$^2$ in their citations.

| Hobein<br>Trapp<br>Koniaris | manuscript R<br>Davies[2]<br>Dübner | manuscript I<br>Heinsius<br>Davies[1] |
|---|---|---|
| 5 | 11 | 30 |
| 6 | 12 | 40 |
| 7 | 13 | 41 |
| 8 | 14 | 26 |
| 9 | 15 | 27 |
| 10 | 16 | 28 |
| 11 | 17 | 1 |
| 12 | 18 | 2 |
| 13 | 19 | 3 |
| 14 | 20 | 4 |
| 15 | 21 | 5 |
| 16 | 22 | 6 |
| 17 | 23 | 7 |
| 18 | 24 | 8 |
| 19 | 25 | 9 |
| 20 | 26 | 10 |
| 21 | 27 | 11 |
| 22 | 28 | 12 |
| 23 | 29 | 13 |
| 24 | 30 | 14 |
| 25 | 31 | 15 |
| 26 | 32 | 16 |
| 27 | 33 | 17 |
| 28 | 34 | 18 |
| 29 | 35 | 19 |
| 30 | 1 | 31 |
| 31 | 2 | 32 |

| Hobein<br>Trapp<br>Koniaris | manuscript R<br>Davies[2]<br>Dübner | manuscript I<br>Heinsius<br>Davies[1] |
|---|---|---|
| 32 | 3 | 33 |
| 33 | 4 | 34 |
| 34 | 5 | 35 |
| 35 | 6 | 36 |
| 36 | 36 | 20 |
| 37 | 37 | 21 |
| 38 | 38 | 22 |
| 39 | 39 | 23 |
| 40 | 40 | 24 |
| 41 | 41 | 25 |

## TITLES OF THE ORATIONS IN MANUSCRIPT R

The titles of the orations adopted in this edition, and listed in the Contents, are those of our archetype manuscript R: although it cannot be determined whether these titles are original or later editorial additions, they are, on the whole, apt descriptions of the speeches. For discussions, see Koniaris (1982, 102–10) and Trapp (1997a, lviii).

# REFERENCES

| | |
|---|---|
| D-K | Diels, H., ed. *Die Fragmente der Vorsokratiker.* 6th ed. rev. W. Kranz. 3 vols. Berlin, 1951–1952. |
| K-A | *Poetae Comici Graeci*. Edited by R. Kassel and C. Austin. Berlin, 1983–2012. |
| L-M | Láks, A., and G. W. Most, eds. *Early Greek Philosophy*. 9 vols. Loeb Classical Library. Cambridge, MA, and London, 2016. |
| Suda | *Suidae lexicon*. Edited by A. Adler. Leipzig, 1928–1938. |
| *SVF* | *Stoicorum veterum fragmenta.* Edited by H. von Arnim. 4 vols. Leipzig, 1905–1924. |
| *TrGF* | *Tragicorum graecorum fragmenta*. Edited by B. Snell, R. Kannicht, and S. Radt. Göttingen, 1971–2004. |

# GENERAL BIBLIOGRAPHY

Brumana, S. I. S. 2019. *Massimo di Tiro Dissertazioni*. Milan: Bompiani.

Dillon, J. 1993. *Alcinous: The Handbook of Platonism*. Oxford: Oxford University Press.

———. 1996. 2nd ed. *The Middle Platonists: 80 B.C. to A.D. 220*. Ithaca: Cornell University Press.

Dürr, K. 1899. "Sprachliche Untersuchungen zu den Dialexeis des Maximus von Tyrus." *Philologus*, suppl. 8:1–156.

Grimaldi, M. 2002. *Due Orazioni di Massimo di Tirio (Diss. 4. 10 Trapp). Traduzione con testo a fronte e commentario*. Napoli: Bibliopolis.

Kindstrand, J. F. 1973. *Homer in der Zweiten Sophistik: Studien zu der Homerlektüre und dem Homerbild bei Dion von Prusa, Maximos von Tyros und Ailios Aristeides*. Acta Universitatis Upsaliensis 7, 45–71. Uppsala: Almquist & Wiksell.

Koniaris, G. L. 1982. "On Maximus of Tyre: Zetemata (I)." *CA* 1:87–121.

———, ed. 1995. *Maximus Tyrius Philosophumena*: ΔΙΑΛΕΞΕΙΣ. Berlin: de Gruyter.

Lauwers, J. 2009. "The Rhetoric of Pedagogical Narcissism: Philosophy, Philotimia and Self-Display in Maximus of Tyre's First Oration." *CQ* 59:593–607.

———. 2012. "Self-Advertising Meta-Poetics in Maximus of Tyre's 25th Oration." *WS* 125:75–84.

———. 2015. *Philosophy, Rhetoric, and Sophistry in the High Roman Empire: Maximus of Tyre and Twelve Other Intellectuals*. Leiden: Brill.

Litwa, M. D. 2021. *Posthuman Transformation in Ancient Mediterranean Thought: Becoming Angels and Demons*. Cambridge: Cambridge University Press.

López Cruces, J. L., and J. Campos Daroca. 2005. *Máximo de Tiro, Disertaciones filosóficas*. 2 vols. Madrid: Gredos.

Pérez-Jean, B., and F. Fauquier. 2014. *Maxime de Tyr: Choix de Conférences Religion et Philosophie, Introduction, traduction et notes*. Paris: Les Belles Lettres.

Puiggali, J. 1983. *Étude sur les* Dialexeis *de Maxime de Tyr, conférencier platonicien du IIème siècle*: Lille.

Roskam, G. 2010. "Socrates' δαιμόνιον in Maximus of Tyre, Apuleius, and Plutarch." In *Tychè et Pronoia: La marche du monde selon Plutarque*, edited by F. Frazier and D. F. Leão, 93–108. Coimbra: Coimbra University Press.

Schönberger, O., and E. Schönberger. 2001. *Maximos von Tyros: Philosophische Vorträge*. Würzburg: Königshausen and Neumann.

Scognamillo, A. F. 1997. *Massimo di Tiro, L'Arte Erotica di Socrate, Orazione XVIII. Edizione critica, traduzione e commento*. Lecce: Congedo.

Trapp, M. B. 1994. *Maximus Tyrius Dissertationes*. Stuttgart and Leiden: Teubner.

———. 1997a. *Maximus of Tyre. The Philosophical Orations. Translated, with an Introduction and Notes*. Oxford: Oxford University Press.

———. 1997b. "Philosophical Sermons: The 'Dialexeis' of Maximus of Tyre." In *ANRW* 2.43.3, pp. 1945–76.

———. 2007a. *Philosophy in the Roman Empire: Ethics, Politics and Society*. Aldershot: Ashgate.

———. 2007b. "Apuleius of Madauros and Maximus of Tyre." In R. Sorabji and R. W. Sharples, *Greek and Roman Philosophy: 100 BC to 200 AD*. *BICS* Suppl. 94, 467–82. London: Institute of Classical Studies, University of London.

Van der Horst, P. W. 1996. "Maximus of Tyre on Prayer: An Annotated Translation of Εἰ δεῖ εὔχεσθαι (*Dissertatio* 5)." In *Geschichte-Tradition-Reflexion: Festschrift für Martin Hengel zum 70 Geburtstag*, edited by H. Cancik, 2:323–38. Tübingen: Mohr Siebeck.

Whittaker, J., and P. Louis. 1990. *Alcinoos: Enseignement des Doctrines de Platon*. Paris: Les Belles Lettres.

# ΜΑΞΙΜΟΥ ΤΥΡΙΟΥ ΠΛΑΤΩΝΙΚΟΥ ΦΙΛΟΣΟΦΟΥ ΤΩΝ ΕΝ ΡΩΜΗΙ ΔΙΑΛΕΞΕΩΝ ΤΗΣ ΠΡΩΤΗΣ ΕΠΙΔΗΜΙΑΣ

# THE DISCOURSES OF THE PLATONIC PHILOSOPHER MAXIMUS OF TYRE, DELIVERED IN ROME DURING HIS FIRST VISIT

# *ORATION* 1

## INTRODUCTION

*Oration* 1, the longest in the collection, is a programmatic statement of Maximus' overall project as a public orator and philosopher.[1] It foregrounds the variety of approaches that will be found in the collection, as the speaker advertises the many voices, personae, and styles needed to convey his ethical philosophy. The kaleidoscope of shifting analogies signals a prominent feature of his style throughout the orations, as do the expansive lists in §5 and the anecdote in §7.

The oration opens with an analogy between a staged drama and the drama of life, where the philosopher must assume various roles and voices to address his audience, and vary his modes as a good musician needs to do (§1). He requires a versatile Muse like Homer's Calliope to address the continuous fluctuation in human affairs. Reason and philosophical discourse (both denoted by the word

[1] In the notes to his 1614 edition, Daniel Heinsius recognized the introductory nature of what is now *Or.* 1 (*Or.* 37 in his ordering). For the three different orderings, see the General Introduction. Lauwers (2009) studies the speaker's self-presentation as a pedagogue.

*logos*) must confront changing circumstances, especially in order to temper fluctuating human emotions (§2). Whereas various occasions call for various forms of speech (as feasts call for bards and courtrooms for orators), philosophical discourse is relevant at all times. It functions like light that illuminates the path of life and prevents people from straying into evil. It acts like a shepherd with his pipes keeping the human flock from scattering. To restrict the philosopher to one occasion would be like preventing a talented soldier from performing all his skills (§3). The philosopher is like an athlete who competes in all the major games (§4).

The speaker's contests, however, are held before audiences of Greeks hoping to acquire virtue. In contrast to physical contests, where the audience is passive, contests of the soul engage the audience in the competition. Whereas physical endowments vary among athletes, nature endows the soul of most people with a foundation upon which to develop the virtues. Moreover, alongside the power of reason, god placed both love and hope. The latter never allows the soul to rest, even for frustrated or immoral ends like those of merchants, mercenaries, and adulterers. But when the soul perceives what is stable through reason and pursues it through both love and hope, it achieves victory. This is what draws the speaker's own audiences (§5). Returning to the analogy of athletics with its passive audience, he begs his audience to compete with him in his intellectual contest, for only then will he be truly victorious. Otherwise, all he wins is praise, like some musical performer (§6). He desires true imitation, not just singing along like trained birds. His discourse can serve

all the needs of the young,[2] who aspire to master rhetoric, poetry, political and deliberative oratory, but philosophy and truth require a much greater champion (§7). Philosophy does not consist merely of sophistic techniques (although these are necessary to know), but the true instructor must temper the passions of his young students by mixing pain and pleasure and inspire them with reasoned discourse imbued with ethical character (*ēthos*) and passion (*pathos*) (§8).

Citing the examples of Socrates and Aristippus, the speaker argues that outward appearances are no true indication of a philosopher (§9). What determines a philosopher is his judgment (*gnōmē*), his discourse (*logos*), and the disposition (*paraskeuē*) of his soul. All externals, like theatrical costumes, do not indicate the character of the person wearing them. What matters is what they actually say, and although the discourse may vary, the good (*kalon*) in it is whole and consistent. In this drama of life, philosophers appear in various guises, as did Pythagoras, Socrates, Xenophon, and Diogenes. He concludes with a sly question as to who might be that worthy performer today (perhaps the speaker himself?) (§10).

2 Only here does he address his audience as young men (ὦ νέοι), as he outlines the verbal skills necessary for a cultured (πεπαιδευμένος) citizen embarking on public speaking and ultimately philosophy.

# *ORATION* 1

## Ὅτι πρὸς πᾶσαν ὑπόθεσιν ἁρμόσεται ὁ τοῦ φιλοσόφου λόγος

1. Τί δήποτε; οἱ ἐν Διονύσου τὰ δράματα ὑποκρινόμενοι, νῦν μὲν τὰς τοῦ Ἀγαμέμνονος ἱέντες φωνάς, νῦν δὲ τὰς τοῦ Ἀχιλλέως, καὶ αὖθις Τήλεφόν τινα ὑποδυόμενοι ἢ Παλαμήδην ἢ ἄλλ' ὅτιπερ ἂν τὸ δρᾶμα ἐθέλῃ, οὐδὲν πλημμελὲς οὐδὲ ἔξω τρόπου νομίζονται ποιεῖν, ἄλλοτε ἄλλοι φαινόμενοι οἱ αὐτοί· εἰ δέ τις τὰ μὲν τοῦ Διονύσου φυλάττει τῇ παιδιᾷ καὶ τῷ θεάτρῳ, ἡγεῖται δέ τι εἶναι αὐτῷ δρᾶμα πολιτικόν, οὐκ ἰαμβείων τινῶν, μὰ Δία, πρὸς ἕνα ἑορτῆς καιρὸν ὑπὸ ποιητοῦ τέχνῃ συντεθέντων, οὐδὲ ᾀσμάτων χορῷ ἐς ἁρμονίαν συνταχθέντων, ἀλλὰ τῆς περὶ τὸν βίον πραγματείας, ὅπερ ἂν εἴη τῷ φιλοσόφῳ δρᾶμα ἀληθέστερον μὲν τῇ ὑποθέσει, διηνεκὲς δὲ τῷ χρόνῳ, διδασκόμενον δὲ ὑπὸ ποιητῇ τῷ θεῷ· κᾆτά τις τὸ δρᾶμα τοῦτο ὑποδυόμενος καὶ τάξας ἑαυτὸν πρωταγωνιστὴν τοῦ χοροῦ, φυλάττοι μὲν τὸ τῶν ποιημάτων ἀξίωμα, σχηματίζοιτο δὲ

[1] Telephus and Palamedes were featured in the *Cypria* and in plays by Euripides.

# *ORATION* 1

## The discourse of a philosopher will adapt itself to every subject

1. How can this be? When actors in the theater of Dionysus at one time speak in Agamemnon's voice and then in Achilles', and in turn play the role of a Telephus or a Palamedes,[1] or whatever else the drama calls for, no one thinks it at all objectionable or unusual for these same men to appear in different guises at different times. Then what about a person who accepts Dionysiac activities as entertainment in the theater, but believes that he himself is involved in a drama of everyday life? But this drama, by Zeus, does not consist of some iambic verses skillfully composed by a poet for a single performance in a festival, nor of songs harmoniously arranged for a chorus, but instead consists of the conduct of life, which for the philosopher would be a drama whose subject is more true, whose performance is continuous, and whose playwright and producer is god.[2] And then, if a man acting in this real drama should cast himself as protagonist of the chorus, and, while maintaining the dignity of the poetry, should

[2] Throughout the orations, I use lower-case god for θεός, even when it refers to the one god, Zeus.

τῷ ἤθει τοῦ λόγου πρὸς τὴν φύσιν τῶν πραγμάτων ὧν δραματουργεῖ ὁ θεός· ἆρ᾽ ἄν τις ἡγήσαιτο τοῦτον πλημμελῆ καὶ πολύφωνον καὶ οἷον τὸν Πρωτέα διηγεῖται Ὅμηρος ἥρω θαλάττιον, πολύμορφόν τινα καὶ παντοδαπὸν τὴν φύσιν; ἢ καθάπερ εἰ μουσικῆς τέχνης καὶ δυνάμεως τοῖς ἀνθρώποις ἔδει πρὸς εὐδαιμονίαν, οὐθεὶς ἂν δήπου λόγος ἦν ἀνδρὸς πρὸς μὲν τὸν Δώριον τρόπον ἡρμοσμένου καλῶς, εἰ δέ που ἐδέησεν Ἰαστὶ[1] ἁρμόσασθαι <ἢ>[2] κατὰ τὸ Αἰόλιον ἦθος, ἀφώνου γιγνομένου ἐν τῇ πολυφωνίᾳ τῆς τέχνης;

2. Ἀλλ᾽ ἐπεὶ ᾠδῆς μὲν καὶ τῆς ἐκ μελῶν ψυχαγωγίας ὀλίγη τοῖς ἀνθρώποις χρεία, δεῖ δέ τινος ἄλλης μούσης ἀνδρικωτέρας, ἣν Ὅμηρος μὲν Καλλιόπην ὀνομάζων χαίρει, ὁ Πυθαγόρας δὲ φιλοσοφίαν, ἄλλος δὲ ἴσως ἄλλο τι, τὸν τῇ μούσῃ ταύτῃ κάτοχον ἄνδρα καὶ λόγον ἆρα ἧττον ἐκείνων τῶν ᾠδικῶν ἡρμόσθαι δεῖ πολυφώνως τε καὶ πολυτρόπως, σώζοντα μὲν ἀεὶ τὸ τῶν ποιημάτων κάλλος, μηδέποτε δὲ ὑπ᾽ ἀφωνίας ἐκπληττόμενον; εἰ μὲν γάρ ἐστιν εἷς χρόνος βίου ἐν τῷ μακρῷ τούτῳ καὶ διηνεκεῖ αἰῶνι ἐνδεὴς φιλοσόφου λόγου, οὐθὲν δεῖ τῆς πολυμεροῦς ταύτης καὶ πολυτρόπου μούσης τε καὶ ἁρμονίας, ἢ εἴπερ τὰ ἀνθρώπινα

[1] Ἰαστὶ Russell, Trapp: Ἰάστιον R
[2] suppl. Dübner, Trapp

adapt the character of his speech to suit the nature of the issues that god is staging, would anyone find him objectionable and many-voiced, and compare him to Proteus the sea hero described by Homer, who assumed many shapes and various natures?[3] Or what if humans needed the art and power of music for their happiness? Surely in that case, with so many tones in the musical art, would not a man who could play well in the Dorian mode be considered worthless, if he fell silent when called upon to perform in the Ionian or Aeolian mode?

2. But since people have limited use for song and the entertainment derived from tunes, they require a different, more vigorous Muse, one whom Homer likes to call Calliope,[4] whom Pythagoras calls Philosophy, and others, perhaps, something else. Must then a man inspired by this Muse attune his speech with less variety of tones and modes than those musicians are allowed, if he is to preserve the beauty of his compositions at all times and never be struck speechless? No, for if, in the long and continuous stretch of time, there were just one certain period of life that needed philosophical discourse, then there would be no call for this multifaceted and versatile[5] Muse and her harmony. The same would be true if human affairs

3 For Proteus' transformations, see *Od.* 4.454–58.

4 Homer never names his Muse. Maximus consistently calls her Calliope, later considered the Muse of epic poetry, probably beginning in the Hellenistic period. However, Pl. *Phdr.* 259d associates Calliope (and Urania) with philosophy, and in the Second Sophistic Calliope became associated with rhetoric and eloquence.

5 The adjective "versatile" (*polytropos*) recalls *polytropos* Odysseus (*Od.* 1.1).

εἰς ἓν σχῆμα συνταχθέντα ὁμοίως πρόεισιν, οὔτε εἰς λύπας ἐξ ἡδονῆς οὔτε εἰς ἡδονὴν ἐκ λύπης μεθιστάμενα, οὔτε πάθος ἀμείβοντα ἐκ πάθους, οὔτε ἄνω καὶ κάτω στρέφοντα καὶ μεταβάλλοντα τὴν ἑκάστου γνώμην·

τοῖος γὰρ νόος ἐστὶν ἐπιχθονίων ἀνθρώπων,
οἷον ἐπ᾿ ἦμαρ ἄγῃσι πατὴρ ἀνδρῶν τε θεῶν τε·

ἀντίστροφα γὰρ ὑπὲρ τῶν ἀνθρωπίνων βουλεύεται τὸ δαιμόνιον, καὶ ἔστιν αὐτῶν ἐφήμερος ἡ φύσις.

Ὥσπερ οὖν τῶν ποταμῶν οὓς ἀφιᾶσιν αἱ ἀέναοι πηγαί, τὸ μὲν ὄνομα ἕν, Σπερχειὸς ἢ Ἀλφειὸς ἢ ἄλλο τι, ἀμείβουσα δὲ ἡ γένεσις τὸ ἐπιὸν πρὸς τὸ οἰχόμενον ἐξαπατᾷ τὴν ὄψιν τῇ συνεχείᾳ τῆς φορᾶς, ὡς ἑνὸς ὄντος ποταμοῦ διηνεκοῦς καὶ ἡνωμένου· οὕτω καὶ τῶν ἀνθρωπίνων πραγμάτων ὥσπερ ἐκ πηγῆς ἀενάου ῥεῖ ἡ γένεσις καὶ ἡ χορηγία, ὀξέως μὲν καὶ μετὰ ἀμηχάνου τάχους, ἀνεπαίσθητος δὲ ἡ φορά, καὶ ἐξαπατᾶται ὁ λογισμὸς ὥσπερ ἐπὶ τοῦ ποταμοῦ ἡ ὄψις, καὶ καλεῖ βίον ἕνα καὶ τὸν αὐτόν· τὸ δέ ἐστιν χρῆμα πολύμορφον καὶ παντοδαπόν, πολλαῖς μὲν τύχαις, πολλοῖς δὲ πράγμασιν, πολλοῖς δὲ καιροῖς ἀλλοιούμενον.

Ἐπιτέτακται δὲ αὐτῷ ὁ λόγος, σχηματιζόμενος ἀεὶ τοῖς παροῦσιν, ὥσπερ ἰατροῦ τέχνη ἐπὶ σώματι οὐχ ἑστῶτι, ἀλλὰ φερομένῳ ἄνω καὶ κάτω καὶ ὑπὸ κενώσεως καὶ πλησμονῆς κυκωμένῳ, οἰκονομοῦσα αὐτοῦ τὴν ἔνδειαν καὶ τὸν κόρον· τοῦτο καὶ τῷ τῶν ἀνθρώπων βίῳ ὁ τῶν φιλοσόφων δύναται λόγος, ξυναρμο-

were arranged in one uniform fashion and progressed consistently, never vacillating from pleasure to pain or from pain to pleasure, nor exchanging one emotion for another, nor shifting and changing each person's judgment this way and that:

> for the mind of men who dwell on earth is such
> as the day the father of men and gods brings them.[6]

This is because divinity is resolved on change and counterchange in the affairs of humans, whose nature it is to change from day to day.

For just as rivers produced by constantly flowing springs have a single name—say Spercheius, Alpheus, and so forth—and deceive our sight by their constant flow, as if the river were one single, continuous entity, whereas its source keeps changing incoming for outgoing water, so too the source and supply of human affairs, as if from an ever-flowing spring, flows forth with unchecked swiftness, but whose motion is not perceived. As a result, our power of reason is deceived, as was our sight in the case of the river, into calling life one and the same event, whereas it is a thing of many shapes and forms, as it is altered by many acts of fortune, many circumstances, and many occasions.

Reason, however, has been put in charge of our lives, ever adjusting to prevailing conditions, like a physician whose skill regulates the deficiencies and excesses of an unstable body that is driven this way and that, in turmoil at filling and emptying itself. This is what the reasoned discourse of philosophers is able to do for human life: it

[6] *Od.* 18.136–37, Odysseus speaking to Amphinomus of the precariousness of human life, also quoted at *Or.* 11.4.

ζόμενος τοῖς πάθεσιν καὶ πεπαίνων μὲν τὰ σκυθρωπά, συνευφημῶν δὲ τοῖς φαιδροτέροις.

3. Εἰ δὲ διὰ βίου τάξις μία καὶ εἶδος ἕν, ἑνὸς ἔδει λόγου καὶ ἤθους ἑνός· νῦν δὲ ἀοιδοῦ μὲν πρὸς κιθάραν μινυρίζοντος καιρὸς εἷς, ἐπειδὰν πλήθωσιν αἱ τράπεζαι

σίτου καὶ κρειῶν, μέθυ δ᾽ ἐκ κρητῆρος ἀφύσσων
οἰνοχόος προχέῃσιν,

καὶ ῥήτορος καιρὸς εἷς, ἐπειδὰν ἀθροισθῇ τὰ δικαστήρια, καὶ ποιητοῦ καιρὸς εἷς ἐν Διονυσίοις, ἐπειδὰν χοροῦ δέῃ· τῷ δὲ φιλοσόφῳ λόγῳ οὐδεὶς ἀποτέτμηται καιρὸς ἴδιος, ἀλλὰ συμπέφυκεν ἀτεχνῶς τῷ βίῳ καὶ ἀνακέκραται, καθάπερ τοῖς ὀφθαλμοῖς τὸ φῶς· τίς γὰρ ἂν ἐπινοήσαι ὀφθαλμοῦ ἔργον, ἀφελὼν τὸ φῶς; ἀλλ᾽ ὄψις μὲν ἤδη καὶ ἐν νυκτὶ θαρσεῖ, ἀμβλὺ μὲν ὁρῶσα, εἰκάζουσα δὲ ἐν τῷ ἀφανεῖ τὴν χειραγωγίαν· τοῦ δὲ τῶν ἀνθρώπων βίου ἂν ἀφέλῃς λόγον, οἰχήσεται κατὰ κρημνῶν τινῶν πονηρὰς καὶ ἀσαφεῖς ὁδοὺς καὶ τραχείας, οἵας ὁδοὺς καὶ τὸ βαρβαρικὸν ἔρχεται, ὅσον αὐτοῦ μὴ μετέσχεν λόγου, τὸ μὲν ληϊζόμενον, †τὸ δὲ μένον†,[3] τὸ δὲ μισθοφοροῦν, τὸ δὲ πλανώμενον. Ἀλλ᾽ αἰπολίου μὲν ἀποστήσας τὸν ποιμένα καὶ ἀφελὼν τὴν σύριγγα, διέλυσας τὸ αἰπόλιον· τῆς δὲ τῶν ἀνθρώπων ἀγέλης ἐὰν ἀποστήσῃς τὸν ἡγεμόνα

[3] obel. Trapp: ‹μαινό›μενον tent. Paccius: ‹χρηματιζό›μενον Meier, Russell: μοιχεῦον Davies[2]

attunes itself to the emotions, as it assuages feelings of sadness and joins in the celebration of more joyful ones.

3. If life maintained a single order and a single form throughout, only one kind of discourse and one style would be needed. But in reality, one occasion calls for a bard crooning to a lyre, when the tables are full

> of bread and meat, and the wine server draws off wine
> from the mixing bowl and pours it out;[7]

another occasion calls for an orator, when the jurors are convened; another for a poet at the Dionysia, when a chorus is needed. But no specific occasion has been set aside for philosophical discourse. It simply coexists with life and is as integral to it as light is to the eyes. Who could imagine an eye functioning, if light is removed? Yet in fact, even at night, vision has the confidence, although seeing dimly, to guess which way will lead through the darkness. But if you remove reasoned discourse from human life, it will go off on paths that are evil, dark, and rugged, down precipices of various kinds, paths like the ones traveled by those barbarians who do not participate in this discourse, as some go plundering, some serve as mercenaries, and some just roam about.

If you remove a herdsman from his flock and take away his pipes, you will scatter the flock. Likewise, if you deprive the human herd of this guiding and unifying dis-

[7] *Od.* 9.9–10.

τοῦτον καὶ συναγωγέα λόγον, τί ἄλλο δρᾷς ἢ λυμαίνῃ καὶ διαλύεις ἀγέλην ἥμερον μὲν τὴν φύσιν, δυσπειθῆ δὲ ὑπὸ πονηρᾶς τροφῆς καὶ δεομένην ποιμένος μουσικοῦ, μὴ μάστιγι μηδὲ κέντρῳ κολάζοντος αὐτῶν τὴν ἀπείθειαν. παραπλήσιον γάρ μοι δοκεῖ δρᾶν ὅστις οὐκ ἀξιοῖ τὸν φιλόσοφον μηδένα παριέναι καιρὸν λόγου, οἷον εἴ τις καὶ ἀνδρὶ δεινῷ τὰ πολέμια, ἀγαθῷ μὲν ὁπλιτεύειν, ἀγαθῷ δὲ ἐκηβολεῖν καὶ ἐφ' ἵππου καὶ ξὺν ἅρματι, ἀποκρίναι καιρὸν ἕνα ἐξελόμενος τῆς ὅλης τοῦ πολέμου χρείας καὶ τύχης, πράγματος οὐχ ἑστῶτος οὐδ' ὡμολογημένου.

4. Ἀθλητῇ μὲν γὰρ ἔστιν Ὀλυμπιάσιν ἀγωνισαμένῳ ἀμελῆσαι τοῦ Ἰσθμοῦ· καίτοι κἀνταῦθα ἐπονείδιστος ἡ ῥᾳθυμία, καὶ οὐκ ἀνέχεται ἡ φιλότιμος ψυχὴ ῥᾳστώνης πόθῳ τὸ μὴ διὰ πάντων ἐλθεῖν, καὶ μετασχεῖν μὴ κοτίνου μόνον Ὀλυμπιάσιν, ἀλλὰ καὶ πίτυος Ἰσθμικῆς καὶ σελίνου Ἀργολικοῦ καὶ μήλων Πυθικῶν· καὶ ταῦτα οὐκ αὐτὴ ἔχουσα ἡ ψυχὴ τὴν αἰτίαν τῆς ἀγωνίας, ἀλλὰ διὰ τὴν συνοίκησίν τε καὶ πρὸς τὸ σῶμα ὁμιλίαν συναπολαύουσα τῆς νίκης αὐτῷ καὶ τῶν κηρυγμάτων· ὅπου δὲ καὶ ὁ πόνος τῆς ψυχῆς αὐτῆς καὶ τὸ ἀγώνισμα τῆς ψυχῆς μόνης καὶ νίκη μόνης, ἐνταῦθα παρόψεταί τινα ἀγῶνος καιρὸν καὶ ῥᾳθυμήσει ἑκοῦσα, ὅπου μήτε μῆλα μήτε κότινος τὸ ἆθλον, ἀλλ' ἀντὶ τούτων ὡραιότερον μὲν πρὸς φι-

course, you do nothing less than scatter and destroy a herd that is naturally docile, but is rendered out of control because of poor rearing, and is in need of a herdsman and his music, not one who punishes its disobedience with whips and goads. I think that anyone who does not allow a philosopher to seize every opportunity to speak is doing much the same as someone who selects one single occasion from all the exigencies and chance events of war, which is an unstable and inconstant enterprise, and there alone constrains a skilled warrior, who is both an excellent infantryman and an excellent archer whether on horseback or on a chariot.

4. Now an athlete who has competed in the Olympics is allowed to skip the Isthmian games, although even then his idleness is open to reproach. But the ambitious soul cannot bear to be prevented by desire for leisure from competing in all the games, and from claiming its share not only of Olympian olive, but also of Isthmian pine, Argive celery, and Pythian apples.[8] Yet in this case the soul does not compete for itself alone, but shares the joy of victory and the official proclamations with the body it inhabits and partners with. But where the effort belongs exclusively to the soul, and the struggle and victory are the soul's alone, do you think that it will be willing to stand idly by and forgo any opportunity to compete, when the prize is not apples or olive leaves, but instead a lovelier object

[8] That is, to become a *periodonikēs*, winner at all four major games. The Olympic, Isthmian, Nemean (here called Argive), and Pythian games awarded prizes of perishable crowns. The Pythian games originally awarded a laurel crown but later apples; cf. Lucian *Anach*. 9.

λοτιμίαν, ἀνυσιμώτερον δὲ τοῖς θεαταῖς πρὸς ὠφέλειαν, εὐδρομώτερον δὲ τῷ λέγοντι πρὸς πίστιν †βίου†;[4]

Οἱ δὲ καιροὶ τῆς ἀγωνίας καὶ οἱ τόποι ἄλλοτε ἄλλοι ἄφνω κηρυττόμενοι καὶ ἀθροίζοντες πλῆθος Ἑλληνικὸν αὐτόκλητον καὶ αὐτεπάγγελτον καὶ ξυνιὸν οὐκ ἐφ' ἡδονῇ ὀφθαλμῶν, ἀλλὰ ἀρετῆς ἐλπίδι, ὅπερ οἶμαι τῇ τοῦ ἀνθρώπου ψυχῇ ἡδονῆς συγγενέστερον. ἰδεῖν γοῦν ἔστιν ἐπὶ μὲν τὰς ἄλλας θέας, ὁπόσαι ῥώμης ἢ τέχνης σωμάτων, ἀφικνούμενον σπουδῇ οὐδένα τῶν θεατῶν ὡς τὸ θέαμα ζηλώσοντα ἢ μιμησόμενον· ἀλλ' ἐκεῖ μὲν ἐξ ἀλλοτρίων πόνων τὰς ἡδονὰς τοῖς ὀφθαλμοῖς ἐρανιζόμεθα, καὶ ἐκ μυρίων θεατῶν οὐδεὶς ἂν εὔξαιτο εἷς εἶναι τῶν ἐν μέσῳ τῷ σταδίῳ κονιωμένων ἢ θεόντων, ἢ ἀγχόντων ἢ ἀγχομένων, ἢ <τυπτόντων ἢ>[5] τυπτομένων, πλὴν εἴ πού τις ἀνδραποδώδης ψυχή· ἐνταῦθα δὲ τοσοῦτον οἶμαι καὶ τὴν ἀγωνίαν τήνδε ἐκείνης τῆς ἀγωνίας φιλοτιμοτέραν εἶναι, καὶ τοὺς πόνους τῶν πόνων ἀνυσιμωτέρους, καὶ τὸ θέατρον τοῦ θεάτρου συμπαθέστερον, ὥστε οὐδεὶς τῶν παρόντων νοῦν ἔχων οὐκ ἂν εὔξαιτο ἀποθέμενος τὸν θεατὴν ἀγωνιστὴς γενέσθαι.

5. Τί δήποτ' οὖν τὸ τούτου αἴτιον; ὅτι τὰς μὲν τῶν σωμάτων τέχνας καὶ τὰς ἐπὶ ταύταις ταλαιπωρίας οὐ πᾶσα ἀνέχεται σαρκῶν φύσις, οὐδέ ἐστιν τὸ χρῆμα

[4] obel. Trapp: *πρὸς σωτειρίαν βίου* tent. Koniaris
[5] suppl. Reiske, Trapp

of ambition, more capable of benefitting the spectators, and more effective for the speaker to carry conviction [in life]?[9]

The times and places for this contest vary. They are announced on the spur of the moment and bring together a crowd of Hellenes, who assemble spontaneously and of their own free will, not for some pleasant spectacle, but in hopes of acquiring virtue, which I consider more akin to the human soul than pleasure. Now in those other spectacles of physical strength and skill, it is impossible to find a single spectator who seriously comes with the intention of imitating or engaging in what he sees, for in this case we take pleasure in watching the exertions of others, and except perhaps for someone with the soul of a slave, not a single person among the myriad spectators would wish to be one of those in the middle of the stadium covered with dust or running, choking or being choked, hitting or being hit. But in this other case, I believe that the soul's contest is so much more worthy of ambition than the physical one, its toils so much more able to be borne, and its audience so much more engaged, that any sensible attendee would wish to be a competitor himself rather than a mere spectator.

5. So, what on earth is the reason for this? It is because athletic skills and the hard work involved in them cannot be sustained by just any physical build, nor is athletic abil-

9 The text and meaning are uncertain. "In life" is corrupt.

κομιδῇ ἑκούσιον, ἀλλὰ αὐτοφυὲς καὶ αὐτόματον καὶ εἰς ὀλίγους ἐκ πολλῶν ἧκον· ἢ γὰρ κατὰ μέγεθος φῦναι δεῖ Τιτόλμῳ ὅμοιον, ἢ κατὰ καρτερίαν Μίλωνι, ἢ κατὰ ῥώμην Πουλυδάμαντι, ἢ κατὰ τάχος Λασθένει· εἰ δέ τις ἀσθενέστερος μὲν ὢν τοῦ Ἐπειοῦ, αἰσχίων δὲ τοῦ Θερσίτου, μικρότερος δὲ τοῦ Τυδέως, βραδύτερος δὲ τοῦ Αἴαντος καὶ πάσας τὰς τοῦ σώματος ἐλαττώσεις ἠθροισμένας ἔχων ζηλῶσαι τὴν ἀγωνίαν, ἦ ἔρωτα ἠράσθη κενὸν καὶ ἀτελεύτητον. τὰ δὲ τῆς ψυχῆς ἀγωνίσματα ἔμπαλιν ἔχει τοῖς ἐκεῖ· ὀλίγον γὰρ καὶ σπάνιον ἐν τῷ τῶν ἀνθρώπων γένει τὸ μὴ πεφυκός· οὐ γὰρ αὐτοφυεῖς αἱ τῆς ψυχῆς ἀρεταί, οὐ γὰρ αὐτόματοι· ἀλλὰ προεξεργάζεται μέν τι καὶ ἡ φύσις, ὅσον ὑποβάλλειν κρηπῖδα ὀλίγην μεγάλῳ τειχίῳ ἢ τρόπιν μικρὰν ὑψηλῇ ὁλκάδι.

Συγκατῴκισεν δὲ ὁ θεὸς τοῖς λογισμοῖς ἔρωτα καὶ ἐλπίδα, τὸν μὲν ὡσπερεὶ πτέρωμά τι κοῦφον καὶ μετάρσιον, ἐπαῖρόν τε καὶ ἀνακουφίζον τὴν ψυχὴν καὶ παρέχον αὐτῇ δρόμον ἐπὶ τὰς αὐτῆς ὀρέξεις· καλοῦσιν δὲ οἱ φιλόσοφοι τὸ πτέρωμα τοῦτο ὁρμὴν ἀνθρωπίνην· αἱ δὲ ἐλπίδες συγκατῳκισμέναι τῇ ψυχῇ

---

10 Elsewhere known as Titormus, a cowherd and rival of Milo, dubbed another Heracles; cf. Ael. *VH* 12.22.

11 A late sixth-century BC wrestler from Croton, famous for supposedly carrying a bull on his shoulders.

12 A late fifth-century BC pancratiast from Scotussa in Thessaly, famous for feats of strength; cf. Paus. 6.5.1–7.

ity simply a matter of willpower, but it is innate, spontaneous, and possessed by very few individuals. One must naturally be as big as Titolmus,[10] as strong as Milo,[11] as powerful as Polydamas,[12] or as fast as Lasthenes.[13] But if someone is weaker than Epeius,[14] more deformed than Thersites,[15] smaller than Tydeus,[16] slower than Ajax,[17] or who has all these physical disadvantages combined, and still competes in this contest, truly he is afflicted with a vain and futile passion. But the soul's contests are the very opposite of these, because few and far between are there human beings not naturally endowed for them. That is because the virtues of the soul are not innate or happen spontaneously. No, natural endowment merely prepares the way to a certain extent, like laying down a small foundation for a great wall, or a small keel for a tall merchant ship.[18]

Moreover, god made love and hope dwell alongside our powers of reasoning. Love is like light and airy wings, which raise and lift up the soul and offer it a speedy approach to the things it desires.[19] Philosophers call these wings human impulse.[20] As for hopes, they too dwell in the

[13] Lasthenes of Thebes won the *dolichos* (long-distance race) at Olympia in 404 BC.

[14] The builder of the Trojan horse. At *Il.* 23.839–40 the Achaeans laugh at his weak attempt to hurl a mass of iron during the funeral games for Patroclus.

[15] His deformities are described at *Il.* 2.216–19.

[16] Cf. *Il.* 5.801.

[17] Cf. *Il.* 11.558–65.

[18] A Platonic example of such natural endowment is that of the slave boy taught geometry in the *Meno*.

[19] The image of the winged soul derives from Pl. *Phdr.* 246e.

[20] The term *hormē* was first used by Stoics in this sense; cf. *SVF* 3.171.

παραμύθιον ταῖς ἑκάστου ὁρμαῖς, οὐ κατὰ τὸν Ἀττικὸν ποιητὴν τυφλαὶ ἀλλὰ ὀξυωπεῖς πάνυ, οὐκ ἐῶσιν αὐτὴν ἀπαγορεῦσαι πονοῦσαν, ὡς τευξομένην πάντως ὧν ἐρᾷ. πάλαι γὰρ ἂν οὐκ οὔσης ἐλπίδος καὶ ὁ χρηματιστὴς ἐπαύσατο χρηματιζόμενος, καὶ ὁ μισθοφόρος στρατευόμενος, καὶ ὁ ἔμπορος πλέων, καὶ ὁ λῃστὴς λῃϊζόμενος, καὶ ὁ ἀκόλαστος μοιχεύων· ἀλλ' οὐκ ἐῶσιν αἱ ἐλπίδες, προστάττουσαι τούτους ἀνήνυτα πονεῖν καὶ ἀτελεύτητα, τὸν μὲν χρηματιστὴν ὡς πλουτήσοντα, τὸν δὲ πολεμοῦντα ὡς νικήσοντα, τὸν δὲ πλέοντα ὡς σωθησόμενον, τὸν δὲ λῃϊζόμενον ὡς κερδανοῦντα, τὸν δὲ μοιχεύοντα ὡς λησόμενον· κᾆτά τις ἕκαστον ὑπολαβοῦσα αἰφνίδιος συμφορὰ ἐσύλησεν μὲν τὸν χρηματιστήν, ἀπέκτεινεν δὲ τὸν μισθοφόρον, κατέδυσεν δὲ τὸν ἔμπορον, ἔλαβεν δὲ τὸν λῃστήν, ἐφώρασεν δὲ καὶ τὸν μοιχόν, καὶ ἀπολώλασιν αὐτοῖς αἱ ὀρέξεις αὐταῖς ἐλπίσιν.

Οὐδὲν γὰρ τούτων περιέλαβεν μέτρῳ οὐδὲ ὥρισεν ὁ θεός, οὔτε πλοῦτον οὔτε ἡδονὰς οὔτε ἄλλο τι τῶν ἀνθρωπίνων ἐπιθυμημάτων, ἀλλ' ἔστιν αὐτῶν ἄπειρος ἡ οὐσία· ἔνθεν που καὶ οἱ διώκοντες ταῦτα ἐμπλησθέντες αὐτῶν διψῶσιν μᾶλλον· ἔλαττον γὰρ τὸ ληφθὲν τοῦ προσδοκωμένου. ὁπόταν δὲ ᾄξῃ ψυχὴ ἐπὶ πρᾶγμα ἑστὸς καὶ ὡμολογημένον καὶ πεπερασμένον καὶ ὡρισμένον, καὶ καλὸν μὲν τῇ φύσει, ἀνυστὸν δὲ τῷ πόνῳ, ληπτὸν δὲ τῷ λογισμῷ, διωκτὸν δὲ τῷ ἔρωτι, καταληπτὸν δὲ τῇ ἐλπίδι, τότε γίγνεται ἡ τῆς ψυχῆς ἀγωνία ἐπιτυχὴς καὶ τελεσιουργὸς καὶ νικηφόρος· ἔστιν δὲ

soul to encourage the individual's impulses—not "blind hopes," as the Athenian playwright describes them,[21] but very clear-sighted ones indeed—and by convincing the soul that it will fully obtain what it desires, they do not allow it to shirk any labors. If hope did not exist, the moneymaker would long since have given up his trade, the mercenary his campaigning, the merchant his travels over the sea, the brigand his plundering, and the libertine his adultery. But hopes do not allow this to happen. They command these men to labor incessantly and to no end, promising the moneymaker that he will be rich, the soldier that he will be victorious, the sailor that he will land safely, the brigand that he will gain plunder, and the adulterer that he will avoid detection. And yet, sudden disaster can strike each one and bankrupt the moneymaker, kill the mercenary, drown the merchant, capture the brigand, and expose the adulterer, making all their desires vanish along with their hopes.

This happens because god has not set a limit or boundary to any of these things, be it wealth, pleasure, or any other object of human longings, for these are essentially limitless. That is precisely why people who pursue such things and get their fill, thirst for them all the more, because what they have acquired is less than what they expect to have. But whenever the soul pursues what is stable and consistent, limited and finite, good by nature, able to be accomplished by hard work and apprehended by the power of reason, able to be pursued by love and attained by hope, then the soul's struggles result in success, fulfillment, and victory. It is for this reason, and for no other,

[21] [Aesch.] *PV* 250.

τοῦτο οὐκ ἄλλο τι ἢ οὗπερ εἵνεκα ταυτὶ τὰ θέατρα οἱ φιλοσοφοῦντες ἀθροίζουσιν.

6. Πάλιν αὖ μοι δεῖ τῆς τῶν ἀθλητῶν εἰκόνος. ἐκείνων μέν γε εὔξαιτ' ἂν ἕκαστος μηδένα ἀγωνιστὴν ἄλλον παρελθεῖν ἐπὶ τὸ στάδιον, ἀλλ' ἀκονιτὶ νικᾶν αὐτός· δεῖ γὰρ νικᾶν ἐκ πολλῶν ἕνα· ἐνταῦθα δὲ οὗτος μάλιστα τῶν ἀγωνιστῶν νικηφόρος ὃς ἂν πολλοὺς ἐπὶ τὴν ἀγωνίαν παρακαλέσῃ. εἰ γάρ, ὦ θεοί, ἐμῶν θεατῶν γένοιτό τις συναγωνιστὴς ἐμοὶ ἐπὶ ταυτησὶ τῆς ἕδρας συγκονιόμενος καὶ συμπονῶν· ἐγὼ τότε εὐδοκιμῶ, στεφανοῦμαι τότε, κηρύττομαι τότ' ἐν τοῖς Πανέλλησιν.

Ἕως δὲ νῦν ἀστεφάνωτος εἶναι ὁμολογῶ καὶ ἀκήρυκτος, κἂν ὑμεῖς βοᾶτε. τί γὰρ ἐμοὶ ὄφελος τῶν πολλῶν λόγων καὶ τῆς συνεχοῦς ταύτης ἀγωνίας; ἔπαινοι; ἅλις τούτων ἔχω· δόξα; διακορής εἰμι τοῦ χρήματος. τὸ δὲ ὅλον, ἐπαινεῖ τις λόγους καὶ οὐ λέγει, φωνὴν ἔχων, ἀκοὴν ἔχων; ἐπαινεῖ τις φιλοσοφίαν καὶ οὐ λαμβάνει, ψυχὴν ἔχων, διδάσκαλον ἔχων; γέγονεν τοίνυν τὸ χρῆμα οἷον αὐλήματα ἢ κιθαρίσματα, ἢ εἴ τις ἄλλη ἐν Διονύσου μοῦσα τραγική τις ἢ κωμῳδική· ἐπαινοῦσιν μὲν πάντες, μιμεῖται δὲ οὐδείς.

7. Ἦ κἀνταῦθα πάμμηκες διαφέρει ἔπαινος ἡδονῆς· ἥδονται μὲν γὰρ πάντες ἀκροώμενοι, ὃς δ' ἂν τῷ ὄντι ἐπαινέσῃ, καὶ μιμήσεται· μέχρι δέ τις μὴ ζηλοῖ, οὐκ ἐπῄνεσεν. ἤδη τις καὶ ὑπὸ αὐλημάτων ἀνὴρ ἄμουσος διετέθη μουσικῶς, καὶ τὰ ὦτα ἔναυλος ὢν διαμέμνη-

that those who practice philosophy assemble these very audiences.

6. I need the analogy of athletes once again. In athletic contests, since there can be only one winner out of many contestants, each athlete would no doubt wish that no other competitor would enter the stadium, and thereby win unopposed. But in this contest of the soul, the preeminent victor is he who can summon many others to compete. O gods, would that one of my spectators might become my competitor and wrestle and toil with me in this very arena. Then I will become famous, then win a crown, and then be proclaimed victor before all the Greeks!

Until now, I must admit, I have received no such crown or proclamation, even though *you* shout your approval. So, what benefit do I get from my many speeches and this constant struggle? Praise? I already have plenty of that. Fame? I have my fill of it. Here's the whole point. Are people to praise speeches, yet give none themselves, although they have voices and hearing? Are they to praise philosophy, but not take it up, although they have souls and teachers? As a result, this whole affair has become like pipe playing or lyre playing, or like any other music performed in tragedy or comedy in the theater of Dionysus: everyone praises the performers, but no one imitates them.

7. But here too there is an enormous difference between praise and mere enjoyment. Everyone can enjoy listening, but whoever gives true praise will also imitate, and to the degree that he does not emulate, he does not truly render praise. In fact, many a person with no musical training can acquire the ability simply by hearing pipe music: as the tune rings in his ears, he memorizes it and

ται τοῦ μέλους καὶ μινυρίζει πρὸς αὐτόν. κἂν τοῦτό τις ὑμῶν τὸ πάθος ζηλωσάτω· τάχα γάρ που ἐρασθήσεται καὶ τῶν αὐλῶν αὐτῶν.

Ἀνὴρ φιλοθρέμμων ὄρνιθας εἶχεν τῶν ἡδὺ μὲν φθεγγομένων τὸ ὄρθριον δὴ τοῦτο, ἄσημον δὲ καὶ οἷον ὄρνιθας εἰκός. ἦν αὐτῷ γείτων αὐλητικός· ἀκροώμενοι δὲ οἱ ὄρνιθες διαμελετωμένου τοῦ αὐλητοῦ καὶ ἀντᾴδοντες αὐτῷ ὁσημέραι, ἐτυπώθησαν τῇ ἀκοῇ πρὸς τὰ αὐλήματα, καὶ τελευτῶντες ἀρξαμένου αὐλεῖν συνεπήχουν πρὸς τὸ ἐνδόσιμον, δίκην χοροῦ. ἄνθρωποι δὲ ὄντες οὐδὲ κατὰ ὄρνιθας ξυνᾴσονται ἡμῖν, ἀκούοντες θαμὰ οὐκ ἀσήμων αὐλημάτων, ἀλλὰ νοερῶν λόγων καὶ διηρθρωμένων καὶ γονίμων καὶ πρὸς μίμησιν εὖ πεφυκότων; ὥστε ἔγωγε τέως καὶ πρὸς ἅπαντας ὑπὲρ τῶν ἡμετέρων σιγὴν ἔχων καὶ μηδὲν σεμνὸν μηδὲ ὑπέραυχον μήτε ἰδίᾳ μήτε εἰς κοινὸν εἰπών, νῦν μοι δοκῶ ὑμῶν εἵνεκεν γαυρότατα ἂν καὶ μεγαλαυχότατα εἰπεῖν.

Παρελήλυθεν εἰς ὑμᾶς, ὦ νέοι, παρασκευὴ λόγων αὕτη πολύχους καὶ πολυμερὴς καὶ πάμφορος, καὶ ἐπὶ πάσας ἐξικνουμένη ἀκοὰς καὶ πάσας φύσεις, καὶ πάσας ζηλώσεις λόγων καὶ πάσας παιδευμάτων ἰδέας, ἀταμίευτος καὶ ἄμισθος καὶ ἀπροφάσιστος καὶ ἄφθονος, ἐν μέσῳ κειμένη τοῖς δυναμένοις λαβεῖν. εἴτε τις ῥητορείας ἐρᾷ, οὗτος αὐτῷ δρόμος λόγου πρόχειρος καὶ πολυαρκὴς καὶ εὔπορος καὶ ὑψηλὸς καὶ ἐκπληκτικὸς καὶ ἄρρατος καὶ ἰσχυρὸς καὶ ἄκμητος· εἴτε τις

can hum it to himself. I wish that some of you here might emulate that experience, and perhaps even come to love the pipes themselves.[22]

There was man who was fond of raising animals and he had some birds of the kind that sing their morning song sweetly, but inarticulately, as birds do. This man had a neighbor who played the pipes, and as the birds listened to him practicing and sang back to him every day, their hearing became attuned to his playing, and eventually, whenever he began to play, they would chime in just like a chorus in response to an instrumental lead-in. But unlike those birds, my audience consists of men. Won't they sing along with me? They are not hearing the repetition of inarticulate piping tunes, but intelligible words that are coherent, stimulating, and well-suited for imitation. So, up to this point I have maintained silence before all men about my accomplishments and have said nothing proud or boastful either in public or in private, but now I am convinced that I ought to speak for your benefit as boastfully and proudly as I can.

Here in your presence, young men, stands this resource for speaking:[23] it is copious, multifaceted, and very productive; it suits all listeners, all temperaments, all pursuits of oratory, and all forms of instruction; it is lavish, free of charge, readily available, unstinting, and open to all who are able to receive it. If anyone is in love with rhetoric, here at hand for him is a copious flow of speech, sufficient for many needs, abundant, lofty, impressive, continuous, strong, and unfailing. And if anyone is in love

22 That is, become philosophers.

23 That is, as exemplified in Maximus' discourses.

ποιητικῆς ἐρᾷ, ἡκέτω πορισάμενος ἄλλοθεν τὰ μέτρα μόνον, τὴν δὲ ἄλλην χορηγίαν λαμβανέτω ἐντεῦθεν, τὸ σοβαρόν, τὸ ἐπιφανές, τὸ λαμπρόν, τὸ γόνιμον, τὸ ἔνθεον, τὴν οἰκονομίαν, τὴν δραματουργίαν, τὸ κατὰ τὰς φωνὰς ἀταμίευτον, τὸ κατὰ τὴν ἁρμονίαν ἄπταιστον. ἀλλὰ πολιτικῆς καὶ τῆς περὶ δήμους καὶ βουλευτήρια παρασκευῆς ἥκεις ἐνδεὴς ὤν; σὺ μὲν καὶ πεφώρακας τὸ ἔργον· ὁρᾷς τὸν δῆμον, ὁρᾷς τὸ βουλευτήριον, τὸν λέγοντα, τὴν πειθώ, τὸ κράτος.

Ἀλλὰ τούτων μέν τις ὑπερορᾷ, φιλοσοφίαν δὲ ἀσπάζεται καὶ ἀλήθειαν τιμᾷ; ἐνταῦθα ὑφαιρῶ τῆς μεγαλαυχίας, ὑφίεμαι, οὐχ ὁ αὐτός εἰμι· μέγα τὸ χρῆμα καὶ δεόμενον προστάτου οὐ δημοτικοῦ, μὰ Δία, οὐδὲ ἐρχομένου χαμαί, οὐδὲ ἀνακεκραμένου τῷ τῶν πολλῶν τρόπῳ.

8. Εἰ μὲν οὖν τις τοῦτ᾽ εἶναι φιλοσοφίαν λέγει, ῥήματα καὶ ὀνόματα, ἢ τέχνας λόγων, ἢ ἐλέγχους καὶ ἔριδας καὶ σοφίσματα καὶ τὰς ἐν τούτοις διατριβάς, οὐ χαλεπὸν εὑρεῖν τὸν διδάσκαλον· πάντα ὑμῖν μεστὰ τοιούτων σοφιστῶν, εὔπορον τὸ χρῆμα καὶ ταχὺ ἀναφαινόμενον· θαρσήσαιμι δ᾽ ἂν ἔγωγε εἰπεῖν ὅτι τῆς τοιαύτης φιλοσοφίας πλείους οἱ διδάσκαλοι τῶν μαθητῶν. εἰ δὲ ταῦτα μὲν ὀλίγη τοῦ φιλοσοφεῖν μοῖρα, καὶ τοσαύτη ὅσην αἰσχρὸν μὲν μὴ εἰδέναι, οὐ σεμνὸν δὲ εἰδέναι, διαφεύγωμεν τὸ αἰσχρὸν καὶ ταῦτα εἰδότες, μὴ καλλωπιζώμεθα δὲ ἐπ᾽ αὐτοῖς· ἢ γὰρ ἂν πολλοῦ ἄξιοι καὶ οἱ γραμματισταὶ εἶεν, πραγματευόμενοι

with poetry, only let him obtain his meter elsewhere, but come here to acquire the rest of poetry's materials: magnificence, clarity, brilliance, creativity, inspiration, composition, theatricality, lavish diction, and impeccable harmony. Or have you come in need of the art of politics and resources for addressing the people and the council chamber? You have found what you seek: here before your eyes are the people, the council chamber, the speaker, the persuasion, and the power.

But is there anyone who disdains all this and instead embraces philosophy and values truth? In this case, I forgo my boasting, I relinquish it. I am not the same person. This mighty work requires no ordinary champion, by Zeus, nor some lowly person, nor anyone imbued with the manners of the multitude.

8. Now anyone who thinks that philosophy consists merely of nouns and verbs, techniques of speaking, refutations, disputations, sophisms, and the waste of time spent on these, has no difficulty finding an instructor. The world around all of you is full of such sophists; their instruction is readily available and is quickly found. In fact, I would go so far as to say that there are more teachers of this kind of philosophy than there are students. If, however, such matters are only a small part of being a philosopher, and if they are important enough that it is shameful not to know them, and at the same time no grand achievement to know them, then let us avoid disgrace by knowing them, but not assume any self-importance because we do, for otherwise grammar teachers would be held in high regard

περὶ τὰς συλλαβὰς καὶ συμψελλίζοντες ἔθνει παίδων ἀνοητοτάτῳ.

Τὸ δὲ ἐν φιλοσοφίᾳ κεφάλαιον καὶ ἡ ἐπ' αὐτὸ ὁδὸς δεῖται διδασκάλου τὰς τῶν νέων ψυχὰς ξυνεπαίροντος καὶ διαπαιδαγωγοῦντος αὐτῶν τὰς φιλοτιμίας, καὶ οὐδὲν ἀλλ' ἢ λύπαις καὶ ἡδοναῖς τὰς ὀρέξεις αὐτῶν συμμετρουμένου· οἷόν που καὶ οἱ πωλευταὶ δρῶσιν, μήτε ἀποσβεννύντες τὸν θυμὸν τῶν πωλευμάτων, μήτε ἐφιέντες αὐτοῖς ἀνέδην χρῆσθαι τῇ γενναιότητι. οἰκονομεῖ δὲ πώλου μὲν θυμὸν χαλινὸς καὶ ῥυτῆρες καὶ ἱππέως καὶ ἡνιόχου τέχνη· ψυχὴν δὲ ἀνδρὸς λόγος οὐκ ἀργὸς οὐδὲ ῥυπῶν οὐδὲ ἠμελημένος, ἀλλὰ ἀνακεκραμένος ἤθει καὶ πάθει καὶ μὴ παρέχων σχολὴν τοῖς ἀκροωμένοις τὰς φωνὰς ἐξετάζειν καὶ τὰς ἐν αὐταῖς ἡδονάς, ἀλλὰ ἀνίστασθαι προσαναγκάζων καὶ συνενθουσιᾶν, ὥσπερ ὑπὸ σάλπιγγι νῦν μὲν τὸ ἐφορμητικὸν φθεγγομένῃ, νῦν δὲ τὸ ἀνακλητικόν.

9. Εἰ τοιούτου δεῖ λόγου τοῖς φιλοσοφίας ἐφιεμένοις, τὸν ἔχοντα ἀθρητέον καὶ δοκιμαστέον καὶ αἱρετέον, ἐάν τε πρεσβύτης οὗτος ᾖ ἐάν τε νέος, ἐάν τε πένης ἐάν τε πλούσιος, ἐάν <τε ἄδοξος ἐάν τε>[6] ἔνδοξος· ἀσθενέστερον δέ, οἶμαι, καὶ νεότητος γῆρας καὶ πλούτου πενία καὶ δόξης ἀδοξία. οἷς δ' ἂν τὰ ἐλαττώματα ταῦτα προσῇ, ῥᾷον ἐπ' αὐτοὺς οἱ ἄνθρωποι παραγίγνονται, καὶ γεγόνασιν αἱ παρὰ τῆς τύχης συμφοραὶ πρὸς φιλοσοφίαν ἐφόδια· καὶ ὅτι μὲν πένης

[6] suppl. Davies[2], Trapp

for busying themselves with syllables and stammering along with an unintelligent class of children.

But the main part of philosophy and the road leading to it require a teacher who uplifts the souls of the young, guides their ambitions, and aims at nothing other than moderating their desires by means of pains and pleasures, much as horse trainers do: they neither snuff out the high spirits of the colts, nor allow them to indulge their natural exuberance unchecked. What controls the colts' high spirits are bits and reins, applied by the skill of riders and charioteers. But what controls a man's soul is reasoned discourse that is not slack, slovenly, or negligent, but so imbued with ethical character and feeling, as not to allow its listeners any time to examine the words for the pleasures they contain, but forces them to rise up and be inspired, as to the call of a trumpet, at one time sounding the charge, at another time the retreat.[24]

9. So, if a discourse like that is needed by those seeking philosophy, we ought to scrutinize, evaluate, and choose the person who possesses it, whether he be old or young, rich or poor, obscure or famous. Now, I consider old age to be inferior to youth, poverty to wealth, and obscurity to fame. But since men in general more readily associate with those who suffer such disadvantages, these calamities caused by fortune have actually paved the way to philoso-

[24] A similar description of Maximus' philosophical discourse that builds on rhetoric but inspires souls to pursue virtue is at *Or.* 25.6.

ἣν ὁ Σωκράτης, ὁ πένης εὐθὺς μιμήσεται τὸν Σωκράτην· ὡς ὠνάμεθα ὅτι μὴ καὶ οἱ σιμοὶ καὶ οἱ προγάστορες ἀμφισβητοῦσιν φιλοσοφίας· ὅτι δὲ Σωκράτης οὐκ ἐπὶ τοὺς πένητας ὠθεῖτο μόνον, ἀλλὰ καὶ ἐπὶ τοὺς πλουσίους καὶ τοὺς ἐνδόξους καὶ τοὺς εὐγενεστάτους, διαμέμνηται οὐδείς. ἡγεῖτο γάρ, οἶμαι, ὁ Σωκράτης Αἰσχίνου μὲν φιλοσοφήσαντος καὶ Ἀντισθένους ὄνασθαι ἂν ὀλίγα τὴν Ἀθηναίων πόλιν· {μᾶλλον δὲ μηδένα τῶν τότε, πλὴν ἡμᾶς τοὺς ἔπειτα, κατὰ τὴν μνήμην τῶν λόγων·}[7] εἰ δὲ Ἀλκιβιάδης ἐφιλοσόφει, ἢ Κριτίας ἢ Κριτόβουλος ἢ Καλλίας, οὐδὲν ἂν τῶν δεινῶν τοῖς τότε Ἀθηναίοις ξυνέπεσεν. οὐδὲ γὰρ ἡ Διογένους ζήλωσις θυλάκιον καὶ βακτηρία, ἀλλ' ἔξεστίν που καὶ ταῦτα περιβεβλημένον Σαρδαναπάλλου εἶναι κακοδαιμονέστερον. ὁ Ἀρίστιππος ἐκεῖνος πορφυρίδι ἀμπισχόμενος καὶ μύροις χριόμενος, οὐχ ἧττον τοῦ Διογένους ἐσωφρόνει. ὥσπερ γάρ, εἴ τις δύναμιν σώ-

7 del. Markland

25 Aeschines from the Attic deme of Sphettus (Aeschines Socraticus) was a student of Socrates. He was present at his trial and death and composed Socratic dialogues. Fragments of his *Alcibiades* are paraphrased in *Orr.* 6.6, 18.4, and 38.4.

26 Socrates' student present at his death, an austere proto-Cynic; cf. Diog. Laert. 6.1–19.

27 This observation is intrusive and is best deleted.

28 Alcibiades championed the disastrous Sicilian Expedition in 415 BC and, when exiled, aided the Spartans. He and Critias

phy. Thus, because Socrates was poor, a poor person will readily imitate Socrates. (How fortunate we are, though, that people with flat noses and pot bellies do not also lay claim to philosophy!) Nobody remembers, however, that Socrates did not associate only with the poor, but also with the rich, the famous, and the most noble. This was because Socrates believed, in my opinion, that the city of Athens would derive little benefit from the philosophizing of Aeschines[25] and Antisthenes,[26] [or rather none of their contemporaries would benefit, although we later generations do for their recording of his words][27] but that if Alcibiades,[28] or Critias,[29] or Critobulus,[30] or Callias[31] had been practicing philosophy, none of those disasters would have befallen their contemporary Athenians. Nor does carrying a sack and staff count as emulating Diogenes,[32] because someone outfitted with these may well be more wretched than Sardanapallus.[33] Indeed, illustrious Aristippus,[34] who was clothed in purple garments and bathed in perfume, exercised no less self-control than Diogenes. Here is the

are often cited as failed students of Socrates; see also *Orr.* 3.8, 7.7, 18.6, and 22.5. [29] Critias became one of the "Thirty Tyrants" and was killed in 403 BC.

[30] A follower of Socrates famed for his beauty; see also *Orr.* 18.4–5, 20.8, and 21.3. [31] A wealthy Athenian (ca. 450–370 BC) and follower of Socrates; see also *Orr.* 14.7, 38.4, and 39.5.

[32] Diogenes the Cynic, fourth-century austere wandering critic of social norms; cf. Diog. Laert. 6.20–80.

[33] A legendary Assyrian king, notorious for his effeminacy and hedonism, who immolated himself; cf. Diod. Sic. 2.23 and 2.27.2. He is also cited at *Orr.* 4.9, 7.7, 14.2, 15.8, 29.1, and 32.3 and 9.

[34] From Cyrene, an associate of Socrates and champion of hedonism.

ματος παρεσκευάσατο οὐδὲν ὑπὸ πυρὸς λυμαινομένην, ἐθάρσει ἄν, οἶμαι, καὶ τῇ Αἴτνῃ αὐτοῦ παραδοὺς τὸ σῶμα, οὕτω καὶ ὅστις πρὸς ἡδονὴν παρεσκεύασται καλῶς, οὐδὲ ἐν αὐταῖς ὧν θάλπεται οὐδὲ ἐμπίμπραται οὐδὲ ἐκτήκεται.

10. Ἐξεταστέον δὴ τὸν φιλόσοφον οὐ σχήματι, οὐχ ἡλικίᾳ, οὐ τύχῃ, ἀλλὰ γνώμῃ καὶ λόγῳ καὶ παρασκευῇ ψυχῆς, ὑφ' ὧν μόνων χειροτονεῖται φιλόσοφος· τὰ δὲ ἄλλα ταυτὶ παρὰ τῆς τύχης σχήματα ἔοικεν τοῖς ἐν Διονύσου περιβλήμασιν. τὸ μὲν γὰρ τῶν ποιημάτων κάλλος ἓν καὶ ταὐτόν, ἐάν τε δυνάστης ὁ λέγων ᾖ ἐάν τε οἰκέτης· αἱ δὲ χρεῖαι τῶν δραμάτων μεταποιοῦσι τὰ σχήματα· ὁ Ἀγαμέμνων τὸ σκῆπτρον φέρει, ὁ βουκόλος διφθέραν, ὁ Ἀχιλλεὺς ὅπλα, Τήλεφος ῥάκια καὶ θύλακον. ἀκροῶνται δὲ οἱ θεώμενοι οὐδὲν μᾶλλον τοῦ Τηλέφου ἢ τοῦ Ἀγαμέμνονος· ἀποτείνεται γὰρ ἡ ψυχὴ ἐπὶ τὰ ποιήματα αὐτά, οὐ τὰς τύχας τῶν λεγόντων.

Νόμιζε δὴ κἀν τοῖς τῶν φιλοσόφων λόγοις, τὸ μὲν καλὸν οὐκ εἶναι παντοδαπὸν οὐδὲ διαπεφορημένον, ἀλλ' ἓν καὶ αὐτὸ αὑτῷ παραπλήσιον· τοὺς δὲ ἀγωνιστὰς αὐτούς, ἄλλον ἄλλῳ σχήματι ὑπὸ τῆς τύχης περιβεβλήμενον, εἰσπέμπεσθαι ἐπὶ τὴν σκηνὴν τοῦ βίου, Πυθαγόραν μὲν πορφυρᾷ ἀμπισχόμενον, τρίβωνι δὲ Σωκράτην, Ξενοφῶντα δὲ θώρακι καὶ ἀσπίδι, τὸν δὲ ἐκ τῆς Σινώπης ἀγωνιστήν, κατὰ τὸν Τήλεφον ἐκεῖνον, βακτηρίᾳ καὶ θυλάκῳ. συνετέλει δὲ αὐτοῖς καὶ τὰ σχήματα αὐτὰ πρὸς τὴν δραματουργίαν, καὶ

point: just as someone who had managed to make his body resistant to fire would, I believe, confidently commit his body even to Aetna, so anyone who is well prepared to resist pleasures would not overheat in their midst, catch on fire, or melt away.

10. Therefore we must not judge a philosopher by his appearance, age, or fortune, but by his judgment, discourse, and the disposition of his soul—by these alone may he be judged a philosopher. All those other attributes determined by fortune are like costumes in the theater of Dionysus. The beauty of the poetry is one and the same, whether spoken by a king or a slave, whereas their trappings vary as required by the play. Agamemnon carries his scepter, the herdsman wears a leather tunic, Achilles has weapons, and Telephus[35] has his rags and sack. Nonetheless, the audience listens just as closely to Telephus as to Agamemnon, for the soul pays attention to the poetry itself, not the fortune of the speakers.

You must then acknowledge that the good in the discourses of philosophers as well is neither variable nor diverse, but is whole and consistent with itself. Yet the performers themselves step onto the stage of life dressed in this or that garb assigned them by fortune—Pythagoras in purple robes, Socrates in his threadbare cloak, Xenophon with his breastplate and shield, and the performer from Sinope,[36] like that character Telephus, with his staff and sack. Their particular trappings contribute to their dramatic performances, and for this reason Pythagoras aston-

[35] A Mysian king wounded by Achilles, famously portrayed in rags by Euripides and parodied in Aristophanes' *Acharnians*.

[36] Diogenes.

διὰ τοῦτο ὁ μὲν Πυθαγόρας ἐξέπληττεν, ὁ δὲ Σωκράτης ἤλεγχεν, ὁ δὲ Ξενοφῶν ἔπειθεν, ὁ δὲ Διογένης ὠνείδιζεν.

Ὦ μακάριοι μὲν τῶν δραμάτων οἱ ὑποκριταί, μακάριοι δὲ τῶν ἀκουσμάτων οἱ θεαταί. τίς ἂν ἡμῖν καὶ νῦν ποιητὴς καὶ ἀγωνιστὴς γένοιτο οὐκ ἀσχήμων οὐδὲ ἄφωνος, ἀλλ᾽ ὁμιλεῖν ἀξιόχρεως θεάτροις Ἑλληνικοῖς; ζητῶμεν τὸν ἄνδρα· τάχα που φανήσεται, καὶ φανεὶς οὐκ ἀτιμασθήσεται.

ished his hearers, Socrates refuted them, Xenophon persuaded them, and Diogenes chastised them.

Oh, blessed were the actors in those plays, and blessed the spectators who heard them! But now, who now might be our own poet and performer, one who is neither inelegant nor speechless, but worthy of playing in the theaters of Hellas? Let us seek that man, and perhaps he will make his appearance. And if he does, he shall not lack due esteem![37]

[37] This is most likely meant to apply to Maximus himself.

# *ORATION* 2

## INTRODUCTION

This oration treats a perennial theological issue, the representation of divinities by means of images (*agalmata*), broadly defined as any physical manifestations associated with divinity. The argument climaxes in §10, with a Platonic (and Stoic) doxology of god as the invisible, ineffable demiurge of the universe, whose essential being is beyond human ken. Therefore, in the desire to know god, humans must resort to names, living creatures, artistic depictions, and natural phenomena as reminders of him.

A major portion of the oration consists of an entertaining anthropological survey of human forms of worship and depictions of god (often with a dose of sarcasm), beginning with the natural world and the association of gods with the sea, mountains, trees, caves, springs, and rivers. As for urban dwellers, the question is posed (but not taken up) as to whether they need images at all, or if words alone suffice (§1). Just as humans invented writing to refresh their memories, they need symbols (*sēmeia*) to awaken their recollection of the gods (§2). Whereas the Greeks honor the gods with artistic depictions of the human form (§3), other cultures worship god through a wide array of symbols, including fire, like the Persians (who sacrifice Greek cities to it!) (§4), or the Egyptians, who worship

animals, including the crocodile, as illustrated by the story of the "god" who killed a mother's son (§5). In the time of Alexander, the Indians worshipped a giant snake that consumed herds of animals dedicated to it (§6). Natural wonders also become manifestations of the divine: a cavern in the Atlas Mountain that never floods (§7), and the Marsyas and Maeander rivers that miraculously divide up sacrifices meant for one or the other, when cast into their common source (§8). After a summary of the universal use of symbols to honor gods, the question is posed: Should one make images of the gods, or not? (§9). Because of human inability to know the ineffable god directly, we must resort to symbols (*symbola*), just like lovers who are reminded of their beloved by seeing physical objects like lyres and javelins associated with him. All these various ways of evoking remembrance of god are acceptable, whether by the Greek artistry of Phidias[1] or by the Egyptian worship of animals, as long as humans know (*ἴστωσαν*) god, love (*ἐράτωσαν*) him, and remember (*μνημονευέτωσαν*) him (§10).

[1] In Dio Chrysostom's *Olympic Oration* (12.55–85), "Phidias" delivers a long defense of his statue of Zeus that shares elements with Maximus' account.

# *ORATION* 2

## Εἰ θεοῖς ἀγάλματα ἱδρυτέον

1. Ἀρωγοὶ ἀνθρώποις θεοί, πάντες μὲν πᾶσιν, ἄλλοι δὲ ἄλλοις ἐνομίσθησαν κατὰ τὴν φήμην τῶν ὀνομάτων, καὶ διένειμαν αὐτοῖς οἱ ἄνθρωποι τιμὰς καὶ ἀγάλματα οἱ ἐς τὰ ἴδια ἕκαστοι ὠφεληθέντες. οὕτω μὲν ναῦται ἐπὶ ἀκλύστου πέτρας ἀνέθηκαν οἴακας θαλαττίοις· οὕτω δέ τις ποιμένων τὸν Πᾶνα τιμᾷ ἐλάτην αὐτῷ ὑψηλὴν ἐξελόμενος ἢ ἄντρον βαθύ· καὶ γεωργοὶ Διόνυσον τιμῶσιν, πήξαντες ἐν ὀρχάτῳ αὐτοφυὲς πρέμνον, ἀγροικικὸν ἄγαλμα· ἱερὰ δὲ Ἀρτέμιδος πηγαὶ ναμάτων καὶ κοῖλαι νάπαι καὶ ἀνθηροὶ λειμῶνες· ἐπεφήμισαν δὲ καὶ Διὶ ἀγάλματα οἱ πρῶτοι ἄνθρωποι κορυφὰς ὀρῶν, Ὄλυμπον καὶ Ἴδην, καὶ εἴ τι ἄλλο ὄρος πλησιάζει τῷ οὐρανῷ. ἔστιν που καὶ ποταμῶν τιμή, ἢ κατ᾽ ὠφέλειαν, ὥσπερ Αἰγυπτίοις πρὸς τὸν Νεῖλον, ἢ κατὰ κάλλος, ὡς Θετταλοῖς πρὸς τὸν Πηνειόν, ἢ κατὰ μέγεθος, ὡς Σκύθαις πρὸς τὸν Ἴστρον, ἢ κατὰ μῦθον, ὡς Αἰτωλοῖς πρὸς Ἀχελῷον, ἢ κατὰ

# *ORATION* 2

## Whether images should be set up for the gods

1. The gods are helpers of mankind. In fact, all the gods provide help to all men, but because of the reputations derived from their various names, different gods have been thought to help different groups of men, and they have assigned honors and images to them according to the particular benefits each group has received.[1] Thus it is that sailors came to dedicate rudders on rocks untouched by waves to the gods of the sea; some shepherds select a tall pine or deep cave to honor Pan; and farmers honor Dionysus by fixing an uncultivated tree trunk in an orchard as a rustic image. Sacred to Artemis are the sources of rivers, deep glens, and flowery meadows. Zeus too had images consecrated to him by the earliest men in the form of mountain peaks such as Olympus, Ida, and any other mountain reaching to heaven. Rivers too receive their honors. The Egyptians revere the Nile for its benefits; the Thessalians the Peneus for its beauty; the Scythians the Ister for its size; the Aetolians the Achelous for its mythol-

[1] The term "image" (ἄγαλμα) refers not just to statues or artistic representations but to any physical manifestation associated with divinity. *Or.* 39.5 also advances the (Stoic) view that god is one, but that we assign various names to his powers.

νόμον, ὡς Σπαρτιάταις πρὸς τὸν Εὐρώταν, ἢ κατὰ τελετήν, ὡς Ἀθηναίοις πρὸς Ἰλισσόν.

Εἶτα ποταμοὶ μὲν διέλαχον τὰς τιμὰς κατὰ τὴν χρείαν τῶν ὠφελουμένων, καὶ αἱ τέχναι τιμῆς θεῶν ἑκάστη εὔπορος,[1] ἄλλο ἄλλη προστησαμένη ἄγαλμα, εἰ δέ πού τι γένος ἀνθρώπων ἐστὶν οὐ θαλάττιον οὐδὲ γεωργικόν, ἀλλ᾽ ἀστυπολοῦν καὶ ἀνακεκραμένον κοινωνίᾳ πολιτικῇ νόμου καὶ λόγου, ἆρα τούτοις ἀγέραστον ἔσται τὸ θεῖον καὶ ἀτίμητον; ἢ τιμήσουσιν μέν, τῇ δὲ φήμῃ μόνῃ, ἀγαλμάτων δὲ καὶ ἱδρυμάτων οὐκ οἰήσονται δεῖν τοῖς θεοῖς; οὐδὲν γὰρ δεῖν τοῖς θεοῖς ἀγαλμάτων οὐδὲ ἱδρυμάτων μᾶλλον ἢ εἰκόνων ἀγαθοῖς ἀνδράσιν.

2. Ὥσπερ δέ, οἶμαι, τῷ κατὰ τὰς φωνὰς λόγῳ οὐδὲν δεῖ πρὸς σύστασιν χαρακτήρων Φοινικείων τινῶν ἢ Ἰωνικῶν ἢ Ἀττικῶν ἢ Ἀσσυρίων ἢ Αἰγυπτίων, ἀλλ᾽ ἡ ἀνθρωπίνη ἀσθένεια ἐξεῦρεν σημεῖα ταῦτα, ἐν οἷς ἀποτιθεμένη τὴν αὑτῆς ἀμβλύτητα ἐξ αὐτῶν ἀναμάττεται τὴν αὖθις μνήμην· οὕτως ἀμέλει καὶ τῇ τοῦ θείου φύσει δεῖ μὲν οὐδὲν ἀγαλμάτων οὐδὲ ἱδρυμάτων, ἀλλὰ ἀσθενὲς ὂν κομιδῇ τὸ ἀνθρώπειον καὶ διεστὸς τοῦ θείου ὅσον οὐρανὸς γῆς, σημεῖα ταῦτα

[1] τιμῆς θεῶν ἑκάστη εὔπορος Hobein, Trapp: τιμῆς θεῶν ἑκάστης ὑπ᾽ ὄρος R: τιμῶσι θεὸν ἑκάστης ἔφορον Markland, Dübner: obel. Koniaris

ogy;[2] the Spartans the Eurotas because of local customs;[3] and the Athenians the Ilissus because of its ritual associations.[4]

So, if rivers have been granted honors according to the uses made of them by their beneficiaries, and if each of the arts capable of honoring the gods has dedicated a different image for each,[5] then what about a class of men who are neither sailors nor farmers, but live in cities and are integrated into a political community based on law and reason? Will their divinities be deprived of offerings and honors? Or will they indeed honor them, but only with words, in the belief that the gods have no need of images and statues, because the gods do not require images or statues any more than good men need portraits?

2. Indeed, it seems to me that just as oral speech is articulated without the need for written characters, be they Phoenician, Ionian, Attic, Assyrian, or Egyptian (for it was human weakness that occasioned the discovery of these symbols, to which people could entrust their obtuseness and later draw upon to refresh their memory),[6] in precisely the same way, the divine nature is such that it has no need for images or statues. It is rather because the human race is so utterly weak—as far from the gods as earth is from heaven—that people devised these symbols, to

[2] The river god Achelous was featured in many myths, including his fight with Heracles over Deianeira.

[3] Spartans bathed in the cold river after strenuous exercise.

[4] Perhaps an allusion to the rape of Orithyia mentioned at Pl. *Phdr*. 229a–d.

[5] The text of this clause is corrupt. I have adopted the emendation of Hobein and Trapp.

[6] This example is adapted from Pl. *Phdr*. 274d–75b.

ἐμηχανήσατο, ἐν οἷς ἀποθήσεται τὰ τῶν θεῶν ὀνόματα καὶ τὰς φήμας αὐτῶν.

Οἷς μὲν οὖν ἡ μνήμη ἔρρωται, καὶ δύνανται εὐθὺ τοῦ οὐρανοῦ ἀνατεινόμενοι τῇ ψυχῇ τῷ θείῳ ἐντυγχάνειν, οὐδὲν ἴσως δεῖ τούτοις ἀγαλμάτων· σπάνιον δὲ ἐν ἀνθρώποις τὸ τοιοῦτο γένος, καὶ οὐκ ἂν ἐντύχοις δήμῳ ἀθρόῳ τοῦ θείου μνήμονι καὶ μὴ δεομένῳ τοιαύτης ἐπικουρίας· καὶ οἷον τοῖς παισὶν οἱ γραμματισταὶ μηχανῶνται ὑποχαράττοντες αὐτοῖς σημεῖα ἀμυδρά, οἷς ἐπάγοντες τὴν χειρουργίαν ἐθίζονται τῇ μνήμῃ πρὸς τὴν τέχνην, δοκοῦσιν δή μοι καὶ οἱ νομοθέται, καθάπερ τινὶ παίδων ἀγέλῃ, ἐξευρεῖν τοῖς ἀνθρώποις ταυτὶ τὰ ἀγάλματα, σημεῖα τῆς πρὸς τὸ θεῖον τιμῆς καὶ ὥσπερ χειραγωγίαν τινὰ καὶ ὁδὸν πρὸς ἀνάμνησιν.

3. Ἀγαλμάτων δὲ οὐχ εἷς νόμος οὐδὲ εἷς τρόπος οὐδὲ τέχνη μία οὐδὲ ὕλη μία· ἀλλὰ τὸ μὲν Ἑλληνικὸν τιμᾶν τοὺς θεοὺς ἐνόμισαν τῶν ἐν γῇ τοῖς καλλίστοις, ὕλῃ μὲν καθαρᾷ, μορφῇ δὲ ἀνθρωπίνῃ, τέχνῃ δὲ ἀκριβεῖ. καὶ οὐκ ἄλογος ἡ ἀξίωσις τῶν τὰ ἀγάλματα εἰς ἀνθρωπίνην ὁμοιότητα καταστησαμένων· εἰ γὰρ ἀνθρώπου ψυχὴ ἐγγύτατον θεῷ καὶ ἐμφερέστατον, οὐ δήπου εἰκὸς τὸ ὁμοιότατον αὐτῷ περιβαλεῖν, τὸν θεόν, σκήνει ἀτοπωτάτῳ, ἀλλ' ὅπερ ἔμελλεν ψυχαῖς ἀθανάτοις εὔφορόν τε ἔσεσθαι καὶ κοῦφον καὶ εὐκίνητον, μόνον τοῦτο τῶν ἐν γῇ σωμάτων ἀνατεῖνον τὴν κορυφὴν ὑψοῦ, σοβαρὸν καὶ γαῦρον καὶ σύμμετρον, οὔτε διὰ μέγεθος ἐκπληκτικόν, οὔτε διὰ χαίτην φοβερόν,

which they could entrust the names of the gods and their reputations.

Now perhaps people with robust memories, who are able to reach straight to heaven with their souls and encounter the divine directly, do not need these images, but such a class of individuals is rare among humans, and you certainly could not encounter an entire population that was so cognizant of the divine as not to need such assistance. And just as grammar teachers contrive to help their pupils by tracing faint letters for them, over which they guide their handwriting and become accustomed to perform this skill from memory,[7] it seems to me that lawmakers likewise came up with these images for humans, as if for some class of boys, to be symbols of the respect owed to divinity, and to serve as a guiding hand, so to speak, and a pathway to recollection.

3. With regard to images in general there is no single rule, no single form, no single artistry, no single material. The Greeks, however, have made it their custom to honor the gods with the most beautiful things on earth: pure materials, human forms, and precise craftsmanship. Indeed, their decision to establish images in human likeness is not irrational, for if the human soul is the closest thing to god and most like him, then it is certainly unreasonable for god to have enclosed that which is most similar to him in some completely alien form, but rather in one needing to be light, agile, and easily borne by immortal souls, namely the only body on earth that holds high its head, that is imposing, proud, and well proportioned; not huge and frightening, not hairy and fearsome, not heavy and

[7] This example is adapted from Pl. *Prt*. 326d.

οὔτε διὰ βάρος δυσκίνητον, οὔτε διὰ λειότητα ὀλισθηρόν, οὔτε διὰ τραχύτητα ἀντίτυπον, οὔτε διὰ ψυχρότητα ἑρπυστικόν, οὔτε ἰταμὸν διὰ θερμότητα, οὔτε νηκτὸν διὰ μανότητα, οὐκ ὠμοφάγον δι' ἀγριότητα, οὐ ποιηφάγον δι' ἀσθένειαν, ἀλλὰ κεκραμένον μουσικῶς πρὸς τὰ αὑτοῦ ἔργα· {φοβερὸν μὲν δειλοῖς, ἥμερον δὲ ἀγαθοῖς,}[2] βαδιστικὸν μὲν τῇ φύσει, πτηνὸν δὲ τῷ λόγῳ, νηκτὸν δὲ τέχνῃ, σιτοφάγον καὶ γεωπόνον καὶ καρποφάγον καὶ εὔχρουν καὶ εὐσταλὲς καὶ εὐωπὸν καὶ εὐγένειον. διὰ τοιούτου σώματος τύπων τοὺς θεοὺς τιμᾶν ἐνόμισαν οἱ Ἕλληνες.

4. Τὸ δὲ βαρβαρικὸν ὁμοίως μὲν ἅπαντες ξυνετοὶ τοῦ θεοῦ, κατεστήσαντο δὲ αὑτοῖς σημεῖα ἄλλοι ἄλλα. Πέρσαι μὲν πῦρ, ἄγαλμα ἐφήμερον, ἀκόρεστον καὶ ἀδηφάγον· καὶ θύουσιν Πέρσαι πυρί, ἐπιφοροῦντες αὐτῷ τὴν πυρὸς τροφήν, ἐπιλέγοντες· "πῦρ δέσποτα, ἔσθιε." ἄξιον δὲ πρὸς τοὺς Πέρσας εἰπεῖν· "ὦ πάντων γενῶν ἀνοητότατον, οἱ τοσούτων καὶ τηλικούτων ἀγαλμάτων ἀμελήσαντες, γῆς ἡμέρου καὶ ἡλίου λαμπροῦ καὶ θαλάττης πλοΐμου καὶ ποταμῶν γονίμων καὶ ἀέρος τροφίμου καὶ αὐτοῦ οὐρανοῦ, περὶ ἓν μάλιστα ἀσχολεῖσθε τὸ ἀγριώτατον καὶ ὀξύτατον, οὐ ξύλων αὐτῷ τροφὴν χορηγοῦντες μόνον οὐδὲ ἱερείων οὐδὲ θυμιαμάτων· ἀλλὰ τούτῳ τῷ ἀγάλματι καὶ τούτῳ τῷ θεῷ καὶ τὴν Ἐρετρίαν ἀναλῶσαι δεδώκατε καὶ τὰς Ἀθήνας αὐτὰς καὶ τὰ Ἰώνων ἱερὰ καὶ τὰ Ἑλλήνων ἀγάλματα."

[2] del. Trapp ut interpolata

cumbersome, not light and slippery, not rough and hard, not cold and creeping, not hot and darting, not slimy and aquatic, not wild and meat eating, not tame and grass eating, but instead harmoniously composed for its proper activities . . .[8] one equipped to walk by virtue of its nature, to take wing by means of its reason, to swim by means of its skill, to cultivate the land for grain and fruit to eat, a being with a lovely complexion, fine proportions, handsome face, and attractive beard. It is with such physical features that the Greeks have seen fit to honor the gods.

4. Barbarians are all just as conscious of god, but different races have established different symbols for themselves. For the Persians it is fire, an image that is transient, voracious, and insatiable. They sacrifice to it by offering heaps of what it feeds on, as they chant, "Lord Fire, eat this." It is fair to say to the Persians, "Most insane race of all, you neglect so many splendid images like the gentle earth, bright sun, navigable sea, life-giving rivers, nourishing air, and the sky itself, and instead devote your energy exclusively to what is most savage and fierce, and the food you supply it is not wood alone, or sacrificial animals, or incense, but you have allowed this image and this god to consume Eretria,[9] Athens itself,[10] Ionian temples,[11] and Greek images!"

[8] An intrusive gloss is deleted by Trapp: "terrifying to cowardly ones, gentle to good ones."

[9] In 490 BC, during the first Persian invasion.

[10] In 480 BC.

[11] During the Ionian revolt, in 494 BC.

5. Μέμφομαι καὶ τὸν Αἰγυπτίων νόμον. βοῦν ἐκεῖνοι τιμῶσιν καὶ ὄρνιν καὶ τράγον καὶ τοῦ ποταμοῦ τοῦ Νείλου τὰ θρέμματα· ὧν θνητὰ μὲν τὰ σώματα, δειλοὶ δὲ οἱ βίοι, ταπεινὴ δὲ ἡ ὄψις, ἀγεννὴς δὲ ἡ θεραπεία, αἰσχρὰ δὲ ἡ τιμή. ἀποθνήσκει θεὸς Αἰγυπτίοις καὶ πενθεῖται θεὸς καὶ δείκνυται παρ' αὐτοῖς ἱερὸν θεοῦ καὶ τάφος θεοῦ. καὶ Ἕλληνες μὲν θύουσιν καὶ ἀνθρώποις ἀγαθοῖς, καὶ τιμῶνται μὲν αὐτῶν αἱ ἀρεταί, ἀμνημονοῦνται δὲ αἱ συμφοραί· παρὰ δὲ Αἰγυπτίοις ἰσομοιρίαν ἔχει τὸ θεῖον τιμῆς καὶ δακρύων.

Γυναικὶ Αἰγυπτίᾳ θρέμμα ἦν κροκοδείλου σκύλαξ. ἐμακάριζον οἱ Αἰγύπτιοι τὴν γυναῖκα, ὡς τιθηνουμένην θεόν· τινὲς αὐτῶν καὶ προσετρέποντο καὶ αὐτὴν καὶ τὸν τρόφιμον. ἦν αὐτῇ παῖς ἄρτι ἡβάσκων, ἡλικιώτης τοῦ θεοῦ, συναθύρων αὐτῷ καὶ συντρεφόμενος. ὁ δὲ τέως μὲν ὑπὸ ἀσθενείας ἦν τιθασός, προελθὼν δὲ εἰς μέγεθος ἤλεγξεν τὴν φύσιν καὶ διέφθειρεν τὸν παῖδα· ἡ δὲ δύστηνος Αἰγυπτία ἐμακάριζεν τὸν υἱὸν τοῦ θανάτου, ὡς γενόμενον δῶρον ἐφεστίῳ θεῷ.

6. Τὰ μὲν Αἰγυπτίων τοιαῦτα. Ἀλέξανδρος δὲ ἐκεῖνος, Πέρσας ἑλὼν καὶ Βαβυλῶνος κρατήσας καὶ Δαρεῖον χειρωσάμενος, ἦλθεν εἰς τὴν Ἰνδῶν γῆν ἄβατον οὖσαν τέως στρατιᾷ ξένῃ, ὡς Ἰνδοὶ ἔλεγον, πλήν γε Διονύσου. {καὶ Ἀλεξάνδρου}[3] ἐστασίαζον Ἰνδοὶ βασιλεῖς Πῶρος καὶ Ταξίλης. Πῶρον μὲν λαμβάνει ὁ Ἀλέ-

[3] del. Koniaris, Trapp

5. I also fault the custom of the Egyptians, for they worship an ox, bird, goat, and those creatures nourished by the Nile, whose bodies are mortal, whose lives are wretched, whose looks are ugly, whose worship is ignoble, and whose veneration is repulsive. The Egyptians have a god[12] who dies and a god who is mourned, and they even point out both the god's temple and his tomb in their country. Greeks indeed sacrifice to heroic men and honor their virtues, but they pass over their misfortunes, whereas in Egypt divinity receives an equal share of honor and lamentation.

An Egyptian woman once raised a baby crocodile. The Egyptians counted the woman blessed for nourishing a god, and some of them even supplicated both her and her nursling. She also had a son just reaching puberty, who was the same age as that god, and had been raised with it and played with it. As long as it was weak it remained tame, but once it grew large, it revealed its true nature and killed the child. And yet the wretched Egyptian mother considered her son blessed by his death, believing that he had been an offering to the household god.[13]

6. So much for Egyptian practices. After Alexander the Great had conquered Persia, taken Babylon, and captured Darius, he went on to the land of India,[14] where, according to the Indians, no foreign army had previously set foot, except for that of Dionysus.[15] At that time the Indian kings Porus and Taxiles were at war with each other. Alexander

12 Osiris, mourned by Isis.

13 Ael. *NA* 10.21 briefly alludes to this story.

14 These events occurred between 331 and 326 BC.

15 A lengthy account of Dionysus' war against the Indians appears in Nonnus (late 4th-c. AD), *Dionysiaca*, Books 13–17.

ξανδρος, Ταξίλην δὲ κατὰ φιλίαν παρεστήσατο. ἐπεδείκνυεν Ἀλεξάνδρῳ Ταξίλης τὰ θαυμαστὰ τῆς Ἰνδῶν γῆς, ποταμοὺς μεγίστους καὶ ὄρνιθας ποικίλους καὶ εὐώδη φυτὰ καὶ εἴ τι ἄλλο ξένον ὀφθαλμοῖς Ἑλληνικοῖς. ἐν δὲ τοῖς ἔδειξε καὶ ζῷον ὑπερφυές, Διονύσου ἄγαλμα, ᾧ Ἰνδοὶ ἔθυον· δράκων ἦν μῆκος πεντάπλεθρον, ἐτρέφετο δὲ ἐν χωρίῳ κοίλῳ, ἐν κρημνῷ βαθεῖ, τείχει ὑψηλῷ ὑπὲρ τῶν ἄκρων περιβεβλημένος· καὶ ἀνήλισκεν τὰς Ἰνδῶν ἀγέλας, χορηγούντων αὐτῷ τροφὴν βοῦς καὶ ὄϊς, καθάπερ τυράννῳ μᾶλλον ἢ θεῷ.

7. Οἱ ἑσπέριοι Λίβυες οἰκοῦσι γῆς αὐχένα στενὸν καὶ ἐπιμήκη καὶ ἀμφιθάλασσον· σχιζομένη γὰρ κατὰ κορυφὴν τοῦ αὐχένος ἡ ἔξω θάλασσα περιλαμβάνει τὴν γῆν κύματι πολλῷ καὶ πελαγίῳ. τοῖς ἀνθρώποις τούτοις ἱερόν ἐστιν καὶ ἄγαλμα ὁ Ἄτλας· ἔστιν δὲ ὁ Ἄτλας ὄρος κοῖλον, ἐπιεικῶς ὑψηλόν, ἀνεῳγὸς πρὸς τὸ πέλαγος ὥσπερ τὰ θέατρα πρὸς τὸν ἀέρα· τὸ δὲ ἐν μέσῳ τοῦ ὄρους χωρίον αὐλὼν βαθύς, εὔγεως καὶ εὔδενδρος· καὶ ἴδοις ἂν καὶ καρποὺς ἐπὶ τῶν δένδρων, καὶ ὀπτεύσαις ἐκ τῆς κορυφῆς ὥσπερ εἰς φρεατίας ἔδαφος· κατελθεῖν δὲ οὔτε δυνατόν, κρημνῶδες γάρ, οὔτε ἄλλως θέμις. τὸ δὲ ἐν τῷ χωρίῳ θαῦμα, ὁ Ὠκεανὸς πλημμύρων ἐμπίπτει τῇ ἠϊόνι, καὶ τῇ μὲν ἄλλῃ ἀναχεῖται ἐπὶ τὰ πεδία, κατὰ δὲ τὸν Ἄτλαντα αὐτὸν κορυφοῦται τὸ κῦμα· καὶ ἴδοις ἂν τὸ ὕδωρ ἀνεστηκὸς ἐφ' ἑαυτοῦ ὥσπερ τειχίον, οὔτε εἰσρέον ἐπὶ τὰ κοῖλα οὔτε ὑπὸ γῆς ἐρειδόμενον, ἀλλ' ἐκ μέσου τοῦ ὄρους

captured Porus and befriended Taxiles, who then showed Alexander the wonders of the land of India: great rivers, multicolored birds, aromatic plants, and whatever else was strange to Greek eyes. Among these he showed him an enormous creature, a sacred image of Dionysus, to which the Indians used to sacrifice. It was a snake five hundred feet long, nourished in a hollow place, in a deep chasm, and it was surrounded by a high wall above the peaks. It would devour the herds and flocks of the Indians, who supplied it with oxen and sheep for its food, as if for a tyrant rather than a god.

7. The western Libyans inhabit a long and narrow neck of land washed by sea water on both sides.[16] The external sea[17] divides at the tip of the peninsula and surrounds the land with its great sea swell. The sacred area and image for the people there is Atlas, which is a cavernous mountain of considerable height, opening onto the sea as a theater opens to the air. The middle portion of the mountain consists of a deep ravine with rich soil and fine trees. You could see fruit on the trees, and could look down from the summit as if into the bottom of a cistern. Because of the steep cliffs descent is impossible, and in any case is forbidden. And the marvel of the place is this. At high tide the Ocean crashes onto the shore and everywhere else inundates the plain, but the wave crests where Atlas itself is located, and you could see the water standing up on itself like a wall, neither flooding the hollow places nor supported by the land, for a mass of air forms a hollow grove

[16] The peninsula opposite Gibraltar.
[17] That is, the Atlantic Ocean.

καὶ τοῦ ὕδατος ἀὴρ πολύς, κοῖλον ἄλσος. τοῦτο Λιβύων καὶ ἱερὸν καὶ θεὸς καὶ ὅρκος καὶ ἄγαλμα.

8. Κελτοὶ σέβουσιν μὲν Δία, ἄγαλμα δὲ Διὸς Κελτικὸν ὑψηλὴ δρῦς. Παίονες σέβουσιν μὲν Ἥλιον, ἄγαλμα δὲ Ἡλίου Παιονικὸν δίσκος βραχὺς ὑπὲρ μακροῦ ξύλου. Ἀράβιοι σέβουσι μὲν <θεόν>,[4] ὅντινα δὲ οὐκ οἶδα· τὸ δὲ ἄγαλμα εἶδον, λίθος ἦν τετράγωνος. Παφίοις ἡ μὲν Ἀφροδίτη τὰς τιμὰς ἔχει· τὸ δὲ ἄγαλμα οὐκ ἂν εἰκάσαις ἄλλῳ τῳ ἢ πυραμίδι λευκῇ, ἡ δὲ ὕλη ἀγνοεῖται. Λυκίοις ὁ Ὄλυμπος πῦρ ἐκδιδοῖ, οὐχ ὅμοιον τῷ Αἰτναίῳ, ἀλλ' εἰρηνικὸν καὶ σύμμετρον, καὶ ἔστιν αὐτοῖς τὸ πῦρ τοῦτο καὶ ἱερὸν καὶ ἄγαλμα. Φρύγες οἱ περὶ Κελαινὰς νεμόμενοι τιμῶσιν ποταμοὺς δύο, Μαρσύαν καὶ Μαίανδρον· εἶδον τοὺς ποταμούς· ἀφίησιν αὐτοὺς πηγὴ μία, ἣ προελθοῦσα ἐπὶ τὸ ὄρος ἀφανίζεται κατὰ νώτου τῆς πόλεως, καὖθις ἐκδιδοῖ ἐκ τοῦ ἄστεος, διελοῦσα τοῖς ποταμοῖς καὶ τὸ ὕδωρ καὶ τὰ ὀνόματα· ὁ μὲν ἐπὶ Λυδίας ῥεῖ, ὁ Μαίανδρος· ὁ δὲ αὐτοῦ περὶ τὰ πεδία ἀναλίσκεται. θύουσιν Φρύγες τοῖς ποταμοῖς, οἱ μὲν ἀμφοτέροις, οἱ δὲ τῷ Μαιάνδρῳ, οἱ δὲ τῷ Μαρσύᾳ· καὶ ἐμβάλλουσιν τὰ μηρία εἰς τὰς πηγάς, ἐπιφημίσαντες τοὔνομα τοῦ ποταμοῦ, ὁποτέρῳ ἔθυσαν· ἀπενεχθέντα δὲ ἐπὶ τὸ ὄρος καὶ ὑποδύντα σὺν τῷ ὕδατι, οὔτ' ἂν ἐπὶ τὸν Μαρσύαν ἐκδοθείη τὰ τοῦ Μαιάνδρου, οὔτ' ἐπὶ τὸν

[4] suppl. Meiser, Trapp

between the mountain and the water. This is the Libyans' temple, the god to whom they swear, and his image.

8. The Celts worship Zeus, and the Celtic image of Zeus is a tall oak tree. The Paeonians worship Helios, and the Paeonian image of Helios is a small disk atop a tall pole. The Arabians worship a god, but which one I don't know; yet I have seen its image, which was a square stone. Aphrodite is honored by the Paphians, but you could only compare her image to a white pyramid of some unknown material.[18] Among the Lycians Mt. Olympus[19] spews fire—not like that of Aetna, but a calm and moderate fire—and this fire is their temple and image. The Phrygians who dwell around Celaenae worship two rivers, the Marsyas and the Maeander. I have seen these rivers. A single source feeds them, but once it reaches the mountain, it disappears beneath the back of the city, only to discharge again from the town, having divided its waters into those rivers with their two names. The Maeander flows on to Lydia, while the other terminates around the plain. Some of the Phrygians sacrifice to both rivers, others to either the Maeander or the Marsyas. They throw the thigh bones of the victims into the waters at their source, calling out the name of whichever river their sacrifice was intended for. Once these thigh bones are borne to the mountain and submerge with the water, the ones meant for the Maeander never emerge in the Marsyas, nor do those meant for the Marsyas ever emerge in the Maean-

18 Paphos on Cyprus was a cult center of Aphrodite. The pyramid was depicted on Cypriot coins of the Roman period.

19 Probably Mt. Chimera.

Μαίανδρον τὰ τοῦ Μαρσύου· εἰ δὲ ἀμφοῖν εἴη, διαιροῦνται τὸ δῶρον. ὄρος Καππαδόκαις καὶ θεὸς καὶ ὅρκος καὶ ἄγαλμα, Μαιώταις λίμνη, Τάναϊς Μασσαγέταις.

9. Ὢ πολλῶν καὶ παντοδαπῶν ἀγαλμάτων· ὧν τὰ μὲν ὑπὸ τέχνης ἐγένετο, τὰ δὲ διὰ χρείαν ἠγαπήθη, τὰ δὲ δι' ὠφέλειαν ἐτιμήθη, τὰ δὲ δι' ἔκπληξιν ἐθαυμάσθη, τὰ δὲ διὰ μέγεθος ἐθειάσθη, τὰ δὲ διὰ κάλλος ἐπῃνέθη. πλὴν οὐδὲν γένος, οὐ βάρβαρον οὐχ Ἑλληνικόν, οὐ θαλάττιον οὐκ ἠπειρωτικόν, οὐ νομαδικὸν οὐκ ἀστυπολοῦν, ἀνέχεται τὸ μὴ καταστήσασθαι σύμβολα ἄττα τῆς τῶν θεῶν τιμῆς. πῶς ἂν οὖν τις διαιτήσαι τὸν λόγον, εἴτε χρὴ ποιεῖσθαι ἀγάλματα θεῶν εἴτε μή;

Εἰ μὲν γὰρ ἄλλοις τισὶν ἐνομοθετοῦμεν ὑπερορίοις ἀνθρώποις ἔξω τοῦ καθ' ἡμᾶς αἰθέρος, ἄρτι ἐκ γῆς ἀναφυομένοις ἢ ὑπό τινος Προμηθέως πλαττομένοις, ἀπείροις βίου καὶ νόμου καὶ λόγου, δέοι ἂν ἴσως τοῦ σκέμματος, πότερα ἐατέον τουτὶ τὸ γένος ἐπὶ τῶν αὐτοφυῶν τούτων ἀγαλμάτων, προσκυνοῦντας οὐκ ἐλέφαντα οὐδὲ χρυσόν, οὐδὲ δρῦν οὐδὲ κέδρον, οὐδὲ ποταμὸν οὐδὲ ὄρνιθα, ἀλλὰ τὸν ἥλιον ἀνίσχοντα, καὶ τὴν σελήνην λάμπουσαν, καὶ τὸν οὐρανὸν πεποικιλμένον, καὶ γῆν αὐτὴν καὶ ἀέρα αὐτόν, καὶ πῦρ πᾶν καὶ ὕδωρ πᾶν, ἢ καὶ τούτους καθείρξομεν εἰς ἀνάγκην τιμῆς ξύλων ἢ λίθων ἢ τύπων; εἰ δέ ἐστιν οὗτος κοινὸς πάντων νόμος, τὰ κείμενα ἐῶμεν, τὰς φήμας τῶν

der.[20] If, however, they are meant for both, then the rivers divide the offering. The Cappadocians have a mountain as the god to which they swear and which serves as his image; the Maeotae have a lake; and the Massagetae have the Tanais River.

9. Oh, how many different images there are! Some are created by artistic skill, some are cherished for their usefulness, some are honored for their benefits, some are admired for their wondrous characteristics, some deified for their size, and some praised for their beauty. Indeed there is not a single race, be it barbarian or Greek, maritime or continental, nomadic or urban, that can refrain from establishing symbols of one kind or another for the honor they pay their gods. So how can we resolve our question, whether one ought to make images of the gods or not?

Now if we were making laws for some foreign people living beyond our own climate, ones who had just sprung from the earth, or were fashioned by some Prometheus, and thus had no experience of life, law, and reason, we might then need to speculate whether these people should be left alone with their natural images, to make obeisance neither to gold or ivory, oak or cedar, river or bird, but instead to worship the rising sun, the resplendent moon, the bespangled heaven, the earth itself and the air itself, and all fire and all water—or whether we should compel them to limit their homage to depictions fashioned of wood or stone. But if such is the custom shared by all peoples, we should leave settled practices alone, accept

[20] Strabo (6.2.9) relates a similar story of the Eurotas and Alpheus rivers.

*θεῶν ἀποδεχόμενοι καὶ φυλάττοντες αὐτῶν τὰ σύμβολα ὥσπερ καὶ τὰ ὀνόματα.*

10. *Ὁ μὲν γὰρ θεός, ὁ τῶν ὄντων πατὴρ καὶ δημιουργός,* {*ὁ*}[5] *πρεσβύτερος μὲν ἡλίου, πρεσβύτερος δὲ οὐρανοῦ, κρείττων δὲ χρόνου καὶ αἰῶνος καὶ πάσης ῥεούσης φύσεως, ἀνώνυμος νομοθέταις*[6] *καὶ ἄρρητος φωνῇ καὶ ἀόρατος ὀφθαλμοῖς· οὐκ ἔχοντες δὲ αὐτοῦ λαβεῖν τὴν οὐσίαν, ἐπερειδόμεθα φωναῖς καὶ ὀνόμασιν καὶ ζῴοις, καὶ τύποις χρυσοῦ καὶ ἐλέφαντος καὶ ἀργύρου, καὶ φυτοῖς καὶ ποταμοῖς καὶ κορυφαῖς καὶ νάμασιν, ἐπιθυμοῦντες μὲν αὐτοῦ τῆς νοήσεως, ὑπὸ δὲ ἀσθενείας τὰ παρ' ἡμῖν καλὰ τῇ ἐκείνου φύσει ἐπονομάζοντες· αὐτὸ ἐκεῖνο τὸ τῶν ἐρώντων πάθος, οἷς ἥδιστον μὲν εἰς θέαμα οἱ τῶν παιδικῶν τύποι, ἡδὺ δὲ εἰς ἀνάμνησιν καὶ λύρα καὶ ἀκόντιον καὶ θῶκός που καὶ δρόμος, καὶ πᾶν ἁπλῶς τὸ ἐπεγεῖρον τὴν μνήμην τοῦ ἐρωμένου.*

*Τί μοι τὸ λοιπὸν ἐξετάζειν καὶ νομοθετεῖν ὑπὲρ ἀγαλμάτων; θεῖον ἴστωσαν γένος, ἴστω*<*σαν*>[7] *μόνον. εἰ δὲ Ἕλληνας μὲν ἐπεγείρει πρὸς τὴν μνήμην τοῦ θεοῦ ἡ Φειδίου τέχνη, Αἰγυπτίους δὲ ἡ πρὸς τὰ ζῷα τιμή, καὶ ποταμὸς ἄλλους καὶ πῦρ ἄλλους, οὐ νεμεσῶ τῆς διαφωνίας· ἴστωσαν μόνον, ἐράτωσαν μόνον, μνημονευέτωσαν.*

[5] del. Markland, Trapp
[6] *νομοθέταις* Reiske, Dübner, Trapp: *νομοθέτης* R
[7] suppl. Reiske, Dübner, Trapp

what is reputed of the gods, and preserve their symbols just as we do their names.

10. For god, the "father and creator"[21] of all that exists, is more ancient than the sun, more ancient than the heavens, mightier than time, eternity, and all the flux of nature. Legislators cannot name him, voices cannot speak of him, eyes cannot see him.[22] Since we are unable to grasp his essential being, we must resort to words, names, and living creatures; to depictions in gold, ivory, and silver; to plants, rivers, mountain peaks, and streams. We desire to know him, but because of our human weakness we denominate his nature by the beautiful things around us. It is precisely what lovers experience: they take the greatest pleasure in seeing depictions of their boyfriends, but they are also pleased when reminded of them by a lyre, javelin, bench, or racetrack—in short, by anything that arouses the memory of their beloved.

Why, then, should I continue this investigation and lay down laws regarding images? Let people know the race of the gods, just let them know it. If the artistry of Phidias awakens the memory of god for the Greeks, if the worship of animals does so for the Egyptians, if it is a river for some, or fire for others, I am not offended by the differences. Just let them know god, just let them love him, just let them remember him.

[21] An echo of Pl. *Ti.* 41a: δημιουργὸς πατήρ τε (creator and father).

[22] Cf. the similar descriptions of the ineffable Platonic god at *Orr.* 11.9 and 41.2.

# *ORATION* 3

## INTRODUCTION

What Socrates did or did not say in his courtroom defense in 399 BC was and is an open question. Two very different versions are extant in the *Apologies* of Plato and Xenophon, but there are indications of many more examples.[1] Maximus, however, argues that Socrates actually remained silent and made no defense at all. It is, in Trapp's words, "plausible . . . to see a neat piece of rhetorical one-upmanship on Maximus' part: how to defend Socrates, while at the same time impugning the legitimacy of everybody else's *Apologies*."[2]

The oration is in fact a clever declamatory exercise, which he calls an inquiry (*skemma*), on a subject of debate that, he claims, continues to his day. It is a rhetorical tour de force marshaling an array of arguments, analogies, hypotheticals, and historical examples.[3] It opens with the question of why a man who expertly fashioned his virtuous life as a work of art should meet with such diverse

[1] See the list at Trapp (1997a, 24).

[2] Trapp (1997a, 25).

[3] The fact that only this oration, besides *Or*. 26, was named in the *Suda* entry on Maximus suggests that it enjoyed subsequent popularity. For the *Suda* text, see the General Introduction.

evaluations (§1). After a précis of Socrates' trial, imprisonment, and execution drawn from Plato's *Apology*, *Crito*, and *Phaedo* (§2), the speaker asks whether or not Socrates did the right thing. First comes an exposition *ex contrario* (in one long sentence) of what Socrates did *not* do, namely, resort to every rhetorical ploy and grovel before the jury to win his acquittal (§3). But that raises the question of what good it would have done Socrates to defend himself before such an unqualified and ill-disposed jury anyway (§4). An interlocutor argues that Socrates should at any rate have defended himself against the charges of corrupting the youth and of introducing new *daimonia*, but the speaker counters that a jury selected by lot in the Heliaea court is incapable of adjudicating such an issue (§5). Furthermore, persuasion would not be effective because honorable conduct can be evaluated only when it actually enjoys respect (*aidōs*) (§6). A second interlocutor says that Socrates should have tried to save his life, but Socrates preserved his virtue in the face of death by refusing to say anything (§7). After comparing Socrates to Leonidas making his stand against Xerxes, the speaker even composes Socrates' counterindictment of the Athenians, accusing them of being the actual corruptors of the youth, specifically of Alcibiades and Critias,[4] thus incurring Zeus' judgment upon themselves with the disasters of the Peloponnesian War (§8).

[4] This reverses the standard accusation that Socrates corrupted his two students, Alcibiades and Critias.

# *ORATION* 3

## Εἰ καλῶς ἐποίησεν Σωκράτης μὴ ἀπολογησάμενος

1. Δεινόν γε τὰς μὲν ἄλλας τέχνας ἀπηλλάχθαι ἑκάστην τοῦ τῶν πολλῶν δικαστηρίου, καὶ μήτε τὸν κυβερνήτην ἐπιλαβόμενον τῆς νεὼς καὶ χρώμενον τῇ τέχνῃ κατὰ τοὺς αὐτοῦ[1] λόγους εὐθύνεσθαι πρὸς τῶν ἀτέχνων, μήτε τὸν ἰατρὸν ἀνέχεσθαι τοὺς κάμνοντας τὰ προστάγματα αὐτοῦ καὶ τὰ ἰάματα καὶ τὰ διαιτήματα ἐπισκοποῦντας καὶ βασανίζοντας, ἀλλ' οὐδὲ κεραμέας οὐδὲ σκυτοτόμους οὐδὲ τοὺς τὰ ἔτι τούτων ἀτιμότερα μεταχειριζομένους ἄλλον τινὰ ἔχειν δικαστὴν τῶν ἔργων πλὴν τῆς τέχνης, Σωκράτη δὲ τὸν μηδὲ τῷ Ἀπόλλωνι παρασχόντα ἀμαθίας αἰτίαν, τῷ τὰς ψάμμους εἰδότι καὶ ‹τὰ μέτρα›[2] καταμαντευσαμένῳ τῆς θαλάττης, οὔπω καὶ νῦν πεπαῦσθαι συκοφαντούμενον καὶ εὐθυνόμενον, ἀλλὰ πικροτέρους αὐτῷ εἶναι τοὺς ἐπιγιγνομένους αἰεὶ {καὶ τοὺς}[3] συκοφάντας Ἀνύτου καὶ Μελήτου, καὶ τοὺς δικαστὰς Ἀθηναίων τῶν τότε.

[1] αὐτοῦ Trapp, Koniaris: αὐτοὺς R: αὐτοῦ R$^2$: ναυτικοὺς Hobein [2] suppl. Meiser, Trapp [3] del. Reiske, Trapp

# *ORATION* 3

## Whether Socrates did the right thing by not defending himself in court

1. This is extraordinary! Of all the other forms of expertise, none is subject to a tribunal of the multitude. A helmsman, when he takes command of his ship and exercises his expertise according to its own principles, is not held to account by people who know nothing of sailing. A doctor does not have to tolerate his sick patients reviewing and questioning his prescriptions, cures, and dietary regimes. Not even potters or shoemakers or those engaged in still less respectable trades must answer to any judge of their works other than the craft itself. And yet Socrates, who was not accused of ignorance even by Apollo,[1] the god who knew the grains of sand and divined the measures of the sea,[2] has not even today stopped being accused and held to account—indeed the succeeding generations of prosecutors and jurors have treated him more harshly than Anytus and Meletus and his contemporary Athenians.

[1] The Pythian oracle declared that no man was wiser than Socrates; see Pl. *Ap.* 21a and Xen. *Ap.* 14.

[2] An adaptation of Apollo's oracle to Croesus at Hdt. 1.47.3: "I know the number of the sands and the measures of the sea."

Καὶ εἰ μὲν γραφεὺς ἦν ἢ δημιουργὸς ἀγαλμάτων οἷον Ζεῦξις ἢ Πολύκλειτος ἢ Φειδίας, παρέπεμπεν ἂν τὰ ἔργα αὐτῷ μετ' εὐφημίας ἡ τῆς τέχνης δόξα· ὁρῶντες γοῦν ἐκεῖνα οἱ ἄνθρωποι μὴ ὅτι αἰτιᾶσθαι ἀλλ' οὐδὲ ἐξετάζειν τολμῶσιν, ἀλλ' εἰσὶν αὐτεπάγγελτοι ἐπαινέται θεαμάτων ἐνδόξων· εἰ δέ τις μὴ κατὰ γραφέας, μηδὲ κατ' ἀγαλμάτων δημιουργοὺς ἀγαθὸς ἦν τὴν χειρῶν τέχνην, ἀλλὰ τὸν αὑτοῦ βίον συμμέτρως καὶ πρὸς τὸ ἀκριβέστατον λόγῳ καὶ πόνῳ καὶ ἐθισμῷ καὶ εὐτελείᾳ καὶ καρτερίᾳ καὶ σωφροσύνῃ καὶ ταῖς ἄλλαις ἀρεταῖς ἡρμόσατο, τοῦτον μὴ τυγχάνειν βεβαίας δόξης μηδὲ ἐπαίνων ὡμολογημένων μηδὲ ὁμοφώνων δικαστῶν, ἀλλὰ ἄλλον ἄλλο τι διατελεῖν ὑπὲρ αὐτοῦ λέγοντας.

2. Ὁποῖόν τι καὶ τὸ παρὸν ἡμῖν νυνὶ σκέμμα. Σωκράτη τοῦτον Μέλητος μὲν ἐγράψατο, Ἄνυτος δὲ εἰσήγαγεν, Λύκων δὲ ἐδίωκεν, κατεδίκασαν δὲ Ἀθηναῖοι, ἔδησαν δὲ οἱ ἕνδεκα, ἀπέκτεινεν δὲ ὁ ὑπηρέτης. καὶ Μελήτου γραφομένου ὑπερεώρα, καὶ Ἀνύτου εἰσάγοντος κατεφρόνει, καὶ Λύκωνος λέγοντος κατεγέλα, καὶ ψηφιζομένων Ἀθηναίων ἀντεψηφίζετο, καὶ τιμωμένων ἀντετιμᾶτο, καὶ δεόντων αὐτὸν τῶν ἕνδεκα τὸ μὲν σῶμα παρεῖχεν, ἀσθενέστερον γὰρ ἦν πολλῶν σωμάτων, τὴν δὲ ψυχὴν οὐ παρεῖχεν, κρείττων γὰρ ἦν Ἀθηναίων ἁπάντων, οὐδὲ τῷ ὑπηρέτῃ ἐχαλέπαινεν, οὐδὲ πρὸς τὸ φάρμακον ἐδυσχέραινεν· ἀλλὰ Ἀθηναῖοι μὲν αὐτὸν οὐχ ἑκόντες κατεδίκασαν, ὁ δὲ ἀπέθνησκεν

And yet, if he had been a painter or sculptor like Zeuxis, Polyclitus, or Phidias, the fame of his expertise would have handed down his works to great acclaim. For when men look at those artists' works, they are so far from finding fault with them, that they do not even dare to examine them carefully, but become spontaneous encomiasts of such celebrated sights. If, however, there was a man[3] who was not good at the skilled use of his hands like painters or sculptors, but who, through his speech, hard work, habits, frugality, endurance, and self-control, along with all the other virtues, fashioned his own life as a work of art, perfectly balanced and precise in every detail, should he not enjoy a secure reputation, universal praise, and unanimous judges, rather than the various opinions of him that people continue to express?

2. Such is the subject of our present inquiry. Meletus indicted that very Socrates, Anytus took him to court, Lycon prosecuted him, the Athenians condemned him, the Eleven[4] imprisoned him, and the executioner put him to death. Yet he disdained Meletus when he indicted him, despised Anytus when he took him to court, laughed at Lycon when he prosecuted him, voted against the Athenians when they found him guilty, and proposed a different punishment when they sentenced him. And when the Eleven bound him, he indeed handed over his body, for it was weaker than the bodies of many, but he withheld his soul, for it was mightier than the souls of all the Athenians combined. Nor did he rebuke the executioner or balk at the proffered poison. No, while the Athenians reluctantly condemned him, he voluntarily accepted his death. His

[3] That is, Socrates.

[4] The Athenian jailers.

ἑκών· ἐλέγχει δὲ τοῦ μὲν τὸ ἑκούσιον, ὅτι ἐξὸν αὐτῷ καὶ χρημάτων τιμήσασθαι καὶ φεύγειν ἐκκλαπέντι, προείλετο ἀποθανεῖν· τῶν δὲ τὸ ἀκούσιον, μετέγνωσαν γὰρ εὐθύς· οὗ τί ἂν εἴη πάθος δικασταῖς καταγελαστότερον;

3. Ἔτ' οὖν ποθεῖς σκέψασθαι περὶ Σωκράτους, εἰ ὀρθῶς ταῦτα ἔδρα ἢ μή; τί οὖν, εἴ τίς σοι παρελθὼν διηγεῖτο ὅτι ἀνὴρ Ἀθηναῖος, γέρων τὴν ἡλικίαν φιλόσοφος τὴν ἐπιτήδευσιν, πένης τὴν τύχην δεινὸς τὴν φύσιν, ἀγαθὸς εἰπεῖν συνετὸς νοῆσαι, ἄγρυπνος καὶ νηφάλιος καὶ οἷος μηδὲν εἰκῇ μήτε ἔργον πρᾶξαι μήτε εἰπεῖν λόγον, βεβιωκὼς μὲν πόρρω ἡλικίας, ἐπαινέτας δὲ σχὼν τοῦ τρόπου Ἑλλήνων μὲν οὐ τοὺς φαυλοτάτους τὴν φύσιν, θεῶν δὲ τὸν Ἀπόλλωνα, οὗτος ἐπαναστάντων αὐτῷ φθόνῳ καὶ ἀπεχθείᾳ καὶ τῇ πρὸς τὰ καλὰ ὀργῇ ἐκ μὲν τοῦ θεάτρου Ἀριστοφάνους, ἐκ δὲ τῶν σοφιστῶν Ἀνύτου, ἐκ δὲ τῶν συκοφαντῶν Μελήτου, ἐκ δὲ τῶν ῥητόρων Λύκωνος, ‹ἐκ δὲ Ἀθηναίων τῶν δικαστῶν,›[4] καὶ τοῦ μὲν κωμῳδοῦντος, τοῦ δὲ γραφομένου, τοῦ δὲ εἰσάγοντος, τοῦ δὲ λέγοντος, τῶν δὲ δικαζόντων, ἐχαλέπαινεν πρῶτα μὲν τῷ Ἀριστοφάνει, καὶ καταστὰς ἐν Ἀθηναίοις ἀντεκωμῴδει τὸν ἄνδρα ἐν Διονυσίοις, ἐπὶ μεθυόντων δικαστῶν· ἔπειτα εἰς τὸ δικαστήριον παρελθὼν ἀντερρητόρευεν

[4] suppl. Russell: ἐκ δὲ τῶν Ἑλλήνων Ἀθηναίων Markland

---

[5] This synopsis takes its details from Plato's *Apology*, *Crito*, and *Phaedo*.

willingness is proved by the fact that while he could have paid a fine and stolen away into exile, he chose instead to die, whereas the reluctance of the Athenians is shown by their immediate regret.[5] What experience could be more humiliating for jurors than that?

3. So, do you still desire to consider whether Socrates' conduct was correct or not? Well, then, what would you say, if someone came and told you how there was an Athenian, a man advanced in age who was a philosopher by profession, a poor man by fortune but astute by nature, a good speaker with a sharp intellect, wakeful and sober,[6] of the sort never to say or do anything at random, of far advanced age, having won as admirers of his conduct men of no mean abilities from the Greeks, and Apollo from the gods; but how because of envy, hatred, and the anger that noble actions provoke, there rose against him Aristophanes from the dramatists, Anytus from the sophists, Meletus from the accusers, Lycon from the orators, <and jurors from the Athenians,> with the first lampooning him,[7] the second bringing charges against him, the third hauling him into court, the fourth speaking against him, and the fifth judging the case; and how first of all this man was so enraged at Aristophanes that he stood up in the midst of the Athenians at the Dionysia and ridiculed him in return in front of the drunken jurors;[8] and how when he entered

[6] A reference to the end of Plato's *Symposium*, where Socrates alone remained awake and sober.

[7] In the *Clouds*, produced in 423 BC.

[8] In contrast, Aelian, at *VH* 5.8 reports that Socrates laughed at being lampooned, and at 2.13 claims that during the performance of the *Clouds*, Socrates obligingly stood up so that the audience could compare him to the actor on stage.

τοῖς λέγουσι καὶ λόγους διεξῄει μακρούς, ἀπολογίαν εὖ μάλα εἰς ἐπαγωγὴν δικαστῶν συγκειμένην, ἐξευμενιζόμενος μὲν τὸ δικαστήριον τοῖς προοιμίοις, πείθων δὲ τοῖς διηγήμασιν, ἀποδεικνὺς δὲ τεκμηρίοις καὶ πίστεσιν καὶ εἰκάσμασιν, ἀναβιβαζόμενος δὲ καὶ μάρτυρας τῶν πλουσίων τινὰς καὶ ἀξιόχρεων ἐν Ἀθηναίων δικασταῖς, κἂν τοῖς ἐπιλόγοις ἱκετεύων καὶ ἀντιβολῶν καὶ δεόμενος καί που καὶ δάκρυα ἐν καιρῷ ἀφιείς, καὶ μετὰ τοῦτο τελευτῶν τὴν Ξανθίππην ἀναβιβασάμενος κωκύουσαν καὶ τὰ παιδία κλαυμυριζόμενα, διὰ τούτων ἁπάντων μετεχειρίσατο τοὺς δικαστάς, καὶ ἀπεψηφίσαντο αὐτοῦ καὶ ᾤκτειραν καὶ ἀφῆκαν;

4. Καλοῦ τοῦ νικηφόρου· ἦ που εἰς Λύκειον ὤσατο ἂν ἐκεῖθεν καὶ εἰς Ἀκαδημίαν αὖθις καὶ τὰς ἄλλας διατριβὰς φαιδρός, ὥσπερ οἱ ἐκ χειμερίου θαλάττης σεσωσμένοι. καὶ πῶς ἂν ἠνέσχετο φιλοσοφία ἐπανιόντα πρὸς ἑαυτὴν τοῦτον τὸν ἄνδρα; οὐ μᾶλλον ἢ παιδοτρίβης ἐκ σταδίου ἀγωνιστὴν μύρῳ κεχρισμένον, ἀνιδρωτὶ καὶ ἀκονιτὶ στεφανωθέντα, ἄπληκτον καὶ ἄτρωτον καὶ μηδὲν ἴχνος ἀρετῆς ἔχοντα.

Τίνος δ' ἂν καὶ εἵνεκα ἀπελογήσατο Σωκράτης ἐπ' ἐκείνων τῶν Ἀθηναίων; ὡς ἐπὶ δικαίων; ἀλλὰ ἄδικοι· ὡς ἐπὶ φρονίμων; ἀλλὰ ἀνόητοι· ὡς ἐπὶ ἀγαθῶν; ἀλλὰ μοχθηροί· ὡς ἐπὶ εὐμενῶν; ἀλλὰ ὠργίζοντο· ὡς ἐπὶ

the courtroom, he spoke against his accusers, and went on at great length with a defense carefully composed to sway the jurors, gained the court's goodwill with his introduction, convinced them with his narrative of what had happened, backed it up with evidence, proofs, and arguments from probability, called forth as character witnesses certain men who were wealthy and respected by the Athenian jurors, and in his peroration supplicated, implored, entreated, perhaps even burst into tears at the right moment, and lastly brought forth Xanthippe wailing and his children weeping; and how by all these means he won over the jurors, who took pity on him, acquitted him, and set him free?

4. What a noble victor! He no doubt would have hastened from the courtroom back to the Lyceum and the Academy and to his other haunts, beaming like people who had just escaped from a storm at sea. But how could philosophy have allowed a man like that to come back to her? About as much as a trainer would welcome an athlete coming from the stadium drenched in fragrance, who had gained his crown without sweat or dust,[9] without a bruise or scar, and bearing no sign of valor.

In any event, what would have been the point of Socrates defending himself before those Athenians? Because he thought them just? No, they were unjust. Because he thought them sensible? No, they were senseless. Because he thought them good? No, they were wicked. Because he thought them sympathetic? No, they were angry. Because he thought them like himself? No, they were completely

9 That is, he won without having to face any opponent; cf. *Or.* 1.6.

ὁμοίων; ἀλλὰ ἀνομοιότατοι· ὡς ἐπὶ κρειττόνων; ἀλλὰ χείρους ἦσαν· ὡς ἐπὶ χειρόνων; καὶ τίς κρείττων χείρονι ἀπελογήσατο; τί δ' ἂν καὶ εἶπεν ἀπολογούμενος; ἆρα ὡς οὐκ ἐφιλοσόφει; ἀλλὰ ἐψεύδετο ἄν· ἢ ὅτι ἐφιλοσόφει; ἀλλὰ ἐπὶ τούτῳ ἐχαλέπαινον.

5. "Ἀλλὰ νὴ Δία τούτων μὲν οὐδέν, ἀπολύεσθαι δ' ἐχρῆν τὴν αἰτίαν ὡς μήτε διέφθειρεν τοὺς νέους μήτε καινὰ δαιμόνια ἐπεισέφερεν." καὶ τίς τεχνίτης τὸν ἄτεχνον πείθει ὑπὲρ τῶν κατὰ τὴν τέχνην; ποῦ γὰρ Ἀθηναίοις συνιέναι τί μὲν διαφθορὰ νέων, τί δὲ ἀρετή, καὶ τί μὲν τὸ δαιμόνιον, πῶς δὲ τιμητέον; οὐ γὰρ τῷ κυάμῳ λαχόντες δικασταὶ χίλιοι ταῦτα ἐξετάζουσιν, οὐδὲ Σόλων τι ὑπὲρ αὐτῶν γέγραφεν, οὐδὲ οἱ Δράκοντος σεμνοὶ νόμοι· ἀλλὰ κλήσεις μὲν καὶ φάσεις καὶ γραφαὶ καὶ εὐθύναι καὶ ἀντωμοσίαι καὶ πάντα τὰ τοιαῦτα ἐν ἡλιαίᾳ εὐθύνεται, ὥσπερ ἐν ταῖς τῶν παίδων ἀγέλαις αἱ περὶ τῶν ἀστραγάλων διαμάχαι †καὶ ῥητορικαί†,[5] ἀφαιρουμένων ἀλλήλους καὶ ἀδικούντων καὶ ἀδικουμένων· ἀλήθεια δὲ καὶ ἀρετὴ καὶ βίος ὀρθὸς ἑτέρων δικαστῶν δεῖται καὶ νόμων ἑτέρων καὶ ῥητόρων ἑτέρων, ἐν οἷς Σωκράτης ἐκράτει καὶ ἐστεφανοῦτο καὶ εὐδοκίμει.

[5] obel. Trapp

---

[10] The interjection of an imagined interlocutor, as in §7 below. *Orr.* 8 and 9 investigate the nature of Socrates' notorious *daimonion*.

different. Because he thought them better than he? No, they were worse. Because he thought them worse? No, what better man defends himself to an inferior? And what would he have said in his defense? That he had not been engaged in philosophy? No, then he would be lying. That he had in fact been practicing philosophy? No, that was why they were angry.

5. "By Zeus, none of that, but still he should have refuted the charge against him by showing that he had not been corrupting the youth or introducing new *daimonia*."[10] Yet what expert can persuade a layman about matters pertaining to his expertise? For how were the Athenians to understand what counts as corrupting the youth and what counts as virtue, or what a *daimon* is and how it should be worshipped? They could not, because these are not matters for a thousand jurors who draw a white bean[11] to examine carefully, nor did Solon prescribe anything about them, nor did Dracon's august laws. But summonses, accusations, indictments, judicial reviews, affidavits, and all such matters taken up in the Heliaea court, are like disputes over knucklebones among gangs of boys,[12] who take them from one another by cheating or being cheated, whereas truth, virtue, and an upright life require different kinds of judges, different laws, and different orators—ones among whom Socrates was victorious, won his crowns, and gained his fame.

[11] Jurors were selected by drawing beans: white, yes; black, no.

[12] See *Or*. 12.10 for a similar depiction of the Athenian court as boys playing knucklebones; cf. also *Or*. 36.5, where the analogy applies to Diogenes' disdain of common pursuits.

6. Πῶς οὖν οὐκ ἂν ἦν καταγέλαστος γέρων ἀνὴρ καὶ φιλόσοφος συναστραγαλίζων τοῖς παισίν; ἢ τίς πώποτε ἰατρὸς ἔπεισεν τοὺς πυρέττοντας ὅτι ἀγαθὸν τὸ διψῆν καὶ λιμώττειν; ἢ τίς τὸν ἀκόλαστον ὅτι πονηρὸν ἡδονή; ἢ τίς τὸν χρηματιστὴν ὅτι οὐδενὸς ἀγαθοῦ ἐφίεται; ἦ γὰρ ἂν καὶ τοῦτο Σωκράτης οὐ χαλεπῶς ἔπεισεν τοὺς Ἀθηναίους, ὡς οὐκ ἔστιν διαφθορὰ νέων ἀρετῆς ἐπιτήδευσις οὐδὲ ἡ τοῦ θείου γνῶσις περὶ δαίμονας παρανομία.

Καὶ γὰρ ἤτοι συνηπίσταντο ταῦτα τῷ Σωκράτει, ἢ ὁ μὲν ἠπίστατο, οἱ δὲ ἠγνόουν. καὶ εἰ μὲν ἠπίσταντο, τί ἔδει λόγων πρὸς τοὺς εἰδότας; εἰ δὲ ἠγνόουν, οὐκ ἀπολογίας αὐτοῖς ἀλλ᾽ ἐπιστήμης ἔδει. τὰς μὲν γὰρ ἄλλας ἀπολογίας μάρτυρες ἀποφαίνουσιν καὶ πίστεις καὶ ἔλεγχοι καὶ τεκμήρια καὶ βάσανοι καὶ ἄλλα τοιαῦτα, ἵνα τὸ ἀφανὲς τέως ἐπὶ δικαστηρίου φωραθῇ· ἀρετῆς δὲ καὶ καλοκἀγαθίας ὁ ἔλεγχος εἷς, ἡ πρὸς ταῦτα αἰδώς, ἧς ἐξεληλαμένης τότε Ἀθήνηθεν τί ἔδει τῷ Σωκράτει λόγου;

7. "Νὴ Δία, ἵνα μὴ ἀποθάνῃ." ἀλλ᾽ εἰ τοῦτο ἐξ ἅπαντος εὐλαβητέον τῷ ἀγαθῷ ἀνδρί, ὥρα ἦν Σωκράτει μὴ <ὅτι>[6] τοῖς Ἀθηναίων δικασταῖς ἀπολογεῖσθαι, ἀλλὰ μήτε Μελήτῳ ἀπεχθάνεσθαι, μήτε ἐλέγχειν Ἄνυτον, μήτε παρέχειν πράγματα τοῖς ἁμαρτάνουσιν Ἀθηναίων, μηδὲ περιιέναι τὴν πόλιν, ἐντυγχάνοντα

[6] suppl. Markland, Trapp

6. Therefore, how could an elderly man who was a philosopher not make himself ridiculous by playing knucklebones with boys? Or what doctor has ever persuaded his patients with fevers that going without food and drink was a good thing? Or who has ever persuaded a libertine that pleasure was a bad thing? Or who has ever persuaded a moneymaker that what he seeks is nothing good? For if such a thing were possible, Socrates would have had no difficulty persuading the Athenians that the practice of virtue is not corrupting the youth, and that knowledge of the divine is not an illegal view of *daimones*.

For in fact, either they had the same understanding of these matters as Socrates did, or he understood them and they did not. Now, if they did understand them, what need was there to tell people what they already knew? But if they were ignorant of them, then what they needed was not a legal defense, but knowledge. That is because these other defenses are conducted with witnesses, arguments, cross-examinations, proofs, testimony under torture, and so forth, in order to clarify for the jury what had previously been unclear, but for virtue and honorable conduct there is only one test, namely the respect that is paid to them; but since that had been banished from Athens at the time, what was the point of Socrates saying anything at all?

7. "For heaven's sake, to avoid death!" But if that is what a good man must see to above all else, then the proper course for Socrates, quite apart from defending himself before the Athenian jury, was not to incur the hatred of Meletus, nor to make a fool of Anytus,[13] nor to annoy those misguided Athenians, nor to go about the city

[13] As at Pl. *Meno* 90a–95a.

πάσαις ἀνδρῶν καὶ τύχαις καὶ τέχναις καὶ ἐπιτηδεύμασιν καὶ ἐπιθυμίαις, σωφρονιστὴν κοινὸν πικρὸν καὶ ἀπαραίτητον, μηδὲν ταπεινὸν μηδὲ θωπικὸν μηδὲ ἀνδραποδῶδες μηδὲ ὑφειμένον πρὸς μηδένα λέγοντα.

Εἰ δὲ θανάτου μὲν ἤδη τις καὶ ἐν πολέμῳ κατεφρόνησεν καὶ κυβερνήτης ἐν θαλάττῃ, ὀρέγονται δὲ ἕκαστοι τῶν ἐν ταῖς τέχναις ἀποθνήσκειν καλῶς σὺν τῇ τέχνῃ, ἦπου τὸν φιλόσοφον ἔδει λιποτάκτην γενέσθαι καὶ λιπόνεων καὶ φιλόψυχον, ῥίψαντα τὴν ἀρετὴν ὡς ἐν πολέμῳ ἀσπίδα; καὶ ταῦτα δρῶντα τίς ἂν αὐτὸν δικαστὴς ἐπῄνεσεν; ἢ τίς ἂν ἠνέσχετο τὸν Σωκράτην ἑστῶτα ἐν δικαστηρίῳ ταπεινὸν καὶ ἐπτηχότα καὶ τὴν ἐλπίδα τοῦ ζῆν ἐρανιζόμενον παρ᾽ ἄλλων; τοῦτο γάρ που τῆς ἀπολογίας τὸ σχῆμα ἦν.

Ἢ λέγειν ἐχρῆν, ταπεινὸν δὲ οὐδὲν οὔτε ἐπτηχὸς οὔτε ὑφειμένον, ἀλλ᾽ ἐλεύθερόν τι καὶ ἄξιον φιλοσοφίας; οὐκ ἀπολογίαν μοι λέγεις, ἀλλ᾽ ὀργῆς ζωπύρωσιν καὶ φλεγμονήν· πῶς γὰρ ἂν ἤνεγκεν τοιαύτην ἀπολογίαν δικαστήριον πονηρὸν καὶ δημοκρατικὸν καὶ ἐκδεδιῃτημένον ὑπ᾽ ἐξουσίας καὶ ἀνήκοον παρρησίας καὶ κολακείᾳ διηνεκεῖ κεχρημένον; οὐ μᾶλλον ἢ ἀκόλαστον συμπόσιον νήφοντα ἄνδρα ἀφαιρούμενον μὲν τὸν κρατῆρα, ἀπάγοντα δὲ τὴν αὐλητρίδα, καθαιροῦντα δὲ τοὺς στεφάνους, παύοντα δὲ τὴν μέθην. τοιγαροῦν ἐσιώπησεν ὁ Σωκράτης ἀσφαλῶς, ὅπου λέγειν οὐκ ἐξῆν καλῶς, φυλάξας μὲν τὴν ἀρετήν, φυλαξάμενος δὲ τὴν ὀργήν, καὶ παρασχὼν τοὔνειδος αὐτοῖς πικρόν, ὅτι καὶ σιωπῶντος αὐτοῦ κατεδίκασαν.

engaging with people of all ranks, trades, occupations, and desires, as a stinging and implacable censor at large, who never spoke a humble, flattering, obsequious, or submissive word to anyone.

But if it is the case that many a man has scorned death in battle, as has many a helmsman at sea, and if every kind of expert hopes to obtain a dignified death while exercising his particular expertise, can it be that a philosopher should desert his post, abandon ship, and cling to life, by throwing away his virtue like a shield in battle? Or what juror would have praised him for doing that? Who would have put up with Socrates standing all humble and cowering in the courtroom, pinning his hopes of survival on what he could beg from others? For that is surely the approach his defense would have taken.

Or should he have spoken, and yet said nothing humble, craven, or submissive, but rather something honest and worthy of philosophy? That is no defense you are speaking of, but igniting a bonfire of anger. For how could a court so debased, so democratic, so corrupted by its power, so unaccustomed to candid speech and so used to constant flattery, have put up with a defense like that? No more than a rowdy drinking party would put up with a sober man taking away their mixing bowl, leading away the pipe player, ripping off their wreaths, and putting a stop to their drunkenness. Therefore Socrates maintained a safe silence where it was impossible to speak nobly, thereby preserving his virtue, guarding against their anger, and casting a stinging reproach on them for condemning him in spite of his silence.

8. Πάνυ γοῦν ἔδει τοῖς τότε Ἀθηναίων δικασταῖς λόγων. Σωκράτη γὰρ ἑβδομήκοντα μὲν ἐτῶν χρόνος καὶ ἐν τούτῳ φιλοσοφία καὶ ἀρετὴ διηνεκής, καὶ ἄπταιστος βίος καὶ ὑγιής, καὶ δίαιτα εἰλικρινής, καὶ ὁμιλίαι χρησταὶ καὶ ἐντεύξεις ὠφέλιμοι καὶ συνουσίαι ἀγαθαί, ταῦτα μὲν αὐτὸν οὐκ ἐξείλετο ἐκ τοῦ δικαστηρίου καὶ τοῦ δεσμωτηρίου καὶ τοῦ θανάτου, ἀμφορεὺς δὲ ἔμελλεν διαμετρηθεὶς πρὸς ῥητορείας καιρὸν βραχὺν ῥύσεσθαι τὸν Σωκράτην; ἀλλ' οὔτε ἠδύνατο, οὔτε δυναμένου ἐδέξατο ἂν ὁ Σωκράτης.

Ἄπαγε, ὦ Ζεῦ καὶ θεοί, ὅμοιον ὡς εἰ καὶ Λεωνίδην τὸν Σπαρτιάτην ἐκεῖνον ἠξίωσεν ἄν τις παραστὰς τοιοῦτος σύμβουλος ὑποχωρῆσαι βραχὺ καὶ ἐνδοῦναι τῇ Ξέρξου ἐμβολῇ ὡς συκοφάντῃ ὡπλισμένῳ· ὁ δὲ οὐκ ἐδέξατο, ἀλλ' αὐτοῦ κεῖσθαι σὺν τῇ ἀρετῇ καὶ τοῖς ὅπλοις μᾶλλον ἢ ζῶν δεῖξαι τὰ νῶτα βασιλεῖ βαρβάρῳ. τί τοίνυν ἦν ἄλλο ἡ Σωκράτους ἀπολογία ἢ νώτων ἀποστροφὴ καὶ φυγὴ βλημάτων καὶ εὐπρεπὴς δειλία; τοιγαροῦν ἔμεινεν καὶ τὴν ἐμβολὴν ἐδέξατο καὶ ἠρίστευσεν· Ἀθηναῖοι δὲ ᾤοντο αὐτοῦ καταψηφίζεσθαι. καὶ γὰρ Ξέρξης ᾤετο νικᾶν Λεωνίδην, ἀλλὰ Λεωνίδης μὲν ἀπέθνησκεν, Ξέρξης δὲ ἡττᾶτο· καὶ Σωκράτης μὲν ἀπέθνησκεν, Ἀθηναῖοι δὲ κατεδικάζοντο, δικαστὴς δὲ ἦν αὐτοῖς θεὸς καὶ ἀλήθεια.

Ἡ δὲ Σωκράτους κατὰ Ἀθηναίων γραφή· "ἀδικεῖ ὁ Ἀθηναίων δῆμος οὓς μὲν Σωκράτης νομίζει θεοὺς οὐ νομίζων, ἕτερα δὲ καινὰ δαιμόνια ἐπεισφέρων· Σωκράτης μὲν γὰρ νομίζει Ὀλύμπιον τὸν Δία, Ἀθηναῖοι

8. Obviously the Athenian jurors of that time needed to hear a speech. But when his span of seventy years, with its continuous practice of philosophy and virtue, and his flawless and sane life, honest conduct, helpful discussions, beneficial conversations, and virtuous relationships, when all this could not save him from the law court, prison, and execution, then was the brief opportunity allotted by the water jar for set speeches going to save Socrates? It could not, nor even if it could, would Socrates have accepted it.

Zeus and the gods forbid this! It would be the equivalent of a similar adviser at the side of Leonidas the famous Spartiate telling him to withdraw just a bit and give way to Xerxes' assault, as if before a prosecutor bearing arms. But Leonidas refused and chose to die there in his armor with his virtue intact, rather than show his back to a barbarian king and go on living. What else would Socrates' defense have been than a turning of his back, flight from his enemies' blows, and cowardice in the name of prudence?[14] Therefore he stood his ground, faced the assault, and triumphed. The Athenians thought that they were condemning Socrates. Just so Xerxes thought that he was defeating Leonidas, but as Leonidas was dying, Xerxes was being defeated; and as Socrates was being put to death, the Athenians were being condemned, for *their* judge was god and truth.

Here, instead, is Socrates' indictment of the Athenians: "The Athenian people break the law by not believing in the gods that Socrates believes in, and by introducing new and different *daimonia*. For Socrates believes that the

[14] The phrase comes from Thuc. 3.82.4: δειλία εὐπρεπής (cowardice with a fine name).

δὲ Περικλέα· καὶ Σωκράτης μὲν πιστεύει τῷ Ἀπόλλωνι, Ἀθηναῖοι δὲ αὐτῷ ἀντιψηφίζονται. ἀδικεῖ δὲ ὁ δῆμος καὶ τοὺς νέους διαφθείρων· οὗτος καὶ Ἀλκιβιάδην διέφθειρεν καὶ Ἱππόνικον καὶ Κριτίαν καὶ ἄλλους μυρίους."

Ὦ γραφῆς ἀληθοῦς καὶ δικαίου δικαστηρίου καὶ καταδίκης πικρᾶς. ὑπὲρ μὲν Διὸς ἀσεβουμένου λοιμὸς ἦλθε καὶ ἐκ Πελοποννήσου πόλεμος· ὑπὲρ δὲ νέων διαφθειρομένων Δεκέλεια καὶ ἡ ἐν Σικελίᾳ τύχη καὶ αἱ ἐν Ἑλλησπόντῳ συμφοραί. οὕτω δικάζει θεός, οὕτω καταψηφίζεται.

Olympian god is Zeus, whereas the Athenians believe that it is Pericles,[15] and Socrates puts his trust in Apollo, but the Athenians vote against the god. The Athenian people also break the law by corrupting the youth, for they corrupted Alcibiades, Hipponicus,[16] Critias,[17] and countless others."

Oh, how truthful this indictment, how just this tribunal, and how bitter the sentence! Because they were impious toward Zeus, the plague came upon them,[18] as did war from the Peloponnesus; and because they corrupted the youth, upon them came Decelea,[19] and the Sicilian debacle,[20] and the disasters in the Hellespont.[21] These are the verdict of god, these are his condemnation.

15 Pericles was nicknamed "the Olympian"; cf. Ar. *Ach.* 530 and Plut. *Per.* 8.

16 A wealthy Athenian, son of Callias, also mentioned at *Or.* 5.7.

17 One of the "Thirty Tyrants," killed in 403 BC.

18 In 430 BC, at the beginning of the Peloponnesian War.

19 A fort in Attica occupied by the Peloponnesians in 413 BC, on the advice of Alcibiades.

20 The Sicilian Expedition (415–413 BC), advocated by Alcibiades, ended in disaster for the Athenians.

21 The battle of Aegospotami in 405 BC sealed the Athenians' defeat.

# *ORATION* 4[1]

## INTRODUCTION

Plato banished Homer from his ideal city in part for portraying the gods as immoral.[2] Consistent with Maximus' view of a uniform tradition stretching from Homer to Plato, this oration seeks a rapprochement between poetry and philosophy in their portrayal of the gods.[3] It opens by declaring that ancient poetry is actually philosophy set to meter and expressed in myth (§1). An analogy for the conduct of this inquiry (*skemma*) is found in medicine, which had to develop from treating the uncomplicated, hardy bodies of Homeric times to the complex and effete ones of the present (§2). Likewise, philosophy treated those simpler souls with a gentler form of philosophy, consisting of myths composed in poetry. But as the soul matured, it could no longer abide poetry's use of hidden

[1] Grimaldi (2002) provides a translation and commentary of this oration. Its theological content connects it with *Orr*. 5, 11, 38, and 41. For these orations (including *Or*. 4), see Pérez-Jean and Fauquier (2014).

[2] *Resp*. 3.388a–91e, summarized at *Or*. 18.5. Homer's banishment is the topic of *Or*. 17.

[3] *Or*. 26 also employs allegory to harmonize Homer's and Plato's views of the gods.

meanings (*ainigmata*), and it stripped that philosophy of its poetic garments and exposed it as naked doctrine. In fact, however, conceptions of the gods have remained constant (§3). With the exception of Epicurus (who counts as neither a philosopher nor a poet), Homer, Plato, Pherecydes, and Heraclitus were all engaged in philosophy (§4). The modern exposé of poetry's hidden meaning in plain prose is like profaning the mysteries, and it prevents the soul from searching for truth in hidden meanings and discovering it on its own (§5). In dealing with divine matters, the poets employed myths that were both entertaining and puzzling, in order to encourage listeners "to seek what truly exists and to investigate it more profoundly." Thus, they hid their philosophy in pleasant myths as doctors put their bitter drugs in pleasant food (§6). As long as they both tell the truth, the speaker will accept the poets' allegories as well as the philosophers' plain prose (§7). If one allegorizes Homer's gods (as Stoics do), by calling Zeus Mind (*nous*), Athena Intelligence (*phronēsis*), Apollo the Sun (*Helios*), and Poseidon Spirit (*pneuma*), the continuity of Greek conceptions of the gods is preserved (§8). Only Epicurus remains outside this tradition, because he holds the absurd view that the gods do not concern themselves with earthly affairs (§9).

# *ORATION* 4

Τίνες ἄμεινον περὶ θεῶν διέλαβον· ποιηταὶ ἢ φιλόσοφοι;

1. Δεινῶς γε οἱ ἄνθρωποι στασιωτικοὶ οὐ μέχρι πολιτείας μόνον οὐδὲ ἀρχῆς οὐδὲ τῶν ἐν μέσῳ κακῶν, ἀλλὰ καὶ ἐπὶ τὰ εἰρηνικώτατα τῶν ὄντων προεληλύθασιν, ποιητικὴν καὶ φιλοσοφίαν· χρῆμα διττὸν μὲν κατὰ τὸ ὄνομα, ἁπλοῦν δὲ κατὰ τὴν οὐσίαν, καὶ διαφέρον αὐτὸ αὑτοῦ[1] οἷον εἴ τις ἢ τὴν ἡμέραν ἄλλο τι ἡγήσαιτο πλὴν ἡλίου φῶς πῖπτον εἰς γῆν, ἢ τὸν ἥλιον ὑπὲρ γῆς θέοντα ἄλλο τι ἢ ἡμέραν· οὕτω τοι καὶ τὰ ποιητικῆς πρὸς φιλοσοφίαν ἔχει. καὶ γὰρ ποιητικὴ τί ἄλλο ἢ φιλοσοφία, τῷ μὲν χρόνῳ παλαιά, τῇ δὲ ἁρμονίᾳ ἔμμετρος, τῇ δὲ γνώμῃ μυθολογική; καὶ φιλοσοφία τί ἄλλο ἢ ποιητική, τῷ μὲν χρόνῳ νεωτέρα, τῇ δὲ ἁρμονίᾳ εὐζωνοτέρα, τῇ δὲ γνώμῃ σαφεστέρα; δύο τοίνυν πραγμάτων χρόνῳ μόνον καὶ σχήματι ἀλλήλοις διαφερομένων πῶς ἄν τις διαιτήσαι τὴν διαφορὰν ἐν οἷς τι περὶ τοῦ θείου ἑκάτεροι λέγουσιν καὶ οἱ ποιηταὶ καὶ οἱ φιλόσοφοι;

2. Ἢ τὸ σκέμμα τουτὶ ἐοικέναι φῶμεν τοιῷδε, οἷον εἴ τις καὶ ἰατρικὴν ἐνθυμηθεὶς τὴν πρώτην ἐκείνην

# *ORATION* 4

## Who has provided a better account of the gods, poets or philosophers?

1. Humans are fiercely contentious, not only about politics, governance, and the common ills of life, but their quarrels even extend to the most peaceable of things, poetry and philosophy. Although these bear two different names, they are essentially a single thing, which differs within itself in much the same way that a person might consider "day" something other than sunlight falling on the earth, or the sun passing over the earth something other than "day." Poetry and philosophy have a similar relationship. For what is poetry other than philosophy that is ancient in time, composed in meter, and expressed in myth? And what is philosophy other than poetry that is more recent in time, composed more loosely, and expressed more clearly? And so, when two things differ from each other only in terms of time and form, how then is one to determine the differences in what poets and philosophers each say about the gods?

2. Should we then say that the present inquiry is like one conducted by a person who compares the early form

1 αὐτὸ αὑτοῦ Davies[2], Trapp, Koniaris: τὸ αὑτοῦ R

πρὸς τὴν νέαν δὴ καὶ τοῖς νῦν σώμασιν ἐπιτεταγμένην, σκοποῖ τὸ ἐν ἑκατέρᾳ βέλτιον καὶ χεῖρον; ἀποκρίναιτο γὰρ ἂν αὐτῷ ὁ Ἀσκληπιὸς ὅτι τὰς μὲν ἄλλας τέχνας οὐ μεταποιοῦσιν οἱ χρόνοι· ὧν γὰρ ἡ αὐτὴ χρεία ἀεί, τούτων παραπλήσια καὶ τὰ ἔργα· ἰατρικὴν δὲ ἀνάγκη ἑπομένην τῇ κράσει τῶν σωμάτων, πράγματι οὐχ ἑστῶτι οὐδὲ ὡμολογημένῳ, ἀλλὰ ταῖς κατὰ τὴν δίαιταν τροφαῖς ἀλλοιουμένῳ καὶ μεταπίπτοντι, ἰάματα καὶ διαίτας αὐτῷ ἐξευρίσκειν ἄλλοτε ἄλλας, προσφόρους τῇ παρούσῃ τροφῇ. μηδὲν οὖν ἡγοῦ τοὺς υἱέας τοὺς ἐμούς, τὸν Μαχάονα ἐκεῖνον καὶ τὸν Ποδαλείριον, ἧττόν τι εἶναι δεξιωτέρους ἰᾶσθαι τῶν αὖθις ἐπιτιθεμένων τῇ τέχνῃ καὶ τὰ σοφὰ ταῦτα καὶ παντοδαπὰ ἰάματα ἐξευρηκότων· ἀλλὰ τότε μὲν ἡ τέχνη σώμασιν ὁμιλοῦσα οὐ θρυπτικοῖς οὐδὲ ποικίλοις οὐδὲ ἐκλελυμένοις παντάπασιν, ῥᾳδίως αὐτὰ μετεχειρίζετο, καὶ ἦν αὐτῆς ἔργον τι ἁπλοῦν

ἰούς τ᾽ ἐκτάμνειν, ἐπί τ᾽ ἤπια φάρμακα πάσσειν·

τελευτῶσα δὲ νῦν, ὑπολισθαινόντων αὐτῇ τῶν σωμάτων εἰς δίαιταν ποικιλωτέραν καὶ κρᾶσιν πονηράν, ἐξεποικίλθη καὶ αὐτή, καὶ μετέβαλεν ἐκ τῆς πρόσθεν ἁπλότητος εἰς παντοδαπὸν σχῆμα.

3. Φέρε καὶ ὁ ποιητικὸς ὁμοῦ καὶ ὁ φιλόσοφος ἀποκρινάσθω κατὰ τὸν Ἀσκληπιὸν ὑπὲρ τῶν ἐπιτη-

of medicine with the modern one that treats present-day bodies, by examining the strengths and weaknesses in each? I think not, for Asclepius would tell this person, "Particular times do not alter the other arts, for when the need is consistent, the practices remain much the same; but in the case of medicine, which is forced to adapt to the dispositions of the bodies it treats—dispositions that are neither stable nor consistent, but are altered and changed by the diets that go along with different lifestyles—it must devise different cures and regimens in different eras that are appropriate for the diets of the time. Therefore do not think that those sons of mine, famous Machaon and Podalirius,[1] were any less skilled in healing than those who subsequently practiced the art and devised their various ingenious cures. For at that earlier time, medicine was not dealing with bodies that were frail, complex, and utterly weakened, but easily treated them because its practice was a simple one, of

cutting out arrows and applying soothing medicines.[2]

But today, as bodies gradually left behind that early practice and adopted a more complex style of life along with an unhealthy disposition, medicine too has become more complex and has changed from its earlier simplicity into a form that is multifaceted."[3]

3. Come, let us then have a poet and a philosopher together defend their respective enterprises as Asclepius

[1] Machaon was the chief physician for the Greek army; he and Podalirius are named as Asclepius' sons at *Il.* 2.731–32.

[2] *Il.* 11.515, said of Machaon.

[3] The complexity of modern medicine is also treated at *Orr.* 28.1 and 39.2.

δευμάτων· οὗτος μὲν καὶ ἄγαν δεινοπαθῶν εἴ τις ἡγήσαιτο Ὅμηρον καὶ Ἡσίοδον ἤ, νὴ Δία, Ὀρφέα ἢ ἄλλον τινὰ τῶν τότε ἀνδρῶν ἧττόν τι εἶναι σοφώτερον Ἀριστοτέλους τοῦ Σταγειρίτου ἢ Χρυσίππου τοῦ Κίλικος ἢ Κλειτομάχου τοῦ Λίβυος ἢ τῶν τὰ πολλὰ καὶ σοφὰ ταῦτα ἡμῖν ἐξευρηκότων, ἀλλὰ οὐχὶ καὶ τούτους ὁμοίως μὲν καὶ τὰ αὐτὰ δεινούς, εἰ μὴ καὶ μᾶλλον.

Καθάπερ δὲ ἐπὶ τῶν σωμάτων τὰ μὲν ἀρχαῖα ὑπὸ διαίτης χρηστῆς εὐμεταχείριστα ἦν τῇ τέχνῃ, τὰ δὲ αὖθις ἐδεήθη ἰατρικῆς ἀλλοιοτέρας, οὕτω καὶ ἡ ψυχὴ πρότερον μὲν δι' ἁπλότητα καὶ τὴν καλουμένην ταύτην εὐήθειαν ἐδεῖτο φιλοσοφίας μουσικῆς τινος καὶ πρᾳοτέρας, ἣ διὰ μύθων δημαγωγήσει αὐτὴν καὶ μεταχειριεῖται, καθάπερ αἱ τιτθαὶ τοὺς παῖδας διὰ μυθολογίας βουκολοῦσιν· προϊοῦσα δὲ εἰς δεινότητα καὶ ἀνδριζομένη καὶ ὑποπιμπλαμένη ἀπιστίας καὶ πανουργίας, καὶ τοὺς μύθους διερευνωμένη καὶ οὐκ ἀνεχομένη τῶν αἰνιγμάτων, ἐξεκάλυψέν τε καὶ ἀπέδυσεν φιλοσοφίαν τοῦ αὐτῆς κόσμου καὶ ἐχρήσατο γυμνοῖς τοῖς λόγοις· οἱ δ' εἰσὶν οὐδὲν ἀλλοιότεροι τῶν προτέρων οἱ ἔπειτα, πλὴν τῷ σχήματι τῆς ἁρμονίας, ἀλλ' αἱ περὶ θεῶν δόξαι ἀρξάμεναι ἄνωθεν διὰ πάσης φιλοσοφίας ἦλθον.

---

4 Aristotle (384–322 BC) founded the Peripatetic school in Athens.

5 Chrysippus of Soli (ca. 280–207) succeeded Cleanthes as head of the Stoic school.

did his. For his part, the poet would complain bitterly if anyone considered Homer and Hesiod, or, by Zeus, Orpheus or any other man of that time, to be any less wise than Aristotle the Stagirite,[4] Chrysippus the Cilician,[5] Clitomachus the Libyan,[6] or any of the others who made those many wise discoveries for our benefit, but would insist that these poets were every bit as skilled in these same matters, if not more so.

We saw in the case of bodies, that those of ancient times were easily treated by medicine because of their wholesome regimen, but in recent times have required a different medical practice. The same is true of the soul. In the past, because of its simplicity and so-called naiveté, it required a gentler kind of philosophy expressed in verse, one that could win it over and guide it by means of myths, just as nurses manage children by telling them stories. But then, as the soul matured and developed shrewdness, it was filled with suspicion and audacity; it took to scrutinizing the myths, and when it could no longer tolerate their use of hidden meanings,[7] it laid bare philosophy, stripped off her adornments, and resorted to the use of naked doctrines. And yet these later doctrines are no different from the earlier myths, except for the form of their composition. In fact, the conceptions of the gods that arose in the distant past have come down through the entire tradition of philosophy.

[6] Clitomachus of Carthage (ca. 187/6–110/9) succeeded Carneades as head of the Middle Academy.

[7] The term *ainigma* can connote "hidden meaning," "riddle," or "allegory."

4. Ἐπίκουρον δὲ ἐξαιρῶ λόγου καὶ ποιητικοῦ καὶ φιλοσόφου, τοῖς δὲ ἄλλοις ἡ πραγματεία ἴση καὶ ἡ αὐτή· πλὴν εἰ μὴ νομίζεις Ὅμηρον ἐντετυχηκέναι τοῖς θεοῖς τοξεύουσιν ἢ διαλεγομένοις ἢ πίνουσιν,[2] ἤ τι ἄλλο δρῶσιν οἷα περὶ αὐτῶν ἐκεῖνος ᾄδει. οὐδὲ γὰρ Πλάτωνα ἡγητέον ἐντετυχηκέναι τῷ Διὶ ἡνιοχοῦντι καὶ φερομένῳ ἐπὶ πτηνοῦ ἅρματος, <οὐδὲ>[3] στρατιᾷ θεῶν κατὰ ἕνδεκα λόχους κεκοσμημένῃ, οὐδέ γε δαινυμένοις τοῖς θεοῖς ἐν Διὸς τοὺς Ἀφροδίτης γάμους, ὅτε Πόρος καὶ Πενία λαθόντε ξυνηλθέτην τε καὶ Ἔρωτα ἐξ ἑαυτῶν ἐγεννησάτην, οὐδέ γε θεατὴν γενέσθαι Πυριφλεγέθοντός τε καὶ Ἀχέροντος καὶ Κωκυτοῦ καὶ τῶν ἄνω καὶ κάτω ποταμῶν ῥεόντων ὕδατι καὶ πυρί, οὐδὲ τὴν Κλωθὼ ἰδεῖν καὶ τὴν Ἄτροπον, οὐδὲ ἐντετυχηκέναι ἑλιττομένῳ τῷ ἀτράκτῳ ἑπτὰ καὶ διαφόρους ἑλιγμούς. ἀλλὰ καὶ τοῦ Συρίου τὴν ποίησιν σκόπει, τὸν Ζῆνα καὶ τὴν Χθονίην καὶ τὸν ἐν τούτοις ἔρωτα καὶ τὴν Ὀφιονέως γένεσιν καὶ τὴν θεῶν μάχην καὶ τὸ δένδρον καὶ τὸν πέπλον· σκόπει καὶ τὸ Ἡρακλείτου, θεοὶ θνητοί, ἄνθρωποι ἀθάνατοι.

5. Πάντα μεστὰ αἰνιγμάτων καὶ παρὰ ποιηταῖς καὶ παρὰ φιλοσόφοις, ὧν ἐγὼ τὴν πρὸς τὸ ἀληθὲς αἰδῶ

[2] *πίνουσιν* Markland: *θύουσιν* R: obel. Trapp, Koniaris
[3] suppl. Markland, Dübner, Trapp

---

[8] Pl. *Phdr.* 246e.
[9] Pl. *Symp.* 203b.

4. I exclude Epicurus from consideration either as a poet or as a philosopher, but all the others were engaged in one and the same endeavor, unless, that is, you believe that Homer was actually present when the gods were shooting arrows, conversing among themselves, drinking, or doing any of the other things he says about them. Nor should one think that Plato was actually present when Zeus was holding the reins as he rode in a winged chariot, or when an army of gods was arrayed in eleven battalions;[8] or indeed when the gods were celebrating the marriage of Aphrodite in the halls of Zeus, at the time when Plenty and Poverty secretly made love and produced Eros;[9] or that he actually saw Pyriphlegethon, Acheron, and Cocytus, and the rivers of water and fire flowing to and fro,[10] or saw Clotho and Atropos, or was present when the spindle was spinning in seven different cycles.[11] Consider as well the "poetry" of the man from Syros,[12] telling of Zeus and Chthonie and the love between them that gave birth to Ophioneus, the battle of the gods, the tree, and the cloak. Consider too Heraclitus' statement, "gods mortal, humans immortal."[13]

5. Hidden meanings are found everywhere, and among both poets and philosophers, but I prefer the earlier au-

10 Pl. *Phd.* 113b–e. 11 Pl. *Resp.* 10.617a–c.

12 Pherecydes of Syros (fl. 544 BC) wrote mythological allegories in prose. For the examples cited, cf. frr. D 3, D 5, and D 8–11 L-M.

13 An adaptation of fr. D 70 L-M (B 62 D-K): *ἀθάνατοι θνητοί, θνητοὶ ἀθάνατοι* (immortals mortal, mortals immortal). The second part of this fragment is quoted at *Or.* 41.4. Heraclitus was notorious for his enigmatic pronouncements.

ἀγαπῶ μᾶλλον ἢ τὴν παρρησίαν τῶν νεωτέρων· πραγμάτων γὰρ ὑπ᾽ ἀνθρωπίνης ἀσθενείας οὐ καθορωμένων σαφῶς εὐσχημονέστερος ἑρμηνεὺς ὁ μῦθος. ἐγὼ δέ, εἰ μέν τι πλέον ἐθεάσαντο τῶν προτέρων οἱ ἔπειτα, μακαρίζω τοὺς ἄνδρας τῆς θέας· εἰ δὲ μηδενὶ πλεονεκτοῦντες κατὰ τὴν γνῶσιν μετέβαλον αὐτῶν τὰ αἰνίγματα εἰς μύθους σαφεῖς, δέδια μή τις αὐτῶν ἐπιλάβηται ὡς ἐξαγορευόντων ἀπορρήτους λόγους. τί γὰρ ἂν ἄλλο εἴη μύθου χρεία ἢ λόγος περισκεπὴς ἑτέρῳ κόσμῳ, καθάπερ τὰ ἱδρύματα οἷς περιέβαλλον οἱ τελεσταὶ χρυσὸν καὶ ἄργυρον καὶ πέπλους, ταύτῃ[4] ἀποσεμνύνοντες αὐτῶν τὴν προσδοκίαν; θρασεῖα γὰρ οὖσα ἡ ἀνθρωπίνη ψυχὴ τὰ μὲν ἐν ποσὶν ἧσσον τιμᾷ, τοῦ δὲ ἀπόντος θαυμαστικῶς ἔχει· καταμαντευομένη δὲ τῶν οὐχ ὁρωμένων καὶ θηρεύουσα ταῦτα τοῖς λογισμοῖς, μὴ τυχοῦσα μὲν σπεύδει ἀνευρεῖν, τυχοῦσα δὲ ἀγαπᾷ ὡς ἑαυτῆς ἔργον.

6. Τοῦτο τοίνυν οἱ ποιηταὶ κατανοήσαντες, ἐξεῦρον ἐπ᾽ αὐτῇ μηχανὴν ἐν τοῖς θείοις λόγοις, μύθους λόγου μὲν ἀφανεστέρους, αἰνίγματος δὲ σαφεστέρους, διὰ μέσου ὄντας ἐπιστήμης πρὸς ἄγνοιαν, κατὰ μὲν τὸ ἡδὺ πιστευομένους, κατὰ δὲ τὸ παράδοξον ἀπιστουμένους, καὶ χειραγωγοῦντας τὴν ψυχὴν ἐπὶ τὸ ζητεῖν τὰ ὄντα, καὶ διερευνᾶσθαι περαιτέρω.

[4] ταύτῃ Davies$^2$: τὰ R: om. I: del. Trapp: obel. Koniaris

thors' respect for the truth to the outspokenness of the moderns, for when it comes to matters that humans cannot clearly perceive with their limited capacity, myth is a more dignified interpreter. In my opinion, if these moderns have perceived something beyond what their predecessors did, I congratulate them for their insight. If, however, they have in no way surpassed their predecessors in knowledge, but have merely converted their hidden meanings into explicit accounts, I fear someone may arrest them for divulging religious secrets. For what would be the use of myth other than as doctrine clothed in different garb, just like the sacred effigies that hierophants cover with gold, silver, and veils, and thereby enhance the anticipation of seeing them? This happens because the human soul, with its impulsive nature, places less value on what is at hand, but is in awe of what is far away. And when it divines what it cannot see and uses its powers of reason to hunt it down, if it is unsuccessful, it intensifies its zeal to discover it, but if it succeeds, it welcomes what it considers to be its own accomplishment.

6. Recognizing this to be the case, poets devised a means for dealing with the soul when discussing divine matters: the use of myths, which are less clear than doctrine but more lucid than riddles, as they occupy the middle ground between knowledge and ignorance. Since myths are both plausible because they are pleasant, and implausible because they are paradoxical, they lead the soul to seek what truly exists and to investigate it more profoundly.[14]

[14] Myth's ability to engage the reader in a search for meaning is also discussed in *Orr*. 17.4 and 18.5.

Ἔλαθον μέχρι πλείστου οἱ ἄνδρες οὗτοι, ἐπιβουλεύσαντες ἡμῶν ταῖς ἀκοαῖς, φιλόσοφοι μὲν ὄντες, ποιηταὶ δὲ καλούμενοι, ἀλλαξάμενοι χρήματος ἐπιφθόνου δημοτερπῆ τέχνην. ὁ μὲν γὰρ φιλόσοφος βαρὺ καὶ πρόσαντες τοῖς πολλοῖς ἄκουσμα, ὡς ἐν πένησιν ὁ πλούσιος θέαμα βαρὺ καὶ ἐν ἀκολάστοις ὁ σώφρων καὶ ἐν δειλοῖς <ὁ>[5] ἀριστεύς· οὐ γὰρ ἀνέχονται αἱ πονηρίαι τὰς ἀρετὰς ἐν αὐταῖς καλλωπιζομένας· ὁ δὲ ποιητὴς ἄκουσμα ἁβρὸν καὶ δήμῳ φίλον, ἀγαπώμενον μὲν καθ' ἡδονήν, ἀγνοούμενον δὲ κατὰ τὴν ἀρετήν. καθάπερ δὲ οἱ ἰατροὶ τοῖς κακοσίτοις τῶν καμνόντων τὰ πικρὰ τῶν φαρμάκων ἀναδεύσαντες προσηνεῖ τροφῇ ἀπέκρυψαν τὴν τοῦ ὠφελοῦντος ἀηδίαν, οὕτως καὶ ἡ παλαιὰ φιλοσοφία καταθεμένη τὴν αὑτῆς γνώμην εἰς μύθους καὶ μέτρα καὶ σχῆμα ᾠδῆς, ἔλαθεν τῇ περιβολῇ τῆς ψυχαγωγίας κεράσασα τὴν ἀηδίαν τῶν διδαγμάτων.

7. Μὴ τοίνυν ἔρῃ πότεροι κρεῖττον περὶ θεῶν διειλήφασιν, ποιηταὶ ἢ φιλόσοφοι, ἀλλὰ σπονδὰς καὶ ἐκεχειρίαν τοῖς ἐπιτηδεύμασιν ποιησάμενος ὡς περὶ μιᾶς καὶ ὁμοφώνου τέχνης σκόπει· κἂν γὰρ ποιητὴν καλῇς, φιλόσοφον λέγεις, καὶ ἂν φιλόσοφον καλῇς, ποιητὴν λέγεις. καὶ γὰρ ἀριστεῖς καλεῖς ὁμοίως μὲν τὸν Ἀχιλλέα μετὰ χρυσῆς καὶ ποιητικῆς ἀσπίδος στρατευόμενον, ὁμοίως δὲ καὶ τὸν Αἴαντα, κἂν ἐκ βύρσης φέρῃ σάκος· ἀμφότερα δὲ ἀριστευτικὰ καὶ

[5] suppl. Markland, Trapp

For the longest time these men, with their seductive designs on our ears, concealed the fact that they were actually philosophers, but by being called poets, they exchanged an activity that was disliked for a skill that the public enjoyed.[15] This is because most people find listening to a philosopher painful and offensive, just as it pains poor people to see a rich man, or rowdy men to see a sober man, or cowards to see a war hero, because human vices cannot stand virtues showing off in their midst. In contrast, a poet makes for soothing listening enjoyed by ordinary people; they welcome it for its pleasantness, and do not notice the virtue that it promotes. And just as physicians, when dealing with squeamish patients, mix their bitter drugs in with pleasant food, in order to conceal the unpleasantness of the remedy, so ancient philosophy put its message into myths, meters, and poetic form, and secretly blended the unpleasantness of its teachings within a coating of entertainment.

7. So do not ask whether poets or philosophers have provided a better account of the gods. Instead, you should call for a ceasefire, declare a truce between their professions, and view them as practicing a single expertise. For when you say poet, you are also saying philosopher; and when you say philosopher, you are also saying poet. After all, you designate as heroes both Achilles going into battle with his poetic shield of gold, as well as Ajax, even though he carries one made of oxhide, because it is their virtue

[15] Protagoras advances a similar argument (about sophists) at Pl. *Prt*. 316d–e.

ἐκπληκτικὰ ὁμοίως ἡ ἀρετὴ ποιεῖ, καὶ οὐδὲν ἐνταῦθα ὁ χρυσὸς πρὸς τὴν βύρσαν.

Εἴκαζε δὴ κἀνταῦθα τὰ μὲν μέτρα καὶ τὴν ᾠδὴν χρυσῷ, τὸν δὲ ψιλὸν λόγον ὕλῃ δημοτικῇ· σκόπει δὲ μήτε τὸν χρυσὸν μήτε τὴν βύρσαν, ἀλλὰ τὴν ἀρετὴν τοῦ χρωμένου. ἀληθῆ λεγέτω, κἂν ποιητὴς λέγῃ, κἂν μῦθον λέγῃ, κἂν ᾄδων λέγῃ· ἕψομαι τοῖς αἰνίγμασιν καὶ διερευνήσομαι τὸν μῦθον καὶ οὐκ ἐκστήσει με ἡ ᾠδή· ἀληθῆ λεγέτω, κἂν ψιλῶς λέγῃ, δέξομαι καὶ ἀγαπήσω τὴν ῥᾳστώνην τῶν ἀκουσμάτων· ἐὰν δὲ ἀφέλῃς ἑκατέρου τὸ ἀληθές, καὶ τοῦ ποιητοῦ καὶ τοῦ φιλοσόφου, ἄμουσον μὲν τὴν ᾠδὴν ποιεῖς, μῦθον δὲ τὸν λόγον· ἄνευ δὲ τοῦ ἀληθοῦς μήτε μύθῳ ποιητοῦ διαπιστεύσῃς τὸ πάμπαν μήτε φιλοσόφου λόγῳ.

8. Καὶ γὰρ Ἐπίκουρος λέγει μὲν λόγους, ἀλλὰ μύθων ἀτοπωτέρους· ὥστε ἔγωγε πιστεύω μᾶλλον Ὁμήρῳ περὶ Διὸς λέγοντι, ὅτι ψυχὰς δυοῖν ἀριστέοιν ἐπὶ πλάστιγγος χρυσῆς ἐταλάντευεν,

τὴν μὲν Ἀχιλλῆος, τὴν δ᾽ Ἕκτορος ἀνδροφόνοιο,

ἀνατείνας τὰ ζυγὰ τῇ δεξιᾷ· ὁρῶ γὰρ τὴν εἱμαρμένην τῶν ἀνδρῶν συναπονεύουσαν τῇ Διὸς δεξιᾷ·

. . . οὐ γὰρ ἐμὸν παλινάγρετον οὐδ᾽ ἀπατηλὸν
οὐδ᾽ ἀτελεύτητον, ὅτι κεν κεφαλῇ κατανεύσω.

---

16 *Il.* 22.211, which has "horse-taming" rather than "manslaying" Hector.

17 *Il.* 1.526–27, spoken by Zeus.

that makes the shields equally heroic and impressive, for in this case the relative value of gold and oxhide is irrelevant.

Likewise, in our present discussion you should understand meters and poetry as gold, and prose as everyday material. Disregard whether the material consists of gold or oxhide, and consider instead the virtue of the one wielding it. Just let him tell the truth, and if a poet says it in a myth and in verse, I will follow his allegories, scrutinize his myth, and not be distracted by his poetry. Just let him tell the truth, and if he says it in plain prose, I will accept it and welcome how easy it is to listen to. But if you deprive either the poet or the philosopher of the truth, you will rob the poem of its poetry and turn the philosopher's discourse into myth. If truth is absent, you should put no faith whatsoever in either the poet's myth or the philosopher's discourse.

8. A case in point is Epicurus, who indeed states his doctrines, but they are more outlandish than any myth, and for that reason I personally put more trust in Homer, when he says that Zeus was weighing the souls of the two heroes in golden scales,

> the one of Achilles, the other of manslaying Hector,[16]

as he held up the balance with his right hand, for I can see the fate of the men swaying in Zeus' hand:

> . . . for no decision of mine may be taken back or proven false
> or nullified, once I nod my head to it.[17]

αἰσθάνομαι τῶν Διὸς νευμάτων· διὰ τούτων γῆ μένει καὶ ἀναχεῖται θάλαττα καὶ ἀὴρ διαρρεῖ καὶ πῦρ ἄνω θεῖ καὶ οὐρανὸς περιφέρεται καὶ ζῷα γίνεται καὶ δένδρα φύεται· τῶν Διὸς νευμάτων ἔργα καὶ ἀνθρώπου ἀρετὴ καὶ εὐδαιμονία.

Συνίημι δὲ καὶ Ἀθηνᾶς, νῦν μὲν τῷ Ἀχιλλεῖ ξυνισταμένης καὶ ἀπαγούσης τοῦ θυμοῦ τὸν ἄνδρα καὶ σπώσης ὀπίσω, νῦν δὲ τῷ Ὀδυσσεῖ παρισταμένης

ἐν πάντεσσι πόνοισιν.

ξυνίημι καὶ τοῦ Ἀπόλλωνος, τοξότης ὁ θεὸς καὶ μουσικός· καὶ φιλῶ μὲν αὐτοῦ τὴν ἁρμονίαν, φοβοῦμαι δὲ τὴν τοξείαν. σείει δὲ καὶ Ποσειδῶν γῆν τριστόμῳ δόρατι, ξυνάγει καὶ Ἄρης στρατοπέδων τάξεις, καὶ ὁ Ἥφαιστος χαλκεύει, ἀλλ᾽ οὐκ Ἀχιλλεῖ μόνῳ, πάσῃ <δὲ>[6] διαπύρῳ χρείᾳ συντάττεται καὶ συνεργάζεται. ταῦτα μὲν οἱ ποιηταὶ λέγουσιν, ταῦτα δὲ καὶ οἱ φιλόσοφοι λέγουσιν· ὧν ἂν μεταβάλῃς τὰ ὀνόματα, εὑρήσεις τὴν ὁμοιότητα καὶ γνωριεῖς τὸ διήγημα. κάλει τὸν μὲν Δία νοῦν πρεσβύτατον καὶ ἀρχικώτατον, ᾧ πάντα ἕπεται καὶ πειθαρχεῖ· τὴν δὲ Ἀθηνᾶν, φρόνησιν· τὸν δὲ Ἀπόλλω, ἥλιον· τὸν δὲ Ποσειδῶ, πνεῦμα διὰ γῆς καὶ θαλάττης ἰόν, οἰκονομοῦν αὐτῶν τὴν στάσιν καὶ τὴν ἁρμονίαν.

[6] suppl. U, Trapp

---

[18] The nods of Zeus are similarly allegorized at *Or.* 41.2.

I can actually experience the effects of Zeus' nods, for through them the earth remains firmly in place, the sea flows over it, the air flows around it, fire rises above it, the heavens revolve about it, creatures are born and trees grow upon it—and human virtue and happiness are also the products of Zeus' nods.[18]

I understand Athena, too, at one time standing with Achilles, when she pulls the man back and dissuades him from his anger,[19] and at another time standing beside Odysseus

amidst all his toils.[20]

I also understand Apollo, the god of music and archery, for I love his harmonies and I fear his arrows. Poseidon shakes the earth with his three-pronged spear, Ares musters the ranks of armies, and Hephaestus performs his metalworking, not only for Achilles,[21] but is at hand and assists wherever fire is being used. This is what poets say, and philosophers say it too. Simply switch the names and you will discover their similarity; you will also realize what they are saying. Call Zeus the most venerable and sovereign Mind that all things follow and obey; call Athena Intelligence;[22] call Apollo the Sun; and Poseidon the Spirit that pervades land and sea, regulating their stability and harmony.[23]

[19] *Il.* 1.193–214. [20] *Od.* 13.301.

[21] In fashioning his golden shield.

[22] Athena is allegorized as a *daimonion* at *Or.* 8.5–6 (quoting *Il.* 1.197) and as virtue at *Or.* 26.8 (quoting *Od.* 13.301).

[23] For these allegorical associations, see the citations of Diogenes of Babylon (ca. 230–ca. 150 BC) at *SVF* 3.33.

9. Κἂν ἐπὶ τὰ ἄλλα ἴῃς, εὑρήσεις πάντα μεστὰ παρὰ μὲν τοῖς ποιηταῖς ὀνομάτων, παρὰ δὲ τοῖς φιλοσόφοις λόγων. τὰ δὲ Ἐπικούρου τίνι μύθων εἰκάσω; τίς οὕτω ποιητὴς ἀργὸς καὶ ἐκλελυμένος καὶ θεῶν ἄπειρος;

τὸ ἀθάνατον οὔτε αὐτὸ πράγματα ἔχει, οὔτε ἄλλῳ παρέχει.

τίς μοι γένηται τοιοῦτος μῦθος; πῶς ἀναπλάσω τὸν Δία; τί δρῶντα καὶ τί βουλευόμενον καὶ ποίαις ἡδοναῖς συνόντα; πίνει μὲν καὶ παρ᾽ Ὁμήρῳ ὁ Ζεύς, ἀλλὰ καὶ δημηγορεῖ καὶ βουλεύεται, ὡς ἡ τῶν περὶ τὴν Ἀσίαν πραγμάτων χορηγία ἐκ βασιλέως ῥεῖ, καὶ ἡ τῶν Ἑλληνικῶν πραγμάτων χορηγία ἐκ τῆς Ἀθηναίων ἐκκλησίας ῥεῖ· βουλεύεται γὰρ ὑπὲρ μὲν τῆς Ἀσίας ὁ μέγας βασιλεύς, περὶ δὲ τῆς Ἑλλάδος ὁ Ἀθηναίων δῆμος.

Βουλεύεται καὶ περὶ νεὼς κυβερνήτης καὶ περὶ στρατοπέδου στρατηγὸς καὶ περὶ πόλεως νομοθέτης· καὶ ἵνα σωθῇ ναῦς καὶ στρατόπεδον καὶ γῆ καὶ οἶκος, πράγματα μὲν ὁ κυβερνήτης ἔχει, πράγματα δὲ ἔχει ὁ στρατηγός, πράγματα δὲ ὁ νομοθέτης· ὑπὲρ δὲ οὐρανοῦ καὶ γῆς καὶ θαλάττης καὶ τῶν ἄλλων μερῶν, τίς, ὦ Ἐπίκουρε, βουλεύεται; τίς κυβερνήτης; τίς στρατηγός; τίς νομοθέτης; τίς γεωργός; τίς οἰκονό-

9. If you proceed to other examples, you will find poetry to be full of proper names and philosophy full of concepts. But when it comes to Epicurus' writings, to what myths can I possibly compare them? What poet is so indolent, so weak, so ignorant of the gods as he is? He actually says,

> what is immortal does not trouble itself, nor does it trouble anyone else.[24]

What myth, I ask, says any such thing? How would I represent such a Zeus—what he does, what he makes plans for, or what pleasures he enjoys? In Homer Zeus does indeed do his drinking, but he also addresses councils and makes plans, just as the administration of Asian affairs emanates from the Persian king, and the administration of Greek affairs emanates from the Athenian assembly, for the Persian king looks out for Asia, while the Athenian people look out for Greece.

A helmsman looks out for his ship, a general for his army, a lawmaker for his city; and in order to insure the safety of their ship, army, land, and home, the helmsman "troubles himself,"[25] the general "troubles himself," and the lawmaker "troubles himself." Who, then, Epicurus, looks out for the sky, earth, sea, and all the other parts of the universe? What helmsman does that? What general? What lawmaker? What farmer? What householder? Not

[24] An adaptation of Principal Doctrine 1 (Diog. Laert. 10.139), substituting "immortal" (*τὸ ἀθάνατον*) for "blessed and eternal" (*τὸ μακάριον καὶ ἄφθαρτον*).

[25] This picks up Epicurus' own words in the quotation (*πράγματα ἔχει*).

μος; ἀλλ' οὐδὲ ὁ Σαρδανάπαλλος ἀπράγμων ἦν, ἀλλ' ἐντὸς θυρῶν κατακεκλεισμένος, ἐπὶ σφυρηλάτου κλίνης κείμενος ἐν γυναικῶν χορῷ, ἐβουλεύετο ὅμως πῶς σωθῇ Νῖνος καὶ πῶς Ἀσσύριοι εὐδαιμονῶσιν· σοὶ δὲ ἡ Διὸς ἡδονὴ καὶ τῆς Σαρδαναπάλλου ἐκείνου ἀργοτέρα; ὢ μύθων ἀπίστων καὶ μηδεμιᾷ ποιητικῇ ἁρμονίᾳ πρεπόντων.

even Sardanapallus[26] remained aloof from affairs,[27] for in spite of being confined indoors, reclining on a bed of hammered gold, and surrounded by his harem, he nonetheless looked out for the safety of Nineveh and the prosperity of the Assyrians. So do you really think that Zeus' pleasure is more indolent than that of Sardanapallus? What absurd myths, and how unfit for any poetic harmony!

26 The legendary hedonistic king of Assyria. For another description of his pleasure seeking, see *Or*. 7.7. He is also cited at *Orr*. 1.9, 14.2, 15.8, 29.1, and 32.3 and 9.

27 Remaining aloof (ἀπράγμων) alludes to Epicurean withdrawal from public life.

## *ORATION* 5[1]

### INTRODUCTION

The oration argues that petitionary prayer (*Bittgebet*) to the gods is useless. It opens with a version of the Midas story as an allegory of foolishly praying for something, regretting it, and then wrongly blaming the gods for the result, wrongly so because the gods give only what is good (§1). Croesus bribed Apollo to get the unfortunate answer he desired, while contradictory examples from the *Iliad* raise the question of whether the gods capriciously grant prayers (§2). Can the gods be "swayed," as Phoenix claims (*Il.* 9.497), or are they unyielding? Unlike humans, the gods do not change their minds. The issue turns on whether the petitioner is deserving (*axios*) of receiving what he prays for: if he is deserving, then he will receive it; if not, then he will not. Prayer will not make a difference (§3).[2]

All the things humans pray for are either overseen by

[1] Van der Horst (1996) provides a translation of this oration with detailed annotation.

[2] The pseudo-Platonic *Second Alcibiades* also treats the danger of ill-considered prayers and endorses the prayer of the Spartans: "King Zeus, give us what is good, whether we pray for it or not; but keep away what is harmful even if we pray for it" (2 *Alc.* 143a).

providence (*pronoia*), or necessitated by fate (*heimarmenē*), or subject to changing fortune (*tychē*), or managed by expertise (*technē*). If something belongs to providence, prayer is useless, because a providential god looks out for the universe as a whole and will not grant anything that goes against the preservation of the whole (§4). Prayer is completely ridiculous if the request goes against fate, for it is like an inflexible tyrant, and even Zeus is subject to it (§5). If the request belongs to fortune, it is like dealing with a capricious, irrational despot. Finally, if it falls under human expertise, there is no need to pray, only to exercise the expertise (§6). Then what *should* one pray for? Not money, for it can be acquired by immoral means. Like a petitioner coming before a tribunal of the gods, they will assess your case on the basis of what is advantageous, not by how pitifully you parade your desires. If you are asking for something for a good purpose, then you will have it because you deserve it: asking is useless (§7). Socrates indeed prayed to the gods, but a philosopher's prayer is not for something he does not have, but is a conversation about what he actually does have, and it exemplifies his own virtue. In fact, only a philosopher truly knows how to pray (§8).[3]

[3] An apt example is Socrates' prayer at the end of the *Phaedrus* (279b–c): "O dear Pan and all you other gods of this place, grant that I may become good (*kalon*) within, and that all I possess outside may accord with what is within me."

# *ORATION* 5

Εἰ δεῖ εὔχεσθαι

1. Ἀνὴρ Φρύξ, ἀργὸς τὸν βίον, ἐραστὴς χρημάτων, λαμβάνει τὸν Σάτυρον, ὥς φησὶν ὁ μῦθος, δαίμονα φίλοινον, κεράσας οἴνῳ κρήνην, εἰς ἣν φοιτῶν διψήσας ἔπινεν. εὔχεται ὁ ἀνόητος Φρὺξ δαίμονι αἰχμαλώτῳ· εὔχεται δὲ εὐχὴν οἵαν εἰκὸς ἦν καὶ τοῦτον αἰτεῖν καὶ ἐκεῖνον τελεσιουργεῖν, γενέσθαι αὐτῷ τὴν γῆν χρυσῆν καὶ τὰ δένδρα χρυσᾶ καὶ τὰ λήϊα καὶ τοὺς λειμῶνας καὶ τὰ ἐν αὐτοῖς ἄνθη. δίδωσιν ταῦτα ὁ Σάτυρος. ἐπεὶ δὲ αὐτῷ ἐκεχρύσωτο ἡ γῆ, λιμὸς εἶχεν Φρύγας· καὶ ὁ Μίδας ὀδύρεται τὸν πλοῦτον καὶ ποιεῖται παλινῳδίαν τῆς εὐχῆς, καὶ εὔχεται Σατύρῳ μὲν οὐκέτι, θεοῖς δὲ καὶ θεαῖς, ἐλθεῖν αὐτῷ τὴν ἀρχαίαν πενίαν, τὴν εὔφορον ἐκείνην καὶ πάμφορον καὶ καρποτρόφον, τὸν δὲ χρυσὸν ἀπελθεῖν εἰς ἐχθρῶν κεφαλάς. ὁ μὲν ταῦτα εὔχετο ποτνιώμενος, ἐτελεῖτο δὲ οὐδὲν μᾶλλον.

# *ORATION* 5

## Whether one ought to pray

1. There is a story about how a Phrygian,[1] who led a lazy life and was a lover of money, once captured Satyrus, a divinity who loved wine, by mixing wine with the water of a spring where he went to drink when he was thirsty. The foolish Phrygian then prayed to his divine captive, and the prayer he made was of the kind one would expect him to make—and the other to fulfill—namely that his land might turn to gold, along with the trees, wheat fields, and meadows with their flowers. So Satyrus granted his wish. But once his land had turned to gold, famine gripped the Phrygians, and Midas lamented this wealth and sought to retract his prayer, yet he no longer prayed to Satyrus, but instead to the gods and goddesses, that his former poverty, which had been so productive and fertile and had nourished his crops, would return to him, and that the gold would leave him and come down on the heads of his enemies. Such was his prayer, but for all his imploring, it remained unfulfilled.

[1] Midas, named below. The capture of Satyrus is briefly mentioned at Xen. *An.* 1.2.13. In the best-known version by Ovid, at *Met.* 11.85–145, Midas turns things to gold by touching them and is ultimately allowed to retract his wish.

Ἐπαινῶ τὸν μῦθον τῆς χάριτος καὶ τῆς πρὸς τἀληθὲς ὁδοῦ. τί γὰρ δὴ ἄλλο αἰνίττεται ἢ ἀνοήτου ἀνδρὸς εὐχὴν ἐπ' οὐδενὶ χρηστῷ, εὐχομένου μὲν ἵνα τύχῃ, μεταγιγνώσκοντος δὲ ἐπειδὰν τύχῃ; τὴν δὲ θήραν τοῦ Σατύρου καὶ τὰ δεσμὰ καὶ τὸν οἶνον ᾐνίξατο ὁ μῦθος ὅτι οἱ μὲν ἀπατήσαντες, οἱ δὲ καὶ βιασάμενοι τυχόντες ὧν εὔξαντο, οὐχ ὧν ἐπεθύμουν,[1] ἀνατιθέασιν θεοῖς τὴν δωρεάν, οὐ παρ' ἐκείνων λαβόντες· οὐδὲν γὰρ τῶν μὴ καλῶν δίδωσιν θεός, ἀλλ' ἔστιν ταῦτα δωρεὰ τύχης, ἄλογος ἀλόγου, οἷαι καὶ αἱ παρὰ τῶν μεθυόντων φιλοφροσύναι.

2. Τί δὲ Λυδός, ὁ τοῦ Φρυγὸς ἀνοητότερος; οὐκ εὔξατο μὲν τῷ Ἀπόλλωνι ἑλεῖν τὴν Περσῶν ἀρχὴν καὶ ἐθεράπευεν χρυσῷ πολλῷ τὸν θεόν, ὥσπερ δωροδόκον δυνάστην, ἀκούων δὲ αὐτοῦ θαμὰ ἐκ Δελφῶν ἐπιστέλλοντος

> Κροῖσος Ἅλυν διαβὰς μεγάλην ἀρχὴν
> καταλύσει,

ἐκδεχόμενος πρὸς ἡδονὴν τὸν χρησμὸν διέβη Ἅλυν, καὶ κατέλυσεν τὴν Λυδῶν μεγάλην ἀρχήν; ἀκούω δὲ καὶ παρ' Ὁμήρῳ εὐχομένου Ἕλληνος ἀνδρός,

[1] εὔξαντο, οὐχ ὧν ἐπεθύμουν Trapp: ἐπεθύμουν, οὐχ ὧν εὔξαντο R

I commend this story both for its charm and for the way it leads to the truth. For what else is it but an allegory about a prayer for nothing worthwhile by a foolish man, who prays to obtain something and then regrets obtaining it? But the story also suggested that the capture of Satyrus, his bondage, and the wine were significant, namely that when people use deception or force to obtain what they pray for—but not what they really want—they attribute the gift to the gods, when in fact it is not from them that they received it, for god never gives things that are not good.[2] No, those are a gift of fortune,[3] a senseless gift from a senseless giver, much like the friendly embraces of drunkards.

2. And what about the Lydian,[4] who was even more foolish than our Phrygian? Did he not pray to Apollo to conquer the empire of the Persians, and court the god with a mass of gold like some corruptible ruler? And when he heard the god's repeated response from Delphi, saying,

> If Croesus crosses the Halys, he will destroy a great
> empire,[5]

did he not interpret the prophecy in the way that pleased him, cross the Halys, and indeed destroy the great empire of the Lydians? In Homer I also hear a Greek man praying,

[2] A basic tenet of Platonists. Cf. Pl. *Ti.* 30a and *Resp.* 2.380c: "God is not responsible for all things, but for good things." See also *Or.* 41.4.

[3] The speaker plays on the verb τυχεῖν (to obtain) and τύχη (fortune): τύχη . . . τύχη . . . τυχόντες . . . τύχης.

[4] Croesus.

[5] Cited at Arist. *Rh.* 3.5.1407a39. Cf. Hdt. 1.53.3 and *Or.* 13.5.

Ζεῦ πάτερ, ἢ Αἴαντα λαχεῖν, ἢ Τυδέος υἱόν,
ἢ αὐτὸν βασιλῆα πολυχρύσοιο Μυκήνης·

καὶ δηλαδὴ ὁ Ζεὺς ἐπιτελεῖ τὴν εὐχήν,

ἐκ δ' ἔθορε κλῆρος κυνέης, ὃν ἄρ' ἤθελον αὐτοί,
Αἴαντος.

καὶ τῷ μὲν Πριάμῳ εὐχομένῳ ὑπὲρ τῆς οἰκείας γῆς, βοῦς καὶ ὄϊς ὁσημέραι τῷ Διὶ καταθύοντι, ἀτελῆ τὴν εὐχὴν τίθησιν· τῷ δὲ Ἀγαμέμνονι

ὑπέσχετο καὶ κατένευσεν

ἐπὶ τὴν ἀλλοτρίαν ἐλθόντι

Ἴλιον ἐκπέρσαντ' εὐτείχεον ἀπονέεσθαι.

καὶ ὁ Ἀπόλλων πρότερον μὲν οὐκ ἐπαμύνει τῷ Χρύσῃ ἀδικουμένῳ, ἐπεὶ δὲ πρὸς αὐτὸν ἐπαρρησιάσατο καὶ ἀνέμνησεν τῆς κνίσης τῶν μηρίων, τότε τοὺς ἰοὺς ἀφίησιν εἰς τὸ Ἑλληνικόν, ἐννῆμαρ ἐποιχόμενος αὐτοὺς καὶ ὀρεῖς καὶ κύνας.

3. Τί ταῦτα, ὦ ποιητῶν ἄριστε; λίχνον καὶ δωροδόκον τὸ θεῖον καὶ μηδὲν διαφέρον τῶν πολλῶν ἀνθρώπων, καί σου τὸ ἔπος τοῦτο ἀποδεξόμεθα,

στρεπτοὶ δέ τε καὶ θεοὶ αὐτοί;

---

[6] *Il.* 7.179–80, as the Greeks were choosing a champion to face Hector. It is also quoted at *Or.* 10.7. [7] *Il.* 7.182–83.

> Father Zeus, may the lot choose Ajax, or Tydeus' son,
> or the king himself, lord of Mycenae rich in gold,[6]

and Zeus clearly fulfilled his prayer, for

> from the helmet sprang the lot they truly wished for,
> that of Ajax.[7]

Yet when Priam prayed for his homeland and sacrificed cattle and sheep every day to Zeus, the god left his prayer unfulfilled,[8] whereas to Agamemnon

> he promised and nodded assent[9]

that after invading another country,

> he would sack well-walled Troy and sail back home.[10]

And although Apollo did not defend Chryses previously when he was being mistreated,[11] once the priest addressed him with candor and reminded him of the savor of the thighbones he had burned for him, the god loosed his arrows on the Greek army, and for nine days attacked the men, mules, and dogs.[12]

3. What does this mean, O greatest of all poets? Is divinity greedy and corruptible, no different from most men, and are we to accept this verse of yours that says,

> the gods themselves can be swayed?[13]

[8] Cf. *Il.* 4.31–49. [9] *Il.* 2.112. [10] *Il.* 2.113.

[11] That is, by Agamemnon, who sent him away and threatened him at *Il.* 1.24–32. [12] *Il.* 1.35–52.

[13] *Il.* 9.497, Phoenix speaking to Achilles. This verse was cited and condemned at Pl. *Resp.* 2.364d–66a.; see also Pl. *Leg.* 10.905d–7b.

ἢ τοὐναντίον ἄστρεπτον τὸ θεῖον καὶ ἀτενὲς καὶ ἀπαραίτητον; μετατίθεσθαι γὰρ καὶ μεταγινώσκειν προσήκει μὴ ὅτι θεῷ, ἀλλ' οὐδὲ ἀνδρὶ ἀγαθῷ· ὁ γὰρ στρεπτὸς ἀνὴρ καὶ μετανοητικός, εἰ μὲν εἰς τὸ βέλτιον ἐκ τοῦ φαυλοτέρου μετατίθεται, πονήρως ἐβουλεύσατο· εἰ δὲ εἰς τὸ χεῖρον ἐκ τοῦ βελτίστου, πονηρῶς μετέθετο· τὸ δὲ θεῖον ἔξω πονηρίας. καὶ γὰρ ἤτοι ὁ εὐχόμενος ἄξιος τυχεῖν ὧν ηὔξατο ἢ οὐκ ἄξιος· εἰ μὲν οὖν ἄξιος, τεύξεται καὶ μὴ εὐξάμενος· εἰ δὲ οὐκ ἄξιος, οὐ τεύξεται οὐδὲ εὐξάμενος. οὔτε γὰρ ὁ ἄξιος μέν, παραλείπων δὲ τὴν εὐχήν, διὰ τοῦτο οὐκ ἄξιος, ὅτι οὐκ εὔξατο· οὔτε ὁ μὴ ἄξιος μὲν τυχεῖν, λαβεῖν δὲ εὐχόμενος, διὰ τοῦτο ἄξιος, ὅτι εὔξατο.

Ἀλλὰ αὐτὸ τοὐναντίον, ὁ μὲν ἄξιος λαβεῖν μὴ ἐνοχλῶν τυχεῖν ἀξιώτερος· ὁ δὲ οὐκ ἄξιος ἐνοχλῶν καὶ διὰ τοῦτο οὐκ ἄξιος· καὶ τῷ μὲν ἀναθήσομεν αἰδῶ καὶ θάρσος, διὰ μὲν τὸ θαρρεῖν πιστεύοντι ὡς τευξομένῳ, διὰ δὲ τὴν αἰδῶ ἡσυχάζοντι κἂν μὴ τύχῃ· τῷ δὲ ἀμαθίαν καὶ μοχθηρίαν, διὰ μὲν ἀμαθίαν εὐχομένῳ, διὰ δὲ μοχθηρίαν οὐκ ἀξιουμένῳ.

Τί δέ, εἰ στρατηγὸς ἦν ὁ θεός, κᾆτα ὁ μὲν σκευοφορεῖν ἄξιος ᾔτει τὸν στρατηγὸν ὁπλίτου χώραν, ὁ δὲ ὁπλιτεύειν ἐπιτήδειος τὴν ἡσυχίαν ἦγεν· ἆρα οὐ κατὰ τὴν χρείαν τῆς τάξεως τὸν μὲν ἀχθοφορεῖν εἴα, τὸν δὲ εἰς τοὺς ὁπλίτας ἔταττεν; ἀλλὰ στρατηγὸς μὲν κἂν

Or is it the opposite, that divinity cannot be swayed and is unyielding and implacable? After all, changing one's mind and repenting is unseemly even for a good man, let alone a god. For in the case of a man who is easily swayed and repentant, if the change is from worse to better, then his decision was faulty in the first place; but if the change is from best to worse, then the change itself is faulty. But divinity is devoid of fallibility. In fact, someone who prays either deserves to get what he prays for, or does not. If he deserves it, then he will get it, even without praying. But if he does not deserve it, then he will not get it, even if he does pray. For neither does someone who is deserving, but fails to pray, become undeserving simply by not praying, nor does someone who does not deserve to have something, but prays to have it, become deserving, just because he prays for it.

In fact, the exact opposite is true. The man who deserves to have something and does not bother the gods for it is all the more deserving, whereas the one who is undeserving and bothers them is even more undeserving for that very reason. To the former we attribute modesty and confidence—because of his confidence he believes that he will succeed, and because of his modesty he keeps quiet even if he fails. To the other we attribute folly and wickedness—because of his folly he prays in the first place, and because of his wickedness he is deemed undeserving.

What if god were a general, and a man qualified only to carry baggage asked the general to be stationed as a hoplite, while a soldier trained as a hoplite remained silent? Would not the general, out of regard for the demands of his battle line, let the one carry baggage and station the other in the ranks of the hoplites? And yet, a

ἀγνοήσαι, κἂν δωροδοκήσαι, κἂν ἐξαπατηθείη· τὸ δὲ θεῖον οὐ τοιοῦτον· οὔτε οὖν εὐχομένοις δώσει παρὰ τὴν ἀξίαν, οὔτε οὐκ εὐχομένοις οὐ δώσει κατὰ τὴν ἀξίαν.

4. Καὶ μὴν τῶν ὅσα οἱ ἄνθρωποι εὔχονται γενέσθαι σφίσι, τὰ μὲν ἡ πρόνοια ἐφορᾷ, τὰ δὲ ἡ εἱμαρμένη καταναγκάζει, τὰ δὲ μεταβάλλει ἡ τύχη, τὰ δὲ οἰκονομεῖ ἡ τέχνη. καὶ ἡ μὲν πρόνοια θεοῦ ἔργον, ἡ δὲ εἱμαρμένη ἀνάγκης, ἡ δὲ τέχνη ἀνθρώπου, ἡ δὲ τύχη τοῦ αὐτομάτου· διακεκλήρωνται δὲ τούτων ἑκάστῳ αἱ ὗλαι τοῦ βίου· ἃ τοίνυν εὐχόμεθα, ἢ εἰς πρόνοιαν συντελεῖ θεοῦ ἢ εἰς εἱμαρμένης ἀνάγκην ἢ εἰς ἀνθρώπου τέχνην ἢ εἰς τύχης φοράν.

Καὶ εἰ μὲν εἰς πρόνοιαν συντελεῖ, τί δεῖ εὐχῆς; εἰ γάρ τοι προνοεῖ ὁ θεός, ἤτοι προνοεῖ τοῦ ὅλου, τῶν δὲ κατὰ μέρος οὐ φροντίζει, ὥσπερ οἱ βασιλεῖς σῴζουσι τὰς πόλεις νόμῳ καὶ δίκῃ, οὐ διατείνοντες ἐφ᾽ ἕκαστον τῇ φροντίδι, ἢ κἂν τοῖς ἐπὶ μέρους ἡ πρόνοια ἐξετάζεται. τί δὴ φῶμεν; βούλει τοῦ ὅλου προνοεῖν τὸν θεόν; οὐκ ἐνοχλητέον ἄρα τῷ θεῷ· οὐ γὰρ πείσεται, ἤν τι παρὰ τὴν σωτηρίαν αἰτῇς τοῦ ὅλου.

Τί γὰρ εἰ καὶ τὰ μόρια τοῦ σώματος φωνὴν λαβόντα, ἐπειδὰν κάμνῃ τι αὐτῶν ὑπὸ τοῦ ἰατροῦ τεμνόμενον ἐπὶ σωτηρίᾳ τοῦ ὅλου, εὔξαιτο τῇ τέχνῃ μὴ φθαρῆναι; οὐκ ἀποκρινεῖται ὁ Ἀσκληπιὸς αὐτοῖς ὡς

---

[14] The argument that preserving the whole entails the de-

general can be ignorant, bribed, or deceived, but divinity is not like that. For this reason, it will not grant anything to undeserving people simply because they pray for it, nor withhold anything from deserving people simply because they do not pray for it.

4. Moreover, of all the things that humans pray to obtain, some are overseen by providence, some are necessitated by fate, some are subject to changing fortune, and some are managed by expertise. Now providence is the work of god, fate the work of necessity, expertise the work of man, and fortune the work of chance. The things that constitute human life are allotted to one or another of these, so that what we pray for belongs either to god's providence, fate's necessity, man's expertise, or fortune's capriciousness.

So, if something belongs to providence, what is the use of prayer? For if god is provident, then either he provides for the universe as a whole, without concern for particulars (just as kings safeguard cities by means of law and justice, but do not extend their concern to each particular instance), or else providence proves to be active in particulars as well. What should we say? Do you want god to provide for the universe as a whole? Then do not bother god, because he will not be persuaded if you ask for anything that goes against the preservation of the whole.[14]

For what would happen if the parts of the body could speak, and whenever one of them was distressed at being amputated by a doctor to save the whole, it would pray to the art of medicine not to be destroyed? Would not Ascle-

struction of individual elements is advanced at *Or*. 41.4. It is both Platonic (*Leg*. 10.903b–c) and Stoic (e.g., Plut. *Stoic. rep*. 1050e).

οὐχ ὑμῶν ἕνεκα, ὦ δείλαια, χρὴ οἴχεσθαι τὸ πᾶν σῶμα, ἀλλὰ ἐκεῖνο σωζέσθω ὑμῶν ἀπολλυμένων; τοῦτο καὶ τῷ σύμπαντι τούτῳ γίγνεσθαι φιλεῖ· Ἀθηναῖοι λοιμώττουσιν, σείονται Λακεδαιμόνιοι, ἡ Θετταλία ἐπικλύζεται, ἡ Αἴτνη φλέγεται· ὧν σὺ μὲν τὴν διάλυσιν φθορὰν καλεῖς, ὁ δὲ ἰατρὸς οἶδεν τὴν αἰτίαν καὶ ἀμελεῖ εὐχομένων τῶν μερῶν, σώζει δὲ τὸ πᾶν· φροντίζει γὰρ τοῦ ὅλου.

Ἀλλὰ καὶ τῶν κατὰ μέρος προνοεῖ ὁ θεός. οὐδὲ ἐνταῦθα τοίνυν εὐκτέον, ὅμοιον ὡς εἰ καὶ ἰατρὸν ᾔτει ὁ κάμνων φάρμακον ἢ σιτίον· τοῦτο γὰρ εἰ μὲν ἀνύτει, καὶ μὴ αἰτοῦντι δώσει, εἰ δὲ ἐπισφαλές, οὐδὲ αἰτοῦντι δώσει. τῶν μὲν δὴ κατὰ τὴν πρόνοιαν οὐδὲν οὔτε αἰτητέον οὔτε εὐκτέον.

5. Τί δὲ τῶν κατὰ τὴν εἱμαρμένην; ἢ κἀνταῦθα ἡ εὐχὴ γελοιότατον· θᾶττον γὰρ ἄν τις βασιλέα ἔπεισεν ἢ τύραννον, τυραννικὸν δὲ ἡ εἱμαρμένη καὶ ἀδέσποτον καὶ ἀμετάστρεπτον, ἣ καθάπερ ψάλιον ἐμβάλλουσα ταῖς τῶν ἀνθρώπων ἀγέλαις βίᾳ σπᾷ καὶ προσαναγκάζει συναπονεύειν ταῖς αὑτῆς ἀγωγαῖς, ὡς Συρακοσίους Διονύσιος, ὡς Πεισίστρατος Ἀθηναίους

---

15 In 430 BC (Thuc. 2.47.3).

16 In 465/4 BC (Thuc. 1.101.2).

17 Cf. Hdt. 7.130.2.

18 In 426/5 BC (Thuc. 3.116.1).

19 For these same examples, see *Or.* 41.4: "these events, which you call destruction . . . I call preservation."

pius reply to these parts in the following way? "O poor things, it is not to save you that the entire body should perish, but for you to perish so that it may be saved." This regularly happens in the whole universe. The Athenians have plagues,[15] the Lacedaemonians have earthquakes,[16] Thessaly has floods,[17] and Aetna erupts.[18] You may call this breaking up "destruction,"[19] but the physician[20] understands the cause, for he disregards the prayers of the parts to preserve the whole, because his concern is for the whole.

But, you object, god's providence extends to particulars as well. Yet here too prayer has no place, for it would be like a sick patient asking his doctor for medicine or food. If it is effective, then the doctor will give it, even if the patient does not ask for it; but if it is unsafe, he will not give it, even if the patient asks for it. Therefore, not a single thing that belongs to providence should be requested or prayed for.

5. Then what about things within the purview of fate? Here too prayer is utterly ridiculous. For although someone might persuade a king sooner than he could a tyrant, fate is in fact a tyrannical power that has no master and cannot be swayed. It casts a bridle and bit, so to speak, on the herds of humans and drags them by force and compels them to comply with its movements,[21] as Dionysius did with the Syracusans,[22] Pisistratus the Athenians,[23] Perian-

20 That is, god.

21 Being dragged by fate is a Stoic image; cf. *SVF* 2.975.

22 Dionysius II ruled 367 to 357 BC.

23 Ruled 546 to 527 BC.

καὶ Περίανδρος Κορινθίους καὶ Θρασύβουλος Μιλησίους. ἐν μὲν γὰρ δημοκρατίᾳ δύναταί τι καὶ πειθὼ καὶ εὐχὴ καὶ θεραπεία καὶ λιταί, ἐν δὲ τυραννίδι ἡ βία κρατεῖ, ὡς ἐν πολέμῳ· {Ὅμηρος}[2]

ζώγρει Ἀτρέος υἱέ, σὺ δ' ἄξια δέξαι ἄποινα.

τίνα τοίνυν ἄποινα δόντες τῇ εἱμαρμένῃ ἐκλυσόμεθα ἑαυτοὺς τῆς ἀνάγκης καὶ τοῦ δεσμοῦ; τίνα χρυσόν; τίνα θεραπείαν; τίνα θυσίαν; τίνα εὐχήν; ἀλλ' οὐδὲ ὁ Ζεὺς αὐτὸς εὕρατο παρ' ἐκείνης ἀποτροπήν, ἀλλ' ὀδύρεται·

ὤ μοι ἐγών, ὅ τέ μοι Σαρπηδόνα φίλτατον
ἀνδρῶν
μοῖρ' ὑπὸ Πατρόκλοιο Μενοιτιάδαο δαμῆναι.

τίνι θεῶν εὔχεται ὁ Ζεὺς ὑπὲρ τοῦ παιδός; καὶ ἡ Θέτις βοᾷ,

ὤ μοι ἐγὼ δειλή· ὤ μοι δυσαριστοτόκεια.

τοιοῦτο χρῆμα ἡ εἱμαρμένη, ἡ Ἄτροπος καὶ ἡ Κλωθὼ καὶ ἡ Λάχεσις, ἄτρεπτον καὶ ἐπικεκλωσμένον καὶ διειληχὸς τοὺς ἀνθρωπίνους βίους. πῶς ἂν οὖν τις εὔξαιτο ἀπαραιτήτῳ εἱμαρμένῃ;

2 del. Stephanus, Davies[2], Dübner, Koniaris

---

24 Ruled ca. 627 to 587 BC.

25 A contemporary of Periander.

der the Corinthians,[24] and Thrasybulus the Milesians.[25] For in a democracy persuasion, prayer, favors, and appeals have some effect, but in a tyranny force prevails, as it does in war:

> Take me alive, son of Atreus, and accept a worthy ransom.[26]

What ransom, then, can we give to fate to free ourselves from its bonds of necessity? What gold? What favor? What sacrifice? What prayer? Not even Zeus himself could find an escape from fate, for he could only lament,

> Woe is me! It is fated for Sarpedon, the man I love best,
> to be killed by Patroclus, son of Menoetius.[27]

To what god can Zeus pray for his son's life? Thetis too cries out,

> O poor me, the wretched mother of the bravest son![28]

Such is the nature of fate—Atropos, Clotho, and Lachesis[29]—the inflexible spinner of destiny, allotted control over human lives. How, then, can anyone ever pray to implacable fate?

26 *Il.* 6.46, Adrastus pleading for his life before Agamemnon dispatches him.

27 *Il.* 16.433–34. Sarpedon was Zeus' son by Laodamia (*Il.* 6.198–99).

28 *Il.* 18.54, Thetis lamenting the fate of Achilles.

29 Atropos (Inflexible), Clotho (Spinner), Lachesis (Allotter). The Stoic Chrysippus similarly allegorized the Fates; cf. *SVF* 2.913–14.

6. Ἀλλ᾿ οὐδὲ ἐν τοῖς κατὰ τὴν τύχην εὐκτέον, καὶ πολὺ μᾶλλον ἐνταῦθα οὐκ εὐκτέον· οὐδὲ γὰρ ἀνοήτῳ δυνάστῃ διαλεκτέον, ἔνθα οὐ βούλευμα οὐδὲ κρίσις οὐδὲ ὁρμὴ σώφρων οἰκονομεῖ τὴν ἀρχήν, ἀλλὰ ὀργὴ καὶ φορὰ καὶ ἄλογοι ὀρέξεις καὶ ἔμπληκτοι ὁρμαὶ καὶ ἐπιθυμιῶν διαδοχαί. τοιοῦτον ἡ τύχη, ἄλογον, ἔμπληκτον, ἀπροόρατον, ἀνήκοον, ἀμάντευτον, Εὐρίπου δίκην μεταρρέον, περιφερόμενον, καὶ οὐδεμιᾶς ἀνεχόμενον κυβερνήτου τέχνης. τί ἂν οὖν τις εὔξαιτο ἀστάτῳ χρήματι καὶ ἀνοήτῳ καὶ ἀσταθμήτῳ καὶ ἀμίκτῳ;

Λοιπὸν δὴ μετὰ τὴν τύχην ἡ τέχνη. καὶ τίς τέκτων εὔξεται περὶ κάλλους ἀρότρου, τὴν τέχνην ἔχων; ἢ τίς ὑφάντης περὶ κάλλους χλανίδος, τὴν τέχνην ἔχων; ἢ τίς χαλκεὺς περὶ κάλλους ἀσπίδος, τὴν τέχνην ἔχων; ἢ τίς ἀριστεὺς περὶ εὐτολμίας, τὴν ἀνδρείαν ἔχων; ἢ τίς ἀγαθὸς περὶ εὐδαιμονίας, τὴν ἀρετὴν ἔχων;

7. Τί τοίνυν ἐστίν, ὑπὲρ ὅτου κἂν εὔξαιτο ἄν τις τοῖς θεοῖς, ὃ μὴ προνοίας ἔχεται ἢ εἱμαρμένης ἢ τέχνης ἢ τύχης; χρήματα αἰτεῖς; μὴ ἐνόχλει θεοῖς, οὐδὲν αἰτεῖς τῶν καλῶν· μὴ ἐνόχλει τῇ εἱμαρμένῃ, οὐδὲν αἰτεῖς τῶν ἀναγκαίων· μὴ ἐνόχλει τῇ τύχῃ, οὐ γὰρ τοῖς δεομένοις δίδωσιν· μὴ ἐνόχλει τῇ τέχνῃ, ἀκούεις γὰρ Μενάνδρου λέγοντος,

---

30 The narrow channel between Boeotia and Euboea, where strong currents shift several times a day, also serves as a symbol of instability in *Orr*. 10.5, 28.3, and 41.3. It already appears at Pl. *Phd*. 90c.

6. Nor should one pray for things within the purview of fortune. Indeed, in this case prayer should be avoided all the more. For there can be no discussion with a senseless despot, whose rule is not based on deliberation, judgment, and reasonable impulses, but on anger, impulsiveness, irrational appetites, capricious urges, and a constant succession of desires. Such is the nature of fortune. It is irrational, capricious, unpredictable, deaf to appeal, inaccessible to prophecy, ebbing and flowing and swirling like the Euripus,[30] and allowing a helmsman no use whatsoever of his expertise. Why then would anyone pray to something so erratic, irrational, unstable, and indifferent?

Lastly, after fortune comes expertise.[31] What carpenter is going to pray for a plow to be beautiful, when he possesses the expertise to make it so? What weaver will pray for a garment to be beautiful, when he possesses the expertise? What smith will pray for a shield to be beautiful, when he possesses the expertise? What war hero will pray for bravery, when he possesses courage? And what good man will pray for happiness, when he possesses virtue?

7. For what, then, should someone pray to the gods that does not depend on providence, fate, expertise, or fortune? Is it money you are asking for? Do not bother the gods for it, because you are not asking for something that is good. Do not bother fate, because you are not asking for something that is necessary. Do not bother fortune, for it does not give to those who beg. Do not bother expertise, because you can hear Menander[32] saying,

31 In this scheme, expertise (*technē*) represents "that which is in our control" (τὸ ἐφ' ἡμῖν).

32 Athenian comic playwright (ca. 344–292 BC).

*οὐ πάνυ τι γηράσκουσιν αἱ τέχναι καλῶς,*
*ἐὰν μὴ λάβωσι προστάτην φιλάργυρον.*

*χρηστὸς εἶ;*[3] *μετάθου τὸν τρόπον, εἶξαι μοχθηρίᾳ,*[4] *ἐπιτήδευσον τὸ πρᾶγμα, καὶ πλοῦτον λάμβανε*[5] *πορνοβοσκῶν ἢ καπηλεύων ἢ ληϊζόμενος ἢ πανουργῶν ἢ ψευδομαρτυρῶν ἢ συκοφαντῶν ἢ δωροδοκῶν. νίκην αἰτεῖς; ἣν δύνασαι λαβεῖν ἐν πολέμῳ μὲν παρὰ μισθοφόρου, ἐν δικαστηρίῳ δὲ παρὰ συκοφάντου. ἐμπορίαν αἰτεῖς; ἣν δίδωσιν ναῦς καὶ θάλαττα καὶ πνευμάτων φορά. ἀγορὰ πρόκειται, ὤνιον τὸ χρῆμα, τί τοῖς θεοῖς ἐνοχλεῖς; μηδὲν τὸ παρὰ τὴν ἀξίαν φοβηθῇς, καὶ πλουτήσεις κἂν Ἱππόνικος ᾖς, νικήσεις κἂν Κλέων ᾖς, αἱρήσεις κἂν Μέλητος ᾖς.*

*Ἐὰν δὲ εἰς τὰς πρὸς τοὺς θεοὺς παρέλθῃς εὐχάς, εἰς δικαστήριον παρελήλυθας ἀκριβὲς καὶ ἀπαραίτητον· οὐδεὶς ἀνέξεταί σου θεὸς εὐχομένου τὰ μὴ εὐκτά, οὐδὲ δώσει τὰ μὴ σοὶ δοτά. ἐξεταστὴς καὶ λογιστὴς ἐφέστηκεν ταῖς ἑκάστου εὐχαῖς πικρός, εὐθύνων τῷ τοῦ συμφέροντος μέτρῳ τὰ σά· οὐδὲ αὐτὸν μεταχειριῇ ἀναβιβασάμενος ὥσπερ εἰς δικαστήριον τὰς ὀρέξεις τὰς σὰς ἐλεεινὰ φθεγγομένας, οἴκτειρον βοώσας,*

[3] *χρηστὸς εἶ* edd.: *ὁ δὲ χρηστὸς ἦν* R
[4] *εἶξαι μοχθηρίᾳ* Trapp: *εὔξαιο μοχθηρίαις* R
[5] *καὶ πλοῦτον λάμβανε* edd.: *καὶ ἢ πλοῦτον καὶ πρᾶγμα λαμβάνεις* R

the arts cannot flourish into maturity
unless they have a patron fond of money.[33]

Are you a decent person? Then you had better change your ways and give in to depravity. Get busy and acquire wealth by running a brothel, or by engaging in trade, or by robbery, crime, perjury, informing, or bribery. Is it victory you are asking for? You can win it in war with the help of mercenaries, or in the courtroom with the help of an informer. Is it commercial success you want? A ship, the sea, and the blowing winds can provide it—the marketplace lies before you and the goods are for sale, so why bother the gods? Have no fear that anything is undeserved, and you will get rich, even if you are a Hipponicus;[34] you will be victorious, even if you are a Cleon;[35] and you will win your case, even if you are a Meletus.[36]

But when you come before the gods with your prayers, you are appearing before a tribunal that is strict and implacable, because no god will put up with your praying for things not to be prayed for, or bestow what should not be given to you. Stern is the examiner and assessor that oversees each person's prayers, scrutinizing your petitions by the standard of what is truly advantageous. You will not influence him by parading your desires, like witnesses in court, wailing piteously, begging for mercy, pouring great

33 Fr. 408 Koerte (= 363 K-A). The text (quoted only here and at Stob. 4.18.14) is in doubt. The point seems to be that art *per se* does not make one rich, only rich patrons do.

34 A wealthy Athenian, also mentioned at *Or*. 3.8.

35 The disgraced Athenian demagogue who was victorious at Pylos in 425 BC.

36 The accuser of Socrates in 399 BC.

*πολλὴν τὴν κόνιν καταχεομένας τῆς κεφαλῆς, εἰ δὲ οὕτω τύχοι καὶ ὀνειδιζούσας τῷ θεῷ,*

*εἴ ποτέ τοι χαρίεντ᾽ ἐπὶ νηὸν ἔρεψα.*

*ἀλλ᾽ ὁ θεὸς λέγει, ἐπὶ ἀγαθῷ αἰτεῖς; λάμβανε· εἶ ἄξιος ὢν*[6] *αἰτεῖς· ταύτῃ ἔχοντί σοι οὐδὲν εὐχῆς δεῖ, λήψῃ καὶ σιωπῶν.*

8. *Ἀλλὰ Σωκράτης εἰς Πειραιᾶ κατῄει προσευξόμενος τῇ θεῷ καὶ τοὺς ἄλλους προετρέπετο, καὶ ἦν ὁ βίος Σωκράτει μεστὸς εὐχῆς. καὶ γὰρ Πυθαγόρας ηὔξατο καὶ Πλάτων καὶ ὅστις ἄλλος θεοῖς προσήγορος· ἀλλὰ σὺ μὲν ἡγεῖ τὴν τοῦ φιλοσόφου εὐχὴν αἴτησιν εἶναι τῶν οὐ παρόντων, ἐγὼ δὲ ὁμιλίαν καὶ διάλεκτον πρὸς τοὺς θεοὺς περὶ τῶν παρόντων καὶ ἐπίδειξιν τῆς ἀρετῆς· ἢ οἴει τοῦτο εὔχετο ὁ Σωκράτης, ὅπως αὐτῷ χρήματα γένηται ἢ ὅπως ἄρξῃ Ἀθηναίων; πολλοῦ γε καὶ δεῖ. ἀλλ᾽ εὔχετο μὲν τοῖς θεοῖς, ἐλάμβανεν δὲ παρ᾽ ἑαυτοῦ συνεπινευόντων ἐκείνων ἀρετὴν ψυχῆς καὶ ἡσυχίαν βίου καὶ ζωὴν ἄμεμπτον καὶ εὔελπιν θάνατον, τὰ θαυμαστὰ δῶρα, τὰ θεοῖς δοτά.*

*Ἐὰν δέ τις παρὰ μὲν τῆς γῆς εὔπλοιαν αἰτῇ, παρὰ δὲ τῆς θαλάττης εὐκαρπίαν, καὶ παρὰ μὲν ὑφάντου ἄροτρον, παρὰ δὲ τέκτονος χλανίδα, ἄπεισιν ἀτελὴς καὶ ἄδωρος καὶ ἄτευκτος. ὦ Ζεῦ καὶ Ἀθηνᾶ καὶ Ἄπολ-*

[6] *εἶ ἄξιος ὢν* scripsi praeeuntibus Acciaiolo, Reiske, Trapp: *εἰ ἄξιος ὢν* R

quantities of dust over their heads, and perhaps even reproaching the god by saying,

> if ever I built a temple that pleased you.[37]

But the god says, "Are you requesting something for a good purpose? If so, then take it, since you deserve what you ask for. If indeed that is the case, you have no need to pray, for you will have it even if you say nothing."

8. But, you object, Socrates went down to the Piraeus to pray to the god,[38] and he urged others to do so as well; indeed Socrates' life was full of prayers. Yes, Pythagoras also prayed, as did Plato and everyone else who was conversant with the gods. You, however, seem to think that a philosopher's prayer is a request for something he does not have, but I consider it a conversation and discussion with the gods about what he actually does have, and is in fact a demonstration of his virtue. Or do you really think that Socrates was praying to have money or to rule over the Athenians? Far from it![39] He certainly prayed to the gods, but it was from himself, with their approval, that he obtained his soul's virtue, his peaceful life, his blameless conduct, and his death full of hope—those extraordinary gifts, the god-given ones.

But if anyone asks the earth for smooth sailing, or the sea for a good harvest, or a weaver for a plow, or a carpenter for a cloak, he will surely go away foiled, empty-handed, and unsuccessful. O Zeus and Athena and Apollo, over-

[37] *Il.* 1.39, Chryses petitioning Apollo; cf. §2 above.

[38] Pl. *Resp.* 1.327a.

[39] Xen. *Mem.* 1.3.2 reports that when Socrates prayed he simply asked for good things (τἀγαθά), in the belief that the gods know best what things are good.

λον, ἐθῶν ἀνθρωπίνων ἐπίσκοποι, φιλοσόφων ὑμῖν μαθητῶν δεῖ, οἳ τὴν ὑμετέραν τέχνην ἐρρωμέναις ψυχαῖς ὑποδεξάμενοι ἄμητον βίου καλὸν καὶ εὐδαίμονα ἐκκαρπώσονται· ἀλλά ἐστιν σπάνιον μὲν τὸ τῆς γεωργίας ταύτης χρῆμα, μόλις δὲ καὶ ὀψὲ παραγινόμενον. δεῖ γε μὴν τοῦ σπανίου τούτου καὶ ὀλίγου ἐναύσματος τῷ βίῳ ἄλλοτε ἐν ἄλλοις σώμασιν φανταζομένου, ὡς ἐν νυκτὶ πολλῇ δεῖ φωτὸς ὀλίγου· τὸ γὰρ καλὸν ἐν ἀνθρωπίνῃ φύσει οὐ πολύ, φιλεῖ γε μὴν πρὸς τοῦ ὀλίγου τούτου σώζεσθαι τὰ πάντα. ἂν δ' ἐξέλῃς τοῦ βίου φιλοσοφίαν, ἐξεῖλες αὐτοῦ τὸ ζώπυρον, τὸ ἔμπνουν, τὸ ζωτικόν, τὸ μόνον εὔχεσθαι ἐπιστάμενον· ὡς ψυχὴν σώματος ἐὰν ἀφέλῃς, ἔπηξας τὸ σῶμα· ὡς καρποὺς γῆς ἐὰν ἀφέλῃς, τὴν γῆν ἐξέτεμες· ὡς ἥλιον ἡμέρας, τὴν ἡμέραν ἔσβεσας.

seers of the ways of men, you need philosophers as your students, ones who will take your expertise into their stout souls and reap a noble and happy harvest of life. But this kind of agriculture is rare, and comes about with effort and belatedly. And yet this rare, small glimmer, which appears now in one body now in another, is as essential to life, as is a small light in the depths of night. For that which is good in human nature may be small, but it is thanks to this small element that the whole is usually preserved. If you remove philosophy from life, you take away its living, breathing spark that alone understands how to pray. So too, if you remove the soul from the body, you render the body inert; if you take away crops from the earth, you cut off its fertility; and if you remove the sun from the day, you extinguish the day.

# *ORATION* 6

## INTRODUCTION

The oration presents a somewhat disjointed examination of knowledge (*epistēmē*) that ends with a discussion of human and divine law. It opens by differentiating human knowledge, which is ephemeral, from divine knowledge, which is eternal (§1). Human knowledge comes about from repeated perception (*aisthēsis*) that leads to experience (*empeiria*), to which the soul applies its power of reasoning (*logismos*). This process resulted in the invention of boats, medicine, and the manual arts (§2). However, not only humans possess this kind of knowledge, because examples of the behavior of cranes and deer prove that animals too can possess a kind of experiential knowledge (§3). What differentiates human knowledge from that of animals is the operation of reason (*logos*), which by means of systematic distinctions and comparisons creates the intellectual arts, such as arithmetic, geometry, and music. The human soul shares its mortal characteristics of nourishment, growth, and perception with animals, while it shares its immortal characteristics of thinking (*noein*), reasoning, and knowing with divinity. Practical intelligence (*phronēsis*) mediates between perception and knowledge, while intellect (*nous*) is its immortal component. The stable certainty (*bebaiotēs*) of knowledge results

from the combined operation of perception, experience, intelligence, reason, and intellect (§4).

Experience leads to the discovery of the arts and crafts that provide for life's needs. Practical intelligence, with the help of reasoning, regulates the emotions, while intellect, the most authoritative element, acts like the laws of a city. But these laws are unwritten, not like the human ones that condemned Socrates and resulted in so many disasters for the Athenians. These divine laws result in peace, knowledge, and philosophy (§5). Historical examples follow. By breaking human laws, Alcibiades was temporarily banished by the Athenians, but when he was banished by philosophy, which never readmits anyone it once banishes, he lost access to knowledge and virtue (§6). Minos' laws embodied the knowledge that was taught to him by Zeus, and as a result the Cretans prospered; Cyrus tried to teach his knowledge of governing, but his successors, Cambyses and Xerxes, did not learn it, and so their people suffered. The text breaks off before Lycurgus' laws as knowledge of music are treated (§7).

# *ORATION* 6

## Τί ἐπιστήμη

1. Τί ποτ' ἐστὶν τοῦτο, ᾧ διαφέρει ἄνθρωπος θηρίου; καὶ τί ποτέ ἐστιν, ᾧ διαφέρει ἀνθρώπου θεός; ἐγὼ μὲν οἶμαι θηρίων μὲν ἀνθρώπους ἐπιστήμῃ κρατεῖν, θεῶν δὲ ἐλαττοῦσθαι σοφίᾳ·[1] θεὸς μὲν γὰρ ἀνθρώπου σοφώτερον, ἄνθρωπος δὲ θηρίου ἐπιστημονέστερον. "ἄλλο τι οὖν ἐπιστήμην σοφίας ἡγεῖ;" οὐ μὰ τὸν Δία, οὐ μᾶλλον ἢ ζωὴν ζωῆς· ἀλλὰ κοινὸν ὑπάρχον τὸ τῆς ζωῆς θνητῇ φύσει πρὸς τὸ ἀθάνατον, κατὰ μὲν τὴν ποιότητα ἰσομοιρεῖ, κατὰ δὲ τὴν βραχύτητα τοῦ βίου σχίζεται· θεοῦ μὲν γὰρ ζωὴ αἰώνιος, ἀνθρώπου δὲ ἐφήμερος.

Ὥσπερ οὖν εἴ τις ἦν δύναμις ὀφθαλμοῖς ὁρᾶν ἀεὶ καὶ ἀποτείνειν διηνεκῶς τὴν ὄψιν καὶ δέχεσθαι τὴν προσβολὴν τοῦ φωτός, καὶ μηδὲν αὐτοῖς ἔδει καλυπτόντων βλεφάρων μηδὲ ὕπνου πρὸς ἀνάπαυλαν μηδὲ νυκτὸς πρὸς ἠρεμίαν, κοινὸν μὲν ἦν τὸ ὁρᾶν ἐκείνοις τοῖς ὀφθαλμοῖς πρὸς ταυτηνὶ τὴν τῶν πολλῶν ὄψιν, διέφερεν δὲ τῷ διηνεκεῖ· οὕτως ἀμέλει καὶ

[1] σοφίᾳ Markland, Trapp: μοχθηρίᾳ R

## *ORATION* 6

### What knowledge is

1. What is it that distinguishes humans from animals? And what distinguishes god from man? In my opinion, humans are superior to animals in knowledge, but are inferior to gods in wisdom: god is wiser than man; man is more knowledgeable than animals. "Do you therefore conclude that knowledge is something other than wisdom?" No, by Zeus, no more than life differs from life. For while the attribute of life is shared by both mortal and immortal nature, and both equally participate in its quality, nonetheless mortal life differs by the brevity of its existence, because the life of god is eternal, whereas that of man is ephemeral.

Now imagine eyes that had the ability to see forever and could maintain their gaze without ceasing and continuously take in the rays of light, and never needed eyelids for cover, or sleep for relaxation, or nighttime for rest. In that case, those eyes would share the faculty of sight with the vision of ordinary people, and the only difference would one of continuity. In exactly the same way divine

ἡ ἐπιστήμη, κοινόν τι οὖσα, διαφορὰν ὅμως ἔχει ἡ θεία πρὸς τὴν ἀνθρωπίνην. καὶ τὴν μὲν θείαν τάχα καὶ αὖθις εἰσόμεθα, νῦν δὲ δὴ ἐπὶ τὰ γνωριμώτατα ἴωμεν· τί ποτ᾽ ἐστὶν τῷ ἀνθρώπῳ τὸ ἐπίστασθαι καὶ εἰδέναι καὶ μανθάνειν, καὶ ὅσα τοιαυτὶ λέγοντες ἕξιν τινὰ θεωρίας τῇ ψυχῇ προστίθεμεν;

2. Ἆρα πᾶν ὅπερ <ἂν>[2] ἡ αἴσθησις ἀθροίσασα τῇ κατὰ βραχὺ θεωρίᾳ, ἐμπειρίαν τοῦτο ὀνομάζουσα, προσαγάγῃ τῇ ψυχῇ, καὶ μετὰ τοῦτο ἐπισφραγίσηται ὁ λογισμὸς τῇ ἐμπειρίᾳ, τοῦτο φῶμεν ἐπιστήμην εἶναι; οἷον τὸ τοιόνδε λέγω· οἱ πρῶτοι ἄνθρωποι οὔπω ναῦν εἰδότες, ἐρῶντες ἐπιμιξίας, ἀγόμενοι μὲν ὑπὸ τῆς χρείας, εἰργόμενοι δὲ ὑπὸ τῆς θαλάττης, εἶδον ὄρνιν ἐξ ἀέρος καταπτάντα νηχόμενον, εἶδον δὲ καὶ φορυτὸν φερόμενον κούφως ὑπὲρ τοῦ κύματος, ἤδη δέ που καὶ δένδρον ἀπενεχθὲν ἐκ ποταμοῦ εἰς κλύδωνα· καὶ τάχα μέν τις καὶ ἄκων κατενεχθείς, κινῶν τὰ ἄρθρα ἐξενήξατο, τάχα δὲ καὶ ἑκὼν ἐν παιδιᾶς μέρει. ἀθροίσασα δὲ ἡ πεῖρα τὴν ἔννοιαν τοῦ πλοῦ σχεδίαν τινὰ φαύλην τὸ πρῶτον ἐξειργάσατο, ὕλην κούφην ξυνδεόντων αὐτοσχέδιον ναῦν· κατὰ βραχὺ δὲ προϊοῦσα ἡ αἴσθησις ὁμοῦ τῷ λογισμῷ ἐσοφίσατο καὶ ἐξεῦρεν ὄχημα κοῖλον, ἐρεσσόμενόν τε καὶ ἐξ ἱστίων πλέον καὶ ὑπὸ ἀνέμων φερόμενον καὶ ὑπὸ οἰάκων εὐθυνόμενον, καὶ ἐπέτρεψεν αὐτοῦ τὴν σωτηρίαν ἐπιστήμῃ μιᾷ τῇ κυβερνητικῇ.

[2] suppl. I, Trapp

knowledge differs from human knowledge, although it is a faculty shared by both.[1] Perhaps at some later time we shall treat divine knowledge,[2] but for now let us turn to what is most familiar. What, then, is it for a human being "to have knowledge," "to know," and "to learn," along with all other such terms we use when we attribute a certain theoretical disposition to the soul?

2. Shall wc then designate as knowledge everything that perception assembles through incremental observation (which is called experience) and presents to the soul, whereupon the power of reasoning puts its confirming stamp on this experience? Here is an example of what I mean. Primitive men, before they had ever seen a ship, longed to socialize with foreigners. They were driven by this need, but were prevented by the sea. They saw a bird descend from the air and begin swimming; they saw wood shavings carried lightly on the waves; and perhaps they even saw a tree carried down a river into the sea. And maybe one of them who inadvertently tumbled into the water began moving his limbs and swam out, or perhaps one intentionally did so in play. Once experience had pieced together the concept of sailing, it first fashioned a flimsy raft, when men tied light materials together to form a makeshift boat. But as perception, along with reasoning, advanced step by step, it came up with the idea and invented a hollow vessel propelled by oars as well as sails, driven by the wind and steered with rudders, and entrusted its safety to the distinct knowledge of navigation.

[1] *Or.* 11.8–9 makes a similar distinction between the divine intellect (*nous*) that is continuous and the human intellect that is intermittent.

[2] This issue is nowhere treated in the orations.

Φασὶν δὲ καὶ ἰατρικὴν εὑρῆσθαι τὸ ἀρχαῖον ὡδί· κομίζοντες οἱ οἰκεῖοι τὸν κάμνοντα εἰς τῶν ἀγυιῶν τὴν ἐντριβῆ, κατετίθεντο· ἐφιστάμενοι δὲ οἱ ἄνθρωποι καὶ ἀνερωτῶντες τὸ ἄλγος, ὅτῳ τὸ αὐτὸ ξυμπεσὸν ἔπειτα ὤνατο ἢ ἐδωδῇ τινι ἢ καύσας ἢ τεμὼν ἢ διψήσας, παρετίθεντο ἕκαστοι ταῦτα τῷ κάμνοντι οἱ πεπονθότες πρότερον καὶ ὠφελημένοι· ἡ δὲ ὁμοιότης τοῦ πάθους συναθροίσασα τὴν τοῦ ὠφελήσαντος μνήμην τῇ κατ' ὀλίγον ἐντεύξει ἐπιστήμην ἐποίησεν τὸ πᾶν. οὕτω καὶ τεκτονικὴ συνέστη καὶ χαλκευτικὴ καὶ ὑφαντικὴ καὶ γραφική, ὑπὸ τῆς πείρας ἑκάστη χειραγωγουμένη.

3. Εἶεν· τοῦτο ἐπιστήμην φῶμεν, ἐθισμὸν ψυχῆς πρὸς ὁτιοῦν τῶν ἀνθρωπίνων ἔργων καὶ ἐπιτηδευμάτων; ἢ τοῦτο μὲν διατείνει καὶ ἐπὶ τὰ θηρία; καὶ αἴσθησις γὰρ καὶ πεῖρα οὐκ ἀνθρώπου ἴδιον, ἀλλὰ καὶ τὰ θηρία αἰσθάνεται καὶ ἐκμανθάνει τι ὑπὸ τῆς πείρας, ὥστε καὶ τούτοις ὥρα μεταποιεῖσθαι σοφίας. αἱ γέρανοι ἐξ Αἰγύπτου ὥρᾳ θέρους ἀνιστάμεναι, οὐκ ἀνεχόμεναι τὸ θάλπος, τείνασαι τὰς πτέρυγας ὥσπερ ἱστία, φέρονται διὰ τοῦ ἀέρος εὐθὺ τῆς Σκυθῶν γῆς. ἅτε δὲ οὐκ ἐν ῥυθμῷ ὂν τὸ ζῷον, ἀλλὰ ἐμβριθὲς μὲν τὰ μέσα, μακρὸν δὲ κατὰ τὸν αὐχένα, κοῦφον δὲ κατὰ τὸ οὐραῖον, ἀραιὸν δὲ κατὰ τὰς πτέρυγας, ἐσχισμένον δὲ κατὰ τὰ κῶλα, κλυδάζεται τὴν πτῆσιν ὥσπερ ναῦς χειμαζομένη. τοῦτο γνοῦσα ἡ γέρανος ἢ αἰσθανομένη ἢ πειραθεῖσα, οὐ πρότερον ἀνίπταται πρὶν ξυλλάβῃ λίθον τῷ στόματι ἕρμα εἶναι αὐτῇ πρὸς τὴν πτῆσιν.

They say that the art of medicine, too, was invented long ago in the following way. The relatives of a sick man would take him to a busy street and leave him there. People would come up to him and ask about his pain, and when anyone afflicted with the same pain had been helped by a certain food, or by cautery, by surgery, or by forgoing liquids, each of them then passed on to the sick man what they themselves had previously found helpful when they were suffering. When similar ailments accumulated a record of what had proved beneficial in each separate encounter, the aggregate produced knowledge. And carpentry, metal working, weaving, and the graphic arts came about in the same way: each one was guided by the hand of experience.

3. So, should we then call knowledge an habituation of the soul to any given human endeavor or pursuit, or does this capacity extend to animals as well? After all, perception and experience are not specific to humans. Animals also have perception and learn some things through experience, so that they too lay claim to wisdom. Take cranes. In summer they migrate from Egypt because they cannot withstand the heat; they spread their wings like sails and are borne through the air on a straight course to the land of the Scythians. But since this animal has a disproportionate body with a heavy midsection, long neck, slight tail, slender wings, and ungainly legs, it can be tossed about in flight like a ship in a storm. Being aware of this either through perception or experience, a crane does not take off without first picking up a stone in its beak to act as ballast during its flight.[3]

[3] Such an account about cranes appears at Ael. *NA* 2.1 and 3.13.

Ἔλαφοι ἐκ Σικελίας ἐπὶ Ῥηγίου περαιοῦνται, νηχόμεναι ὥρᾳ θέρους ἐπιθυμίᾳ καρπῶν· ἅτε δὲ ἐν μακρῷ πλῷ, ἐξασθενεῖ ἡ ἔλαφος ἀνέχουσα τὴν κορυφὴν ὑπὲρ τοῦ ὕδατος· κουφίζονται δὴ τὸν κάματον ὧδέ πως· νήχονται ἐπὶ μιᾶς τεταγμέναι, ἀλλήλαις ἑπόμεναι ὥσπερ στρατόπεδον ἐπὶ κέρως βαδίζον· νήχονται δὲ ἐπιθεῖσα ἑκάστη τὴν κορυφὴν τῇ τῆς ἡγουμένης ἰξύϊ· ἡ δὲ στρατηγοῦσα τῆς τάξεως, ἐπειδὰν κάμῃ, ἐπὶ οὐραῖον μεθίσταται, καὶ ἡγεῖται ἄλλη καὶ οὐραγεῖ ἄλλη, ὡς ἐν τοῖς στρατοπέδοις Ξενοφῶν μὲν οὐραγεῖ, ἡγεῖται δὲ Χειρίσοφος· ὥστε καὶ στρατηγίας τακτικῆς μεταποιεῖται ταυτὶ τὰ θηρία.

4. Μήποτε οὖν αἴσθησις μὲν καὶ πεῖρα οὐκ ἀνθρώπου ἴδιον, λόγος δὲ ἀνθρώπου ἴδιον, καὶ οὐδὲν ἂν εἴη ἄλλο ἐπιστήμη πλὴν βεβαιότης λόγου ὁδεύοντος κατὰ τὰ αὐτά, ἐκθηρωμένου τὰ συγγενῆ τῶν πραγμάτων, καὶ διακρίνοντος τὰ ἀνόμοια καὶ τὰ ὅμοια συγκρίνοντος, καὶ τὰ οἰκεῖα συντιθέντος καὶ τὰ ἀλλότρια χωρίζοντος, καὶ τὰ συγκεχυμένα διαιροῦντος καὶ τὰ ἄτακτα συντάττοντος καὶ τὰ ἀνάρμοστα ἁρμοζομένου. τοιοῦτον γὰρ ἀμέλει καὶ ἀριθμητικὴ καὶ γεωμετρία καὶ μουσική, καὶ ὅσαι ἄλλαι χειρουργίας ἀδεεῖς τῇ τοῦ λόγου ῥώμῃ ἐπεξῆλθον τοῖς αὐτῶν νοήμασιν καὶ ἐξειργάσαντο.

---

[4] Similar accounts of deer appear at Aristid. 2.378, Ael. *NA* 5.56, and Opp. *Cyn*. 2.217–32.

Deer, too, swim from Sicily across to Rhegium in summer, driven by desire for food. But since on a long crossing deer become weak from holding their heads above water, they lessen their fatigue in the following way. They swim in a line, one after the other, like an army advancing in a column. As they swim, each one rests its head on the hind quarter of the one in front.[4] When the leader of the formation becomes exhausted, it moves to the tail end, so that a different deer takes the lead and another brings up the rear, just as Xenophon brings up the rear in his army while Cheirisophus takes the lead.[5] So it is that these animals can lay claim to the tactics of a general.

4. Perhaps, then, although perception and experience are not unique to humans, reason is, and thus knowledge would be nothing other than a stable certainty produced by reason as it proceeds in a consistent manner, hunting down related phenomena, distinguishing things that are different and comparing ones that are similar; combining things that belong together and separating ones that do not; dividing up things that are jumbled together, putting into order things that are disordered, and harmonizing things that are discordant.[6] Such is precisely the case with arithmetic, geometry, music, and all other disciplines not dependent on any physical procedure, that through the power of reason have developed their own concepts and brought them to completion.

[5] Cf. Xen. *An.* 3.2.37, etc.

[6] This process of division (*diairesis*) and combination (*synagōgē*) is sketched at Pl. *Phdr.* 265d–66b. *Or.* 11.8 offers an elaborate example.

Καὶ μὴν Ὅμηρος οὐ ταύτας πρεσβυτάτας ἐπιστημῶν λέγει, παλαιὸς ἀνὴρ καὶ ἀξιόχρεως δήπου πιστεύεσθαι, ἀλλὰ θαυμάζει τούτους μόνους ὡς σοφούς,

> μάντιν ἢ ἰητῆρα κακῶν ἢ τέκτονα δούρων,
> <ἢ> καὶ θέσπιν ἀοιδόν.

ὢ τῆς ἰσοτιμίας· ὁ μάντις σοφὸς καὶ ὁ τέκτων σοφὸς καὶ ὁ Ἀπόλλων δήπου καὶ ὁ ἰατρός, καὶ ὁ Ἀσκληπιὸς δήπου ὁμοίως τίμιος καὶ ὁ Φήμιος. μήποτ᾽ οὖν Ὅμηρος μὲν ταῖς ἐπιστήμαις τὰς τιμὰς νέμει κατὰ τὴν εὕρεσιν μᾶλλον ἢ κατὰ τὴν χρείαν αὐτῶν, ἡμῖν δὲ οὐ ταύτῃ θηρατέον, ἀλλὰ ὡδὶ λέγωμεν· ὅτι ἡ τοῦ ἀνθρώπου ψυχὴ τὸ εὐκινητότατον οὖσα τῶν ὄντων καὶ ὀξύτατον, κεκραμένη ἐκ θνητῆς καὶ ἀθανάτου φύσεως, κατὰ μὲν τὸ θνητὸν αὐτῆς ξυντάττεται τῇ θηριώδει φύσει, καὶ γὰρ τρέφεται καὶ αὔξει καὶ κινεῖται[3] καὶ αἰσθάνεται· κατὰ δὲ τὸ ἀθάνατον τῷ θείῳ καὶ ξυνάπτει, καὶ γὰρ νοεῖ καὶ λογίζεται καὶ μανθάνει καὶ ἐπίσταται· καθὸ δὲ ξυμβάλλουσιν αὐτῆς αἱ θνηταὶ φύσεις τῷ ἀθανάτῳ, τοῦτο πᾶν καλεῖται φρόνησις, διὰ μέσου οὖσα ἐπιστήμης πρὸς αἴσθησιν. καὶ ἔστιν ἔργον ψυχῆς, ὡς μὲν ἀλόγου, αἴσθησις· ὡς δὲ θείας, νοῦς· ὡς δὲ ἀνθρωπίνης, φρόνησις.

[3] τρέφεται . . . κινεῖται Markland, Trapp: τρέφει . . . κινεῖ R

And yet, you say, Homer—that ancient authority who is surely deserving of belief—does not mention these as the most venerable kinds of knowledge, but the only practitioners he admires as wise are

> a prophet, or healer of ills, or fashioner of wood,
> or a divine bard.[7]

O, what egalitarianism! A prophet is wise, a carpenter is wise, Apollo no doubt is, so too a physician, and evidently Asclepius is just as esteemed as Phemius.[8] Perhaps, then, Homer confers esteem on these kinds of knowledge for their discovery rather than for their usefulness, but we must not conduct our investigation on that basis. No, let us put it this way: the human soul, being the fastest moving and most acute of all things, is composed of a nature both mortal and immortal. Because of its mortal component, it shares its nature with that of animals, for it experiences nourishment, growth, movement, and perception,[9] but because of its immortal component, it is closely linked with the divine, for it is capable of thinking, reasoning, learning, and knowing. To the extent that its mortal elements interact with the immortal part, this conjunction as a whole is called practical intelligence, which exists in between perception and knowledge. The function of the soul's irrational component is perception, of its divine component is intellect, and of its human component is intelligence.

[7] *Od.* 17.384–85, Eumaeus speaking.

[8] The bard on Ithaca.

[9] Cf. *Or.* 11.8: "the entire soul is a kind of aggregate that includes nourishment, growth, mobility, emotion, and intellection."

Ἀθροίζει δὲ αἴσθησις μὲν ἐμπειρίαν, φρόνησις δὲ λόγον, νοῦς δὲ βεβαιότητα· τὴν δὲ ἐξ ἁπάντων ἁρμονίαν ἐπιστήμην καλῶ. εἰ δέ τοι δεῖ καὶ εἰκόνος τῷ λόγῳ, ἔστω ἡ μὲν αἴσθησις κατὰ τὴν ἐν τεκτονικῇ χειρουργίαν, ὁ δὲ νοῦς κατὰ γεωμετρίαν, ἡ δὲ φρόνησις οἵα καὶ τῶν ἀρχιτεκτόνων ἡ δὲ τέχνη, διὰ μέσου οὖσα γεωμετρίας καὶ τεκτονικῆς, πρὸς μὲν τὴν χειρουργίαν ἐπιστήμη τις οὖσα, πρὸς δὲ γεωμετρίαν ἐλαττουμένη κατὰ τὴν βεβαιότητα.

5. Διείληχε δὴ καὶ τὰς τῶν ἀνθρώπων δυνάμεις ἐπιστήμη καὶ φρόνησις καὶ ἐμπειρία. καὶ ἡ μὲν ἐμπειρία, περὶ πῦρ καὶ σίδηρον καὶ ἄλλας ὕλας πραγματευομένη παντοδαπάς, ἐρανίζει τὰς χρείας τοῦ βίου ταῖς εὐπορίαις τῶν τεχνῶν. ἡ δὲ φρόνησις ἐπιτεταγμένη τοῖς τῆς ψυχῆς παθήμασιν καὶ οἰκονομοῦσα ταῦτα τῷ λογισμῷ, πρὸς μὲν ἐμπειρίαν ἐπιστήμης ἔχει λόγον, ἀπολείπεται δὲ ἐπιστήμης, καθ' ὅσον περὶ πρᾶγμα οὐχ ἑστὸς οὐδὲ ὡμολογημένον πραγματευομένη σχηματίζεται τῇ τούτου φύσει.

Ὁ δὲ νοῦς τὸ τιμιώτατον ἐν ψυχῇ καὶ ἀρχικώτατον, καθάπερ ἐν πόλει νόμος, οὐκ ἐπ' ἀξόνων γεγραμμένος, οὐδὲ ἐπὶ στήλης ἐγκεχαραγμένος, οὐδὲ ὑπὸ ψηφισμάτων κεκυρωμένος, οὐδ' ὑπ' ἐκκλησίας κεχειροτονημένος, οὐδ' ὑπὸ δήμου ἐπῃνημένος, οὐδ' ὑπὸ δικαστηρίου δεδοκιμασμένος, οὐδ' ὑπὸ Σόλωνος ἢ Λυκούργου τεθείς· ἀλλὰ θεὸς μὲν ὁ νομοθέτης, ἄγραφος δὲ ὁ νόμος, ἀχειροτόνητος δὲ ἡ τιμή, ἀνυπεύθυ-

Perception, then, builds up experience, intelligence builds up reasoned argument, and intellect builds up stable certainty. I call knowledge the harmonious coordination of all three operations. But if an analogy is needed for our discussion, then let perception correspond to the physical operation of carpentry, intellect to geometry, and intelligence to the expertise possessed by architects, which exists in between geometry and carpentry, being a kind of knowledge when compared with the physical operation of carpentry, but inferior to geometry in terms of stable certainty.

5. In fact, our human capacities fall under the separate spheres of knowledge, intelligence, and experience. Experience, which deals with fire, iron, and many other kinds of materials, provides for the needs of life through the productivity of its crafts. Intelligence, which is placed in charge of the soul's emotions and manages them by means of reasoning, assumes the role of knowledge when compared with experience, but falls short of actual knowledge, insofar as it deals with a matter[10] that is neither stable nor consistent and must adapt itself to the nature of that matter.

Intellect, however, is both the most highly respected and authoritative element of the soul. It is analogous to law in a city, but it is not written on tablets or inscribed on stone markers, or ratified by decrees, passed by an assembly, approved by the people, sanctioned by a court, or laid down by a Solon or Lycurgus.[11] No, its lawmaker is god, and the law is unwritten; respect for it is not subject to a

[10] That is, human emotions.

[11] Lawgivers, respectively, of Athens and Sparta.

*νος δὲ ἡ ἐξουσία. καὶ μόνος ἂν εἴη οὗτος νόμος· οἱ δὲ ἄλλοι, οἱ καλούμενοι, δόξαι ψευδεῖς καὶ διημαρτημέναι καὶ σφαλλόμεναι. κατ' ἐκείνους τοὺς νόμους καὶ Ἀριστείδης ἔφευγεν καὶ Περικλῆς ἐζημιοῦτο καὶ Σωκράτης ἀπέθνησκεν· κατὰ δὲ τὸν θεῖον τοῦτον νόμον καὶ Ἀριστείδης δίκαιος ἦν καὶ Περικλῆς ἀγαθὸς ἦν καὶ Σωκράτης φιλόσοφος. ἐκείνων τῶν νόμων ἔργον δημοκρατία καὶ δικαστήρια καὶ ἐκκλησίαι καὶ δήμου ὁρμαὶ καὶ δημαγωγῶν δωροδοκίαι καὶ τύχαι παντοδαπαὶ καὶ συμφοραὶ ποικίλαι· τούτου τοῦ νόμου ἔργον ἐλευθερία καὶ ἀρετὴ καὶ βίος ἄλυπος καὶ ἀσφαλὴς εὐδαιμονία. ὑπ' ἐκείνων τῶν νόμων ἀθροίζεται μὲν τὰ δικαστήρια, πληροῦνται δὲ αἱ τριήρεις, ἐκπέμπονται δὲ οἱ στόλοι, τέμνεται γῆ, πολεμεῖται θάλαττα, Αἴγινα ἀνίσταται, Δεκέλεια τειχίζεται, Μῆλος ἀπόλλυται, Πλαταιαὶ ἁλίσκονται, Σκιώνη ἀνδραποδίζεται, Δῆλος καθαίρεται· ὑπὸ τούτων τῶν νόμων ἀρετὴ ἀθροίζεται, πληροῦται ψυχὴ μαθημάτων, οἰκεῖται οἶκος καλῶς, εὐνομεῖται πόλις, εἰρήνην ἄγει γῆ καὶ θάλαττα, οὐδὲν σκαιὸν οὐδὲ ἀπάνθρωπον οὐδὲ βαρβαρικόν, πάντα εἰρήνης μεστὰ καὶ ἐκεχειρίας καὶ ἐπιστήμης καὶ φιλοσοφίας καὶ λόγων μουσικῶν.*

6. *Ὦ νόμοι νόμων πρεσβύτεροι, καὶ νομοθέται νομοθετῶν ἡμερώτεροι, οἷς ὁ μὲν ἑκὼν ὑπορρίψας ἑαυ-*

---

[12] *Or.* 28 discusses the relationship between psychological pain of the soul (primarily at issue here) and physical pain of the body.

vote, nor is its authority subject to review. This is the only true law, whereas the other so-called laws are mere opinions that are false, flawed, and fallacious. Under these laws Aristides was banished, Pericles was fined, and Socrates was put to death, but according to this divine law Aristides was a just man, Pericles a good man, and Socrates a philosopher. The products of these human laws are democracy, law courts, assemblies, impulsive masses, corrupt demagogues, mishaps of every kind, and disasters of all sorts, whereas the products of divine law are freedom, virtue, a life free from pain,[12] and happiness that is secure. Under human laws courts are assembled, triremes are filled with men, expeditions are launched, the land is devastated, the sea is a theater of war, Aegina is overthrown,[13] Decelea is fortified,[14] Melos is destroyed,[15] Plataea is captured,[16] Scione is enslaved,[17] and Delos is obliterated.[18] Under divine laws virtue is assembled, the soul is filled with learning, households are well managed, the city is well governed, the land and sea enjoy peace; nothing is devious, inhumane, or cruel; all is filled with peace, armistice, knowledge, philosophy, and literary pursuits.

6. O how much more venerable are the divine laws than the human ones! O how much more humane the

[13] In 431 BC (Thuc. 2.27).

[14] In 413 BC (Thuc. 7.19).

[15] In 415 BC (Thuc. 5.116).

[16] In 427 BC (Thuc. 3.52).

[17] In 421 BC (Thuc. 5.32).

[18] In 426/5 BC the Athenians "purified" Delos (Thuc. 3.104), but there is no record of its destruction.

τὸν ἐλεύθερος καὶ εὔπορος καὶ ἀδεὴς ἐφημέρων νόμων καὶ ἀνοήτων δικαστῶν· εἰ δέ τινες παράνομοι ἐν τούτοις καὶ ὑβρισταὶ ἄνδρες, ἔχουσιν τὴν δίκην, οὐκ Ἀθηναίων καταψηφιζομένων, οὐδὲ τῶν ἕνδεκα ἀπαγόντων, οὐδὲ τοῦ δημίου προσφέροντος τὸ φάρμακον, ἀλλ' αὐτόθεν ἐξ αὐτοφυοῦς καὶ ἑκουσίου μοχθηρίας·

αὐτῶν γὰρ σφετέρῃσιν ἀτασθαλίῃσιν ὄλοντο.

τοῦτον παραβὰς τὸν νόμον Ἀλκιβιάδης ἐδυστύχει, οὐχ ὁπότε αὐτὸν Ἀθηναῖοι ἐκ Σικελίας ἐκάλουν, οὐδ' ὁπότε

ἐπηράσαντο αὐτῷ κήρυκες καὶ Εὐμολπίδαι,

οὐδ' ὁπότε ἔφευγεν ἔξω τῆς Ἀττικῆς. μικρὰ ταῦτα καὶ καταδίκη εὐκαταφρόνητος· κρείττων γὰρ ἦν καὶ φεύγων Ἀλκιβιάδης τῶν οἴκοι μενόντων· οὗτος παρὰ Λακεδαιμονίοις φεύγων εὐδοκίμει, οὗτος Δεκέλειαν ἐπετείχισεν, οὗτος Τισσαφέρνῃ φίλος καὶ Πελοποννησίων ἡγεῖτο.

Ἀλλ' ἡ ἀληθὴς Ἀλκιβιάδου δίκη πρεσβυτέρα μακρῷ, πρεσβυτέρου νόμου καὶ πρεσβυτέρων δικαστῶν·

---

[19] The Athenian jailers.

[20] *Od.* 1.7, referring to Odysseus' companions.

[21] In 415 BC (Thuc. 6.53).

[22] An anonymous citation (cf. *Suda* s.v. ἐπηράσαντο et Εὐμολπίδαι) concerning Alcibiades' alleged profanation of the mysteries in 415 BC; cf. Plut. *Alc.* 22. The Eumolpidae were priests at Eleusis. Maximus alludes to this incident at *Or.* 39.4.

divine lawmakers than the human ones! Whoever willingly submits to these true laws becomes free, well provided for, and unafraid of ephemeral laws and stupid judges. But any men who transgress or violate these laws suffer punishment, not because they are condemned by the Athenians, or led off by the Eleven,[19] or served poison by the executioner, but are condemned from within by their own willful depravity,

> for they perished by their own acts of recklessness.[20]

It was because he transgressed this divine law that Alcibiades was truly unfortunate—not when the Athenians recalled him from Sicily,[21] not when

> the heralds and the Eumolpidae cursed him,[22]

not when he went into exile from Attica.[23] Those were but minor matters and the sentence was negligible, because even in exile Alcibiades was more powerful than those who stayed home,[24] for during his banishment he had the respect of the Lacedaemonians, fortified Decelea,[25] befriended Tissaphernes,[26] and led the Peloponnesian armies.

No, the true trial of Alcibiades was far more authoritative, one conducted under a more venerable law and by

[23] In 415/4 BC (Thuc. 6.88).

[24] "Even in exile . . . stayed home" is adapted from Aeschin. *Alc*. fr. 50, 34–35 [Giannantoni].

[25] The Spartans fortified Decelea in Attica in 413 BC on the advice of Alcibiades.

[26] The Persian satrap, in 412/1 BC (Thuc. 8.45).

ἡνίκα ἐξῆλθεν Λυκείου καὶ ὑπὸ Σωκράτους κατεγινώσκετο καὶ ὑπὸ φιλοσοφίας ἐξεκηρύττετο, τότε φεύγει Ἀλκιβιάδης, τότε ἁλίσκεται. ὢ καταδίκης πικρᾶς καὶ ἀμειλίκτου ἀρᾶς καὶ ἐλεεινῆς πλάνης. τοιγαροῦν Ἀθηναῖοι μὲν αὐτὸν καὶ δεηθέντες κατεδέξαντο· φιλοσοφία δὲ καὶ ἐπιστήμη καὶ ἀρετὴ τοῖς ἅπαξ φεύγουσιν ἄβατος μένει καὶ ἀδιάλλακτος. τοιοῦτον ἡ ἐπιστήμη, τοιοῦτον ἡ ἀμαθία.

7. Ἐγὼ δὲ καὶ τοὺς Μίνω νόμους ἐπιστήμην καλῶ, ἣν ἐδίδασκεν μὲν ὁ Ζεὺς ἐν ἐνναετεῖ χρόνῳ, ἐμάνθανεν δὲ ὁ Μίνως, εὐδαιμόνει δὲ τὸ Κρητῶν γένος. καὶ τὴν Κύρου ἀρετὴν ἐπιστήμην καλῶ βασιλικήν, ἣν ἐδίδασκεν μὲν Κῦρος, Καμβύσης δὲ οὐκ ἐμάνθανεν οὐδὲ Ξέρξης ἐμάνθανεν. Κῦρος μὲν γὰρ ἡγεῖτο Περσῶν ὡς ποιμὴν θρεμμάτων, σώζων τὸ αἰπόλιον καὶ τρέφων, καὶ Μήδοις πολεμῶν καὶ Βαβυλωνίους λαμβάνων καὶ μηδενὶ ἐφιεὶς λύκῳ βαρβάρῳ καὶ ἀγρίῳ ἀναμιχθῆναι τῷ ἀγέλῃ. Καμβύσης δ᾽ ἦν καὶ αὖθις Ξέρξης ἐκ ποιμένων ἀγαθῶν πονηροὶ λύκοι, κείροντες τὴν ἀγέλην καὶ τῆς ἐπιστήμης ἀπεληλαμένοι. ἐγὼ καὶ τοὺς Λυκούργου νόμους ἐπιστήμην καλῶ μουσικήν ⟨. . .⟩

more venerable judges. It was when he left the Lyceum, condemned by Socrates and banished by philosophy, that Alcibiades truly went into exile and was truly convicted. O what a bitter sentence, implacable curse, and pitiful exile! To be sure, the Athenians took him back and even begged him to return,[27] but philosophy, knowledge, and virtue remain inaccessible and irreconcilable to those they have once banished. Such is knowledge, such is ignorance.

7. I myself call the laws of Minos knowledge, which Zeus taught him over the course of nine years:[28] Minos learned it and the people of Crete enjoyed happiness. I also call the virtue of Cyrus regal knowledge, which Cyrus taught, but which neither Cambyses nor Xerxes learned. For Cyrus led the Persians as a shepherd leads his sheep, preserving and nurturing his flock by fighting the Medes and conquering the Babylonians, thereby allowing no savage foreign wolf to mingle with his sheep. But Cambyses, and after him Xerxes, changed from good shepherds into wicked wolves. They strayed from that knowledge and ravaged their flocks. I also call the laws of Lycurgus musical knowledge . . .[29]

[27] In 411 BC (Thuc. 8.97) and again in 407 (Xen. *Hell*. 1.4.10–20).

[28] Cf. Pl. *Leg*. 1.624a–b, where, however, as in *Or*. 38.2, the instruction occurred every ninth year.

[29] The oration breaks off here. It is doubtful that much more remained. For the importance of music in Spartan life, see Plut. *Inst. Lac*. 238b–c and *Lyc*. 21.

# *ORATION* 7

## INTRODUCTION

Health in both body and soul consists of a proper balance of the constituents in each, and illness occurs when some elements become unruly and upset that balance. The question then becomes which is worse, illness of the body or of the soul (§1).[1] An elaborate political analogy of soul as ruler and body as *demos* argues that the unruly body needs a governing soul to check its bad impulses. Accordingly, if its ruler is in good health, a city remains healthy, but when the ruler becomes ill, the city loses its freedom. Medicine heals the body's misfortunes, but it is virtue that heals the soul's depravity (§2). Disease of the soul results in disdain for law and leads to wars and crime. Disease of the body affects only one person, whereas disease of the soul distresses those around (§3).[2] During the Peloponnesian War when the Athenian populace was sick with the plague, Pericles remained healthy and was able

[1] *Or.* 28.4 poses the same question with regard to pain of the body or of the soul.

[2] This last point is made at *Mor.* 501e in Plutarch's incomplete essay, "Whether the affections of the soul are worse than those of the body." Although the two essays are in general agreement, they share little common material.

to steady them. But then when Pericles died, the subsequent rulers became sick with infatuation, the infection spread to the populace, and disasters resulted (§4). The example of Pherecydes, whose soul was released at death from his terrible skin disease, leads to an analogy of the good soul being imprisoned in the body and eager to free itself from its confining garment of flesh. When the body suffers, the soul suffers as well, but the good soul regards death as a healer (§5). Philoctetes serves as an example of a man with a diseased body but a healthy soul who brings salvation to his comrades (§6). The oration ends with examples of men with healthy bodies but sick souls. Sardanapallus, the paradigm of hedonism, exhausts his body in pleasures; Alcibiades flees from the teaching of Socrates and roams feverishly about; Critias contracts a cruel disease and becomes a hated tyrant of Athens. It would have been better for these men to have had sick bodies, because wickedness is unmanageable once it invades the soul and latches on to the vicious matter there, namely unrestrained license and audacity (§7).

## *ORATION 7*

Πότερα χαλεπώτερα νοσήματα,
τὰ τοῦ σώματος, ἢ τὰ τῆς ψυχῆς;

1. Ἄιδεταί τι ἐξ ἀρχαίου ᾆσμα ἐν εὐχῆς μέρει,

> Ὑγεία πρεσβίστα μακάρων, μετὰ σοῦ
> ναίοιμι τὸ λειπόμενον βιοτᾶς.

ἐρωτῶ δὴ τὸν ποιητὴν τοῦ ᾄσματος τίνα καὶ οὖσαν τὴν ὑγείαν ταύτην ξύνοικον αὐτῷ ἐλθεῖν παρακαλεῖ κατὰ τὴν εὐχήν. ἐγὼ μὲν γὰρ ὑποπτεύω δαιμόνιόν τι εἶναι χρῆμα καὶ εὐχῆς ἄξιον· οὐ γὰρ ἂν εἰκῇ οὐδὲ ἐκ τοῦ προστυχόντος κατηξιώθη ᾠδῆς καὶ ἔμεινεν ᾀδόμενον. εἰ δὲ καὶ τοιοῦτόν ἐστιν ὁποῖον αὐτὸ ὑποπτεύω εἶναι, ἀποκρινάσθω ἡμῖν ὑπὲρ τοῦ ποιητοῦ ὁ λόγος αὐτός.

Δύο γὰρ ὄντοιν ἐν τῇ τοῦ ἀνθρώπου ἁρμονίᾳ, ψυχῆς καὶ σώματος, εἰ μὲν οὐ πέφυκεν ψυχὴ νοσεῖν, ἦν ἂν δήπου τὸ ᾆσμα τοῦτο εὐχὴ σώματος, τοῦ καὶ πεφυκότος νοσεῖν καὶ ὑγείας ἐρῶντος·[1] εἰ δὲ ἀμφοῖν

[1] ὑγείας ἐρῶντος Davies², Dübner: ὑγειατερωννος R: ὑγιαίνειν U: obel. Trapp, Koniaris

# *ORATION 7*

Which illnesses are more grave,
those of the body or those of the soul?

1. There is a song from long ago in the form of a prayer,

> O Health, most venerable of the blessed gods,
> may I dwell with you for the rest of my life.[1]

But I would ask the composer of this song, what exactly he means by this health that he entreats in his prayer to come dwell with him. I ask because I suspect that it is something divine and worth praying for, because it would not have been by accident or for no good reason that it was deemed worthy of song and has continued to be sung of. If it is such as I suspect it is, then let reason itself answer us on the composer's behalf.

There are two components in the makeup of a human being, soul and body. Now if the soul were naturally immune to illness, then obviously this song would be a body's prayer, since it is naturally prone to illness and longs for

[1] Ariphron of Sicyon, "Paean to Health," fr. 813.1–2 PMG.

ὁμοίως συγκεκραμένων μὲν πρὸς τὸ κάλλιστον ὑπὸ τῆς φύσεως, ταραττομένων δὲ ὑπὸ τῆς παροινίας τῶν μερῶν, ἐπειδὰν πλεονεκτήσῃ τι ἐν αὐτοῖς ὡς ἐν πόλει δῆμος ἢ τύραννος, κωλύει τὰ ἄλλα καὶ λυμαίνεται αὐτῶν τῇ συμμετρίᾳ, καλοῦμεν δὲ ἑκατέραν τὴν πλεονεξίαν, τὴν μὲν ψυχῆς <νόσον>,[2] τὴν δὲ σώματος, καὶ πρὸς μὲν αὑτὸ ἑκάτερον ὁμοίως ὑγείας ἐνδεές, πρὸς δὲ τὸ πλησίον οὐ κατ᾽ ἰσηγορίαν τάττεται· τὴν ποτέρου αὐτοῖν συμμετρίαν καὶ σωτηρίαν πρεσβίσταν μακάρων ὀνομάζωμεν; ἵνα δὴ καὶ τὴν ἑκατέρου νόσον ἐκ τοῦ ἐναντίου θεασώμεθα, ποτέρα τῷ ἀνθρώπῳ μεῖζον κακόν, φέρε δὴ οὑτωσὶ τὸ πᾶν διαιτήσωμαι.

2. Ψυχὴ καὶ σῶμα ὁ ἄνθρωπος, τὸ μὲν αὐτοῦ ἄρχον, τὸ δὲ ἀρχόμενον, ὡς ἐν πόλει ἄρχων καὶ ἀρχόμενος· καὶ ἔστιν καὶ ὁ ἄρχων πόλεως μέρος καὶ οἱ ἀρχόμενοι παραπλησίως· πότερον δὴ τῶν μερῶν τούτων πρᾶττον κακῶς λυμαίνεται τῇ πόλει; νοσείτω δῆμος ἐν δημοκρατίᾳ, ἀλλὰ Περικλῆς ὑγιαίνων, ἄρχων ἀγαθός, ἐπανορθοῖ τὴν τοῦ δήμου νόσον· νοσείτω Συρακοσίοις Διονύσιος τυραννικὴν νόσον, ἀλλ᾽ ὁ δῆμος ὑγιαίνων ἐξασθενεῖ πρὸς τὴν σωτηρίαν. βούλει δὴ τὸ μὲν σῶμα εἶναί σοι οἷον δῆμον, τὴν δὲ ψυχὴν ὥσπερ δυνάστην; θέασαι τοίνυν καὶ παράβαλε τὴν εἰκόνα.

[2] suppl. Trapp

health. But even when body and soul are both excellently constituted by nature, they can be disturbed by the violent behavior of their constituent parts, when some part within them takes over, like the people or a tyrant in a city, and impedes the other parts and damages their proper balance. We call this takeover an illness, whether of the soul or of the body. And although both soul and body are equally in need of good health for themselves, each is not of equal status with respect to its counterpart. So, of these two components, which one's proper balance and security should we call "most venerable of the blessed gods"? In order for us to consider the illness of each component by comparison with its opposite, and thus to determine which one constitutes the greater evil for humans, let me set forth the entire issue as follows.

2. Man consists of soul and body. The former is the ruling element, the latter is subject to it, like rulers and subjects in a city, where both the ruler and the subjects are parts of a city in much the same way. Which, then, of these two constituents, when unwell, damages a city? In a democracy it may happen that the people become ill, but as long as a good ruler like Pericles remains healthy, he can alleviate the people's illness. Conversely, should Dionysius[2] in Syracuse come down with the illness of a tyrant, even the healthy people are too weak to protect themselves. So, are you willing to compare the body to the people and the soul to their ruler? Then keep it in mind and develop the analogy.

[2] Dionysius II (ca. 397–343 BC), the cultured tyrant of Syracuse, whom Plato tried, unsuccessfully, to reform; cf. Pl. *Ep.* 7 and Diog. Laert. 3.18–23. Plato's brave opposition to Dionysius is cited at *Orr.* 15.9, 34.9, and 36.6.

Ὁ δῆμος πλέον ἢ ὁ ἄρχων, καὶ τὸ σῶμα πλέον ἢ ἡ ψυχή· δῆμος ἔμπληκτον, καὶ τὸ σῶμα ὅμοιον· δῆμος πολυμερὲς καὶ πολύφωνον καὶ πολυπαθές, ‹καὶ τὸ σῶμα πολυμερὲς καὶ πολύφωνον καὶ πολυπαθές.›[3] δῆμος ἐξ ἀνομοίων πολλῶν καὶ παντοδαπῶν συγκεκραμένον, καὶ τὸ σῶμα ἐξ ἀνομοίων πολλῶν καὶ παντοδαπῶν συγκεκραμένον· δῆμος χρῆμα ὀξὺ ἐν ὀργαῖς, ἰσχυρὸν ἐν ἐπιθυμίαις, ὑγρὸν ἐν ἡδοναῖς, δύσθυμον ἐν λύπαις, χαλεπὸν ἐν θυμοῖς· ταὐτὰ καὶ σώματος πάθη, καὶ γὰρ ἐπιθυμητικὸν καὶ ἰτητικὸν καὶ φιλήδονον καὶ ὁρμητικόν.

Φέρε καὶ τὸν ἄρχοντα τῷ ἄρχοντι εἰκάζωμεν. ἄρχων ἐν πόλει προστακτικώτατον καὶ τιμιώτατον καὶ ἰσχυρότατον, ψυχὴ ‹ἐν›[4] ἀνθρώπῳ προστακτικώτατον καὶ τιμιώτατον καὶ ἰσχυρότατον· ἄρχων τῇ φύσει φροντιστικώτατον καὶ λογιστικώτατον, τὸ δὲ αὐτὸ καὶ ἡ ψυχή· ὁ ἄρχων αὐτεξούσιον, καὶ ἡ ψυχή. τούτων τοίνυν οὕτως ἐχόντων, τὴν ποτέρου νόσον χαλεπωτέραν φήσομεν καὶ ἐν ἀνθρώπῳ καὶ ἐν πόλει; οὐ τὸ κρεῖττον νοσοῦν ἀνιαρότερον τῷ ὅλῳ; δῆμος μὲν γὰρ κάμνων, ὑγιαίνοντος ἄρχοντος, ἐν ἐλευθέρᾳ τῇ πόλει νοσεῖ· ἄρχοντος δὲ νοσοῦντος, δουλεία πόλεως.

Συνελόντι δ' εἰπεῖν, ψυχὴ σώματος τιμιώτερον· τὸ δὲ τοῦ τιμιωτέρου ἀγαθὸν μεῖζον· τὸ δὲ τῷ μείζονι ἀγαθῷ ἐναντίον, μεῖζον κακόν· ἀγαθὸν δὲ μεῖζον ὑγεία ψυχῆς ὑγείας σώματος· μεῖζον οὖν κακὸν νόσος

[3] suppl. Markland, Hobein, Koniaris [4] suppl. edd.

The people are more numerous than the ruler, and the body is larger than the soul. The people are impulsive, and so is the body. The people consist of many parts, many voices, and many passions, <and the body consists of many parts, many voices, and many passions>. The people are a mixture of many dissimilar constituents, and the body is a mixture of many dissimilar constituents. The people constitute a component that is quick to anger, vehement in its desires, dissolute in its pleasures, dispirited when distressed, and dangerous when enraged. The passions of the body are the same: it is appetitive, reckless, hedonistic, and impetuous.

Let us also compare the two rulers. In a city the ruler is the most authoritative, respected, and powerful element; in a human being the soul is the most authoritative, respected, and powerful element. A ruler is by nature the most reflective and rational component; so too the soul. The ruler acts on his own authority, and the soul does too. Since such is the case, which constituent's illness should we consider more grave, both for an individual and for a city? Does not the more powerful element, when it falls sick, cause greater distress for the whole? For when the people are sick, but the ruler remains healthy, the city remains free in spite of their illness. But when the ruler falls ill, it means slavery for the city.

In sum, the soul is more valuable than the body, and the good of the more valuable entity is the greater good; and conversely, the opposite of the greater good is the greater evil. Since the health of the soul is a greater good than the health of the body, then disease of the soul is a

ψυχῆς νόσου σώματος. ὑγεία μὲν σώματος τέχνης ἔργον, ὑγεία δὲ ψυχῆς ἀρετῆς ἔργον· νόσος ψυχῆς μοχθηρία, νόσος σώματος δυστυχία· ἑκούσιον ἡ μοχθηρία, ἀκούσιον ἡ δυστυχία· ἐλεεῖται τὰ ἀκούσια, μισεῖται τὰ ἑκούσια· τὰ ἐλεούμενα βοηθεῖται, τὰ μισούμενα κολάζεται· τὰ βοηθούμενα μέτρια, τὰ κολαζόμενα χείρω.

3. Πάλιν αὖ τὴν ὑγείαν ἐφ᾽ ἑκατέρου σκόπει. ἡ μὲν πάντων ἀδεής, ἡ δὲ πάντων ἐνδεής· ἡ μὲν εὐδαιμονίαν χορηγεῖ, ἡ δὲ <κακοδαιμονίαν>[5] πορίζεται· ἡ μὲν ἄμοιρος κακοῦ, ἡ δὲ ἐπισφαλὴς εἰς μοχθηρίαν· τῇ μὲν ἀέναος ὑγεία, τῷ δὲ ἐφήμερος· τῇ μὲν βέβαιος, τῷ δὲ ἄστατος· τῇ μὲν ἀθάνατος, τῷ δὲ θνητή.

Σκόπει καὶ τὰς νόσους· νόσος σώματος εὐαπάλλακτος τῇ τέχνῃ, νόσος ψυχῆς δυσμετάβλητος τῷ νόμῳ· ἡ μὲν τὸν ἔχοντα ἀνιῶσα ποιεῖ πρὸς τὴν ἴασιν εἰκτικώτερον, ἡ δὲ ἐξαναλοῦσα τὸν ἔχοντα ὑπερορᾶν τῶν νόμων παρασκευάζει· τῇ μὲν βοηθοῦσιν θεοί, τὴν δὲ μισοῦσιν· πόλεμον οὐ κινεῖ νόσος σώματος, διὰ δὲ ψυχῆς νόσον οἱ πολλοὶ πόλεμοι· οὐδεὶς νοσῶν τὸ σῶμα συκοφαντεῖ ἢ τυμβωρυχεῖ ἢ ληΐζεται ἤ τι ἄλλο

5 suppl. Acciaiolus, Davies$^{2}$, Dübner: lacunam stat. Trapp: *πορίζεται* obel. Koniaris

---

3 The meaning of this contrast is unclear. Others interpret *μέτρια* (moderate) to mean "limited in its ill effects" (Trapp), "limited in scope" (López Cruces), or "pardonable" (Koniaris).

4 That is, through the line of doctors from Asclepius.

greater evil than disease of the body. Health in the body is brought about by medical expertise, whereas health in the soul is brought about by virtue. The soul's illness is depravity, the body's is misfortune; depravity is voluntary, misfortune is involuntary. Involuntary evils are pitied, voluntary ones are hated. What is pitiful elicits help, what is hated elicits punishment. What calls for help is moderate,[3] what elicits punishment is worse.

3. Then again, consider the condition of health in each case. The soul needs nothing, whereas the body needs everything; the soul brings happiness, whereas the body brings <unhappiness>. The soul is free of evil, whereas the body is at risk of falling into depravity. The health of the soul lasts forever, that of the body is short-lived. The soul's health is stable, the body's is unstable; the soul's health is immortal, the body's is mortal.

Consider too their diseases. Disease of the body is easy for medical expertise to remove; disease of the soul is difficult for laws to treat. The body's disease, by causing distress, makes the patient more likely to seek a cure; the soul's disease, by completely wearing down the patient, accustoms him to disdain the laws. The gods lend assistance to the one,[4] they hate the other. Disease of the body starts no wars, whereas most wars are caused by disease of the soul. No one, just because he has a physical disease, gives false testimony, robs graves, engages in piracy, or commits any other major crime . . .[5] disease of the body

[5] To maintain the parallel comparison, Reiske adds "those are the diseases of the soul." Trapp suggests "whereas sickness of the soul is at the root of all such offences." Other editors indicate a lacuna.

δρᾷ κακὸν μέγα· <. . .>[6] νόσος σώματος ἀνιαρὸν τῷ ἔχοντι, νόσος ψυχῆς ἀνιαρὸν καὶ τῷ πλησίον.

4. Θέασαι τὸ λεγόμενον ὡδὶ σαφέστερον ἐπὶ πολιτικῆς εἰκόνος. Ἀθήνησιν ἐν δημοκρατουμένῃ πόλει καὶ ἀκμαζούσῃ πλήθει ἀνδρῶν καὶ μεγέθει ἀρχῆς καὶ δυνάμει χρημάτων καὶ εὐπορίᾳ στρατηγῶν, ὑπὸ Περικλεῖ δυναστεύοντι, λοιμὸς ἐμπεσών, ἐξ Αἰθιοπίας ἀρξάμενος καὶ καταβὰς διὰ τῆς βασιλέως γῆς καὶ τελευτήσας ἐκεῖ καὶ ἱδρυθεὶς αὐτόθι, ἔφθειρε τὴν πόλιν· συνεπελάμβανεν δὲ τῇ τοῦ κακοῦ ἐπιδημίᾳ καὶ ἐκ Πελοποννήσου πόλεμος. δῃουμένης δὲ τῆς γῆς καὶ φθειρομένης τῆς πόλεως καὶ ἀναλισκομένων τῶν σωμάτων καὶ μαραινομένης τῆς δυνάμεως καὶ ἀπαγορεύοντος τῇ πόλει τοῦ σώματος, εἷς ἀνὴρ οἷον ψυχὴ πόλεως, ὁ Περικλῆς ἐκεῖνος, ἄνοσος καὶ ὑγιὴς μένων, ἐξώρθου τὴν πόλιν καὶ ἀνίστη καὶ ἀνεζωπύρει καὶ ἀντετάττετο τῷ λοιμῷ καὶ τῷ πολέμῳ.

Θέασαι δὴ καὶ τὴν δευτέραν εἰκόνα· ὅτε μὲν ὁ λοιμὸς ἐπέπαυτο καὶ τὸ πλῆθος ἔρρωτο καὶ ἡ δύναμις ἤκμαζεν, τότε δὴ τὸ ἀρχικὸν μέρος τῆς πόλεως ἐνόσει νόσον δεινὴν καὶ ἐγγύτατα μανίᾳ, <ἣ>[7] καὶ κατελάμβανεν τὸ πλῆθος καὶ τὸν δῆμον συννοσεῖν προσηνάγκαζεν. ἦ γὰρ οὐχ οὗτος ὁ δῆμος καὶ Κλέωνι συνεμαίνετο καὶ Ὑπερβόλῳ συνενόσει καὶ Ἀλκιβιάδῃ

[6] lacunam indic. Markland, Dübner, Trapp: <ψυχῆς ταῦτα τὰ νοσήματα> suppl. Reiske

[7] suppl. Trapp praeeunte Koniaris

causes grief only for the sick person, but disease of the soul causes grief for those around as well.

4. You may see more clearly what I mean with the following analogy drawn from politics. When democratic Athens was at its peak under the leadership of Pericles with its large population, extensive empire, financial strength, and many good generals, it was afflicted by a plague that originated in Ethiopia, progressed through the land of the Persian king, and came to rest there in the city and was ravaging it. Concurrent with the arrival of this pestilence was an invasion from the Peloponnesus. As the land was being laid waste, the city being ravaged, bodies dying, the city's strength diminishing, and the body politic failing, one man—the city's soul, as it were—that famous Pericles, who remained free of the disease and in good health, set about lifting up the city, putting it on its feet, rekindling its spirit, and enabling it to resist both the plague and the war.[6]

Consider as well this second analogy. When the plague had run its course, and the populace had recovered and their strength was at its height, at that point the ruling element in the city came down with a terrible illness very near to insanity, which gripped the populace and forced the people to sicken as well. Were these not the people who came down with Cleon's madness,[7] Hyperbolus' sick-

[6] Pericles' steadying control over the Athenians at the beginning of the Peloponnesian War is detailed at Thuc. 2.13–14, 21–22, 34–46, and 59–65.

[7] A bellicose demagogue who captured Spartan soldiers on Sphacteria in 425 BC and was killed in battle in 422.

συνεφλέγετο, καὶ τελευτῶν τοῖς δημαγωγοῖς συνετήκετο καὶ συνεσφάλλετο καὶ συναπωλλύετο, ἄλλου ἄλλοσε τὴν δειλαίαν καλοῦντος,

δεῦρ' ἴθι, νύμφα φίλη, ἵνα θέσκελα ἔργα ἴδηαι;

καὶ δείκνυσι μὲν Ἀλκιβιάδης Σικελίαν, δείκνυσι δὲ Κλέων Σφακτηρίαν καὶ ἄλλος ἄλλην γῆν ἢ θάλατταν, ὡς πυρέττοντι πηγὰς καὶ φρέατα. ταῦτά ἐστιν ὑμῶν, ὦ πονηροί, τὰ θέσκελα ἔργα; φθορὰ καὶ ἀνάστασις καὶ κακῶν ἀκμὴ καὶ φλεγμονὴ νόσου; τοῦτο δύναται καὶ ψυχῆς νόσος πρὸς σώματος νόσον παραβαλλομένη. νοσεῖ σῶμα καὶ ταράττεται καὶ φθείρεται· ἀλλ' ἐὰν ἐπιστήσῃς αὐτῷ ψυχὴν ἐρρωμένην, ἀμελεῖ τῆς νόσου καὶ ὑπερφρονεῖ τοῦ κακοῦ· ὡς Φερεκύδης ὑπερεφρόνει ἐν Σύρῳ κείμενος, τῶν μὲν σαρκῶν αὐτῷ φθειρομένων, τῆς δὲ ψυχῆς ἑστώσης ὀρθῆς καὶ καραδοκούσης τὴν ἀπαλλαγὴν τοῦ δυσχρήστου τούτου περιβλήματος.

5. Φαίην δ' ἂν ἔγωγε οὐδὲ ἀκούσῃ εἶναι τῇ γενναίᾳ ψυχῇ φθορὰν σώματος· οἷον εἰ καὶ δεσμώτην ἐννοήσαις ὁρῶντα σηπόμενον καὶ διαρρέον τὸ τειχίον τοῦ δεσμωτηρίου, ἀναμένοντα τὴν ἔκδυσιν καὶ τὴν ἐλευθερίαν τοῦ εἱργμοῦ, ἵνα ἐκ πολλοῦ καὶ ἀφεγγοῦς ζόφου, οὗ τέως κατορώρυκτο, ἀναβλέψῃ πρὸς τὸν αἰθέρα

[8] An Athenian demagogue, executed in 411 BC (Thuc. 8.73).

[9] Alcibiades championed the disastrous Sicilian Expedition in 415 BC. His feverish adventurism is summarized in §7 below.

ness,[8] and Alcibiades' feverishness,[9] and who ended up wasting away, going astray, and perishing with these demagogues, as each of them summoned the wretched city to one place or another?

> Come here, dear bride, to see these marvelous deeds.[10]

Alcibiades points to Sicily, Cleon to Sphacteria, others to this land or that sea, as if pointing a person with a fever to springs and cisterns. You scoundrels, are these your "marvelous deeds"—ruin, destruction, consummate evils, and feverish illness? Such is the power of sickness of the soul compared to sickness of the body. The body may become ill, disturbed, and waste away, but if you place a robust soul in charge of it, it makes light of its illness and disdains the malady, just as Pherecydes disdained his when he lay sick on Syros: his flesh was wasting away, but his soul stood fast and waited for its release from that troublesome wrapping of skin.[11]

5. In fact, I would say that the noble soul does not even regret the body's demise. Imagine, if you will, a prisoner watching the walls of his cell rotting and crumbling away, as he awaits his release and freedom from his confinement, so that he might emerge from the deep and gloomy darkness in which he has hitherto been buried, and look up at the sky and bask in the bright light. Or do you think that

[10] *Il.* 3.130, Iris disguised as Laodice, summoning Helen to the wall to see the contending armies.

[11] Pherecydes of Syros (fl. 544 BC) is also cited in *Orr.* 4.4 and 13.5. For various accounts of his lingering death from skin disease, see Diog. Laert. 1.118–22.

καὶ ἐμπλησθῇ λαμπροῦ φωτός· ἢ οἴει ἄνδρα ἠσκημένον καλῶς καὶ διαπεπονημένον τῷ σώματι ταραχθῆναι ἂν τῶν χλανιδίων αὐτῷ διαρρηγνυμένων, ἀλλ' οὐκ ἂν ἀπορρίψαι αὐτὰ ἄσμενον καὶ παραδοῦναι τὸ σῶμα τῷ ἀέρι, γυμνὸν γυμνῷ, φίλον φίλῳ, ἐλεύθερον ἐλευθέρῳ; τί οὖν ἄλλο ἡγεῖ τῇ ψυχῇ εἶναι τὸ δέρμα τοῦτο καὶ τὰ ὀστᾶ καὶ τὰς σάρκας ἢ χλανίδια ἐφήμερα καὶ ῥακία ἀσθενῆ καὶ τρύχινα; ταῦτα καὶ σίδηρος διαρρήγνυσιν καὶ πῦρ τήκει καὶ ἕλκη ἐπινέμεται.

Ἡ μὲν οὖν ἀγαθὴ ψυχὴ καὶ διαπεπονημένη καὶ ἠσκημένη ἀμελεῖ καὶ ὡς τάχιστα ἐφίεται γυμνωθῆναι· ὥστε κἂν ἐπιφθέγξαιτό τις τῷ γενναίῳ ἀνδρί, νοσοῦντα τῷ σώματι θεασάμενος, τὸ τοῦ Ὀδυσσέως ἐκεῖνο,

οἵην ἐκ ῥακέων ὁ γέρων ἐπιγουνίδα φαίνει.

ἡ δὲ δειλὴ ψυχὴ κατορωρυγμένη ἐν σώματι, ὡς ἑρπετὸν νωθὲς εἰς φωλεόν, φιλεῖ τὸν φωλεὸν καὶ οὐδεπώποτε θέλει ἀπαλλαγῆναι αὐτοῦ οὐδὲ ἐξερπύσαι, ἀλλὰ καιομένῳ συγκάεται καὶ σπαραττομένῳ συσπαράττεται, καὶ ἀλγοῦντι τῷ σώματι συναλγεῖ καὶ βοῶντι συμβοᾷ.

ὦ πούς, ἀφήσω σε;

ὁ Φιλοκτήτης λέγει. ἄνθρωπε, ἄφες καὶ μὴ βόα, μηδὲ λοιδοροῦ τοῖς φιλτάτοις, μηδὲ ἐνόχλει τὴν Λημνίων γῆν.

a man with a well disciplined and thoroughly conditioned body would be upset if his garments were being torn open? Would he not happily rip them off himself and hand over his body to the air, a naked and free body to the friendly embrace of the naked and free air? For what else do you think that this skin, these bones, and this flesh are for the soul other than temporary garments, flimsy tattered rags, that iron can pierce, fire can melt, and festering wounds can consume?

The good soul, then, that has been disciplined and thoroughly conditioned, does not care about its clothes, and longs to strip them off as quickly as possible. Thus, when someone sees a noble man with a diseased body, he could quote him that famous verse about Odysseus:

> what a thigh the old man reveals under his rags![12]

In contrast, the cowardly soul that is buried in its body like a sluggish reptile in its lair, loves that lair and never wishes to leave or crawl out of it. And yet that soul is burned when its body is burned, is torn when its body is torn, is pained when its body is in pain, and screams out when its body screams, like Philoctetes,

> O my foot! Shall I lose you?[13]

Get rid of it, my friend, and stop screaming. Stop railing against your dearest friends, and stop disturbing the land of the Lemnians.

[12] *Od.* 18.74, spoken by one of the suitors, when the disguised Odysseus girds himself to box with Irus.

[13] Aesch. *Phil.* fr. 254 Nauck$^2$, quoted only here.

ὦ θάνατε παιάν·

εἰ μὲν ταῦτα λέγεις ἀλλαττόμενος κακὸν κακοῦ, οὐκ ἀποδέχομαι τῆς εὐχῆς· εἰ δὲ ἡγεῖ τῷ ὄντι τὸν θάνατον παιᾶνα εἶναι καὶ ἀπαλλακτὴν κακοῦ καὶ ἀπλήστου καὶ νοσεροῦ θρέμματος, ἡγεῖ καλῶς· εὔχου καὶ κάλει τὸν παιᾶνα.

6. Καὶ δὴ φέρων με ὁ λόγος εἰς παράδειγμα ἐμβέβληκεν σαφέστερον οὗ πάλαι ποθῶ ἐνδείξασθαι ὑμῖν. ἐν γὰρ τοῖς Ἀχαιοῖς τότε ἦν που σώματα μυρία,

ὅσσα τε φύλλα καὶ ἄνθεα γίνεται ὥρῃ,

ὑγιῆ πάντα, ἄνοσα καὶ ἰσχυρὰ καὶ ἄρτια, τῷ τῶν πολεμίων τείχει περιχεόμενα· ἐν <δὲ>[8] δεκαέτει χρόνῳ ἐπέραινεν οὐδὲν οὐχ ὁ Ἀχιλλεὺς διώκων, οὐχ ὁ Αἴας μένων, οὐχ ὁ Διομήδης ἀναιρῶν, οὐχ ὁ Τεῦκρος τοξεύων, οὐχ ὁ Ἀγαμέμνων βουλευόμενος, οὐχ ὁ Νέστωρ λέγων, οὐχ ὁ Κάλχας μαντευόμενος, οὐχ ὁ Ὀδυσσεὺς σοφιζόμενος. ἀλλ᾽ ὁ θεὸς λέγει· "ὦ καλὰ καὶ γενναῖα γῆς Ἑλλάδος θρέμματα, μάτην πονεῖτε, μάτην διώκετε, κενὰ τοξεύετε, κενὰ βουλεύεσθε· οὐ γὰρ ἂν ἄλλως ἕλοιτε τουτὶ τὸ τεῖχος, πρὶν ὑμῖν ἐπίκουρος ἔλθῃ ψυχὴ μὲν ἐρρωμένη, σῶμα δὲ νοσοῦν, ὀδωδὸς καὶ χωλεῦον καὶ διαβεβρωμένον ὑπὸ τῆς νό-

[8] suppl. Trapp

14 Aesch. *Phil.* fr. 255.1 Nauck[2].

> O death, my healer![14]

If you say that merely to exchange one malady for another, then I reject the premise of your prayer. But if you believe that death truly is a healer that will liberate you both from your malady and from a creature that is insatiable and diseased, then you are correct. Keep praying and invoking this healer!

6. I see now that the train of my argument has led me to a clearer illustration of what I have wanted to make plain for you[15] all along. For back then in the Achaean army there were some ten thousand bodies,

> as many as the leaves and flowers in springtime,[16]

that were surrounding the walls of the enemy, all of them healthy, free of disease, strong, and fit. But over the span of ten years they accomplished nothing, not with Achilles on the attack or Ajax on defense, not with Diomedes wreaking slaughter, Teucer launching arrows, Agamemnon making plans, Nestor speaking his mind, Calchas prophesying, or Odysseus scheming. The god,[17] however, said: "O good and noble progeny of the land of Hellas, your efforts and pursuits are in vain, and your arrows and plans are futile, because there is no other way for you to take this wall until there comes to your aid a vigorous soul, but one with a body that is sick, foul-smelling, lame, and

[15] This plural ὑμῖν speaks to the wider audience; elsewhere in this oration (and generally so), "you" is singular and addresses a member of the audience or a fictional interlocutor.

[16] *Il.* 2.468, describing the size of the Greek army at Troy.

[17] Apollo, as in Sophocles' *Philoctetes*.

*σου.” οἱ δὲ ἐπείσθησαν τῷ θεῷ, καὶ ἤγαγον ἐκ Λήμνου σύμμαχον ψυχὴν μὲν ὑγιᾶ, σῶμα δὲ νοσοῦν.*

7. Εἰ δὲ *βούλει, σκέψαι μεταβαλὼν τῆς ψυχῆς νόσον ἐν σώματι ὑγιεινῷ. νοσεῖ ψυχὴ τὴν ἡδονῆς νόσον, τήκεται καὶ μαραίνεται· τί χρήσῃ τῷ νοσοῦντι; τίς ὄνησις σώματος τοιαύτῃ ψυχῇ;* Σαρδανάπαλλος *νοσεῖ· οὐχ ὁρᾷς ὡς καὶ ἐπὶ τὸ σῶμα αὐτῷ τὸ κακὸν ἔρχεται; ἐντρίβεται ὁ δύστηνος καὶ λεαίνεται καὶ τὼ ὀφθαλμὼ συντήκεται, καὶ οὐκ ἀνεχόμενος τὴν νόσον ἐπὶ πῦρ ἦλθεν. νοσεῖ* Ἀλκιβιάδης· *πῦρ αὐτὸν ἐπινέμεται πολὺ καὶ ἄγριον καὶ τοὺς λογισμοὺς ἐπιταράττει ἐγγύτατα μανίας καὶ περιφέρει πανταχοῦ, ἀπὸ μὲν* Λυκείου *ἐπὶ τὴν ἐκκλησίαν, ἀπὸ δὲ τῆς ἐκκλησίας ἐπὶ τὴν θάλατταν, ἀπὸ δὲ τῆς θαλάττης ἐπὶ* Σικελίαν, *κἀκεῖθεν εἰς* Λακεδαίμονα, *εἶτα παρὰ τοὺς* Πέρσας, *καὶ ἀπὸ* Περσῶν *ἐπὶ* Σάμον, *καὶ ἀπὸ* Σάμου *ἐπὶ τὰς* Ἀθήνας, *καὶ ἐπὶ τὸν* Ἑλλήσποντον *αὖθις, καὶ πανταχοῦ. νοσεῖ* Κριτίας *νόσον πικρὰν καὶ παντοδαπὴν καὶ οὐκ ἰάσιμον, οὐδὲ ἀνασχετὴν τῇ πάσῃ πόλει. καίτοι τούτοις τὰ σώματα ὑγιῆ καὶ ἄρτια· ἁβρὸς μὲν γὰρ ὁ* Σαρδανάπαλλος, *καλὸς δὲ ὁ* Ἀλκιβιάδης, *ἰσχυρὸς δὲ ὁ* Κριτίας· *ἀλλὰ τὴν ὑγείαν ἐπὶ τούτων μισῶ. νοσείτω* Κριτίας, *ἵνα μὴ τυραννῇ· νοσείτω* Ἀλκιβιάδης, *ἵνα μὴ*

[18] The Assyrian king, notorious for his hedonism, eventually immolated himself. He is also cited at *Orr.* 1.9, 4.9, 14.2, 15.8, 29.1, and 32.3 and 9.

[19] The place where Socrates taught.

being eaten away by its disease." They then obeyed the god and brought from Lemnos a healthy soul in a diseased body to be their ally.

7. Consider, if you will, the converse, namely a sick soul in a healthy body. Say the soul suffers from the disease of pleasure seeking, and is pining and wasting away. What will you do with this patient? What help is the body to a soul in this condition? Sardanapallus has this disease.[18] Do you not see how the malady extends to his body as well? The poor wretch puts on cosmetics, removes his facial hair, and fills his eyes with erotic desire, until he is unable to endure this disease and ends his life in flames. Alcibiades falls ill. A raging, fiery fever consumes him, confounds his reasoning to the point of madness, and sends him hither and yon: from the Lyceum[19] to the assembly, from the assembly to the sea, from the sea to Sicily, and from there to Lacedaemon, then to Persia, and from Persia to Samos, from Samos to Athens, then back to the Hellespont, and all over the place.[20] Critias contracts a disease that is cruel and incurable, one that takes on many forms and proves unendurable for the entire city.[21] And yet, all their bodies are healthy and fit. Sardanapallus is elegant, Alcibiades is handsome, and Critias is strong. But in these cases I hate their health. Let Critias be so ill that he does not become a tyrant; let Alcibiades be so ill that

[20] For the far-ranging career of Alcibiades from 415 BC until his death in 403, cf. Thuc. Books 6–8, Xen. *Hell.* 1.1.5–2.1.26, and Plut. *Alc.* 18–39. His activities during his exile from Athens are listed at *Or.* 6.6.

[21] Leader of the "Thirty Tyrants" in Athens. He was killed in 403 BC. For his last days, see Xen. *Hell.* 2.3.2–2.4.19.

ἐπὶ Σικελίαν Ἀθηναίους ἄγῃ· νοσείτω Σαρδανάπαλλος, βέλτιον γὰρ αὐτῷ διὰ νόσον κεῖσθαι μᾶλλον ἢ διὰ ἡδονήν· μᾶλλον δὲ φθειρέσθω πᾶς ὅτῳ ἐπιρρεῖ ἀέναος πονηρία.

Ὥσπερ γὰρ τὰ ἑρπυστικὰ τῶν ἑλκῶν τοῖς σώμασιν ἐμπεσόντα πρόσω νέμεται καὶ τοῦ ὑγιαίνοντός τι ἀεὶ προσαπόλλυσιν καὶ πρὸς τὰς ἰάσεις ἀγριαίνει, ἕως ἂν ἡ τέχνη τὴν κρηπῖδα καὶ τὴν ἕδραν τοῦ νοσήματος ἐκτέμῃ· ὧδε καὶ ὅτῳ ὕπουλος καὶ διαβεβρωμένη καὶ σαθρὰ οὖσα ἡ ψυχὴ ἐπινέμεται πρόσω τε καὶ τὰ πλησίον ἀεὶ καταλαμβάνει, ἐκτμητέον δὴ αὐτῆς καὶ ἀφαιρετέον τὰς δυνάμεις τῶν σωμάτων, ὡς λῃστοῦ χεῖρας, ὡς ἀκολάστου ὀφθαλμούς, ὡς λίχνου γαστέρα. κἂν γὰρ ἐπιστήσῃς τῇ νόσῳ δικαστὰς καὶ δεσμωτήρια καὶ δημίους, τὸ κακὸν φθάνει καὶ ἕρπει καὶ προλαμβάνει· ἀμήχανος γὰρ ἡ πονηρίας ὀξύτης, ἐπειδὰν ἅπαξ ἤθει ψυχῆς ἐμπεσοῦσα ἐπιλάβηται ὕλης πονηρᾶς, καὶ ἐξουσίας ἀδεοῦς, καὶ ἀνεπιτιμήτου τόλμης.

he does not lead the Athenians against Sicily; let Sardanapallus be ill, because it is better for him to die from illness than from pleasure seeking. Better still, let anyone perish who is flooded with constant wickedness.

Just as when creeping diseases attack the body and spread ever further, and continually destroy some healthy part and stubbornly resist any cures, until medical expertise excises the root and seat of the disease, so too when someone's soul festers and rots with a devouring disease, which spreads ever further and continually seizes on anything around it, then the powers of the body must be cut off and taken from it, like hands from a robber, eyes from a lecher, or the belly from a glutton. For even if you institute juries, prisons, and executioners to deal with this disease, the malady outstrips them, continues to creep, and stays one step ahead. For wickedness is too quick to manage, once it has invaded the very character of the soul and latched on to vicious material there: license without fear, and audacity without constraint.

# *ORATION* 8

## INTRODUCTION

This oration forms a pair with *Or.* 9 (explicitly signaled in §7) and treats an issue of importance in Platonic circles in the second century, as evidenced by Plutarch's *De genio Socratis* and especially by Apuleius' *De deo Socratis*, among others,[1] namely the nature of Socrates' personal *daimonion*.[2] It opens with an extensive survey of the many ways in which humans communicate with divinity through oracles and prophecy (§§1–2). Since people believe in these oracles and act on their advice, there should be no doubt that a good man like Socrates could be in contact with the divine realm through voices and a *daimonion* (§3). But to understand the nature of his *daimonion* requires a discussion of *daimonia* in general (§4). Homer believed in *daimonia*, as shown by allegorical interpretations of seven passages where a god (*daimonion*) assists mortals (§5). In contrast to Socrates' *daimonion* that was his alone, Homeric *daimonia* take on many forms and many voices. The speaker argues that the Homeric gods must not be understood merely as poets and sculptors

[1] For surveys, see Roskam (2010) and Litwa (2021).

[2] The diminutive *daimonion* is specific to individuals, in contrast to *daimones* in general.

depict them, but allegorically as daemonic powers. If that is accepted, and if Socrates is deemed worthy of receiving such divine assistance, the question remains as to what *daimones* in general really are (§6). As humans compete to win virtue in the stadium of life and travel down an obstacle-filled road to attain it, they need divine assistance because of their limited powers and the opposition of their adversary, fortune (*tychē*) (§7). Sincc god remains in one place, he needs a secondary race of *daimones* to bridge the immense gulf between the divine and mortal realms. They act as intermediaries, and, like translators, enable communication between the two. There is an immense number of them. Many give advice, or disclose the future, or assist in various ways, and some inhabit individual bodies, as in the cases of Socrates, Plato, Pythagoras, Zeno, and Diogenes (notably heads of philosophical schools). They are as diverse as men are, and inhabit virtuous souls, but are absent from depraved ones (§8).

# *ORATION* 8

Τί τὸ δαιμόνιον Σωκράτους. α′

1. Θαυμάζεις εἰ Σωκράτει συνῆν δαιμόνιον φίλον, μαντικόν, ἀεὶ παρεπόμενον, καὶ μόνον οὐ τῇ γνώμῃ αὐτοῦ ἀνακεκραμένον, ἀνδρὶ καθαρῷ μὲν τὸ σῶμα, ἀγαθῷ δὲ τὴν ψυχήν, ἀκριβεῖ δὲ τὴν δίαιταν, δεινῷ δὲ φρονεῖν, μουσικῷ δὲ εἰπεῖν, εἰς δὲ τὸ θεῖον εὐσεβεῖ, ὁσίῳ δὲ τὰ ἀνθρώπινα. τί δήποτε οὖν τοῦτο μὲν θαυμάζεις, γύναιον δὲ τὸ τυχὸν Δελφικὸν Πυθοῖ, ἢ Θέσπρωτον ἄνδρα ἐν Δωδώνῃ, ἢ Λίβυν ἐν Ἄμμωνος, ἢ Ἴωνα ἐν Κλάρῳ, ἢ Λύκιον ἐν Ξάνθῳ, ἢ Βοιωτὸν ἐν Ἰσμηνίου, τούτους ἅπαντας οὐ θαυμάζεις τῷ δαιμονίῳ ὅσαι ἡμέραι συγγιγνομένους, καὶ οὐ τὰ σφίσιν μόνον πρακτέα ἢ μὴ γιγνώσκοντας, ἀλλὰ καὶ τοῖς ἄλλοις χρησμῳδοῦντας καὶ ἰδίᾳ καὶ δημοσίᾳ; ἢ διότι ἡ μὲν πρόμαντις καθίζουσα ἐπὶ τρίποδος, ἐμπιμπλαμένη δαιμονίου πνεύματος, χρησμῳδεῖ, ὁ δὲ ἐν

---

[1] A fictitious interlocutor.

[2] Human interactions with *daimones* are rendered by the verb *συγγίγνεσθαι* (to be in contact with), which occurs seven times, and by the noun *συνουσία* (relationship), which occurs twice.

# *ORATION* 8

## What Socrates' *daimonion* was. Part I

1. You[1] act surprised that a benevolent *daimonion* with prophetic powers was a constant companion of Socrates, and was all but integral to his mind, even though the man was pure in body, virtuous in soul, scrupulous in conduct, a formidable thinker, an accomplished speaker, pious toward the gods, and righteous in his dealings with other men. Why then does this surprise you? You don't seem surprised when all sorts of people are in contact with[2] the daemonic realm every day, not only to ascertain what they themselves should or should not do, but also to prophesy to others, both privately and publicly. These include an ordinary Delphian woman at Pytho,[3] a Thesprotian man in Dodona, a Libyan in the temple of Zeus Ammon, an Ionian at Claros, a Lycian in Xanthus, and a Boeotian in the temple of Ismenian Apollo.[4] Or are these different because the Pythian priestess sits on a tripod and is filled with daemonic inspiration when she prophesies; and the

[3] That is, the Pythia. Plut. *De Pyth. or.* 405c reports that she came from poor, uneducated peasants.

[4] At Thebes.

Ἰωνίᾳ ὑποφήτης, ὕδωρ ἐκ πηγῶν ἀρυσάμενος καὶ πιών, μαντικῶς ἔχει, οἱ δὲ χαμεῦναι καὶ ἀνιπτόποδες ἐν Δωδώνῃ θεραπεύοντες δρῦν, παρ' ἐκείνης, ὡς ὁ Θεσπρωτῶν λόγος, μαθόντες χρησμῳδοῦσιν;

2. Ἐν Τροφωνίου γε μήν (καὶ γὰρ τοῦτο μαντεῖόν ἐστιν ἐν Βοιωτίᾳ ἥρωος Τροφωνίου περὶ Λεβαδίαν πόλιν) ὁ δεόμενος συγγενέσθαι τῷ δαιμονίῳ, ἐνσκευασάμενος ὀθόνῃ ποδήρει καὶ φοινικίδι, μάζας τε ἐν χεροῖν ἔχων, εἰσδύεται ὕπτιος κατὰ στομίου στενοῦ· καὶ τὰ μὲν ἰδών, τὰ δὲ ἀκούσας, ἄνεισιν αὖθις ὑποφήτης αὐτάγγελος. ἦν δέ που τῆς Ἰταλίας κατὰ τὴν μεγάλην Ἑλλάδα περὶ λίμνην Ἄορνον οὕτω καλουμένην μαντεῖον ἄντρον καὶ θεραπευτῆρες τοῦ ἄντρου ἄνδρες ψυχαγωγοί, οὕτως ὀνομαζόμενοι ἐκ τοῦ ἔργου. ἐνταῦθα ὁ δεόμενος ἀφικόμενος, εὐξάμενος, ἐντεμὼν σφάγια, χεάμενος χοάς, ἀνεκαλεῖτο ψυχὴν ὅτου δὴ τῶν πατέρων ἢ φίλων· καὶ αὐτῷ ἀπήντα εἴδωλον, ἀμυδρὸν μὲν ἰδεῖν καὶ ἀμφισβητήσιμον, φθεγκτικὸν δὲ καὶ μαντικόν· καὶ συγγενόμενος ὑπὲρ ὧν ἐδεῖτο ἀπηλλάττετο. τοῦτό μοι δοκεῖ τὸ μαντεῖον καὶ Ὅμηρος γνούς, προσθεὶς τῷ Ὀδυσσεῖ τὴν ἐπ' αὐτὸ ὁδόν, ἐκτοπίσαι τὸ χωρίον ποιητικῶς μάλα τῆς καθ' ἡμᾶς θαλάττης.

---

5 The Selloi; cf. *Il.* 16.235: "prophets with unwashed feet who sleep on the ground."

6 Pausanias gives a detailed description of this elaborate ritual at 9.39.5–14.

priest in Ionia waxes prophetic after drawing water from a spring and drinking it; and the men in Dodona, who sleep on the ground with unwashed feet and watch over an oak tree,[5] are said by the Thesprotians to learn what to prophesy from that tree?

2. Then too, in the precinct of Trophonius—for here is the oracle of the hero Trophonius in Boeotia near the city of Lebadeia—any person wishing to make contact with the daemonic realm puts on a linen robe reaching his feet and a scarlet cloak, holds bread in his hands, and enters the oracle by descending on his back through a narrow opening. After seeing and hearing various things in there, he reemerges as the prophet of his own oracle.[6] And somewhere in Italian Magna Graecia there used to be an oracular cave near the lake called Aornos,[7] attended by psychagogues,[8] so-named because of their function. Anyone seeking an oracle would come there, pray, sacrifice a victim, pour libations, and call up the soul of some forebear or friend. A phantom would then appear to him, albeit indistinct and difficult to make out, that could nonetheless speak and prophesy. After consulting on the matters for which he sought answers, he would depart. I believe that Homer knew of this oracle, but in depicting Odysseus' journey to it he used poetic license to locate it far beyond our sea.[9]

[7] Virgil's Avernus near Cumae; cf. *Aen*. 6.236–63.

[8] Literally, "soul conductors."

[9] In the land of the Cimmerians (*Od*. 11.13–22), where Odysseus conversed with the souls of his mother Anticlea, Tiresias, and his dead companions.

3. Εἰ δὲ ταῦτα ἀληθῆ, ὥσπερ ἐστίν—καὶ σώζεται καὶ νῦν τὰ μὲν αὐτὰ ἐκεῖνα οἷα ἦν, τῶν δὲ ἴχνη σαφῆ ἔτι λέλειπται τῆς περὶ αὐτὰ θεραπείας τε καὶ κομιδῆς—θαυμαστὸν εἰ ταῦτα μὲν οὐδεὶς ἡγεῖται ἄτοπά τε εἶναι καὶ ἔξω τρόπου οὐδὲ ἀμφισβητεῖ περὶ αὐτῶν, ἀλλὰ τὴν πίστιν παραδοὺς τῷ χρόνῳ εἴσεισιν ἕκαστος μαντευσόμενος, καὶ ἀκούσας διαπιστεύει καὶ πιστεύσας χρῆται καὶ χρησάμενος τιμᾷ· εἰ δὲ ἀνὴρ φύσει τε κεχρημένος γενναιοτάτῃ καὶ παιδείᾳ σωφρονεστάτῃ καὶ φιλοσοφίᾳ ἀληθεστάτῃ καὶ τύχῃ δεξιωτάτῃ, συγγίγνεσθαι τῷ δαιμονίῳ ἠξιώθη πρὸς τοῦ θεοῦ, θαυμαστὸν δοκεῖ καὶ ἄπιστον, καὶ τοῦτο ὅσον αὐτῷ ἱκανὸν εἶναι χρησμῳδεῖν, οὐκ Ἀθηναίοις, μὰ Δία, περὶ τῶν Ἑλληνικῶν κακῶν βουλευομένοις, οὐδὲ Λακεδαιμονίοις περὶ στρατείας μαντευομένοις, οὐδὲ εἴ τις Ὀλυμπίαζε ἀγωνιούμενος περὶ νίκης ἠρώτα, οὐδ' εἴ τις εἰς δικαστήριον καθιστάμενος εἰ αἱρήσει διεπυνθάνετο, οὐδ' εἴ τις ἤρα χρημάτων εἰ πλουτήσει, οὐδὲ ἄλλο τι τῶν ἐπὶ μηδεμιᾷ προφάσει ἀξιόχρεῳ πραγματευομένων, ὑπὲρ ὧν ὁσημέραι ἐνοχλοῦσιν οἱ ἄνθρωποι τοὺς θεούς.

Τάχα μὲν γὰρ καὶ ταῦτα ἦν ἱκανὸν καὶ τὸ Σωκράτους δαιμόνιον διειδέναι, εἴπερ ἦν μαντικόν· καὶ γὰρ ἰατρῶν ὅστις αὐτῷ ἱκανός, καὶ ἄλλῳ ὁ αὐτός, καὶ τεκτόνων καὶ σκυτοτόμων καὶ τῶν ἄλλων ἑξῆς καὶ

3. Now if all these practices are true, as indeed they are—since some oracles are preserved to this day exactly as they were, while clear traces still remain of how others were tended and maintained—then it is astonishing that, on the one hand, no one considers these to be strange or unusual practices, or takes issue with them, but individuals put their trust in the antiquity of oracles and go there to receive prophecies, and they fully believe what they hear, act on this belief, and revere the oracles for their advice; and yet, on the other hand, when it comes to a man with a most noble nature, most proper upbringing, possessing the truest philosophy, and most favored by fortune, who is deemed worthy by god to be in contact with the daemonic realm, that this is somehow considered astonishing and unbelievable, as well as the fact that his *daimonion* was capable of prophesying to him, but not, by Zeus, to the Athenians deliberating about troubles in Greece, or to the Lacedaemonians seeking an oracle about a military campaign, or to some athlete going to compete at Olympia, asking whether he would be victorious, or to someone on trial, inquiring if he would win his case, or to some lover of money asking if he would become rich, or inquiries concerning any other matters with no valid justification whatsoever, about which humans bother the gods every single day.[10]

Now, perhaps Socrates' *daimonion* was capable of knowing these things as well, since it had prophetic powers. After all, any doctor able to treat himself can also treat someone else, and the same can be said for carpenters,

[10] For the futility of bothering the gods with such matters, see *Or.* 5.

ἐπιστημῶν καὶ δυνάμεων· ἀλλὰ ταύτῃ γε ὁ Σωκράτης ἐπλεονέκτει, τῷ νῷ ταῖς τῶν θεῶν φωναῖς συγγιγνόμενος, {τε}[1] ὅτι τὰ αὑτοῦ ἐν καλῷ διατιθέμενος τῇ πρὸς τὸ δαιμόνιον συνουσίᾳ, τοῖς ἄλλοις ἀνεπιφθόνως τε καὶ ὅσα ἀνάγκη προσεφέρετο.

4. Εἶεν· "τοῦτο μέν," φήσει τις, "πείθομαι ὅτι κατ' ἀρετὴν τρόπου καὶ φύσεως γενναιότητα ἠξιώθη ὁ Σωκράτης δαιμονίου συνουσίας· τί δὲ καὶ ἦν τὸ δαιμόνιον ποθῶ μαθεῖν." ἐὰν πρῶτον, ὦ τάν, ἀποκρίνῃ μοι, πότερον ἡγεῖ τι εἶναι δαιμονίων γένος ἐν τῇ φύσει, ὡς θεῶν, ὡς ἀνθρώπων, ὡς θηρίων, ἢ μή· γελοῖον γὰρ ἂν <ἦν>[2] ἐρωτᾶν τί ἦν τὸ δαιμόνιον Σωκράτους, τὸ πᾶν ἀγνοοῦντα· οἷον εἰ καὶ νησιώτης ἀνήρ, ἀθέατος τοῦ ἵππων γένους καὶ ἀμαθέστατος, ἀκούων ὅτι ἦν Μακεδόνι βασιλεῖ κτῆμα ὁ Βουκεφάλας, ὄχημα ἐκείνῳ μὲν τιθασόν, τοῖς δὲ ἄλλοις ἄβατον, ἔπειτα ἀνερωτῴη, τί ἦν πρᾶγμα ὁ Βουκεφάλας· ἠπόρησεν γὰρ ἂν ὁ διηγούμενος πρὸς ἄνδρα ἀθέατον τῆς ἵππων φύσεως εἰκόνος σαφοῦς.

5. Τί δέ; οἱ νῦν ἀποροῦντες περὶ τοῦ δαιμονίου τοῦ Σωκράτους Ὁμήρῳ <οὐ>[3] συνεγένοντο διηγουμένῳ αὐτὰ ἐκεῖνα ἃ διηγεῖτο, περὶ μὲν τοῦ Ἀχιλλέως ὅτι ἐν ἐκκλησίᾳ στρατιωτικῇ δημηγορῶν, διενεχθεὶς πρὸς

[1] del. $R^2$, U
[2] suppl. Russell
[3] suppl. Markland, Dübner, Trapp

cobblers, and all the other skills and abilities. But Socrates was exceptional in that he had contact with divine voices in his mind,[11] and it was by means of this relationship with his *daimonion* that he put his own affairs in good order and treated others as generously as he found necessary.[12]

4. Well and good. But someone will retort, "I can believe that Socrates was deemed worthy of a relationship with a *daimonion* because of his virtuous character and noble nature, but I want to learn what his *daimonion* actually was." I will oblige, my friend, if first you tell me whether or not you believe that there is a race of *daimonia* in nature as there are races of gods, humans, and animals. For it would be ridiculous to ask what Socrates' *daimonion* is, without any knowledge of what they are in general. It would be like an islander, who had never seen horses and knew nothing of the species, being told that a Macedonian king[13] had a thing in his possession called Bucephalus, that was tame enough to carry him, but allowed no others to mount, then asking what sort of thing Bucephalus was. His informant would be at a loss for a clear description when faced with a man who had never seen an actual horse.

5. Furthermore, can it be that those who are now in doubt about Socrates' *daimonion* were never acquainted with Homer and his famous account of how Achilles, when he was speaking before the assembled army, quarreled

[11] For the voice of god speaking to Socrates, see Xen. *Ap.* 12; for the voice of his *daimonion*, see Pl. *Theag.* 128e.

[12] According to Xen. *Ap.* 13 and *Mem.* 1.1.4–5, he often advised his friends with what he learned from his *daimonion*.

[13] Alexander the Great.

τὸν Ἀγαμέμνονα, σπώμενος τὸ ξίφος ὡς παίσων, κωλύεται ὑπὸ δαιμονίου; Ἀθηνᾶν καλεῖ τὸ δαιμόνιον· αὕτη γάρ, φησίν, ὀργιζομένῳ αὐτῷ παρεγένετο,

> στῆ δ᾽ ὄπιθεν, ξανθῆς δὲ κόμης ἕλε Πηλείωνα.

τὴν δὲ αὐτὴν ταύτην Ἀθηνᾶν λέγειν καὶ <ἐπὶ>[4] τοῦ Διομήδους φησίν·

> ἀχλὺν δ᾽ αὖ τοι ἀπ᾽ ὀφθαλμῶν ἕλον, ἣ πρὶν ἐπῆεν,
> ὄφρ᾽ εὖ γινώσκοις[5] ἠμὲν θεὸν ἠδὲ καὶ ἄνδρα.

πάλιν αὖ τῷ Τηλεμάχῳ μέλλοντι συγγίγνεσθαι βασιλεῖ πρεσβυτέρῳ, αἰδουμένῳ καὶ ἀπορουμένῳ, ὁ ἑταῖρος λέγει·

> Τηλέμαχ᾽, ἄλλα μὲν αὐτὸς ἐνὶ φρεσὶ σῇσι νοήσεις,
> ἄλλα δὲ καὶ δαίμων ὑποθήσεται·

καὶ προστίθησιν τὴν αἰτίαν τῆς παρὰ τοῦ δαιμονίου ἐλπίδος·

> οὐ γὰρ ὀΐω
> οὐδέ σε θεῶν ἀέκητι γενέσθαι τε τραφέμεν τε.

καὶ ἐπ᾽ ἄλλου αὖθις,

[4] suppl. Trapp

[5] γινώσκοις Davies[2], Dübner, Koniaris: γινώσκοι R: γιγνώσκῃς Homerus

with Agamemnon and began drawing his sword to strike him, whereupon he was restrained by a *daimonion*? Homer calls that *daimonion* Athena. For it was she, he says, who appeared to the angry hero,

> and stood behind him, and seized Peleus' son by his fair hair.[14]

And he states that this same Athena said, apropos of Diomedes,

> Moreover, I have taken from your eyes the mist that was upon them before,
> so that you might recognize who is god and who is man.[15]

Then again, when Telemachus was about to converse with the king who was his elder,[16] and was bashful and at a loss, his companion said,

> Telemachus, some things you will devise in your own mind,
> and other things a *daimon* will suggest,[17]

and he then adds why he expects help from the *daimonion*,

> for I do not think
> that you were born and raised without the care of the gods.[18]

And then in another case:

[14] *Il.* 1.197. [15] *Il.* 5.127–28. [16] Nestor.
[17] *Od.* 3.26–27, spoken by Athena disguised as Mentor.
[18] *Od.* 3.27–28.

τῷ γὰρ ἐπὶ φρεσὶ θῆκε θεὰ λευκώλενος Ἥρη,

καὶ ἐπ' ἄλλου,

Τυδεΐδῃ Διομήδεϊ Πάλλας Ἀθήνη
δῶκε μένος καὶ θάρσος,

καὶ ἐπ' ἄλλου,

γυῖα δ' ἔθηκεν ἐλαφρά, πόδας καὶ χεῖρας
ὕπερθεν.

ὁρᾷς τὸ πλῆθος τῶν συγγιγνομένων τῷ δαιμονίῳ;

6. Βούλει τοίνυν τὸν Σωκράτην ἐάσας Ὁμήρου πυθέσθαι, τί σοι ταυτὶ ἐθέλει, ὦ ποιητῶν γενναιότατε; τὸ μὲν γὰρ Σωκράτους δαιμόνιον ἓν καὶ ἁπλοῦν καὶ ἰδιωτικὸν καὶ δημοτικόν,[6] ἢ ποταμὸν διαβαίνοντα ἀνακαλούμενον, ἢ Ἀλκιβιάδου ἐρῶντα ἀναβαλλόμενον, ἢ ἀπολογεῖσθαι βουλόμενον <κωλῦον>,[7] ἢ ἀποθνήσκειν προαιρούμενον οὐ κωλῦον. Ὁμήρῳ δὲ τὸ δαιμόνιον συνίσταται οὔτε ἑνὶ οὔτε ἐφ' ἑνὶ οὔτε ἓν οὔτε ἐπὶ σμικροῖς, ἀλλὰ καὶ παντοδαπὸν καὶ πολλάκις, καὶ ἐν πολλοῖς ὀνόμασιν καὶ ἐν πολλοῖς φαντάσμασιν καὶ ἐν παντοδαπαῖς φωναῖς.

[6] καὶ δημοτικόν R, Hobein, Trapp: {καὶ} <οὐ> δημοτικόν Markland, Dübner: obel. Koniaris
[7] suppl. Markland, Dübner, Koniaris

---

[19] *Il.* 1.55, of Hera prompting Achilles to call an assembly.
[20] *Il.* 5.1–2. [21] *Il.* 5.122, of Athena assisting Diomedes.

> for Hera the white-armed goddess had put it in his
> mind.[19]

And in another:

> to Tydeus' son Diomedes Pallas Athena
> gave strength and courage.[20]

And in another:

> She lightened his limbs, his feet, and his hands
> above.[21]

Do you not see the multitude of those in contact with the daemonic realm?

6. If you will allow me, let us set aside Socrates for now and ask Homer, "What do *you* mean by these incidents, O most noble of poets?" I ask because the *daimonion* of Socrates was a single entity and of a single nature, personal to an ordinary individual, whether it called him back when he was crossing a river,[22] or postponed his love affair with Alcibiades,[23] or <opposed> him when he wanted to defend himself in court,[24] or did not oppose him when he chose to die.[25] But in Homer, the *daimonion* is not a single entity, nor does it assist just one individual on a specific occasion involving trivial matters, but it assumes many forms and intervenes frequently under many names, in many manifestations, and with many different voices.

22 Pl. *Phdr.* 242b–c. 23 [Pl.] 1 *Alc.* 103a and 105e.

24 If the supplement of κωλῦον (opposed) is correct, Maximus is following Xen. *Ap.* 4, where Socrates' divine sign opposed his defending himself.

25 Pl. *Ap.* 40b–c.

Ἆρ᾽ οὖν καὶ ἀποδέχῃ τι τούτων, καὶ ἡγεῖ τι εἶναι τὴν Ἀθηνᾶν καὶ τὴν Ἥραν καὶ τὸν Ἀπόλλωνα καὶ Ἔριν, καὶ ὅστις ἄλλος δαίμων Ὁμηρικός; μή με οἵου πυνθάνεσθαι εἰ τοιαύτην ἡγεῖ τὴν Ἀθηνᾶν οἵαν Φειδίας ἐδημιούργησεν, οὐδὲν τῶν Ὁμήρου ἐπῶν φαυλοτέραν, παρθένον καλήν, γλαυκῶπιν, ὑψηλήν, αἰγίδα ἀνεζωσμένην, κόρυν φέρουσαν, δόρυ ἔχουσαν, ἀσπίδα ἔχουσαν· μηδὲ αὖ τὴν Ἥραν οἵαν Πολύκλειτος Ἀργείοις ἔδειξεν, λευκώλενον, ἐλεφαντόπηχυν, εὐῶπιν, εὐείμονα, βασιλικήν, ἱδρυμένην ἐπὶ χρυσοῦ θρόνου· μηδέ γε αὖ τὸν Ἀπόλλωνα οἷον γραφεῖς καὶ δημιουργοὶ εἰκάζουσιν, μειράκιον γυμνὸν ἐκ χλαμυδίου, τοξότην, διαβεβηκότα τοῖς ποσὶν ὥσπερ θέοντα.

Οὐ τοῦτο ἐρωτῶ, οὐδὲ ἡγοῦμαί σε φαῦλον εἶναι τἀληθῆ εἰκάζειν, ὥστε μὴ μεταβάλλειν τὸ αἴνιγμα εἰς λόγον· ἀλλ᾽ εἰ τῷ ὄντι ἡγεῖ ταυτὶ τὰ ὀνόματα καὶ τὰ σώματα αἰνίττεσθαί τινας δαιμονίους δυνάμεις καὶ συνισταμένας τῶν ἀνθρώπων τοῖς εὐμοιροτάτοις καὶ ὕπαρ καὶ ὄναρ. εἰ μὲν γὰρ μηδεμίαν ἡγεῖ, ὥρα σοι καὶ Ὁμήρῳ πολεμεῖν καὶ τὰ μαντεῖα ἀναιρεῖν καὶ ταῖς φήμαις ἀπιστεῖν καὶ τὰ ὀνείρατα φεύγειν, καὶ Σωκράτην δὲ ἐᾶν. εἰ δὲ ταῦτα μὲν οὔτε ἄπιστα ἡγεῖ οὔτε ἀδύνατα, ἀπορεῖς δὲ περὶ Σωκράτους, μεταβαλὼν ἐρήσομαί σε πότερα οὐκ ἄξιον ἡγεῖ τὸν Σωκράτην

---

26 Paus. 2.17.4 provides a brief description of this chryselephantine statue.

So, do you then accept any of this, and believe in the existence of Athena, Hera, Apollo, Strife, and all the other *daimones* in Homer? Please do not think that I am asking whether you believe that Athena is exactly the way Phidias sculpted her, as a being every bit as impressive as she is in Homer's verses, namely a beautiful, tall virgin with gray eyes, girded with an aegis, wearing a helmet, and holding a spear and shield. Nor in turn whether Hera is such as Polyclitus represented her for the Argives, namely with white arms, forearms of ivory, beautiful eyes, splendid garments, regal bearing, and seated on a golden throne.[26] Nor yet whether Apollo is like the images made by artists and sculptors, namely a youth, naked beneath his military cloak, carrying a bow and arrows, and with feet apart as if running.

That is not my question, nor do I consider you so poor at surmising the truth that you are unable to convert the allegory into its rational meaning.[27] No, I wish to know whether you believe that these names and physical forms refer allegorically to certain daemonic powers that actually exist, ones that assist especially fortunate humans, whether openly or in dreams. But if you think that no such power exists, then it is high time for you to do battle with Homer, do away with oracles, put no trust in prophetic utterances, discount dreams, and dismiss Socrates. If, however, you consider these phenomena to be neither inconceivable nor impossible, but still remain unsure about Socrates, then I shall change tack and ask whether you consider Socrates unworthy of being allotted a *daimonion*,

[27] Cf. *Or.* 2, where representations of the divine serve as reminders of the gods, not literal depictions.

*μοίρας δαιμονίου, ἢ τὸ δυνατὸν ἄλλοθι ἐνταῦθα ἐξασθενεῖ. ἀλλὰ τὸ μὲν δυνατὸν διδοὺς κἀνταῦθα δώσεις, τὸ δὲ ἄξιον οὐκ ἀφαιρήσεις τοῦ Σωκράτους. εἰ τοίνυν καὶ δυνατὸν τὸ πρᾶγμα καὶ ἄξιος Σωκράτης, λείπεταί σοι μὴ περὶ Σωκράτους ἀμφισβητεῖν, ἀλλὰ καθόλου σκοπεῖν τίς ἡ τοῦ δαιμονίου φύσις.*

7. *Καὶ τοῦτο μέν σοι παρ' ἐμοῦ καὶ αὖθις λελέξεται· νῦν δὲ ἴθι αὐτὸς πρὸς αὐτὸν ἐκκαθηράμενος ταυτηνὶ τὴν δόξαν, ἵνα σοι καὶ προτέλεια γένηται ταῦτα τοῦ μέλλοντος λόγου· ὅτι θεοὶ ἀνθρώποις ἀρετὴν καὶ κακίαν ἔνειμαν, ὥσπερ ἐν σταδίῳ ἀγωνισταῖς, τὴν μὲν ἆθλον μοχθηρᾶς φύσεως καὶ γνώμης πονηρᾶς, τὴν δὲ ἐπινίκιον γνώμης ἀγαθῆς καὶ φύσεως ἐρρωμένης, ὅταν κρατῶσιν καλοκἀγαθίᾳ. τούτοις καὶ τὸ θεῖον ἐθέλει ξυνίστασθαί τε καὶ συνεπιλαμβάνειν τοῦ βίου, ὑπερέχον χεῖρα καὶ κηδόμενον· τὸν μὲν φήμαις σώζει, τὸν δὲ οἰωνοῖς, τὸν δὲ ὀνείρασιν, τὸν δὲ φωναῖς, τὸν δὲ θυσίαις. ἀσθενὴς γὰρ ἡ ἀνθρωπίνη ψυχὴ πρὸς πάντα ἐξικνεῖσθαι τοῖς λογισμοῖς, ἅτε περιβεβλημένη ἐν τῷ δεῦρο βίῳ πολλὴν καὶ σκοτεινὴν ἀχλύν, καὶ ἐν πολλῷ ψόφῳ καὶ θορύβῳ τῶν δεῦρο κακῶν διατρίβουσα καὶ ταραττομένη ὑπ' αὐτῶν.*

*Τίς γὰρ οὕτω ταχὺς καὶ ἀσφαλὴς ὁδοιπόρων, ὡς μὴ ἐντυχεῖν βαδίζων χαράδρᾳ ἀφανεῖ ἢ χάρακι ἀδήλῳ ἢ κρημνῷ ἢ τάφρῳ; τίς δὲ οὕτω κυβερνήτης ἀγαθὸς καὶ εὔστοχος, ὡς ἀπείρατος διελθεῖν κλύδω-*

[28] It is taken up in *Or.* 9.

or if you think that what is possible in those other cases is not valid in his. If, however, you concede the possibility in those other instances, then you must grant it in his case as well, and you will not deprive Socrates of his worthiness. Therefore, if the thing is possible and Socrates is worthy of it, your only recourse is to stop arguing about Socrates and instead consider in general what *daimones* actually are.

7. That, however, is a topic for me to take up with you at a later time.[28] For now, come, purify yourself by accepting the following premise, in order to prepare yourself for initiation into the argument that follows, namely that the gods have apportioned virtue and vice to humans, as if to competitors in a stadium. Vice is the reward for a depraved nature and a wicked mind, whereas virtue is the prize for a good mind and a strong nature, when individuals are victorious by dint of their noble character. These are the ones that divinity wishes to assist and to participate in their lives, as it holds over them a protective hand and cares for them. It saves one person through prophetic utterances, another through flights of birds, another through dreams, another through voices, another through sacrificial omens. They do so because the human soul is too weak to accomplish everything through its powers of reason, as it is surrounded in its life here by a dark and dense fog, and is confounded by living amid the great din and tumult caused by the ills that exist here on earth.

What traveler, I ask, is so fast or sure-footed as never to encounter in his path some hidden gully, unseen trench, cliff, or ditch? What helmsman is so good and skillful as to complete his voyage without ever experiencing high seas,

νος καὶ ζάλης καὶ πνευμάτων ἐμβολῆς καὶ ἀέρος τεταραγμένου; τίς δὲ οὕτω ἰατρὸς τεχνικός, ὡς μὴ ἐπιταραχθῆναι ἀφανεῖ καὶ ἀνελπίστῳ νοσήματι, ἄλλου ἄλλοθεν ὑποφυομένου καὶ ὑποτεμνομένου τοὺς τῆς τέχνης λόγους; τίς δὲ <οὕτως>[8] ἀνὴρ ἀγαθός, ὡς διελθεῖν βίον ἀπταίστως καὶ ἀσφαλῶς, ὡς σῶμα νοσερόν, ὡς πλοῦν ἄδηλον, ὡς ὁδὸν διεσκαμμένην, καὶ μὴ δεηθῆναι ἐν τούτοις κυβερνήτου καὶ ἰατροῦ καὶ χειραγωγοῦ θεοῦ;

Καλὸν μὲν γὰρ ἡ ἀρετὴ καὶ εὐπορώτατον καὶ δραστικώτατον· ἀλλ' ἀνακέκραται ὕλῃ πονηρᾷ καὶ ἀσαφεῖ καὶ μεστῇ πολλοῦ τοῦ ἀδήλου, ἣν δὴ καλοῦσιν οἱ ἄνθρωποι τύχην, χρῆμα τυφλὸν καὶ ἀστάθμητον. ἀντιφιλοτιμεῖται τῇ ἀρετῇ καὶ ἀντιστατεῖ καὶ ἀνταγωνίζεται καὶ πολλάκις αὐτὴν ἀναταράττει, ὡς νέφη αἰθέρι ὑποδραμόντα τὴν ἡλίου ἀκτῖνα ἀπέκρυψεν αὐτοῦ τὸ φῶς, καὶ ἐστὶν μὲν καὶ τότε ἥλιος καλός, ἀλλὰ ἡμῖν ἄδηλος· οὕτω καὶ ἀρετὴν ὑποτέμνεται τύχης ἐμβολή, καὶ καλὴ μὲν ἡ ἀρετὴ τά γε ἄλλα, ἐμπεσοῦσα δὲ εἰς νεφέλην ἄδηλον ἐπισκιάζεται καὶ διατειχίζεται, ἔνθα δὴ αὐτῇ θεοῦ δεῖ συλλήπτορος καὶ συναγωνιστοῦ καὶ παραστάτου.

8. Θεὸς μὲν οὖν αὐτὸς κατὰ χώραν ἱδρυμένος οἰκονομεῖ τὸν οὐρανὸν καὶ τὴν ἐν οὐρανῷ τάξιν· εἰσὶ δ' αὐτῷ φύσεις ἀθάνατοι δεύτεραι, οἱ καλούμενοι δαίμονες, ἐν μεθορίᾳ γῆς καὶ οὐρανοῦ τεταγμένοι· θεοῦ μὲν ἀσθενέστεροι, ἀνθρώπου δ' ἰσχυρότεροι· θεῶν μὲν

squalls, blasts of wind, and tempests? What doctor is so expert as never to be confounded by some unseen and unexpected disease, when various diseases develop from various sources and thwart the tenets of medicine? And what man is so good as to travel safely through life without a stumble, and—as we saw in the case of a diseased body, an uncertain voyage, and a road full of pitfalls—never in need at such times of a divine helmsman, doctor, and guide?

Now even though virtue is a noble thing and is most resourceful and effective, it nonetheless intermingles with a harmful element that is dark and full of uncertainty, which men call fortune, an entity that is inscrutable and unstable. It is virtue's adversary, opposing it, fighting against it, and frequently confounding it. It acts like clouds in the sky that float beneath the sun's rays and conceal its light. For even though the sun itself remains beautiful, it becomes invisible to us. Such is the way that a stroke of fortune thwarts virtue, for although virtue remains beautiful in other respects, once it falls into an obscuring cloud, it becomes overshadowed and walled off. This is precisely when virtue needs a god to take up its cause, fight on its behalf, and stand by its side.

8. While god himself remains in one place, as he governs the heavens and maintains order in them, he has a race of secondary immortal beings, the so-called *daimones*, that are stationed in the space between the earth and heaven. They are less powerful than god, but stronger than a man; they are servants of the gods, but overseers of

---

[8] suppl. Trapp praeeunte Stephano

ὑπηρέται, ἀνθρώπων δὲ ἐπιστάται· θεῶν μὲν πλησιαίτατοι, ἀνθρώπων δὲ ἐπιμελέστατοι. ἦ γὰρ ἂν τῷ διὰ μέσου πολλῷ τὸ θνητὸν πρὸς τὸ ἀθάνατον διετειχίσθη τῆς οὐρανίου ἐπόψεώς τε καὶ ὁμιλίας, ὅτι μὴ τῆς δαιμονίου ταύτης φύσεως, οἷον ἁρμονίας, κατὰ τὴν πρὸς ἑκάτερον συγγένειαν καταλαβούσης δεσμῷ τὴν ἀνθρωπίνην ἀσθένειαν πρὸς τὸ θεῖον κάλλος.

Καθάπερ γάρ, οἶμαι, τὸ βαρβαρικὸν τοῦ Ἑλληνικοῦ διῄρηται φωνῆς συνέσει, ἀλλὰ τὸ τῶν ἑρμηνέων γένος τὰς παρ᾽ ἑκατέρων φωνὰς ὑποδεχόμενον καὶ διαπορθμεῦον πρὸς ἑκατέρους, συνῆψεν αὐτῶν καὶ συνεκέρασεν τὰς ὁμιλίας· οὕτω {δ᾽ ἂν}[9] καὶ τὸ δαιμόνων γένος ἐπίμικτον νοεῖται {καὶ}[10] θεοῖς τε καὶ ἀνθρώποις. τοῦτο γάρ ἐστιν τὸ ἀνθρώποις προσφθεγγόμενον καὶ φανταζόμενον καὶ εἱλούμενον ἐν μέσῃ τῇ θνητῇ φύσει καὶ ἐπωφελοῦν ὅσα ἀνάγκη δεῖσθαι θεῶν τὸ θνητῶν γένος. πολλὴ δὲ ἡ δαιμόνων ἀγέλη·

τρὶς γὰρ μύριοί εἰσιν ἐπὶ χθονὶ πουλυβοτείρῃ,
ἀθάνατοι Ζηνὸς πρόπολοι.

οἱ μὲν ἰατροὶ νοσημάτων, οἱ δὲ τῶν ἀπόρων σύμβουλοι, οἱ δὲ τῶν ἀφανῶν ἄγγελοι, οἱ δὲ τέχνης συνεργάται, οἱ δὲ ὁδοῦ συνέμποροι· οἱ μὲν ἀστικοί, οἱ δὲ ἀγροικικοί, οἱ δὲ θαλάττιοι, οἱ δὲ ἠπειρωτικοί· εἴλη-

9 delevi praeeunte Koniaris: obel. Trapp, Koniaris in textu: δ᾽αὖ Stephanus
10 del. Trapp

men; they are very closely related to the gods, but deeply concerned for humans. In fact, because of the great distance between them, the mortal realm would have been walled off from the immortal realm and from any view of heaven or any association with it, were it not for the nature of these *daimones*, who, like harmony, bind together human weakness and divine beauty by virtue of their kinship with both.[29]

For in my opinion, just as barbarians are separated from Greeks because their languages are incomprehensible, but then when the race of translators takes in what one party says and conveys it to the other, it connects them and enables their interaction, so too the race of *daimones* is thought to mingle with both gods and men, for it is this race that speaks to humans and appears to them, that roams in the midst of the mortal realm and lends assistance whenever the human race is forced to need the gods.[30] *Daimones* form an immense group,

> for over the fruitful earth there are thirty thousand
> immortal servants of Zeus.[31]

Some heal diseases, others advise those who are bewildered, some disclose what cannot be seen, others assist craftsmen in their trade, some accompany travelers; some are in cities, others in the countryside; some are on the

[29] For the mediating role of *daimones*, see. Pl. *Symp.* 202e–3a. Their harmonizing function is described in *Or.* 9.1–4.

[30] This passage, including *daimones* as translators who convey messages to the gods, is closely based on Pl. *Symp.* 202e–3a.

[31] Hes. *Op.* 252–53, where the text has "guardians (φύλακες) ‹of mortal men›" instead of "servants of Zeus."

χεν δὲ ἄλλος ἄλλην ἑστίαν σώματος, ὁ μὲν Σωκράτην, ὁ δὲ Πλάτωνα, ὁ δὲ Πυθαγόραν, ὁ δὲ Ζήνωνα, ὁ δὲ Διογένην· ὁ μὲν φοβερός, ὁ δὲ φιλάνθρωπος, ὁ δὲ πολιτικός, ὁ δὲ τακτικός· ὅσαι φύσεις ἀνδρῶν, τοσαῦται καὶ δαιμόνων·

καί τε θεοὶ ξείνοισιν ἐοικότες ἀλλοδαποῖσιν,
παντοῖοι τελέθοντες, ἐπιστρωφῶσι πόληας.

ἐὰν δέ που μοχθηρὰν δείξῃς ψυχήν, ἀνέστιος αὕτη καὶ ἀνεπιστάτητος.

sea, others on land. Different ones are allotted different bodies to inhabit, be it Socrates', Plato's, Pythagoras', Zeno's, or Diogenes'. One *daimon* is terrifying, another benevolent;[32] one is concerned with political affairs, another with military tactics. There are as many kinds of *daimones* as there are kinds of men:

> and gods, in the guise of all sorts of strangers,
> take on various forms and visit the cities of men.[33]

Show me a depraved soul, and you can be certain that it has no resident *daimon* and overseer.

[32] *Daimones* can avenge and punish wrongdoing as well as aid good people; cf. *Or*. 9.6.

[33] *Od*. 17.485–86, the suitors speaking of gods in disguise observing the behavior of humans.

# *ORATION* 9

## INTRODUCTION

The oration opens by investigating the nature of *daimones* in general, as promised in *Or.* 8.7. A Homeric quotation ("Are you a god or a mortal?") opens the discussion. If a *daimon* is simply a god, then there is nothing more to be said, but if it is a being that spends time on earth and shares our emotions and speech, then what is its place in nature? Assuming that animate nature progresses through an unbroken chain from god to plants, then *daimones* must logically occupy some intermediate place, like middle notes in musical harmony (§1). Positing that god is unemotional and immortal, whereas man is emotional and mortal, then if *daimones* are intermediate beings, they must be immortal and emotional (§2). An analogy from the four elements and their properties shows that opposing elements such as fire and water have a mediating element in air, which takes heat from fire and moisture from water. Such is the case with *daimones*, who share immortality with god but emotion with humans (§3). In sum, wherever in nature there is harmony, there must be intermediate terms that sustain it, again demonstrating that *daimones* are immortal and emotional (§4).

*Daimones* are defined as souls that have shed their human bodies, and since souls themselves must be immortal,

so too are *daimones* (§5). When the soul leaves behind its storm-tossed body and becomes a *daimon*, it migrates to heaven, where it can directly behold beauty itself.[1] But while the *daimon* experiences joy at its new status, it also pities the condition of humans and wishes to join them because of its love for men (*philanthrōpia*). So god orders it to aid people of all kinds and to enforce justice (§6). Specific examples of *daimones* helping humans include Asclepius, Heracles, Dionysus, Amphilochus, the Dioscuri, and Minos. There is evidence of their continued existence. Achilles' presence on Leuce is attested by numerous sightings and one fabulous account, and Hector has been seen bounding across the Trojan plain. Remarkably, the speaker claims to have witnessed not only the Dioscuri as stars guiding a ship but also to have seen Asclepius and Heracles with his very own eyes (§7).

[1] The soul's vision of heaven draws on numerous Platonic texts (e.g., *Phdr.* 247c–e, *Symp.* 210e–11b, and *Phd.* 82d–84b).

# *ORATION* 9

Ἔτι περὶ τοῦ Σωκράτους δαιμονίου. β′

1. Φέρε ἐρώμεθα τὸ δαιμόνιον· φιλάνθρωπον γὰρ καὶ εἰωθὸς ἀποκρίνεσθαι διὰ σωμάτων ἀνθρωπίνων, ὡς ἡ Ἰσμηνίου τέχνη διὰ τῶν αὐλῶν· ἐρώμεθα δὲ ὧδέ πως κατὰ τὸν Ὁμήρου Ὀδυσσέα·

> θεός νύ τις ἦ βροτός ἐσσι;
> εἰ μέν τις θεός ἐσσι, τοὶ οὐρανὸν εὐρὺν ἔχουσιν,

οὐδὲν δεῖ λόγων· ἴσμεν γὰρ τὰ σά·

> εἰ δέ τίς ἐσσι βροτῶν, τοὶ ἐπὶ χθονὶ ναιετάουσιν,

ἆρα τοιοῦτον χρῆμα οἷον ὁμοπαθές τε εἶναι ἡμῖν καὶ ὁμόφωνον καὶ ὁμογενὲς καὶ σύγχρονον; ἢ κατὰ μὲν τὴν δίαιταν ἐφέστιον τῇ γῇ, κατὰ δὲ τὴν οὐσίαν κρεῖττον αὐτῆς; οὐ γὰρ σάρκες αἱ δαιμόνων φύσεις (ἀποκριτέον γάρ τοι ὑπὲρ αὐτῶν, κελεύουσι γάρ), οὐδὲ ὀστᾶ, οὐδὲ αἷμα, οὐδὲ ἄλλο τι σκεδαστέον ἢ λυόμενον ἢ τηκόμενον ἢ διαρρέον.

---

[1] A fourth-century BC aulos player.

# *ORATION* 9

## More on Socrates' *daimonion*. Part II

1. Come, then, let us ask the *daimon* itself, for it is benevolent and accustomed to giving answers through human bodies, just as Ismenias[1] performed his skill through his pipes. Let us pose our questions in much the same way that Homer's Odysseus does:

> Are you a god or a mortal?
> If you are one of the gods who inhabit the broad heaven,[2]

then nothing more need be said, since we know all about you.

> But if you are one of the mortals who dwell on earth,[3]

then are you a kind of being that shares our emotions and our speech, belongs to the same race, and has the same lifespan? Or is it that you spend time living on earth, but in essence belong to a higher realm? After all, *daimones* (and here I must answer for them, since they order me to do so) are not beings of flesh, bones, blood, or anything else that can be dispersed, dissolved, melted, or made to waste away.

[2] *Od.* 6.149–50, addressed to Nausicaa.

[3] *Od.* 6.153.

Ἀλλὰ τί μήν; οὑτωσὶ πρῶτον θεασώμεθα τὸ ἀναγκαῖον τῆς δαιμόνων οὐσίας· τὸ ἀπαθὲς τῷ ἐμπαθεῖ ἐναντίον, καὶ τὸ θνητὸν τῷ ἀθανάτῳ, καὶ τὸ ἄλογον τῷ λογικῷ, καὶ τὸ ἀναίσθητον τῷ αἰσθητικῷ, καὶ τὸ ἔμψυχον τῷ ἀψύχῳ. πᾶν τοίνυν ψυχὴν ἔχον, ‹ἐξ›[1] ἑκατέροιν συγκεκραμένον· ἢ γὰρ ἀπαθὲς {τὸ}[2] ἀθάνατον, ἢ ἀθάνατον ἐμπαθές, ἢ ἐμπαθὲς θνητόν, ἢ ἄλογον αἰσθητικόν, ἢ ἔμψυχον ἀπαθές· καὶ διὰ τούτων ὁδεύει ἡ φύσις κατὰ βραχὺ ἀπὸ τῶν τιμιωτάτων ἐπὶ τὰ ἀτιμότατα καταβαίνουσα ἑξῆς· ἐὰν δέ τι τούτων ἐξέλῃς, διέκοψας τὴν φύσιν· ὥσπερ ἐν ἁρμονίᾳ φθόγγων τὴν πρὸς τὰ ἄκρα ὁμολογίαν ἡ μέση ποιεῖ· ἀπὸ γὰρ τοῦ ὀξυτάτου φθόγγου ἐπὶ τὸ βαρύτατον ταῖς διὰ μέσου φωναῖς ἐπερειδομένην τὴν μεταβολὴν ἐμμελῆ ποιεῖ καὶ τῇ ἀκοῇ καὶ τῇ χειρουργίᾳ.

2. Τοῦτό τοι νόμιζε γίγνεσθαι καὶ ἐν τῇ φύσει, ὥσπερ ἐν ἁρμονίᾳ τελεωτάτῃ· καὶ τίθεσο θεὸν μὲν κατὰ τὸ ἀπαθὲς καὶ ἀθάνατον, δαίμονα δὲ κατὰ τὸ ἀθάνατον καὶ ἐμπαθές, ἄνθρωπον δὲ κατὰ τὸ ἐμπαθὲς καὶ θνητόν, θηρίον δὲ κατὰ τὸ ἄλογον καὶ αἰσθητικόν, φυτὸν δὲ κατὰ τὸ ἔμψυχον καὶ ἀπαθές. καὶ τὰ μὲν ἄλλα ἡμῖν τὸ νῦν ἔχον κατὰ χώραν ἔστω· ἐπεὶ δὲ τῆς δαιμονίων φύσεως πέρι σκοπούμεθα, ἣν φαμὲν μεσότητα εἶναι πρὸς ἄνθρωπον καὶ θεόν, ἴδωμεν εἴ πῃ

[1] suppl. Stephanus, Trapp
[2] del. Trapp

Then what are they? Let us begin by considering in the following way what the essential nature of *daimones* must necessarily be. The opposite of unemotional is emotional, of mortal is immortal, of irrational is rational, of impassive is sentient, and of animate is inanimate. Now every living thing[4] is compounded of two qualities drawn from these different pairs, and must be either unemotional and immortal, or immortal and emotional, or emotional and mortal, or irrational and sentient, or animate and unemotional. For it is through these qualities that nature proceeds in a gradual order that descends in unbroken fashion from the most esteemed beings to the least,[5] and if you remove any one of these stages, you will split nature in two. In just the same way, it is the middle range in musical harmony that produces an agreement between the extremes, for when the transition from the highest note to the lowest one is based on the intermediate notes, the resulting transformation becomes harmonious for the ear to hear and the hand to play.

2. You must recognize that this happens in nature, just as it does in the most perfect harmony. Posit that god is unemotional and immortal, a *daimon* is immortal and emotional, a man is emotional and mortal, an animal is irrational and sentient, and a plant is animate and unemotional. For the time being, let us set aside all the other categories of beings. But since we are focusing our examination on *daimones*, whose nature, we say, is intermediate between that of man and god, let us ascertain

4 Literally, "everything possessing soul."

5 That is, in a progression from god, to *daimon*, man, animal, and plant.

δυνατὸν ἐξελέσθαι αὐτὴν καὶ διασῶσαι τὰ ἄκρα. ἆρ' οὖν ὁ θεὸς ἀθάνατον μέν, ἐμπαθὲς δέ; οὐδαμῶς, ἀλλὰ ἀθάνατον μέν, ἀπαθὲς δέ· τί δὲ ἄνθρωπος; θνητὸν μέν, ἀπαθὲς δέ; οὐδὲ τοῦτο· ἀλλὰ θνητὸν μέν, οὐ μὴν ἀπαθές. ποῦ τοίνυν ἡμῖν οἰχήσεται τὸ ἀθάνατον ὁμοῦ καὶ ἐμπαθές; δεῖ γὰρ συστῆναι ἐξ ἀμφοῖν οὐσίαν κοινήν, κρείττονα μὲν ἀνθρώπου, θεοῦ δὲ ἐλάττονα, εἰ μέλλει ἔσεσθαι τῶν ἄκρων πρὸς ἄλληλα ἀναλογία· δύο γὰρ πραγμάτων κεχωρισμένων τῇ φύσει χωρισθήσεται καὶ ἡ ἐπιμιξία παντάπασιν, ἐὰν μή τις κοινὸς ὅρος ἀμφότερα ὑποδέξηται.

3. Οἷον τὸ τοιόνδε λέγω· καλοῦμέν τι πῦρ ξηρόν τε καὶ θερμόν· ἐναντίον δὲ θερμῷ μὲν ψυχρόν, ‹ξηρῷ δὲ ὑγρόν· καλοῦμεν δέ τι ὕδωρ ψυχρόν τε›[3] καὶ ὑγρόν· ἀδύνατον δὴ μεταβάλλειν πῦρ εἰς ὕδωρ, καὶ ὕδωρ εἰς πῦρ· οὔτε γὰρ ψυχρὸν εἰς θερμότητα, οὔτε ὑγρὸν εἰς ξηρότητα μεταβάλοι ἄν. οὕτω δὴ τὸν τούτων πόλεμον μετεχειρίσατο ἡ φύσις· ἔδωκεν αὐτοῖς ὥσπερ ἐκεχειροφόρον τὸν ἀέρα, ὃς λαβὼν παρὰ μὲν τοῦ πυρὸς τὴν θερμότητα, παρὰ δὲ τοῦ ὕδατος τὴν ὑγρότητα, συνεκέρασεν αὐτῶν καὶ συνῆψεν τὰς ὁμιλίας, καὶ γίνεται μεταβολὴ καὶ πρόσβασις, ποτὲ μὲν τοῦ πυρὸς εἰς ἀέρα κατὰ θερμότητα, ποτὲ δὲ τοῦ ἀέρος εἰς ὕδωρ κατὰ ὑγρότητα. πάλιν αὖ ἀὴρ θερμόν τε καὶ ὑγρόν, γῆ δὲ ψυχρόν τε καὶ ξηρόν· ἐναντίον δὲ ξηρότης μὲν ὑγρότητι, ψυχρότης δὲ θερμότητι· οὐκ ἂν οὖν μετέβαλέν ποτε ἀὴρ εἰς γῆν, ὅτι μὴ τῆς φύσεως καὶ τούτοις δούσης τὴν τοῦ ὕδατος οὐσίαν, διαιτῶσάν τε

whether it is at all possible to remove their nature from this arrangement and still preserve the two extremes. So, then, is god immortal but emotional? Hardly. He is immortal and unemotional. What about man? Is he mortal, but unemotional? No again. He is mortal, but certainly not unemotional. Where, then, shall we find something that is both immortal and emotional? It must be a being that combines both qualities and is superior to man and inferior to god, if there is to be any relationship between these two extremes. For when two entities have completely distinct natures, any association between them is precluded, unless they share some boundary that is receptive to both.

3. Let me explain with the following analogy. We call fire something both dry and hot; the opposite of hot is cold, <and the opposite of dry is wet. We call water something both cold> and wet. It is impossible for fire to become water, or for water to become fire, because cold cannot become heat, nor wet become dry. Nature, however, has managed the war between these two elements in the following way. It has given them air as a kind of truce maker, which draws heat from the fire and moisture from the water, and combines them and enables their interaction. Thus comes about their transformation and transition, at one time of fire into air through its heat, at another of air into water through its moisture. Then again, air is both hot and wet, while earth is cold and dry. But since dry and wet are opposites, as are cold and heat, air could never change into earth, had not nature also given these two the element of water, which acts as a mediator and

3 suppl. Trapp: τε addidi

*αὐτὰ καὶ ξυνάγουσαν, παρὰ μὲν ἀέρος λαβοῦσαν τὴν ὑγρότητα, παρὰ δὲ γῆς τὴν ψυχρότητα.*

*Σκόπει δὴ τὸ πᾶν οὕτως συγκεφαλαιωσάμενος βραχεῖ λόγῳ· ἐπειδὴ ἕκαστον τούτων ἀνὰ δύο συνέστηκεν φύσεων ἐναντίων, ὧν ἀεὶ τὴν ἑτέραν ἀφαιρῶν μοῖραν, προστιθεὶς τῶν ἔπειτα τῇ ἑτέρᾳ, καθ' ἥμισυ μὲν χωρίζεις ἑκατέρου ἑκάτερον, καθ' ἥμισυ δὲ συντάττεις ἑκατέρῳ ἑκάτερον, τοῦτον τὸν τρόπον τὰ ἐναντία ἀλλήλοις ἄμικτα ὄντα κοινωνεῖ ὅμως καὶ ἀνακίρνανται καὶ πῦρ ἀέρι κατὰ θερμότητα, καὶ ἀὴρ ὕδατι κατὰ ὑγρότητα, καὶ ὕδωρ γῇ κατὰ ψυχρότητα, καὶ γῆ πυρὶ κατὰ ξηρότητα· οὕτω κἀνταῦθα κοινωνεῖ θεὸς μὲν δαίμονι κατὰ τὸ ἀθάνατον, δαίμων δὲ ἀνθρώπῳ κατὰ τὸ ἐμπαθές, ἄνθρωπος θηρίῳ κατὰ τὸ αἰσθητικόν, θηρίον φυτῷ κατὰ τὸ ἔμψυχον.*

4. Εἰ *δὲ βούλει, καὶ τὴν οἰκονομίαν τοῦ σώματος θέασαι, ὡς οὐδὲ ἐνταῦθα ἡ φύσις μεταπηδᾷ ἀθρόως, ἀλλὰ καὶ ταύτῃ μεσοτήτων τινῶν δεῖ πρὸς τὴν χειραγωγίαν τῆς κράσεως τῶν σωμάτων· θρὶξ γάρ που καὶ ὄνυξ ὀστοῦ μαλακώτερον καὶ νεύρου ἀραιότερον καὶ αἵματος ξηρότερον καὶ σαρκὸς τραχύτερον. συνελόντι δὲ εἰπεῖν, παντὶ χρήματι ἐν ᾧ τὸ ἡρμοσμένον καὶ τεταγμένον μεσότητος δεῖ, ἐν φωναῖς, ἐν χρόαις, ἐν χυμοῖς, ἐν ὀσμαῖς,*[4] *ἐν ῥυθμοῖς, ἐν σχήμασιν, ἐν πάθεσιν, ἐν λόγοις. εἶεν· οὕτω τούτων ἐχόντων, εἰ ὁ μὲν θεὸς ἀπαθὴς καὶ ἀθάνατος, ὁ δὲ ἄνθρωπος θνητός*

[4] *ὀσμαῖς* Markland, Trapp, Koniaris (*ὀδμαῖς*): *σώμασιν* R

reconciles them, by taking moisture from the air and cold from the earth.

Come, then, consider the entire matter in brief with the following summary. Each of these four elements consists of two properties, each of which in turn has an opposing property. When you take away a property from one element and add it to one of the remaining elements, while you take away half of that element's property and add it to another's half, the result is that although the elements themselves cannot mix with one another, they can nonetheless share properties and thereby intermingle—fire with air through their heat, and air with water through their moisture, and water with earth through their coolness, and earth with fire through their dryness. In the same way, in our case, god shares immortality with *daimones*, *daimones* share emotion with humans, humans share sensation with animals, and animals share life[6] with plants.

4. Also consider, if you will, the organization of the human body. Here too nature makes no complete leaps, but needs certain intermediate terms to bring about a coherent composition of bodies. For example, hairs and nails are softer than bones, thinner than sinews, dryer than blood, and tougher than flesh. In sum, wherever there is harmony and order, there must be intermediate terms, whether in sounds, colors, flavors, smells, rhythms, shapes, emotions, or speech. So then, if such is the case, and god is unemotional and immortal, whereas man is mortal and

[6] Or more literally, "soul."

τε καὶ ἐμπαθής, ἀνάγκη τὸ διὰ μέσου τούτων ἢ ἀπαθὲς θνητὸν εἶναι ἢ ἀθάνατον ἐμπαθές· ὧν τὸ μὲν ἀδύνατον, οὐ γὰρ ἂν ξυνέλθοι ποτὲ οὐδὲ ὁμολογῆσαι τῷ θνητῷ τὸ ἀπαθές· λείπεται δὴ τὴν δαιμόνων φύσιν ἐμπαθῆ τε εἶναι καὶ ἀθάνατον, ἵνα τοῦ μὲν ἀθανάτου κοινωνῇ τῷ θεῷ, τοῦ δὲ ἐμπαθοῦς τῷ ἀνθρώπῳ.

5. Πῶς οὖν καὶ ἐμπαθὲς καὶ ἀθάνατον τὸ δαιμόνιον γένος ὥρα λέγειν, καὶ πρῶτόν γε περὶ τοῦ ἀθανάτου. τὸ φθειρόμενον πᾶν ἢ τρέπεται ἢ διαλύεται ἢ τήκεται ἢ κόπτεται ἢ ῥήγνυται ἢ μεταβάλλει· ἢ διαλύεται, ὡς πηλὸς ὑπὸ ὕδατος· ἢ ῥήγνυται, ὡς ὑπὸ ἀρότρου γῆ· ἢ τήκεται, ὡς ὑπὸ ἡλίου κηρός· ἢ κόπτεται, ὡς ὑπὸ σιδήρου φυτόν· ἢ μεταβάλλει καὶ τρέπεται, ὡς ὕδωρ εἰς ἀέρα καὶ ἀὴρ εἰς πῦρ. δεῖ δὴ τὴν οὐσίαν τοῦ δαιμονίου, εἰ μέλλει ἔσεσθαι ἀθάνατος, μὴ διαλύεσθαι, μὴ σκεδάννυσθαι, μὴ ῥήγνυσθαι, μὴ τρέπεσθαι καὶ μεταβάλλειν, μὴ κόπτεσθαι· εἰ γὰρ πείσεταί τι τούτων, ἀπολεῖ τὸ ἀθάνατον. πῶς δ' ἂν καὶ θάνοι, εἴπερ ἐστὶν τὸ δαιμόνιον αὐτὸ ψυχὴ ἀποδυσαμένη τὸ σῶμα; ἣ γὰρ καὶ τῷ σώματι τῷ φύσει φθειρομένῳ παρέχει τὸ μὴ φθείρεσθαι ἡνίκ' ἂν αὐτῷ συνῇ, πολλοῦ γε δεῖ φθαρῆναι αὐτή.

Ἐν γοῦν τῇ συστάσει τὸ μὲν σῶμα συνέχεται, ἡ δὲ ψυχὴ συνέχει· εἰ δὲ καὶ τὴν ψυχὴν ἕτερόν τι συνέχει, ἀλλὰ μὴ αὐτὴ αὑτήν, τί τοῦτο ἔσται καὶ τίς ἂν ἐπινοήσαι ψυχὴν ψυχῆς; ὅταν γὰρ ἕτερον ὑφ' ἑτέρου σῴζηται συνεχόμενον, ἀνάγκη που παύσασθαι τὴν

emotional, then whatever is intermediate between them must either be an unemotional mortal or an emotional immortal. One of these is impossible, for lacking emotion could never be an attribute of or accord with a mortal being.[7] That leaves the conclusion that *daimones* are by nature emotional and immortal, with the result that they share immortality with god and emotion with man.

5. The time has come to explain how *daimones* as a race are both emotional and immortal. Let us begin with immortality. Everything that perishes does so because it is transformed, dissolved, melted, cut down, broken up, or changed—dissolved like mud in water, broken up like earth with a plow, melted like wax in the sun, cut down like a plant with an iron implement, or changed and transformed like water into air or air into fire. Consequently, if the essential nature of *daimones* is for them to remain immortal, then they cannot be dissolved, dispersed, broken up, transformed, changed, or cut down, for if they experience any of these events, they will lose their immortality. How, then could they possibly die, if in fact *daimones* themselves are souls that have shed their bodies? For an entity which keeps a naturally perishable body from perishing so long as it remains with it, can hardly perish itself.

Obviously, in this arrangement, it is the body that is sustained and the soul that sustains it. If something else sustains the soul besides the soul itself, then what could this be? Who could imagine the soul of a soul? For when one thing is preserved because another sustains it, it is

[7] Trapp (1997a, 80n7) points out that this formulation would omit plants, which are emotionless and mortal.

*συνοχὴν ἐπὶ πρᾶγμα προελθοῦσαν συνέχον μὲν ἄλλο, συνεχόμενον δὲ ὑφ᾽ ἑαυτοῦ· εἰ δὲ μή, ποῖ στήσεται ὁ λογισμὸς προϊὼν εἰς ἄπειρον; οἷον εἰ ξυνείη τις ὁλκάδα ἐν κλύδωνι ἐκ πέτρας ποθὲν καθωρμισμένην διὰ πολλῶν κάλων, ὧν ἕτερον ἐξ ἑτέρου συνεχόμενον τῇ ξυνδέσει τελευτᾷ ἐπὶ τὴν πέτραν, χρῆμα ἑστὸς καὶ ἑδραῖον.*

6. *Τοιοῦτον ἡ ψυχή· σῶμα ἐν σάλῳ ἀεὶ καὶ κλύδωνι νηχόμενον καὶ κραδαινόμενον καὶ σειόμενον συνέχει αὐτὴ καὶ καθορμίζει καὶ ἵστησιν· ἐπειδὰν δὲ ἀποκάμῃ τὰ νεῦρα ταυτὶ καὶ τὸ πνεῦμα καὶ τὰ ἄλλα τὰ ὥσπερ καλώδια ἐξ ὧν τέως προσώρμιστο τῇ ψυχῇ τὸ σῶμα, τὸ μὲν ἐφθάρη καὶ κατὰ βυθοῦ ᾤχετο, αὐτὴ δὲ ἐφ᾽ ἑαυτῆς ἐκνηξαμένη συνέχει τε αὑτὴν καὶ ἵδρυται. καὶ καλεῖται ἡ τοιαύτη ψυχὴ δαίμων ἤδη, θρέμμα αἰθέριον, μετοικισθὲν ἐκ γῆς ἐκεῖ, ὥσπερ ἐκ βαρβάρων εἰς Ἕλληνας καὶ ἐξ ἀνόμου καὶ τυραννουμένης καὶ στασιωτικῆς πόλεως εἰς εὐνομουμένην καὶ βασιλευομένην καὶ εἰρηνικὴν πόλιν. ἐγγύτατα γάρ μοι δοκεῖ ἔχειν τὸ γιγνόμενον Ὁμηρικῇ εἰκόνι· οἷόν φησιν ἐκεῖνος χαλκεῦσαι τὸν Ἥφαιστον ἐπὶ χρυσῆς ἀσπίδος πόλεις δύο·*

*ἐν τῇ μέν ῥα γάμοι τ᾽ ἔσαν εἰλαπίναι τε,*

*καὶ χοροὶ καὶ παιᾶνες καὶ δᾳδουχίαι· ἐν δὲ τῇ πόλεμοι καὶ στάσεις καὶ ἁρπαγαὶ καὶ μάχαι καὶ ὀλολυγαὶ καὶ οἰμωγαὶ καὶ στόνοι. τοῦτο δύναται καὶ γῆ πρὸς αἰθέρα· ὁ μὲν γὰρ εἰρηναῖόν τι χρῆμα καὶ παιάνων*

necessary that this series terminate at some concrete thing which sustains something else, but which sustains itself. Otherwise, where will this infinite regress end? One might compare a barge in a stormy sea tethered to some distant rock by many connected ropes, each one sustained by its attachment to another, and terminating at that rock, an entity that is stable and firm.

6. Such is the nature of the soul. It sustains the body as it swims in the ever-pitching waves of life, mooring and steadying it, as it is shaken and tossed about. But when its sinews and breath give out, along with what we might call the rest of its rigging, which up to that point had tethered the body to the soul, then it perishes and sinks into the depths, while the soul swims out on its own, sustains itself, and remains firm. At that point such a soul is called a *daimon*, an ethereal being that has emigrated up there from earth, as from barbarians to Hellenes, or from a lawless, strife-torn city ruled by a tyrant to one that is law-abiding, at peace, and ruled by a king. Indeed it seems to me very similar to what Homer depicts, when he says that Hephaestus fashioned two cities on the golden shield.

> In the one city were weddings and feasts,[8]

and choruses, songs, and processions by torchlight. In the other city were wars, strife, looting, fighting, shouting, wailing, and groaning. Such is the difference between earth and heaven: the latter is a peaceful place full of songs

[8] *Il.* 18.491.

μεστὸν καὶ θείων χορῶν, ἡ δὲ πολυφωνίας καὶ πολυεργίας καὶ διαφωνίας.

Ἐπειδὰν γὰρ ἀπαλλαγῇ ψυχὴ ἐνθένδε ἐκεῖσε, ἀποδυσαμένη τὸ σῶμα καὶ καταλιποῦσα αὐτὸ τῇ γῇ φθαρησόμενον τῷ αὐτοῦ χρόνῳ καὶ νόμῳ, δαίμων <ἀν>[5]τ' ἀνθρώπου, ἐποπτεύει μὲν αὕτη τὰ οἰκεῖα θεάματα καθαροῖς τοῖς ὀφθαλμοῖς, μήτε ὑπὸ σαρκῶν ἐπιπροσθουμένη, μήτε ὑπὸ χρωμάτων ἐπιταραττομένη, μήτε ὑπὸ σχημάτων παντοδαπῶν συγχεομένη, μήτε ὑπὸ ἀέρος θολεροῦ διατειχιζομένη, ἀλλὰ αὐτὸ κάλλος αὐτοῖς ὀφθαλμοῖς ὁρῶσα καὶ γανυμένη, οἰκτείρουσα μὲν αὐτὴν τοῦ πρόσθεν βίου, μακαρίζουσα δὲ τοῦ παρόντος, οἰκτείρουσα δὲ καὶ τὰς συγγενεῖς ψυχάς, αἳ περὶ γῆν στρέφονται ἔτι, καὶ ὑπὸ φιλανθρωπίας ἐθέλουσα αὐταῖς συναγελάζεσθαι καὶ ἐπανορθοῦν σφαλλομένας. προστέτακται δὲ αὐτῇ ὑπὸ τοῦ θεοῦ ἐπιφοιτᾶν τὴν γῆν καὶ ἀναμίγνυσθαι πάσῃ μὲν ἀνδρῶν φύσει, πάσῃ δὲ ἀνθρώπων τύχῃ καὶ γνώμῃ καὶ τέχνῃ, καὶ τοῖς μὲν χρηστοῖς συνεπιλαμβάνειν, τοῖς δὲ ἀδικουμένοις τιμωρεῖν, τοῖς δὲ ἀδικοῦσιν προστιθέναι τὴν δίκην.

7. Ἀλλ' οὐχὶ δαιμόνων πᾶς πάντα δρᾷ, ἀλλ' αὐτοῖς διακέκριται κἀκεῖ τὰ ἔργα, ἄλλο ἄλλῳ. καὶ τοῦτο ἔστιν ἀμέλει τὸ ἐμπαθές, ᾧ ἐλαττοῦται δαίμων θεοῦ· ἧς γὰρ εἶχον φύσεως ὅτε περὶ γῆν ἦσαν, οὐκ ἐθέλουσιν ταύτης παντάπασιν ἀπαλλάττεσθαι, ἀλλὰ καὶ Ἀσκληπιὸς ἰᾶται νῦν καὶ ὁ Ἡρακλῆς ἰσχυρίζεται καὶ Διόνυσος βακχεύει καὶ Ἀμφίλοχος μαντεύεται καὶ οἱ

and divine choruses, whereas the former is replete with clamorous voices, much toil, and discord.

For when a soul sheds its body and leaves it behind on the earth to waste away in its own time and fashion, and departs this world for that, being now a *daimon* instead of a human, it beholds with unobstructed eyes the sights akin to its nature,[9] being no longer impeded by flesh, or perplexed by colors, or confused by all kinds of shapes, or obstructed by murky air. No, as it looks upon beauty itself with its very own eyes, it rejoices, and pities itself for its previous life, while counting itself blessed for its present one. But it also pities its kindred souls that still roam about the earth, and out of its love for humans wishes to rejoin their company and to put them on track when they go astray. And it has been ordered by god to travel over the earth and to mingle with individuals of every nature and with humans of every status, intellect, and skill, aiding those who are good, avenging those who are wronged, and punishing those who are unjust.

7. And yet each *daimon* does not perform every function, for in their case, as in ours, different ones have separate tasks. And it is precisely their emotion that makes a *daimon* inferior to god, because they are unwilling to rid themselves entirely of the natures they had when they were on earth, and so still today Asclepius heals the sick, Heracles lends his strength, Dionysus leads his revels,

[9] Cf. *Or*. 11.7 of the soul's proper sights (τὰ αὑτοῦ θεάματα) and Pl. *Phd*. 84b: "after death, the soul reaches what is akin (τὸ συγγενές) to it."

---

[5] suppl. $U^{pc}$, Trapp

Διόσκουροι ναυτίλλονται καὶ Μίνως δικάζει καὶ Ἀχιλλεὺς ὁπλίζεται. Ἀχιλλεὺς νῆσον οἰκεῖ εὐθὺ Ἴστρου κατὰ τὴν Ποντικὴν θάλατταν, <οὗ>[6] Ἀχιλλέως ναὸς καὶ βωμοὶ Ἀχιλλέως· καὶ ἑκὼν μὲν οὐκ ἄν τις προσέλθοι ὅτι μὴ θύσων· θύσας δὲ ἐπιβαίνει τῆς νεώς. εἶδον ἤδη ναῦται πολλάκις ἄνδρα ἠΐθεον, ξανθὸν τὴν κόμην, πηδῶντα ἐν ὅπλοις· τὰ ὅπλα χρυσᾶ· οἱ δὲ εἶδον μὲν οὐδαμῶς, ἤκουσαν δὲ παιωνίζοντος· οἱ δὲ καὶ εἶδον καὶ ἤκουσαν. ἤδη δέ τις καὶ κατέδαρθεν ἄκων ἐν τῇ νήσῳ, καὶ αὐτὸν Ἀχιλλεὺς ἀνίστησιν καὶ ἐπὶ σκηνὴν ἄγει καὶ εὐωχεῖ· ὁ Πάτροκλος ᾠνοχόει, Ἀχιλλεὺς ἐκιθάριζεν, παρεῖναι δὲ ἔφη καὶ τὴν Θέτιν καὶ ἄλλων δαιμόνων χορόν. ὁ δὲ Ἕκτωρ κατὰ χώραν μένει, ὡς ὁ Ἰλιέων λόγος, καὶ φαντάζεται πηδῶν ἀνὰ τὸ πεδίον καὶ ἀστράπτων. ἐγὼ δὲ τὸν μὲν Ἀχιλλέα οὐκ εἶδον, οὐδὲ τὸν Ἕκτορα εἶδον· εἶδον δὲ καὶ Διοσκούρους ἐπὶ νεώς, ἀστέρας λαμπρούς, ἰθύνοντας τὴν ναῦν χειμαζομένην· εἶδον καὶ τὸν Ἀσκληπιόν, ἀλλ' οὐχὶ ὄναρ· εἶδον καὶ τὸν Ἡρακλέα, ἀλλ' ὕπαρ.

[6] suppl. Reiske

Amphilochus prophesies,[10] the Dioscuri sail the sea, Minos renders judgments,[11] and Achilles dons his armor—Achilles who dwells on an island[12] in the Black Sea opposite the mouth of the Ister, where his temple and altars are located. No one would go there without intending to offer sacrifices, and after sacrificing he boards his ship.[13] Indeed, sailors passing the island have often seen a young man with fair hair performing a war dance in his armor made of gold. Even those who have not seen him, have nonetheless heard him singing a paean. Some have both seen and heard him. Indeed, one person, who inadvertently fell asleep on the island, was awakened by Achilles, who led him to his tent and feasted him, where Patroclus poured the wine, Achilles played the lyre, and where, he said, even Thetis attended with her chorus of other *daimones*.[14] And as the people of Ilium tell it, Hector remains in their land and can be seen bounding across the plain flashing light. I myself have never seen Achilles or Hector, but I have seen the Dioscuri aboard a ship, appearing as shining stars and keeping it on course during a storm. I have also seen Asclepius, but not in a dream,[15] and I have also seen Heracles, but while awake.

10 His mantic shrine was at Mallus in Cilicia.

11 As a judge in the underworld (*Od.* 11.568–71).

12 Leuce, the "White Island."

13 This ritual of sacrificing and then boarding one's ship is described at Philostr. *Her.* 55.10–11.

14 That is, Nereids.

15 Normally, one "saw" Asclepius while sleeping in his temple, in the ritual of incubation.

# *ORATION* 10[1]

## INTRODUCTION

This oration treats the Platonic doctrine of learning (*mathēsis*) as recollection (*anamnēsis*). The main treatments are at *Meno* 81c–86c, *Phd.* 72e, and *Phdr.* 249b–c. The theory is dependent upon the immortality of the human soul, with its ability to escape physical nature and perceive reality directly. The oration opens with three such examples, beginning with Epimenides' decades-long dream (§1), Pythagoras' soul having previously been that of the Trojan Euphorbus, and the flight of Aristeas' soul as he lay dying and its reporting of all it had seen (§2). These examples suggest that when the soul of a good man escapes the turmoil of the body and "turns its intellect (*nous*) in on itself," it soars into the ether to contemplate truth. Is this phenomenon then "learning" or "recollection"? Like a doctor restoring vision by removing an obstruction of the eye, reason (*logos*) awakens the soul's drowsy knowledge (*epistēmē*) (§3). Maximus takes up Plato's analogy of midwifery of the pregnant soul at *Tht.* 150b–51c and adds an elaborate analogy of the immortal seeds of truth flowering in the soul (§4).[2]

[1] Grimaldi (2002) provides a translation and commentary.

[2] The closest Platonic parallel would be the words planted in the soul at *Phdr.* 276d–77a.

Pythagoras, Plato, and Homer all recognized that the soul is immortal. It is "self-taught" (like Homer's bard) and possesses innate knowledge, as do all other animals with their innate survival skills. The question is where that knowledge came from. Humans cannot have learned it from someone else, because then by an infinite regress someone had to have discovered it in the first place[3] (§5). In fact, the soul's power of discovery lies within itself and consists of awakening true opinions.[4] As Agamemnon woke up and organized his troops, reason awakens and organizes the thoughts (*noēmata*) in the soul: their awakening is recollection (§6). Just as Demodocus' song awakened Odysseus' recollection of his experiences at Troy, so in everyday life a small impulse from our senses, like the sight of a boyfriend's lyre, awakens our memory, as the mind rapidly traverses a series of connected events (§7). It is by asking questions that Socrates guides souls in search of virtue to recollect the truth (§8). When the soul quits this tumultuous earthly domain for the bright ethereal realm, and joins the gods and Zeus himself, it commits to memory what is real, but back on earth it must recollect it. A soul with a good *daimon* can free itself from the body and awaken the memory of what it had witnessed there (§9).

3 Cf. the skeptical dilemma posed at *Meno* 80d–e and resolved at 85d–86c.

4 Cf. *Meno* 85c.

## *ORATION* 10

Εἰ αἱ μαθήσεις ἀναμνήσεις

1. Ἀφίκετό ποτε Ἀθήναζε Κρὴς ἀνήρ, ὄνομα Ἐπιμενίδης, κομίζων λόγον οὑτωσὶ ῥηθέντα πιστεύεσθαι χαλεπόν· ἐν τοῦ Διὸς τοῦ Δικταίου τῷ ἄντρῳ κείμενος ὕπνῳ βαθεῖ ἔτη συχνά, ὄναρ ἔφη ἐντυχεῖν αὐτοῖς θεοῖς καὶ θεῶν λόγοις καὶ ἀληθείᾳ καὶ δίκῃ. τοιαῦτα ἄττα διαμυθολογῶν ᾐνίττετο, οἶμαι, ὁ Ἐπιμενίδης ὡς ἄρα ὁ ἐν γῇ βίος ταῖς τῶν ἀνθρώπων ψυχαῖς ὀνείρατι ἔοικεν μακρῷ καὶ πολυετεῖ. πιθανώτερος δ' ἦν ἂν καὶ τὰ Ὁμήρου ἔπη προστιθεὶς τῷ αὐτοῦ λόγῳ, ἃ περὶ ὀνείρων ἐκεῖνος. λέγει γάρ που Ὅμηρος δύο εἶναι πύλας ἀμενηνῶν ὀνείρων, τὴν μὲν ἐξ ἐλέφαντος, τὴν δὲ ἐκ κεράτων· τοὺς μὲν οὖν διὰ κεράτων ἰόντας ἀτρεκεῖς τε εἶναι καὶ πιθανοὺς πιστεύεσθαι· τοὺς δὲ ἑτέρους σφαλεροὺς καὶ ἀπατεῶνας καὶ μηδὲν ὕπαρ ἐπὶ τὴν ψυχὴν φέροντας. ταύτῃ τοι ἔτεινεν καὶ ὁ Ἐπιμενίδου εἴτε μῦθος εἴτε καὶ ἀληθὴς λόγος. ἐνύπνιον

[1] A philosopher, poet, and prophet from Cnossus ca. 600 BC, famous for his paradoxical statement, "all Cretans are liars," and

# *ORATION* 10

## Whether learning is recollection

1. A man from Crete named Epimenides[1] once came to Athens bearing a story difficult to believe—if taken literally. He claimed that while lying in a deep sleep for many years in the cave of Dictaean Zeus, he encountered the gods themselves in his dreams, conversed with them, and met with Truth and Justice too. By telling such a tale, I believe that Epimenides was suggesting that life on earth for human souls is indeed like one long dream lasting many years. He would have been more convincing, had he included in his story the verses of Homer in which he speaks about dreams. For Homer says at one point that there are two gateways for "insubstantial dreams," one made of ivory, the other of horn.[2] Those issuing through the gates of horn are true and worthy of belief, whereas the others are treacherous, deceptive, and convey to the soul nothing real about the waking world. This is what Epimenides was trying to convey, whether you call it a tale or a true story, namely that this life here on earth is really

who was said to have slept for fifty-seven years (Diog. Laert. 1.109). He is also cited at *Or.* 38.3. [2] Penelope says this to the disguised Odysseus at *Od.* 19.562–67.

*γάρ τί ἐστιν ἀτεχνῶς οὑτοσὶ ὁ δεῦρο βίος, καθ' ὃν ἡ ψυχὴ κατορωρυγμένη ἐν σώματι ὑπὸ κάρου*[1] *καὶ πλησμονῆς μόγις πως ὀνειρώττει τὰ ὄντα. ἔρχονται δὲ ταῖς μὲν τῶν πολλῶν ψυχαῖς ὄνειροι δι' ἐλεφαντίνων πυλῶν· εἰ δέ πού τίς ἐστιν καθαρὰ ψυχὴ καὶ νηφάλιος καὶ ὀλίγα ὑπὸ τοῦ δεῦρο κάρου καὶ τῆς πλησμονῆς ἐπιταραττομένη, εἰκός που ταύτῃ δι' ἑτέρων ἰόντα ἀπαντᾶν ὀνείρατα σαφῆ καὶ διακεκριμένα καὶ ἐγγύτατα τῷ ἀληθεῖ. οὗτος ἦν ὁ Ἐπιμενίδου ὕπνος.*

2. *Πυθαγόρας δὲ ὁ Σάμιος πρῶτος ἐν τοῖς Ἕλλησιν ἐτόλμησεν εἰπεῖν ὅτι αὐτῷ τὸ μὲν σῶμα τεθνήξεται, ἡ δὲ ψυχὴ ἀναπτᾶσα οἰχήσεται ἀθανὴς καὶ ἀγήρως· καὶ γὰρ εἶναι αὐτὴν πρὶν ἥκειν δεῦρο. ἐπίστευον δὲ αὐτῷ οἱ ἄνθρωποι ταῦτα λέγοντι καὶ ὅτι ἤδη πρότερον γένοιτο ἐν γῇ ἐν ἄλλῳ σώματι,* Εὔφορβος *δὲ εἶναι ὁ* Τρὼς *τότε. ἐπίστευον δὲ ὧδε· ἀφίκετο εἰς* Ἀθηνᾶς *νεών, οὗ πολλὰ ἦν καὶ παντοδαπὰ ἀναθήματα, ἐν δὲ τοῖς καὶ ἀσπὶς τὸ μὲν σχῆμα* Φρυγία, *ὑπὸ δὲ χρόνου ἐξίτηλος· εἶπεν οὖν ὅτι γνωρίζω τὴν ἀσπίδα, ἀφείλετο δέ με ὅσπερ καὶ ἀπέκτεινεν τότε ἐν* Ἰλίῳ *ἐν τῇ μάχῃ. θαυμάσαντες οἱ ἐπιχώριοι τὸν λόγον καθεῖλον τὸ ἀνάθημα, καὶ ἦν ἐπίγραμμα,*

Παλλάδι Ἀθηνᾷ Μενέλεως ἀπὸ Εὐφόρβου.

Εἰ *δὲ βούλει καὶ ἄλλον αὖ λόγον διέξειμί σοι.*

[1] *κάρου* Wakefield, Dübner, Koniaris: *κόρου* R

a kind of dream, during which the soul, buried in a body and overcome with stupor and surfeit, barely even dreams about reality. Most men's souls receive dreams that come through the gates of ivory, but if somewhere there exists some pure and sober soul little befuddled by earthly stupor and surfeit, it might reasonably be met with dreams coming through the gates of horn that are clear, distinct, and very close to the truth. Such was the sleep of Epimenides.

2. Pythagoras of Samos was the first Greek who dared to say that his own body would die, but that his soul would fly up and away, because it was deathless and ageless, since it had also existed before it came here to earth. People believed him when he said this, and believed his claim that he had once before been on earth in another body, back when he was Euphorbus the Trojan. They were persuaded for the following reason. He came to a temple of Athena, where many dedications of all sorts were housed. Among these was a shield of Phrygian design, worn down by time. He declared, "I recognize that shield. It was taken from me by the man who slew me in battle back then at Troy." The local residents were astonished at what he claimed, so they took down the dedication on which was inscribed:

> To Pallas Athena Menelaus ‹dedicates this taken›
> from Euphorbus.[3]

If you are willing, I will tell you yet another story. The

[3] Menelaus kills Euphorbus and strips him of his armor at *Il.* 17.59–60. A slightly different version of this story is told at Diog. Laert. 8.4–5.

Προκοννησίῳ ἀνδρὶ τὸ μὲν σῶμα ἔκειτο ἔμπνουν μέν, ἀλλ' ἀμυδρῶς καὶ ἐγγύτατα θανάτου· ἡ δὲ ψυχὴ ἐκδῦσα τοῦ σώματος ἐπλανᾶτο ἐν τῷ αἰθέρι ὄρνιθος δίκην πάντα ὕποπτα θεωμένη, γῆν καὶ θάλατταν καὶ ποταμοὺς καὶ πόλεις καὶ ἔθνη ἀνδρῶν καὶ παθήματα καὶ φύσεις παντοίας· καὶ αὖθις εἰσδυομένη τὸ σῶμα καὶ ἀναστήσασα, ὥσπερ ὀργάνῳ χρωμένη, διηγεῖτο ἅττα εἶδέν τε καὶ ἤκουσεν, παρ' ἄλλοις ἄλλα.

3. Τί δήποτ' οὖν Ἐπιμενίδης καὶ Πυθαγόρας καὶ Ἀριστέας ἐθέλουσιν αἰνίττεσθαι; ἄλλο τι ἢ τὴν σχολὴν τῆς ψυχῆς τοῦ ἀγαθοῦ ἀνδρὸς ἀπὸ τῶν τοῦ σώματος ἡδονῶν καὶ παθημάτων, ὅταν ἀπαλλαγεῖσα τοῦ περὶ ἐκεῖνο ταράχου καὶ ἐπιστρέψασα εἰς ἑαυτὴν τὸν νοῦν ἔμπαλιν ἐντυγχάνει τῷ ἀληθεῖ αὐτῷ, ἀφεμένη τῶν εἰδώλων; τοῦτο ἔοικεν μὲν ὕπνῳ καλῷ καὶ μεστῷ ἐναργῶν ὀνειράτων, ἔοικεν δὲ ψυχῆς πτήσει μεταρσίῳ, οὐχ ὑπὲρ ἄκρων φερομένης τῶν ὀρῶν ἐν ἀχλυώδει καὶ ταραττομένῳ τῷ ἀέρι, ἀλλ' ὑπὲρ τοῦτον ὑψοῦ ἐν σταθερῷ αἰθέρι, γαλήνης καὶ ἠρεμίας αὐτὴν παραπεμπούσης ἀλύπως ἐπὶ τὸ ἀληθές, ἐπὶ τὴν ὄψιν.

Τίς δὲ ὁ τῆς παραπομπῆς τρόπος καὶ τί ἂν αὐτὴν ἐμμελῶς ὀνομάζοιμεν; ἆρά γε μάθησιν, ἢ Πλάτωνι ὁμοφώνως ἀνάμνησιν; ἢ δύο θησόμεθα ὀνόματα πράγματι ἑνί, μάθησιν καὶ ἀνάμνησιν; τὸ δέ ἐστιν τοιοῦτον οἷον τὸ περὶ τὸν ὀφθαλμὸν πάθος· σύνεστιν μὲν γὰρ αὐτῷ ἡ ὄψις ἀεί, ἤδη δέ που ὑπὸ συμφορᾶς

body of a man from Proconnesus[4] lay still breathing, but barely so, and on the brink of death. At that point his soul left his body and wandered about the ether like a bird, surveying everything it could see below—the land and sea and rivers, the cities and nations of men, their experiences and natures of all sorts. Then, when it reentered his body and revived it, it used it as an instrument to relate what it had seen and heard among the various peoples.

3. What is it, then, that Epimenides, Pythagoras, and Aristeas wish to suggest? What else but the respite of a good man's soul from the pleasures and sufferings of its body, when it escapes from the turmoil surrounding that body and turns its intellect in on itself, and once again encounters truth itself, having freed itself from mere semblances? This state is like a beautiful sleep full of lucid dreams; it resembles a lofty flight of the soul, not borne above mountain peaks in the cloudy and turbulent air, but far beyond these in the serene ether, where calmness and tranquility transport it effortlessly to truth and to its contemplation.

What is the nature of this transport, and what should we properly call it? Should we call it learning, or, in Plato's terminology, recollection? Or should we apply both names, learning and recollection, to this one event? Regardless, the phenomenon itself is similar to what happens to the eye. Although it continually possesses the power of sight, occasionally through some misfortune darkness covers

[4] Aristeas (ca. 7th c. BC), named below. He supposedly composed a poem called "Arimaspea," detailing his journeys in the far north. Hdt. 4.13–15 provides an early version of this story. A longer description of his soul's travels appears at *Or*. 38.3.

ἐπιχυθεῖσα ἀχλὺς καὶ ἀμφιέσασα τὸ ὄργανον διετείχισεν αὐτοῦ τὴν πρὸς τὰ ὁρώμενα ὁμιλίαν· ἡ δὲ τέχνη παρελθοῦσα ὄψιν μὲν οὐκ ἐνεποίησε τῷ ὀφθαλμῷ, τὸ δὲ ἐνοχλοῦν παραναγαγοῦσα ἀπεκάλυψεν αὐτοῦ τὸν ἔξω δρόμον.

Νόμιζε δὴ καὶ τῇ ψυχῇ ὄψιν τινὰ εἶναι διορατικὴν τῶν ὄντων φύσει καὶ ἐπιστήμονα, ὑπὸ δὲ τῆς τῶν σωμάτων συμφορᾶς ὑποκεχύσθαι αὐτῇ πολλὴν ἀχλύν, ‹ἣν›[2] καὶ συγχεῖν τὴν θέαν καὶ ἀφαιρεῖσθαι τὴν ἀκρίβειαν καὶ ἀποσβεννύναι τὸ οἰκεῖον φῶς· προσιόντα δὲ αὐτῇ τεχνίτην λόγον ὥσπερ ἰατρὸν οὐ προστιθέναι αὐτῇ φέροντα ἐπιστήμην, πρᾶγμα ὃ μήπω ἔχει, ἀλλ᾽ ἐπεγείρειν ἣν ἔχει μέν, ἀμυδρὰν δὲ καὶ ξυνδεδεμένην καὶ καρηβαροῦσαν.

4. Ὅνπερ οὖν τρόπον καὶ ταῖς κυούσαις προσάγουσα ἡ μαιευτικὴ τὰς χεῖρας σὺν τῇ τέχνῃ ὑποδέχεται τὸ κυούμενον καὶ θεραπεύει τὰς ὠδῖνας, καὶ ἐξάγει τὸ τελεσφορηθὲν εἰς φῶς καὶ ἀπαλλάττει τῆς ὀδύνης τὴν φέρουσαν, τοῦτον τὸν τρόπον καὶ λόγος μαιεύεται ψυχὴν κύουσαν καὶ ὠδίνων μεστήν· ἀλλὰ πολλαὶ ἀμβλισκάνουσιν, ἢ δι᾽ ἀτεχνίαν τῶν μαιουμένων ἢ διὰ σφοδρότητα τῶν ὠδίνων ἢ διὰ ἀμβλύτητα τῶν σπερμάτων· ὀλίγαι δέ που καὶ σπάνιοι ψυχαὶ τελεσφόροι, ὧν τὰ ἔκγονα σαφῆ καὶ διηρθρωμένα καὶ γνήσια τῶν πρώτων πατέρων· ὄνομα δὲ τῇ μὲν ψυχῆς κυήσει νοῦς, τῇ δὲ ὠδῖνι αἴσθησις, τῇ δὲ ἀποτέξει ἀνάμνησις.

[2] suppl. Reiske, edd.

and surrounds the organ of vision, thus obstructing its contact with objects of sight. Then, when medical expertise comes to the rescue, it does not implant vision in the eye, but instead removes the impediment and opens up its passage to the outside.

You must understand that the soul too possesses a kind of vision naturally capable of discerning and understanding the things that truly exist, but because of the misfortune of its embodiment, a deep darkness covers it, which confounds its vision, takes away its acuity, and extinguishes its innate brightness. But then, when reason comes to the soul with its expertise like a doctor, it does not bring knowledge and add it to the soul, like something it does not already possess, but instead awakens the knowledge it already has, but which is faint, constricted, and drowsy.

4. Just as a midwife lends helping hands to pregnant women, and uses her expertise to care for the fetus, ease the labor pains, deliver the fully developed baby into the light, and relieve the mother of her pains, in just that way reason acts as a midwife for a pregnant soul beset by labor pains.[5] And yet, many souls miscarry, either because of the incompetence of their midwives, or because of the intensity of their pains, or because of the weakness of their seed. Few and far between are there souls able to bring their pregnancy to term, with progeny that are distinct, well-formed, and genuine offspring of their original parents. The name for the soul's conception is intellection, for its labor pains is perception, and for its delivery is recollection.

[5] This is an adaptation of the trope of Socrates as a midwife for pregnant souls at *Tht*. 150b–51c.

Κύουσιν δὲ πᾶσαι μὲν ψυχαὶ φύσει, ὠδίνουσιν δὲ ἔθει, τίκτουσιν δὲ λόγῳ. ὥσπερ οὖν ἀδύνατον φῦναί τι ἄνευ σπέρματος καὶ ἀλλοῖον ἢ οἷα τὰ σπέρματα, <ἀνάγκη δὲ φῦναι>[3] ἄνθρωπον μὲν ἐξ ἀνθρώπου, βοῦν δὲ ἐκ βοός, καὶ ἐξ ἐλαίας ἐλαίαν καὶ ἐξ ἀμπέλου ἄμπελον, οὕτω καὶ εἴ τι ἀληθὲς ἡ ψυχὴ ξυνίησιν,[4] ἀνάγκη ἀληθῆ εἶναι ταυτὶ τὰ σπέρματα ἐμπεφυτευμένα τῇ ψυχῇ· εἰ δὲ ἦν, καὶ ἀεὶ ἦν· ἀεὶ δὲ ὄντα, καὶ ἀθάνατα ἦν. καὶ τοῦτό ἐστιν ἀμέλει τὸ περὶ τὰς ἐπιστήμας γιγνόμενον, σπερμάτων ψυχῆς ἄνθος καὶ τελεσφόρησις· ὃ δὲ καλοῦσιν οἱ ἄνθρωποι ἄγνοιαν, τί ἂν εἴη ἄλλο ἢ ἀργία τῶν σπερμάτων;

5. Εἰ μὲν οὖν τοιοῦτόν ἐστιν ἡ ψυχὴ οἷον καὶ τὸ σῶμα, θνητὸν καὶ φθειρόμενον καὶ λυόμενον καὶ σηπόμενον, οὐδὲν ἔχω περὶ αὐτῆς σεμνὸν εἰπεῖν· οὐδὲ γὰρ περὶ σώματος σεμνὸν οὐδὲν εἰπεῖν ἔχω· ἐφήμερον γὰρ τὸ θρέμμα καὶ ἀκροσφαλές, φερόμενον, ἄπιστον, ἀσαφὲς καὶ ἔμπληκτον. εἰ τοιοῦτον ἡ ψυχή, οὔτε τι οἶδεν οὔτε ἀναμιμνήσκεται οὔτε μανθάνει· θᾶττον γὰρ ἂν φυλάξαι σφραγῖδος τύπους κηρὸς ὑπὸ ἡλίου τηκόμενος ἢ ψυχὴ μάθημα, εἴπερ ἐστὶν σῶμα· πᾶν γὰρ σῶμα ῥεῖ καὶ φέρεται ὀξέως Εὐρίπου δίκην ἄνω καὶ κάτω, νῦν μὲν ἐκ νηπιότητος εἰς ἥβην οἰδαῖνον, νῦν δὲ ἐξ ἥβης εἰς γῆρας ὑπονοστοῦν καὶ ὑποφερόμενον.

[3] suppl. Koniaris: <ἀλλ᾽ ἀνάγκη φῦναι> Reiske: <ἀλλ᾽> Dübner: lacunam stat. Trapp [4] ξυνίησιν R, Davies[2], Dübner, Koniaris: ἐξανίησιν Reiske, Trapp: ἀνίησιν Markland

All souls conceive by nature, go into labor by custom, and give birth by means of reason. And just as it is impossible for anything to be born except from seed, or to be of a nature different from its seed (<since it is necessary that> man come from man, ox from ox, olive tree from olive tree, and vine from vine), just so, if the soul comprehends some truth, it is necessary that the seeds of it implanted in the soul must themselves be true, and if they existed, then they always existed; and if they always existed, then they were immortal. This is precisely what takes place with forms of knowledge, namely the flowering of seeds in the soul and their coming to fruition. And as for what men call ignorance, what else can it be but the sluggishness of those seeds to develop?

5. Now if the soul is anything like the body—something mortal that perishes, disintegrates, and rots away—then I have nothing commendable to say about it, any more than I can say anything commendable about the body, a creature that is short-lived and highly unsteady, unstable, unreliable, baffling, and impulsive. If that is the nature of the soul, then it has no ability to know, recollect, or learn anything. For, if it is corporeal, sooner would wax melting in the sun preserve the imprints of a seal than a soul retain what it has learned, because every physical body is in constant flux and like the Euripus[6] is swiftly borne this way and that, at one time surging from infancy to adolescence, at another subsiding and receding from adolescence to old age.

[6] For the Euripus strait as a symbol of instability, see *Or*. 5.6.

Ἀλλ᾿ οὐ τοιοῦτον χρῆμα εἶναι τὴν ψυχὴν μαντεύεται οὔτε Πυθαγόρας οὔτε Πλάτων, ἀλλ᾿ οὐδὲ ὁ πρὸ τούτων Ὅμηρος, ᾧ καὶ ἐν Ἅιδου διαλέγονται αἱ ψυχαὶ καί εἰσιν μαντικαὶ τότε. λέγει δέ που αὐτῷ καὶ ἀοιδὸς ἀνήρ,

αὐτοδίδακτος δ᾿ εἰμί, θεοὶ δέ μοι ὤπασαν ὀμφήν.

καὶ ἀληθῆ λέγει· αὐτοδίδακτον γάρ τι χρῆμα ἀτεχνῶς ἡ ψυχὴ καὶ τοῦ εἰδέναι παρὰ θεῶν τῇ φύσει εὖ ἔχον. ἢ τὰ μὲν ἄλλα ζῷα αὐτοδίδακτα πρὸς τὰ αὑτῶν ἔργα καὶ οὐδεὶς εἰπεῖν ἔχει διδασκάλους, οὐ λεόντων πρὸς ἀλκήν, οὐκ ἐλάφων πρὸς φυγήν, οὐχ ἵππων πρὸς δρόμον· ἀλλὰ καὶ ὀρνίθων γένος αὐτοδίδακτον ἐπ᾿ ἄκρων φυτῶν ἐμηχανήσαντο καλιάδας αὐτουργῷ τέχνῃ, καὶ ἀράχναι αὐτοφυεῖ μίτῳ θήρατρα ἐν ἀέρι καὶ ἑρπετὰ φωλεοὺς καὶ ἰχθύες χηραμούς, καὶ ὅσαι ἄλλων ζῴων τέχναι πρὸς σωτηρίαν ἑκάστῳ γένει ξύμφυτοι· ἀνθρώπῳ δὲ ἄρα τῷ νοερωτάτῳ τῶν ὄντων ἐπίκτητον ἥξει τὸ εἰδέναι; οὔκουν ἥξει ποτέ· ἀνάγκη γὰρ ἢ εὑρόντα εἰδέναι ἢ μαθόντα· ὧν ἑκάτερον ἀσθενὲς οὐχ ὑπούσης ἐπιστήμης φύσει· ὅ τε γὰρ εὑρὼν πῶς ἂν χρήσαιτο τῷ εὑρεθέντι, μὴ γνωρίσας τὴν χρείαν αὐτοῦ; κἂν γὰρ ἠπειρώτης ἀνὴρ καθ᾿ Ὅμηρον οἴακι ἐντύχῃ,

But neither Pythagoras nor Plato surmised that the soul was any such thing—nor did Homer before them, who portrays souls even in Hades conversing and uttering prophecies.[7] And at one point he has a singer say,

I am self-taught, and the gods gave me my voice.[8]

He is telling the truth here, because the soul really is a self-taught entity, well empowered by the gods and by its very nature to possess knowledge. Now other living creatures are self-taught with respect to their proper functions, and no one can claim that anyone taught lions their bravery, deer their ability to flee, or horses their speed. Birds as well are a self-taught species: they build their nests atop trees with innate skill. Spiders too spin their webs in the air with self-generated threads, and reptiles make their lairs and fish their hideouts, not to mention all the other instinctive skills that creatures use to preserve their own species. But in the case of man, the most intelligent of all beings, can it be that the knowledge he acquires comes to him from elsewhere? If that is true, then it will never come to him, because knowledge must necessarily result either from discovery or from learning, both of which are ineffective without a basis of innate knowledge to support them. For how could anyone who discovers something ever put it to use, if he cannot recognize its use? For according to Homer, if a landlubber encounters a steering oar,

[7] *Od.* 11.51–227 and 24.98–204.

[8] An adaptation of *Od.* 22.347–48, Phemius speaking, also quoted at *Or.* 38.1.

φήσει ἀθηρηλοιγὸν ἔχειν ἀνὰ φαιδίμῳ ὤμῳ.

ὁ δὲ μαθὼν παρὰ μὲν τοῦ οὐκ εἰδότος οὐκ ἂν μάθοι, παρὰ δὲ τοῦ εἰδότος κἂν μάθοι, ἐρήσομαι τὸν διδάξαντα, πῶς καὶ οὗτος ἔγνω. οὐκοῦν καὶ οὗτος ἢ εὗρεν ἢ ἔμαθεν; καὶ εἰ μὲν εὗρεν, τὰ αὐτὰ ἐρήσομαι, πῶς ἐχρήσατο τῷ εὑρεθέντι μὴ γνωρίσας; εἰ δὲ ἔμαθεν παρ' ἄλλου, πάλιν ἤδυ ἐκεῖνον διέρεσθαι. καὶ ποῖ στησόμεθα ἄλλον ἄλλου διδάσκαλον ἀνερωτῶντες; ἀφίξεται γάρ ποτε λογισμὸς προϊὼν ἐπὶ τὸν οὐ μαθόντα ἀλλ' εὑρόντα, πρὸς ὃν τὰ αὐτὰ ἐκεῖνα ῥητέον.

6. Ἥκει τοίνυν ἡμᾶς ὁ λόγος φέρων ἐπὶ τὸ ζητούμενον. ἡ γὰρ δὴ ψυχῆς εὕρεσις, αὐτογενής τις οὖσα καὶ αὐτοφυὴς καὶ ξύμφυτος, τί ἄλλο ἐστὶν ἢ δόξαι ἀληθεῖς ἐπεγειρόμεναι, ὧν τῇ ἐπεγέρσει τε καὶ συντάξει ἐπιστήμη ὄνομα; εἰ δὲ βούλει, καὶ ταύτῃ εἴκαζέ μοι τὸ λεγόμενον, στρατιώτῃ πλανωμένῳ καὶ διακεχυμένῳ· ἢ καθ' Ὅμηρον μᾶλλον, νὺξ μὲν ἔστω καὶ ἡσυχία πολλὴ κατὰ τὸ στρατόπεδον καὶ ὕπνος βαθὺς τῶν ἄλλων ἁπάντων κειμένων ἑξῆς·

he will say that you have a winnowing fan on your
strong shoulder.[9]

When someone learns something, he obviously cannot learn it from someone who does not know it. But if he learns it from someone who does know it, then I shall ask his teacher how *he* came to know it. Did he discover it himself or did he learn it? If he discovered it, I shall repeat the question, namely how could he put to use what he discovered without recognizing its use? If he learned about it from someone else, then I shall enjoy interrogating *him* in turn. So where can our questioning one teacher after another ever end? It will logically arrive, eventually, at the one who made the discovery rather than the one who learned of it—and we shall have to ask *him* those same questions.

6. At this point, the argument has brought us to the object of our inquiry. Now given that the soul's power of discovery is self-generated, spontaneous, and innate, what can it consist of other than true opinions that have been awakened to consciousness? And what is knowledge other than the name we give to the awakening and organizing of these true opinions?[10] And, if you will, compare this process to that of a soldier wandering about out of formation[11]—or still better, as Homer describes it, let it be nighttime and deep calm throughout the camp, when all the others without exception were fast asleep,

[9] *Od.* 11.128, Tiresias prophesying to Odysseus.

[10] A reprise of the argument at Pl. *Meno* 85c–86a.

[11] In this analogy, the wandering soldier represents a true opinion.

ἀλλ᾽ οὐκ Ἀτρεΐδην Ἀγαμέμνονα, ποιμένα λαῶν,
ὕπνος ἔχεν·

ἀλλ᾽ ἐπιὼν καὶ ἐξανιστὰς ἕκαστον καὶ συντάττων,

ἱππῆας μὲν πρῶτα, σὺν ἵπποισιν καὶ ὄχεσφιν·
πεζοὺς δ᾽ ἐξόπιθε στῆσεν πολέας τε καὶ ἐσθλούς,
ἕρκος ἔμεν πολέμοιο, κακοὺς δ᾽ ἐς μέσσον
ἔλασσεν.

τοιοῦτον ἡγοῦ καὶ περὶ τὴν ψυχὴν γίγνεσθαι· νύκτα πολλὴν καὶ ὕπνον βαθὺν τῶν τῆς ψυχῆς νοημάτων· τὸν δὲ λόγον αὐτόν, τὸν στρατηγὸν ὄντα ἢ βασιλέα ἢ ὅτιπερ ὀνομάζων χαίρεις, ἐπιόντα τούτων ἕκαστον καὶ ἐπεγείροντα καὶ συντάττοντα. κάλει δὲ τὸν μὲν ὕπνον λήθην, τὴν δὲ ἀνάστασιν αὐτῶν ἀνάμνησιν, μνήμην δὲ τὴν φυλακὴν καὶ τὴν σωτηρίαν τῶν συνταχθέντων. γίγνεται δὲ ἡ ἀνάμνησις κατὰ βραχὺ ἕτερον ἐξ ἑτέρου θηρευούσης τῆς ψυχῆς καὶ χειραγωγουμένης ὑπὸ τοῦ παρόντος ἐπὶ τὸ μέλλον, ὁποῖον ἀμέλει περὶ τὰς τῶν δεῦρο πραγμάτων ἀναμνήσεις γίγνεται.

7. Ἄιδει ὁ Δημόδοκος ἐν τῇ Φαιάκων δαιτὶ

νεῖκος Ὀδυσσῆος καὶ Πηλεΐδεω Ἀχιλῆος·

Ὀδυσσεὺς παρών, ἀκούων τῆς ᾠδῆς, γνωρίσας δακρύει. ἆρ᾽ οὖν οὐκ εἰκὸς ἐπιλαβομένην αὐτῷ τὴν ψυ-

---

12 *Il.* 10.3–4.
13 *Il.* 4.297–99, actually said of Nestor marshaling his troops.
14 *Od.* 8.75.

> except for Agamemnon, son of Atreus, shepherd of the army,
> who was not asleep,[12]

but went about awakening each soldier and stationing him in rank:

> the horsemen first in line with their horses and chariots,
> then behind them he stationed the many good infantrymen
> to be the bulwark of battle, while putting cowards in the middle.[13]

You may be certain that something similar takes place in the soul. Its thoughts are fast asleep in the dark of night. Reason itself, acting as a general, or king, or whatever you wish to call it, approaches each of them, awakens them, and organizes them in their ranks. Call their sleep forgetfulness, their arousal recollection, and the guarding and preservation of their organization memory. Recollection occurs step by step, as the soul hunts down one thing after another in sequence, and is led by each new one on to the next, precisely as recollection occurs in everyday life.

7. During the banquet with the Phaeacians, Demodocus sings of

> the quarrel between Odysseus and Peleus' son Achilles.[14]

Being present and listening to the song, Odysseus recognizes the event and begins to weep. Is it not reasonable that his soul seized on such a starting point and made its

χὴν τοιαύτης ἀρχῆς ὁδεύειν ἐπὶ τὰ ἐκεῖ ἔργα, καὶ τὸ μὲν σῶμα αὐτῷ συμπίνειν τοῖς Φαίαξιν αὐτοῦ μένον, τὴν δὲ ψυχὴν γίγνεσθαι τῇ μνήμῃ ἐκεῖ ἐν Ἰλίῳ, ἀναπεμπαζομένην ἕκαστον ὧν εἶδεν τέως καὶ ἰοῦσαν ἐπὶ πολλὰ τῶν ἑαυτῆς θεαμάτων ἀπὸ μικρᾶς ἀρχῆς;

Ἤδη τις καὶ λύραν ἰδὼν ἐμνήσθη τῶν παιδικῶν τῶν χρησαμένων τῇ λύρᾳ· κοῦφον γάρ τι χρῆμα ἀνάμνησις καὶ εὔκολον, καὶ ὥσπερ τὰ εὐκίνητα τῶν σωμάτων τοῦ χειρὶ προάγοντος δεῖται, καὶ παραλαβόντα τὴν ἐξ ἐκείνου ἀρχὴν φυλάττει ἐπὶ πολὺ τὴν κίνησιν, οὕτω καὶ ὁ νοῦς ἐπιλαβόμενος πρὸς μνήμην βραχείας ἀρχῆς, ἣν ἡ αἴσθησις αὐτῷ ὀρέγει, ἐπὶ πολλὰ χωρεῖ προϊὼν κατὰ ἀνάμνησιν.

Ἕκαστον γὰρ οἶμαι τῶν ὄντων ἢ γεγονότων, οἷς ἡ ψυχὴ ἐνέτυχεν, ἀκολουθίαν ἔχει, ἢ κατὰ χρόνον, ὡς ἐπὶ ἡμέρᾳ νὺξ καὶ ἐπὶ νεότητι γῆρας καὶ ἐπὶ χειμῶνι ἔαρ, ἢ κατὰ πάθος, ὡς κάλλει ἔρως ἐπιγίνεται καὶ προπηλακισμῷ ὀργὴ καὶ ἡδονὴ εὐτυχίαις καὶ λύπη συμφοραῖς· ἢ κατὰ τόπον,

Φᾶρίν τε Σπάρτην τε πολυτρήρωνά τε Θίσβην·

ἢ κατὰ νομόν,

Βοιωτῶν μὲν Πηνέλεως καὶ Λήϊτος ἦρχον,
Ἀρκεσίλαός τε Προθοήνωρ τε Κλονίος τε·

ἢ κατὰ δύναμιν,

way back to what had happened in that place, and while his body remained there drinking with the Phaeacians, his memory transported his soul way back to Troy, as it went back over each thing it had seen in the meantime, and, prompted by this small impulse, passed in review the many things it had itself witnessed?

In fact, the mere sight of a lyre has reminded many a person of the boyfriend who used to play it, for recollection is a lively faculty and easily set in motion. Just as mobile objects need but a push of the hand to move them forward, and once they receive its impulse maintain their motion over a long distance, just so, once the mind receives a small stimulus to its memory provided by the senses, it travels great distances through recollection.

For I believe that each thing the soul encounters, whether present or past, exists in a sequence, either in order of time, as night after day, old age after youth, and spring after winter; or in order of emotions, as love follows beauty, anger follows insult, pleasure follows success, and distress follows disaster; or in order of location, as in

> Pharis and Sparta and Thisbe, home of doves;[15]

or in order of rank, as in

> Peneleus and Leitus led the Boeotians
> along with Arcesilaus, Prothoenor, and Clonius;[16]

or in order of strength, as in

[15] *Il.* 2.582. The third city is Messe, not Thisbe, in the standard Homeric text. Cf. *Il.* 2.502.

[16] *Il.* 2.494–95.

Ζεῦ πάτερ, ἢ Αἴαντα λαχεῖν, ἢ Τυδέος υἱόν,
ἢ αὐτὸν βασιλῆα πολυχρύσοιο Μυκήνης.

8. Ἅτε οὖν ἐν προθύροις τῆς ψυχῆς αἱ αἰσθήσεις ἱδρυμέναι, ἐπειδάν τινος ἐφάψωνται ἀρχῆς καὶ παραδῶσιν τῷ νῷ, ἐπιλαβόμενος ταύτης διορᾷ τὰ λοιπὰ καὶ διεξέρχεται ἐπὶ τὰ ἀκόλουθα, ἢ χρόνῳ ἢ φύσει ἢ νομῷ ἢ τόπῳ ἢ τιμῇ ἢ δυνάμει. ὥσπερ γὰρ ἐπὶ τῶν μακρῶν καὶ λεπτῶν δοράτων, ὁ τὸν στύρακα κλονήσας παρέπεμψε τὴν κίνησιν διὰ παντὸς τοῦ δόρατος μέχρι τῆς αἰχμῆς· καὶ ὥσπερ τῶν μακρῶν καὶ διατεταμένων κάλων ὁ διασείσας τὴν ἀρχὴν παραδίδωσιν τὴν κίνησιν τῷ ὅλῳ βαδίζουσαν ἐπὶ τὸ πέρας· οὕτω καὶ τῷ νῷ βραχείας ἀρχῆς δεῖ πρὸς ἔννοιαν τῶν πραγμάτων ὅλων.

Ὁ μὲν δὴ εὖ πεφυκὼς ἀνὴρ καὶ πρὸς ἀρετὴν εὐδρομώτατος, αὐτὸς παρ' αὑτοῦ τὴν ἀρχὴν λαβών, πορεύεται καὶ ἐφοδεύει καὶ ξυλλαμβάνει καὶ ἀναπεμπάζεται τῇ μνήμῃ τὰ τοῦ νοῦ θεάματα· ὁ δὲ ἧττον δεινὸς δεῖται τοῦ Σωκράτους, αὐτοῦ μὲν διδάσκοντος οὐδέν, διερωτῶντος δὲ καὶ διαπυνθανομένου· ὁ δὲ ἀποκρίνεται τἀληθῆ αὐτά. τίς ἂν οὖν ἀποκρίναιτο ἃ μήπω οἶδεν; πλὴν εἰ μὴ καὶ τὸν βαδίζοντα χειραγωγοῦντος ἑτέρου φήσει τις μὴ βαδίζειν αὐτόν. τί τοίνυν διαφέρει ὁ χειραγωγῶν τοῦ ἀνερωτῶντος, καὶ τί δια-

Father Zeus, may the lot choose Ajax, or Tydeus' son,
or the king himself, lord of Mycenae rich in gold.[17]

8. Just so, when our senses, located in the vestibule of the soul, catch hold of some stimulus, they pass it on to the mind, which in turn takes hold of it, discerns the rest of the sequence, and moves on through what follows in order of time, or in order of nature, or in order of command, location, rank, or strength. For just as when someone propels the bottom end of a long thin javelin and passes on the motion through the entire shaft right up to its point; or when someone gives a shake to one end of a long taut rope and passes on the motion that traverses its entire length to the other end, so the mind needs only a small stimulus to form a conception of things in their entirety.

Now someone who is naturally gifted and swift in his pursuit of virtue, can seize the impulse within himself and journey on and on, gathering together and going back over in his memory what his mind has seen. But someone less capable needs a Socrates, who teaches nothing himself, but instead keeps asking questions and cross-examining, as his respondent answers with the truth itself. Who, then, could give answers, if he does not already know them? Unless, that is, someone will claim that a person is not really walking, when another is leading him by the hand. But what difference is there between someone leading by the hand and someone asking questions, or between someone walking in the one example and someone answering questions

[17] *Il.* 7.179–80, one of the Achaeans speaking, also quoted at *Or.* 5.2.

φέρει ὁ βαδίζων τοῦ ἀποκρινομένου; ὁ μὲν γὰρ ἑαυτῷ παρέχει τὴν ἐνέργειαν, ὁ δὲ ἐκείνῳ τὴν ἀσφάλειαν. ἀλλ᾽ οὔτε ὁ χειραγωγούμενος μανθάνει βαδίζειν, οὔτε ὁ ἀνερωτώμενος ἀποκρίνεσθαι μανθάνει· ἀλλ᾽ ἑκάτερος ὁ μὲν βαδίζει, δύναται γάρ· ὁ δὲ ἀποκρίνεται, οἶδε γάρ· ξυνεπιλαμβάνουσιν δὲ πρὸς ἀσφάλειαν ἑκατέρῳ ἑκάτερος.

9. Σῶμα μὲν βαδιστικὸν τῇ φύσει, ψυχὴ δὲ λογιστικὴ τῇ φύσει· εἰ δ᾽ ἐστὶν ἀθάνατος, ὥσπερ ἐστίν, ἀνάγκη που αὐτῇ τοῦτο ἐξ ἀϊδίου ἐνεῖναι, τὰς νοήσεις τε καὶ ἐπιστήμας τῶν πραγμάτων. ἅτε δὲ οἶμαι διττῷ βίῳ ἡ ψυχὴ συνεχομένη, τῷ μὲν καθαρῷ καὶ διαυγεῖ καὶ ὑπὸ μηδεμιᾶς συμφορᾶς ἐνοχλουμένῳ, τῷ δὲ θολερῷ καὶ τεταραγμένῳ καὶ ἐν παντοίαις τύχαις φυρομένῳ, ἐνταῦθα μὲν ἀσαφείας ἐμπέπλησται καὶ καρηβαρεῖ, αὐτὸ ἐκεῖνο τὸ τῶν μεθυόντων πάθος· τούτοις γάρ που φλεγμαίνουσα ἡ ψυχὴ ὑπὸ τοῦ ἀνέδην πότου ἐγγύτατα μὲν τείνει μανίας· ἤδη δέ που ἀνακαλεῖται αὑτήν, καὶ οὔτε ἀκριβῶς σφάλλεται οὔτε σαφῶς λογίζεται, ἀλλ᾽ ἐν μεθορίῳ μένει ἀγνοίας καὶ λογισμοῦ.

Ἐπειδὰν δὲ ἀπαλλαγῇ ἡ ψυχὴ ἐνθένδε ἐκεῖσε, ὥσπερ ἐκ τῆς Κιμμερίων γῆς ἐπὶ λαμπρὸν αἰθέρα ἐξελθοῦσα, ἐλευθέρα μὲν γενομένη σαρκῶν, ἐλευθέρα δὲ ἐπιθυμιῶν, ἐλευθέρα νόσων, ἐλευθέρα συμφορῶν, τότε διορᾷ καὶ λογίζεται τἀληθῆ αὐτά, θεοῖς καὶ θεῶν παισὶν συγγιγνομένη ὑπὲρ ἄκραν τὴν οὐρανοῦ ἁψῖδα, συμπεριπολοῦσα καὶ συντεταγμένη στρατιᾷ θεῶν ὑφ᾽ ἡγεμόνι καὶ στρατηγῷ τῷ Διί· καὶ μέμνηται μὲν ἀλη-

in the other? Each one provides his own effort, while the other provides steadiness. Neither is the one being led by the hand learning how to walk, nor is the one being questioned learning how to answer. In the one case, he is walking because he has the ability; in the other, he answers because he has the knowledge. In each case, the one assists the other with steadiness.

9. The body is naturally endowed to walk; the soul is naturally endowed to use reason. Now, if the soul is immortal, as it most certainly is, then its thoughts and knowledge of existing things must always have been in it. For I believe that the soul is constrained to live in two different realms: the one is pure, bright, and undisturbed by any mishap whatsoever; the other is murky, disrupted, and confounded by all sorts of chance events. In this latter realm the soul is filled with uncertainty and becomes drowsy, just like what happens to drunkards, for when their souls are inflamed by excessive drinking they reach the point of madness. And yet, sometimes the soul can get a grip on itself, when it does not exactly stumble nor yet reason clearly, but remains in a middle state between ignorance and reason.

But when the soul quits this earthly realm for the other one—as if leaving the land of the Cimmerians[18] for the bright ether—it becomes free of its flesh, and freed from its desires, diseases, and misfortunes. Then it discerns and ponders things as they really are, as it joins the gods and the gods' offspring high above the vault of the sky, and takes its place in the ranks of the gods and makes its rounds under the guidance and command of Zeus. At that

[18] A mythical land where the sun never shines (*Od.* 11.14–19).

θείας τότε, ἀναμιμνήσκεται δὲ νῦν· καὶ θαρσεῖ μὲν τότε, σφάλλεται δὲ νῦν.

Ἡ δὲ ἐρρωμένη ψυχὴ καὶ χρηστῷ δαίμονι συγκεκληρωμένη κἀνταῦθα ἀντέχει τῷ κυκηθμῷ, καὶ κατὰ δύναμιν ἀπαλλάττουσα αὐτὴν τῆς πρὸς τὸ σῶμα ὁμιλίας, τὴν μνήμην ἐγείρει ἐκείνων τῶν θεαμάτων καὶ ἐκείνων τῶν ἀκουσμάτων. τοῦτο ἄρα καὶ οἱ ποιηταὶ τὴν Μνημοσύνην αἰνίττονται Μουσῶν μητέρα, Μούσας μὲν τὰς ἐπιστήμας ὀνομάζοντες, ἠγάθεον χορὸν καὶ ἔργον Διός, ὑπὸ Μνημοσύνης δὲ γεννωμένας καὶ συντατττομένας. θεραπεύωμεν τὰς Μούσας, θεραπεύωμεν τὴν Μνημοσύνην.

time the soul truly remembers reality, but now it must recollect it; then the soul has confidence; now it stumbles along.

But the robust soul that has been allotted a good *daimon* resists the confusion here on earth, and by freeing itself as much it can from its association with the body, awakens the memory of what it saw and heard up there. That indeed is what the poets are suggesting when they call the Muses' mother Mnemosyne (Memory) and the Muses themselves forms of knowledge.[19] They are a holy chorus, the work of Zeus, but brought to birth and kept in order by Mnemosyne. Let us worship the Muses; let us worship Mnemosyne.

[19] The nine Muses came to be associated with different types of literature and learning.

# *ORATION* 11

## INTRODUCTION

This oration is the second longest in the collection and was placed first in manuscript I. It opens with a lengthy *captatio benevolentiae* expressing the difficulty of treating such a lofty and difficult subject as the gods, especially when even Plato's eloquence has failed to convince people on the subject. Explaining Plato's view of god is like offering a paltry drink to a thirsty man, when a clear and mighty river is at hand (§1). Better still, a first reading of Plato is like a miner coming across gold ore, who needs the expertise of an assayer (that is, reasoned discourse) to refine the gold to make it useful (§2). Zeus is not such as Homer depicts him, for the representations of poets, artists, and philosophers are products of our human weakness to see god (§3).[1] Although all people disagree about most everything, there is universal belief that there is one father god, with other gods as his offspring, whose works are evident in nature. Even Leucippus, Democritus, Epicurus, and Protagoras tacitly acknowledge god's existence (§§4–5). So Plato himself is summoned to speak on behalf of god (§6).

Plato divides the soul into two faculties that allow com-

[1] The need for representations of gods occasioned by human weakness is treated in *Orr*. 2 and 4.

prehension (*synesis*): perception (*aisthēsis*) and intellect (*nous*). The deluge of sensations overwhelms the intellect so that it cannot concentrate on its proper, intelligible objects (§7). In the hierarchy of being, god must be at the pinnacle, situated in the intellect itself (§8). Whereas the divine intellect sees everything all at once and all the time, the human intellect sees only partially and intermittently. According to Plato, the divine intellect is the "father and begetter (*gennētēs*)" of the whole universe: it has no physical attributes, and the human intellect alone can "see" and "hear" it (§9). Only an intellect in a strong soul can perceive it by turning from the tumultuous physical realm and allowing itself to be guided by reason and spurred on by eros to make its ascent into the heavens (§10). You will truly see god when he calls you at death, but in the meantime you can recognize that he is the ever-flowing source of all beauty. As a lover strips off the clothing to behold his beloved, you must use reason to remove the earthly tumult that blocks your view of god (§11). If you are unable to see "the father and creator (*dēmiourgos*)," at least you can behold his works and worship his celestial offspring and *daimones*. The universe is like a great empire, where the king remains motionless and his subjects are various gods that exist in a hierarchy descending to earth (§12).[2]

[2] The oration has several points of contact with Alcinous' *Didascalicus*, ch. 10 (which work was preserved with the *Orations* in manuscript R). These include a transcendent, ineffable, and immobile god grasped only by the intellect and reached by three ways of apprehension (*Didasc.* 10.165.16–34): preeminence in §8, analogy in §9, and negation in §9.

# *ORATION* 11

## Τίς ὁ θεὸς κατὰ Πλάτωνα

1. Περὶ μὲν δαιμόνων ἀμφισβητοῦντα λόγον λόγῳ φέρω, καὶ ἀνέχομαι τὴν στάσιν, καὶ οὐδὲν δεινὸν οὐδὲ πλημμελὲς οὐδὲ ἔξω τρόπου ἡγοῦμαι δρᾶν τὸν ἀμφισβητοῦντα πρὸς ἑαυτὸν καὶ πρὸς ἄλλον, εἰ ἔστιν τὸ δαιμόνιον καὶ τί καὶ ὁποῖον· καὶ γὰρ ἦν ἐνταῦθα τὸ μὲν ὄνομα ἄδηλον, ἡ δὲ οὐσία ἀφανής, ἡ δὲ δύναμις ἀμφισβητήσιμον. νῦν δὲ δὴ τίς γένωμαι περὶ θεοῦ λέγων; ποῖον κάλλος ῥημάτων περιβαλόμενος, ἢ ποῖον φῶς ἐξ ὀνομάτων σαφεστάτων πορισάμενος, ἢ τίνα ἁρμονίαν ᾠδῆς ἐκλόγου ἁρμοσάμενος, δείξαιμι ἂν ἐμαυτῷ καὶ ἄλλῳ τὸ νῦν ζητούμενον;

Ὁπότε γὰρ οὐδὲ ὁ εὐφωνότατος τῶν ὄντων Πλάτων, εἰ καὶ πρὸς Ὅμηρον παραβάλλειν ἐθέλοις, οὔπω καὶ νῦν ἀξιόχρεως πιστεύεσθαι περὶ θεοῦ λέγων, ἀλλ' ἑτέρωθέν τις πυθέσθαι ποθεῖ τὴν Πλάτωνος δόξαν, σχολῇ γ' ἄν τις ἐπιτολμήσαι τῷ λόγῳ νοῦν καὶ βραχὺν ἔχων· πλὴν εἰ μὴ καὶ ἀνδρὶ διψῶντι ποταμοῦ

# *ORATION* 11

## What god is according to Plato

1. When it comes to *daimones*, I can accept one account disagreeing with another and can tolerate the discord. I do not consider it at all shocking, inappropriate, or unusual behavior, if someone disagrees with himself, or with someone else, about the existence, nature, and qualities of the race of *daimones*, because in this case their very name has proved to be[1] uncertain, their essence obscure, and their powers a matter of dispute. But now that my subject is god, what am I to say about it? In what beautiful language can I clothe it, what light can I shed by the use of perfectly clear terms, or what harmony of exquisite poetry can I compose, so that I might elucidate the object of this present inquiry both for myself and anyone else?

For when Plato himself, the most eloquent of men (even if you should choose to compare him to Homer), still to this day fails to carry conviction when he speaks of god, and since people feel the need to learn of Plato's doctrine from other sources, scarcely would anyone with even a modicum of sense venture upon this subject—unless, that

[1] The past tense of ἦν suggests a reference to the preceding discussions of *daimones* in *Orr.* 8 and 9.

παρόντος καθαροῦ καὶ πολλοῦ, ἰδεῖν ἡδίστου καὶ πιεῖν προσηνεστάτου καὶ θρέψαι γονιμωτάτου, ἄλλοθέν ποθεν ἐκ πηγῆς ἀσθενοῦς καὶ ἧττον τὰ ἄλλα ἀγαθῆς ἀρυσάμενοι κομίζοιμεν τῷ διψῶντι ἀναγκαῖον ποτόν. Ὁποῖόν φασι τὴν γλαῦκα πάσχειν, πρὸς μὲν τὸν ἥλιον ἀμαυρουμένην, θηρεύουσαν δὲ ἐν νυκτὶ ἐκ πυρὸς φῶς· εἰ γάρ τις ἐς τὰς Πλάτωνος φωνὰς ἐμπεσὼν ἑτέρων δεῖται λόγων, καὶ εἴ τῳ τὸ ἐκεῖθεν φῶς ἀμαυρὸν δοκεῖ καὶ ἥκιστα μετέχον αὐγῆς σαφοῦς, οὗτος οὐδ' ἂν τὸν ἥλιον ἴδοι ἀνίσχοντα, οὐδὲ τὴν σελήνην λαμπρυνομένην, οὐδὲ τὸν Ἕσπερον καταδυόμενον, οὐδὲ τὸν Ἑωσφόρον φθάνοντα.

2. Ἔχε ἀτρέμας· νῦν γάρ τοι ἠρέμα ἐννοῶ οἷον ἂν εἴη τὸ πάθος τοῦ τοιοῦδε λόγου· αὐτὸ ἐκεῖνο οἷον τὸ τῶν μεταλλέων· οὗτοι γάρ που κόπτοντες τὴν γῆν, ὀρύσσοντες τὸν χρυσόν, οὐχ ἱκανοὶ διαγιγνώσκειν τὴν τοῦ χρυσοῦ φύσιν, ἀλλὰ ἔστιν ἔργον βασανιζόντων[1] τὸν χρυσὸν ἐν πυρί. εἰκάζω δὴ τὴν μὲν πρώτην ὁμιλίαν τῶν Πλάτωνος λόγων μετάλλῳ τινὶ ἀτεχνῶς χρυσοῦ· τὸ δὲ ἐπὶ τούτῳ ἑτέρας δεῖται τέχνης, ἣ τὸ ληφθὲν δοκιμάζουσα καὶ ἐκκαθαίρουσα λόγῳ, οὐ πυρί, χρῆσθαι ἤδη δύναται ἀκηράτῳ καὶ βεβασανισμένῳ τῷ χρυσῷ. εἰ τοίνυν δήλη μὲν ἡ μεταλλεία τοῦ ἀληθοῦς καὶ μεγαλόδωρος καὶ ἄφθονος, δεῖ δὲ ἡμῖν τέχνης ἑτέρας πρὸς βάσανον τοῦ ληφθέντος, φέρε παρακαλῶμεν τὴν τέχνην ταύτην ξυνεπιλαβέσθαι ἡμῖν τοῦ παρόντος λόγου, τί ποτέ ἐστι τὸ θεῖον κατὰ Πλάτωνα σκοπουμένοις.

is, when encountering a thirsty man while there is a pure and mighty river at hand, one most pleasant to behold, very refreshing to drink, and most nourishing, we should draw off just enough drink from some other weak and wholly inferior source to quench his thirst.

Something similar is said to happen to an owl: when blinded by the light of the sun, it seeks out firelight at night. So, if someone who has encountered Plato's own words still needs further explanation, and if the light coming from them seems to him dim and wholly devoid of clear illumination, then such a person would be incapable of seeing the rising sun, the shining moon, the Evening Star when it sets, or the Morning Star when it appears.

2. But wait—for I am now truly coming to realize what sort of experience this kind of discourse would resemble: one just like the work of miners. For when they cut into the ground and dig up the gold, they are incapable of distinguishing the quality of the gold, because that is the job of those who assay the gold with fire. In fact, I would compare one's first acquaintance with Plato's writings to mining for gold ore. What comes next requires a different expertise, one that uses reason, rather than fire, to examine and purify what has been extracted, and only then can the refined and assayed gold be put to use. If, therefore, this mine of truth is in plain sight, and its yield is generous and unstinting, but if we still need an additional expertise to test what we have extracted, then let us summon this other expertise to assist us in our present discourse, as we investigate what divinity is according to Plato.

[1] *βασανιζόντων* Paccius, Stephanus, Trapp: *βασανίζον* R

3. Εἰ οὖν ἔροιτο ἡμᾶς ἡ τέχνη φωνὴν λαβοῦσα, πότερα τοίνυν οὐχ ἡγούμενοι αὐτοί τι εἶναι θεῖον ἐν τῇ φύσει οὐδὲ ἔχοντες καθάπαξ ἔννοιαν θεοῦ ἀμφισβητοῦμεν περὶ Πλάτωνος, ἢ αὐτοί τινας ἔχοντες οἰκείας δόξας ἕτερ' ἄττα ἡγούμεθα παρὰ ταύτας δοξάζειν ἐκεῖνον, κᾆτα ἡμῶν φασκόντων ἔχειν, ἀξίωσαι ἀποκρίνασθαι ὁποῖόν τινα ἡγούμεθα εἶναι τὸν θεόν, τί τοίνυν ἂν ἀποκρινοίμεθα; ὅτι ἐστὶν ὁ θεὸς

γυρὸς ἐν ὤμοιϊν, μελανόχροος, οὐλοκάρηνος;

καταγέλαστος ἡ ἀπόκρισις, κἂν εἰ μειζόνως χαρακτηρίζοις τὸν Δία, κυανᾶς μὲν ὀφρύας, χρυσᾶς δὲ χαίτας, ἐλελιζόμενον δὲ ὑπ' αὐτῶν τὸν οὐρανόν. πάντα γάρ που τὰ τοιαῦτα ἀπορίᾳ ὄψεως καὶ ἀσθενείᾳ δηλώσεως καὶ γνώμης ἀμβλύτητι, ἐφ' ὅσον δύνανται ἕκαστοι ἐξαιρόμενοι τῇ φαντασίᾳ πρὸς τὸ κάλλιστον δοκοῦν ‹καὶ γραφεῖς ἀπεργάζονται, καὶ ἀγαλματοποιοὶ διαπλάττουσιν, καὶ ποιηταὶ αἰνίττονται,›[2] καὶ φιλόσοφοι καταμαντεύονται.

4. Εἰ δὲ συναγαγὼν ἐκκλησίαν τῶν τεχνῶν τούτων κελεύοις ἅπαντας ἀθρόους διὰ ψηφίσματος ἑνὸς ἀποκρίνασθαι περὶ τοῦ θεοῦ, οἴει ἄλλο μὲν ἂν τὸν γραφέα εἰπεῖν, ἄλλο δὲ {καὶ}[3] τὸν ἀγαλματοποιόν, καὶ τὸν ποιητὴν ἄλλο, καὶ τὸν φιλόσοφον ἄλλο; ἀλλ' οὐδὲ μὰ

[2] suppl. Hobein
[3] om. U, Koniaris: del. Trapp

3. Now if this expertise could talk and were to ask us whether, as we dispute about Plato, we ourselves do not believe that there is any divine element in nature and simply have no concept of god at all, or whether we hold some personal opinions and believe that Plato holds others that differ from ours; and then, if we reply that we do indeed have opinions of our own, it should ask us to respond with what *we* think god is like, then what would we answer? That god is

> round-shouldered, dark-skinned, curly-haired?[2]

What a ridiculous response, even if you should depict Zeus more majestically, with dark brow and golden hair, at whose nod heaven quakes.[3] For surely all such representations result from our inability to see god, our incapacity to explain him to others, and the dullness of our intelligence, such that individuals, inspired by their imaginations, portray as best they can what seems to them most beautiful: <such are the works of painters, the images of sculptors, the allegories of poets,> and the surmises of philosophers.[4]

4. But if you were to convene an assembly of experts in these arts and demand that they answer all together with one single vote what god is, do you think that the painter, sculptor, poet, and philosopher would all say something

[2] *Od.* 19.246, describing Eurybates.

[3] An adaptation of *Il.* 1.528–30. According to Dio Chrys. *Or.* 12.25–26, these verses were the inspiration for Phidias' chryselephantine statue of Zeus at Olympia.

[4] The text is corrupt; the supplement is Hobein's. The need to depict the divine through images because of human weakness is discussed at *Or.* 2.2–3.

Δία τὸν Σκύθην, οὐδὲ τὸν Ἕλληνα, οὐδὲ τὸν Πέρσην ἢ τὸν Ὑπερβόρεον· ἀλλὰ ἴδοις ἂν ἐν μὲν τοῖς ἄλλοις †ἐν δὲ τοῖς ἄλλοις†[4] <οὐ>[5] ταὐτὸ ψηφιζομένους τοὺς ἀνθρώπους, πάντας δὲ πᾶσιν διαφερομένους· οὐ τὸ ἀγαθὸν τὸ αὐτὸ πᾶσιν, οὐ τὸ κακὸν ὅμοιον, οὐ τὸ αἰσχρόν, οὐ τὸ καλόν· νόμος μὲν γὰρ δὴ καὶ δίκη ἄνω καὶ κάτω φέρεται[6] διασπώμενα καὶ σπαρασσόμενα· μὴ γὰρ ὅτι γένος γένει ὁμολογεῖ ἐν τούτοις, ἀλλ' οὐδὲ πόλις πόλει, ἀλλ' οὐδὲ οἶκος οἴκῳ, οὐδὲ ἀνὴρ ἀνδρί, οὐδὲ αὐτὸς αὑτῷ·

> τοῖος γὰρ νόος ἐστὶν ἐπιχθονίων ἀνθρώπων,
> οἷον ἐπ' ἦμαρ ἄγῃσι πατὴρ ἀνδρῶν τε θεῶν τε.

5. Ἐν τοσούτῳ δὴ πολέμῳ καὶ στάσει καὶ διαφωνίᾳ ἕνα ἴδοις ἂν ἐν πάσῃ γῇ ὁμόφωνον νόμον καὶ λόγον, ὅτι θεὸς εἷς πάντων βασιλεὺς καὶ πατήρ, καὶ θεοὶ πολλοί, θεοῦ παῖδες, συνάρχοντες θεῷ. ταῦτα καὶ ὁ Ἕλλην λέγει καὶ ὁ βάρβαρος λέγει, καὶ ὁ ἠπειρώτης καὶ ὁ θαλάττιος, καὶ ὁ σοφὸς καὶ ὁ ἄσοφος· κἂν ἐπὶ τοῦ Ὠκεανοῦ ἔλθῃς τὰς ἠϊόνας, κἀκεῖ θεοί, τοῖς μὲν ἀνίσχοντες ἀγχοῦ μάλα, τοῖς δὲ καταδυόμενοι. <οἴ>ει[7] δὴ τούτοις Πλάτωνα ἀντιχειροτονεῖν καὶ ἀντινομοθετεῖν, ἀλλὰ οὐχ ὁμόφωνον εἶναι καὶ ὁμοπαθῆ καλλίστης φωνῆς καὶ ἀληθεστάτου πάθους; τί τοῦτο; ἥλιος,

[4] obel. Trapp [5] suppl. Markland
[6] φέρεται Acciaiolus, Trapp, Koniaris: φύρεται R
[7] suppl. Acciaiolus, edd.

different? No, by Zeus, nor would any Scythian, Greek, Persian, or Hyperborean. In all other matters, though, you would never find people voting for the same thing, but all would disagree with everyone else, because not all of them share the same concept of good, evil, ugliness, or beauty. For in fact law and justice are pulled this way and that, separated and torn to pieces, so that not only do nations disagree with nations in these matters, but cities with cities, families with families, one man with another, and even one man with himself,

> for the mind of men who dwell on earth is such
> as the day the father of men and gods brings them.[5]

5. Nonetheless, in the midst of so much conflict, discord, and disagreement, you can discern one law and one account agreed upon over all the earth, that there is one god, the king and father of all, and that there are many other gods who are his offspring and who share in his rule. That is what Greeks and barbarians, those dwelling inland and on the coast, wise men and fools, all say. And even if you go to the shores of the Ocean, there too are gods, who rise near one people and set near the other.[6] Do you really think that Plato votes against all these witnesses and lays down some other law, rather than agreeing with their most beautiful affirmation and sharing their most truthful experience? What is this? we ask. "The sun," our eyes tell us.

[5] *Od.* 18.136–37, Odysseus speaking to Amphinomus, also cited in *Or.* 1.2.

[6] This refers to the eastern and the western Ethiopians, thought to inhabit the ends of the earth, whose gods are celestial.

ὀφθαλμὸς λέγει· τί τοῦτο; βρονταί, ἀκοὴ λέγει· τί ταῦτα ὡραῖα καὶ καλά, καὶ περίοδοι καὶ μεταβολαὶ καὶ κράσεις ἀέρων καὶ ζώων γενέσεις καὶ καρπῶν φύσεις; θεοῦ πάντα ἔργα, ἡ ψυχὴ λέγει, καὶ τὸν τεχνίτην ποθεῖ καὶ καταμαντεύεται τῆς τέχνης.

Εἰ δὲ ἐξεγένοντο ἐν τῷ ξύμπαντι αἰῶνι δύο που καὶ τρεῖς, ἄθεον καὶ ταπεινὸν καὶ ἀναισθὲς γένος, καὶ πεπλανημένον μὲν τοῖς ὀφθαλμοῖς, ἐξηπατημένον δὲ ταῖς ἀκοαῖς, ἐκτετμημένον δὲ τὴν ψυχήν, ἄλογον καὶ ἄγονον καὶ ἄκαρπον, ὡς ἄθυμος λέων, ὡς βοῦς ἄκερως, ὡς ὄρνις ἄπτερος, καὶ παρὰ τούτου ὅμως τοῦ γένους πεύσει τὸ θεῖον· ἴσασιν γὰρ οὐχ ἑκόντες, καὶ λέγουσιν ἄκοντες, κἂν ἀφέλῃς αὐτοῦ τὸ ἀγαθόν, ὡς Λεύκιππος· κἂν προσθῇς τὸ ὁμοπαθές, ὡς Δημόκριτος· κἂν ὑπαλλάξῃς τὴν φύσιν, ὡς Στράτων· κἂν δῷς τὴν ἡδονήν, ὡς Ἐπίκουρος· κἂν μὴ εἶναι φῇς, ὡς Διαγόρας· κἂν ἀγνοεῖν τι φῇς, ὡς Πρωταγόρας.

6. Τούτους μὲν οὖν ἐῶμεν χαίρειν, μὴ δυναμένους ἐπαύρασθαι τοῦ ἀληθοῦς ὅλου καὶ ἀρτίου, ἰόντας δὲ

---

[7] A late fifth-century BC atomist; cf. fr. B 2 D-K (= D 73 L-M): He says in his *On Mind*, "Nothing happens at random, but everything for a reason and by necessity."

[8] A fifth-century BC atomist. The concept does not appear in his extant works.

[9] A late fourth-century BC peripatetic philosopher. Cicero says of him (*Nat. D.* 1.35): "In his view the sole repository of divine power is nature, which contains in itself the causes of birth,

And this? "Thunder," say our ears. And what are all these lovely and beautiful things, the natural cycles and changes and temperate climates, the birth of creatures and growth of crops? "All are the works of god," our soul tells us, and it yearns for the craftsman and divines the presence of his craft.

And even if throughout all time there have emerged some two or three individuals belonging to a group that is godless, base, and insensitive, who are led astray by their eyes, deceived by their ears, and emasculated in their souls; who are as irrational, sterile, and unproductive as a lion without courage, a bull without horns, a bird without wings—yet, even from this group you will learn about divinity. For they know god without wishing to and speak of him and without meaning to—even if you take away god's goodness like Leucippus;[7] or add shared sensation like Democritus;[8] or change his nature like Strato;[9] or allow him pleasure like Epicurus;[10] or deny his existence like Diagoras;[11] or admit your own ignorance like Protagoras.[12]

6. Let us leave these men well enough alone, for they are incapable of grasping the truth whole and complete,

growth and decay, but is entirely devoid of sensation and of form" (trans. H. Rackham).

10 He argued that the gods had a blissful existence (Diog. Laert. 10.123 and 139). He is criticized at *Orr.* 4.4–9, 15.8, 30.3–4, 33.3, and 41.2.

11 Late fifth-century BC lyric poet from Melos, renowned for his atheism; cf. Cicero, *Nat. D.* 1.2: "Diagoras of Melos . . . believed that there were no gods at all."

12 Fifth-century BC sophist, famous for his statement, fr. B 4 D-K (= D 10 L-M): "I cannot know whether the gods exist or not."

ἐπ' αὐτὸ ἀσαφεῖς ὁδοὺς καὶ πεπλανημένας· αὐτοὶ δὲ δὴ τί δράσωμεν; ἀπείπωμεν ἐκ τοῦ λοξοῦ οὐδὲ[8] ἴχνη αὐτοῦ σκεψάμενοι, οὐδὲ ὅσον εἰδώλοις ἐντυχόντες; ἀλλ' ὁ μὲν Ὀδυσσεὺς προσχὼν τῇ ξένῃ, εἰς περιωπὴν ἀνελθών, ἐσκέπτετο τὰ ἴχνη τῶν ἐχόντων,

ἦ ῥ' οἵγ' ὑβρισταί τε καὶ ἄγριοι οὐδὲ δίκαιοι,
ἠὲ φιλόξενοι, καί σφιν νόος ἐστὶ θεουδής·

ἡμεῖς δὲ ἆρα οὐ τολμήσομεν ἀναβιβασάμενοι τὸν λογισμὸν εἴς τινα περιωπὴν ἄνω τῆς ψυχῆς περισκέψασθαι τὰ τοῦ θεοῦ ἴχνη, τίνα χώραν ἔχει, τίνα φύσιν· ἀγαπήσομεν δὲ ἀμυδρῶς ἰδόντες;

Εἴθε μοι μαντεῖον ἦν ἐκ Διὸς ἢ Ἀπόλλωνος, οὐ λοξὰ χρησμῳδοῦν οὐδὲ ἀμφίβολα. ἠρόμην ἂν τὸν θεὸν οὐ τὸν Κροίσου λέβητα, τοῦ βασιλέων ἀνοητοτάτου καὶ μαγείρων δυστυχεστάτου, ἀλλ' οὐδὲ θαλάττης μέτρα, οὐδὲ ἀριθμὸν ψάμμου· ἠμέλησα δ' ἂν καὶ τῶν σεμνῶν τούτων ἐρωτημάτων· "ἐπίασιν Μῆδοι, πῶς φυλάξομαι;" κἂν ὁ θεὸς μὴ συμβουλεύῃ, τὰς τριήρεις ἔχω· "ἐπιθυμῶ Σικελίας, πῶς λάβω;" κἂν γὰρ ὁ

[8] ἀπείπωμεν ἐκ τοῦ λοξοῦ οὐδὲ Dübner: ηδεπιμεν ἐκ τοῦ λοξίου δὲ R: obel. Trapp, Koniaris

---

[13] Traces of the divine in images is the subject of *Or.* 2.

[14] Cf. *Od.* 10.97 and 148, when Odysseus lands on Circe's island.

[15] *Od.* 6.120–21, 9.175–76, and 13.201–2.

[16] For Croesus' testing of the oracle at Delphi and Apollo's

but instead make their way toward it down blind and wandering paths. But then what are we ourselves to do? Are we to give up and not even search for oblique traces of the divine, nor so much as encounter it in images?[13] After all, when Odysseus went ashore in a foreign land, he would climb up to a lookout[14] and search for the traces of the inhabitants, wondering,

> are they violent, savage, and lawless,
> or hospitable with minds that fear the gods?[15]

Shall we not then have the courage to take our power of reason onto a lookout, so to speak, high up in the soul, to look all around for the traces of god and ascertain his location and nature? Are we to be satisfied with an indistinct view?

If only I could have an oracle from Zeus or Apollo, whose answer was not indirect or ambiguous. I would not ask the god about the caldron of Croesus, that most foolish king and unfortunate cook, nor about the measures of the sea or the number of grains of sand.[16] I would have disregarded as well these weighty questions: "The Medes are coming; how can I defend myself?"[17] Even if god does not give his advice, I still have my triremes. "I long to possess Sicily; how can I capture it?"[18] Even if god is not opposed,

response, see Hdt. 1.47.3 and 1.48.2. This incident is also referred to at *Orr.* 13.3 and 29.7.

[17] The Athenians consulted the Pythian oracle in 480 BC (Hdt. 7.140–43). The rationalization of this ambiguous oracle is treated at *Or.* 13.1.

[18] A reference to the Athenians' foolhardy passion to invade Sicily in 415 BC, but there is no record of any oracle being consulted.

θεὸς μὴ κωλύῃ, ἡ Σικελία πολλή· ἐμοὶ δὲ σαφῶς ὁ Ἀπόλλων ἐκ Δελφῶν περὶ τοῦ Διὸς ἀποκρινάσθω ἢ ὁ Ζεὺς αὐτός· ὑπὲρ αὐτοῦ τίς; ἐξ Ἀκαδημίας ὑποφήτης τοῦ θεοῦ, ἀνὴρ Ἀττικός, μαντικός· ἀποκρίνεται δὲ ὧδε.

7. "Τῇ τοῦ ἀνθρώπου ψυχῇ δύο ὀργάνων ὄντων πρὸς σύνεσιν, τοῦ μὲν ἁπλοῦ ὃν καλοῦμεν νοῦν, τοῦ δὲ ποικίλου καὶ πολυμεροῦς καὶ πολυτρόπου ἃς αἰσθήσεις καλοῦμεν, συνῆπται μὲν αὐτῶν ἡ ἐργασία, κεχώρισται δὲ ἡ οὐσία· ὡς δὲ ταῦτα πρὸς ἄλληλα ἔχει, οὕτω κἀκεῖνα ὧν ἐστι ταῦτα ὄργανα, καὶ διαφέρει νοητὸν αἰσθητοῦ ὅσον νοῦς αἰσθήσεως. ἔστιν δὲ τούτων κατὰ μὲν τὴν ὁμιλίαν θἄτερον γνωριμώτερον, τὸ αἰσθητόν, τὰ δὲ νοητὰ ἄγνωστα μὲν ταῖς ὁμιλίαις, γνωριμώτερα δὲ τῇ φύσει.

"Ζῷα γάρ που καὶ φυτὰ καὶ λίθοι καὶ φωναὶ καὶ χυμοὶ καὶ ὀδμαὶ καὶ σχήματα καὶ χροιαί, ὑπὸ τοῦ ἔθους ξυναγειρόμενα καὶ τῇ καθ' ἡμέραν διαίτῃ ἀνακιρνάμενα, παρεσκεύακεν τὴν ψυχὴν καὶ ἀναπέπεικεν μηδὲν ἄλλο ἡγεῖσθαι εἶναι ὅτι μὴ ταῦτα· τὸ δὲ νοητόν, ἀπηλλαγμένον τῆς τούτων ἐπαφῆς καὶ ἐπερείσεως, αὐτὸ καθ' ἑαυτὸ ὁρᾶσθαι πέφυκεν ὑπὸ τοῦ νοῦ· ὁ δὲ τῇ πάσῃ ψυχῇ ἐμπεφυτευμένος διασπᾶται ὑπὸ τῶν αἰσθήσεων καὶ ταράττεται καὶ ἀσχολίαν ἄγει, ὥστε μὴ διορᾶν τὰ αὐτοῦ θεάματα, ἤδη δὲ καὶ δημαγωγηθεὶς ἀναπείθεται ὥστε συμφθέγγεσθαι ταῖς τῶν αἰσθήσεων φωναῖς, καὶ μηδὲν ἡγεῖσθαι ἄλλο εἶναι

Sicily is still enormous. No, let Apollo in Delphi give me a clear answer about Zeus, or indeed Zeus himself. But who can speak on his behalf? From the Academy comes a spokesman of god,[19] a man from Attica, who is divinely inspired. He answers in the following way.

7. "The human soul has two faculties that enable comprehension. The one is simple, which we call intellect; the other is complex, multifaceted, and variable, which we call perception. They operate together, but their essential natures are distinct. They differ from each other in terms of their objects: what is intelligible differs from what is perceptible to the extent that intellect differs from perception. Of these two objects, what is perceptible is more familiar because of our everyday involvement with it, whereas the objects of the intellect are unknown to us in everyday experience, but are actually more knowable by their very nature.

"That is because animals, plants, stones, sounds, flavors, smells, shapes, and colors, being gathered together by habituation and inseparable from daily life, have conditioned the soul and persuaded it to believe that nothing exists besides these things. But what is intelligible is free from contact with or dependence on these things, and its nature is such that it can be seen, all on its own, by the intellect. But because the intellect is implanted in the soul as a whole, it is distracted by its sense of perception, and becomes so confused and preoccupied that it is unable to discern its proper sights,[20] and is seduced and won over to such an extent that it assents to the clamor of the senses,

[19] Plato. [20] The soul's proper sights when freed from the body are described at *Orr.* 9.6 and 16.6.

*παρὰ τὰ ὁρατὰ καὶ ἀκουστὰ καὶ ὀσφραντὰ καὶ γευστὰ καὶ ἁπτά.*

"Ὥσπερ οὖν ἐν συμποσίῳ μεστῷ κνίσσης πολλῆς καὶ οἴνου χεομένου καὶ αὐλῶν ἤχου καὶ συρίγγων καὶ ψαλμάτων καὶ θυμιαμάτων, ἀνδρὸς ἂν εἴη καρτεροῦ, συναγείραντος ‹ἑαυτὸν›[9] καὶ συστείλαντος, καὶ τὰς αἰσθήσεις ἀποστρέψαντος[10] ‹πρὸς τὸ›[11] νηφάλιον καὶ κόσμιον, οὕτως ἀμέλει καὶ ἐν τῇ τῶν αἰσθήσεων πολυφωνίᾳ χαλεπὸν εὑρεῖν νήφοντα νοῦν καὶ δυνάμενον προσβλέπειν τοῖς αὑτοῦ θεάμασιν. καὶ μὲν δὴ καὶ ἡ τῶν αἰσθητῶν φύσις, πολυειδής τε οὖσα καὶ συμπεφορημένη καὶ ῥέουσα, ἐν μεταβολῇ παντοίᾳ συνδιατίθησιν αὑτῇ τὴν ψυχήν, ὥστε καὶ μεταβιβάζουσαν αὐτὴν ἐπὶ τὴν τοῦ νοητοῦ φύσιν, στάσιμόν τε οὖσαν καὶ ἑδραίαν, μὴ δύνασθαι διορᾶν ἀσφαλῶς ὑπὸ τοῦ σάλου καὶ τοῦ ταράχου κραδαινομένην· οἷόν που ξυμβαίνειν φιλεῖ καὶ τοῖς ἐκ νεὼς εἰς ἤπειρον ἀποβᾶσιν· μόγις γάρ που καὶ τούτοις ἵσταται τὸ σῶμα, ὑπὸ τοῦ ἐν τῷ κλύδωνι ἔθους κινούμενόν τε καὶ περιφερόμενον καὶ σειόμενον.

8. "Ἐν ποτέρᾳ δὴ τῶν φύσεων τούτων τὸν θεὸν τακτέον; ἆρα οὐκ ἐν τῇ στασιμωτέρᾳ καὶ ἑδραιοτέρᾳ καὶ ἀπηλλαγμένῃ τοῦ ῥεύματος τούτου καὶ τῆς μεταβολῆς; τί γὰρ ἂν καὶ τῶν ὄντων σταίη, ὅτι μὴ τοῦ θεοῦ ἐπαφησαμένου τῆς ἐκείνου φύσεως; εἰ δέ σοι πρὸς τὸ πᾶν ὥσπερ τινὸς χειραγωγίας δεῖ, ἐφέπου[12]

[9] suppl. Reiske, Trapp

and comes to believe that nothing exists but what can be seen, heard, smelled, tasted, and touched.

"So, just as during a symposium, when the air is full of savory smells and the wine is being poured, as flutes, pipes, and lyres ring out, and incense burns, it would take a man of great fortitude, who could pull himself together and restrain himself, as he turns away his senses to a state of sobriety and order; in just the same way, amid the great clamor of the senses, it is difficult to find a sober intellect able to maintain its gaze on its own proper objects. Moreover, things that are perceptible, coming by nature in various forms, all jumbled together, and in constant flux, embroil the soul in all their various changes, so that when it turns to what is intelligible, whose nature is stable and firm, it is unable to discern it steadily because it is shaken by the pitching and turbulence, as commonly happens to those who step off a ship onto dry land: their bodies are barely able to stand, since they are still moving, spinning, and shaking from their habituation to the tossing waves.

8. "In which of these two realms,[21] then, should god be located? Must it not be in the one that is more stable and firm, and which is free from all that flux and change? For what existing thing could remain stable, without god upholding its nature? But if you need some kind of guidance in order to grasp the whole matter, then follow reason. It

[21] That is, perception or intellect.

---

[10] ἀποστρέψαντος Reiske, Trapp: ἀποστρέφοντος R
[11] suppl. Reiske
[12] Koniaris: ἔφη R: obel. Trapp

τῷ λόγῳ· ὁ δὲ ἡγήσεται, διαιρούμενος τὰς γνωριμωτάτας φύσεις δίχα καὶ τὴν ἑτέραν τὴν τιμιωτέραν τέμνων ἀεί, ἔστ᾽ ἂν ἐφίκηται τοῦ νῦν ζητουμένου.

"Τῶν ὄντων τοίνυν τὰ μὲν ἄψυχα, τὰ δὲ ἔμψυχα· καὶ τὰ μὲν ἄψυχα, λίθοι καὶ ξύλα καὶ ὅσα τοιαῦτα· τὰ δὲ ἔμψυχα, φυτὰ καὶ ζῷα· κρεῖττον δ᾽ ἔμψυχον ἀψύχου· τοῦ δ᾽ ἐμψύχου τὸ μὲν φυτικόν, τὸ δὲ αἰσθητικόν· τὸ <δὲ>[13] αἰσθητικὸν τοῦ φυτικοῦ κρεῖττον· τοῦ δὲ αἰσθητικοῦ τὸ μὲν λογικόν, τὸ δὲ ἄλογον· κρεῖττον δὲ τὸ λογικὸν τοῦ ἀλόγου· ἀλλὰ καὶ ἐν λογικῇ ψυχῇ, ἐπειδήπερ ἐστὶν ἡ πᾶσα ὥσπερ ἄθροισμά τι, θρεπτικόν, αὐξητικόν, κινητικόν, παθητικόν, νοητικόν· ὃν οὖν ἔχει λόγον τὸ ἄψυχον πρὸς τὸ ἔμψυχον, <τὸν αὐτὸν>[14] τοῦτον ἔχει καὶ ἡ ἔννους ψυχὴ {αὐτὸ τοῦτο}[15] πρὸς τὴν ὅλην ψυχήν· καὶ δῆλα δὴ ὡς κρεῖττον ἡ ἔννους ψυχὴ τῆς ἐξ ἁπάντων τούτων ἠθροισμένης.

"Ποῦ τοίνυν τούτων τὸν θεὸν τάττωμεν; πότερα ἐν τῷ ἀθροίσματι; ἀλλὰ εὐφημεῖν ἄξιον. λείπεται δὴ ὥσπερ εἰς ἀκρόπολιν ἀναβιβασαμένους τῷ λόγῳ τὸν θεὸν ἱδρῦσαι κατὰ τὸν νοῦν αὐ<τόν>,[16] τὸν ἀρχηγικώτατον· ἀλλὰ καὶ ἐνταῦθα διαφυὴν ὁρῶ· τοῦ γὰρ νοῦ ὁ μὲν νοεῖν πέφυκεν, καὶ μὴ νοῶν, ὁ δὲ καὶ νοεῖ· ἀλλὰ

[13] suppl. Schott, Trapp
[14] suppl. Acciaiolus, Trapp
[15] del. Acciaiolus, Trapp
[16] suppl. Reiske, Trapp: αὖ R

will lead you by dividing the most familiar realms into two parts, and then by repeatedly dividing the more important part in each case, until it arrives at the object of our present inquiry.[22]

"Accordingly, of all things that exist, some are inanimate, others animate. Inanimate are stones, sticks, and so forth; animate are plants and animals. Animate is superior to inanimate. Animate includes what is vegetative and perceptive, and perceptive is superior to vegetative. Perceptive includes rational and irrational, and rational is superior to irrational. However, even in a rational soul, there is a further distinction, since the entire soul is a kind of aggregate that includes nourishment, growth, mobility, emotion, and intellection. Therefore, the same relationship that exists between inanimate and animate holds as well between the intellective part of the soul and the soul as a whole, and it is obvious that the soul's intellective part is superior to the aggregate of all its other faculties.[23]

"In which of these, then, are we to locate god? In this aggregate? It is not worth discussing! Our only recourse is, so to speak, to take god up to the acropolis in our argument and situate him with the intellect itself, the highest ruling element. Yet here too I see a distinction. One kind of intellect is naturally capable of thinking, although it really does not think; the other one actually does think. And yet, even the latter one is still not perfect, unless you grant it the capacity to think of everything all the time—

[22] This procedure corresponds to Alcinous' "way of preeminence" (*hyperochē*) at *Didasc.* 10.165.27–34.

[23] Cf. Alcin. *Didasc.* 10.164.18–19: "intellect is superior to soul" (ψυχῆς νοῦς ἀμείνων).

*καὶ οὗτος οὔπω τέλειος, ἂν μὴ προσθῇς αὐτῷ τὸ καὶ νοεῖν ἀεὶ καὶ πάντα νοεῖν καὶ μὴ ἄλλοτε ἄλλα· ὥστε εἴη ἂν ἐντελέστατος ὁ νοῶν ἀεὶ καὶ πάντα καὶ ἅμα.*

9. "Εἰ δὲ βούλει, τῇδε εἴκαζέ μοι τὸ λεγόμενον· τὸν μὲν θεῖον νοῦν τῷ ὁρᾶν, τὸν δὲ ἀνθρώπινον τῷ λέγειν· ὀφθαλμοῦ μὲν γὰρ βολὴ ὀξύτατον, ἀθρόως σπῶσα τὴν αἴσθησιν τοῦ ὁρωμένου· λόγου δὲ ἐνέργεια ἔοικεν σχολαίῳ βαδίσματι. μᾶλλον δὲ ταύτῃ· εἰκαζέσθω ὁ μὲν θεῖος νοῦς κατὰ τὴν περιβολὴν τοῦ ἡλίου πάντα ἐφορῶντος τὸν ἐν γῇ τόπον ἀθρόως, ὁ δὲ ἀνθρώπινος κατὰ τὴν πορείαν αὐτοῦ, ἄλλοτε ἄλλα μέρη τοῦ ὅλου ἐπιπορευομένου."

Τοῦτον μὲν δὴ ὁ ἐξ Ἀκαδημίας ἡμῖν ἄγγελος δίδωσιν πατέρα καὶ γεννητὴν τοῦ ξύμπαντος· τούτου ὄνομα μὲν οὐ λέγει, οὐ γὰρ οἶδεν· οὐδὲ χρόαν λέγει, οὐ γὰρ εἶδεν· οὐδὲ μέγεθος λέγει, οὐ γὰρ ἥψατο· φύσεις αὗται, σαρκῶν καὶ ὀφθαλμῶν συνέσεις. τὸ δὲ θεῖον αὐτὸ ἀόρατον ὀφθαλμοῖς, ἄρρητον φωνῇ, ἀναφὲς σαρκί, ἀπευθὲς ἀκοῇ, μόνῳ δὲ τῷ τῆς ψυχῆς καλλίστῳ καὶ καθαρωτάτῳ καὶ νοερωτάτῳ καὶ κουφοτάτῳ καὶ πρεσβυτάτῳ ὁρατὸν δι' ὁμοιότητα καὶ ἀκουστὸν

---

24 Cf. Alcin. *Didasc.* 10.164.19–20 of the actualized intellect, "which cognizes everything simultaneously and eternally" (trans. Dillon).

25 The following corresponds to Alcinous' "way of analogy" (*analogia*) at *Didasc.* 10.165.20–26.

not just of different things at different times. Thus the most perfect intellect would be that which thinks of all things all the time and all of them simultaneously.[24]

9. "If you are willing, make the following comparison to illustrate what I am saying:[25] the divine intellect is like seeing, the human intellect like speaking. The emission of light from the eye is extremely swift, and takes in the sensation of the visible object all at once, whereas the operation of speech is like a leisurely stroll. Better still, compare the divine intellect to the encirclement by the sun, as it beholds the entire surface of the earth all at once, and the human intellect to the sun's journey, as it passes over different parts of the whole at different times."[26]

It is in fact this intellect that our messenger from the Academy[27] informs us is "the father and begetter of all."[28] He does not tell us its name,[29] for he does not know what it is. He does not tell us its color, for he has not seen it. He does not tell us its size, because he has not touched it. These are physical attributes comprehended by our flesh and eyes. Divinity itself cannot be seen by eyes, spoken of by voice, touched by flesh, or heard by ears, but it can be seen only by the most beautiful, purest, most intelligent, most subtle, and most venerable aspect of the soul because of their similar nature, and heard because of their

[26] The difference between the divine and human intellect is also treated at *Or*. 13.2–3. [27] Plato.

[28] A version of Pl. *Ti*. 28c: "the maker and father" and of *Ti*. 41a: "creator and father." Variations of this famous formulation appear in §12 below and in *Orr*. 2.10 and 41.2.

[29] The following corresponds to Alcinous' "way of negation" (*aphairesis*) at *Didasc*. 10.165.16–19.

διὰ συγγένειαν, {ὅλον}[17] ἀθρόον ἀθρόᾳ συνέσει παραγινόμενον. ὥσπερ οὖν εἴ τις ἐπιθυμεῖ ἰδεῖν τὸν ἥλιον, οὐχὶ ταῖς ἀκοαῖς θηρᾶται αὐτοῦ σύνεσιν· οὐδὲ εἴ τις τῆς ἐν φωναῖς ἁρμονίας ἐρᾷ, τοῖς ὀφθαλμοῖς αὐτὴν μεταδιώκει· ἀλλ' ὄψις μὲν ἐρᾷ χρωμάτων, ἀκοὴ δὲ ἀκουστῶν· οὕτω καὶ νοῦς νοητὰ ὁρᾷ καὶ νοητῶν ἀκούει.

10. Τοῦτ' ἔστιν ἀμέλει τὸ τοῦ Συρακοσίου αἴνιγμα,

νοῦς ὁρῇ καὶ νοῦς ἀκούει.

πῶς οὖν ὁρᾷ νοῦς, καὶ πῶς ἀκούει; ὀρθῇ τῇ ψυχῇ καὶ ἐρρωμένῃ, πρὸς τὸ ἀκήρατον ἐκεῖνο φῶς ἀντιβλέπων καὶ μὴ σκοτοδινιῶν μηδὲ εἰς γῆν καταφερόμενος· ἀλλὰ ἀποφράττων μὲν {καὶ}[18] τὰ ὦτα, ἀποστρέφων δὲ τὰς ὄψεις καὶ τὰς ἄλλας αἰσθήσεις ἔμπαλιν πρὸς ἑαυτόν, καὶ ἐκλαθόμενος μὲν τῶν κάτω οἰμωγῶν καὶ στόνων καὶ ἡδονῶν καὶ δοξῶν καὶ τιμῆς καὶ ἀτιμίας, ἐπιτρέψας δὲ τὴν ἡγεμονίαν αὐτοῦ λόγῳ ἀληθεῖ καὶ ἔρωτι ἐρρωμένῳ, τῷ μὲν λόγῳ φράζοντι ᾗ χρὴ ἰέναι, τῷ δὲ ἔρωτι ἐφισταμένῳ καὶ τοὺς πόνους τῆς πορείας πειθοῖ καὶ χάρισιν ἐπελαφρύνοντι· ἰόντι δὲ ἐκεῖσε καὶ ἀφισταμένῳ τῶν κάτω, ἀεὶ τὰ πρόσθεν σαφῆ καὶ εὐλαμπέστατα[19] καὶ τὴν τοῦ θεοῦ φύσιν προοιμιαζόμενα· καὶ πορευόμενος μὲν ἀκούει τὴν φύσιν τοῦ θεοῦ, ἀνελθὼν δὲ ὁρᾷ. τέλος δὲ τῆς ὁδοῦ οὐχ ὁ οὐρανὸς

[17] del. Trapp [18] del. Markland, Trapp
[19] εὐλαμπέστατα R: εὐλαμπέστερα Russell, Trapp

close kinship, when it is wholly accessible to an all-inclusive act of comprehension. So, just as anyone who desires to see the sun does not seek to comprehend it with his ears, or anyone who longs for harmonious sounds does not pursue them with his eyes—for sight longs for colors and hearing longs for sounds—just so, the intellect both "sees" and "hears" what is intelligible.

10. This is precisely the point of the Syracusan's riddle:

> intellect sees and intellect hears.[30]

How then does the intellect see, and how does it hear? It is by having an upright and strong soul, and by gazing straight at that pure light and not becoming dizzy, nor being drawn back down to earth, but by stopping up its ears, and turning its eyes and the other senses back into itself, and by forgetting all the wailing and groaning, pleasures and fancies, honors and dishonors down below, and turning over its guidance to true reason and powerful eros, with reason showing where it ought to go, and with eros on hand lightening the hardships of the journey with its persuasive charms. As the intellect ascends there and distances itself from things down below, the clear and perfect brilliance that lies ever ahead of it serves as a prelude to the nature of god. On its way, it hears of god's nature; upon completing its ascent, it sees it. But the end of the journey is not the heavens nor the heavenly bodies. For although

[30] Epicharmus, early fifth-century BC comic playwright, fr. B 12 D-K, quoted at Plut. *Alex. Fort.* 336b, etc.

οὐδὲ τὰ ἐν τῷ οὐρανῷ σώματα· καλὰ μὲν γὰρ ταῦτα καὶ θεσπέσια, ἅτε ἐκείνου ἔγγονα ἀκριβῆ καὶ γνήσια καὶ πρὸς τὸ κάλλιστον ἡρμοσμένα· ἀλλὰ καὶ τούτων ἐπέκεινα ἐλθεῖν δεῖ καὶ ὑπερκύψαι τοῦ οὐρανοῦ ἐπὶ τὸν ἀληθῆ τόπον καὶ τὴν ἐκεῖ γαλήνην,

ἔνθ' οὐκ ἔστ' οὔτ' ἂρ χειμὼν πολύς, οὐδέ ποτ' ὄμβρῳ
δεύεται,

ἀλλὰ μάλ' αἴθρη
πέπταται ἀννέφελος, λευκὴ δ' ἐπιδέδρομεν αἴγλη,

μηδενὸς ἐνοχλοῦντος τὴν θέαν πάθους σαρκίνου, οἷα δεῦρο ἐνοχλεῖ τὴν δειλαίαν ψυχήν, ὅσον αὐτῇ τοῦ φρονεῖν ἔνεστιν ὑπὸ τοῦ κυκηθμοῦ καὶ τοῦ θορύβου καταβάλλοντα. πῶς γὰρ ἄν τις συνείη θεοῦ[20] ὑπὸ πλήθους ἐπιθυμιῶν καὶ λογισμῶν ἀλλοκότων ταραττόμενος; οὐ μᾶλλον <ἢ> ἐν δημοκρατίᾳ πολυφώνῳ καὶ συντεταραγμένῃ συνείη ἄν τις νόμου καὶ ἄρχοντος·

ἀνδρῶν δὲ ἐν πολλῷ ὁμάδῳ πῶς κέν τις ἀκούσαι;

καταπεσοῦσα γὰρ ἡ ψυχὴ εἰς τουτονὶ τὸν θόρυβον καὶ δοῦσα ἑαυτὴν ἐπ' ἀμηχάνου φορεῖσαι κύματος, νήχεται δυσέκνευστον πέλαγος, ἐστ' ἂν αὐτὴν φιλοσοφία ὑποδέξηται ὑποβαλοῦσα τοὺς ἑαυτῆς λογισμούς, ὥσπερ τὸ κρήδεμνον τῷ Ὀδυσσεῖ ἡ Λευκοθέα.

[20] θεοῦ Markland, Trapp: θεὸν R

they are indeed beautiful and wondrous, since they are god's true and legitimate offspring and are in harmony with what is most beautiful, yet the intellect must go beyond even these and pass beyond the heavens to that realm of truth where tranquility reigns,

> where there are no heavy storms, and rainfall never drenches it,
>
> but cloudless skies
> spread all around, flooded with bright radiance,[31]

where no sensations of the flesh disturb its vision, like those that trouble the wretched soul here on earth, tearing down whatever ability to think it possesses with their noise and confusion. For how could anyone perceive god when being buffeted by a multitude of unseemly desires and thoughts? No more than someone in a raucous and disorderly democracy could hear the voice of law and authority:

> and how can anyone hear in this great din of men?[32]

For when the soul falls into this tumult and lets itself be carried on an overpowering wave, it swims in deep waters with no escape in sight, until Philosophy takes it in hand and supports it with her arguments, as Leucothea buoyed up Odysseus with her veil.[33]

31 An adaptation of *Od.* 4.566 (describing the Elysian Field) and 6.43–45 (describing Olympus), also quoted at *Or.* 30.4.

32 *Il.* 19.81, Agamemnon speaking.

33 *Od.* 5.333–53.

11. Πῶς ἂν οὖν τις ἐκνήξαιτ᾽ ἂν καὶ ἴδοι τὸν θεόν; τὸ μὲν ὅλον, ὄψει τότε, ἐπειδὰν πρὸς αὑτὸν καλῇ· καλέσει δὲ οὐκ εἰς μακράν· ἀνάμεινον τὴν κλῆσιν. ἥξει σοι γῆρας ὁδηγοῦν ἐκεῖ, καὶ θάνατος, ὃν ὁ μὲν δειλὸς ὀδύρεται καὶ προσιόντα δέδιεν, ὁ δὲ ἐραστὴς τοῦ θεοῦ ἐκδέχεται ἄσμενος, καὶ προσιόντος θαρσεῖ. εἰ δὲ καὶ νῦν ἤδη μαθεῖν ἐρᾷς τὴν ἐκείνου φύσιν, πῶς τις αὐτὴν διηγήσεται; καλὸν μὲν γὰρ εἶναι τὸν θεὸν καὶ τῶν καλῶν τὸ φανότατον· ἀλλ᾽ οὐ σῶμα καλόν, ἀλλ᾽ ὅθεν καὶ τῷ σώματι ἐπιρρεῖ τὸ κάλλος· οὐδὲ λειμῶνα καλόν, ἀλλ᾽ ὅθεν καὶ ὁ λειμὼν καλός· καὶ ποταμοῦ κάλλος καὶ θαλάττης καὶ οὐρανοῦ καὶ τῶν ἐν οὐρανῷ θεῶν, πᾶν τὸ κάλλος τοῦτο ἐκεῖθεν ῥεῖ, οἷον[21] ἐκ πηγῆς ἀενάου καὶ ἀκηράτου· καθόσον δὲ αὐτοῦ μετέσχεν ἕκαστα, καλὰ καὶ ἑδραῖα καὶ σωζόμενα, καὶ καθόσον αὐτοῦ ἀπολείπεται, αἰσχρὰ καὶ διαλυόμενα καὶ φθειρόμενα.

Εἰ μὲν ταῦτα ἱκανά, ἑώρακας τὸν θεόν· εἰ δὲ μή, πῶς τις αὐτὸν αἰνίξηται; ἐννόει γάρ μοι μήτε μέγεθος μήτε χρῶμα μήτε σχῆμα μήτε ἄλλο τι ὕλης πάθος, ἀλλ᾽ ὥσπερ ἂν εἰ καὶ σῶμα καλὸν ἀπεκρύπτετο πρὸς τὴν θέαν ὑπὸ ἐσθήτων πολλῶν καὶ ποικίλων, ἀπέδυσεν αὐτὸ ἐραστὴς ἵνα ἴδῃ σαφῶς, οὕτω καὶ νῦν ἀπόδυσον καὶ ἄφελε τῷ λόγῳ τὴν περιβολὴν ταύτην καὶ τὴν ἀσχολίαν τῶν ὀφθαλμῶν, καὶ τὸ καταλειπόμενον ὄψει, αὐτὸ ἐκεῖνο οἷον ποθεῖς.

21 ῥεῖ, οἷον Reiske: ῥεῖ, ὃν R: ῥεῖν Russell, Trapp

11. How then can anyone swim to safety and see god? In a word, you will see him when he calls you to him. He will call before long, so await his summons. Old age will come and lead you there, as will death, which cowards lament and whose approach they fear, whereas the lover of god awaits death gladly and faces its approach with confidence. But if you still long to learn of god's nature right now, how can anyone explain it? For although god is beautiful, and is the most splendid of all beautiful things, he is not a beautiful body, but rather he is the source of the beauty that flows into that body. Nor is he a beautiful meadow, but the source of the meadow's beauty. The beauty of a river, of the sea, of the heavens, and of the celestial gods—all this beauty flows from him as from a pure and ever-flowing source.[34] To the extent that individual things have a share of it, they are beautiful, stable, and secure; but to the extent that they lack it, they are ugly and subject to degeneration and destruction.

So, if this account suffices, then you have seen god; but if not, how might one intimate his nature? Please do not imagine his size, color, form, or any other attribute of matter. Instead, just as when a beautiful body is hidden from view by many layers of fancy clothing, and a lover removes the clothing so as to see it clearly, so now too you should use reason to strip off and remove this covering that obstructs your vision, and you will see what remains, namely the very thing for which you yearn.

[34] For the descent of Beauty into the physical world, see *Or.* 21.7–8.

12. Εἰ δὲ ἐξασθενεῖς πρὸς τὴν τοῦ πατρὸς καὶ δημιουργοῦ θέαν, ἀρκεῖ σοι τὰ ἔργα ἐν τῷ παρόντι ὁρᾶν καὶ προσκυνεῖν τὰ ἔγγονα, πολλὰ καὶ παντοδαπὰ ὄντα, οὐχ ὅσα Βοιώτιος ποιητὴς λέγει· οὐ γὰρ τρισμύριοι μόνον θεοί, θεοῦ παῖδες καὶ φίλοι, ἀλλ' ἄληπτοι ἀριθμῷ· τοῦτο μὲν κατ' οὐρανὸν αἱ ἀστέρων φύσεις· τοῦτο δ' αὖ κατ' αἰθέρα αἱ δαιμόνων οὐσίαι.

Βούλομαι δέ σοι δεῖξαι τὸ λεγόμενον σαφεστέρᾳ εἰκόνι. ἐννόει μεγάλην ἀρχὴν καὶ βασιλείαν ἐρρωμένην, πρὸς μίαν ψυχὴν βασιλέως τοῦ ἀρίστου καὶ πρεσβυτάτου συμπάντων νενευκότων ἑκόντων· ὅρον δὲ τῆς ἀρχῆς οὐχ Ἅλυν ποταμὸν οὐδὲ Ἑλλήσποντον οὐδὲ τὴν Μαιῶτιν οὐδὲ τὰς ἐπὶ τῷ Ὠκεανῷ ἠϊόνας· ἀλλὰ οὐρανὸν καὶ γῆν, τὸν μὲν ὑψοῦ, τὴν δ' ἔνερθεν· οὐρανὸν μὲν οἷον τεῖχός τι ἐληλαμένον ἐν κύκλῳ ἄρρηκτον, πάντα χρήματα ἐν ἑαυτῷ στέγον, γῆν δὲ οἷον φρουρὰν καὶ δεσμοὺς ἀλιτρῶν σωμάτων, βασιλέα δὲ αὐτὸν δὴ τὸν μέγαν ἀτρεμοῦντα ὥσπερ νόμον, παρέχοντα τοῖς πειθομένοις σωτηρίαν ὑπάρχουσαν ἐν αὐτῷ· καὶ κοινωνοὺς τῆς ἀρχῆς πολλοὺς μὲν ὁρατοὺς θεούς, πολλοὺς δὲ ἀφανεῖς, τοὺς μὲν περὶ τὰ πρόθυρα αὐτὰ εἱλουμένους, οἷον εἰσαγγελέας τινὰς καὶ βασιλεῖ συγγενεστάτους, ὁμοτραπέζους αὐτοῦ καὶ συνεστίους, τοὺς δὲ τούτων ὑπηρέτας, τοὺς δὲ ἔτι τούτων καταδεεστέρους. διαδοχὴν ὁρᾷς καὶ τάξιν ἀρχῆς καταβαίνουσαν ἐκ τοῦ θεοῦ μέχρι γῆς.

12. But if you are not strong enough to see "the father and creator,"[35] at least for the present you can be satisfied with looking upon his works and worshiping his many and various offspring, who are more numerous than the Boeotian poet claims,[36] for there are not just thirty thousand divine beings that are the children and intimates of god, but an incalculable number—not only celestial bodies in the heavens, but also *daimones* in the ether.

I wish to illustrate my argument with a clearer analogy. Imagine a great empire and mighty kingdom, where all the inhabitants willingly bow down to one soul belonging to the best and most venerable king. The boundary of that realm is not the Halys River, the Hellespont, the Maeotis lake, or the shores of the Ocean, but the heavens above and the earth below. The sky is like a circular and impenetrable wall that encloses and protects everything within it, whereas the earth is like a guard post[37] and prison for sinful bodies. The great king himself remains motionless and, like the law, bestows his inherent protection on his subjects. Sharing in his reign are many gods, both visible and invisible. Some gather around the very doors of his chambers, like a king's attendants and close relatives who live and dine with him; others are their subordinates, and still others are beneath them. This is the chain of command and the hierarchy you can see descending from god to earth.

35 An echo of Pl. *Ti.* 41a; see §9 above.

36 Hes. *Op.* 252–53: "Thirty thousand are Zeus' immortal guardians of mortal men."

37 The image of the guard post derives from Pl. *Phd.* 62b.

# *ORATION* 12

## INTRODUCTION

The Platonic basis of the oration is that the good man never returns wrong for wrong.[1] It opens with a quotation from an unidentified poem by Pindar that appears to question whether deceit is as effective as justice,[2] a notion an ethical person must reject (§1). Would a just person, if wronged, choose to retaliate in kind? No, because doing wrong and being wronged are different acts altogether and cannot be attributed to the same individual (§2). Is then wrongdoing to be attributed to a bad person and being wronged to a good one? No, because wrongdoing requires removing some good, and since the only good is virtue, which is inalienable, it cannot be taken away. Then too a bad man cannot be wronged because he has nothing good, namely virtue, that can be taken away (§3). Perhaps, then, wrongdoing must be attributed to the corrupt intention of the perpetrator, as it is in law, when an unsuccess-

[1] Cf. *Cri.* 49b: "Nor should one return wrong (ἀνταδικεῖν) when wronged (ἀδικούμενον), since one should never do wrong (ἀδικεῖν)."

[2] The only citation of this fragment before Maximus is at Pl. *Resp.* 2.365b, where it also serves as a springboard to a discussion of the nature of justice.

ful attempt is still punishable. If so, the good man, who never intends to do wrong, cannot do wrong, whereas the bad man may commit wrong because of his wickedness (§4). When a bad man attempts to wrong a good man, the good man cannot wrong him in return, because the bad man has nothing good to be taken away. Furthermore, whoever retaliates puts himself on the same low level as the perpetrator (§5).

Retaliation creates an endless succession of wrongdoing, all in the name of perverted justice, since vengeance is a pretext for further acts of vengeance, as exemplified by the series of abductions leading up to the Trojan War and by the many disasters suffered by Greeks in the Peloponnesian and Theban wars (§§6–7). On an individual level, Socrates did not retaliate against his accusers because he understood that a good man cannot be harmed by a bad one, a principle that is the very essence of justice. Like a spreading disease, vengeance unchecked destroys families and devastates nations (§8). In fact, the one who retaliates is even worse than the perpetrator, because he absolves the other of blame for having acted first and engages in an unequal competition that only sullies him, since it is conducted under unfair rules (§9). A just and good man may indeed be mistreated, even condemned to die, but like Socrates, would laugh at people's childish attempts to harm him and would bear them no resentment (§10).

# *ORATION* 12

Εἰ τὸν ἀδικήσαντα ἀνταδικητέον

1. Πότερον δίκα[1] τεῖχος ὕψιον,
ἢ σκολιαῖς ἀπάταις ἀναβαίνει
ἐπιχθόνιον γένος ἀνθρώπων,
δίχα μοι νόος ἀτρέκειαν εἰπεῖν.

σὺ μέν, ὦ Πίνδαρε, ἀμφισβητεῖς πρὸς ἑαυτὸν περὶ ἀπάτης καὶ δίκης, παραβάλλων χρυσὸν χαλκῷ· ποιητὴς γὰρ ἦσθα καὶ δεινὸς ᾠδὴν συντιθέναι χορῷ καὶ τυράννοις ποιεῖν ἐπινίκια ᾄσματα, καί σοι ἐμέλησεν ὀνομάτων μέτρου καὶ ἁρμονίας μελῶν καὶ ῥυθμοῦ σχημάτων· ἀνδρὶ δὲ ὅτῳ χορὸς μὲν καὶ ᾠδὴ καὶ ἡ ἐκ μελῶν ἡδονὴ χώραν ἔχει ὅσηνπερ καὶ τοῖς παισὶν τὰ ἀθύρματα, μέλει δὲ αὐτῷ μέτρου ψυχῆς καὶ ῥυθμοῦ καὶ μέλους, καὶ σχήματος τοῦ περὶ τὰς πράξεις καὶ τὸν ἄλλον βίον, οὐδ' ἂν τὴν ἀρχὴν εἰς νοῦν ἔλθοι τουτὶ τὸ ἀπόρημα

πότερον δίκα τεῖχος ὕψιον

[1] δίκα R: δίκᾳ Plato, *Resp.* 2.365b et alii

# *ORATION* 12

## Whether a wrongdoer should be wronged in return

1. Whether justice is a higher wall,
or if the earthly race of men
scale it by crooked deceit,
my mind is divided in telling precisely.[1]

O Pindar, in debating with yourself about deceit and justice, you are comparing gold to bronze. You were indeed a skillful poet in composing odes for choruses and victory songs for tyrants, and you took great care with the meter of words, musical harmonies, and rhythmical arrangements. But for a man who finds choruses, odes, and pleasant songs equivalent to children's toys, and who cares instead for the meter, rhythm, and melody of his soul, and for the proper arrangement of his actions and of his life in general, the question,

Whether justice is a higher wall,

[1] Pind. fr. 213 Maehler. Manuscript R has δίκα in the nominative, whereas Plato and most other citations have the dative. At Pl. *Resp.* 2.365b, Adeimantus embeds the first two lines in a question: "Whether by justice or by crooked deceit I should ascend the higher wall and thus fortify myself for the rest of my life." Maximus' version is grammatically difficult and its precise meaning is in doubt.

ἢ μή· ἀλλ᾽ οὑτωσὶ φαίη ἂν μεταβαλὼν τὸ ᾆσμα τὸ σόν, ὅτι

> καὶ δίκα τεῖχος ὕψιον
> καὶ σκολιαῖς ἀπάταις ἀναβαίνει
> ἐπιχθόνιον γένος ἀνθρώπων,

ἀλλ᾽ ἀπρόσβατόν τι χρῆμα τῇ ἀπάτῃ ἡ δίκη, ὥσπερ τοῖς Ἀλωείδαις ὁ οὐρανός, καὶ ὤνησεν αὐτοὺς οὐδὲν ἡ Ὄσσα ἐπιτεθεῖσα τῷ Ὀλύμπῳ καὶ ὁ Ὄλυμπος τῷ Πηλίῳ, ἀλλὰ ἀπεῖχον τοῦ οὐρανοῦ ὅσον ἀπέχει ἀπάτη δίκης. οὐκοῦν τῶν μὲν ἀγαθῶν ἡ δίκη, τῶν δὲ μοχθηρῶν ἡ ἀπάτη· καὶ δόκιμον μὲν ἡ δίκη, κίβδηλον δέ τι ἡ ἀπάτη· καὶ ἰσχυρὸν μὲν ἡ δίκη, ἀσθενὲς δὲ ἡ ἀπάτη· καὶ τὸ μὲν ὠφέλιμον, τὸ δὲ οὔ.

2. Ὅτῳ δὴ μέλει δίκης καὶ περιβέβληται τουτὶ τὸ Πινδάρου τειχίον, οὗτος ἕλοιτο ἄν ποτε ἀδικηθεὶς ἀμύνασθαι ἐκ τῆς ἴσης; φέρε ἴδω τί καὶ λέγω· μὴ γὰρ οὐδὲ ἀδικεῖσθαι αὐτῷ θέμις ᾖ. εἰ μὲν γὰρ τὸ ἀδικεῖν καὶ τὸ ἀδικεῖσθαι τοιοῦτόν ἐστιν ὁποῖον τὸ τύπτειν καὶ τύπτεσθαι καὶ τέμνειν καὶ τέμνεσθαι, οὐδὲν δεινὸν τὸν αὐτὸν καὶ δραστικὸν ὁμοῦ εἶναι ἀδικίας καὶ παθητικόν· εἰ δ᾽ ἐνταῦθα ὁ αὐτὸς μὲν τῇ κοινότητι τῆς φύσεως ἐνέργειαν καὶ πάθος, ἑκάτερον αὐτῶν, καταδέχεται, ἔοικεν δὲ τὸ ἀδικεῖν καὶ ἀδικεῖσθαι πολὺ μᾶλλον τῷ ὁρᾶν καὶ ὁρᾶσθαι· ὁ<ρᾶται>[2] μὲν γὰρ τὸ μετέχον ὄψεως, τὸ δὲ ὁρώμενον οὐ πάντως καὶ ὁρᾷ·

[2] suppl. Davies[2], Dübner, Trapp

or not, would not have occurred to him in the first place. He might instead rephrase your poem this way:

> justice is indeed a higher wall,
> and also with crooked deceit
> the earthly race of men scale it,

but he would insist that justice is something as inaccessible to deceit as heaven was to the Aloidae,[2] whose piling of Ossa on Olympus and Olympus on Pelion did them no good, for they remained as far from heaven as deceit remains from justice. So it is that justice belongs to what is good, whereas deceit belongs to what is wicked; justice is genuine, whereas deceit is counterfeit; justice is strong, deceit weak; the one is beneficial, the other not.

2. Would then the man who truly cares about justice and is protected by this wall of Pindar's ever choose, if wronged, to retaliate in kind? But let me consider what I am actually saying, since perhaps it is not even permitted for him to be wronged at all. For if doing wrong and being wronged are like hitting and being hit, or cutting and being cut, then it is not surprising that the same person can both inflict and suffer a wrongful act. But although in these examples the same person is the agent and recipient of each action because these actions share the same nature, in fact wronging and being wronged are much more like seeing and being seen: what possesses sight can also be seen, but what is seen does not in all cases also see. Or

[2] Otus and Ephialtes, sons of Poseidon who tried to scale heaven by piling up these mountains.

*μᾶλλον οὑτωσὶ λέγωμεν, ὅτι ἔοικεν τὸ <ἀδικεῖν καὶ>*[3] *ἀδικεῖσθαι τῷ ἐλέγχειν καὶ ἐλέγχεσθαι· ἐλέγχει μὲν γὰρ ὁ τὸ ἀληθὲς εἰδώς, ἐλέγχεται δὲ ὁ ἀγνοῶν· καὶ ὡς οὐκ ἂν εἴη οὔτε τοῦ τἀληθὲς εἰδότος τὸ <ἐλέγχεσθαι, οὔτε τοῦ ἀγνοοῦντος τὸ>*[4] *ἐλέγχειν, οὕτως οὐδὲ τὸ ἀδικεῖν εἴη ἂν καὶ τὸ ἀδικεῖσθαι τοῦ αὐτοῦ.*

3. *Ἐπεὶ τοίνυν οὐ τοῦ αὐτοῦ ἀλλ' ἑτέρου, ὁ δὲ χρηστὸς τῷ πονηρῷ οὐχ ὁ αὐτός, ποτέρῳ πότερον προσθήσομεν; ἆρα τὸ μὲν ἀδικεῖν τῷ πονηρῷ, τὸ δὲ ἀδικεῖσθαι τῷ χρηστῷ; ἢ τὸ μὲν ἀδικεῖν τοῦ μοχθηροῦ, τὸ δὲ ἀδικεῖσθαι οὔπω δῆλον ὁποτέρου αὐτοῖν; οὑτωσὶ δὲ θεασώμεθα.*

*Ἀδικία ἐστὶν ἀφαίρεσις ἀγαθοῦ· τὸ δὲ ἀγαθὸν τί ἂν εἴη ἄλλο ἢ ἀρετή; ἡ δὲ ἀρετὴ ἀναφαίρετον. οὐκ ἀδικηθήσεται τοίνυν ὁ τὴν ἀρετὴν ἔχων, ἢ οὐκ ἔστιν ἀδικία ἀφαίρεσις ἀγαθοῦ· οὐδὲν γὰρ ἀγαθὸν ἀφαιρετόν, οὐδὲ ἀποβλητὸν οὐδὲ ἑλετὸν οὐδὲ ληϊστόν. εἶεν· οὐκ ἀδικεῖται ὁ χρηστὸς οὔτε ὑπὸ <τοῦ χρηστοῦ οὔτε ὑπὸ>*[5] *τοῦ μοχθηροῦ· ἀναφαίρετος γὰρ <ἡ ἀρετὴ αὐτοῦ>.*[6] *λείπεται τοίνυν ἢ μηδένα ἀδικεῖσθαι καθάπαξ ἢ τὸν μοχθηρὸν ὑπὸ τοῦ ὁμοίου· ἀλλὰ τῷ μοχθηρῷ οὐδενὸς μέτεστιν ἀγαθοῦ, ἡ δὲ ἀδικία ἦν ἀγαθοῦ*

[3] suppl. Acciaiolus, edd.
[4] suppl. Acciaiolus, edd.
[5] suppl. Trapp
[6] suppl. Heinsius

rather let us put it this way: wronging and being wronged are like refuting someone else and being refuted oneself. The one who refutes knows the truth, whereas the one being refuted does not know it. And so, just as neither the one knowing the truth could be refuted, nor the one not knowing it could refute someone else, in the same way doing wrong and being wronged could not be attributed to the same individual.

3. Now, since these two actions cannot be attributed to the same person, but to different ones, and since a good man and a bad man are not identical, which attribute should we assign to which individual? Should we attribute doing wrong to the bad person and being wronged to the good one? Or should we say that doing wrong certainly applies to the bad person, but that it is not yet clear to which of them being wronged applies? Let us look at it this way.

Wrongdoing is the removal of good. But what else could the good be but virtue, which itself is inalienable? Therefore either a person in possession of virtue will never suffer wrongdoing, or else wrongdoing is not the removal of good, for nothing good can be removed, "thrown away,"[3] "seized, or plundered."[4] Therefore the good man cannot be wronged either by <a good man or by a bad man>, because <his virtue> is inalienable. We are therefore left with this conclusion: either no one can be wronged at all, or else only a bad person by another like himself. However, the bad person has no share of any good, whereas wrongdoing was shown to be the removal of good. What-

[3] *Il.* 3.65, Paris speaking of the gods' gifts.

[4] *Il.* 9.408–9, Achilles speaking of one's life.

ἀφαίρεσις· ὁ δὲ μὴ ἔχων ὅ τι {μὴ}[7] ἀφαιρεθῇ, οὐδὲ εἰς ὅ τι ἀδικηθῇ ἔχει.

4. Μήποτε οὖν οὐ κατὰ τὴν ἀφαίρεσιν τοῦ πάσχοντος ἡ ἀδικία τέτακται, ἀλλὰ κατὰ τὴν γνώμην τοῦ δράσαντος· καὶ ὁ μοχθηρὸς ὑπὸ τοῦ μοχθηροῦ ἀδικεῖται, κἂν μὴ ἔχῃ τὸ ἀγαθόν, καὶ ὁ χρηστὸς ὑπὸ τοῦ μοχθηροῦ, κἂν ἔχῃ ἀναφαίρετον τὸ ἀγαθόν. ἀποδέχομαι τοῦ λόγου τῆς γνώμης τῷ ἡμαρτημένῳ προστιθέντος τὴν ἀδικίαν μᾶλλον ἢ τῷ ἐπιτυχεῖ τοῦ ἔργου· καὶ γὰρ μοιχὸν κολάζει ὁ νόμος οὐ τὸν δράσαντα μόνον ἀλλὰ καὶ τὸν βουληθέντα, καὶ τοιχώρυχον τὸν ἐπιχειρήσαντα, κἂν μὴ λάβῃ,[8] καὶ προδότην τὸν μελλήσαντα, κἂν μὴ πράξῃ.

Ἥξει τοίνυν ὁ σύμπας λόγος εἰς τὸ δέον. ὁ μὲν γὰρ ἀγαθὸς οὔτε ἀδικεῖ οὔτε ἀδικεῖται· οὐκ ἀδικεῖ μὲν διὰ τὴν βούλησιν, οὐκ ἀδικεῖται δὲ διὰ τὴν ἀρετήν. ὁ δὲ μοχθηρὸς ἀδικεῖ μέν, οὐκ ἀδικεῖται δέ· ἀδικεῖ μὲν διὰ μοχθηρίαν, <οὐκ ἀδικεῖται δὲ δι' ἀπουσίαν>[9] ἀγαθοῦ. ἔτι τοίνυν, εἰ μὲν ἀγαθὸν ἀρετὴ μόνον καὶ οὐκ ἄλλο τι, ὁ μοχθηρὸς τὴν ἀρετὴν οὐκ ἔχων οὐδ' εἰς ὅ τι ἀδικηθῇ ἔχει· εἰ δὲ πρὸς τῇ ἀρετῇ καὶ ταυτὶ ἀγαθά, τὰ περὶ σῶμα καὶ τὴν ἐκτὸς τύχην καὶ περιβολήν, ἀρετῆς μὴ παρούσης βέλτιον ἀπεῖναι ταῦτα ἢ μή· ὥστε οὐδ' ὣς ἀδικηθείη ἂν ὁ μοχθηρός, ἀφαιρούμενός

[7] del. Stephanus, Trapp
[8] λάβῃ Meiser, Trapp: φθάσῃ Markland, Dübner: λάθῃ R
[9] suppl. Schenkl, Hobein, Trapp, Koniaris

ever someone does not possess cannot be taken away from him, so he has nothing in which to be wronged.

4. Perhaps then wrongdoing is not defined by the removal of anything from the victim, but by the intention of the perpetrator. A bad person may then be wronged by another bad person, even if he does not possess the good, and a good man by a bad man, even if he possesses the good that is inalienable.[5] I accept this account that attributes wrongdoing to the corrupt nature of the intention rather than to the success of the attempt. For example, the law punishes an adulterer not only for committing the act, but also for intending to do so; the housebreaker for making the attempt, even if he does not take anything; and the would-be betrayer, even if he does not carry it out.

The whole argument, then, will come down to this necessary conclusion: the good man neither commits wrong nor suffers wrong. He does no wrong because he does not intend to; he does not suffer wrong because his virtue is inalienable. The bad man can indeed do wrong, but he cannot suffer wrong: he commits wrong because of his wickedness, but he does not suffer wrong through loss of any good. Furthermore, if virtue is the one and only good, then because the bad man does not possess virtue, he has nothing in which he can suffer wrong. But if in addition to virtue there are these other goods, namely physical attributes, external fortune, and surrounding circumstances, then without virtue these would be better absent than present, so that not even then would the bad man suffer wrong for being deprived of any of these assets that he in

[5] That is, virtue.

τι τούτων οἷς χρῆται κακῶς. οὐκοῦν ἀδικεῖ μέν, οὐκ ἀδικεῖται δέ, προστιθέντων ἡμῶν τῇ βουλήσει τὸ ἄδικον.

5. Οὕτως ἐρῶ <περὶ> πονερῶ<ν> νῦν·[10] βούλεται μὲν ὁ μοχθηρὸς ἀδικεῖν, οὐ μὴν δυνατός. βουλόμενος δέ, ἢ πρὸς τὸν ὅμοιον ἀποτείνεται ἢ πρὸς τὸν κρείττονα. τί δὲ τῷ κρείττονι δραστέον; ἢ ἀνταδικητέον τὸν μοχθηρόν; καὶ μὴν εἰς ὅ τι ἀδικηθῇ οὐκ {ἀδικῇ ὅτι οὐκ}[11] ἔχει· ἀπουσίᾳ γὰρ ἀγαθοῦ μοχθηρός ἐστιν. οὔτ᾽ οὖν κατὰ τὸ ἔργον ἀνταδικήσει ὁ νοῦν ἔχων τὸν μοχθηρόν, οὐ γὰρ ἔχει εἰς ὅ τι ἀδικηθήσεται, οὔτε κατὰ τὴν βούλησιν, οὐ γὰρ ἐθέλει ἀδικεῖν χρηστὸς ὤν, οὐ μᾶλλον ἢ αὐλητικὸς παρὰ μέλος αὐλεῖν.

Καθόλου δέ, εἰ τὸ ἀδικεῖν πονηρόν, καὶ τὸ ἀνταδικεῖν ὅμοιον· οὐ γὰρ τῷ ὑπάρξαι πλεονεκτεῖ κατὰ πονηρίαν ὁ ἀδικῶν, ἀλλὰ τῷ ἀμύνασθαι ἐξισοῦται κατὰ μοχθηρίαν ὁ ἀνταδικῶν. καὶ μὴν εἰ ὁ ἀδικῶν κακῶς ποιεῖ, ὁ ἀντιποιῶν κακῶς οὐδὲν ἧττον ποιεῖ κακῶς, κἂν ἀμύνηται· ὥσπερ γὰρ ὁ ἀποδιδοὺς χάριν τῷ προϋπάρξαντι οὐδὲν ἧττον εὖ ποιεῖ κἂν προπεπονθὼς ᾖ, οὕτως ὁ μετατιθεὶς τὴν ἀμοιβὴν εἰς κάκωσιν οὐδὲν ἧττον κακῶς δρᾷ κἂν προπεπονθὼς ᾖ.

6. Τί δὲ τοίνυν ἔσται καὶ πέρας τοῦ κακοῦ; εἰ γὰρ ὁ ἀδικηθεὶς ἀμύνεται, ἀεὶ μεταβαίνει τὸ κακὸν ἀπ᾽ ἄλλου πρὸς ἄλλον καὶ μεταπηδᾷ καὶ διαδέχεται ἀδι-

[10] supplevi praeeuntibus Hernández Muñoz et Heinsio: *οὕτωσερωπονηρωνυν* R: alia alii [11] del. Acciaiolus, Trapp

fact misuses. Therefore, if we attribute wrongdoing to intention, the bad man can indeed commit wrong, but he cannot suffer it.

5. Here is what I shall say about bad men at this point.[6] A bad man intends to do wrong, even though he cannot do it, and so he intends it either against an equal or against someone better than he. What is the better man to do? Will he wrong thc bad man in return? Surely not, because the bad man does not possess anything wherein he can be wronged, since the absence of good is why he is bad in the first place. Therefore, a sensible man will neither do anything to wrong a bad man in return, since he has nothing good in which to wrong him; nor will he intend to do so, since a good man has no wish to do wrong, any more than a pipe player wishes to play out of tune.

If, in general, doing wrong is bad, then returning a wrong is equally bad. For the one doing wrong is not the more wicked one for being the first to act, but rather the one returning the wrong is equally bad for retaliating. Furthermore, if the one doing wrong is acting badly, then the one who reciprocates is acting no less badly, even though he is retaliating. For just as someone who repays a favor to the person who gave it is acting no less better for having received the prior benefit, so a person returning harm for harm acts no less badly for having been harmed first.

6. And then, what limit will there be to this evil? For if the wronged person retaliates, the evil continues forever as it reverts from one party to the other, and one wrong

[6] This is a tentative reconstruction of the corrupt text.

κία ἀδικίαν. ᾧ γὰρ δικαίῳ συγχωρεῖς τῷ παθόντι ἐπεξιέναι, τῷ αὐτῷ τούτῳ δικαίῳ ἐπαναχωρεῖ αὖθις ἀπ᾽ ἐκείνου πρὸς τὸν αὐτὸν ἡ τιμωρία· τὸ γὰρ δίκαιον ἐπ᾽ ἀμφοῖν ἴσον.

Ὦ Ζεῦ, οἷον καὶ πεποίηκας· δικαιοσύνην ἐξ ἀδικημάτων. καὶ ποῖ βαδιεῖται τὸ κακόν; καὶ ποῦ στήσεται; οὐκ οἶσθα ὅτι πηγὴν ταύτην ἀέναον κινεῖς πονηρίας καὶ γράφεις νόμον ἀρχέκακον τῇ πάσῃ γῇ; τοῦτο γὰρ ἀμέλει ἐστὶν τὸ τῶν πάλαι κακῶν τοῖς ἀνθρώποις ἡγησάμενον, στόλων βαρβαρικῶν καὶ Ἑλληνικῶν ἐπ᾽ ἀλλήλους περαιουμένων, ἁρπαζόντων καὶ πολεμούντων καὶ ληϊζομένων, προκάλυμμα ποιουμένων τῆς παρούσης ἀδικίας τὴν φθάσασαν.

Φοίνικες ἐξ Ἄργους βασιλικὴν κόρην ἄγουσιν, Ἕλληνες ἐκ Κόλχων βαρβαρικὴν παρθένον ἄγουσιν, καὶ αὖθις Φρύγες ἐκ Πελοποννήσου Λακωνικὴν γυναῖκα. ὁρᾷς τὴν διαδοχὴν τῶν κακῶν καὶ τὰς προφάσεις τῶν πολέμων καὶ τὸν πολυπλασιασμὸν τῶν ἀδικημάτων; τοῦτο καὶ τὴν Ἑλλάδα συνέτριψεν αὐτὴν {ἡ}[12] περὶ ἑαυτήν, δόξα ἀδικίας διαβαίνουσα ἐπὶ τοὺς πλησίον καὶ ἄπαυστοι θυμοὶ καὶ ὀργαὶ ἀθάνατοι καὶ τιμωρίας ἔρως καὶ ἀμαθία δίκης.

7. Ἀλλ᾽ εἴπερ οἱ ἀδικούμενοι ἠπίσταντο ὅτι τοῖς

[12] del. Reiske, Trapp

act follows another. For the very same justification by which you allow the victim to exact vengeance also permits vengeance to revert from the victim to the original perpetrator, because the justification applies equally in both cases.

O Zeus! What a situation you have brought about by creating justice out of wrongful acts! How far indeed will the evil go? Where will it stop? Do you not realize that you are opening up this floodgate of wickedness and are laying down a law that marks the "beginning of evil"[7] for the entire world? This is precisely what brought upon mankind those evils of long ago: the expeditions of Greeks and barbarians crossing the sea to attack each other, the abductions, wars, and plundering, as they made the previous wrongdoing an excuse for each new one.

The Phoenicians abduct a princess from Argos; the Greeks abduct a barbarian girl from Colchis; and in turn the Phrygians abduct a Spartan wife from the Peloponnesus.[8] Can you not see the succession of evils, the pretexts for wars, and the multiplication of wrongful acts? This process even tore Greece itself apart from within, as a sense of being wronged passed on to neighbors, along with its unstoppable anger, undying rage, lust for retribution, and ignorance of justice.[9]

7. If only those who suffered wrong had understood

[7] The word *archekakon* (beginning of evil) occurs at *Il.* 5.63, alluding to Paris' ships that brought Helen to Troy.

[8] Hdt. 1.1–4 lists these abductions of Io, Medea, and Helen as pretexts for the ensuing wars.

[9] A reference to the Peloponnesian War, with examples to follow of what the Athenians and Spartans suffered.

ἀδικοῦσιν μέγιστον κακὸν ἡ ἀδικία αὐτή, τοῦτ᾽ εἶναι πολέμου μεῖζον καὶ τειχῶν καθαιρέσεως καὶ γῆς δῃώσεως καὶ τυραννίδος καταστάσεως, οὐκ ἂν ἐμπέπληστο ἡ Ἑλλὰς τοσούτων κακῶν. Ποτίδαιαν Ἀθηναῖοι πολιορκοῦσιν· ἔασον, ὦ Λακεδαιμόνιε· μεταγνώσονταί ποτε· μὴ μιμήσῃ τὸ κακόν, μὴ μεταλάβῃς τοῦ ψόγου. ἐὰν δὲ ἀγαπᾷς μὲν τὴν πρόφασιν καὶ ἐπὶ Πλαταιὰς ἔλθῃς, ἀπόλωλέ σοι Μῆλος νῆσος γείτων, ἀπόλωλεν Αἴγινα νῆσος φίλη, ἀπόλωλεν Σκιώνη πόλις σύμμαχος· μίαν πόλιν λαβὼν πολλὰς πορθήσεις.

Ὥσπερ γὰρ τῶν ἐπὶ χρηματισμῷ παραβαλλομένων ἐν θαλάττῃ οἱ τόκοι μεγάλοι τῶν δανεισμάτων, οὕτω καὶ τῶν ἐπεξιόντων τοῖς θυμοῖς οἱ τόκοι μεγάλοι τῶν συμφορῶν. καὶ πρὸς τὸν Ἀθηναῖον λέγω· Σφακτηρίαν ἔχεις, ἀπόδος τῇ Σπάρτῃ τοὺς ἄνδρας· ἕως εὐτυχεῖς, σωφρόνησον. εἰ δὲ μή, τοὺς μὲν ἄνδρας ἕξεις, τὰς δὲ τριήρεις οὐχ ἕξεις. Λύσανδρος περὶ Ἑλλήσποντον εὐτυχεῖ καὶ ἡ Σπάρτη μεγάλη· ἀλλὰ ἀπέχου Θηβῶν. εἰ δὲ μή, δακρύσεις τὴν ἐν Λεύκτροις τύχην καὶ τὴν ἐν Μαντινείᾳ συμφοράν.

8. Ὦ δίκης ἀφανοῦς καὶ πλανωμένης. διὰ τοῦτο

---

10 All are examples of what Athens suffered in the Peloponnesian War.

11 The Athenian siege of Potidea (432 BC), the Spartan seizure of Plataea (427), the Athenian destruction of Melos (415), and seizure of Aegina (431) and of Scione (421).

that wrongdoing itself is the greatest evil for those who commit it—that it is worse than war, the demolition of fortifications, the devastation of land, and the establishment of tyranny[10]—then Greece would not have been flooded with so many evils. The Athenians are besieging Potidaea. Let them be, Spartan! They will be sorry soon enough. Do not imitate their wrongdoing; do not share in their blame. But if you welcome the pretext and attack Plataea, then you will lose the neighboring island of Melos, the friendly island of Aegina, and the allied city of Scione. By seizing one city, you will cause the destruction of many.[11]

For just as merchants, who risk their lives at sea for money, must pay huge interest on their loans, so those who take vengeance out of anger must pay huge interest on the disasters they cause. And to the Athenian I say: You have Sphacteria; give Sparta back its men.[12] While you enjoy success, control yourself! If you do not do so, you may have their men, but you won't have your triremes. Lysander achieves success in the Hellespont and Sparta is mighty,[13] but you, Spartan, stay away from Thebes, for if you do not, you will rue your misfortune at Leuctra and disaster at Mantinea.[14]

8. O what a blind and misguided kind of justice! For

[12] Cleon captured three hundred Spartans on Sphacteria in 425, and the Athenians refused to return them.

[13] An allusion to Lysander's defeat of the Athenian fleet at Aegospotami in the Hellespont in 405.

[14] The Thebans under Epaminondas defeated the Spartans at Leuctra (371 BC) and Mantinea (362).

ὁ Σωκράτης οὐκ Ἀριστοφάνει ὠργίζετο, οὐ Μελήτῳ ἐχαλέπαινεν, οὐκ Ἄνυτον ἐτιμωρεῖτο, ἀλλὰ ἐβόα μέγα· "ἐμὲ δὲ Ἄνυτος καὶ Μέλητος ἀποκτεῖναι μὲν δύνανται, βλάψαι δὲ οὐ δύνανται· οὐ γὰρ θέμις ἀγαθῷ ἀνδρὶ ὑπὸ πονηροῦ βλαβῆναι." αὕτη φωνὴ δίκης, ἣν εἴπερ ἅπαντες ταύτην ἐφθέγγοντο, οὐκ ἂν ἦσαν αἱ τραγῳδίαι, οὐδὲ τὰ ἐπὶ τῇ σκηνῇ δράματα, οὐδὲ αἱ πολλαὶ καὶ παντοδαπαὶ συμφοραί.

Ὥσπερ γὰρ ἐπὶ τῶν τοῦ σώματος νοσημάτων χαλεπὰ τὰ ἑρπυστικά, καὶ δεῖ τούτοις ἐπικουρίας στασίμου ἵνα τὸ περιλειφθὲν σωθῇ, οὕτως ἐπειδὰν ἐμπέσῃ οἴκῳ ἢ πόλει ἀδικίας ἀρχή, στῆσαι δεῖ τὸ κακόν, εἰ μέλλει τὸ περιλειφθὲν σωθήσεσθαι. τοῦτο Πελοπίδας ἐξέτριψεν, τοῦτο Ἡρακλείδας ἠφάνισεν, τοῦτο τὴν Κάδμου οἰκίαν, τοῦτο Πέρσας ἀπώλεσεν, τοῦτο Μακεδόνας, τοῦτο Ἕλληνας.

9. Ὦ νοσήματος διηνεκοῦς καὶ ἐπὶ πολλὰς περιόδους χρόνων καταλαβόντος τὴν γῆν. ἐπιτολμήσαιμι δ᾽ ἂν ἔγωγε εἰπεῖν ὅτι εἴπερ ἐστὶν ἀδικίας πρὸς ἀδικίαν ὑπερβολή, ὁ τιμωρῶν τοῦ προϋπάρξαντος ἀδικώτερος. ὁ μὲν γὰρ ὑπὸ ἀμαθίας ἐπὶ τὸ ἀδικεῖν ἐλθὼν ἔχει τὴν δίκην ἐκ τοῦ ψόγου· ὁ δὲ ἐπεξιών, προσλαβὼν ἐκ τοῦ ὁμοίου τὸ ἄδικον, ἀφῄρηκεν ἐκείνου τὸ ἐπίψογον. ὥσπερ γὰρ τῷ μαρίλης ἐμπεπλησμένῳ τὸν συμπλεκέντα ἀνάγκη καὶ αὐτὸν συναισχῦναι τὸ σῶμα,

[15] An adaptation of Pl. *Ap.* 30d.

this very reason Socrates would not become angry with Aristophanes, or resent Meletus, or take revenge on Anytus, but instead declared, "Anytus and Meletus may have the power to kill me, but they cannot harm me, because it is not permitted for a good man to be harmed by a bad man."[15] That is the very voice of justice. If everyone said it out loud, there would be no tragedies or plays on the stage, nor those many and various disasters.

For just as in the case of bodily diseases, where the kind that spread are difficult to treat and require a cure to halt them in order to save the rest of the body, so when wrongdoing first strikes a household or a city, it is necessary to halt the evil, if the rest is to be saved. This is the disease that wiped out the Pelopidae, that annihilated the Heraclidae, that destroyed the house of Cadmus,[16] the Persians, the Macedonians, and the Greeks.[17]

9. Oh what an unrelenting disease! It has infected the world in age after age throughout time! I would venture to assert that if one form of wrongdoing exceeds another, then whoever takes revenge is more unjust than the original wrongdoer. For the wrongdoer is led to do evil through ignorance, and his just punishment is the censure he receives; but the one who exacts vengeance, by committing wrongdoing in equal measure, actually frees the wrongdoer from his exposure to censure. For just as anyone who wrestles with someone covered with soot necessarily dirties his own body, so anyone who sees fit

[16] Three legendary families destroyed by cycles of revenge, the subjects of numerous tragedies.

[17] The Persians were defeated in 479 BC; the references to Macedonians and Greeks are vague.

οὕτω καὶ ὅστις ἀδίκῳ ἀνδρὶ συμπλέκεσθαι καὶ συγκυλινδεῖσθαι ἀξιοῖ, ἀνάγκη τοῦτον συναπολαύειν τοῦ κακοῦ καὶ συναναπίμπλασθαι τῆς μαρίλης.

Ἀθλητῇ μὲν οὖν ἀνδρὸς προσφερομένου ἀθλητοῦ ἐκ τῆς ἴσης ἀγωνίας καὶ φιλοτιμίας ἀποδέχομαι· ὁρῶ γὰρ αὐτοῖς ὁμοίαν μὲν τὴν φύσιν, παραπλησίαν δὲ τὴν μελέτην, ἰσότιμον δὲ τὴν ἐπιθυμίαν τοῦ νικᾶν· ὅταν δὲ ἀγαθὸς ἀνὴρ πονηρῷ συμπέσῃ, οὐκ ἐκ τῆς αὐτῆς παλαίστρας προεληλυθὼς ἑκάτερος, οὐδὲ ὑπὸ τῷ αὐτῷ παιδοτρίβῃ ἀσκηθείς, οὐδὲ τὴν αὐτὴν τέχνην ἐκμαθών, οὐδὲ τοῖς αὐτοῖς παλαίσμασιν ἐντεθραμμένος, οὐδὲ τοῦ αὐτοῦ στεφάνου ἐρῶν οὐδὲ τοῦ αὐτοῦ κηρύγματος, οἰκτείρω τὴν μάχην, ἄνισος ἡ ἀγωνία. ἀνάγκη τὸν πονηρὸν κρατεῖν ἀγωνιζόμενον ἐν τοιούτῳ σταδίῳ, οὗ πονηροὶ μὲν θεαταί, ἄδικοι δὲ οἱ ἀθλοθέται· ὁ δὲ ἀγαθὸς ἐν τούτοις ἄτεχνος καὶ ἀμαθὴς καὶ ἄπειρος ἀπιστίας καὶ πανουργίας καὶ ἀπάτης, καὶ τῶν ἄλλων παλαισμάτων ὑφ᾽ ὧν μοχθηρία κρατύνεται καὶ ἰσχυρίζεται, ὥστε καὶ καταγέλαστος ἂν γίγνοιτο ἀντεπιχειρῶν ἀδικεῖν ὁ μὴ πεφυκὼς τὸν ἄδικον καὶ τῇ φύσει καὶ τῇ τέχνῃ καὶ τῷ ἔθει.

10. Ἀλλὰ διὰ τοῦτο, φαίη ἄν τις, ὁ δίκαιος ἀνὴρ προπηλακίζεται καὶ συκοφαντεῖται καὶ διώκεται, καὶ χρήματα ἀφαιρεῖται καὶ εἰς δεσμωτήριον ἐμβάλλεται, καὶ φεύγει καὶ ἀτιμοῦται καὶ ἀποθνήσκει. τί οὖν, εἰ καὶ οἱ παῖδες νόμους πρὸς ἀλλήλους θέμενοι, καθίσαντες δικαστήριον ἑαυτῶν, ὑπάγοιεν ἄνδρα κατὰ τοὺς αὑτῶν νόμους, κᾆτα, εἰ δόξαι ἀδικεῖν, ψηφίζοιντο

to wrestle and roll around with an unjust man necessarily participates in his wrongdoing and is contaminated with the same soot.

I am delighted when two athletes compete who are equally matched and share the same aspirations, for I can see their similar builds, comparable training, and equally matched desire to win. But when a good man falls in with a bad one, and they do not come from the same palaestra, have not trained with the same trainer, have not learned the same techniques, have not been taught the same wrestling holds, and do not desire the same crown and the same victory proclamation, then the fight moves me to tears, for the contest is unequal. The bad man cannot help but win when competing in a kind of stadium where the spectators are immoral and the organizers are unjust. Under these conditions the good man proves to be unskilled and ignorant, since he is inexperienced in bad faith, dirty tricks, and deceit[18]—not to mention all the other ploys that give wickedness its power and strength. As a result, a man would make a fool of himself by undertaking to wrong the wrongdoer, when he lacked the nature, skill, and habit to do so.

10. But that is precisely why, someone might say, the just man is insulted, slandered, and prosecuted, stripped of his money, thrown in prison, driven into exile, deprived of his rights, and executed. So? What then if children were to make laws for one another and establish their own tribunal, and then were to charge an adult for breaking their laws, and if they then determined that he had indeed bro-

[18] The word "deceit" recalls the Pindaric quote and the discussion in §1.

αὐτὸν ἄτιμον εἶναι ἐν τῷ τῶν παίδων δήμῳ, δημεύοιεν δὲ αὐτοῦ τὰ παιδικὰ χρήματα, τοὺς ἀστραγάλους καὶ τὰ παίγνια, τί εἰκὸς πρᾶξαι τὸν ἄνδρα; <ἢ οὐ καταγελάσασθαι τοῦ>[13] τοιούτου δικαστηρίου αὐταῖς ψήφοις καὶ καταδίκαις αὐταῖς;

Οὕτω καὶ ὁ Σωκράτης Ἀθηναίων κατεγέλα, ὡς παιδαρίων ψηφιζομένων καὶ κελευόντων ἀποθνήσκειν ἄνδρα θνητόν. καὶ ἄλλος ὅστις ἀγαθὸς ἀνὴρ καὶ δίκαιος καταγελάσεται γέλωτα ἀκραιφνῆ, ὁρῶν τοὺς ἀδίκους ἐπ᾽ αὐτὸν ὡρμημένους σπουδῇ, οἰομένους τι δρᾶν, δρῶντας δὲ οὐδέν· ἀλλὰ καὶ ἀτιμαζόντων ἐκείνων βοήσεται τὸ τοῦ Ἀχιλλέως,

φρονέω δὲ τετιμῆσθαι Διὸς αἴσῃ·

καὶ ἀφαιρουμένων τὰ χρήματα προήσεται ὡς παίγνια καὶ ἀστραγάλους ἀφαιρούμενος, καὶ ἀποθανεῖται ὡς ὑπὸ πυρετοῦ καὶ λίθου, οὐδὲν ἀγανακτῶν πρὸς τοὺς ἀποκτειννύντας.

[13] suppl. Markland, Reiske: ἐκ (τοιούτου) R

ken their laws and then voted to deprive him of his rights in the land of children, and confiscated his childhood possessions, to wit his knucklebones and toys, what would be reasonable for a grown man to do? Would he not laugh at such a tribunal, along with its votes and convictions?

That is how Socrates made fun of the Athenians, as if they were children voting and ordering a man to die who was mortal anyway.[19] And any other good and just man will laugh wholeheartedly, when he sees wrongdoers earnestly attacking him, thinking that they are accomplishing a mighty deed, when in fact they are achieving nothing. No, when they are depriving him of his honor, he will cry out in the words of Achilles,

> I know that I am honored in the ordinance of Zeus.[20]

And when they are confiscating his property, he will hand it over as if they were taking his toys and knucklebones, and finally he will die—as if from fever or a kidney stone—without a resentful word to his executioners.[21]

[19] Cf. Xen. *Ap.* 27, Socrates speaking after his trial, "Haven't you known all along that from the moment I was born nature had condemned me to death?" (trans. Henderson).

[20] *Il.* 9.608, Achilles responding to Phoenix' appeal to let go his anger at Agamemnon for having dishonored him.

[21] Cf. the testimony of Socrates' executioner at Pl. *Phd.* 116c.

# *ORATION* 13

## INTRODUCTION

The oration explores the role of human intelligence (*gnōmē*) and what is within our control (*to eph' hēmin*) in the face of divine intelligence that is cognizant of the order of the universe.[1] The riddling Delphic oracle in 480 BC, advising the Athenians to fortify the city with a "wooden wall," was unnecessary, when a sensible man could correctly advise them with rational arguments (§1). Why, then, do men consult oracles when they have intellect (*nous*) and intelligence (*gnōmē*)? One reason is that prophecy is not always accurate, nor is human intelligence always inaccurate (§2). Human intellect is distinct from divine intellect only in terms of its accuracy and certainty. A series of analogies depicts the place of prophecy in the order of things. First, the universe is a harmonious whole with god as its conductor (§3). Second, the universe is like a machine hauling up a ship or dragging a boulder, whose parts all pull in the direction that fate (*heimarmenē*) determines. A general, ship captain, or doctor can predict the results of his ef-

[1] At issue is the opposition between Stoic determinism and Platonic ethical responsibility, as seen in [Plut.] *de fato*. See the discussions of Puiggali (1983, 283–304), Dillon (1996, 44–45 and 208–11), and Trapp (1997a, 115–24).

forts by considering his resources and maintaining vigilance, but what is within our control is also integrated into fate, so that prophecy too has its place in this larger scheme (§4).

The oracles to Laius and Croesus show that god can prophesy about events that are within our control, by stating them as conditions that depend on human choice. Thus divine prophecy and human intellect (*nous*) can act in harmony (§5). Humans are part of an integrated universe of gods and men (§6). An analogy of human life as a sea voyage compares the use of reason with the ship's tackle, the sea and winds with circumstances, and the captain's expertise with prophecy. A quotation from Plato's *Laws* demonstrates that although god, chance (*tychē*), and occasion (*kairos*) are in charge of everything, human expertise too plays a role (§7). Human existence involves both autonomy (*exousia*) and necessity (*anankē*). The autonomy is that of a man in chains going of his own free choice (*authairetōs*) where necessity pulls him (a Stoic image of determinism). Necessity, however, is not to be equated with the ambiguous term destiny (*peprōmenē*) or with the Fates, *daimones*, and Erinyes in Homer and tragedy (§8). These in fact provide specious excuses for human wickedness. The true sources of wickedness, mistrust, and intemperance are in the soul, and their consequences were foretold by Socrates with the approval of Apollo (§9).

## *ORATION* 13

Εἰ, μαντικῆς οὔσης, ἔστιν τι ἐφ' ἡμῖν

1. Ὅτε οἱ Μῆδοι ἐπὶ τὴν Ἑλλάδα ἐστρατεύοντο, ἐχρῶντο οἱ Ἀθηναῖοι τῷ θεῷ, τί χρὴ δρᾶν ἐπιόντος αὐτοῖς βαρβαρικοῦ στόλου, ἵππου Μηδικῆς, ἁρμάτων Περσικῶν, ἀσπίδων Αἰγυπτίων· εἵποντο δὲ καὶ σφενδονῆται Κᾶρες καὶ ἀκοντισταὶ Παφλαγόνες καὶ πελτασταὶ Θρᾷκες καὶ ὁπλῖται Μακεδόνες καὶ Θετταλικὸν ἱππικόν· ἐχρῶντο οὖν τῷ θεῷ οἱ Ἀθηναῖοι τί χρὴ δρᾶν ἐπιόντος ταῖς Ἀθήναις τοσούτου κακοῦ. ὁ δὲ αὐτοῖς χρᾷ φράττεσθαι τὸ ἄστυ ξυλίνῳ τείχει. Θεμιστοκλῆς λέγει ὅτι οἱ δοκεῖ τὸ ξύλινον τεῖχος αἱ τριήρεις εἶναι. συνεδόκει ταῦτα τοῖς Ἀθηναίοις καὶ ἀναστάντες ἐκ τοῦ ἄστεος ἐς τὸ τεῖχος τοῦ θεοῦ μετῳκίσθησαν.

Εἰ οὖν οἱ Ἀθηναῖοι τότε τῷ μὲν θεῷ συμβουλεύεσθαι περὶ τούτων οὐκ ἤθελον, νοῦν δὲ ἔχοντι ἀνδρὶ καὶ δυναμένῳ ἐκλογίζεσθαι καὶ τὴν παροῦσαν δύναμιν καὶ τὴν ἐπιοῦσαν παρασκευὴν καὶ τὸν μέλλοντα κίνδυνον καὶ τὴν ὑποφαινομένην ἀσφάλειαν, τί εἰκὸς συμβουλεῦσαι ἂν τὸν ἄνδρα τοῦτον καταδεέστερον

# *ORATION* 13

## Whether, given the existence of prophecy, anything is within our control

1. When the Medes were invading Greece, the Athenians asked the god[1] what they should do about the barbarian expedition advancing against them with its Median cavalry, Persian chariots, and Egyptian infantry, all reinforced by Carian slingers, Paphlagonian javelin throwers, Thracian peltasts, Macedonian hoplites, and Thessalian cavalry. So when the Athenians sought the god's advice on how to deal with so great a threat advancing against Athens, the god told them to fortify their city with a wooden wall. Themistocles said that he thought the wooden wall meant their triremes. The Athenians concurred with this, left their city, and migrated into the god's "wall."

Now if the Athenians at that time had not seen fit to seek advice from the god about this but instead from a sensible man, one capable of taking into account the forces they had, the resources of the attacking army, the impending danger, and the prospect of safety, what is the likelihood that this man's advice would have been at all

[1] That is, Apollo at Delphi in 480 BC. For the oracle and its interpretations, see Hdt. 7.141–43.

τῆς χρησμῳδίας τοῦ θεοῦ; ἐγὼ μὲν οἶμαι οὐδὲ αἰνίγματος ἂν ἐδεήθη πρὸς αὐτοὺς οὐδὲ τείχους ἀμφισβητησίμου, ἀλλ' εἶπεν ἂν ὧδέ πως· "ὦ Ἀθηναῖοι, τῶν μὲν λίθων καὶ τῶν οἰκοδομημάτων ἐξίστασθε τῷ βαρβάρῳ, αὐτοὶ δὲ πανοικησίᾳ, αὐτοῖς παισὶν καὶ ἐλευθερίᾳ καὶ νόμοις, ἴτε ἐπὶ τὴν θάλατταν· ὑποδέξονται δὲ ὑμᾶς τριήρεις ἱκαναὶ καὶ σώζειν φέρουσαι καὶ νικᾶν μαχόμεναι."

2. Τί δήποτ' οὖν οἱ ἄνθρωποι ἐπὶ τὰ μαντεῖα παραγίγνονται, ἀμελήσαντες τῆς παρὰ τοῦ ὁμοίου συμβουλῆς; ἢ διότι γνώμη μὲν ἀνθρώπου ἐπισφαλὲς καὶ ἄπιστον καὶ ἐπίφθονον καὶ κίβδηλον καὶ οὐκ ἀεὶ ὅμοιον καὶ οὐκ ἐν παντὶ εὔστοχον, τὸ δὲ θεῖον κατὰ μὲν τὴν ὑπεροχὴν πιστόν, κατὰ δὲ τὴν ἀλήθειαν δόκιμον, κατὰ δὲ τὴν πεῖραν εὔστοχον, κατὰ δὲ τὴν τιμὴν ἀνεπίφθονον; θεοῦ δὲ μαντεία καὶ ἀνθρώπου νοῦς (τολμηρὸν μὲν εἰπεῖν, φράσω δὲ ὅμως) χρῆμα συγγενές, καὶ εἴπερ τι ἄλλο ἄλλῳ ὅμοιον, οὐδὲν ἂν εἴη ἐμφερέστερον ἀρετῆς ἀνθρωπίνης γνώμῃ θεοῦ.

Μὴ τοίνυν ἀπόρει μηθ' ὅντινα τρόπον τὸ αὐτεξούσιον τῆς ἀνθρωπίνης γνώμης χρῆται μαντικῇ, μήθ' ὅπως ἀληθευούσης τῆς μαντικῆς δύναταί τι καὶ ἀνθρώπου γνώμη· περὶ γὰρ ὁμοίου πράγματος σκοπεῖς· τὸ γὰρ αὐτὸ ἐρωτᾷς καὶ ἀπορεῖς καὶ ἀναστρέφεις, ἐξὸν τὸ πᾶν διελέσθαι ὡς δεῖ· οὔτε τὸ θεῖον πάντων εὔστοχον, οὔτε τὸ ἀνθρώπινον πάντων ἄστοχον.

---

2 Intelligence (*gnōmē*) connotes sound judgment, good sense.

inferior to the god's oracle? In my opinion, he would not even needed to tell them a riddle or speak of some enigmatic wall, but would have said something along these lines: "Men of Athens, leave behind these stones and buildings for the barbarians, and with your entire households—children, freedom, laws, and all—take to the sea. You will be received by triremes capable of carrying you to safety and of fighting for victory."

2. Why in the world, then, do humans go to oracles and neglect the advice from one of their own kind? Is it because human intelligence[2] is risky, unreliable, open to criticism, fraudulent, not always consistent, and not accurate every time, whereas divinity is trustworthy because of its preeminence, esteemed because of its truthfulness, accurate because it has been tested, and beyond criticism because of the respect it enjoys? Now, prophecy belongs to god, whereas intellect belongs to man. Even though this is a bold assertion, I shall make it nonetheless: these two faculties are akin, for if any one thing resembles another, nothing could be more similar to divine intelligence than human virtue.

Therefore, stop wondering how autonomous human intelligence can make use of prophecy, or, conversely, how human intelligence retains any validity, when prophecy tells the truth, because you are considering two similar things. For what you are questioning, doubting, and pondering is one and the same thing, while the whole issue can be properly resolved in this way: neither is divinity accurate in all matters,[3] nor is humanity inaccurate in all matters.

[3] Cf. *Or.* 5.4, where god's providence does not extend to particulars.

3. Καὶ περὶ μὲν τοῦ ἀνθρωπίνου {νόμου}[1] καὶ αὖθις ῥητέον· τὸ δὲ θεῖον δοκεῖ σοι γινώσκειν πάντα ἑξῆς, καὶ τὰ καλὰ καὶ τὰ αἰσχρά, καὶ τὰ τίμια καὶ τὰ ἄτιμα; φείδομαι τῶν ῥημάτων καὶ αἰδώς με τοῦ θείου ἔχει· σεμνὸν γάρ τι τὸ πάντα εἰδέναι, καὶ ἀριθμὸν ψάμμων καὶ θαλάττης μέτρα, καὶ ξυνιέναι ἀτόπου λέβητος ἑψομένου ἐν Λυδοῖς· καὶ δηλαδὴ πᾶσι τοῖς δεομένοις θεσπίζει ὁ θεός, καὶ συμφέρει τὸ ἀληθὲς μαθεῖν,[2] κἂν μέλλῃ ὁ μαθὼν ἄδικος ὢν πλεονεκτήσειν.

Δεινῶς τινα πολυπράγμονα ἡγεῖ τὸν θεὸν καὶ περίεργον καὶ εὐήθη, καὶ μηδὲν τῶν ἐν τοῖς κύκλοις ἀγειρόντων διαφέροντα, οἳ δυοῖν ὀβολοῖν τῷ προστυχόντι ἀποθεσπίζουσιν· ἐγὼ δὲ μὴ ὅτι θεὸν ἀλλ᾽ οὐδὲ ἄνδρα ἀγαθὸν ἀξιῶ ἐπιπηδᾶν τῷ ἀληθεῖ· οὐδὲν γὰρ σεμνὸν τὸ τἀληθῆ λέγειν, εἰ μὴ γίγνοιτο ἐπ᾽ ἀγαθῷ τοῦ μαθόντος. οὕτω καὶ ἰατρὸς νοσοῦντα ἐξαπατᾷ καὶ στρατηγὸς στρατόπεδον καὶ κυβερνήτης ναύτας, καὶ δεινὸν οὐδέν· ἀλλὰ ἤδη καὶ ψεῦδος ὤνησεν ἀνθρώπους καὶ τἀληθὲς ἔβλαψεν.

Εἰ μὲν οὖν ἄλλο τι ἡγεῖ εἶναι τὴν μαντικὴν ἢ νοῦν θεῖον, διαφέροντα τοῦ ἀνθρωπίνου ἀκριβείᾳ καὶ βεβαιότητι, νόμιζε πολεμεῖν λόγον λόγῳ· εἰ δέ ἐστιν οὐδὲν ἀλλοιότερον ἢ ὅσον τὸ ἐξ ἡλίου φῶς τοῦ ἐκ

[1] del. Markland, Trapp: νοῦ Heinsius: obel. Koniaris: alia alii

[2] καὶ συμφέρει τὸ ἀληθὲς μαθεῖν coni. Trapp: τὸ ἀληθὲς μαθεῖν καὶ συμφέρει R: locus conclamatus

3. We must discuss the human situation again later.[4] But do you really think that divinity knows everything without exception, including what is beautiful and ugly, honorable and disgraceful? You may say, "I refrain from disputing this, and reverence for divinity overcomes me, for it is a wonderful thing to know everything—the number of grains of sand and the measures of the sea—and to be aware of a bizarre cauldron cooking in Lydia.[5] It is also apparent that the god gives his oracles to all those who inquire, and that it is beneficial to learn the truth, even if an unjust person will take advantage of what he has learned."

But what a terribly meddlesome, simpleminded busybody you take god to be—no different from those who go begging in crowds and tell fortunes for two obols to anyone they meet. For my part, I consider it unworthy of a good man, let alone a god, to rush straight to the truth, because there is nothing admirable in telling the truth, unless it benefits the one who learns it. For this reason, it is not unusual for a doctor to deceive his patient, or a general his army, or a captain his crew, for many a lie has helped men while the truth has harmed them.

If then you think that prophecy is anything other than divine intellect, and that it differs from its human counterpart only because of its precision and certainty, then you must recognize that reason is therefore at war with itself. For if in fact these two entities differ only to the degree that sunlight differs from firelight—when both are

[4] In §§4–5 below.

[5] A reference to the famous testing of oracles by Croesus at Hdt. 1.47–48, also referred to in *Orr*. 3.1 and 11.6.

πυρός, φῶς δὲ ἑκάτερον, ἀγάπα μὲν τὸ λαμπρότερον, μὴ ἀτίμαζε δὲ τῇ διαιρέσει τὸ ἀμαυρότερον. ἀλλ' ἡγοῦ τὸ πᾶν τοῦτο ἁρμονίαν τινὰ εἶναι ὀργάνου μουσικοῦ, καὶ τεχνίτην μὲν τὸν θεόν, τὴν δὲ ἁρμονίαν αὐτὴν ἀρξαμένην παρ' αὐτοῦ, δι' ἀέρος ἰοῦσαν καὶ γῆς καὶ θαλάττης καὶ ζῴων καὶ φυτῶν, ἐμπεσοῦσαν μετὰ τοῦτο εἰς πολλὰς καὶ ἀνομοίους φύσεις, συντάττειν τὸν ἐν αὐταῖς πόλεμον· ὡς κορυφαίου ἁρμονία, ἐμπεσοῦσα εἰς πολυφωνίαν χοροῦ, συντάττει τὸν ἐν αὐτῇ θόρυβον.

4. Τίς δὲ ὁ τρόπος τῆς θείας τέχνης, ὀνόματι μὲν εἰπεῖν οὐκ ἔχω, εἴσῃ δὲ αὐτῆς τὴν δύναμιν ἐξ εἰκόνος τοιᾶσδε· ἤδη ποτὲ[3] ἐθεάσω νεῶν ἐρύσεις ἐκ θαλάττης ἄνω καὶ λίθων ἀγωγὰς ὑπερφυῶν κατὰ μέγεθος παντοδαποῖς ἑλιγμοῖς καὶ ἀναστροφαῖς ὀργάνων· ὧν ἕκαστον πρὸς τὸ πλησίον τὴν ῥώμην νειμάμενον, ἕτερον ἐξ ἑτέρου διαδεχόμενον τὴν ἀγωγήν, κινεῖ τὸ πᾶν· καὶ τὸ μὲν ὅλον ἔχει τὴν αἰτίαν τοῦ ἔργου, συνεπιλαμβάνει δέ τι αὐτῷ καὶ τὰ μέρη. κάλει τοίνυν τεχνίτην μὲν τὸν θεόν, ὄργανα δὲ τοὺς λογισμοὺς τοὺς ἀνθρωπίνους, τέχνην δὲ τὴν μαντικὴν σπῶσαν ἡμᾶς ἐπὶ τὴν ἀγωγὴν τῆς εἱμαρμένης.

Εἰ δέ σοι καὶ σαφεστέρας εἰκόνος δεῖ, νόει μοι στρατηγὸν μὲν τὸν θεόν, στρατείαν δὲ τὴν ζωήν, ὁπλίτην δὲ τὸν ἄνθρωπον, σύνθημα δὲ τὴν εἱμαρ-

[3] τοιᾶσδε· ἤδη ποτὲ Dübner: ἢ οἷα δήποτε R: obel. Trapp, Koniaris

light—then go ahead and revere the brighter one, but do not despise the one that is dimmer by this distinction. Instead, consider the whole universe to be like the harmony from a musical instrument: god is the artist, and the very harmony originating from him spreads throughout the air, land, sea, animals, and plants, and then permeates the many dissimilar elements of nature and settles their warfare with one another, just as the harmonious notes of a chorus master permeate the many voices of a chorus and bring order to the dissonance within it.

4. I am unable to tell you in exact terms the nature of this divine expertise, but you can grasp its effect from the following analogy. You have at some point observed ships being hauled up out of the sea, and immense boulders being towed by the various twistings and turnings of machines, when each component transmits its force to its neighbor, and one receives the pull from the other, so as to move the entire load. The whole machine is responsible for accomplishing the work, but its parts also make their contribution. So, call the engineer god, the machinery human powers of reasoning, and the engineer's expertise the art of prophecy that draws us in the direction that fate pulls.[6]

If you require an even clearer analogy, imagine, if you will, god as a general, life as a campaign, man as a hoplite, fate as the watchword, human faculties as weapons, mis-

[6] The notion of fate (*heimarmenē*) pulling individuals along is Stoic; cf. *Or.* 5.5. The image is reprised in §8 below.

μένην, ὅπλα δὲ τὰς εὐπορίας, πολεμίους δὲ τὰς συμφοράς, σύμμαχον δὲ τὸν λογισμόν, ἀριστείαν δὲ τὴν ἀρετήν, ἧτταν δὲ τὴν μοχθηρίαν, μαντικὴν δὲ τὴν τέχνην αὐτὴν τὴν ἐκ τῆς παρασκευῆς ἐπισταμένην τὸ μέλλον. καὶ γὰρ κυβερνήτης ναῦν ἔχων καὶ εἰδὼς τὰ ὄργανα καὶ τὴν θάλατταν ὁρῶν καὶ αἰσθανόμενος τῶν πνευμάτων, οἶδεν τὸ ἀποβησόμενον· καὶ στρατηγὸς στρατόπεδον ἔχων καὶ τὰ ὅπλα εἰδὼς καὶ τῆς παρασκευῆς μεμνημένος καὶ τῶν πολεμίων αἰσθανόμενος, οἶδεν τὸ ἀποβησόμενον· καὶ ἰατρὸς τὸν κάμνοντα ἰδὼν καὶ τῆς τέχνης ξυνεὶς καὶ τῆς νόσου αἰσθανόμενος, οἶδεν τὸ ἀποβησόμενον.[4]

Ὁρᾷς τὸ πλῆθος τῶν μάντεων, ὡς σαφές, ὡς τεχνικόν, ὡς εὔστοχον; εἰ μὲν οὖν τὸ ἐφ' ἡμῖν αὐτὸ ἦν καθ' αὑτό, ἀπήλλακτο δὲ εἱμαρμένης, οὐδὲν ἔδει μαντικῆς· εἰ δὲ ἀνακέκραται τὸ ἐφ' ἡμῖν τοῖς ὅλοις, μέρος ὅσον καὶ τοῦτο τῆς εἱμαρμένης, κατὰ μὲν τὸ ἀναγκαῖον ἡ μαντικὴ στήσεται, κατὰ δὲ τὸ δῆλον ἢ μὴ βουλεύσεται.[5]

5. Ἤδη δὲ καὶ τοῦ ἀναγκαίου ἡ γνώμη †μαντικῇ δηλωτική†.[6] πῶς καὶ τίνα τρόπον ἑκατέρα; αὐχμοὺς μὲν καὶ ἀνομβρίας καὶ σεισμοὺς γῆς καὶ πυρὸς ἐκβολὰς καὶ πνευμάτων ἐμβολὰς καὶ ἀέρων μεταβολὰς

[4] τέχνης . . . νόσου transp. Trapp: νόσου . . . τέχνης R

[5] δῆλον ἢ μὴ βουλεύσεται obel. Trapp

[6] γνώμη <εἰκαστική, καὶ τοῦ ἐφ' ἡμῖν ἡ> μαντικὴ δηλωτική tent. Trapp: alia alii

fortunes as enemies, the power of reasoning as ally, virtue as victory, wickedness as defeat, and prophecy as the very art of predicting the future on the strength of available resources. Then too, the captain of a ship who knows his ship's equipment, observes the sea and keeps an eye on the winds, knows what the result will be. Likewise, the general in command of an army, who knows the capability of his armaments, is mindful of his resources, and who keeps track of the enemy, knows what the result will be. Then too, a doctor who examines his patient, and understands his medical art, and keeps an eye on the disease, knows what the result will be.

Do you see how reliable, skillful, and accurate this multitude of prophets is? If in fact what is in our control were completely independent and free from fate, then there would be no need of prophecy. But if what is in our control is integrated into the entire system, being as much a part of fate as all else, but only a part, then the necessity of prophecy will be established, though the question of its clarity or lack of clarity will remain to be discussed.[7]

5. Moreover, intelligence of what is necessary <. . .>.[8] How does this come about in each case? In the first instance, droughts, lack of rainfall, earthquakes, volcanic eruptions, windstorms, and changes of weather, are known

[7] I am relying on Trapp's translation and interpretation of this difficult sentence.

[8] Trapp emends the text and translates: "We must also observe both that <human> intellect can foresee events brought about by necessity, and that prophecy can reveal <actions brought about by human Free Will>."

οὐ θεὸς οἶδεν μόνος, ἀλλὰ καὶ ἀνθρώπων ὅσοι δαιμόνιοι· οὕτω καὶ Φερεκύδης σεισμὸν Σαμίοις προεμήνυσεν, καὶ Ἱπποκράτης Θετταλοῖς προσιόντα λοιμόν, καὶ Τιμησίας Κλαζομενίοις ἐκλείποντα ἥλιον, καὶ ἄλλος ἄλλο τι. πῶς δὲ δὴ καὶ θεὸς τῶν ὅσα ἐφ' ἡμῖν καταμαντεύεται;

μὴ σπεῖρε τέκνων ἄλοκα δαιμόνων ἄτερ,

ὁ θεὸς λέγει·

ἢν γὰρ φυτεύσῃς παῖδ', ἀποκτενεῖ σ' ὁ φύς.

ταῦτα λέγει μέν, ἀλλὰ οἶδεν ἀνδρὶ συμβουλεύων ἀκολάστῳ καὶ ἀκρατεῖ μέθης, καὶ διὰ τοῦτο προλέγει τὴν συμφοράν, ἧς παρέσχεν μὲν τὴν ἀρχὴν ὁ Λάϊος, ἐγνώρισεν δὲ τὴν αἰτίαν ὁ θεός.

Κροῖσος Ἅλυν διαβὰς μεγάλην ἀρχὴν
καταλύσει.

ὅτι μὲν διαβήσεται οὐ λέγει, τί δὲ πείσεται διαβὰς λέγει. εἰ δὲ ἀπαλλάξεις τῆς συμπλοκῆς καὶ διοικίσεις μαντικὴν θεοῦ καὶ ἀνθρώπου νοῦν, καὶ διέλυσας ἁρμονιῶν τὴν μουσικωτάτην.

---

[9] Cf. Diog. Laert. 1.116. [10] Cf. Plin. *HN* 7.123.

[11] Timesius of Clazomenae founded Abdera; cf. Hdt. 1.168. His prediction of an eclipse is mentioned only here.

[12] Adaptations of Eur. *Phoen.* 18–19, where Jocasta is reporting what Apollo's oracle said to Laius, who, in a drunken stupor, went on to impregnate Jocasta with Oedipus. Alcin. *Didasc.*

not only by god, but also by those many men who are divinely inspired, like Pherecydes, who predicted an earthquake for the Samians;[9] Hippocrates, who predicted a plague coming to the Thessalians;[10] Timesius, who predicted a solar eclipse for the Clazomenians;[11] and so on. And how, in the second instance, does god divine those many matters that are in our control?

> Do not sow a furrow of children without divine consent,

the god says,

> for if you beget a child, that begotten child will kill you.[12]

He indeed says this, but he knows full well that he is advising a licentious man given to intemperate drinking, and for this reason he foretells the catastrophe for which Laius provided the impetus, but it was god who discerned the true cause.

> If Croesus crosses the Halys, he will destroy a great empire.[13]

The god does not say that he *will* cross the river; he simply says what will happen to him if he does. If you break their bond and separate divine prophecy from human intellect, then you will have destroyed the most beautiful of all harmonies.

26.179.15–19 quotes the same passage to make the point that the oracle is merely stating a premise; it is its consequence that is fated.

13 Spoken by Apollo's oracle (Hdt. 1.53.3), also cited at *Or.* 5.2.

6. Οἶκος οὗτος εἷς θεῶν καὶ ἀνθρώπων, οὐρανὸς καὶ γῆ, δυοῖν ἑστίαιν[7] ὀχήματα {τὰ}[8] ἀθάνατα· ὧν τὸν μὲν νέμονται θεοὶ καὶ θεῶν παῖδες, τὴν δὲ ὑποφῆται θεῶν ἄνθρωποι, οὐ χαμαιεῦναι καθ' Ὅμηρον οὐδὲ ἀνιπτόποδες, ἀλλὰ ἄνω εἰς τὸν οὐρανὸν ὁρῶντες ὀρθῇ ψυχῇ καὶ ἀνηρτημένοι τῇ γνώμῃ πρὸς τὸν Δία. διέλαχον δὲ αὐτῶν τοὺς βίους ἐπιστάται θεοί· γῆν τε γὰρ θεοὶ ἐπιβόσκονται, σώζοντες τὰ τῆς γῆς ἔγγονα, οὐχ ὁρώμενοι, οὐδὲ τοξεύοντες ἢ τιτρωσκόμενοι,

οὐ γὰρ σῖτον ἔδουσ', οὐ πίνουσ' αἴθοπα οἶνον.

ἄνθρωποι δὲ εἰς τὸν οὐρανὸν ἀφορῶντες, ᾗ θέμις, ὁρῶσιν[9] τὸν τοῦ Διὸς περιλαμπῆ οἶκον, οὐ χρυσοῖς καθ' Ὅμηρον κόσμοις καὶ κόροις δᾷδας μετὰ χεῖρας φέρουσιν λαμπόμενον, ἀλλὰ ἡλίῳ καὶ σελήνῃ καὶ τῶν τούτοις συντεταγμένων ἀκμαίῳ πυρὶ καταφεγγόμενον. στρατὸν ὁρᾷς ἡγεμόνων ἀγαθῶν καὶ θεραπόντων ἀναγκαίων· τοῦτό μοι φύλαττε τὸ σύνθημα, καὶ ὄψει μὲν τὴν μαντικήν, συνήσεις δὲ τὴν ἀρετήν, γνωριεῖς δὲ τὴν ἑκατέρου ἐπιμέλειαν καὶ κοινωνίαν.

7. Πορείαν ὁρᾷς τὸν ἀνθρώπινον βίον, οὐχ ἑδραίαν οὐδὲ ἠπειρωτικήν, ἀλλὰ νεὼς ὁλκάδος ἐν πελάγει

[7] ἑστίαιν Schenkl, Trapp: ἑστία ἢ R: ἑστίαι ἢ Acciaiolus
[8] del. Markland, Trapp
[9] ὁρῶσιν Heinsius, Koniaris: ὁρᾶν R, edd.

6. Gods and men share this single abode, heaven and earth, these immortal supports of their two homes. The former is inhabited by the gods and children of the gods, while the latter is inhabited by humans, the gods' interpreters, who do not sleep on the ground with unwashed feet, as Homer has it,[14] but who look up to heaven with upright souls and depend upon Zeus with their intelligence. And gods have been appointed to oversee their lives, for gods do indeed roam the earth and preserve the earth's offspring. They are not visible, nor do they shoot arrows or suffer wounds,[15]

for they do not eat bread or drink dark wine.[16]

And when humans look up to heaven, they behold, to the extent that they are permitted, the radiant home of Zeus, not, however, lit, as Homer says, by golden furnishings and youths bearing torches in their hands,[17] but illuminated by the sun, the moon, and the intense fire of the other celestials arrayed with them. It is an army of good leaders and their indispensable subordinates that you see there. I ask you to keep this arrangement in mind, and you will see what prophecy is, understand what virtue is, and recognize the bond and partnership of the two.

7. This human life that you see is a journey—not, however, one over solid ground on the mainland, but instead on board a cargo ship traversing a deep and wide sea,

[14] Said of the Selloi at Dodona at *Il.* 16.235, also cited at *Or.* 8.1. [15] Iliadic references to Apollo shooting arrows at the Greek camp in Book 1 and Aphrodite being wounded by Diomedes in Book 5. [16] *Il.* 5.341.

[17] Said of Alcinous' palace at *Od.* 7.100–102.

πλατεῖ περαιουμένης· σώζει δὲ αὐτὴν οὐ μόνον κυβερνήτου τέχνη, ἀλλὰ καὶ πνευμάτων καιροὶ καὶ ὑπηρεσία ναυτῶν καὶ εὐκολία ὀργάνων καὶ θαλάττης φύσις. τάττε δέ μοι κατὰ μὲν τὰ ὄργανα καὶ τὰς ὑπηρεσίας τοὺς λογισμοὺς τῆς ψυχῆς, κατὰ δὲ θάλατταν καὶ τὰ πνεύματα τὸ ἄδηλον τῶν ἀνθρωπίνων, κατὰ δὲ τὸ προορατικὸν τῆς κυβερνητικῆς τέχνης τὸ εὔστοχον τῆς μαντικῆς. εἰ δέ σου †ἀντετύχει τῷ λογισμῷ τῆς πολιτείας κράσεις†[10] ἀκούσῃ Πλάτωνος ὡδὶ λέγοντος,

> ὡς θεὸς μὲν πάντα, καὶ μετὰ θεοῦ τύχη καὶ καιρὸς τὰ ἀνθρώπινα κυβερνῶσιν τὰ ξύμπαντα· ἡμερώτερόν γε μὴν τρίτον ἐπὶ τούτοις προσθεῖναι δεῖν ἕπεσθαι τὴν τέχνην. καιρῷ γὰρ χειμῶνος συλλαβέσθαι κυβερνητικὴν ἢ μή, μέγα πλεονέκτημα ἔγωγ᾽ ἂν θείην.

8. Ταῦτά μου τὰ μαντεύματα τὴν ψυχὴν ταράττει, καὶ οὔτε καθαρῶς εἰς ὑπεροψίαν ἄγει τῆς μαντικῆς, οὔτε καθαρῶς τοῖς λογισμοῖς διαπιστεύει· ἀλλ᾽ ὥσπερ τῶν ἀμφιβίων ζῴων οἱ ὄρνιθες κοινωνοῦσιν τοῦ ἐν ἀέρι δρόμου τοῖς μεταρσίοις ‹καὶ τῆς ἐπὶ γῆς σιτήσεως τοῖς χερσαίοις›,[11] τοιαύτην ὁρῶ καὶ τῷ ἀνθρώπῳ τὴν διαγωγὴν τοῦ βίου, ἀμφίβιον καὶ κεκραμένην ὁμοῦ ἐξουσίᾳ καὶ ἀνάγκῃ, οἷα γένοιτ᾽ ἂν καὶ δεσμώτῃ

[10] obel. edd. [11] suppl. Trapp: καὶ τοῖς νηκτοῖς τῆς ἐν ὕδατι διαίτης suppl. Reiske

whose safety depends not only on the captain's expertise, but also on opportune winds, the rowing of the sailors, the functionality of the rigging, and the condition of the sea. Consider, if you will, that the rigging and rowing represent the soul's powers of reasoning, that the sea and winds represent what is uncertain in human affairs, and that the foresight provided by the captain's expertise represents the accuracy of prophecy. But if you . . .[18] you will hear Plato saying this:

> God controls everything, and chance and occasion cooperate with god to govern all human affairs. And yet a third factor, one more amenable, must be added to these, namely expertise. For on the occasion of a storm I would consider it of great consequence whether or not navigational expertise is involved.[19]

8. These oracular pronouncements present my soul with a dilemma, leading me neither to despise prophecy entirely, nor to put complete trust in human reasoning. For just as birds, which belong to the class of animals living in two realms, share their flight through the air with creatures of the sky <and share their food on the ground with animals of the earth>, so I see that humans too have a double manner of living, consisting of both autonomy and necessity, like the autonomy of a man in chains who

[18] The text of six words is corrupt.

[19] Pl. *Leg.* 4.709b–c, the Athenian stranger speaking. This is the only quotation from Plato of more than a few words in the entire corpus.

ἀνδρὶ ἐξουσία ἑπομένῳ αὐθαιρέτως τοῖς ἄγουσιν· ὥστε ἐγὼ ὑποπτεύω μὲν τὴν ἀνάγκην, ὀνομάσαι δὲ αὐτὴν εὐπόρως οὐκ ἔχω. κἂν γὰρ πεπρωμένην φῶ, ὄνομα λέγω πλανώμενον ἐν ἀνθρώπων δόξαις· τίς γὰρ ἡ πεπρωμένη; ποίας φύσεως; τίνος οὐσίας;

εἰ μέν τοι θεός ἐσσι, τοὶ οὐρανὸν εὐρὺν ἔχουσιν,

οὐδὲν τῶν δεινῶν σὸν ἔργον, οὐδὲ καθ' εἱμαρμένην αἱ ἀνθρώπιναι συμφοραί· οὐ γὰρ θέμις ἀνάπτειν θεῶν αἰτίαν κακοῦ·

εἰ δέ τίς ἐσσι βροτῶν, τοὶ ἐπὶ χθονὶ ναιετάουσιν,

ψεύδεται μὲν ὁ Ἐλπήνωρ λέγων,

ἆσέ με δαίμονος αἶσα κακή·

ψεύδεται δὲ ὁ Ἀγαμέμνων λέγων,

ἐγὼ δ' οὐκ αἴτιός εἰμι,
ἀλλὰ Ζεὺς καὶ Μοῖρα καὶ ἠεροφοῖτις Ἐρινύς.

9. Ἔοικεν δὲ καὶ ταυτὶ τὰ ὀνόματα εἶναι μοχθηρίας ἀνθρωπίνης εὔφημοι ἀποστροφαί, ἀναθέντων αὐτῆς τὴν αἰτίαν τῷ δαιμονίῳ καὶ ταῖς Μοίραις καὶ ταῖς Ἐρινύσιν. οἱ δὲ ἐν μὲν ταῖς τραγῳδίαις ἐχέτωσαν χώραν (οὐ νεμεσῶ τοῖς ποιηταῖς τῶν ὀνομάτων), ἐν δὲ

---

20 The term *peprōmenē* is post-Homeric and is not used by Plato. It does occur in tragedy and Stoic texts.

21 *Od.* 6.150, addressed to Nausicaa by Odysseus, also quoted at *Or.* 9.1.

follows, of his own free choice, those who are pulling him. This being the case, I suspect I know what necessity is, but cannot readily come up with a name for it. If I call it destiny,[20] I am using a term that shifts its meaning in the opinions of men. For what exactly is destiny? What is its nature? What is its essence?

> If you are one of the gods who inhabit the broad
> heaven,[21]

then nothing terrible can come of your work, and so human disasters do not occur because of fate, since it is not permitted to hold the gods responsible for evil.[22]

> But if you are one of the mortals who dwell on
> earth,[23]

then Elpenor is lying, when he says,

> an evil doom sent by a *daimon* confounded me;[24]

as is Agamemnon, when he says,

> I am not to blame,
> but Zeus, Fate, and the Erinys that walks in
> darkness.[25]

9. These names too look like specious excuses for human wickedness, as men place the blame for it on divine powers, the Fates, and the Erinyes. Let these entities have their place in tragedies (I do not begrudge the poets the

[22] For the doctrine that nothing evil comes from the gods, see *Orr.* 5.1 and 41.2–4. [23] *Od.* 6.153.

[24] *Od.* 11.61, said to excuse himself for having fallen off a roof when drunk. [25] *Il.* 19.86–87, said to excuse himself for having insulted Achilles.

τῷ βίου δράματι μήποτε ταῦτα κενά, ἥ τε Ἐρινὺς καὶ ἡ Αἶσα καὶ οἱ δαίμονες καὶ ὅσα ἄλλα διανοίας ἡμαρτημένης[12] ὀνόματα, ἔνδον ἐν τῇ ψυχῇ καθειργμένα. ‹ταῦτα›[13] καὶ τὸν Ἀγαμέμνονα ἐνοχλεῖ,

ὅτ' ἄριστον Ἀχαιῶν οὐδὲν ἔτισεν·

ταῦτα καὶ τὸν Ἐλπήνορα εἰς μέθην ἄγει, ταῦτα καὶ τὸν Θυέστην ὠθεῖ ἐπὶ τὸν τοῦ ἀδελφοῦ γάμον, ταῦτα καὶ τὸν Οἰδίποδα ἐπὶ τὸν τοῦ πατρὸς φόνον, ταῦτα καὶ τὸν συκοφάντην ἐπὶ τὰ δικαστήρια, καὶ τὸν λῃστὴν ἐπὶ τὴν θάλατταν, καὶ τὸν ἀνδροφόνον ἐπὶ τὸ ξίφος, καὶ τὸν ἀκόλαστον ἐφ' ἡδονάς.

Αὗται πηγαὶ συμφορῶν ἀνθρωπίνων, ἐντεῦθεν ῥεῖ τὸ τῶν κακῶν πλῆθος, ὡς ἀπὸ τῆς Αἴτνης τὸ πῦρ ῥεῖ, ὡς ἐξ Αἰθιοπίας ὁ λοιμὸς ῥεῖ· καὶ τὸ μὲν πῦρ ἐπὶ γῆν ῥεῖ, καὶ ὁ λοιμὸς μέχρι τῶν Ἀθηνῶν προελθὼν ἔστη· οἱ δὲ ὀχετοὶ τῆς μοχθηρίας πολλοὶ καὶ ἀέναοι, καὶ δεόμενοι μαντείων πολλῶν καὶ χρησμῶν μυρίων. τίς ἂν οὖν ἁμάρτοι μαντευόμενος τί τέλος μοχθηρίας, τί τέλος ἀπιστίας, τί τέλος ἀκολασίας; ταῦτα καὶ Σωκράτης προὔλεγεν, οὐχ ὁ Ἀπόλλων μόνον· διὰ τοῦτο ὁ Ἀπόλλων ἐπῄνει Σωκράτην, ὅτι ἦν ὁμότεχνος αὐτῷ.

[12] ἡμαρτημένης Heinsius, Trapp: εἱμαρμένης R
[13] suppl. Heinsius, Trapp

---

[26] *Il.* 1.412, Achilles speaking of Agamemnon's disparagement of him.

[27] Thyestes seduced Atreus' wife, Aërope.

use of their names), but never in the drama of life let them be mere empty names, for Erinys, Fate, *daimones*, and all other such names for misguided intentions, are confined within the soul. They are what trouble Agamemnon,

> because he paid no honor to the best of the
> Achaeans.[26]

They also lead Elpenor to his drunkenness, and impel Thyestes to defile his brother's marriage;[27] they lead Oedipus to murder his father; and they lead a slanderer to court, a pirate to the sea, a murderer to his sword, and an intemperate man to his pleasures.

They are the wellsprings of human disasters: from them flows the flood of ills, as the fire flows from Aetna and as the plague flows from Ethiopia. And yet, the lava merely flows onto the land and the plague stopped once it came as far as Athens,[28] but the sluices of wickedness are many and unceasing, and stand in need of many oracles and countless prophecies. Who then would fail to learn the truth when inquiring about the consequences of wickedness, the consequences of mistrust, and the consequences of intemperance? Socrates too kept foretelling these,[29] not just Apollo: for this reason Apollo praised Socrates[30] for practicing the same expertise as he did.[31]

28 At the beginning of the Peloponnesian War, in 430 BC.

29 An example is Socrates' prophecy to the jurors at Pl. *Ap.* 39c–d.

30 Apollo's oracle declared that no one was wiser than Socrates; cf. Pl. *Ap.* 21a and Xen. *Ap.* 14.

31 "The lecture thus ends with one more assertion of the affinity and the joint indispensability of divine prophecy and human intelligence, to foresee the results that will inevitably follow from the misuse of human autonomy" (Trapp 1997a, 124n41).

# *ORATION* 14

## INTRODUCTION

The oration seeks to define friendship by differentiating it from its counterfeit, flattery. As such, it is part of a longstanding philosophical interest in friendship.[1] Maximus refashions Prodicus' famous myth of young Heracles at the crossroads of Virtue and Vice as that of a good man at the crossroads of friendship and flattery (§1). Four historical figures are said to have chosen flattery and to have come to bad ends (§2). How then to test friendship and flattery? By the outcome? No, that would be too late. By pleasure or pain? No, flatterers can bring pleasure and friends can share pain. By harm and benefit? No, because a friend often shares in a friend's misfortunes (§3). Furthermore, friends, like doctors, parents, and teachers, can inflict pain for a good reason, as Odysseus did by tearing away his companions from the Lotus-Eaters. In contrast,

[1] Examples include Xen. *Mem.* 2.4–5, Pl. *Lysis*, Arist. *Eth. Nic.* 8–9, and Arr. *Epict. diss.* 2.22. Closer in time is Plutarch's *De ad. et am.* 48e–74e and *De am. mult.* 93a–97b. Alcin. *Didasc.* 33 provides a brief treatment: for its various sources, see Dillon (1993, 198–204). Puiggali (1983, 410–15) provides a detailed list of parallels with this oration. *Or.* 35 also treats friendship.

Eurymachus flattered his fellow suitors and joined them in their wickedness (§4).

Purpose, performance, and disposition of the soul must serve to distinguish the friend from the flatterer. A citizen soldier and a mercenary may perform the same activity, but the one fights for his friends and homeland, the other for whoever pays him (§5). In a series of contrasts, friends are distinguished from flatterers by their purpose and by their dispositions. The friend bases the relationship on equality, candor, and sharing, the flatterer on inequality, deceit, and self-advantage (§6). The discussion broadens to friendship and flattery with respect to the gods: the virtuous man approaches them with confidence; the flatterer lives in superstitious fear of them as tyrants. In governments, friendship is dominant in an aristocracy, whereas flattery is rampant in a democracy, where the demos is flattered by demagogues and led into disasters, as happened in Athens (§7). Monarchies too are subject to flatterers, as was Xerxes, convinced by Mardonius to invade Greece, and Alexander, flattered by the Macedonians into adopting Persian customs and disregarding his ancestral heritage from Heracles. In a tyranny, where friendship is simply suppressed, flattery flourishes most of all. Flattery exists as well in the professions and arts, when debased forms imitate valid ones, as happens in music, medicine, law, and worst of all in philosophy (§8).

# *ORATION* 14

Τίσιν χωριστέον τὸν κόλακα τοῦ φίλου

1. Πρόδικος μὲν Ἡρακλέα ἄγει ἐν τῷ μύθῳ ἄρτι ἡβάσκοντα καὶ ἀνδριζόμενον ἐπὶ διττὰς ὁδούς, Ἀρετὴν καὶ Ἡδονὴν ἐπιστήσας ἡγεμόνας ἑκατέρᾳ τῇ ὁδῷ, ἡ μὲν αὐτῷ σοβαρὰ τῶν ἡγεμόνων, {ἡ δὲ}[1] εὐσχήμων ἰδεῖν, βαδίζουσα ἠρέμα, φθεγγομένη μουσικῶς, βλέμμα πρᾶον, ἀμπεχόνη λιτή, ἡ δὲ δευτέρα θρυπτική, ἐπίχριστος, χλανιδίοις ἐξηνθισμένη, βλέμμα ἰταμόν, βάδισμα ἄτακτον, φωνὴ ἄμουσος. ταῦτα ὁρᾷ καὶ ὁ Ἡρακλῆς, ἅτε Διὸς παῖς καὶ ἀγαθὸς τὴν φύσιν, καὶ χαίρειν τῇ Ἡδονῇ φράσας ἐπιτρέπει ἑαυτὸν τῇ Ἀρετῇ ἄγειν.

Φέρε καὶ ἡμεῖς πλάττωμεν μῦθον, διττὰς ὁδοὺς καὶ ἄνδρα ἀγαθὸν καὶ ἡγεμόνας ταῖν ὁδοῖν, ἀντὶ μὲν τῆς Ἀρετῆς τὸν φίλον, ἀντὶ δὲ τῆς Ἡδονῆς τὸν κόλακα. οὐκοῦν καὶ τούτω διαφέρετον σχήματι καὶ βλέμματι καὶ ἀμπεχόνῃ καὶ φωνῇ καὶ βαδίσματι· ὁ μὲν ὡς ἥδιστος ἰδεῖν ὤν, ὁ δὲ ὡς ἀληθέστατος· καὶ ὁ μὲν σεσηρώς, ὀρέγων δεξιάν, παρακαλείτω τὸν ἄνδρα ἕπεσθαι

[1] del. Boissonade, Dübner, Trapp

# *ORATION* 14

## By what means one should distinguish a flatterer from a friend

1. In his myth, Prodicus brings Heracles, an adolescent just reaching manhood, to a place where two roads part.[1] He stations Virtue and Pleasure as guides for each road. One of his guides is imposing, with a dignified bearing, steady gait, pleasant voice, calm expression, and simple clothing; the other is dainty, with makeup, gaudy garments, a brazen look, mincing gait, and unpleasant voice. Heracles surveys these two, and, being the son of Zeus and a good man by nature, bids farewell to Pleasure and entrusts himself to the guidance of Virtue.

Come, let us too make up a myth, one with two roads, a good man, and guides for each of the roads, but instead of Virtue let us have a friend, and instead of Pleasure a flatterer. Accordingly, let us differentiate the two by their bearing, expressions, clothing, voices, and gaits, with the one as pleasant as possible to look at, the other as truthful as can be. Let the one grin, extend his right hand, and

[1] Cf. Xen. *Mem.* 2.1.21–34, where Virtue and Vice (Κακία), not Pleasure, are the guides. Prodicus was a contemporary of Socrates.

αὐτῷ ἐπαινῶν καὶ κυδαίνων καὶ ἀντιβολῶν καὶ δεόμενος καὶ διηγούμενος ἐκτόπους τινὰς ἡδονάς, ᾗ λαβὼν αὐτὸν ἄξει, λειμῶνας ἀνθοῦντας καὶ ποταμοὺς ῥέοντας καὶ ὄρνιθας ᾄδοντας καὶ αὔρας προσηνεῖς καὶ δένδρα ἀμφιλαφῆ καὶ λείας ὁδοὺς καὶ δρόμους εὐπετεῖς καὶ κήπους εὐθαλεῖς, ὄγχνας ἐπ' ὄγχναις καὶ μῆλα ἐπὶ μήλοις καὶ σταφυλὴν σταφυλῇ ἐπιφυομένην· ὁ δὲ ἕτερος τῶν ἡγεμόνων λέγει μὲν ὀλίγα, τὰ δὲ ἀληθῆ αὐτά, ὅτι πολλὴ μὲν τῆς ὁδοῦ ἡ τραχεῖα, ὀλίγη δὲ ‹ἡ›[2] εὐπετής, καὶ χρὴ τὸν ἀγαθὸν ὁδοιπόρον ἥκειν παρεσκευασμένον, ἵνα δεῖ πόνου μοχθήσοντα, τὴν δὲ ῥᾳστώνην ἐκ περιουσίας ληψόμενον.

2. Ταῦτά τοι λεγόντων ποτέρῳ πείσεται καὶ ποτέραν ἄπεισιν; ἀποκρινώμεθα τῷ ποιητῇ τοῦ μύθου ὅτι εἰ μὲν Ἀσσύριός τις οὗτος εἴη, κακοδαίμων ἀνήρ, ἢ Φοῖνιξ Στράτων ἢ Νικοκλῆς ὁ Κύπριος ἢ ὁ Συβαρίτης ἐκεῖνος, τὸν μὲν καὶ μισήσει τῶν ἡγεμόνων καὶ ἡγήσεταί τινα εἶναι ἄξεινον καὶ ἀηδῆ καὶ ἄμουσον, τὸν δὲ ἕτερον χαρίεντα καὶ προσηνῆ καὶ φιλάνθρωπον δεινῶς. ἀγέτω δὴ λαβὼν τὸν ἄνδρα τοῦτον ὁ καλὸς ἡγεμών· οὐκοῦν ἄξει τελευτῶν ἢ ἐπὶ πῦρ, ὡς τὸν Ἀσσύριον, ἢ ἐπὶ πενίαν, ὡς τὸν Φοίνικα, ἢ ἐπὶ

[2] suppl. Trapp

---

[2] An adaptation of *Od.* 7.120–21, describing the fruit in Alcinous' orchard, also cited at *Or.* 25.5.

[3] Sardanapallus, the legendary king devoted to pleasure, who

invite the man to follow him, all the time praising, complimenting, entreating, and begging him, as he describes certain extraordinary pleasures to which he will take and lead him—flowery meadows, flowing rivers, singing birds, gentle breezes, spreading trees, smooth roads, easy strolls, and flourishing gardens, where there are "pears upon pears, apples upon apples, and grapes upon grapes."[2] The other guide says little, but tells the very truth, that the rough stretch of the road is long and the easy part is short, and that the good traveler must come well prepared to work hard where toil is needed and to consider ease as something superfluous.

2. These being their claims, which one will he believe, and which road will he take? Let us answer the inventor of this myth by saying that if the man is some wretched Assyrian,[3] or Strato the Phoenician,[4] or Nicocles the Cypriot,[5] or that notorious Sybarite,[6] then he will loathe the one guide and consider him to be some unfriendly, unpleasant, and boorish sort, but will find the other to be charming, affable, and extremely humane. Then let this good-looking guide take the man and lead him off. And so, in the end he will lead him to a pyre like the Assyrian, or to poverty like the Phoenician, or to prison like the Cyp-

immolated himself on a pyre. He is frequently cited as an exemplar of hedonism; see *Orr*. 1.9, 4.9, 7.7, 15.8, 29.1, and 32.9.

[4] Strato I, king of Sidon (4th c. BC).

[5] Ruler of Cyprus after his father, Evagoras, was assassinated in 374 BC. He is paired with Strato as a rival sensualist, both of whom died violent deaths, at Ath. 12.531a–e and Ael. *VH* 7.2.

[6] Smindyrides (6th c. BC), famous for luxuriousness; cf. Ael. *VH* 9.24. He is also mentioned at *Or*. 32.9.

δεσμά, ὡς τὸν Κύπριον, ἢ ἐπί τι ἄλλο διὰ ψευδοῦς ἡδονῆς ἀληθὲς κακόν. εἰ δὲ εἴη ἀνὴρ κατὰ τὸν Ἡρακλέα, αἱρήσεται τὸν ἀληθῆ τῶν ἡγεμόνων, τὸν φίλον, ὥσπερ ἐκεῖνος τὴν Ἀρετήν.

3. Καὶ ὁ μὲν μῦθος ὡδὶ τελευτᾷ· μεταλαβὼν δὲ ὁ λόγος πρὸς αὐτὸν σκοπείτω τῷ ἄν τις διακρίναι τὸν κόλακα τοῦ φίλου. τὸν μὲν γὰρ χρυσὸν βασανίζει λίθος προστριβόμενον αὐτῇ· φιλίας δὲ δὴ καὶ κολακείας τίς ἔσται βάσανος; ἆρα τὸ ἐξ ἑκατέρου τέλος; ἀλλ' εἰ ἀναμενοῦμεν τὸ τέλος, {ἀλλ'}[3] ἡ βλάβη φθήσεται τὴν γνῶσιν· δεῖ δὲ κρῖναι πρὶν ἄρξασθαι χρῆσθαι· ἐὰν δὲ ὑστερῇ τῆς χρήσεως ἡ κρίσις, ὁ χρήσασθαι φθάσας καὶ μεταγνοὺς εἰς οὐδὲν δέον τὴν κρίσιν κατατίθεται.

Βούλει τοίνυν ἡδονῇ καὶ λύπῃ κρινοῦμεν τὸν φίλον καὶ τὸν κόλακα; καὶ μὴν καὶ ὁ κόλαξ ὑπερβολὴν λαβὼν ἀνιαρότατον καὶ ἐπαχθέστατον, καὶ ὁ φίλος ἥδιστον εὐτυχίαν προσλαβών. μήποτε οὖν βλάβῃ καὶ ὠφελείᾳ τοὺς ἄνδρας κριτέον. ἀμφισβητήσιμον καὶ τοῦτο λέγεις. ὁ μὲν γὰρ κόλαξ κἂν βλάψῃ, ἢ εἰς χρήματα ἐζημίωσεν ἢ εἰς ἡδονὴν ἐξέχεεν· ὧν τὸ μὲν εἰς χρήματα κουφότατον, τὸ δὲ εἰς ἡδονὴν τερπνότατον· διὰ δὲ φιλίας πολλοὶ ἤδη καὶ φυγῆς ἐκοινώνησαν καὶ ἀτιμίας συναπέλαυσαν καὶ θανάτῳ περιέπεσον.

[3] del. Trapp

riot, or to some other evil that is real, brought about by pleasure that is false. But if the man is anything like Heracles, he will choose the true guide, the one who is the friend, just as Heracles chose Virtue.

3. So ends our myth. Now let reasoned argument take over and investigate on its own how someone can distinguish a flatterer from a friend. Gold is tested by being rubbed against a touchstone, but what in fact will be the test for friendship and flattery? Will it be the ultimate outcome that each brings about? No, because if we wait for the outcome, the harm will arrive before our knowledge of it. We must make the assessment before beginning a relationship. If the assessment comes after the relationship is established, then anyone who first enters a relationship and then regrets it invests in a worthless assessment.[7]

Do you prefer, then, for us to distinguish a friend from a flatterer on the basis of pleasure and pain? But yet, a flatterer is most distressing and offensive when he goes to excessive lengths, while a friend is most pleasant when he also has good fortune. Perhaps then, you say, these men should be judged on the basis of harm and benefit. But this claim of yours can also be disputed, because when a flatterer causes harm, he does so either by damaging the other financially, or by involving him in pleasure. The financial harm is very easily borne, and indulgence in pleasure is very enjoyable, whereas for the sake of friendship many before now have joined their friends in exile, shared their loss of citizenship, and met their own deaths.

[7] Cf. Plut. *De ad. et am.* 49d–e: "But one's friend, like a coin, should have been examined and approved before the time of need, not proved by the need to be no friend" (trans. F. C. Babbit).

4. Τῷ οὖν διακρινοῦμεν τὸν κόλακα τοῦ φίλου, εἰ μήτε τῷ τέλει μήτε ἡδονῇ μήτε βλάβῃ; φέρε χωρὶς ἑκάτερον θεασώμεθα. ἆρά γε ὁ πρὸς ἡδονὴν ὁμιλῶν φίλος; καὶ πάνυ εἰκός· καὶ μὴν εἰ ἐχθρὸς ὁ λύπης παρασκευαστικός, φίλος ἂν εἴη ὁ ἡδονῆς παρασκευαστικώτατος. τὸ δὲ οὐχ οὕτως ἔχει· καὶ γὰρ ἰατρῶν ὁ φιλάνθρωπος λυπηρότατος, καὶ στρατηγῶν ὁ ἀκριβέστατος, καὶ κυβερνητῶν ὁ ἀσφαλέστατος. φιλοῦσιν δέ που καὶ παῖδας πατέρες καὶ διδάσκαλοι μαθητάς· καὶ τί ἂν εἴη ἀνιαρότερον ἢ παιδὶ πατὴρ καὶ μαθητῇ διδάσκαλος; ἐπεὶ καὶ Ὀδυσσεὺς ἐφίλει δήπου τοὺς ἑαυτοῦ ἑταίρους, ὃς πολλὰ καὶ δεινὰ ἀνέτλη

ἀρνύμενος ἥν τε ψυχὴν καὶ νόστον ἑταίρων·

ἀλλ᾽ ἐντυχὼν ἀνδρῶν γένει ἀκολάστῳ καὶ φιληδόνῳ, οἳ διῆγον καθάπερ τὰ θρέμματα,

λωτὸν ἐρεπτόμενοι μελιηδέα

(οὕτω γάρ που τὴν ἡδονὴν ὀνομάζει Ὅμηρος), ἀναμιχθέντας αὐτῷ τοὺς ἑταίρους τῇ τούτων τρυφῇ καὶ γευσαμένους τῆς ἀτοπίας τοῦ λωτοῦ, ἄκοντας καὶ δακρύοντας λαβὼν ἐπὶ ναῦν ἄγει. ἀλλ᾽ οὐχ ὁ Εὐρύμαχος τοῖς μνηστῆρσι τοιοῦτος, ἀλλὰ τοῦ ἑτέρου γένους τοῦ κολακευτικοῦ, οἷον σιάλους σῦς ἢ αἶγας εὐτραφεῖς συγκατακόπτειν αὐτοῖς καὶ τοῦ οἴνου ἄδην συν-

4. How, then, are we to distinguish a flatterer from a friend, if we cannot do so on the basis of outcome, pleasure, or harm? Come, let us consider each of these terms separately. Is a friend, then, one whose company is meant to provide pleasure? It seems most likely, for if an enemy is someone who is able to cause pain, then a friend would be someone best able to provide pleasure. But in fact this is not the case. A humane doctor inflicts enormous pain, as does the most scrupulous general and the most trustworthy helmsman. Fathers certainly are friends to their children, as are teachers to their students, yet who could be more distressing to a son than his father and to a student than his teacher? Odysseus certainly was a friend to his comrades, since he suffered many terrible things,

> striving to save his own life and bring his comrades home.[8]

But when he came upon a dissolute, pleasure-loving race of men who lived like animals,

> feeding on honey-sweet lotus[9]

(for "lotus" is no doubt Homer's term for pleasure), and when his comrades had fallen in with their luxuriousness and tasted the extraordinary nature of the lotus, he seized them against their will and dragged them back to their ship in tears. In contrast, Eurymachus behaved very differently toward his fellow suitors. He belonged to the other class, that of flatterers, inasmuch as he joined them in slaughtering fat pigs and well-fed goats and in guzzling

[8] *Od.* 1.5.

[9] A combination of *Od.* 9.94 and 97.

εκροφεῖν, καὶ συγκυλινδεῖσθαι ἐᾶν τῆς νυκτὸς θεραπαινιδίοις καὶ κείρειν οἶκον ἀνδρὸς βασιλέως καὶ διεπιβουλεύειν τῷ γάμῳ.

5. Βούλει δὴ συνελὼν τὸν μὲν κόλακα κατὰ τὴν μοχθηρίαν τάξαι, τὸν δὲ φίλον κατὰ τὴν ἀρετήν, λύπην δὲ καὶ ἡδονὴν χαίρειν ἐᾶν; οὔτε γὰρ τὸ φιλεῖν ἡδονῆς ἀτυχὲς οὔτε τὸ κολακεύειν λύπης ἄμοιρον, ἀλλ' ἑκάτερον ἐν ἑκατέρῳ φύρεται, καὶ ἡδονὴ ἐν φιλίᾳ καὶ λύπη ἐν κολακείαις· ἐπεὶ καὶ αἱ μητέρες καὶ αἱ τιτθαὶ φιλοῦσιν τὰ βρέφη καὶ πρὸς ἡδονὴν αὐτὰ θεραπεύουσιν, καὶ οὐκ ἀφαιρήσεις αὐτῶν τὸ φιλεῖν διὰ τὴν ἡδονήν. ὁ Ἀγαμέμνων τῷ Μενελάῳ παραινεῖ,

πάντας κυδαίνειν, μηδὲ μεγαλίζεο θυμῷ·

ἢ οἴει κολακείαν αὐτῷ ὑποτίθεται; ὁ Ὀδυσσεύς, ἐκνηξάμενος τῆς θαλάττης εἰς τὴν Φαιάκων γῆν, γυμνὸς διαναστὰς ἐκ τῆς εὐνῆς, ἐντυχὼν παιζούσαις κόραις, τὴν βασιλίδα γνωρίσας, Ἀρτέμιδι εἰκάζει αὐτὴν καὶ αὖθις φυτῷ καλῷ, καὶ οὐδεὶς ἂν διὰ ταῦτα κόλακα εἴποι τὸν Ὀδυσσέα. προθέσει γὰρ καὶ χρείᾳ καὶ διαθέσει ψυχῆς ὁ κόλαξ διακρίνεται τοῦ φίλου. καὶ γὰρ ὁ ἀριστεὺς ὅπλοις χρῆται καὶ ὁ μισθοφόρος, καὶ οὐδεὶς αὐτῶν εἰκάζει τὰ ἔργα κατὰ τὴν χειρουργίαν, ἀλλὰ χωρίζει τὴν ἑκατέρου χρείαν κατὰ τὴν πρόθεσιν· ὁ μὲν γὰρ διασωστικὸς διὰ τὴν φιλίαν, ὁ δὲ μι-

down great quantities of wine, and allowed them to roll around with the maids at night, to ravage a king's household, and to carry out a plot against his marriage.

5. Putting all this together then, are you willing to classify the flatterer on the basis of wickedness and the friend on the basis of virtue, and dismiss pain and pleasure? After all, being a friend is not devoid of pleasure, nor is being a flatterer without its share of pain, but there is a mixture of each in both relationships, pleasure in friendship, and pain in flattery. Mothers and nurses certainly are friends to their infants and try to bring them pleasure as they care for them. You surely would not deny them their friendship because they provide pleasure. When Agamemnon advises Menelaus

> to compliment everyone and not be proud at heart,[10]

do you really think that he is instructing him to use flattery? And when Odysseus swam from the sea onto the land of the Phaeacians, and emerged naked from his bed of leaves, and came upon young girls playing, and upon recognizing their princess, compared her to Artemis and then to a beautiful tree,[11] no one would call Odysseus a flatterer for saying that. This is because a flatterer is distinguished from a friend on the basis of his purpose, performance, and the disposition of his soul. A war hero uses weapons as does a mercenary soldier, yet no one equates their activities simply because they both use arms, but distinguishes each one's performance in terms of its purpose—the one defending his own people out of friendship, the

[10] *Il.* 10.69, advice for summoning the leaders of the army.
[11] *Od.* 6.149–63.

σθαρνικὸς τῶν βουλομένων· καὶ ὁ μὲν αὐθαίρετος, ὁ δὲ ὤνιος· καὶ ὁ μὲν τοῖς ἐνσπόνδοις πιστός, ὁ δὲ καὶ τοῖς φίλοις ἄπιστος.

6. Ταύτῃ νόμιζε καὶ τὸν κόλακα διαφέρειν τοῦ φίλου, καὶ συμπίπτειν μὲν ἑκάτερον ἑκατέρῳ πολλάκις εἰς τὰς αὐτὰς πράξεις καὶ τὰς ὁμιλίας, διαφέρειν δὲ ἑκάτερον ἑκατέρου τῇ χρείᾳ καὶ τῷ τέλει καὶ τῇ διαθέσει τῆς ψυχῆς.

Ὁ μὲν γὰρ φίλος τὸ φαινόμενον αὐτῷ ἀγαθὸν εἰς κοινὸν καταθέμενος τῷ φίλῳ, ἐάν τε λυπηρὸν τοῦτο ᾖ ἐάν τε ἡδύ, συναπολαύει αὐτῷ ἐκ τῆς ἴσης· ὁ δὲ κόλαξ ἐπακολουθῶν τῇ αὑτοῦ ὀρέξει οἰκονομεῖ τὴν ὁμιλίαν πρὸς τὸ ἴδιον πλεονέκτημα· καὶ ὁ μὲν φίλος ὀρέγεται τοῦ ἴσου, ὁ δὲ κόλαξ τοῦ ἰδίου· καὶ ὁ μὲν ἰσοτιμίας κατὰ τὴν ἀρετήν, ὁ δὲ πλεονεξίας κατὰ τὴν ἡδονήν· καὶ ὁ μὲν ἰσηγορίας κατὰ τὴν ὁμιλίαν, ὁ δὲ ταπεινότητος κατὰ τὴν θεραπείαν· ὁ μὲν ἀληθείας ἐν τῇ κοινωνίᾳ, ὁ δὲ ἀπάτης· καὶ ὁ μὲν ὠφελείας τῆς εἰς τὸ μέλλον, ὁ δὲ χάριτος τῆς ἐν τῷ παρόντι· ὁ μὲν δεῖται μνήμης ὧν ἔπραξεν, ὁ δὲ λήθης ὧν ἐπανούργησεν· ὁ μὲν ὡς κοινῶν κήδεται, ὁ δὲ ὡς ἀλλότρια λυμαίνεται· ὁ μὲν φίλος καὶ εὐτυχίας κοινωνὸς κουφότατος, καὶ συμφορῶν κοινωνὸς ἰσότατος· ὁ δὲ κόλαξ εὐτυχίας μὲν κοινωνὸς ἀπληστότατος, ἐν δὲ ταῖς συμφοραῖς ἀμικτότατος.

Φιλία μὲν ἐπαινετόν, κολακεία δὲ ἐπονείδιστον· φιλία γὰρ ἑκατέρου πρὸς ἑκάτερον ἴσην ἔχει τὴν

other up for hire by those who want him; the one acting of his own volition, the other because he is being paid. The one is faithful to his allies, the other unfaithful even to his friends.

6. You must recognize that a flatterer differs from a friend in just this way, and that although the two often resemble each other, since they engage in the same activities and associate with the same people, they differ from each other when it comes to performance, purpose, and disposition of the soul.

For the friend shares with his friend what he considers to be good, whether it is painful or pleasant, and participates in it equally with him; the flatterer follows his own desires and manipulates their relationship with a view to his own advantage. The friend aims for equality, the flatterer for his own interest. The friend aims for an equal status in virtue, the flatterer for gains in pleasure. The friend aims for candor in the relationship, the flatterer for subservience by way of obsequiousness. The friend aims for truth in their shared activities, the flatterer for deceit. The friend wants what is beneficial for the future; the flatterer wants gratification in the present. The friend needs his achievements to be remembered; the flatterer needs his misdeeds to be forgotten. The friend cares for his friend's possessions as belonging to both of them; the flatterer plunders the other's possessions as belonging to someone else. The friend is both the least demanding sharer of good fortune and the most equal sharer of adversity; the flatterer is the greediest sharer of good fortune, but the most distant in times of adversity.

Friendship is praiseworthy; flattery is disgraceful, for friendship maintains an equal reciprocity between both

ἀντίδοσιν, ἡ δὲ κολακεία χωλεύει· ὁ γάρ του ἐνδεὴς θεραπεύων τὸν ἔχοντα κατὰ τὴν χρείαν, καθόσον οὐκ ἀντιθεραπεύεται ἐλέγχει τὸ ἄνισον. ὁ φίλος λανθάνων δυστυχεῖ, ὁ κόλαξ μὴ λανθάνων. φιλία βασανιζομένη κρατύνεται, κολακεία ἐλεγχομένη θραύεται· φιλία χρόνῳ αὔξεται, κολακεία χρόνῳ ἐλέγχεται· φιλία χρείας ἀδεής, κολακεία χρείας ἐνδεής. εἰ δέ ἐστιν καὶ ἀνθρώποις πρὸς θεοὺς ἐπιμιξία, ὁ μὲν εὐσεβὴς φίλος θεῷ, ὁ δὲ δεισιδαίμων κόλαξ θεοῦ· καὶ μακάριος <ὁ>[4] εὐσεβὴς {φίλος θεοῦ},[5] δυστυχὴς δὲ ὁ δεισιδαίμων.

7. Ὅνπερ οὖν τρόπον ὁ μὲν θαρσῶν τῇ ἀρετῇ πρόσεισιν τοῖς θεοῖς ἄνευ δέους, ὁ δὲ ταπεινὸς διὰ μοχθηρίαν μετὰ πολλοῦ δέους, δύσελπις καὶ δεδιὼς τοὺς θεοὺς ὥσπερ τοὺς τυράννους, τοῦτον οἶμαι τὸν τρόπον καὶ πρὸς ἀνθρώπους εὔελπι μὲν καὶ θαρσαλέον ἡ φιλία, δύσελπι δὲ καὶ ἐπτηχὸς ἡ κολακεία. τυράννῳ οὐδεὶς φίλος, βασιλεῖ δὲ οὐδεὶς κόλαξ· βασιλεία δὲ τυραννίδος θειότερον.

Εἰ δέ ἐστιν ἡ φιλία ἰσότης τρόπου, τὸ δὲ μοχθηρὸν οὔτε αὐτὸ αὐτῷ οὔτε τῷ χρηστῷ ἴσον, ὁ μὲν ἀγαθὸς τῷ ἀγαθῷ φίλος, ἴσος γάρ· ὁ δὲ κόλαξ τοῦ μὲν ἀγαθοῦ πῶς ἂν εἴη κόλαξ; οὐ γὰρ ἂν λάθοι· τοῦ δὲ μοχθηροῦ κόλαξ ὤν, εἰ μὲν εἴη ἴσος ἐκείνῳ, οὐκ ἂν εἴη

[4] suppl. Markland, Dübner, Trapp
[5] del. Davies[2], Trapp

individuals, whereas flattery cripples it, because when someone fawns on another who possesses something which that person lacks and wants for his own use, he proves the inequality of their relationship insofar as his fawning is not returned. A friend is unfortunate if his deeds are unnoticed; the flatterer is unfortunate if his really are noticed. When put to the test, friendship strengthens; when examined, flattery shatters. Over time friendship increases; over time flattery is put to shame. Friendship is independent of need; flattery cannot do without it. And if men have any dealings with gods, the pious man is a friend to god, whereas the superstitious man[12] is a flatterer of god. Happy is the pious man; miserable is the superstitious one.

7. Therefore, just as the man confident in his own virtue approaches the gods without fear, whereas the man debased by wickedness does so full of dread, being despondent and afraid of the gods as if they were tyrants; in the same way, I believe, when it comes to relationships with other men, friendship is hopeful and confident, whereas flattery is despondent and cowering. A tyrant has no friends, and a king[13] has no flatterers, for kingship is more divine than tyranny.

If friendship is based on equality of ethical character, and wickedness is neither equal to itself nor to the good, then a good man is a friend to a good man, since he is his equal. But then how could the flatterer be a flatterer of a good man? He would be exposed for what he is. But if he were to flatter a wicked man as his equal, he would not be

[12] Literally, he who lives in fear of god (*deisidaimōn*). See Plut. *De. superst.* 164e–71f. [13] That is, an ideal king, in contrast to the monarchs cited in §8 below.

κόλαξ· οὐ γὰρ ἀνέχεται κολακεία ἰσηγορίας· εἰ δὲ οὐκ εἴη ἴσος, οὐκ ἂν εἴη φίλος.

Ἀλλὰ καὶ τῶν πολιτειῶν ἡ μὲν ἀριστοκρατία φιλίας μεστή, δημοκρατία δὲ κολακείας ἀνάπλεως· κρείττων δὲ ἀριστοκρατία δημοκρατίας. οὐδεὶς ἐν Λακεδαίμονι Κλέων ἦν, οὐδὲ Ὑπέρβολος, κόλακες πονηροὶ τρυφῶντος δήμου. ἀλλὰ Καλλίαν μὲν ἐν Διονυσίοις ἐκωμῴδει Εὔπολις, ἰδιώτην ἄνδρα ἐν συμποσίοις κολακευόμενον, ὅπου τῆς κολακείας τὸ ἆθλον ἦν κύλικες καὶ ἑταῖραι καὶ ἄλλαι ταπειναὶ καὶ ἀνδραποδώδεις ἡδοναί· τὸν δὲ δῆμον αὐτόν, τὸν τῆς Εὐπόλιδος στωμυλίας θεατήν, ποῦ τις ἐλθὼν κωμῳδήσει, ἐν ποίῳ θεάτρῳ; ποίοις Διονυσίοις; καὶ τοὺς πολλοὺς ἐκείνους κόλακας, οἷς τὰ ἆθλα ἦν οὐ ταπεινὰ οὐδὲ μέχρι γαστρὸς καὶ ἀφροδισίων ἥκοντα, ἀλλὰ αἱ τῆς Ἑλλάδος συμφοραί; εἰ δὲ ἤθελον Ἀθηναῖοι παρωσάμενοι τοὺς κόλακας πείθεσθαι Περικλεῖ καὶ Νικίᾳ, εἶχον ἂν δημαγωγοὺς ἀντὶ κολάκων φίλους.

8. Ἂν δὲ ἐπὶ τὰς μοναρχίας ἔλθῃς, κολακεύει καὶ Ξέρξην Μαρδόνιος, βάρβαρος βάρβαρον, ἀνόητος ἀνόητον, δειλὸς οἰκέτης δεσπότην τρυφῶντα· τὰ δὲ τῆς κολακείας τέλη, ἀνίσταται ἡ Ἀσία, μαστιγοῦται ἡ θάλαττα, Ἑλλήσποντος ζεύγνυται, Ἄθως ὀρύττεται·

[14] Notorious Athenian demagogues during the Peloponnesian War.

[15] In his play *Flatterers*, Eupolis, a contemporary of Aristophanes, lampooned Callias (ca. 450–370 BC), a wealthy and extravagant Athenian also mentioned in *Orr.* 1.9, etc.

a flatterer, since flattery cannot abide an equal status. And so if he was not his equal, then he could not be his friend.

When it comes to governments, aristocracy is full of friendship, whereas democracy is replete with flattery, for aristocracy is superior to democracy. In Sparta there was no Cleon or Hyperbolus,[14] those malicious flatterers of a pampered demos. To be sure, at the Dionysia Eupolis lampooned Callias,[15] who as a private citizen was flattered in symposia, where the rewards of flattery were cups of wine, courtesans, and other base and servile pleasures. But where can someone go to ridicule the demos itself, the very audience for Eupolis' mockery? In what kind of theater? In what kind of Dionysiac festival? Where can one ridicule all those flatterers, whose rewards were not the base ones confined to food and sex, but instead involved catastrophes for Greece? For if the Athenians had been willing to reject the flatterers[16] and listen to Pericles and Nicias,[17] they would have had friends leading the demos instead of flatterers.

8. And if you turn your attention to monarchies, you will see Mardonius flattering Xerxes,[18] a barbarian flattering a barbarian, a fool flattering a fool, a despicable servant flattering a pampered master. As a result of this flattery Asia is depopulated, the sea is lashed, the Hellespont is bridged, and Athos is dug through. And the results of all

[16] Prime examples are Cleon and Hyperbolus, mentioned above. [17] Both cautious generals.

[18] Mardonius persuaded Xerxes to invade Greece in 480 BC, during which campaign Xerxes lashed the Hellespont for resisting his march, built pontoon bridges across it, and dug a canal through the Athos peninsula. After Xerxes' retreat back to Persia, Mardonius himself was killed at the Battle of Plataea in 479 BC.

τέλος δὲ τῆς σπουδῆς ἧττα καὶ φυγὴ καὶ θάνατος αὐτοῦ κόλακος. κολακεύουσιν καὶ Ἀλέξανδρον Μακεδόνες· τῆς δὲ κολακείας τὰ ἔργα ἀναξυρίδες Περσικαὶ καὶ προσκυνήσεις βαρβαρικαὶ καὶ λήθη τοῦ Ἡρακλέους καὶ τοῦ Φιλίππου καὶ τῆς Ἀργεάδων ἑστίας. τὰς δὲ τυραννίδας τί χρὴ λέγειν; ὅπου γὰρ δέος καὶ ἐξουσία δεσποτικὴ τὸ ἀρχόμενον ἄγχει, ἀνάγκη δεῦρο κολακείαν μὲν ἀνθεῖν, φιλίαν δὲ κατορωρύχθαι.

Ἔστιν καὶ ἐν ἐπιτηδεύμασιν καὶ τέχναις κολακείας ἰδεῖν, ὁμοίας μὲν ταῖς τέχναις κατὰ τὸ σχῆμα, ἀνομοίους δὲ κατὰ τὰ ἔργα. ἐκολάκευσεν ἀνθρώπους καὶ μουσικὴ νόθος, ὅτε Δωριεῖς τὴν πάτριον ἐκείνην καὶ ὄρειον μουσικὴν καταλιπόντες, ἣν ἐπ᾽ ἀγέλαις καὶ ποίμναις εἶχον, αὐλημάτων καὶ ὀρχημάτων ἐρασταὶ γενόμενοι ἐνόθευσαν ὁμοῦ τῇ μουσικῇ καὶ τὴν ἀρετήν. ἐκολάκευσεν ἀνθρώπους καὶ ἰατρικὴ νόθος, ὅτε τὴν Ἀσκληπιοῦ καὶ τὴν Ἀσκληπιαδῶν ἴασιν καταλιπόντες οὐδὲν διαφέρουσαν ἀπέφηναν τὴν τέχνην ὀψοποιϊκῆς, πονηρὰν κόλακα πονηρῶν σωμάτων. κολακεύει καὶ συκοφάντης ῥήτορα, λόγον λόγῳ ἐπανιστὰς καὶ ἐπιτειχίζων τὸ ἄδικον τῷ δικαίῳ καὶ τὸ αἰσχρὸν τῷ καλῷ. κολακεύει καὶ σοφιστὴς φιλόσοφον· οὗτος μὲν κολάκων ἀκριβέστατος <. . .>

---

19 Alexander adopted Persian customs in place of Greek traditions represented by Heracles, Alexander's father Philip II, and his lineage of the Argeadae.

this effort are defeat, retreat, and the death of the flatterer himself. The Macedonians also flattered Alexander, and the products of this flattery were Persian trousers, the barbarian ritual of prostration, and the failure to remember Heracles, Philip, and the ancestral home of the Argeadae.[19] Why speak only of tyrannies? Wherever fear and despotic authority throttle their subjects, there flattery is bound to flourish, while friendship is suppressed.

Forms of flattery[20] can also be seen in professions and in areas of expertise, where they outwardly resemble the expertise, but differ in their products. Men were flattered by a fraudulent form of music, when the Dorians abandoned their native rustic music, which they used to play while guarding their flocks and herds, and instead became enamored of pipe playing and dancing, thus corrupting their virtue along with their music.[21] Men were flattered by a fraudulent form of medicine, when they abandoned the cures of Asclepius and the Asclepiadae and rendered the medical art no different from that of gourmet cookery,[22] a debased flattery of debased bodies. The slanderer flatters the orator by countering argument with argument and by fortifying injustice against justice and what is shameful against what is good. The sophist flatters the philosopher. He is the most meticulous flatterer of them all . . .[23]

20 Here flattery has the sense of a specious imitation that corrupts the practice.

21 The same example is cited at *Or*. 37.4.

22 Cf. Pl. *Grg*. 465b: "cookery is flattery disguised as medicine" (trans. W. R. M. Lamb).

23 The *μέν* (on the one hand) in this last sentence indicates that the oration continued.

# *ORATION* 15

## INTRODUCTION

This and the following oration present opposite sides of a longstanding debate over the superiority of the active or the contemplative life. The issue is raised in Plato's *Gorgias* at 484c–86d by Callicles, the notorious representative of the active life; is treated in *Republic*, Books 6–7; and is discussed at length by Aristotle in *Eth. Nic.* 10.7–8. Closer to Maximus' time, Alcinous' *Didascalicus*, ch. 2 provides a brief overview.[1]

The oration opens with the general observation that no life is perfect, as is evident from people's dissatisfaction with their particular lives (§1). Philosophers too disagree as to what kind of life to live, in spite of their claims to be experts on the subject. A proponent of the active life will first present his defense (§2). He argues that everyone entering life, like someone seeking entry into a city, comes with some skill to contribute to the overall good (§3). What contribution, then, does the philosopher bring with him? He says that he leads a quiet life and fills himself with truth. However, a city, like a ship, needs workers to sustain it (§4). Every organized entity, be it a human body, city, building, or army, needs the support of individual contri-

[1] See the commentary of Dillon (1993, 53–57).

butions to survive. So what good to others is theoretical knowledge if it is hoarded in the soul (§5)? The wisdom of Nestor, Odysseus, and Heracles is apparent in their actions, and Zeus himself never rests in maintaining the universe (§6). Virtue consists of action in the public realm (§7). Citing the dangers of engagement in politics can be no deterrent, for that leads to a life of indolence like that of Sardanapallus, in contrast to that of Cyrus the Great, who liberated the Persians, and to the life of Epicurus, in contrast to the active lives led by Plato, Xenophon, and Diogenes the Cynic (§§8–9). Finally, like Socrates, a philosopher must stand his ground and never embolden bad men by retreating under pressure from such opponents as Anytus and Meletus (§10).

# *ORATION* 15

Τίς ἀμείνων βίος, ὁ πρακτικὸς ἢ ὁ θεωρητικός· ὅτι ὁ πρακτικός

1. Χαλεπὸν εὑρεῖν ἀκριβῆ βίον, ὥσπερ ἄνδρα· ἀλλὰ παντὶ ἀνακέκραται ἔνδειά τις πρὸς τὸ ἄκρως καλόν, καὶ πλεονεκτεῖ ἕτερος ἑτέρου, ὅτῳ ἂν ἐλάττω τὰ ἐνδέοντα ᾖ. καὶ ἴδοις ἂν τὸν μὲν γεωργικὸν μακαρίζοντα τοὺς ἀστικούς, ὡς συνόντας βίῳ χαρίεντι καὶ ἀνθηρῷ, τοὺς δὲ ἀπὸ τῶν ἐκκλησιῶν καὶ τῶν δικαστηρίων, καὶ τοὺς πάνυ ἐν αὐτοῖς εὐδοκίμους, ὀδυρομένους τὰ αὑτῶν καὶ εὐχομένους ἐπὶ σκαπάνῃ βιῶναι καὶ γηδίῳ σμικρῷ· ἀκούσῃ δὲ τοῦ μὲν στρατιωτικοῦ τὸν εἰρηνικὸν εὐδαιμονίζοντος, τοῦ δὲ ἐν εἰρήνῃ τὸν στρατιωτικὸν τεθηπότος.

Καὶ εἴ τις θεῶν, ὥσπερ ἐν δράματι ὑποκριτάς, ἀποδύσας ἕκαστον τοῦ παρόντος βίου καὶ σχήματος μεταμφιέσει τὰ τοῦ πλησίον, αὖθις αὖ οἱ αὐτοὶ ἐκεῖνοι ποθήσουσι μὲν τὰ πρότερα, ὀδυροῦνται δὲ τὰ παρόντα. οὕτω δυσάρεστόν τί ἐστιν ὁ ἄνθρωπος κομιδῇ καὶ φιλαίτιον καὶ δεινῶς δύσκολον, καὶ οὐδὲν τὰ αὑτοῦ ἀσπάζεται.

2. Καὶ τὰς μὲν τῶν πολλῶν ὀρέξεις τε καὶ δυσαρε-

# *ORATION* 15

Which life is better, the active or the contemplative?
The active.

1. It is difficult to find a perfect life, just as it is difficult to find a perfect man, because every life has some inherent deficiency when compared to the highest good, and one life surpasses another merely by having fewer shortcomings. Consequently, you will find the farmer counting townsmen blessed for their refined and colorful life, while at the same time you will find townsmen who serve in assemblies and courts of law, even the most celebrated among them, lamenting their own lot and praying for life with a spade and a small patch of land. You will also hear the soldier praising the good fortune of the man at peace, and the man during peacetime expressing his admiration of the soldier.

And yet if some god were to strip each of these men of his present style of life and dress him in the garb of his neighbor, like actors in a drama, these same men will long to have their former roles back again and lament their current ones. So utterly dissatisfied a creature is man: so censorious, so terribly bad-tempered, and not at all content with his own lot!

2. But what need is there to examine the desires and

στήσεις τί χρὴ σκοπεῖν; οὐ μᾶλλον ἢ τὰς τῶν θρεμμάτων. τοὺς δὲ ἐν φιλοσοφίᾳ καὶ πάνυ ἄν τις ἢ μέμψαιτο ἢ οἰκτείραι, οἳ κομῶντες ἐπὶ φρονήσει καὶ τέχνῃ βίου καὶ ἐπιστήμῃ λόγου οὔπω γε νῦν παύονται στασιάζοντες πρὸς αὑτοὺς καὶ πρὸς ἄλλους καὶ ἀμφισβητοῦντες ποίῳ σχήματι βίου φέροντες αὑτοὺς ἐγχειριοῦσιν, ἀλλὰ ἀτεχνῶς ἐοίκασιν κυβερνήταις παρεσκευασμένοις μὲν πρὸς πλοῦν καλῶς, μεγέθει ὁλκάδος καὶ κατασκευῇ ὑγιεῖ καὶ πλήθει ὀργάνων καὶ ὑπηρεσίας ἀκριβείᾳ καὶ τέχνης ἀσφαλείᾳ καὶ ἕρματος συμμετρίᾳ, ἐν δὲ τῇ τοῦ πλοῦ χρείᾳ πλανωμένοις καὶ ἀποροῦσιν πῇ τράπωνται, πολλῶν μὲν ὑποφαινομένων λιμένων, πάντων δὲ ἀπιστουμένων.

Τοὺς μὲν ἄλλους ἐῶμεν χαίρειν αὐτοῖς βίοις, τὸν μὲν ἐν ἡδονῇ τηκόμενον, τὸν δ᾽ ἐν γῇ πονούμενον, τὸν δὲ ἐν θαλάττῃ πλανώμενον, τὸν δὲ ἐν ὅπλοις μισθοφοροῦντα, τὸν δὲ ἐν ἐκκλησίαις βοῶντα, τὸν δὲ ἐν δικαστηρίοις φυρόμενον· ὥσπερ δὲ ἐν ἀγῶνι σωμάτων οἱ μὲν ἀσθενεῖς καὶ παρὰ τὸ εἰκὸς ἐπιτολμήσαντες τῇ τοῦ νικᾶν ἐλπίδι ταχὺ ἀπεῖπον, οἱ δὲ ἐφάμιλλοι ἀρετῇ μένουσιν καὶ καρτεροῦσιν καὶ διαγωνίζονται περὶ τῆς νίκης, οὕτω κἂν τῇ τῶν βίων ἀγωνίᾳ οἱ μὲν ἄλλοι ἡμῖν ἐκκηρυχθέντες τε καὶ ἀπαγορεύσαντες οἰχέσθωσαν, †οἱ δὲ θεωρητικοῖς†[1] ἐφαμίλλω ὄντε καὶ ἀμφισβητησίμω δεῦρο ἰόντων ἀγωνιουμένω τὰ νῦν τῷ λόγῳ. πότερος τοίνυν πρότερος ἡμῖν τοῖς δικασταῖς τὰ αὑτοῦ δίεισιν; ἐγὼ μὲν οἶμαι ὅτι ὁ πρακτι-

dissatisfactions of the masses? No more than we should those of animals. However, those engaged in philosophy fully deserve either our blame or our pity, since they pride themselves on their intelligence, their expertise in how to live life, and their knowledge of argumentation, yet still today have not stopped disputing among themselves and with others, as they debate what style of life they should adopt for themselves. They are just like helmsmen who are excellently prepared for a voyage, with a large freighter, sound tackle, lots of equipment, a disciplined crew, reliable navigational skill, and a balanced ballast, but during the actual voyage they become adrift and do not know where to turn, for although many ports come into view, they distrust them all.

Let us bid farewell to all the others, along with their lives, including the man immersed in pleasure, or laboring on the land, or wandering on the sea, or hiring out as a mercenary, or shouting in assemblies, or engaged in courts of law. Just as in athletic competitions, those with weak bodies, who against all odds are emboldened by their hope of victory, soon give up, whereas competitors with true ability stand their ground, persevere, and fight through to victory, so in our contest of lives, let all the other competitors depart—those who gave up and were disqualified by us—and let two disputing contestants come forward to debate the topic at hand. Which of them, then, will be the first to present his case to us jurors? I think that it should be the advocate of the active life, for he is bold, more

[1] obel. Trapp, Koniaris: ὁ δὲ θεωρητικὸς καὶ ὁ πρακτικὸς coni. Acciaiolus

κός· θαρσαλέος γὰρ καὶ ἰτητικώτερος καὶ ἐθὰς ὁμιλεῖν τοῖς πολλοῖς· λέγει δὲ ὧδε.

3. "Εἴ τις ἡμᾶς παριόντας εἰς τὸν βίον ὥσπερ ἄρχων πόλεως ἢ οἰκιστὴς οὐκ εἴα βαδίζειν εἴσω πυλῶν, πρὶν πυθέσθαι τί ἑκάστῳ ἔργον καὶ τίνα ἕκαστος ἥκει χρείαν εἰς κοινὸν φέρων τῇ πόλει, οἶμαι ἂν εἰπεῖν τὸν μὲν οἰκοδόμον ὅτι λίθους ἐν τάξει διὰ τέχνης ἁρμόσας, πρός τε χειμῶνα καὶ θάλπος ἀποχρῶντα μηχανήσεται τοῖς οἰκοῦσιν ἐρύματα· τὸν δὲ ὑφάντην ὅτι μίτοις καὶ στημονίοις συνυφῇ[2] ἐσθήματα ἐργασάμενος, σκέπην ὁμοῦ ποριεῖ καὶ εὐσχημοσύνην τοῖς σώμασιν· τέκτων δὲ ἄροτρον φήσει ἢ σκίμποδα ἤ τι ἄλλο τῶν ὅσα ἡ τέχνη παρέχει ξυνεισφέρειν, καὶ ὁ χαλκεὺς ὅσα χαλκοῦ ἢ σιδήρου δεῖσθαι πολεμιστήριά τε καὶ εἰρηναῖα τῆς τέχνης ἔργα.

"Καὶ ὅσα πρὸς ἡδονὴν δημιουργεῖται, καὶ ταῦτα ὡς τὸ εἰκὸς εἰσδέξεται· γραφέας μὲν καὶ δημιουργοὺς ἀγαλμάτων, ἐπὶ εὐφροσύνῃ ὀφθαλμῶν· μυροπώλας δὲ καὶ ὀψοποιούς, χυμῶν καὶ ὀδμῶν δημιουργοὺς γενναίους, καὶ ὅσοι δι' αὐλημάτων ἢ δι' ᾠδῆς ἢ ψαλμάτων ἢ χορῶν τὸ τερπνὸν μηχανῶνται τῇ ἀκοῇ. ἤδη δέ τις καὶ ἐπὶ γελοίου χρείᾳ παρελεύσεται καὶ ἄλλος ἐπὶ θαυμάτων καὶ ἄλλος λόγων. Ὁμήρῳ δὲ καὶ τὸ τοῦ Νιρέως κάλλος χώραν ἔσχεν καὶ ταῦτα ἐν στρατοπέδῳ. ἀσύμβολος δέ, ὡς ἔπος εἰπεῖν, παρέρχεται οὐδεὶς εἰς τὸν βίον, ἀλλ' ὁ μὲν χρείαν τινὰ παρεχόμενος, ὁ δὲ τέχνην, ὁ δὲ ἡδονήν.

[2] συνυφῇ Markland, Trapp: σὺν ὕφει R: obel. Koniaris

assertive than his opponent, and used to mingling with the masses. Here is what he says.

3. "Suppose that someone like a ruler or founder of a city were to meet us as we come forward to enter our lives, and would not allow us to pass through the gates, before asking what each person's occupation was and what service each brought with him for the common good of the city. I think that the mason would say that he would use his skill to arrange stones and build structures sufficient to protect the inhabitants from both winter cold and summer heat. The weaver would say that he would make clothing woven together with threads of warp and weft and provide covering both to protect and to adorn their bodies. The carpenter would say that he is contributing a plow, or couch, or anything else his skill produces, and the metal worker would mention all the products of his craft made of bronze or iron that were needed in war and peace.

"It is also likely that goods created for our enjoyment would be admitted: painters and sculptors of statues to delight the eyes; perfumers and chefs, noble creators of tastes and smells; and all those who contrive pleasure for the ears with pipe playing, songs, lyre playing, and choruses. And surely someone too will enter to provide laughter; another to perform amazing feats of skill, and another to entertain with words. In Homer, Nireus' beauty too had its place, even in an army camp![1] All told, no one enters life without some contribution to make: one provides a service, another a skill, and yet another provides pleasure.

[1] At *Il.* 2.671–74, Homer devotes four verses of his catalogue to Nireus, the most handsome Greek except for Achilles.

4. "Εἶεν· εἰς τί τούτων τὸ τοῦ φιλοσόφου ἔργον καταστησόμεθα; ὅτι μὲν γὰρ οὐκ ἀχρεῖος ἡμῖν οὐδὲ κηφὴν παρέρχεται, ἄνθρωπος δὲ ὢν ξύννομος καὶ συνεργάτης κοινοῦ νομοῦ,[3] παντὶ δῆλον. τί δέ ἐστίν ποτ' αὐτῷ τὸ τῆς κοινωνίας συμβόλαιον, καὶ ποῦ τάττωμεν τὸν ἄνδρα; εἰς τοὺς δημιουργούς, ὡς τὸν Τυχίον; εἰς τοὺς ὀψοποιούς, ὡς Μίθαικον; εἰς τοὺς εὐφραίνοντας, ὡς Φρυνίωνα; εἰς τοὺς γελωτοποιούς, ὡς Φίλιππον; εἰς τοὺς δημαγωγούς, ὡς Κλέωνα; ἢ ἄφιλος καὶ ἀνέστιος ἡμῖν ἀνὴρ πλανήσεται; ἀλλ' ἔστιν μέν τι αὐτοῦ ἔργον, ὅ τι δέ ἐστιν τοῦτο, οὐκ ἴσμεν.

"'Ἡσυχίαν ἄγω,' φησίν, 'καὶ ἀνασκοπῶ πρὸς ἐμαυτὸν τὰ ὄντα καὶ ἀληθείας ἐμπίμπλαμαι.' μακάριος τῆς πολλῆς σχολῆς· σύ μοι δοκεῖς καὶ νεὼς ἐπιβὰς μὴ ὅτι κυβερνήτης γενέσθαι, ἀλλ' οὐδὲ ἐρέτης, οὐδέ τις τῶν διαθεόντων καὶ ξυνεπιλαμβανόντων τῇ σωτηρίᾳ τῆς νεώς, ἀλλ' οὐδὲ ἐπιβάτης εὐκίνητος, οἷος ἢ καλωδίου ἐπιλαβέσθαι ἢ προσάψασθαι κώπης ἐν γαλήνῃ, ἀλλά τις τῶν εἰκῇ κειμένων καὶ φερομένων, αὐτὸ τοῦτο, ἄχθος νεώς.

"Ἢ οἴει ἧττόν τι δεῖσθαι πόλιν τῶν ξυλληψομένων αὐτῇ πρὸς τὴν σωτηρίαν ἢ ναῦν ἐν θαλάττῃ; καὶ πολύ

[3] *νομοῦ* Reiske, Trapp, Koniaris: *νόμου* R

---

[2] The maker of Ajax' shield at *Il.* 7.220.

[3] A Syracusan author of a cookbook, mentioned by Plato at *Grg.* 518b and by Maximus in *Orr.* 17.1–2 and 33.5.

4. "Well then, to which one of these groups are we to assign the occupation of the philosopher? For it is perfectly clear that he is not coming before us as a useless drone, but as a human being and a partner and fellow worker in our shared community. But then what exactly is his engagement with our society, and in which group are we to place this man? Among the artisans like Tychius?[2] Among the chefs like Mithaecus?[3] Among the entertainers like Phrynion?[4] Among the comedians like Philip?[5] Among the demagogues like Cleon?[6] Or will this man just wander about our city without friends or any home? He must have *some* occupation, but what that is we do not know.

"He says, 'I lead a quiet life and contemplate in solitude what really exists and fill myself with truth.' Lucky man, to enjoy so much leisure! However, it seems to me that if you were to board a ship, far from becoming the helmsman, or an oarsman, or one of the deckhands who hustle and bustle and lend a hand to keep the ship safe, or even a passenger agile enough to handle the ropes or manage an oar in calm water, you would be one of those who lie about here and there and are carried along, a mere burden on the ship.[7]

"Or do you think that a city is in any less need of people lending a hand to keep it safe than is a ship at sea? Much

[4] He is unattested elsewhere.

[5] Philip is a comedian in Xenophon's *Symposium*.

[6] The notorious Athenian demagogue during the Peloponnesian War frequently censured by Maximus.

[7] Perhaps an allusion to Achilles' calling himself "a useless burden on the earth" for his inactivity at *Il.* 18.104.

γε οἶμαι μᾶλλον· ἐν νηὶ μὲν γὰρ ὀλίγον τὸ ἐνεργόν, ὁ δὲ φόρτος πολύς· πόλις δέ ἐστιν πρᾶγμα ἀνακεκραμένον πάντων ξυνεργατῶν, καθάπερ καὶ ἡ τοῦ σώματος χρεία, πολυμερής τε οὖσα καὶ πολυδεής, σώζεται τῇ συντελείᾳ τῶν μερῶν πρὸς τὴν ὑπηρεσίαν τοῦ ὅλου· φέρουσιν πόδες, ἐργάζονται χεῖρες, ὁρῶσιν ὀφθαλμοί, ἀκούουσιν ἀκοαί, καὶ τἄλλα, ἵνα μὴ διατρίβω λέγων.

5. "Εἰ δὲ θελήσαι λογοποιὸς Φρὺξ μῦθον πλάττειν, ὅτι ἄρα δυσχεράνας ὁ ποὺς τῷ ἄλλῳ σώματι καὶ ἀπαγορεύσας πρὸς τὸν κάματον, φέρων καὶ αἰωρῶν μετέωρον τοσοῦτον ἄχθος, σχολὴν ἄγειν καὶ ἡσυχίαν ἐπανείλετο· ἢ αὖ τὼ γομφίω, ὡς ἀλοῦντε καὶ ἐργαζομένω τροφὴν τοσούτῳ ὄχλῳ σαρκῶν †κᾆτα ἔροιντο†[4] ἀπειπαμένω τὸ ἔργον τὸ αὑτῶν σκοπεῖν· εἰ ταῦτα ἄρα γίγνοιτο, ἄλλο τι ἢ φθαρήσεται ὁ ἄνθρωπος ἐν τῷ μύθῳ; τοιοῦτο ἀμέλει ἐστὶν τὸ περὶ τὴν κοινωνίαν τὴν πολιτικὴν γιγνόμενον· εἰ γὰρ ἐθελήσαι ἕκαστος ὄκνῳ τοῦ πονεῖν ἀφέμενος τοῦ παράγειν ἐπαναχωρεῖν ἐκ τῆς κοινωνίας πρὸς τὴν αὑτοῦ σχολήν, τί κωλύει διαλυθῆναι τὸ πᾶν καὶ φθαρῆναι;

"Ἢ τὰ μὲν ἰσχυρὰ τῶν οἰκοδομημάτων τῇ πρὸς ἀλλήλους ξυννεύσει τῶν ἐν αὐτοῖς λίθων ξυνδέδεται καὶ ἕστηκεν καὶ μένει, εἰ δὲ ἐξέλοις ὁτιουν τῆς ἁρμονίας, διαλύσεις τὸ πᾶν· τὸν δὲ ξύμπαντα βίον οὐχ ἡγεῖ τὴν σωτηρίαν ἔχειν ἐκ τῆς πρὸς ἑαυτὰ ξυννεύ-

[4] obel. Trapp, Koniaris

more so, I would say. For on a ship the crew is small and the cargo is large. A city, however, is an enterprise involving all its fellow workers. It functions like a human body with its many parts and numerous needs, and is sustained by the contributions of its parts in service to the whole: feet to carry, hands to work, eyes to see, ears to hear, and so on and so forth.

5. "Suppose that some Phrygian storyteller[8] should decide to make up a fable, to the effect that the foot, becoming angry with the rest of the body and tired of all its effort in carrying and holding up so great a burden, chose to live in peace and leisure; or, in an alternate version, that the molars, after grinding food to produce nourishment for such a mass of flesh, refused to see to their proper work.[9] Now, if such were to happen, what else would the man in the fable do but die? That is precisely the case with society in a city. If each person out of an aversion to hard work should decide to stop participating and to withdraw from the community to enjoy his own leisure, what prevents the entire enterprise from breaking down and being destroyed?

"Or again, sturdy buildings owe their structure, stability, and durability to the interdependence of their stones, and if you remove any one part of this construction, you will destroy the entire structure. And do you not think human life as a whole owes its preservation to the interde-

[8] That is, one like Aesop.

[9] The last part of this sentence is corrupt.

σεως τῶν ἐν αὐτῷ μερῶν; καὶ τῶν μὲν ἄλλων τοῦ πράττειν ἐξισταμένων οὐδεὶς λόγος· οὐδὲ γὰρ ὁ Θερσίτης λιποτακτῶν ἐλύπησεν ἂν τὸ Ἑλληνικόν· ὁ δὲ Ἀχιλλεὺς ὁ μηνίσας καὶ ἐπὶ σκηνῆς ἀναπαυόμενος καὶ δοὺς αὑτὸν σχολῇ καὶ κιθάρᾳ καὶ τῇ ᾠδῇ ἀνέπλησεν τὸ στρατόπεδον πολλῶν κακῶν· οὗ γὰρ παρόντος ὠφελεῖσθαι ὑπάρχει, ἀπόντος τούτου βλάπτεσθαι ἀνάγκη.

"Καὶ τὸ νῦν ὁ θεωρίαν καὶ ἀλήθειαν καὶ σχολὴν ἀσπαζόμενος τίς ἂν εἴη ἄλλος ἢ ὁ φρόνιμος καὶ νοῦν ἔχων; ἀλλὰ τί οὖν; μὴ ὁ κυβερνητικώτατος ἐξίσταται τῆς αὑτοῦ ἕδρας τοῖς ἀτεχνοτάτοις, καὶ ὁ στρατηγὸς ἐξίσταται τῆς ἀρχῆς τοῖς ἀναρχοτάτοις; τί δὲ καὶ τὴν ἀρχὴν σεμνὸν τὸ τἀληθῆ εἰδέναι καὶ τεταμιεῦσθαι ἐν τῇ ψυχῇ θησαυρὸν ἄγονον καὶ ἀργὸν καὶ ἄκαρπον, μηδὲν αὐτοῦ ὀνήσεσθαι μέλλοντα μηδὲ ὠφελήσειν ἑτέρους; πλὴν εἰ μὴ καὶ ἀκοὴ καλὸν ἵνα ἔχωμεν, οὐχ ἵνα ἁρμονίας καὶ φωνῆς συνιῶμεν· καὶ ὄψις καλὸν ἵνα ἔχωμεν, οὐχ ἵνα ἴδωμεν τὸ τοῦ ἡλίου φῶς· καὶ ὁ πλοῦτος καλὸν κἂν ἔχει τις αὐτὸν κατορύξας ἐν γῇ, θησαυρὸν ἀργόν.

6. "Συνελόντι δ' εἰπεῖν, τίς ὄνησις τοῦ εἰδέναι, ‹μὴ χρωμένῳ›[5] εἰς ἅπερ συντελεῖ τὸ εἰδέναι; τίς χρεία ἰατρῷ τῆς τέχνης, μὴ ὑγιάζοντι κατὰ τὴν τέχνην; τίς χρεία Φειδίᾳ τῆς τέχνης, μὴ προστιθέντι αὐτὴν τῷ ἐλέφαντι καὶ τῷ χρυσῷ; σοφὸς ἦν δήπου καὶ ὁ Νέ-

[5] suppl. Meiser: alia alii: lacunam statuit Trapp

pendence of its constituent parts, one with another? Now the fact that some people abandon their role in that order is of no importance. Thus the desertion of Thersites would have done no harm to the Greek army, but when Achilles became angry and lingered by his tent and indulged in the leisure of lyre and song, he inflicted many evils on the army, because when one's presence is beneficial, his absence is bound to cause harm.

"So in the present case, what should we call the man who embraces theoretical speculation, truth, and leisure other than a prudent and sensible person? But what then? Should a highly skilled helmsman turn over his station to those least skilled, and a general turn over his command to those least able to exercise it? And what in the first place is so splendid in knowing the truth and hoarding a sterile, useless, and unproductive treasure in the soul, that will be of no use to oneself or beneficial to others? Unless, that is, hearing is a good thing to have, but not so that we can perceive harmony and sound; and that sight is a good thing to have, but not so that we can see the light of the sun; and that wealth is a good thing, even if its possessor buries it in the ground as a useless treasure.

6. "In sum, what good is knowledge, if no use is made of what that knowledge can contribute? Of what use is expertise to a doctor, if he does not heal with it? Of what use is expertise to Phidias,[10] if he does not apply it to ivory and gold? Nestor was certainly wise, but I can see the

[10] Sculptor of the chryselephantine statues of Zeus at Olympia and of Athena in Athens.

στωρ· ἀλλὰ ὁρῶ τὰ τῆς σοφίας ἔργα, σωτηρίαν στρατοπέδου, εἰρήνην πόλεως, παίδων πειθώ, δήμου ἀρετήν. σοφὸς ἦν ὁ Ὀδυσσεύς· ἀλλ' ὁρῶ τὰ ἔργα, τοῦτο μὲν ἐν γῇ, τοῦτο δὲ ἐν θαλάττῃ·

πολλῶν δ' ἀνθρώπων ἴδεν ἄστεα καὶ νόον ἔγνω,
ἀρνύμενος ἥν τε ψυχὴν καὶ νόστον ἑταίρων.

καὶ πρὸς τούτῳ ἔτι ἦν σοφὸς ὁ Ἡρακλῆς· ἀλλὰ οὐχ αὑτῷ σοφός, ἀλλὰ ἐπὶ πᾶσαν γῆν καὶ θάλατταν ἡ σοφία ἔτεινεν. οὗτος ὁ θηρίων καθαρτής, οὗτος ὁ τυράννων σωφρονιστής, ὁ δουλείας ἐλευθερωτής, ὁ ἐλευθερίας νομοθέτης, ὁ δικαιοσύνης βεβαιωτής, εὑρετὴς νόμων, ἀληθευτὴς λόγων, κατορθωτὴς ἔργων. εἰ δὲ ἤθελεν ὁ Ἡρακλῆς ἐπαναχωρήσας καθ' ἡσυχίαν βιοῦν καὶ σχολὴν ἄγειν καὶ διώκειν σοφίαν ἀπράγμονα, ἦν ἂν δήπου ἀνθ' Ἡρακλέους σοφιστής, καὶ οὐδεὶς ἂν αὐτὸν ἐτόλμησεν εἰπεῖν παῖδα Διός.

"Οὐδὲ γὰρ ὁ Ζεὺς σχολὴν ἄγει· ἦ γὰρ ἂν ἐπαύσατο καὶ οὐρανὸς περιφερόμενος καὶ γῆ τρέφουσα καὶ ποταμοὶ ῥέοντες καὶ ἀναχεομένη θάλαττα καὶ ὧραι ἀμείβουσαι καὶ Μοῖραι διαλαγχάνουσαι καὶ Μοῦσαι ᾄδουσαι· ἐπαύσαντο δ' ἂν καὶ αἱ ἀνθρώπων ἀρεταὶ καὶ ζῴων σωτηρίαι καὶ καρπῶν γενέσεις, καὶ τὸ πᾶν τοῦτο αὖθις ἂν περὶ αὐτῷ σφαλλόμενον συνεχύθη καὶ συνεταράχθη. ἀλλ' ἡ Διὸς πραγματεία ἄτρυτος οὖσα καὶ διηνεκὴς καὶ ἀκοίμητος, καὶ μηδέποτε ἀπαγο-

products of his wisdom: the safety of the army, peace in his city, obedient children, and virtuous townsmen.[11] Odysseus was wise, but I can see his accomplishments on both land and sea:

> He saw the cities of many men and learned their minds . . .
> striving to save his own life and bring his comrades home.[12]

And as a further example, Heracles was wise, but he was not wise for himself alone, for his wisdom extended to every land and sea. It was he who purged the earth of savage beasts, chastised tyrants, liberated enslaved peoples, legislated freedom, secured justice, created laws, spoke the truth, and accomplished great deeds. But if Heracles had chosen to retire and live a quiet life of leisure in pursuit of wisdom divorced from action, he surely would have been a sophist rather than Heracles, and no one would have dared to speak of him as the son of Zeus.

"Nor does Zeus himself lead a life of leisure, for if he did, the heavens would have stopped revolving, the earth producing crops, the rivers flowing, the sea spreading its waters, the seasons rotating, the Fates allocating destinies, and the Muses singing their songs. Then too, human virtues would have ceased, along with the survival of animals and the growth of crops, and our entire universe would have collapsed back again upon itself in turmoil and confusion. But because Zeus' diligence is unabating, constant,

[11] Nestor's military acumen is detailed throughout the *Iliad*, and his civic virtue is displayed in the *Odyssey*, Book 3.

[12] *Od.* 1.3 and 5.

ῥεύουσα μηδὲ ἐπαναχωροῦσα τοῦ ἑαυτῆς ἔργου, ἀέναον χορηγεῖ τὴν σωτηρίαν τοῖς οὖσιν. οὕτω που καὶ βασιλέων τοῖς ἀγαθοῖς καὶ Διὶ ὁμοίοις παραινεῖ δι' ὀνειράτων ὁ Ζεύς,

οὐ χρὴ παννύχιον εὕδειν βουληφόρον ἄνδρα,
ᾧ λαοί τ' ἐπιτετράφαται καὶ τόσσα μέμηλεν.

7. "Πρὸς ταῦτα ἀπιδὼν ὁ φιλόσοφος, μὴ τὸν Δία μιμείσθω, μὴ τὸν Ἡρακλέα, μὴ τοὺς ἀγαθοὺς βασιλεῖς, μὴ τοὺς ἄρχοντας, ἀλλὰ βιούτω βίον ἀνδρὸς ἐν ἐρημίᾳ γεννηθέντος, μονωτὴν βίον, οὐκ ἀγελαστικόν, Κυκλώπιον βίον, οὐκ ἀνθρώπινον. ἀλλὰ καὶ τούτοις ἔφερεν μὲν ἡ γῆ πυροὺς καὶ κριθάς,

οὔτε φυτεύουσιν χερσὶν φυτὸν οὔτ' ἀρόωσιν·

ἀλλὰ θεμιστεύει ἕκαστος ὅμως καὶ παίδων καὶ γυναικῶν, καὶ οὐ παντάπασιν ἀπράγμων ἦν. τὸ δὲ ὅλον, ἀπραγμοσύνη τίνος ἄλλου εἴη πλὴν νεκροῦ; εἰ μὲν οὖν τὸ πράττειν ἔρημον ἦν ἀρετῆς, καλῶς εἶχε διώκοντας τὴν ἀρετὴν ἀπολείπεσθαι αὐτοῦ· εἰ δ' ἔστιν ἀνθρώπου ἀρετὴ οὐ λόγος, ἀλλ' ἔργον καὶ πρᾶξις ἐν κοινωνίᾳ καὶ χρῆσις βίου πολιτική, διωκτέον ταῦτα μεθ' ὧν ἄν τις καὶ τὴν ἀρετὴν λάβοι.

τὴν μὲν γὰρ κακότητα καὶ ἰλαδὸν ἔστιν ἑλέσθαι,

---

[13] For Zeus' tireless preservation of the cosmos, see also *Orr.* 4.9 and 41.2.

ever vigilant, never flagging or shirking its proper work, it preserves the universe forever.[13] That is why, I think, Zeus gives this advice in dreams to good kings who are Zeus-like:[14]

> a counselor should not sleep all night long,
> who has an army in his care and so many concerns.[15]

7. "After he considers all this, let our philosopher still refuse to imitate Zeus, Heracles, good kings, and commanders, and instead live the life of a man born in the wilderness, living a solitary life apart from the herd, the life of a Cyclops, not of a man. Yet, even though the earth bore wheat and barley for the Cyclopes,

> for they neither sow with their hands nor plow,[16]

nevertheless each was in charge of his own wife and children,[17] and was not entirely inactive. In a word, what is total inactivity but the characteristic of a corpse? Now if action itself were devoid of virtue, then it would be well for those who pursue virtue to abandon it altogether. But if in fact human virtue does not consist of words but of deeds, and of action in the common realm and engagement in political life, then these things, whereby a man may actually attain virtue, must be pursued.

> For evil can be had in abundance,

[14] An allusion to the Homeric epithets of "Zeus-nurtured" and "Zeus-born," used of kings and heroes.

[15] *Il.* 2.24–25, said by the dream sent to Agamemnon by Zeus.

[16] *Od.* 9.108.

[17] An adaptation of *Od.* 9.114–15.

ὁ Βοιώτιος ποιητὴς λέγει,

τῆς δὲ ἀρετῆς ἱδρῶτα θεοὶ προπάροιθεν ἔθηκαν.

καλός γε ὁ ἀγωνιστὴς ἡμῖν ἀνιδρωτὶ στεφανοῦσθαι ἐθέλων.

8. "Ἀλλὰ τῷ προσαπτομένῳ πραγμάτων κίνδυνος ἕπεται καὶ ζημία καὶ ἐπιβουλαὶ καὶ φθόνοι καὶ φυγαὶ καὶ θάνατοι καὶ ἀτιμίαι. φέρε οὖν, εἰ καὶ τῷ κυβερνήτῃ ὁ λογισμὸς οὗτος ἦν, ὅτι τὸ πλεῖν ἐπισφαλές, κινδύνων μεστὸν καὶ πόνων καὶ πολλοῦ τοῦ ἀδήλου καὶ χειμώνων καὶ πνευμάτων· φέρε, εἰ καὶ τῷ στρατηγῷ τοιοῦτος λογισμὸς ἦν, ὅτι ἄδηλοι μὲν αἱ τοῦ πολέμου τύχαι, τὸ δὲ σφαλερὸν ἐπ᾽ ἀμφοῖν ἴσον, ἐν ποσὶν δὲ ὁ κίνδυνος καὶ ὁ θάνατος πλησίον· τί τοίνυν ἐκώλυεν ἐκ τούτων τῶν λογισμῶν ἄπλουν μὲν εἶναι τὴν θάλατταν, ἐλευθερίας δὲ μηδὲ ὄναρ μετέχειν τοὺς πολλοὺς ἀπορίᾳ στρατηγῶν, τὸν δὲ ξύμπαντα βίον εἶναι μηδὲν σκωλήκων διαφέροντα, δειλὸν καὶ ἀργὸν καὶ ἐπτηχότα; Σαρδαναπάλλου μοι βίον λέγεις, Ἐπικούρου μοι βίον λέγεις. ἀντιθῶμεν αὐτοῖς, Κῦρον μὲν Σαρδαναπάλλῳ, τὸν Πέρσην τῷ Ἀσσυρίῳ, ὅς, ἐξὸν αὐτῷ σχολὴν ἄγειν καὶ καθ᾽ ἡσυχίαν βιοῦν, εἵλετο ἐλευθεροῦν τὸ Περσῶν γένος, πονῶν καὶ στρατευόμενος καὶ διψῶν καὶ λιμώττων, καὶ μὴ ἀνεὶς τὸν κάματον μήτε νύκτωρ μήτε μεθ᾽ ἡμέραν. ἀντίθες καὶ Ἐπικούρῳ πολλούς, Ἕλληνι Ἕλληνας, ἐκ μὲν Ἀκαδημίας

as the Boeotian poet says,

> but the gods have placed sweat in front of virtue.[18]

Some noble competitor it is, who wants us to crown him without his even breaking a sweat!

8. "But, you may say, anyone engaging in public affairs is exposed to danger, punishment, plots, envy, exile, death, and disgrace. Come then, what if every helmsman were to reason in this way, namely that sailing is hazardous, full of danger, toil, and much that is unpredictable, including storms and winds? And what if every general thought the same way, namely that the fortunes of war are unpredictable, that both sides are equally liable to lose, that danger lies before him and death is nearby? On the basis of this reasoning, what then would have prevented the sea from being devoid of ships; what would have prevented the populace from entertaining even a dream of freedom because they lacked generals; or what would have prevented human life as a whole from becoming no different from that of worms—craven, sluggish, and cringing? You are describing to me the life of Sardanapallus, the life of Epicurus.[19] Let us contrast others to each of these. To the Assyrian Sardanapallus, let us contrast the Persian Cyrus, who could have enjoyed leisure and led a quiet life, but chose instead to liberate the Persian people by toiling, campaigning, and enduring thirst and hunger, never relaxing his labors day or night. As for Epicurus the Greek, there are many other Greeks you can contrast with him—

[18] Hes. *Op.* 287 and 289.

[19] Cf. *Or.* 4.9 for Sardanapallus as representing Epicureanism.

Πλάτωνα, ἐκ δὲ στρατοπέδου Ξενοφῶντα, ἐκ δὲ τοῦ Πόντου Διογένην.

9. "Οὐκοῦν ὁ μὲν ὑπὲρ ἀνδρὸς φίλου, φυγάδος καὶ πένητος, μεγάλῃ καὶ ἰσχυρᾷ τυραννίδι ἀντετάξατο, γῆν πολλὴν βαδίζων καὶ πελάγη περαιούμενος καὶ ἀπεχθανόμενος τῷ τυράννῳ καὶ ἐκπίπτων καὶ κινδυνεύων, ἵνα μὴ προδῷ τὸ φιλοσοφίας ἦθος· ἐξῆν δέ που αὐτῷ ἐν Ἀκαδημίᾳ θεωρεῖν καὶ ἀληθείας ἐμπίμπλασθαι. Ξενοφῶντα δὲ καλεῖ μὲν Πρόξενος, παραπέμπει δὲ ὁ Ἀπόλλων, συνεκπέμπει δὲ ὁ Σωκράτης ἐκ τῆς πολλῆς σχολῆς καὶ θεωρίας ἐπὶ στρατείαν καὶ στρατηγίαν καὶ σωτηρίαν Ἑλλήνων μυρίων. τὰ δὲ Διογένους τί χρὴ λέγειν; ὃς ἀφέμενος τῆς αὑτοῦ σχολῆς περιῄει ἐπισκοπῶν τὰ τῶν πλησίον, οὐκ ἀργὸς οὐδὲ ἠμελημένος ἐπιστάτης, ἀλλὰ κατὰ τὸν Ὀδυσσέα ἐκεῖνον,

ὅντινα μὲν βασιλῆα καὶ ἔξοχον ἄνδρα κιχείη,
τόν ῥ' ἀγανοῖς ἐπέεσσιν ἐρητύσασκε
  παραστάς . . .
ὃν δ' αὖ δήμου τ' ἄνδρα ἴδοι, βοόωντά τ' ἐφεύροι,
τὸν σκήπτρῳ ἐλάσασκεν·

ἀλλ' οὐδ' ἑαυτοῦ ἀπείχετο, ἀλλ' ἐκόλαζεν καὶ παρεῖχεν ἑαυτῷ πράγματα,

Plato from the Academy, Xenophon from the army, and Diogenes from Pontus.[20]

9. "And so, on behalf of his friend who was penniless in exile,[21] Plato stood up to a great and powerful tyranny, traveling great distances over land and crossing open seas, incurring the tyrant's hatred and enduring exile and danger, so as not to betray the moral character of philosophy. Yet he surely could have remained in the Academy engaged in contemplation and filling himself with truth. As for Xenophon, Proxenus summoned him and Apollo sent him off, as did Socrates, from his life of much leisure and contemplation to go on campaign, command an army, and save ten thousand Greeks.[22] As for Diogenes' deeds, what need I say? He gave up his own leisure and went all around examining the conduct of his neighbors. No lazy or careless supervisor was he, but like famous Odysseus,

> whenever he encountered a king or a prominent man,
> he would go up to him and restrain him with gentle words . . .
> but whenever he saw a common man and found him bellowing,
> he would strike him with his scepter.[23]

Nor did he spare himself, but chastised himself and endured indignities,

[20] Diogenes the Cynic hailed from Sinope (of Pontus).

[21] That is, Dion, whom Plato defended against Dionysius II, tyrant of Syracuse; cf. Pl. *Ep.* 7, and *Or.* 34.9.

[22] These events are narrated in Xenophon's *Anabasis*.

[23] *Il.* 2.188–89 and 198–99, also quoted at *Or.* 26.5, where they describe Socrates' conduct.

αὐτόν μιν πληγῇσιν ἀεικελίῃσι δαμάσσας,
σπεῖρα κάκ' ἀμφ' ὤμοισι βαλών.

10. "Ἐῶ λέγειν ὅτι ὁ μὲν ἀγαθὸς ἀνὴρ πράττων καὶ μὴ ἐπαναχωρῶν μηδὲ ἐξιστάμενος τοῖς μοχθηροῖς ἑαυτὸν ἂν σώζοι καὶ τοὺς ἄλλους ἐπὶ τὸ βέλτιστον τρέποι· ἐπαναχωρῶν δὲ καὶ δεικνὺς τὰ νῶτα, θρασύτητος μὲν καὶ ἀπειροκαλίας καὶ τόλμης τὸ μοχθηρὸν πᾶν ἀνέπλησεν,[6] τὸ δὲ ἑαυτοῦ προΐεται.

πῇ φεύγεις μετὰ νῶτα βαλὼν κακὸς ὣς ἐν ὁμίλῳ;

μένε καὶ ἵστασο καὶ ἀνέχου τῶν βλημάτων καὶ μηδὲν ἐκπλαγῇς· δειλὸν τὸ τῶν πολεμίων στρατόπεδον, κενὰ τὰ βλήματα, ἐπιόντα σε οὐδεὶς δέξεται, φεύγοντα πάντες βαλοῦσιν, ὡς τὸν Αἴαντα οἱ Τρῶες, ὡς τὸν Σωκράτην Ἀθηναῖοι ἔβαλλον, καὶ οὐκ ἀπέσχοντο αὐτοῦ πρὶν κατέβαλον.

"Πῶς ἂν οὖν τις βιώῃ ἀσφαλῶς ἐν μέσοις ὢν τοῖς πολεμίοις; οὐδὲν γὰρ πολεμιώτερον ἀνδρὸς ἀρετῇ μοχθηρίας ἀμφιλαφοῦς. συνυποσταλείς, φησὶν ὁ Σωκράτης, ὑπὸ τειχίον, τοὺς ἄλλους ὁρῶν ζάλῃ καὶ ἀμηχανίᾳ κυκωμένους. δεῖξον, ὦ Σώκρατες, ἀσφαλὲς τειχίον, ἔνθα στὰς ὑπερόψομαι τῶν βλημάτων· ἐὰν δέ μοι τοιοῦτον τειχίον λέγῃς ᾧ καὶ σὺ ὑπεστάλης, ὁρῶ τὰ βλήματα, Ἀνύτους πολλούς, Μελήτους πολλούς· ἁλώσιμον τὸ τειχίον."

[6] ἀνέπλησεν Acciaiolus, Trapp: ἂν ἀπέπλησεν R: obel. Koniaris

> subjecting himself to degrading blows
> and throwing a shabby garment about his shoulders.[24]

10. "I shall not dwell on the fact that when the good man engages in action and does not retreat or yield to wicked men, he will save himself and direct others toward what is best. But when he shows his back and retreats, then he fills all wicked men with boldness, vulgarity, and daring, and throws away what good he has.

> Where are you fleeing with your back turned like a
> coward in the midst of battle?[25]

Stay put, stand your ground, endure their missiles and have no fear. The enemy army is cowardly, and their missiles are ineffective. If you advance, no one will oppose you, but if you retreat, then everyone will shoot at you, as the Trojans shot at Ajax,[26] and as the Athenians shot at Socrates and never relented until they had brought him down.

"How, then, can anyone live safely in the midst of these enemies, when there is no greater enemy to a man's virtue than the wickedness that surrounds him? It is by crouching behind a low wall, says Socrates,[27] while watching the others helplessly confounded by the storm. Show me, Socrates, that safe wall, where I can take my stand and scorn their missiles. If you tell me that it is the kind of wall where *you* took shelter, then I can see those missiles—many an Anytus, many a Meletus.[28] That wall can be breached."

[24] *Od.* 4.244–45, said by Helen describing Odysseus' disguised entry into Troy. [25] *Il.* 8.94, said by Diomedes to Odysseus. [26] Cf. *Il.* 11.544–74. [27] Pl. *Resp.* 6.496d.
[28] The accuser and prosecutor of Socrates.

# *ORATION* 16

## INTRODUCTION

The spokesman for the contemplative life is Anaxagoras (ca. 500–428 BC), who is depicted as defending himself before his fellow Clazomenians for neglecting his lands and not participating in public life.[1] Many points of contact with Plato's *Apology* indicate that it is largely based on Socrates' defense in 399 BC. It begins with a fictional indictment of Anaxagoras by his fellow Clazomenians for refusing to participate in their civic life (§1). In his defense, Anaxagoras explains that he is naturally unfit for public office, so he instead devotes his life to contemplating reality and pursuing the truth (§2). He argues that his pursuit of the truth and of what is best and most just benefits the city by promoting political order and virtue through reasoned argument. He urges the citizens to observe his work for themselves before voting but vows that whatever the outcome of the trial, he will continue to seek the truth (§3). The speaker acknowledges that Anaxagoras

[1] Diog. Laert. 2.7 reports that when Anaxagoras' relatives accused him of neglecting his estate, he simply turned the estate over to them to care for and withdrew from civic life to study nature. He later came to Athens, where he was actually put on trial for impiety and went into exile ca. 437 BC.

would probably lose his case with the Clazomenians, but not before an ideal juror, who was not chosen by lot, but because he possessed knowledge. In front of such a judge, philosophers like Heraclitus, Pythagoras, Democritus, Xenophanes, Parmenides, and Diogenes of Apollonia would not need to defend themselves before their cities as though they were criminals. This ideal juror would hold a tripartite theory of the soul: a deliberative and ruling element, a subordinate active element, and an unruly element. These correspond to monarchies, aristocracies, and democracies (§4). In determining which is best, the democratic element is ruled out of contention, but in deciding between the soul's contemplative and active elements, when both lay claim to priority, one must take into account different people's natures. Some are contemplative, others active. Then too, young people tend to be active, but more mature ones contemplative, as in the case of Plato and Xenophon, while fortune confers positions of authority on some that require action and grants leisure to others for contemplation (§5). The connection of "seeing" with contemplation, *theōria*, leads to the sights the philosopher sees as his soul travels the world over and goes up into the heavens, where it all but joins Zeus as he maintains order in the universe (§6).

# *ORATION* 16

*Ὅτι ὁ θεωρητικὸς βίος ἀμείνων τοῦ πρακικοῦ*

1. Ἀλλ' εἰ μὲν δίκην ἐφεύγομεν, ἠχθόμεθα ἂν τῷ δικαστῇ μὴ παρέχοντι ἑκατέρῳ ἐκ τῆς ἴσης τὴν ἀπολογίαν, ἀλλ' ἐοικότι τυράννῳ μᾶλλον ἢ δικαστῇ· ἐπεὶ δὲ ἡ μὲν ἐν δικαστηρίοις ψῆφος καὶ τύχη ἔξω τοῦ κατὰ φιλοσοφίαν ἤθους καὶ τρόπου, κατήγορος δὲ λόγος λόγου, φίλος φίλου, ἐπὶ θήρᾳ τοῦ ἀληθοῦς γίγνεται {γοῦν},[1] καὶ δικαστηρίῳ τινὶ ἔοικεν ἡ τοιαύτη βάσανος, φέρε δῶμεν τήμερον τὴν ἀπολογίαν τῷ ἑτέρῳ τῶν λόγων καὶ τῶν ἀνδρῶν τῷ θεωρητικῷ, ἀτεχνῶς ὥσπερ ἐπὶ δικαστῶν καθισταμένῳ καὶ ἀποτεινομένῳ πρὸς τὴν γραφήν. καὶ ἡ μὲν γραφὴ τοιάδε τις ἔστω, ἢ ὅτι ἐγγυτάτω·

> Ἀδικεῖ Ἀναξαγόρας, γεγονὼς μὲν ἐν τῇ Κλαζομενίων γῇ καὶ πόλει καὶ μετασχὼν ἱερῶν καὶ ὁσίων καὶ νόμων καὶ τροφῆς καὶ τῶν ἄλλων ὧν καὶ οἱ λοιποὶ Κλαζομένιοι, ἐπαναχωρῶν δὲ

[1] delevi praeeunte Koniaris: *γίγνεται γοῦν* obel. (vel del.) Trapp: *γοῦν* post *θήρᾳ* transp. Markland

# *ORATION* 16

## That the contemplative life is superior to the active one

1. If we were on trial, we would be vexed with any juror who would not allow each side an equal opportunity to plead its case, but acted more like a tyrant than a juror. Now, the vote in a law court and the element of chance it involves are both contrary to the character and conduct of philosophy, but since in this case we find argument disputing argument and friend accusing friend, all in the pursuit of the truth, and since such a means of testing does in some respects resemble a trial, let us today permit the opposing argument and the man espousing the contemplative life to offer his defense, just as if he were standing before a jury and responding to an indictment. So, let us then present such an indictment, or one most like it.

> Anaxagoras[1] is guilty of the following offense: although being a resident in the land and city of Clazomenae, and having shared in the same sacrifices, rites, laws, upbringing, and everything else with the rest of the Clazomenians, flees from them

[1] This natural philosopher and close associate of Pericles was tried for impiety in Athens, where he had immigrated from Clazomenae. Cf. Pl. *Ap.* 26d–e, *Phd.* 97b–98b, and Plut. *Per.* 32.

ὥσπερ ἐκ θηρίων, καὶ μήτε ταῖς ἐκκλησίαις ἀναμιγνύμενος μήτε εἰς Διονύσια ἀπαντῶν μήτε εἰς δικαστήρια μήτε ἄλλοθι Κλαζομενίοις, ἀλλὰ αὐτῷ ἡ μὲν γῆ μηλόβοτος, ἡ δὲ ἑστία ἄοικος, διατελεῖ δὲ καθ' αὑτὸν τὴν θαυμαστὴν σοφίαν ἄνω καὶ κάτω στρέφων καὶ διερευνώμενος.

2. Ἡ μὲν δὴ γραφὴ ταύτῃ ἐχέτω· ἀπολογείσθω δὲ Ἀναξαγόρας ὧδέ πως· "Ὅτι μὲν πολλοῦ δέω ἀδικεῖν ὑμᾶς, ὦ ἄνδρες Κλαζομένιοι, εὖ τοῦτο οἶδα· οὔτε γὰρ εἰς χρημάτων λόγον ἐπλημμελεῖσθέ τι ὑπ' ἐμοῦ, οὔτε τὸ ἐμαυτοῦ μέρος ἀδοξοτέραν ὑμῖν τὴν πόλιν ἐν τοῖς Ἕλλησιν παρασκευάζω· ἔν τ' αὖ τοῖς πρὸς ἕκαστον ὑμῶν συμβολαίοις ἀλυπότατον ἐμαυτὸν παρέχειν οἶμαι καὶ μέτριον, τῶν τε νόμων τῶν κειμένων καὶ τῆς πολιτείας ὑφ' ἧς κοσμούμεθα, οὐκ ἔστιν ὅτου ἐλάττω ἔχω λόγον. λείπεται δή, εἰ μηδὲν ἀδικῶν ὑμᾶς ἐγὼ ἐν τοῖς καθ' ἡμέραν ἐμαυτοῦ διαιτήμασι καὶ τῷ τοῦ βίου σχήματι, γνώμῃ ἔτι ἁμαρτάνω, τοῦ μὲν ἔχειν αἰτίαν ὡς ἀδικῶ δημοσίᾳ τὴν πόλιν ἀφεῖσθαί με, τυχεῖν δὲ εἰς τὰ ἐμαυτοῦ ἰδίᾳ διδασκάλων ἀλλ' οὐ κατηγόρων. φράσω δὴ πρὸς ὑμᾶς οἷον τοὐμὸν πρᾶγμά ἐστιν οὐδὲν ὑποστειλάμενος, εἰ καὶ μέλλει γέλωτα ὀφλισκάνειν τὸ ἐπιτήδευμα τοὐμὸν ῥηθέν.

"Ἐγὼ γάρ, ὅτι μέν ἐστιν πολλοῦ ἄξιον δύναμις ἐν πόλει καὶ κοινωνία βίου καὶ ἔργων ἐπιφάνεια καὶ χρῆσις πραγμάτων, σαφῶς οἶδα· εὖ γε μὴν ἐπίστα-

as if from wild animals, neither attending their assemblies, nor being present at festivals of Dionysus, or in law courts, or anywhere else with the Clazomenians; his lands are left for sheep to graze,[2] and his home is derelict, for he spends all his time in solitude, mulling over and over and investigating that strange wisdom of his.

2. Let such be our indictment, and let Anaxagoras defend himself along these lines. "I know full well that I am very far from wronging you, men of Clazomenae, for neither have you suffered any financial loss at my hands, nor for my part do I render your city any less respected among the Greeks at large. Moreover, in my interactions with each one of you, I believe that I show myself to be entirely inoffensive and fair. And as for our established laws and the constitution under which we order our lives, there is nothing in them that I hold in contempt. The conclusion, then, must be that if I do you no wrong either in my daily conduct or in my way of life, but that I am still guilty of poor judgment, then I should be acquitted of the charge of wronging the city at large, and should be assigned advisors for my private affairs instead of public prosecutors. Let me explain my situation to you with no holding back, even though the way I spend my time is likely to provoke your laughter once I describe it.

"Now I am well aware that political power in a city is of great worth, as is communal life, distinction through deeds, and the administration of public affairs. And I also

[2] This detail is also mentioned by Plut. *Per.* 16 and Philo, *Vit. Contemp.* 14.

μαι ταυτὶ τὰ πολλοῦ ἄξια, μετὰ μὲν τρόπου ἀρετῆς καὶ καλοκἀγαθίας, εἰς μέγα πάνυ συντελοῦντα τῷ σχόντι· εἰ δὲ μή, εἰς τοὐναντίον κατασμικρύνοντα καὶ καταβάλλοντα, καὶ μηδὲ τὸ λαθεῖν τοῖς ἔχουσιν, μοχθηροῖς οὖσιν, παρεχόμενα. ἐκλαμπρύνουσι γὰρ αἱ δυνάμεις τοὺς ἄνδρας· καθόσον δ' ἄν τις ἁμάρτῃ τοῦ καλοῦ, κατὰ τοσοῦτον αὐτοὺς ἐξήλεγξαν. εἰ μὲν δή τις γνώμης ἔχοι καλῶς, τὴν ἐπιφάνειαν ἐν τῷ ἀσφαλεῖ κτησάμενος, τῆς δυνάμεως ὤνατο· εἰ δὲ ταύτῃ ἐνδέων ἐπιθοῖτο οἷς αὕτη χρῆται, ἀνάγκη πολλὴ ἀμαθίᾳ τέχνης καὶ εὐπορίᾳ[2] ὀργάνων σφαλῆναι τὸν χρώμενον.

"Ταῦτά τοι ἐννοῶν, ἡγούμην δεῖν φροντιστέον εἶναί μοι μᾶλλον ἄλλου μὴ λάθω, προσιὼν παρὰ δύναμιν τοῖς κοινοῖς, πταίων περὶ αὐτὰ καὶ σφαλλόμενος· οὐδὲ γὰρ εἰ ἐν χορῷ ξυνᾴδειν ὑφ' ὑμῶν ἐταττόμην, ἠδίκουν ἂν πρὶν ἔχειν φωνῆς ἐμμελῶς οὐκ ἐθέλων ἐγκαταμίγνυσθαι τῷ χορῷ. διά τοι ταῦτα τῆς μὲν γῆς ὅπως μοι ἕξει καλῶς ὀλίγα ἐφρόντιζον, κατεθέμην δὲ ἐμαυτὸν φέρων εἰς τοῦτον τὸν βίον ἐξ οὗ τὸ εἰδέναι τῇ ψυχῇ παραγενόμενον, ὥσπερ φῶς ὀφθαλμοῖς, τὴν ἀσφάλειαν τῇ λοιπῇ πορείᾳ παρασκευάσει. τοῦτό γε μὴν τὸ φῶς κτητόν ἐστιν ‹. . .›[3] †οἷς τε λέγομεν παθηναια†[4] ὁδοὶ αἱ ἐπ' αὐτὴν τετμημέναι, οὐ λῆροι οὐδὲ φλυαρίαι οὐδ' ἐπιμέλειαι γεωργικαὶ οὐδὲ ἀγοραῖοι

[2] εὐπορίᾳ R, Trapp: ἀπορίᾳ Heinsius, Davies², Dübner
[3] lacunam stat. Hobein [4] obel. Trapp, Koniaris

understand full well that when these very worthwhile activities are matched with a virtuous and honorable character, they are of enormous benefit to their practitioner, but that when they are not, they produce the opposite effect, and demean and ruin those who engage in them, and do not even allow them to hide their deficiencies. That is because positions of power shine a bright light on the men holding them, and expose them to the degree that any fall short of the good. Thus anyone who has sound judgment and possesses a secure reputation will benefit from that office. But if anyone who lacks these qualities should engage in the very affairs that require them, it is quite certain that he will fail for not having learned the required skills, regardless of abundant means.[3]

"So, with all this in mind, I concluded that I, more than anyone, needed to be wary of thoughtlessly entering public life beyond my abilities and thus make mistakes and fail. By the same token, if I were being appointed by you to sing in a chorus, I would do no wrong by refusing to join the chorus until I could sing in tune. For that reason I have given little thought to keeping my lands in good condition, but instead have devoted myself to this present life, whereby knowledge will come to my soul, like light to my eyes, and provide security for my life's journey ahead. And yet this light is a possession . . .[4] the paths leading to this do not consist of frivolous talk or nonsense, or involve the concerns of farmers, the pursuits of business, or interac-

[3] Or, reading ἀπορίᾳ (and for lack of means). The text of the last phrase is uncertain.

[4] No satisfactory conjecture has been proposed to fill the lacuna and corrupt text.

σπουδαὶ οὐδὲ δημώδεις κοινωνίαι, ἀλλ' ἀληθείας ἔρως καὶ ἡ τῶν ὄντων θέα καὶ ἡ περὶ ταῦτα φιλοτιμία. ταύτῃ νομίσας ἰέναι δεῖν εἰπόμην τοῖς ἄγουσιν λόγοις καὶ τὰ ἴχνη τῆς ὁδοῦ διεσκόπουν.

3. "Καὶ τὰ μὲν ἐμὰ ταύτῃ ἔχει· ὅτι δὲ καὶ περὶ ὑμᾶς τὰ ἄριστα καὶ τὰ δικαιότατα βουλεύομαι ταύτῃ ἰών, νῦν ἐρῶ. τὰ γὰρ κοινὰ σώζεσθαι φιλεῖ, οὐκ ἐὰν τὰ τείχη ὑμῖν ἀραρότα ᾖ οὐδὲ νεώσοικοι σωζόμενοι οὐδὲ νῆες αὐταὶ πλέουσαι, οὐδέ γε στοαὶ καὶ ἄλση καὶ γυμνάσια καὶ τεμένη καὶ πομπεῖα (ταῦτα γὰρ δὴ εἰ καὶ μὴ οἱ πολέμιοι μηδὲ πῦρ μηδὲ ἄλλη τις συμφορά, ἀλλ' ὅ γε χρόνος λαβὼν οἰχήσεται)· τὸ δὲ σῶζον τὰς πόλεις ἡ ἁρμονία καὶ ὁ τῆς πολιτείας κόσμος· {φημὶ κἀγὼ}[5] ταῦτα δὲ ὑπὸ τῆς εὐνομίας γίγνεται, τὴν δὲ εὐνομίαν ἡ τῶν χρωμένων ἀρετὴ φυλάττει, τὴν δὲ ἀρετὴν διδόασιν οἱ λόγοι, τοὺς δὲ λόγους ἡ ἄσκησις, τὴν δὲ ἄσκησιν ἡ ἀλήθεια, τὴν δὲ ἀλήθειαν ἡ περὶ αὐτὴν σχολή. οὐ γάρ ἐστιν, οὐκ ἔστιν ἄλλο ὄργανον ᾧ κτητὸν ἀρετὴ πλὴν ἀληθὴς λόγος, ὑφ' οὗ παροξύνεται ἡ ψυχὴ καὶ ζωπυρεῖται, καὶ οὐκ εἰδυῖα μὲν μανθάνει, μαθοῦσα δὲ φυλάττει ἃ ἔμαθεν, φυλάττουσα δὲ χρῆται, χρωμένη δὲ οὐ σφάλλεται. τοῦτο ἡ διατριβή, τοῦτο ἡ σχολή, ἀληθείας μελέτη καὶ τέχνη βίου καὶ ῥώμη λόγου καὶ παρασκευὴ ψυχῆς καὶ ἄσκησις καλοκἀγαθίας.

"Εἰ μὲν οὖν ταῦτα ἐπ' οὐδὲν συντελεῖ τῶν καλῶν,

[5] del. Meiser, Trapp ut interpolata

tions with the common people, but rather the love of truth, the contemplation of reality, and the zealous pursuit of these. Because I concluded that I had to take this journey, I followed where the arguments led me and searched all about for the traces of their path.

3. "So much for my pursuits. Now I shall explain that by proceeding in this fashion it is also for your benefit that I try to determine what is best and most just. For the preservation of the community does not depend on your having well-constructed city walls, well-preserved shipyards, actual ships on the sea, porticos, groves, gymnasia, temple sanctuaries, or sacred vessels—all of which, even if they survive hostile armies, fires, and other disasters, time itself will seize and carry off. No, what truly preserves cities is harmony and political order. These come about through adherence to the laws. But adherence to the laws is maintained by the virtue of those who live under them, while their virtue is the product of reasoned arguments, the reasoned arguments are the products of practice, the practice is the product of truth, and the truth is the product of the leisure devoted to studying it. For there is, indeed there can be, no other means for acquiring virtue than by true reason, which stimulates and inflames the soul: what it does not know, it seeks to learn; what it has learned, it seeks to retain; what it retains, it puts into practice; and when putting it into practice, it does not go wrong. This is how I spend my time, and this is what occupies my leisure: the pursuit of truth, an expertise in living life, the power of reason, a preparation of the soul, and a training in honorable conduct.

"Now if these things have nothing good to contribute,

ἢ συντελοῦντά γε οὐ δεδίδακται οὐδὲ ἤσκηται, ἀλλὰ εἰκῇ καὶ εἰ ἔτυχεν παραγίγνεται,[6] σκηνὴ τὸ χρῆμα, εἰσαγγελίας ἄξιον καὶ γραφῆς·[7] εἰ δὲ τοῦτο μὲν οὐδεὶς φήσει, οὐχ οὕτω μέμηνεν, ἀλήθειαν δὲ καὶ ὑγιῆ λόγον καὶ ἀρετὴν καὶ γνῶσιν νόμου καὶ δίκης οὐκ ἔστιν ἑτέρως λαβεῖν ἢ περὶ αὐτὰ πραγματευόμενον, οὐ μᾶλλον ἢ τὰ σκυτοτομικὰ μὴ περὶ αὐτὰ ἄγοντας σχολήν, ἢ τὰ χαλκευτικὰ μὴ πρὸς τῷ βαύνῳ καὶ τῷ πυρὶ διημερεύοντας, ἢ τὰ κυβερνητικὰ μὴ θαλαττουργοῦντας καὶ ναυτιλλομένους, πράττοντες μὲν ταῦτα ἀδικοῦμεν οὐδέν, ἀπολειπόμενοι δὲ αὐτῶν καὶ μηλόβοτον ἐῶντες τὴν ψυχὴν καὶ ἄγονον, ἦμεν ἂν γραφῆς καὶ εἰσαγγελίας <ἄξιοι>.[8]

"Ἐγὼ μὲν ἃ νομίζω καὶ δίκαια ἅμα καὶ ἀληθῆ εἶναι ἀπελογησάμην πρὸς ὑμᾶς, ὦ ἄνδρες Κλαζομένιοι. ἀξιῶ δὲ ὑμᾶς μὴ αὐτόθεν διενέγκαι τὴν ψῆφον, ἀλλ' ἐπισχεῖν τὸ νῦν ἔχον· αὐτόπτας δὲ καὶ θεατὰς γενομένους τῶν αὐτῶν ἐμοί, εἰ μέν τι χρηστὸν περιγίγνεσθαι δόξετε διδαχθέντες ἔργῳ, ἀφεῖναι τῆς γραφῆς· εἰ δὲ μή, τότε ὑμεῖς μὲν ψηφιεῖσθε τὰ ὑμῖν δοκοῦντα, ἡμεῖς δὲ καὶ ὧς περὶ αὐτῶν καλῶς βουλευσόμεθα."

4. Ταῦτα λέγοντος καὶ ἀπολογιζομένου τοῦ Ἀναξαγόρου γελάσονται, ὡς τὸ εἰκός, οἱ Κλαζομένιοι· οὐ

[6] παραγίγνεται Markland, Trapp: παραγιγνόμενα R
[7] καὶ γραφῆς Trapp: ὄντα φῇς R
[8] hic suppl. Trapp: post γραφῆς Acciaiolus

or even if they do make some contribution, they do not come about by teaching or training but instead happen randomly and by chance,[5] then the whole endeavor is an empty show and truly deserves an indictment and criminal prosecution. But if no one is mad enough to claim that such is indeed the case, and if it is a fact that there is no other way to acquire truth, sound reason, virtue, and a knowledge of law and justice than by spending time and effort on them—any more than people can learn shoemaking without devoting time to it, or metalworking without spending days at forges and fires, or seamanship without going to sea and sailing—then I do nothing wrong by pursuing these matters. On the contrary, if I should abandon them and allow my soul to become a barren field for sheep to graze, then I really would be liable to indictment and prosecution.

"Men of Clazomenae, I have offered you a defense that I consider both just and true. I request, however, that you not render your verdict right away, but withhold your decision for the time being, and instead become eyewitnesses and observers of the same things I observe, and if you think that anything good results from what you learn from this experience, you should acquit me of this charge. But if not, then you will vote what seems right to you, and I shall nonetheless continue my rightful deliberations on these matters."

4. The Clazomenians will undoubtedly laugh at Anaxagoras for saying such things in his defense, for they will

[5] This issue is taken up in *Orr.* 27 ("Whether virtue is an art") and 38 ("Whether one can become good by divine dispensation").

γὰρ δὴ πιθανώτερός γε δόξει εἶναι τῆς γραφῆς, ἀληθῆ δὲ οὐδὲν ἧττον αὐτῷ λελέξεται, κἂν ἐκεῖνοι καταψηφίσωνται. εἰ δέ πού τις οἷος δικαστοῦ χώραν ἔχειν μὴ κυάμῳ λαχόντος, ἀλλ' ἥπερ δὴ χειροτονία δικαστοῦ μόνη, αὐτῷ τῷ εἰδέναι, πρὸς τοῦτον οὐχ ὡς ἀδικῶν, οὐδ' ὡς φεύγων γραφὴν ἀπολογιεῖται εἴτε Ἀναξαγόρας ἐν Κλαζομεναῖς, εἴτε ἐν Ἐφέσῳ Ἡράκλειτος, εἴτε ἐν Σάμῳ Πυθαγόρας, εἴτε ἐν Ἀβδήροις Δημόκριτος, εἴτε ἐν Κολοφῶνι Ξενοφάνης, εἴτε ἐν Ἐλέᾳ Παρμενίδης, εἴτε ἐν Ἀπολλωνίᾳ Διογένης, εἴτε τις ἄλλος τῶν δαιμονίων ἐκείνων ἀνδρῶν, ἀλλ' ἐξ ἰσοτιμίας οὑτωσὶ πείθων καὶ διαλεγόμενος, συνετὰ συνετοῖς λέγων καὶ πιστὰ πιστοῖς καὶ ἔνθεα ἐνθέοις· ὅτι τῇ τοῦ ἀνθρώπου ψυχῇ ἔνειμεν θεὸς δυνάμεις τρεῖς καὶ χώρας καὶ φύσεις, ὥσπερ τινὰ ἀθροίζων ξυνοίκησιν πόλεως· ἧς τὸ μὲν ἄρχον καὶ προβουλευόμενον εἰς ἀκρόπολιν ἀναγαγών, ἱδρύσας αὐτοῦ, πλέον οὐδὲν αὐτῷ προσέταξεν λογισμοῦ· τὸ δ' ἀκμάζον καὶ πράττειν δεινὸν καὶ τελεσιουργεῖν ἱκανὸν τὰ βουλευθέντα, συνῆψέν τε καὶ ξυνεκέρασεν δι' ὑπηρεσίας προσταγμάτων τῷ βουλευτικῷ· τρίτον δ' αὖ, τὸ ἀργὸν τοῦτο πλῆθος καὶ ἀκόλαστον καὶ βάναυσον, καὶ μεστὸν μὲν ἐπιθυμιῶν, μεστὸν δὲ ἐρώτων, μεστὸν δὲ ὕβρεως, μεστὸν δὲ ἡδονῶν παντοδαπῶν, τρίτην ἔχειν μοῖραν, οἷον δῆμόν τινα ἀργὸν καὶ πολύφωνον καὶ πολυπαθῆ καὶ ἔμπληκτον.

not find him more convincing than the charges brought against him. All the same, he will have spoken the truth, even if they condemn him. But what if there existed somewhere a person able to serve as a juror, one not chosen by a bean,[6] but appointed by the only true criterion for selecting a juror, knowledge itself? Before such a juror neither Anaxagoras in Clazomenae, nor Heraclitus in Ephesus, Pythagoras on Samos, Democritus in Abdera, Xenophanes in Colophon, Parmenides in Elea, Diogenes in Apollonia,[7] nor any other of these divinely inspired men will need to present his case like some lawbreaker or defendant in a criminal trial, but instead will seek to persuade by conversing on an equal basis, by making intelligent arguments to intelligent men, trustworthy ones to trustworthy men, and inspired ones to inspired men. He will say, in effect, that god allotted to the human soul three faculties with their specific locations and natures, as if he were bringing them together to found a city. He led the ruling and deliberative component up to the acropolis and situated it there, allotting to it the faculty of reasoning and reasoning alone. A second component that is vigorous, skilled to act, and able to put deliberations into effect, he attached to and combined with the deliberative faculty as a subordinate to execute its commands. The third component, a lazy, unruly, low-class multitude filled with desires, lusts, violence, and pleasures of all kinds, occupies third place, like some lazy, raucous, impassioned, and impulsive populace.

[6] Jurors in Athens were selected by drawing beans from an urn: white, yes; black, no—a procedure also mentioned at *Or*. 3.5.

[7] A fifth-century BC Ionian philosopher, not to be confused with Diogenes the Cynic; cf. Diog. Laert. 9.57.

Ταύτῃ δὴ νενεμημένης τῆς ψυχῆς, τῇ οἰκονομίᾳ τῆς τοῦ ἀνθρώπου συντάξεως στάσις ἐγγίγνεσθαι φιλεῖ, αὐτὸ ἐκεῖνο τὸ ἐν πόλει πάθος· ὧν ἡ μὲν εὐδαίμων πόλις βασιλεύεται, τῶν ἄλλων μερῶν εἰκόντων κατὰ τὸν τοῦ θεοῦ νόμον τῷ δυναμένῳ καὶ πεφυκότι ἐξηγεῖσθαι· ἡ δὲ ταύτης ἐλλειπεστέρα κατ' εὐδαιμονίαν πόλις, ἀριστοκρατίαν ὀνομάζουσα τὴν τῶν ἐν δυνάμει ξυνεληλυθότων ἀρχήν, ἐλάττων μέν ἐστιν βασιλευομένης, κρείττων δὲ δημοκρατουμένης, ἰσχυρὰ μέν τις καὶ πρακτική, κατὰ τὴν Λακωνικὴν ἢ Κρητικὴν ἢ Μαντινικὴν ἢ Πελληνικὴν ἢ Θετταλικὴν πολιτείαν ἱσταμένη, φιλότιμος δὲ ἄγαν καὶ φιλόνεικος, καὶ δύσερις καὶ πολυπράγμων καὶ ἰτητικὴ καὶ θαρσαλέα. τρίτον δ' αὖ πολιτείας γένος, ᾗ ὄνομα μὲν εὔφημον δημοκρατία, τὸ δὲ ἀληθὲς ὀχλοκρατία, κατὰ τὴν Ἀττικὴν ἢ Συρακοσίαν ἢ Μιλησίαν ἤ τινα ἄλλην πλήθους ἰσχύν, πολύφωνόν τε καὶ ἀκόλαστον καὶ παντοδαπόν.

5. Τριῶν δὴ πολιτειῶν τρία ταυτὶ μιμήματα {βίων}[9] ἴδοις ἂν ἐν ἀνθρώπου ψυχῇ· κατὰ μὲν τὸ βουλευτικὸν καὶ ἀρχικὸν καὶ ἐκποδὼν τῇ πράξει τε καὶ χειρουργίᾳ, τὸ θεωρητικὸν ψυχῆς γένος· τὸ δὲ πρακτικὸν δεύτερον, δευτέρως τιμώμενόν τε καὶ δοκιμαζόμενον· τήν τε ἐν ἀνδρὶ δημοκρατίαν οὐ χαλεπὸν ἰδεῖν· πολὺ γὰρ τὸ τῆς πολιτείας τοῦτο γένος ἐπινέμεται πᾶσαν ψυχήν.

Καὶ τοῦτο μὲν ἐατέον καὶ ἀποχειροτονητέον τοῦ ἀρίστου· θεωρίαν δὲ πράξει παραβαλλομένην, ἑκα-

Because the soul is divided up in this fashion, factions all too often arise within the organization of the human constitution, just as it happens in a city. Now, happy is the city governed by a king, when, in accordance with divine law, all the other elements yield to the one that is naturally capable of leading them. Second to it with respect to happiness is the city that gives the name of aristocracy to the rule of men who have joined together to hold power. It is inferior to a city ruled by a monarch, but superior to a democratic one. It is strong and active with a constitution like that of Sparta, Crete, Mantinea, Pellene, or Thessaly, but it also can be excessively ambitious and competitive, contentious, meddlesome, reckless, and audacious. The third type of government, euphemistically called a democracy but in reality an ochlocracy, is like that of Athens, Syracuse, Miletus, or any other kind of mass rule that is raucous, unruly, and heterogeneous.

5. You can find counterparts of these three forms of governance in the human soul. Corresponding to the deliberative and ruling component, which does not engage in action or in manual crafts, is the contemplative element of the soul. Second is the active element, which takes second place in honor and esteem. Finally, democracy is not difficult to find in an individual, for this form of governance is numerous and spreads throughout every soul.

We can simply dismiss this third element and reject it as unqualified for first place. But when contemplation is

---

[9] del. Markland, Trapp

τέραν τυγχάνουσαν τοῦ καλοῦ, τὴν μὲν θεωρίαν κατὰ τὴν γνῶσιν, τὴν δὲ πρᾶξιν κατὰ τὴν ἀρετήν, ποτέραν προτιμητέον; ἀποκρίνεται ὁ λόγος ὅτι εἰ μὲν κατὰ τὴν χρείαν αὐτῶν ἱστάμεθα, τιμητέον τὴν πρᾶξιν, εἰ δὲ κατὰ τὴν αἰτίαν τοῦ γενομένου καλῶς, προτιμητέον τὴν θεωρίαν. ὥστε καὶ σπονδὰς ἑκατέρῳ σπεισάμενοι νείμωμεν τὰς δυνάμεις καὶ τὸ σχῆμα τοῦ βίου τοῖς ἀνδράσιν ἢ κατὰ φύσιν ἢ καθ' ἡλικίαν ἢ κατὰ τύχην.

Καὶ γὰρ φύσει διαφέρει ἕτερος ἑτέρου, ὁ μὲν ἐν πράξει ἐξασθενῶν, εὐχερὴς δέ τις ὢν κατὰ τὴν ψυχὴν πρὸς θεωρίαν, ὁ δὲ ἐν μὲν θεωρίᾳ καματηρὸς ὤν, πράττειν δὲ ἐρρωμένος. διίστησιν δὲ καὶ ἡλικία τοὺς ἄνδρας· νεότητος μὲν γὰρ ἡ πρᾶξις· Ὅμηρος λέγει, κἀγὼ πείθομαι,

νέῳ δέ τε πάντ' ἐπέοικεν . . .

νέος μὲν γὰρ ὢν ὁ φιλόσοφος πραττέτω, λεγέτω, πολιτευέσθω, στρατευέσθω, ἀρχέτω. καὶ γὰρ οἱ Πλάτωνος ἐπὶ Σικελίαν δρόμοι καὶ πόνοι καὶ περὶ Δίωνα σπουδὴ κατὰ τὴν ἀκμὴν ἐγίγνοντο τῆς ἡλικίας· γηράσαντα δ' αὐτὸν ὑπεδέξατο Ἀκαδημία καὶ βαθεῖα σχολὴ καὶ λόγοι καλοὶ καὶ θεωρία ἄπταιστος, ἐν πολλῇ καὶ ἀμφιλαφεῖ ἀληθείᾳ κατατιθέμενον τὸ τοῦ βίου τέλος. καὶ Ξενοφῶντα νεανιευόμενον μὲν ἐν τοῖς

compared to action, with each having a share of the good—contemplation for its acquisition of knowledge, action for its exercise of virtue, then which should be preferred? Reason's answer is that if our evaluation of them is based on utility, then we must choose action, but if it is based on what causes a noble action, then we must prefer contemplation. As a result, let us declare a truce between them both and instead assign men their capabilities and appropriate ways of life on the basis of their natures, ages, or fortunes.

People differ from one another by their natures. One person is utterly feeble when it comes to action, but has an unflinching soul for contemplation, whereas another grows weary when it comes to contemplation, but is tireless in action. Age also differentiates men. Youth is a time of action, and here I agree with Homer:

> it is altogether proper for a young man . . .[8]

When he is young, a philosopher may well lead an active life, make speeches, engage in politics, go on campaign, and hold office. For example, Plato's trips to Sicily and his labors and zeal on behalf of Dion all took place in the prime of his life.[9] But once he grew old, he was welcomed into the Academy with its profound leisure, noble discussions, and uninterrupted contemplation, where he spent the end of his life in the quest for abundant and spacious truth. I admire Xenophon for spending his youth in action,

[8] *Il.* 22.71. Priam is telling Hector that "it is altogether proper for a young man" to die in battle, but disgraceful for an old man like himself.

[9] The trips of Plato to Syracuse were between 367 and 361 BC.

ἔργοις φιλῶ, γηράσκοντα δὲ ἐν τοῖς λόγοις ἐπαινῶ. διίστησιν δὲ ἤδη καὶ τύχη· τὸν μὲν γὰρ δυνάμει καὶ πράξει ἀναγκαίᾳ περιέβαλεν, τὸν δὲ σχολῇ καὶ ἡσυχίᾳ προσηνεῖ· ὧν τὸν μὲν ἐπαινῶ ἐν τῷ ἀναγκαίῳ ἀνδριζόμενον, τὸν δὲ καὶ μακαρίζω καὶ ἐπαινῶ· μακαρίζω μὲν τῆς σχολῆς, ἐπαινῶ δὲ τῆς ἱστορίας.

6. Ἀλλὰ τὸν μὲν ἐκ τῆς Εὐρώπης ἐπὶ τὴν Ἀσίαν πλέοντα, ἵνα ἴδῃ τὴν Αἰγυπτίων γῆν καὶ τοῦ Νείλου τὰς ἐκβολάς, ἢ πυραμίδας ὑψηλὰς ἢ ὄρνεις ξένους ἢ βοῦν ἢ τράγον, μακαρίζομεν τῆς θέας, κἂν ἐπὶ τὸν Ἴστρον τις ἔλθῃ, κἂν τὸν Γάγγην ἴδῃ, κἄν τις αὐτόπτης γένηται Βαβυλῶνος κειμένης, ἢ τῶν ἐν Σάρδεσιν ποταμῶν, ἢ τῶν ἐν Ἰλίῳ τάφων, ἢ τῶν ἐν Ἑλλησπόντῳ τόπων· καὶ ‹ἐκ›[10] τῆς Ἀσίας ἐπὶ τὴν Ἑλλάδα περαιοῦνται στόλοι, ἢ ἐπὶ τὰς Ἀθήνησιν τέχνας, ἢ ἐπὶ τοὺς Θήβησιν αὐλούς, ἢ ἐπὶ τοὺς ἐν Ἄργει τύπους.

Ὁμήρῳ δὲ καὶ Ὀδυσσεὺς σοφὸς διὰ πολλὴν πλάνην,

πολλῶν δ᾽ ἀνθρώπων ἴδεν ἄστεα καὶ νόον ἔγνω·

τὰ δὲ Ὀδυσσέως θεάματα ἢ Θρᾷκες ἦσαν, ἢ Κίκονες οἱ ἄγριοι, ἢ Κιμμέριοι οἱ ἀνήλιοι, ἢ Κύκλωπες οἱ ξενοκτόνοι, ἢ γυνὴ φαρμακίς, ἢ τὰ ἐν Ἅιδου θεάματα, ἢ Σκύλλα, ἢ Χάρυβδις, ἢ Ἀλκινόου κῆπος, ἢ ἡ Εὐμαίου αὐλή· πάντα θνητά, πάντα ἐφήμερα, πάντα ἄπιστα.

10 suppl. Trapp praeeunte Davies[2]

but I also praise him for spending his old age in his philosophical pursuits. Finally, fortune too differentiates people by investing one person with authority and the action it necessitates, but another with leisure and pleasant tranquility. I praise the former for manfully doing what needs to be done, but I count the latter both blessed and praiseworthy—blessed for his leisure, praiseworthy for his investigations.

6. When someone sails from Europe to Asia in order to see the land of Egypt and the Nile Delta, or the great pyramids, or the exotic birds, or the ox, or the goat, we congratulate him on the sights he has seen, as we do when someone travels to the Ister, or sees the Ganges, or inspects firsthand the ruins of Babylon, or the rivers of Sardis, or the tombs at Troy, or sites on the Hellespont. And there are excursions that cross over from Asia to Greece, either to see the arts in Athens, or the reed pipes in Thebes,[10] or the sculptures in Argos.[11]

According to Homer, Odysseus became wise through his wide travels:

> he saw the cities of many men and learned their
> minds.[12]

But the sights that Odysseus saw included Thracians, savage Cicones, sunless Cimmerians, Cyclopes who kill strangers, a woman who serves drugs,[13] the sights in Hades, Scylla, Charybdis, the gardens of Alcinous, or the hut of Eumaeus—all mortal, all ephemeral, and all incredible.

[10] Boeotian Thebes was famous for crafting *auloi* (reed pipes), also mentioned at *Or*. 29.1. [11] Polyclitus (5th c. BC) was the most celebrated Argive sculptor.

[12] *Od*. 1.3. [13] Circe.

Τὰ δὲ τοῦ φιλοσόφου ἀνδρὸς θεάματα τῷ εἰκάσω; ὀνείρῳ, νὴ Δί', ἐναργεῖ καὶ πανταχοῦ περιφερομένῳ· οὗ τὸ μὲν σῶμα οὐδαμοῦ στέλλεται, ἡ δὲ ψυχὴ πρόεισιν πᾶσαν γῆν, ἐκ γῆς ἐπ' οὐρανόν, πᾶσαν μὲν περαιουμένη θάλατταν, πᾶσαν δὲ διερχομένη γῆν, πάντα δὲ ἀέρα ἀνιπταμένη, συνθέουσα ἡλίῳ, συμπεριφερομένη σελήνῃ, συνδεδεμένη τῷ τῶν ἄλλων ἄστρων χορῷ καὶ μονονουχὶ τῷ Διὶ συνοικονομοῦσα τὰ ὄντα καὶ συντάττουσα. ὦ στόλου μακαρίου, καὶ θεαμάτων καλῶν καὶ ὀνείρων ἀληθινῶν.

But to what can I compare the sights of a man pursuing philosophy? To a dream, by Zeus, but one that is clear-sighted and roams everywhere.[14] His body remains stationary, but his soul goes forth over the entire earth, travels from earth to heaven, crosses every sea, traverses every land, flies up through every region of the air, keeps pace with the sun, revolves with the moon, takes its place in the chorus of the other heavenly bodies, and all but joins with Zeus in controlling and ordering all that exists. What a blessed journey, what beautiful sights, what truthful dreams!

[14] Cf. *Or.* 10.3 and 9 for the philosophical dreamlike state and the flight of the soul over the earth and into the heavens.

# *ORATION* 17

## INTRODUCTION

This oration defends Plato's notorious decision to banish poetry from his ideal state (*Resp.* 3.398a–b).[1] It opens with an analogous situation of the Spartan magistrates banishing Mithaecus the chef, because they had no need for his expertise, whereas he was welcomed elsewhere for the pleasure and utility he provided (§1).[2] Since pursuits and customs differ greatly from one people to another and cannot be interchanged, the citizens in Plato's ideal state are justified in determining what is beneficial to them (§2). The problem for the speaker is how to respect Plato's writings while at the same time maintain his admiration for Homer.[3] He argues that Plato fashioned his republic like a sculptor, who selects features from many different bodies and combines them into one harmonious whole. If, theoretically, humans could fashion perfect bodies that never needed medical attention, they could not be blamed for sending off doctors to other peoples, who would need

[1] Plato's specific criticisms are listed in *Or.* 18.5.

[2] The criteria of pleasure and utility form the basis of the entire argument.

[3] An aspect of Maximus' overall project is reconciling Homer with Plato; cf. *Or.* 41.2: "I believe Homer and I trust Plato."

and welcome them (§3). Likewise, the citizens in Plato's republic, having been fashioned by a strict upbringing, have no need of a Homer to give them pleasure and magnify in his verses their already established ideas of the gods. Moreover, since one pleasure sets off a chain of further pleasures, Plato banned poetry from the very start as unnecessary and corrupting (§4). Many peoples have sound governments who lack any knowledge of Homer. Spartans and Cretans were renowned for their virtue long before they heard rhapsodic performances. Barbarians also possess virtue that is completely independent of Homer. If Homer's verses were simply a source of pleasure, then rhapsodes would not be the sorry bunch that they are. If his poetry were welcomed exclusively for the pleasure it provides, then Homer would be banished not only from ideal states but from actual ones, where hard work and virtue are held in esteem (§5).

# *ORATION* 17

Εἰ καλῶς Πλάτων Ὅμηρον τῆς πολιτείας παρῃτήσατο

1. Ἦλθεν εἰς Σπάρτην Συρακόσιος σοφιστής, οὐ κατὰ τὴν Προδίκου καλλιλογίαν, οὐδὲ κατὰ τὴν Ἱππίου γενεαλογίαν, οὐδὲ κατὰ τὴν Γοργίου ῥητορείαν, οὐδὲ κατὰ τὴν Θρασυμάχου ἀδικίαν, οὐδὲ κατ᾽ ἄλλην πραγματείαν λόγου παρεσκευασμένος· ἀλλ᾽ ἦν τῷ Συρακοσίῳ σοφιστῇ ἡ τέχνη αὐτὸ ἔργον, κεκραμένον ὁμοῦ χρείᾳ καὶ ἡδονῇ. τὰ γὰρ ὄψα καὶ τὰ σιτία ἡδυσμάτων συμμετρίαις καὶ κράσεσιν καὶ ποικιλίαις καὶ τῇ διὰ πυρὸς ὁμιλίᾳ αὐτὰ ἑαυτῶν προσφορώτατα εἶναι παρεσκεύαζεν· καὶ ἦν πολὺ τὸ Μιθαίκου κλέος ἐν τοῖς Ἕλλησιν κατὰ ὀψοποιΐαν, ὥσπερ τὸ Φειδίου κατὰ ἀγαλματουργίαν.

Ἧκεν δὴ καὶ εἰς τὴν Σπάρτην οὗτος ἀνὴρ δυναστεύουσαν τότε, ἐν ἀρχούσῃ τῇ πόλει καὶ δύναμιν

---

[1] Mithaecus (late 5th c. BC), named below, wrote a cookbook that is mentioned at Pl. *Grg.* 518b; he is also cited at *Or.* 15.4.

[2] A contemporary of Socrates, famous for making fine distinctions between words; cf. Pl. *Meno* 75e, *Euthd.* 277e, *La.* 197d,

# *ORATION* 17

## Whether Plato was right to exclude Homer from his republic

1. A Syracusan sophist[1] once came to Sparta. He was no expert in elegant language like Prodicus,[2] or in genealogies like Hippias,[3] or in rhetoric like Gorgias,[4] or in injustice like Thrasymachus,[5] or in any other intellectual endeavor, but the art of this sophist from Syracuse was an activity that combined both utility and pleasure. For by balancing, blending, and varying seasonings and by heating them together, he was able to make both delicacies and staples so much more palatable than they otherwise were. Indeed, Mithaecus enjoyed as much fame among the Greeks for his cuisine as Phidias did for his sculpture.

This man came to Sparta when it was the foremost city in Greece,[6] with high hopes that in this leading city in-

and *Chrm.* 163d. He also authored the fable of Heracles at the crossroads, cited at *Orr.* 14.1 and 25.7.

[3] Cf. Pl. *Hp. mai.* 285d. Hippias of Elis was a fifth-century BC polymath.

[4] The famous rhetorician and sophist who appears in Plato's *Gorgias*.

[5] Thrasymachus' arguments in favor of practicing injustice are refuted at Pl. *Resp.* 1.336b–54a.

[6] That is, after the end of the Peloponnesian War in 403 BC.

γενναίαν περιβεβλημένῃ εὔελπις ὢν εὐδόκιμον αὐτῷ φανεῖσθαι τὴν τέχνην. τὸ δὲ ἦν ἄρα οὐ τοιοῦτον, ἀλλὰ τῶν Λακεδαιμονίων τὰ τέλη ἀνακαλεσάμενοι τὸν ἄνδρα ἐκέλευον αὐτῷ ἐξιέναι τῆς Σπάρτης αὐτίκα μάλ' εἰς ἄλλην γῆν καὶ ἀνθρώπους ἄλλους· εἰθίσθαι[1] γὰρ ὑπὸ τοῦ πονεῖν δεῖσθαι τροφῆς ἀναγκαίας μᾶλλον ἢ τεχνικῆς, καὶ τὰ σώματα ἔχειν ἀκολάκευτα καὶ ἁπλᾶ καὶ μηδὲν ὀψοποιοῦ δεόμενα, οὐ μᾶλλον ἢ τὰ τῶν λεόντων· ἀπιέναι δὲ ἐκεῖσε ἔνθα καὶ εἰκὸς τιμηθήσεσθαι αὐτῷ τὴν τέχνην, δι' ἡδονῆς καὶ χρείας τοὺς δημιουργοὺς αὐτῆς ἀσπαζομένων. οὕτω Μίθαικος ἐξῆλθεν Σπάρτης αὐτῇ τέχνῃ· παρεδέξαντο δὲ αὐτὸν οὐχ ἧττον οἱ ἄλλοι Ἕλληνες, κατὰ τὴν ἑαυτῶν ἡδονὴν ἀσπαζόμενοι, οὐ κατὰ τὴν παρὰ Λακεδαιμονίοις ἀτιμίαν ὑπεριδόντες.

2. Εἰ δὲ δεῖ καὶ ἄλλας παρακαλέσαι εἰκόνας τῷ παρόντι λόγῳ σεμνοτέρας τῆς Μιθαίκου τέχνης, Θηβαῖοι αὐλητικὴν ἐπιτηδεύουσιν καὶ ἔστιν ἡ δι' αὐλῶν μοῦσα ἐπιχώριος τοῖς Βοιωτοῖς· Ἀθηναῖοι λέγειν, καὶ ἔστιν ἡ περὶ λόγους σπουδὴ τέχνη Ἀττική· ἐπιτηδεύματα Κρητικὰ θῆραι, ὀρειβασίαι, τοξεῖαι, δρόμοι· τὰ Θετταλικὰ ἱππική, τὰ Κυρηναϊκὰ διφρεῖαι, τὰ Αἰτωλικὰ λῃστεῖαι· ἀκοντίζουσιν Ἀκαρνᾶνες, πελτάζουσιν Θρᾷκες, νησιῶται πλέουσιν. ἐὰν δὲ μεταθῇς τὰ ἐπιτηδεύματα ἄλλων πρὸς ἄλλους, νοθεύσεις τὰς τέχνας. τί γὰρ δεῖ ἠπειρώταις νεῶν, ἢ ἀμούσοις αὐλῶν, ἢ ὀρείοις ἵππων, ἢ πεδιάδα οἰκοῦσιν δρόμων, ἢ ὁπλίταις τόξων, ἢ τοξόταις ἀσπίδων;

vested with noble power he and his art would become famous. It did not turn out that way, however, for the Spartan magistrates summoned him and ordered him to leave Sparta immediately for some other land and different people. Their own regimen of hard work, they said, required food that was nutritious rather than artificial, and they had unpampered and simple bodies no more in need of chefs than the bodies of lions. So he should go where he and his art were likely to win respect, where people welcomed such practitioners to provide both pleasure and utility. And so Mithaecus left Sparta and took his art with him. The other Greeks received him no less warmly for all that, welcoming him for the sake of their own pleasure, rather than spurning him because of his rebuff in Sparta.

2. But I may need to adduce some other examples on this topic more impressive than Mithaecus and his art. The Thebans practice pipe playing, and pipe music is indigenous to the Boeotians; the Athenians practice speaking, and the study of oratory is the art of Attica. The Cretans practice hunting, mountaineering, archery, and running; the Thessalians horsemanship, the Cyrenaeans chariot racing, and the Aetolians banditry. The Acarnanians are javelin throwers, the Thracians peltasts, and the islanders are sailors. If, however, you transfer the pursuits of one community to another, you will corrupt the arts themselves. For what need do inland dwellers have for ships, or those with no knowledge of music for pipes, or mountain dwellers for horses, or plains dwellers for racecourses, or hoplites for bows and arrows, or archers for infantry shields?

---

1 εἰθίσθαι Russell: ἐφίεμεν R

Ὥσπερ οὖν ἐνταῦθα διεκληρώσαντο τὰς τέχνας οἱ τόποι ἢ αἱ φύσεις τῶν χρωμένων ἢ αἱ φιλίαι τῶν ἀπ' ἀρχῆς ἐπιτηδευθέντων, καὶ οὐ <κατὰ>[2] ταὐτὰ ἕκαστον οὔτε πᾶσιν τίμιον διότι ἐνίοις οὔτε ἄτιμον πᾶσιν ὅτι μή τισιν, ἀλλὰ εὐδοκιμεῖ ἕκαστον κατὰ τὴν χρείαν τῶν λαβόντων, τί κωλύει τοὺς τῆς καλῆς ταύτης πόλεως πολίτας, οὓς Πλάτων θρεψάμενος τῷ λόγῳ ὑπὸ νόμοις ξένοις καὶ οὐ καθωμιλημένοις τῷ τῶν πολλῶν ἔθει κατῴκισεν, αὖθις αὖ λόγῳ ἔχειν καὶ τούτους ἐπιχώρια ἄττα αὐτῶν νόμιμά τε καὶ ἐπιτηδεύματα, ξυμπεφυκότα τῇ ἐκ παίδων τροφῇ, τιμώμενα μὲν αὐτοῖς κατὰ τὴν χρείαν αὐτῶν ἐκείνων, οὐκ ἀτιμαζόμενα δὲ παρὰ τοῖς ἄλλοις ἐπεὶ μὴ κἀκείνοις ἥρμοσεν;

Εἰ μὲν γὰρ πόλιν πόλει παραβάλλομεν καὶ πολιτείαν πολιτείᾳ καὶ νόμους νόμοις καὶ νομοθέτην νομοθέτῃ καὶ τροφὴν τροφῇ, ἔχοι ἄν τινα ἡμῖν λόγον ἡ ἐξέτασις τοιάδε, διερευνωμένοις τὸ παρ' ἑκάστοις ἐνδέον· εἰ δέ τις μέρος τοῦ ὅλου ἀποτεμόμενος καθ' αὑτὸ σκοπεῖ διὰ μαρτύρων τῶν χρωμένων τούτῳ ἢ μή—οὕτω γὰρ ἂν καὶ τὰ ἄλλα πάντα ὅσα ἄνθρωποι χρῶνται κατ' ἴσον ἂν τύχοι τιμῆς καὶ ἀτιμίας καὶ διατελοῖ ἐν ἀμφισβητησίμῳ κρίσει πλανώμενα· καὶ γὰρ αἱ τροφαὶ καὶ τὰ φάρμακα καὶ τὰ διαιτήματα καὶ τἆλλα ὅσα τῇ τῶν ἀνθρώπων χρείᾳ ἀνακέκραται, οὐ πᾶσιν ἑξῆς ὅμοια πάντα, ἀλλὰ τὸ αὐτὸ ἤδη τὸν μὲν ἔβλαψεν, τὸν δὲ ὤνησεν, καὶ τὸν μὲν εὔφρανεν, τὸν δὲ

[2] suppl. Schenkl, Meiser, Trapp

If therefore, as these examples show, the arts are distributed according to their locations, or the natural abilities of those engaging in them, or the affinities of those who first practiced them, and for this reason no one of them is universally respected because a few respect it, nor universally disrespected because a few disrespect it, but each is respected by those who have taken it up and find it useful, then what is to prevent the citizens of Plato's noble city, whom he educated with his arguments and organized under novel laws that did not conform to ordinary practice, from having in theory their own native customs and pursuits naturally conforming to their upbringing since childhood? Should not these practices be held in honor by the very people who find them useful and not be despised by others for not conforming to their own practices?

Now if we were comparing cities with cities, constitutions with constitutions, laws with laws, lawmakers with lawmakers, and upbringings with upbringings, then such an examination on our part would make some sense, so long as we were investigating what is lacking in each. If, however, anyone isolates one component from the whole and examines it all by itself on the basis of testimonies from those who practice it and those who do not, then, if they are examined in this way, absolutely all human practices would meet with equal amounts of respect and disrespect, and would remain in limbo, with no evaluation that was conclusive. For example, diets, medicines, regimens, and everything else pertaining to human needs, are not all the same for everyone without exception, but the very same thing has often harmed one person and helped another, or given joy to one and grief to another. That is

ἠνίασεν· ἕκαστον γὰρ τούτων ἡ χρεία καὶ ὁ καιρὸς καὶ ἡ ὑπόθεσις τοῦ βίου ἕτερον ἑτέρῳ φαίνεσθαι ποιεῖ.

3. Οὕτω τοίνυν ἐχόντων τούτων, μεταβάντες αὖ περὶ Ὁμήρου σκοπῶμεν ἀδεκάστως μάλα, οὔθ' ὅστις Πλάτωνι χαίρει ἀτιμάζων Ὅμηρον, οὔθ' ὅστις Ὅμηρον θαυμάζει μεμφόμενος Πλάτωνι· οὐ γὰρ διακεκλήρωται οὐδὲ ἀπέσχισται ἑκάτερον θατέρου, ἀλλ' ἔξεστίν που καὶ τὰ Πλάτωνος τιμᾶν καὶ θαυμάζειν Ὅμηρον· ἔξεστιν δὲ ὧδε.

Πόλιν οἰκίζει Πλάτων τῷ λόγῳ οὐ Κρητικὴν οὐδὲ Δωρικὴν οὐδὲ Πελοποννησίαν οὐδὲ Σικελικὴν οὐδέ, μὰ Δί', Ἀττικήν· ἦ γὰρ ἂν τοιαύτην οἰκίζων πόλιν μὴ ὅτι Ὁμήρου ἂν ἐδεήθη μόνου, ἀλλὰ καὶ πρὸς Ὁμήρῳ Ἡσιόδου καὶ Ὀρφέως, καὶ εἴ τις ἄλλη παλαιὰ μοῦσα ποιητική, κατεπᾴδειν ἱκανὴ τὰς τῶν νέων ψυχὰς καὶ δημαγωγεῖν καὶ ἡδονῇ συνήθει ἀνακιρνάναι πράως ἀληθεῖς λόγους· ἀλλ' ἔστιν αὐτῷ <ἡ>[3] ξυνοίκησις καὶ ἡ πολιτεία γιγνομένη λόγῳ, κατὰ τὸ ἀκριβέστατον μᾶλλον ἢ χρειωδέστατον, ὅνπερ τρόπον καὶ τοῖς τὰ ἀγάλματα τούτοις διαπλάττουσιν, οἳ πᾶν τὸ παρ' ἑκάστου καλὸν συναγαγόντες, κατὰ τὴν τέχνην ἐκ διαφόρων σωμάτων ἀθροίσαντες εἰς μίμησιν μίαν, κάλλος ἓν ὑγιὲς καὶ ἄρτιον καὶ ἡρμοσμένον αὐτὸ αὑτῷ ἐξειργάσαντο· καὶ οὐκ ἂν εὕροις σῶμα ἀκριβῶς κατὰ ἀλήθειαν ἀγάλματι ὅμοιον· ὀρέγονται μὲν γὰρ αἱ τέχναι τοῦ καλλίστου, αἱ δὲ ἐν ποσὶν ὁμιλίαι καὶ χρεῖαι ἀπολείπονται τῶν τεχνῶν.

because needs, circumstances, and ways of life make each of these things appear different to different people.

3. Such being the case, let us proceed to examine the situation of Homer with utmost impartiality, neither being someone who likes Plato and scorns Homer, nor who admires Homer and criticizes Plato, for these two sentiments are not completely divorced or separated from each other, since it is surely possible to respect the writings of Plato and also to admire Homer. Here is how.

The city Plato founds in his dialogue is not Cretan, nor Dorian, nor Peloponnesian, nor Sicilian, nor, by Zeus, Athenian. For if he had been founding a city like those, he would have needed not only Homer, but in addition to him Hesiod and Orpheus, along with any other ancient form of poetry able to enchant and guide the souls of the young, as it subtly mixes truthful arguments with its customary pleasure. No, Plato's community and his republic are established in theory according to what is most perfect rather than what is most practicable, just as those sculptors of statues do, who collect all that is beautiful from each individual, then use their art to combine these elements from different bodies into one representation, and thus produce a single work of beauty that is sound, complete, and harmoniously proportioned. You could not find any single body that truly and exactly matched that statue, because the arts aim for what is most beautiful, whereas the familiar items we use every day fall short of what the arts can produce.

[3] suppl. Reiske, Trapp

Οἶμαι δέ, εἰ καί τις ἦν ἐν ἀνθρώποις δύναμις πλαστικὴ σωμάτων σαρκίνων, ξυμφορήσαντες ἂν οἱ δημιουργοὶ τὰς δυνάμεις ξυμμέτρως γῆς καὶ πυρός, καὶ τῶν ὅσα τούτοις ἁρμοσθέντα τε καὶ ὁμολογήσαντα συνίστησιν τὴν σωμάτων φύσιν, ἀπέφηναν ὡς τὸ εἰκὸς ἂν σῶμα ἀδεὲς φαρμάκου καὶ μαγγανευμάτων καὶ διαιτημάτων ἰατρικῶν. εἰ οὖν τις ἐκείνων τινὸς τῶν δημιουργῶν ἀκούσας νομοθετοῦντος τοῖς ὑπ᾽ αὐτοῦ πλασθεῖσιν τῷ λόγῳ, ὅτι ἄρα δεήσονται οὐδὲ Ἱπποκράτους ἰωμένου σφᾶς, ἀλλὰ χρὴ στέψαντας ἐρίῳ τὸν ἄνδρα καὶ χρίσαντας μύρῳ ἀποπέμπειν παρ᾽ ἄλλους, εὐδοκιμήσοντα ἐκεῖ ὅπου τὴν τέχνην παρακαλεῖ ἡ νόσος, κᾆτα ἀγανακτοίη πρὸς αὐτὸν ὡς ἀτιμάζοντα τὴν Ἀσκληπιοῦ καὶ τὴν Ἀσκληπιάδων τέχνην, ἆρα οὐ καταγέλαστος ἂν γίγνοιτο, αἰτίαν προσφέρων τῷ μὴ κατὰ ἀτιμίαν παραιτουμένῳ ἰατρικήν, ἀλλὰ μήτε κατὰ χρείαν δεομένῳ αὐτῆς μήτε καθ᾽ ἡδονὴν ἀσπαζομένῳ;

4. Δύο γὰρ ὄντων τούτων, ὑφ᾽ ὧν Ὅμηρος καὶ Ἡσίοδος καὶ ὅστις ἄλλος ἐν ἁρμονίᾳ ποιητικῇ εὐδόκιμοι ἦσαν, χρείας καὶ ἡδονῆς, κατ᾽ οὐδέτερον αὐτοῖν ἐπιτήδεια τὰ ἔπη τῇ Πλάτωνος πολιτείᾳ, οὔτε κατὰ τὴν χρείαν, οὔτε κατὰ τὴν ἡδονήν. ἥ τε γὰρ χρεία ξυνελήλαται αὐτοῖς εἰς τροφὴν ἀκριβῆ καὶ ἀκούσματα ἀναγκαῖα, οὐδὲν αὐθαίρετον οὐδὲ αὐτεξούσιον οὐδὲ οἷον ἂν δέξαιντο παρὰ μητέρων παῖδες ὑπὸ

I think that if humans possessed the ability to fashion bodies of flesh and blood, then craftsmen could combine in correct proportions the properties of earth and fire and of all the other elements that, when harmonized and coordinated with them, make up the nature of human bodies, they would presumably produce a body that never needed medicines, quack remedies, or medical regimes. Suppose then that someone heard one of these craftsmen laying down the law to his theoretical creations, explaining that they in fact would not need any Hippocrates to heal them, but instead should crown the man with a woolen fillet, anoint him with myrrh, and send him off to other people,[7] to win fame wherever sicknesses required his expertise. Then suppose that this person became angry with the craftsman for disrespecting the art of Asclepius and the Asclepiadae. Would he not then be ridiculous if he brought charges against someone who banned the art of medicine, not out of disrespect, but because he neither needed it for its utility, nor welcomed it for its pleasure?

4. These two factors, utility and pleasure, were what made Homer, Hesiod, and all the other composers of poetic harmony famous, but on neither account, be it utility or pleasure, are their verses suitable for Plato's republic. That is because its citizens' needs have been limited by a meticulous upbringing and restrictions on what they may hear, with no room for spontaneity or autonomy, or for the kind of story made up of nonsensical tales that children

[7] An allusion to the sendoff of a poet at Pl. *Resp.* 3.398a: "We would send him away to another city after anointing his head with oil and wreathing it with woolen bands" (trans. Emlyn-Jones and Preddy). It is also alluded to at *Or.* 18.5.

φήμης ἀλόγου πλασθέντα μῦθον· οὐδὲν γὰρ εἰκῇ οὐδὲ ἐκ τοῦ προστυχόντος, οὔτε ἄκουσμα οὔτε παίδευμα οὔτε ἄθυρμα, παρέλθοι ἂν εἰς τοιαύτην πόλιν, ὥστε καὶ δεηθῆναι Ὁμήρου τὰς οὔσας περὶ θεῶν δόξας ἐμμελῶς μεγαλύνοντος, καὶ τρέποντος[4] τὰς τῶν πολλῶν ψυχὰς ἐκ ταπεινῆς φαντασίας εἰς ἔκπληξιν.

Τοῦτο γάρ τοι δύναται ποιητοῦ λόγος ἐμπεσὼν ἀκοαῖς τεθραμμέναις κακῶς, περιβομβεῖν αὐτὰς καὶ μὴ παρέχειν σχολὴν διαπιστεύειν τοῖς εἰκῇ θρυλουμένοις λόγοις, ἀλλ' εἰδέναι μὲν ὅτι ποιητικὴ πᾶσα αἰνίττεται, καταμαντεύεσθαι δὲ τῶν αἰνιγμάτων μεγαλοπρεπῶς κατὰ τὴν θεῶν δίκην. ὁπόθεν δὲ ἐξελήλαται τὸ ταπεινὸν πᾶν καὶ τὸ ἠμελημένον, τί δεῖ ἐνταῦθα τοιούτου φαρμάκου;

Τὸν Ἀνάχαρσιν ἐκεῖνον ἤρετο Ἕλλην ἀνὴρ εἰ ἔστιν αὐλητικὴ ἐν Σκύθαις· "οὐδὲ ἄμπελοι," ἔφη. ἄλλη γὰρ ἄλλην παρακαλεῖ ἡδονὴν καὶ ἔστιν ξυμφυὲς τὸ χρῆμα καὶ ἄπαυστον καὶ ἀέναον, ἐπειδὰν ἄρξηται ῥεῖν· καὶ μία μηχανὴ πρὸς σωτηρίαν, στῆσαι τὰς πηγὰς καὶ ἀποφράξαι τὴν ἡδονῶν γένεσιν. ἡ δὴ τοιαύτη πόλις, ἣν συνεστήσατο ὁ Πλάτων, ἄβατος ἡδονῇ καὶ θε-

[4] τρέποντος Acciaiolus, Davies[2], Dübner, Koniaris: τρέφοντος R, Hobein, Trapp

---

[8] Or, reading *τρέφοντος* with manuscript R, "nourish."

[9] For the ability of Homeric verse to elevate the imagination of listeners, see *Or.* 18.5.

might hear from their mothers. For nothing random or left to chance—no literature, education, or play—could enter this kind of city, so as to need a Homer to magnify established ideas about the gods in his melodious verse and turn[8] the souls of the populace from a low-grade imagination to a sense of awe.[9]

For this is indeed what a poet's words can do when they fall on ears that have been poorly brought up:[10] they resound within them and afford no leisure to put full trust in the randomly repeated stories, but instead compel the listeners to recognize that all poetry contains hidden meanings and to divine its allegories in accordance with the majesty that befits the gods.[11] But in a community where everything low-grade and haphazard has been excluded, what need is there for a remedy like that?

A Greek once asked famous Anacharsis[12] if they played the pipes in Scythia, to which he answered, "We don't even have grape vines."[13] So it is that one pleasure invites another, and once this process starts to flow, it is self-generating, unstoppable, and unending. There is only one way to escape from it: stop the sources and block the pleasures' origin. This is in fact the kind of city that Plato es-

[10] That is, lacking the strict upbringing in Plato's republic.

[11] A similar discussion of poetry's hidden meaning beneath its aesthetic appeal is at *Or*. 18.5. The topic is also treated in *Orr*. 4 and 26.

[12] A Scythian philosopher of the time of Solon (early 6th c. BC) whose satiric observations on Athenian customs prefigured those of Diogenes the Cynic (4th c. BC). Another anecdote about him is told at *Or*. 25.1.

[13] Piping traditionally followed hard drinking at symposia.

αμάτων καὶ ἀκουσμάτων, ὥστε οὔτε εἰ ποιητικὴ παρασκευαστικὸν ἡδονῆς εἰσδέξαιτο ἂν αὐτήν, καὶ πολὺ μᾶλλον κατὰ τὴν χρείαν.

5. Ἐῶ λέγειν ὅτι καὶ τῶν ἐν ἀνθρώποις γενῶν οὐ λόγῳ μόνον πλαττόμεναι πόλεις ἀλλὰ καὶ ἔργῳ γενόμεναι πολλαί, καὶ πολιτευθεῖσαι ὑγιῶς καὶ ξυνοικισθεῖσαι νομίμως, ἀγνοοῦσιν τὸν Ὅμηρον. ὀψὲ μὲν γὰρ ἡ Σπάρτη ῥαψῳδεῖ, ὀψὲ δὲ καὶ ἡ Κρήτη, ὀψὲ δὲ καὶ τὸ Δωρικὸν ἐν Λιβύῃ γένος· ἐπαινοῦνται δὲ οὐκ ὀψέ, ἀλλ' ἐκ παλαιᾶς ἀρετῆς. τὰ δὲ τῶν βαρβάρων τί χρὴ λέγειν; σχολῇ γὰρ ἂν ἐκεῖνοι τὰ Ὁμήρου μάθοιεν, ἀλλ' εὕροις ἂν ὅμως καὶ ἐν βαρβάροις ἀρετὴν ἀπεσχισμένην τῶν Ὁμήρου ἐπῶν· ἦ γὰρ ἂν καὶ τὸ τῶν ῥαψῳδῶν γένος τὸ ἀνοητότατον εὐδαιμόνει κατὰ τὴν συνουσίαν τῆς τέχνης· τὸ δὲ οὐχ οὕτως ἔχει.

Καλὰ μὲν γὰρ τὰ Ὁμήρου ἔπη καὶ ἐπῶν τὰ κάλλιστα καὶ φανότατα καὶ ᾄδεσθαι Μούσαις πρέποντα· ἀλλ' οὐ πᾶσιν καλὰ οὐδὲ ἀεὶ καλά· οὐδὲ γὰρ τῶν ἐν μουσικῇ μελῶν εἷς νόμος οὐδὲ εἷς χρόνος. καλὸν μὲν ἐν πολέμῳ τὸ ὄρθιον, καλὸν δὲ ἐν συμποσίῳ τὸ παροίνιον, καὶ καλὸν μὲν Λακεδαιμονίοις τὸ ἐμβατήριον, καλὸν δὲ Ἀθηναίοις τὸ κύκλιον, καὶ καλὸν μὲν ἐν διώξει τὸ ἐγκελευστικόν, καλὸν δὲ ἐν φυγῇ τὸ ἀνακλητικόν. ἡδεῖα μὲν πᾶσα μοῦσα, ἀλλὰ τὸ τῆς χρείας οὐχ ὅμοιον πᾶσιν.

tablished, one that barred the pleasure of both sights and sounds.[14] As a result, it would not admit poetry, even as a source of pleasure, much less as something useful.

5. I shall pass over the fact that among the races of men there are many cities, not just ones devised in theory, but actual ones with sound governments and law-abiding citizens, that lack any knowledge of Homer. For rhapsodic recitations came late to Sparta as well as to Crete and to the Dorians of Libya, whereas they have been celebrated for their virtue not just of late, but from ancient times. And what need is there to bring up barbarian examples? They could hardly have learned Homer's poetry, and yet you can also find virtue among barbarians that has nothing to do with Homer's verses. Otherwise, that idiotic race of rhapsodes would be living happy lives thanks to their familiarity with Homer's artistry—which, of course, is not the case![15]

Yes, Homer's verses are beautiful. Indeed they are the most beautiful and splendid of all verses, and worthy to be sung by the Muses, but they are not beautiful at all times or for all people, nor for that matter is there one single mode or one single occasion that suits all the strains of music. Beautiful in war is the martial mode; at a symposium drinking music. Beautiful to the Lacedaemonians is marching music; to the Athenians choral music. Beautiful is the charging song when attacking, but beautiful is the retreat when giving ground. Every type of music is pleasant, but not all of them have the same utility.

[14] That is, spectacles (like plays) and sounds (like certain musical and poetic performances).

[15] The vain pretensions of rhapsodes are the subject of Plato' *Ion* and Xen. *Symp.* 3.6.

Ἂν τοίνυν καθ' ἡδονὴν κρίνῃς Ὅμηρον, δεινὰ δρᾷς· εἰσκυκλεῖς ποιητῶν χορὸν ἀκόλαστον καὶ βακχεύοντα, κρατοῦντα ἡδονῇ τῆς Ὁμήρου ᾠδῆς. "ἀποχειροτονεῖς τῆς ἡδονῆς τὸν ἄνδρα;" ἡδὺς μὲν γάρ, ἡδύς, ἀλλὰ τὸ κάλλος ἀκμαιότερον τῆς ἡδονῆς καὶ μὴ παρέχον σχολὴν εὐφραίνεσθαι, ἀλλὰ ἐπαινεῖν. "ἀλλ' ἔπαινος σὺν ἡδονῇ μέν, ἀλλ' οὐκ αὐτὸ ἡδονή." εἰ δὲ καθ' ἡδονὴν τὰ Ὁμήρου ἀσπαζόμεθα, ὡς αὐλήματα, ὡς κιθαρίσματα, ἐξελαύνεις Ὅμηρον οὐκ ἐκ τῶν Πλάτωνος τροφίμων μόνον, ἀλλὰ καὶ ἐκ τῶν Λυκούργου καὶ ἐκ τῶν Κρητικῶν, καὶ παντὸς χωρίου καὶ πάσης πόλεως ὅπου μετὰ ἀρετῆς εὐδοκιμοῦσιν οἱ πόνοι.

If, therefore, you judge Homer's worth solely on the basis of pleasure, you are making a terrible mistake. You are wheeling on stage a rowdy, raving chorus of poets,[16] who surpass Homer's own song in the pleasure they provide.[17] "Are you denying the man his claim to provide pleasure?"[18] Yes, he gives pleasure, of course he does, but the beauty of his poetry is greater than its pleasure, and it leaves no room for enjoyment, but only for praise.[19] "Yet it is praise combined with pleasure, not pleasure pure and simple." But if we welcome Homer's verses just for their pleasure, as we would pipe playing and lyre playing, then you are effectively banishing Homer not only from the citizens brought up by Plato, but also from those brought up by Lycurgus and by the Cretans,[20] and also from those in every region and every city where hard work combined with virtue is held in esteem.

[16] That is, rhapsodes.

[17] That is, their theatrical performances eclipse the poetry itself.

[18] An interruption by a fictitious interlocutor.

[19] Cf. *Or.* 25.7: "I understand the pleasure of Homer's poetry, but I praise it for its more venerable qualities."

[20] At Pl. *Leg.* 3.680c–d the Cretan and Spartan representatives express reservations about the relevance of Homer's poetry in their states.

# *ORATION* 18

## INTRODUCTION

This is the first of four lectures on the art of love, of which Socrates claims to be an expert (Pl. *Theag*. 108b).[1] It opens with two examples of "unjust,"[2] pederastic love, one by an unnamed Corinthian, the other by Periander of Ambracia, both driven by political power and wine to abuse the boys (§1). Two examples of "just" love follow: the love between Harmodius and Aristogeiton that brought down the Pisistratid tyranny in Athens, and the Sacred Band of lovers formed by Epaminondas that liberated Thebes from Sparta (§2). The term love (*erōs*) is ambiguous, designating both the god Love and the sickness of lust. Genuine love is distinguished from its counterfeit, when it is the love of true, not just apparent, beauty (§3). Socrates openly acknowledges his reactions to beautiful boys (an extensive list of his statements found in Plato, Xenophon, and Aeschines follows) and claims that love is the one subject he understands and practices (§4). The question becomes whether Socrates was speaking ironically or al-

[1] Scognamillo (1997) provides a text, translation, and commentary of this oration.

[2] Unjust love in the *Orations* denotes an abusive relationship enabled by an imbalance of power.

legorically. After all, he[3] banished Homer from his ideal republic for his depiction of offensive behavior. Furthermore, Socrates' erotic feelings have nothing to do with his other activities, especially his bravery at Delium and his courageous opposition to the Thirty Tyrants (§5).

In defense of Socrates, the speaker notes that of all the accusations brought against him by the Athenians, there was no mention whatsoever of his erotic affairs (§6). In fact, the views of love that Socrates expressed are not his alone, but are found in the tradition of Homer, Sappho, and Anacreon (§7). In particular, Homer depicts all kinds of good and bad loves: Agamemnon represents obsessive love; Paris represents adulterous love; Hector and Andromache represent "just" marital love; and, finally, Patroclus and Achilles represent manly (*andreion*) love that endures until death (§8). The final section draws parallels between Sappho's love of girls and Socrates' love of boys and concludes with Anacreon's self-control (*sōphrosynē*), as he looks to the character (*ēthos*) of his boyfriends and wins their love by his charming speech, as Socrates does (§9).

[3] That is, the character of Socrates in Plato's *Republic*.

## *ORATION* 18

Τίς ἡ Σωκράτους ἐρωτική. αʹ

1. Κορινθίῳ ἀνδρί, ὄνομα Αἰσχύλῳ, παῖς ἦν Ἀκταίων, μειράκιον Δωρικὸν ὥρᾳ διαφέρον. ἐρᾷ Ἀκταίωνος νεανίας Κορίνθιος, γένους τοῦ <τῶν>[1] Βακχιαδῶν· Βακχιάδαι δὲ Κορίνθου ἐδυνάστευον. ὡς δὲ ἐσωφρόνει τὸ μειράκιον καὶ ὑπερεφρόνει ὑβριστοῦ ἐραστοῦ, ἐκώμασεν εἰς Ἀκταίωνος ὁ ἐραστὴς ὁμοῦ τοῖς Βακχιάδαις νεανίσκοις, οἳ θαρσοῦντες μέθῃ καὶ τυραννίδι καὶ ἔρωτι, εἰσπεσόντες εἰς τὸ δωμάτιον, οἱ μὲν ἐπειρῶντο ἀπάγειν, οἱ δὲ οἰκεῖοι κατέχειν. σπώμενον τὸ μειράκιον ὑπ' ἀμφοῖν βίᾳ διαφθείρεται ἐν χερσὶν αὐτῶν. καὶ εἰκάσθη τὸ ἐν Κορίνθῳ τοῦτο πάθος τῷ Βοιωτίῳ διὰ τὴν ὁμωνυμίαν τῶν μειρακίων, ἀπολομένου ἑκατέρου, τοῦ μὲν ὑπὸ κυνῶν ἐν θήρᾳ, τοῦ δὲ ὑπὸ ἐραστῶν ἐν μέθῃ.

[1] suppl. Koniaris, Scognamillo

---

[1] Versions of this story are at Plut. *Amat*. 772e–73a and Diod. Sic. 8, fr. 10, where the father is Melissus, and the lover is called Archias.

# *ORATION* 18

## What Socrates' art of love was. Part I

1. A Corinthian man named Aeschylus had a son called Actaeon,[1] a Dorian boy[2] who was exceptionally handsome. A Corinthian youth,[3] a member of the Bacchiad family that at the time ruled over Corinth,[4] was in love with Actaeon. When the boy proved chaste and rejected his overbearing lover, the suitor went on a revel with other Bacchiad youths to Actaeon's home, and they, emboldened by wine, tyrannical power, and love, broke into the house and tried to drag him out, while his family tried to hold him back. The boy, forcefully pulled apart by both sides, died in their hands. This incident in Corinth was compared to the one in Boeotia,[5] because both boys shared the same name and were both killed, the one by dogs when hunting, the other by lovers when drunk.

[2] *meirakion* generally applies to an adolescent in his later teens. It is used of Apollo (*Or.* 8.6), of Paris (*Or.* 20.7), and of Achilles (*Or.* 26.5).

[3] *neanias* applies to a mature young man.

[4] The Bacchiadae were a Dorian clan that ruled over Corinth in the mid-seventh century BC.

[5] In the Boeotian myth, Actaeon was changed into a deer by Artemis and torn apart by his own hunting dogs.

Περιάνδρῳ τῷ Ἀμβρακιώτῃ τυράννῳ παιδικὰ ἦν μειράκιον πολιτικόν· ἅτε δὲ οὐ σὺν δίκῃ τὴν ὁμιλίαν συστησαμένῳ ὕβρις ἦν τὸ χρῆμα, οὐκ ἔρως. θαρσῶν δὲ ὁ Περίανδρος τῇ ἐξουσίᾳ παροινεῖ εἰς τὸ μειράκιον. ἡ δὲ παροινία αὕτη Περίανδρον μὲν ἔπαυσεν ὑβρίζοντα, τὸ δὲ μειράκιον ἐποίησεν ἐξ ἐρωμένου τυραννοκτόνον. αὕτη δίκη ἀδίκων ἐρώτων.

2. Βούλει σοι λέγω καὶ τοῦ ἑτέρου τρόπου τῶν ἐρώτων, τοῦ δικαίου, μίαν γέ τινα ἢ δευτέραν εἰκόνα; μειρακίῳ Ἀττικῷ δύο ἦσαν ἐρασταί, ἰδιώτης καὶ τύραννος· ὁ μὲν δίκαιος ἦν διὰ ἰσοτιμίαν, ὁ δὲ ἄδικος δι' ἐξουσίαν. ἀλλὰ τό γε μειράκιον ὄντως ἦν καλὸν καὶ ἐρᾶσθαι ἄξιον, ὥστε ὑπεριδὸν τοῦ τυράννου τὸν ἰδιώτην ἠσπάζετο. ὁ δὲ ὑπ' ὀργῆς ἄλλα τε ἀμφοτέρους προὐπηλάκισεν, καὶ ἀδελφὴν Ἁρμοδίου Παναθηναίοις ἥκουσαν ἐπὶ τὴν πομπὴν κανηφοροῦσαν ἐξήλασεν ἐπ' ἀτιμίᾳ. διδόασιν δίκην ἐκ τούτου Πεισιστρατίδαι, καὶ ἦρξεν ἐλευθερίας Ἀθηναίοις ὕβρις τυράννου καὶ μειρακίου θάρσος καὶ ἔρως δίκαιος καὶ ἐραστοῦ ἀρετή.

Ἐλευθεροῖ τὰς Θήβας Ἐπαμεινώνδας ἀπὸ Λακεδαιμονίων στρατηγήματι ἐρωτικῷ. μειρακίων πολλῶν

---

[6] A just relationship in Maximus is based on equality and mutual affection; see esp. *Or.* 14.6.

[7] *hybris* denotes abusive behavior, including insults, violence, or rape, resulting from a power imbalance.

[8] Plut. *Amat.* 768f reports that when Periander asked the boy if he was pregnant yet, he flew into a rage and killed him. Cf. also Arist. *Pol.* 5.8.1311a40–b1. This occurred ca. 580 BC.

Periander the Ambracian tyrant had as his lover a boy who was an ordinary citizen. But since he had not based their relationship on justice,[6] it was a matter of abuse,[7] not love. Emboldened by his political power and with too much to drink, Periander insulted the boy. This very taunt put a stop to Periander's abuse and turned the boy from a sexual object into a tyrannicide.[8] Such is the punishment for unjust love.

2. Would you like me to give you one or two examples of the other kind of love, the just one? An Athenian boy[9] had two lovers, a private citizen and a tyrant. The one lover was just because of their equal status, whereas the other was unjust because of his superior power. Now the boy, who was truly beautiful and worthy of love, consequently rejected the tyrant and gave his affection to the private citizen. In a rage, the tyrant insulted both of them in various ways, but most of all when he sent Harmodius' sister away in humiliation, when she came to carry the sacred basket in the Panathenaic procession. But the Pisistratids paid the price for this: Athenian freedom had its beginning in a tyrant's abuse, a boy's bravery, a just love, and a lover's virtue.

Epaminondas employed a military strategy based on love to liberate Thebes from the Lacedaemonians.[10] There

[9] Harmodius. He and his lover, Aristogeiton, assassinated the Pisistratid Hipparchus in 514 BC at the Panathenaic festival, which led to the establishment of democracy six years later. The whole episode is related at Thuc. 6.54–57. The two lovers are cited as exemplars of friendship at *Or*. 35.4.

[10] He defeated the Spartans at the battles of Leuctra (371 BC) and Mantinea (362 BC).

*καλῶν ἐρασταὶ ἦσαν Θήβησιν πολλοὶ νεανίαι· ὅπλα δοὺς Ἐπαμεινώνδας τοῖς ἐρασταῖς καὶ τοῖς ἐρωμένοις συνέταξεν λόχον ἱερὸν τοῦ ἔρωτος, δεινὸν καὶ ἄμαχον καὶ συνασπίζοντα ἀκριβῶς καὶ ἄρρηκτον, οἷον οὔτε ὁ Νέστωρ περὶ τὸ Ἴλιον συνεστήσατο, ὁ δεινότατος τῶν στρατηγῶν, οὔτε Ἡρακλεῖδαι περὶ Πελοπόννησον οὔτε Πελοποννήσιοι περὶ τὴν Ἀττικήν. ἔδει γὰρ ἕκαστον τῶν ἐραστῶν ἀριστεύειν, καὶ διὰ φιλοτιμίαν ἐν ὄψει τῶν παιδικῶν μαχόμενον καὶ δι' ἀνάγκην ὑπερμαχοῦντα τῶν φιλτάτων· ἦν δὲ καὶ τὰ μειράκια ἐφάμιλλα ταῖς ἀρεταῖς τοῖς ἐρασταῖς, ὥσπερ ἐν θήρᾳ σκύλακες συμπαραθέοντες τοῖς πρεσβυτέροις τῶν κυνῶν.*

3. *Τί δή μοι βούλεται ὁ Ἐπαμεινώνδας καὶ ὁ Ἁρμόδιος καὶ οἱ περὶ τοῦ ἀδίκου ἔρωτος λόγοι; ὅτι πρᾶγμα διττόν, τὸ μὲν ἀρετῆς ἐπήβολον, τὸ δὲ μοχθηρίᾳ συμπεφυκός, φωνῇ μιᾷ οἱ ἄνθρωποι ἐπονομάζοντες ἔρωτα, οὑτωσὶ καλοῦντες καὶ τὸν θεὸν καὶ τὴν νόσον, καλλωπίζονται μὲν οἱ μοχθηροὶ ἐρασταὶ διὰ τὴν πρὸς τὸν θεὸν ὁμωνυμίαν, ἀπιστοῦνται δὲ οἱ χρηστοὶ διὰ τὸ ἀμφίβολον τοῦ πάθους.*

*Ἀλλ' ὥσπερ, ‹εἰ›*[2] *τοὺς ἀργυρογνώμονας ἐξετάζειν ἔδει, ὁπότερος αὐτῶν γνωριστικὸς τοῦ δοκίμου καὶ μή, τὸν μὲν ‹ἂν›*[3] *πρὸ τοῦ δοκίμου τὸ φαινόμενον*

[2] suppl. Acciaiolus, Trapp
[3] suppl. Trapp

were many young men in Thebes who were lovers of just as many handsome boyfriends. Epaminondas gave weapons to both the lovers and their beloveds and formed a Sacred Band of love that was formidable and invincible, one keeping such a tight formation of shields as to be impenetrable.[11] Neither Nestor, that most formidable general, mustered such a unit at Troy, nor did the Heraclidae in the Peloponnesus,[12] nor did the Peloponnesians in Attica.[13] Every one of the lovers had to perform bravely, both from a love of honor, since he was fighting before the eyes of his beloved, and out of necessity, since he was defending what he loved best. Then too, the boys competed with their lovers in bravery, just as puppies keep up alongside the older dogs during a hunt.

3. What is my point in telling of Epaminondas and Harmodius and in relating these other stories of unjust love? It is because when people take a twofold phenomenon, where one form possesses virtue and the other is imbued with wickedness, and they give it the single name of love, thus calling it both the god and the sickness, then wicked lovers flaunt their love because it shares its name with the god, while virtuous lovers are mistrusted because of the ambiguous nature of the emotion.

Suppose that we were required to examine assayers of silver, to determine which one could and could not discern genuine silver. We would consider far from expert the one

[11] As long as its formation of shields remains unbroken, a hoplite phalanx will be victorious. [12] The legendary "sons of Heracles" invaded the Peloponnesus ca. 1000 BC.

[13] The Peloponnesians invaded Attica during the Peloponnesian War (431–404 BC).

ἀσπαζόμενον πόρρω πάνυ ἐτίθεμεν τῆς τέχνης, τὸν δὲ τἀληθῆ αὐτὰ γνωρίζοντα, τοῦτον καὶ συνιέναι αὐτῆς, ταύτῃ καὶ τὴν ἐρωτικὴν προσθῶμεν φέροντες ὥσπερ τινὰ νομίσματα τῇ τοῦ καλοῦ φύσει. ἐὰν γὰρ τούτου τὸ μὲν ᾖ φαινόμενον καλόν, οὐχ οὕτως ἔχον, τὸ δὲ καλὸν καὶ ὂν καὶ φαινόμενον, ἀνάγκη τοὺς μὲν τοῦ φαινομένου κάλλους καὶ μὴ ὄντος γλιχομένους νόθους τινὰς εἶναι καὶ κιβδήλους ἐραστάς, τοὺς δὲ τοῦ καὶ ὄντος καὶ φαινομένου γνησίους ἐραστὰς κάλλους ἀληθινοῦ.

4. Εἶεν· ἐπεὶ ταύτῃ βασανιστέον τε καὶ ἀθρητέον τὸν ἐρωτικὸν καὶ λόγον καὶ ἄνδρα, ἐπιτολμητέον τοι καὶ περὶ Σωκράτους ἐκλογίσασθαι, τί ἦν αὐτῷ ταυτὶ τὰ θρυλούμενα ἐν τοῖς λόγοις, ὁποῖα ἄττα φησὶν περὶ αὑτοῦ ἐκεῖνος, ὅτι ἐστὶν θεράπων τοῦ ἔρωτος καὶ λευκὴ στάθμη πρὸς τοὺς καλοὺς καὶ τὴν τέχνην δεινός. ἀλλὰ καὶ διδασκάλους ἐπιγέγραπται τῆς τέχνης, Ἀσπασίαν τὴν Μιλησίαν καὶ Διοτίμαν τὴν Μαντινικήν, καὶ μαθητὰς λαμβάνει τῆς τέχνης, Ἀλκιβιάδην τὸν γαυρότατον καὶ Κριτόβουλον τὸν ὡραιότατον καὶ Ἀγάθωνα τὸν ἁβρότατον καὶ Φαῖδρον τὴν θείαν κεφαλὴν καὶ Λῦσιν τὸ μειράκιον καὶ Χαρμίδην τὸν καλόν.

Ἀποκρύπτεται δὲ οὐδὲν τῶν τοῦ ἔρωτος, οὔτε ἔργον

---

14 For Socrates as the lover of true beauty perceived through the medium of human bodies, see *Or*. 21.8.

15 Nowhere in Plato or Xenophon does Socrates actually call himself a servant of love. At Pl. *Chrm*. 154b he calls himself a

who accepted the apparent over the genuine silver, but would conclude that the one who recognized what was really true understood his craft. In the same way, let us take the art of love and assess it, like some silver coins, against the nature of the beautiful. If one sample appears to be beautiful, but actually is not, while the other both appears to be beautiful and actually is, then we must conclude that those who yearn for apparent rather than true beauty are debased and counterfeit lovers, whereas those who yearn for the beauty that is both real and apparent are genuine lovers of true beauty.[14]

4. So, since this is the way both the lover and erotic discourse should be examined and tested, we must boldly take up the case of Socrates and consider what he meant by all those statements he so often makes about himself in his conversations, such as his claims of being a servant of love, "a white line when it comes to beautiful young men," and skilled in his art.[15] Moreover, he cites those who taught him his art, Aspasia of Miletus[16] and Diotima of Mantinea,[17] and also takes on students of his art, namely conceited Alcibiades, gorgeous Critobulus,[18] elegant Agathon,[19] "divinely inspired" Phaedrus,[20] young Lysis, and handsome Charmides.

He hides no aspect of his erotic experiences, neither

"white line" for measuring beautiful young men, because almost all young men seem beautiful to him. A white chalk line (as opposed to a red one) is useless for leaving a mark on white stone. For his claim to be skilled (*deinos*) in matters of love, see Pl. *Theag*. 128b.

16 Pl. *Menex*. 235e.

17 Pl. *Symp*. 201d.

18 Cf. Xen. *Symp*. 4.10–11.

19 Host of Plato's *Symposium*, notorious for his refinement.

20 Pl. *Phdr*. 234d.

*οὔτε πάθος, ἀλλὰ ἔοικεν πάντα ἑξῆς παρρησιαζομένῳ· πηδᾶν μὲν αὐτῷ τὴν καρδίαν ἐπὶ Χαρμίδῃ καὶ ἰδίειν τὸ σῶμα, ἐπτοῆσθαι δὲ καὶ ἐνθουσιᾶν καθάπερ τὰς βάκχας ἐπὶ Ἀλκιβιάδῃ, ἐπεστράφθαι δὲ ἐπ' Αὐτόλυκον τὰ ὄμματα ὥσπερ ἐν νυκτὶ ἐπὶ φέγγος. πόλιν δὲ οἰκίζων ἀγαθῶν ἀνδρῶν, τιθεὶς νόμους τοῖς ἀριστεῦσιν οὐ στέφανον οὐδὲ εἰκόνας, τὰς Ἑλληνικὰς φλυαρίας, δωρεῖται, ἀλλ' ἐξεῖναι φιλεῖν τῷ ἀριστεῖ ὅντινα ἂν θέλῃ τῶν καλῶν. ὢ τοῦ θαυμαστοῦ γέρως.*

*Αὐτὸς δὲ δὴ τὸν ἔρωτα, ἀναπλάττων ἐπ' αὐτῷ μῦθον, οἷον καὶ εἶναι λέγει, αἰσχρὸν ἰδεῖν καὶ πένητα, ἐγγυτάτω τῆς ἑαυτοῦ τύχης, ἀνυπόδητον, χαμαιεύνην, ἐπίβουλον, θηρευτικόν, φαρμακέα, σοφιστήν, γόητα—ἀτεχνῶς οἷα εἰς αὐτὸν Σωκράτην ἔσκωπτον ἐν Διονυσίοις οἱ κωμῳδοί. ἔλεγε δὲ ταῦτα μόνον οὐκ ἐν μέσοις τοῖς Ἕλλησιν, ἀλλὰ καὶ οἴκοι καὶ δημοσίᾳ, ἐν συμποσίοις, ἐν Ἀκαδημίᾳ, ἐν Πειραιεῖ, ἐν ὁδῷ, ὑπὸ πλατάνῳ, ἐν Λυκείῳ. καὶ τὰ μὲν ἄλλα ἅπαντα ἀποποιεῖται εἰδέναι, καὶ τοὺς περὶ ἀρετῆς λόγους καὶ τὰς περὶ θεῶν δόξας, καὶ τὰ ἄλλα ἅπαντα ἐφ' οἷς οἱ σοφισταὶ ἐκόμων· τὴν δὲ ἐρωτικὴν τέχνην ὑποδύς, ταύτης καὶ ἐπιστήμων εἶναι καὶ πραγματεύεσθαι περὶ αὐτὴν ἔλεγεν.*

---

21 Loosely based on Pl. *Chrm.* 155d and Alcibiades' pounding heart at Pl. *Symp.* 215e. 22 Adapted from Aeschin. *Alc.* fr. 53, 22–24 [Giannantoni] = Aristid. 2.74: "Thanks to the love I happened to feel for Alcibiades I had experienced exactly what happens to the Bacchants" (trans. Trapp).

his actions nor his emotions, but appears to state every detail frankly—how his heart pounded and his body broke out in a sweat at the sight of Charmides,[21] how he was terrified and raved like a Bacchant over Alcibiades,[22] and how his eyes turned to Autolycus as to a beacon in the night.[23] And when founding his city of noble men and establishing laws for war heroes, he did not reward them with crowns or statues (those frivolous Greek awards), but instead allowed the hero to kiss any beautiful boy that he wished.[24] What a truly wonderful reward!

And the way he himself describes Love in the myth he fashions about him![25] Ugly and poor (so like himself!), barefoot, sleeping on the ground, a schemer, hunter, enchanter, sophist, and wizard—precisely the kinds of jibes that the comic playwrights hurled at Socrates himself at the Dionysia. And yet, except at large gatherings of Greeks, he said all this everywhere—at home and in public, at symposia, in the Academy, in the Piraeus, on the road, under a plane tree, and in the Lyceum.[26] Of all other matters he denied having any knowledge, such as theories about virtue and doctrines about the gods, and all the other topics that the sophists prided themselves on, but the art of love he made his own, and claimed that he understood it and devoted himself to it.[27]

[23] Adapted from Xen. *Symp.* 1.9. Autolycus was the victor in the boys' pancratium at the Panathenaic games in 422 BC.

[24] Pl. *Resp.* 5.468b–c.

[25] Pl. *Symp.* 203b–e.

[26] Academy and Lyceum, Pl. *Lys.* 203a–b, *Symp.* 223d; Piraeus, *Resp.* 1.327a; on the road, *Phdr.* 227a; under a plane tree, *Phdr.* 230b.

[27] Pl. *Symp.* 177d–e: "I claim to understand nothing but matters of love."

5. Τί βούλεται τῷ Σωκράτει ταυτὶ τὰ κομψά, εἴτε αἰνίγματα εἴτε εἰρωνεύματα; ἀποκρινάσθω ἡμῖν ὑπὲρ τοῦ Σωκράτους Πλάτων ἢ Ξενοφῶν ἢ Αἰσχίνης, ἤ τις ἄλλος τῶν ὁμοφώνων αὐτῷ. ἐγὼ μὲν γὰρ θαυμάζω καὶ ἐκπλήττομαι, ὅπως τὰ μὲν Ὁμήρου ἔπη τῆς θαυμαστῆς πολιτείας καὶ τροφῆς τῶν νέων ἀπεπέμψατο αὐτῷ Ὁμήρῳ, στεφανώσας τὸν ποιητὴν καὶ χρίσας μύρῳ, αἰτιασάμενος τὴν παρρησίαν τῶν ἐπῶν, ὅτι ὁ Ζεὺς πεποίηται αὐτῷ τῇ Ἥρᾳ μισγόμενος ἐν τῇ Ἴδῃ, νεφέλης αὐτοὺς καλυπτούσης ἀθανάτου, καὶ Ἄρεως καὶ Ἀφροδίτης συνουσία καὶ Ἡφαίστου δεσμά, καὶ θεοὶ πίνοντες καὶ γελῶντες θεοὶ ἄσβεστον γέλωτα, καὶ Ἀπόλλων φεύγων καὶ Ἀχιλλεὺς διώκων,

αὐτὸς θνητὸς ἐὼν θεὸν ἄμβροτον,

καὶ ὀδυρόμενοι θεοί·

ὤ μοι ἐγών, ὅ τέ μοι Σαρπήδονα, φίλτατον ἀνδρῶν,

ὁ Ζεὺς λέγει· καὶ αὖθις αὖ,

ὤ μοι ἐγὼ δειλή, ὤ μοι δυσαριστοτόκεια,

ἡ Θέτις λέγει· καὶ ὅσα ἄλλα ἐπὶ τούτοις Ὅμηρος μὲν ᾐνίξατο, Σωκράτης δὲ ἐμέμψατο.

---

[28] Aeschines, the follower of Socrates, who wrote numerous Socratic dialogues, only fragments of which are extant. He is paraphrased in §4 above and mentioned in *Orr.* 1.9 and 22.6.

[29] Pl. *Resp.* 3.398a, also alluded to at *Or.* 17.3.

5. What did Socrates intend by all these clever remarks, whether meant as allegories or as irony? Let us hear an answer on Socrates' behalf from Plato, Xenophon, Aeschines,[28] or another of his devotees. For my part, I must say that I am surprised and shocked at how he excluded Homer's poetry from his marvelous republic and from the education of the young, and sent off Homer himself, after crowning the poet and anointing him with myrrh,[29] all because he condemned the frankness of his verses, in which he portrayed Zeus making love to Hera on Ida, when they were concealed by an immortal cloud,[30] and the intercourse of Ares and Aphrodite and the snares of Hephaestus,[31] and the gods drinking and bursting into "unquenchable laughter,"[32] and Apollo fleeing from the pursuit of Achilles,

> a mortal pursuing an immortal god;[33]

and the gods lamenting, when Zeus says,

> O wretched me, that Sarpedon, dearest of men to me, [must die];[34]

and again, when Thetis says,

> O wretched me, how bitter to have borne the best of men;[35]

and all the other allegorical things Homer said about the gods that Socrates censured.

[30] *Il.* 14.292–353; cf. Pl. *Resp.* 3.390b–c.
[31] *Od.* 8.266–366; cf. Pl. *Resp.* 3.390c.
[32] *Il.* 1.597–600, cited at Pl. *Resp.* 3.389a.
[33] *Il.* 22.9.
[34] *Il.* 16.433, cited at Pl. *Resp.* 3.388c.
[35] *Il.* 18.54; cited at Pl. *Resp.* 3.388b–c.

Αὐτὸς δὲ δὴ Σωκράτης, ὁ ἐραστὴς μὲν σοφίας, πενίας δὲ κρείττων, ἡδονῆς δὲ ἐχθρός, ἀληθείας δὲ φίλος, οὕτω σφαλεροὺς καὶ κινδυνώδεις λόγους ταῖς αὑτοῦ ὁμιλίαις ἀνεκέρασεν, ὥστε τὰ Ὁμήρου αἰνίγματα πόρρω πάνυ εἶναι τῆς αἰτίας τοῖς ἐκείνου παραβαλλόμενα. αὐτίκα καὶ ὁ μὲν περὶ τοῦ Διὸς τοιαῦτα ἀκούσας καὶ τοῦ Ἀπόλλωνος καὶ τῆς Θέτιδος καὶ τοῦ Ἡφαίστου, καταμαντεύεται τοῦ λόγου ὡς φησὶ μὲν ταῦτα, ἕτερα δὲ αἰνίττεται· καὶ παρεὶς τῇ ἀκοῇ τὸ τερπνόν, συναγωνίζεται τῷ ποιητῇ καὶ συνεξαίρεται τῇ φαντασίᾳ καὶ συναναπλάττει τὸν λόγον, ἀπιστῶν ὁμοῦ καὶ χαίρων τῇ τῆς μυθολογίας ἐξουσίᾳ.

Ὁ δὲ Σωκράτης ἡμῖν ἐπ' ἀληθείᾳ διατεθρυλημένος ἐπισφαλέστερος ἐν οἷς αἰνίττεται, διὰ τὸ ἀξιόπιστον μὲν ἐν τοῖς λόγοις, δυνατὸν δ' ἐν τῇ μιμήσει, ἀνόμοιον δ' ἐν τοῖς ἔργοις. οὐδὲν γὰρ αὐτὸς αὑτῷ ὅμοιος ὁ Σωκράτης ἐρῶν τῷ σωφρονοῦντι καὶ ὁ ἐκπληττόμενος τοὺς καλοὺς τῷ ἐλέγχοντι τοὺς ἄφρονας, ὁ Λυσίου τῶν ἐρωτικῶν ἀντίτεχνος, ὁ Κριτοβούλου ἁπτόμενος, ὁ ἀπὸ κυνηγεσίου τῆς Ἀλκιβιάδου ὥρας παραγινόμενος, ὁ Χαρμίδην τεθηπώς. πῶς γὰρ ὅμοια ταῦτα φιλοσόφῳ βίῳ; οὐ τῇ πρὸς τὸν δῆμον παρρησίᾳ, οὐδὲ τῇ πρὸς τοὺς τυράννους ἐλευθερίᾳ, οὐδὲ τῇ ἐπὶ Δηλίῳ

36 A similar account of divining poetry's hidden meanings is at *Or*. 17.4.

37 For Socrates' resistance to Alcibiades' advances, see Pl. *Symp*. 219b–d.

But in fact, Socrates himself, the lover of wisdom, the victor over poverty, the enemy of pleasure, and the friend of truth, included such risky and dangerous stories in his own conversations, that in comparison, Homer's allegories deserve far less censure than do his. That is because anyone hearing such stories about Zeus, Apollo, Thetis, and Hephaestus immediately divines that the story is saying one thing, but suggesting something else. And so, leaving its pleasure for the ear to enjoy, he teams up with the poet, soars with him in his imagination, and joins him in fashioning the story, simultaneously withholding belief and delighting in the license allowed to mythological discourse.[36]

But it is Socrates, the one we constantly hear credited with the truth, who is actually more dangerous with his allegories, because his stories are so convincing, his descriptions so powerful, and yet his actions are so inconsistent with one another. For Socrates in love is nothing like Socrates who remains chaste,[37] nor is Socrates dumbfounded by beautiful boys anything like Socrates who refutes foolish men, or at all like the one who competes with Lysias in the arts of love,[38] who rubs shoulders with Critobulus,[39] who joins a party after pursuing beautiful Alcibiades,[40] or who is stunned at the sight of Charmides.[41] How can all this accord with the philosophical life? It certainly does not match Socrates' outspokenness before the Athenian people, his assertion of freedom in the face

[38] Pl. *Phdr*. 234d–57c.
[39] Xen. *Symp*. 4.27–28.
[40] Pl. *Prt*. 309a.
[41] Pl. *Chrm*. 155d.

ἀριστείᾳ, οὐδὲ τῇ πρὸς τοὺς δικαστὰς ὑπεροψίᾳ, οὐδὲ τῇ ἐπὶ τὸ δεσμωτήριον ὁδῷ, οὐδὲ τῇ πρὸς τὸν θάνατον παρασκευῇ. πολλοῦ γε καὶ δεῖ.

Εἰ μὲν γὰρ ἀληθῆ ταῦτα, εὐφημεῖν ἄξιον· εἰ δὲ αἰνίττεται δι' αἰσχρῶν ῥημάτων πράξεις καλάς, δεινὸν καὶ σφαλερὸν τὸ χρῆμα. τὸ γὰρ ὑποβαλεῖν αἰσχρῷ καλὸν καὶ τὰ ὠφελοῦντα διὰ τῶν βλαπτόντων ἐπιδείκνυσθαι, οὐκ ὠφελεῖν βουλομένου ἔργον, τὸ γὰρ ὠφελοῦν ἀφανές, ἀλλὰ βλάπτειν, πρόχειρον γὰρ τοῦτο. ταῦτα οἶμαι Θρασύμαχον ἂν εἰπεῖν ἢ Καλλίαν ἢ Πῶλον, ἢ ὅστις ἄλλος τῇ Σωκράτους φιλοσοφίᾳ ἐπολέμει.

6. Φερ' ἐπαμύνωμεν τῷ λόγῳ, μὴ κενὰ[4] φλυαρῶμεν. καὶ δή μοι δοκῶ βούλεσθαι μὲν ταῦτα, δύνασθαι δὲ ἧττον· χρὴ δὲ ὁμοῦ τῷ βούλεσθαι καὶ δύνασθαι. ὧδε τοίνυν δράσωμεν περι<ποιοῦντες>[5] ῥᾳστώνην τοιαύτην τῷ λόγῳ, οἵαν καὶ εἰς τὰ δικαστήρια εἰσαγγελλόμενοι οἱ κινδυνεύοντες· οὐ περὶ τοῦ πράγματος ἀπολογοῦνται μόνον ὑπὲρ ὅτου ἡ εἰσαγγελία ἐγένετο, ἀλλ' ἠρέμα εἰς ἄλλους ἀξιοχρεωτέρους τρέπουσι τὴν αἰτίαν, τῇ πρὸς ἐκείνους κοινωνίᾳ κατασμικρύνοντες τὰ αὑτῶν. οὐκοῦν καὶ ἡμεῖς περὶ Σωκράτους εἰ μὲν ὀρθῶς ταῦτα ἔδρα ἢ μή, σκοπεῖν ἀναθησόμεθα σμικρόν,

[4] *κενὰ* Reiske, Dübner, Trapp: *ἱκανὰ* R: obel. Koniaris
[5] suppl. Stephanus

of the tyrants,[42] his bravery at Delium,[43] his disdain for his jurors, his willingness to go to jail, and his readiness to face death. They are completely at odds.

If all this is true, then better to stay silent. If, on the other hand, he is using shameful language to hint at honorable actions, then it is a shocking and dangerous enterprise. For hiding what is good under what is shameful, and portraying what is beneficial through what is harmful, is not the work of someone who wishes to be helpful (since the benefit remains hidden), but the work of someone who intends to do harm (since the harm is apparent). In my opinion, that is what Thrasymachus, Callias, Polus, or any other opponent of Socrates' philosophy would have said.[44]

6. Come, let us mount a defense, and waste no time in pointless chatter. I do want to do this, but I sense that my ability is lacking, and one must be both willing and able. So then, let us adopt the following course and allow our argument such license as is permitted defendants on trial in a courtroom. They not only defend themselves against what is alleged in the indictment, but also subtly shift the blame onto other more prominent individuals, and by this association with them, they diminish their own crimes. Therefore we shall postpone, but only for the time being, our examination as to whether or not Socrates was right to

[42] He refused to carry out an unjust order by the "Thirty Tyrants" in 403 BC (Pl. *Ap.* 32c–e). [43] In 424 BC (Pl. *Symp.* 221a–c). [44] Thrasymachus' inversions of ethical terms are exposed in Pl. *Resp.* Book 1; Polus appears at *Grg.* 461b–80e. Callias (the wealthy sponsor of sophists mentioned at *Or.* 1.9) is undoubtedly a mistake for Callicles (cf. *Grg.* 481b–527e), who is listed with Thrasymachus and Polus at *Or.* 26.5.

ὅσον τὸ νῦν ἔχον, λέγωμεν δὲ ὡδὶ πρὸς τουτουσὶ τοὺς δεινοὺς κατηγόρους, ὅτι·

Ἡμῖν δοκεῖτε, ὦ ἄνδρες, ἀτοπώτεροι εἶναι συκοφάνται Ἀνύτου καὶ Μελήτου· ἐκεῖνοι μέν γε ἀδικεῖν γραψάμενοι Σωκράτην καὶ τοὺς νέους διαφθείρειν, καὶ ὅτι μὲν Κριτίας ἐτυράννησεν, τοῦτο ἀδικεῖν ἔλεγον τὸν Σωκράτην, καὶ ὅτι Ἀλκιβιάδης ἐξύβριζεν, καὶ ὅτι τὸν ἥττω λόγον κρείττω ποιεῖ καὶ ὀμνύει τὴν πλάτανον καὶ τὸν κύνα· τῶν δὲ ἐρωτικῶν τῶν Σωκράτους ἀπέσχοντο καὶ οἱ δεινοὶ οὗτοι συκοφάνται. ἀλλ' οὐδὲ Ἀριστοφάνης τὰ Σωκράτους ἐν Διονυσίοις κωμῳδῶν, ὁ δεινότατος τῶν κατηγόρων, ἐλοιδορήσατο τῷ ἔρωτι τοῦ Σωκράτους, καίτοι πένητα εἰπὼν καὶ ἀδολέσχην καὶ σοφιστήν, καὶ πάντα μᾶλλον ἢ κακῶς ἐρῶντα. οὐ γὰρ ἦν, ὡς ἔοικεν, τὸ πρᾶγμα οὔτε τοῖς συκοφάνταις οὔτε τοῖς κωμῳδοῖς ἐπιλήψιμον.

7. Διὸ δὴ τὸ μὲν Ἀθηναίων θέατρον καὶ τὸ δικαστήριον ἐκεῖνο διαπέφευγεν· πρὸς τουτουσὶ δὲ τοὺς νυνὶ κατηγόρους (οὐ γάρ εἰσιν ἐκείνων ἀμαχώτεροι) διαγωνισώμεθα τὸ πρῶτον τῇδε, ὡς οὐκ ἴδιον Σωκράτους τὸ ἐρωτικὸν ἐπιτήδευμα, ἀλλὰ μακρῷ πρεσβύτερον. μάρτυρα δὲ αὐτὸν Σωκράτην παραστησώμεθα, ἐπαινοῦντα μὲν τὸ ἔργον καὶ θαυμάζοντα, ἐξαρνούμενον δὲ αὐτοῦ τὴν εὕρεσιν. ἐπιδειξαμένου γὰρ αὐτῷ τοῦ Μυρρινουσίου Φαίδρου λόγον ὑπὸ Λυσίου τοῦ

act as he did. Let us address these formidable accusers in the following way.

You seem to us, Gentlemen, to be accusers more outlandish than Anytus and Meletus, for when they accused Socrates in their indictment of wrongdoing and of corrupting the young, they based their accusations on the fact that Critias became a tyrant, that Alcibiades abused his power,[45] that he himself made the weaker argument appear to be the stronger, and that he swore by the plane tree[46] and by the dog.[47] And yet these fearsome accusers never mentioned Socrates' erotic affairs. Nor did Aristophanes, the fiercest of all his accusers, when lampooning Socrates' eccentricities at the Dionysia, ever rail against his sexual conduct, although he called him a pauper, an endless talker, a sophist, and everything else besides a malicious lover. Apparently neither his accusers nor the comic playwrights found this matter to be reprehensible.

7. Thus this subject passed without a word in the Athenian theater and in the courtroom. So, in response to these present-day accusers (who are no less combative than the former ones), let us begin to contest the issue in the following way. Now an involvement in affairs of love was not unique to Socrates, but was much older. So let us summon Socrates himself as a witness, who praises and expresses his admiration for this pursuit, but denies that he invented it. For when Phaedrus of Myrrhene recited to him a

45 Accusers cited the harmful actions of these two "students" as examples of Socrates' corrupting influence; cf. Xen. *Mem.* 1.2.12.

46 Pl. *Phdr.* 236d–e.

47 Pl. *Ap.* 21e, etc. Such oaths presumably indicated the worship of gods not sanctioned by the city.

Κεφάλου συγγεγραμμένον ἐρωτικόν, οὐκ ἔφη θαυμάζειν, πλῆρες τὸ στῆθος ἔχων ὥσπερ ἀγγεῖον ἀλλοτρίων ναμάτων, ἤ που Σαπφοῦς τῆς καλῆς (οὕτω γὰρ αὐτὴν ὀνομάζων χαίρει διὰ τὴν ὥραν τῶν μελῶν, καίτοι μικρὰν οὖσαν καὶ μέλαιναν), ἢ Ἀνακρέοντος, φησίν, τοῦ σοφοῦ. τὸν δὲ ἐν τῷ συμποσίῳ λόγον, εἰς ἔρωτα ἔπαινον, Μαντινικῇ γυναικὶ ἀνατίθησιν· ἀλλὰ εἴτε Μαντινικὴ εἴτε καὶ Λεσβία τις ἦν ἡ τοῦ λόγου μήτηρ, πάντως γε οὐκ ἴδιοι οἱ τοῦ Σωκράτους ἐρωτικοὶ λόγοι οὐδὲ πρῶτου. θεασώμεθα γὰρ οὕτως ἀπὸ Ὁμήρου ἀρξάμενοι.

8. Οὗτος γάρ μοι δοκεῖ πολυφωνότατος ὢν καὶ δεινὸς ὁμοῦ τοῖς καλοῖς τὰ αἰσχρὰ ἱστορεῖν, τὰ μὲν ὅπως ἔχωμεν, τὰ δὲ ὅπως φεύγωμεν, τὰ μὲν ἄλλα εὐήθως πάνυ καὶ ἀρχαίως ἐκδιδάσκειν, ἰᾶσθαι καὶ ἡνιοχεῖν καὶ τάττειν στράτευμα, ἐν νύσσῃ μὲν παραινῶν ἐγχριμφθῆναι τὸν ἐπὶ λαιᾷ ἵππον, κυκεῷ δὲ Πραμνίου διδοὺς τοῖς κάμνουσιν, τοὺς δὲ κακοὺς ἐν μέσῳ τάττων τῶν ἀγαθῶν καὶ τοὺς ἱππεῖς διακρίνων τῶν πεζῶν (ἦ γὰρ ἂν γέλωτα ὄφλοι τὰ σοφὰ ταῦτα τοῖς νῦν τακτικοῖς καὶ ἰατροῖς καὶ ἡνιόχοις), τὰ δὲ τοῦ ἔρωτος πάντα ἑξῆς δίεισιν, καὶ ἔργα καὶ ἡλικίας καὶ

[48] Pl. *Phdr.* 230e–34c. [49] Pl. *Phdr.* 235c.

[50] Pl. *Symp.* 201c–12b. [51] Cf. Dion. Hal. *Comp.* 16: "Homer, the poet with the most voices (πολυφωνότατος)."

[52] For Homer's juxtaposition of good and bad examples of behavior, see *Or.* 26.5–6.

speech on love composed by Lysias, son of Cephalus,[48] he said that he was not surprised to have his chest filled like a pitcher with streams that flowed from other sources, "perhaps from the lovely Sappho" (so he delighted to call her because her songs were so beautiful, even though she was short and dark), or, as he says, "from the wise Anacreon."[49] He also attributes his own speech during the symposium in praise of Love to a woman from Mantinea.[50] But whether the "mother" of the discourse was from Mantinea or from Lesbos, it is perfectly clear that Socrates' discussions of love were neither entirely his own nor was he their inventor. Let us then consider this topic in the following way, beginning with Homer.

8. Now it seems to me that Homer has the widest range of voices[51] and is skillful in juxtaposing what is noble with what is shameful in his narrative, so that we might hold on to the one and avoid the other,[52] but when it comes to other matters like medicine, chariot racing, and military tactics, his teachings are utterly naive and primitive. He recommends that the left-hand horse should barely miss the turning post;[53] he gives a concoction with Pramnian wine to wounded soldiers;[54] he stations the cowardly troops in the midst of the brave ones and separates the cavalry from the infantry[55]—"wise" advice that would be found laughable by today's generals, doctors, and charioteers. But when it comes to love, he discusses all of its aspects in detail, including its acts, times of life, types, and

[53] *Il.* 23.338, Nestor advising Antilochus.
[54] *Il.* 11.638–41.
[55] *Il.* 4.297–307, said of Nestor marshaling his troops.

εἴδη καὶ πάθη, τὰ καλά, τὰ αἰσχρά, τὸν σώφρονα ἔρωτα, τὸν ἀκόλαστον, τὸν δίκαιον, τὸν ὑβριστήν, τὸν ἐπιμανῆ, τὸν πρᾶον, καὶ ἔστιν ἐν τοιούτοις οὐκέτι ἀρχαῖος ἀλλὰ τεχνίτης δεινός,

οἷοι νῦν βροτοί εἰσιν.

Αὐτίκα ἐν πρώτῳ λόγῳ ἐπὶ αἰχμαλώτῳ ἐρασταὶ δύο, ὁ μὲν θρασὺς καὶ ἐπιμανής, ὁ δὲ ἥμερος καὶ ἐμπαθής· ὁ μὲν ἀποφλογοῦται τὰ ὄμματα καὶ λοιδορεῖται πᾶσιν καὶ ἀπειλεῖ· ὁ δὲ ἀναχωρεῖ ἐφ' ἡσυχίας καὶ δακρύει κείμενος καὶ ἀλύει καὶ ἀπελεύσεσθαί φησιν καὶ οὐκ ἄπεισιν. ἄλλη εἰκὼν ἀκολάστου ἔρωτος· τοιοῦτος αὐτῷ ὁ Ἀλέξανδρος οἷος ἐκ μάχης ἐπανιέναι εἰς τὸν θάλαμον καὶ ἀεὶ μοιχῷ ἐοικέναι. ἔστιν αὐτῷ καὶ δίκαιος ἔρως παρ' ἀμφοῖν ἴσος οἷον <ὁ>[6] τῆς Ἀνδρομάχης καὶ τοῦ Ἕκτορος· ἡ μὲν πατέρα καὶ ἀδελφὸν καλεῖ τὸν ἄνδρα καὶ ἐραστὴν καὶ πάντα δὴ τὰ φίλτατα ὀνόματα· ὁ δὲ οὐδὲ μητρὸς τοσουτονὶ αὐτῷ μέλειν ὅσον ἐκείνης λέγει.

Ἔδειξεν καὶ τὸν χαμαιεύνην ἔρωτα ἐπὶ τῆς Ἥρας καὶ τοῦ Διός, καὶ τὸν ὑβριστὴν ἐπὶ τῶν μνηστήρων, καὶ τὸν γόητα ἐπὶ τῆς Καλυψοῦς, καὶ τὸν φαρμακέα ἐπὶ τῆς Κίρκης, καὶ τὸν ἀνδρεῖον ἐπὶ τοῦ Πατρόκλου, τὸν πόνῳ κτητὸν καὶ χρόνῳ καὶ μέχρι θανάτου προερχόμενον, νέων καὶ καλῶν ἀμφοτέρων καὶ σωφρόνων,

[6] suppl. Markland, Trapp

emotions; what is noble, what is shameful; chaste love, licentious love, just love, abusive love, obsessive love, and gentle love. In all this he is no longer some old-fashioned man, but a skilled practitioner,

such as men are today.[56]

For instance, in his first book there are two lovers quarreling over a prisoner of war:[57] one is rash and obsessed, the other gentle and affectionate. The one flashes fire from his eyes and rails against everyone and threatens them all; the other withdraws to solitude and remains there crying and distraught, saying that he is going to sail away—and yet never leaves. Homer offers a second example, one of licentious love, in Alexander,[58] the type of person who leaves the fighting for his bed chamber like a perpetual adulterer. But he also portrays a just love shared equally between two people, like that of Andromache and Hector. She calls her husband "father," "brother," "lover," and all the dearest names; and for his part, he says that she matters more to him than even his own mother.[59]

Homer also described lovemaking on a bed of grass in his portrayal of Hera and Zeus,[60] abusive love in his portrayal of the suitors, bewitching love in the person of Calypso, spell-induced love in the example of Circe, and manly love in the person of Patroclus, a love that is won through long toil and endures until death, where both lovers are young, beautiful, and virtuous, where one in-

[56] *Il.* 5.304, etc. [57] Agamemnon and Achilles quarrel over Briseis at *Il.* 1.130–307. [58] That is, Paris; cf. *Il.* 3.380–448. [59] *Il.* 6.429–30, 450–55. [60] *Il.* 14.346–53, cited in §5 as a reason to exclude Homer from Plato's republic.

τοῦ μὲν παιδεύοντος, τοῦ δὲ παιδευομένου· ὁ μὲν ἄχθεται, ὁ δὲ παραμυθεῖται· ὁ μὲν ᾄδει, ὁ δὲ ἀκροᾶται· ἐρωτικὸν δὲ καὶ τὸ τυχεῖν ἐθέλοντα ἐξουσίας πρὸς μάχην δακρῦσαι ὡς οὐκ ἀνεξομένου τοῦ ἐραστοῦ· ὁ δὲ ἐφίησιν καὶ τοῖς αὑτοῦ ὅπλοις κοσμεῖ, καὶ βραδύνοντος περιδεῶς ἔχει, καὶ ἀποθανόντος ἀποθανεῖν ἐρᾷ, καὶ τὴν ὀργὴν κατατίθεται· ἐρωτικὰ δὲ καὶ τὰ ἐνύπνια καὶ τὰ ὀνείρατα καὶ τὰ δάκρυα καὶ τὸ τελευταῖον δῶρον ἤδη θαπτομένῳ ἡ κόμη. ταῦτα μὲν τὰ Ὁμήρου ἐρωτικά.

9. Ἡσιόδῳ δὲ ἀείδουσιν αἱ μοῦσαι τί ἄλλο ἢ γυναικῶν ἔρωτας καὶ ἀνδρῶν καὶ ποταμῶν ἔρωτας καὶ βασιλέων καὶ φυτῶν; τὸν δὲ Ἀρχιλόχου ἔρωτα, ὑβριστὴς γάρ, χαίρειν ἐῶ. ὁ δὲ τῆς Λεσβίας (εἴ τοι χρὴ πρεσβύτερα τοῖς νέοις εἰκάσαι) τί ἂν εἴη ἄλλο ἢ αὐτὸ ἡ Σωκράτους τέχνη ἐρωτική; δοκοῦσιν γάρ μοι τὴν καθ᾽ αὑτὸν ἑκάτερος φιλίαν, ἡ μὲν γυναικῶν, ὁ δὲ ἀρρένων, ἐπιτηδεῦσαι. καὶ γὰρ πολλῶν ἐρᾶν ἔλεγον, καὶ ὑπὸ πάντων ἁλίσκεσθαι τῶν καλῶν· ὅ τι γὰρ ἐκείνῳ Ἀλκιβιάδης καὶ Χαρμίδης καὶ Φαῖδρος, τοῦτο τῇ Λεσβίᾳ Γύριννα καὶ Ἀτθὶς καὶ Ἀνακτορία· καὶ ὅτιπερ Σωκράτει οἱ ἀντίτεχνοι, Πρόδικος καὶ Γοργίας καὶ Θρασύμαχος καὶ Πρωταγόρας, τοῦτο τῇ Σαπφοῖ Γοργὼ καὶ Ἀνδρομέδα. νῦν μὲν ἐπιτιμᾷ ταύταις, νῦν δὲ ἐλέγχει, καὶ εἰρωνεύεται αὐτὰ ἐκεῖνα τὰ Σωκράτους·

structs and the other learns; one grieves and the other consoles; one sings and the other listens. It is also a sign of love for Patroclus to weep when desiring to obtain permission to enter the battle, fully expecting that his lover will be unable to refuse him.[61] And the other does indeed give in, outfits him in his own armor, is terrified when he is slow to return, wishes to die when his friend has died, and ultimately lets go of his anger. Additional signs of love are his dreams, visions, tears, and his final gift at the burial, a lock of his hair.[62] Such are Homer's depictions of love.

9. What do the Muses in Hesiod sing of other than the loves of men and women, and of rivers, kings, and plants?[63] I make no mention of love in Archilochus because it is abusive,[64] but is the love of the Lesbian poetess (if one may compare old things to new) in any way different from Socrates' art of love? It seems to me that they each pursued their particular affection, the one for women, the other for men. In fact, both claimed to have many beloveds and to be captivated by all beautiful individuals. What Alcibiades, Charmides, and Phaedrus were to him, Gyrinna, Atthis, and Anactoria were to the woman from Lesbos. And just as Socrates' rivals were Prodicus, Gorgias, Thrasymachus, and Protagoras, so Sappho's were Gorgo and Andromeda. At one time she reproaches them, at another refutes them, and she uses irony just as Socrates does. He says,

61 *Il.* 16.1–45. 62 *Il.* 23.65–151.

63 In his *Catalogues*. "Kings" here is probably corrupt.

64 Cf. fr. 196a, which describes the seduction of a young girl.

τὸν Ἴωνα χαίρειν

φησὶν ὁ Σωκράτης·

πόλλα μοι τὰν
Πωλυανάκτιδα παῖδα χαίρην,

Σαπφὼ λέγει. οὐ προσιέναι φησὶν ὁ Σωκράτης Ἀλκιβιάδῃ, ἐκ πολλοῦ ἐρῶν, πρὶν ἡγήσατο ἱκανὸν εἶναι πρὸς λόγους·

σμίκρα μοι πάϊς ἔτι φαίνεο κἄχαρις

Σαπφὼ λέγει. κωμῳδεῖ σχῆμά που καὶ κατάκλισιν σοφιστοῦ· καὶ αὕτη

τίς δὲ . . . ἀγροΐωτιν ἐπεμμένα στόλαν . . .

τὸν ἔρωτά φησιν ἡ Διοτίμα τῷ Σωκράτει οὐ παῖδα, ἀλλὰ ἀκόλουθον τῆς Ἀφροδίτης καὶ θεράποντα εἶναι· λέγει που καὶ Σαπφοῖ ἡ Ἀφροδίτη ἐν ᾄσματι,

σύ τε κἄμος θεράπων Ἔρως.

ἡ Διοτίμα λέγει ὅτι θάλλει μὲν ἔρως εὐπορῶν, ἀποθνήσκει δὲ ἀπορῶν· τοῦτο ἐκείνη ξυλλαβοῦσα εἶπεν γλυκύπικρον καὶ ἀλγεσίδωρον. τὸν ἔρωτα Σωκράτης

---

65 The opening words of Plato's *Ion* (530a), where Socrates goes on to make a fool of Ion. 66 Fr. 155 Campbell.

67 Cf. [Pl.] 1 *Alc*. 103a and esp. 105e. His delay is also mentioned at *Orr*. 8.6 and 38.4.

Greetings, Ion[65]

while Sappho says,

warmest greetings to
the daughter of the house of Polyanax.[66]

Socrates claims that, in spite of being in love with Alcibiades for a long time, he did not approach him until he considered him ready to engage in dialogue.[67] Sappho says,

you seem to me still to be a graceless little girl.[68]

Socrates mocks a sophist's appearance and way of reclining;[69] she sings,

Who is this dressed in a rustic garment?[70]

Diotima tells Socrates that Love is not Aphrodite's child, but rather her follower and attendant,[71] while Aphrodite tells Sappho in one of her poems,

you and my attendant Love.[72]

Diotima says that love flourishes in abundance, but dies in poverty.[73] Sappho encapsulates this in her characterization of love as "bittersweet" and "a gift of pain."[74] Socrates

68 Fr. 49.2 Campbell (adapted).

69 Probably a reference to Prodicus lying in bed, wrapped up in blankets, at Pl. *Prt*. 315d–16a.

70 Fr. 57.1–2 Campbell (adapted).

71 A paraphrase of Pl. *Symp*. 203c.

72 Fr. 159 Campbell.

73 Pl. *Symp*. 203e.

74 Frr. 130.2, 172, 188 Campbell.

σοφιστὴν λέγει, Σαπφὼ μυθοπλόκον. ἐκβακχεύεται ἐπὶ Φαίδρῳ ὑπὸ τοῦ ἔρωτος, τῇ δὲ ὁ ἔρως ἐτίναξεν τὰς φρένας,

ὡς ἄνεμος κὰτ ὄρος δρύσιν ἐμπέτων.

ἄχθεται[7] τῇ Ξανθίππῃ ὀδυρομένῃ ὅτι ἀπέθνησκεν, ἡ δὲ τῇ θυγατρί·

οὐ γὰρ θέμις ἐν μουσοπόλων οἰκίᾳ
θρῆνον ἔμμεν'· οὔ κ' ἄμμι πρέποι τάδε.

Ἡ δὲ τοῦ Τηΐου σοφιστοῦ τέχνη τοῦ αὐτοῦ ἤθους καὶ τρόπου· καὶ γὰρ πάντων ἐρᾷ τῶν καλῶν καὶ ἐπαινεῖ πάντας· μεστὰ δὲ αὐτοῦ τὰ ᾄσματα τῆς Σμέρδιος κόμης καὶ τῶν Κλεοβούλου ὀφθαλμῶν καὶ τῆς Βαθύλλου ὥρας. ἀλλὰ κἂν τούτοις τὴν σωφροσύνην ὁρᾷς·

ἔραμαί τοι συνηβᾶν,

φησίν,

χαρίεν γὰρ ἔχεις ἦθος·

καὶ αὖθις,

καλὸν εἶναι τῷ ἔρωτι τὰ δίκαια,

[7] ἄχθεται Meiser, Trapp: ἀνάθεται R

calls Love a sophist, Sappho calls Love a "weaver of tales."[75] Love drives Socrates into a bacchic frenzy over Phaedrus;[76] love buffeted Sappho's mind,

> like a wind in the mountains assailing oak trees.[77]

Socrates is annoyed at Xanthippe for lamenting his impending death;[78] Sappho advises her daughter that

> lamentation is not permitted in the house of the Muses'
> followers, nor would it befit us.[79]

The art of the Teian sophist[80] is of the same kind and manner. He too loves all beautiful boys and sings their praises. His poems are full of Smerdies' hair, Cleobulus' eyes, and Bathyllus' youthful charms.[81] But even in these you can find self-control, for he says,

> I want to be young with you . . .
> because you have a charming character,[82]

and again he says that

> just deeds are beautiful when it comes to love.[83]

75 Fr. 188 Campbell.
76 Pl. *Phdr.* 234d.
77 Fr. 47 Campbell.
78 Pl. *Phd.* 60a.
79 Fr. 150 Campbell.
80 Anacreon.
81 Cf. Anac. frr. 357, 359, and 366 Campbell.
82 Fr. 402 (a) Campbell.
83 Fr. 402 (b) Campbell.

φησίν. ἤδη δέ που καὶ τὴν τέχνην ἀπεκαλύψατο·

ἐμὲ γὰρ λόγων εἵνεκα παῖδες ἂν φιλοῖεν·
χαρίεντα μὲν γὰρ ᾄδω, χαρίεντα δ' οἶδα λέξαι.

τοῦτο καὶ περὶ Σωκράτους Ἀλκιβιάδης ἔλεγεν, εἰκάζων αὐτοῦ τὴν χάριν τοῖς Ὀλύμπου καὶ Μαρσύου αὐλήμασιν. τίς ἄν, ὦ θεοί, μέμψαιτο ἐραστὴν τοιοῦτον, πλὴν Τιμάρχου;

And at one point he actually revealed his art:

boys would love me because of what I say,
for I know how to sing charming songs and speak
charming words.[84]

Alcibiades said the same thing of Socrates, when he compared his charm to the pipe playing of Olympus and Marsyas.[85] Who then, by the gods, would blame such a lover except Timarchus?[86]

[84] Fr. 402 (c) Campbell.
[85] Pl. *Symp.* 215c.
[86] Accused of prostitution in Aeschines' *Or.* 1 in 346 BC.

# *ORATION* 19

## INTRODUCTION

This second oration in the series differentiates Socrates' love for boys from that of wicked lovers.[1] It turns out that Socrates' amorous pursuits actually aim to protect the boys (*meirakia*) from the abuse (*hybris*) of unjust young men (*neaniskoi*) (§1). A fable explains how. A shepherd and a butcher spot a lamb separated from its flock and each take after it. The lamb, upon learning the professions of the two, entrusts himself to the shepherd, who will look out for him, rather than to the butcher, who will destroy him. So Socrates outstrips would-be murderers by getting to the boys first. The wicked lover is impelled by a desire for the youthful bloom (*anthos*) of the body, whereas Socrates' love is based on virtue and is inspired by the youthful bloom of the soul shining through a beautiful body, a soul that presages virtue in the eyes of a philosopher (§2). The philanthropic lover cares for his boyfriend with a view to sharing virtue. The wicked lover aims for pleasure; Socrates for virtue (§3). Virtuous love is differentiated from wicked love in a series of oppositions similar to the distinc-

[1] The argument here and in the following two orations draws on Plato's *Phaedrus* and *Symposium* for imagery and for descriptions of virtuous and wicked love.

tions between a friend and a flatterer in *Or.* 14.6. The virtuous lover openly displays his love; the wicked lover conceals his. The virtuous lover is like a shepherd; the wicked lover is like a thief who plunders a farmer's fruit and damages the stalk (§4). The oration concludes with the example of Agesilaus, who resisted taking advantage of the beautiful Megabates. His bravery in this regard is praised even above that of Leonidas at Thermopylae, and above Agesilaus' own exploits, for it is owed to the Spartan training of his soul (§5).

## *ORATION* 19

Ἔτι περὶ ἔρωτος. β′

1. Ἀναλαβόντες αὖθις αὖ τοὺς περὶ ἔρωτος λόγους, ὥσπερ ἀρχὴν μακρᾶς ὁδοῦ, μετ᾽ ἀνάπαυλαν βαδίζωμεν ἐπὶ τὸ τέλος, ἡγεμόνας παρακαλέσαντες τῆς ὁδοῦ Ἑρμῆν τὸν Λόγιον καὶ Πειθὼ καὶ Χάριτας καὶ τὸν Ἔρωτα αὐτόν. οὐ γάρ τι σμικρὸν οὐδ᾽ ὑπὲρ τῶν τυχόντων τὸ κινδύνευμα· παραθεῖ μὲν γὰρ τῇ λεωφόρῳ τοῦ περὶ ἔρωτος λόγου κρημνὸς βαθὺς καὶ χρὴ δυοῖν θάτερον, ἢ καλῶς ἐρῶντας ἰέναι ἀσφαλῶς, ἢ ἐκτραπομένους τῆς ὁδοῦ κακῶς ἐρᾶν καὶ ἐνεχθῆναι κατὰ τοῦ κρημνοῦ.

Τοῦτό τοι δείσας καὶ Σωκράτης ἐκεῖνος, εὑρὼν τὸ πάθος ἐνακμάζον τῇ τε ἄλλῃ Ἑλλάδι καὶ πολὺ μάλιστα ταῖς Ἀθήναις, καὶ μεστὰ πάντα ἀδίκων ἐραστῶν καὶ μειρακίων ἐξηπατημένων, οἰκτείρας τοῦ πάθους ἑκατέραν τὴν ἀγέλην, καὶ μήτε παῦσαι δυνάμενος τὴν ὕβριν νόμῳ (οὐ γὰρ ἦν Λυκοῦργος οὐδὲ Σόλων οὐδὲ Κλεισθένης, οὐδέ τις ἄλλος τῶν {διὰ}[1] δύναμιν ἀρχικὴν πιστευομένων ἐν τοῖς Ἕλλησι), μήτε δι᾽ ἐξουσίας

[1] del. Dübner, Trapp

# *ORATION* 19

## More on love. Part II

1. Let us resume our discussion of love, as if at the beginning of a long journey, and after catching our breath let us travel on to the end, having summoned Hermes Logios,[1] Persuasion, the Graces, and Love himself to guide us on our way, because the danger is not slight, nor are mundane matters at stake. For alongside the roadway of any speech on love runs a steep cliff that necessitates one of two alternatives: either to travel in safety by loving virtuously, or to veer off the road by loving wickedly and plunge down the cliff.

This latter alternative alarmed our Socrates, when he discovered that this passion was raging throughout Greece and most of all in Athens, and that everywhere there were lovers who were unjust and boys[2] who were deceived. Although he pitied what both groups were suffering, he was unable to stop the abuse by means of legislation (for he was no Lycurgus, Solon, Cleisthenes,[3] or any other person entrusted with political power in Greece). Nor did he have

[1] Hermes as the patron of messengers and orators.

[2] *meirakia* generally designates adolescents in their teens; cf. *Or*. 18.1.

[3] The Athenian lawgiver who instituted democratic reforms in 508 BC.

βιάσασθαι πρὸς τὰ κρείττω (Ἡρακλέους γὰρ αὐτοῖς πρὸς τοῦτο ἔδει ἢ Θησέως ἤ τινος ἄλλου σωφρονιστοῦ ἰσχυροῦ), μήτε πεῖσαι λόγῳ (ἀπειθὲς γὰρ χρῆμα ἐπιθυμία προσλαβοῦσα οἶστρον καὶ προελθοῦσα ἐγγύτατα μανίας)· οὕτω δὴ ὁ Σωκράτης τὸ μὲν ὑπεριδεῖν παντάπασιν τῶν νεανίσκων καὶ τῶν μειρακίων οὐκ ἠνέσχετο οὐδὲ πρὸς τὴν σωτηρίαν αὐτῶν ἐξέκαμεν, ἐξεῦρεν δὲ μηχανὴν ἑκουσίου ἀγωγῆς τοιάνδε τινά.

2. Φράσω δὲ αὐτὴν κατὰ τοὺς τοῦ Φρυγὸς λόγους μῦθον πλάττων. ποιμὴν ἀνὴρ καὶ μάγειρος ἐβάδιζον ἄμφω κοινὴν ὁδόν. ἰδόντες δὲ ἐκ ποίμνης ἄρνα εὐτραφῆ πλανώμενον, ἀπολειφθέντα τῶν συννόμων, ὤσαντο ἐπ' αὐτὸν ἄμφω. ἦν ἄρα τότε ὁμόφωνα καὶ τὰ θηρία τοῖς ἀνθρώποις· ἐρωτᾷ ὁ ἀμνός, τίς ὢν ἑκάτερος ἐθέλει αὐτὸν μεταχειρίσασθαι καὶ ἄγειν. ὡς δὲ ἐπύθετο τἀληθῆ αὐτά, τὴν ἀμφοῖν τέχνην, φέρων ἑαυτὸν ἐπιτρέπει τῷ ποιμένι· "σὺ μὲν γὰρ δήμιός τις εἶ καὶ μιαιφόνος τῆς ἀρνῶν ποίμνης, τούτῳ δὲ ἐξαρκέσει ἂν καλῶς τὰ ἡμέτερα ἔχῃ." εἴκαζε, εἰ βούλει, κατὰ τὸν μῦθον, τοὺς μὲν ἐραστὰς ἐκείνους μαγείροις πολλοῖς, τὸν δὲ Σωκράτην ποιμένι ἑνί, τὰ δὲ μειράκια τὰ Ἀττικὰ θρέμμασιν πλανωμένοις, ὁμοφώνοις ἀληθῶς, οὐ κατὰ τὴν ἐν τοῖς μύθοις ἐξουσίαν.

Τί ἂν οὖν δράσαι ὁ ποιμὴν οὗτος ὁρῶν τοὺς δημίους τῆς τῶν μειρακίων ὥρας ἐφιεμένους καὶ δρόμῳ ἐπ' αὐτὴν ὠθουμένους; ἆρα ἀνέξεται καὶ τὴν ἡσυχίαν ἄγων στήσεται; οὕτω μὲν εἴη ἂν μιαιφονώτερος αὐτῶν

the power of authority to compel them to reform (for that would have required a Heracles, or a Theseus, or some other mighty enforcer of morals to do that). Nor could he persuade them with reasoned argument (for desire that has been goaded and driven to the brink of insanity is not something amenable to persuasion). Consequently, since Socrates could not bear to ignore the young men[4] and their boyfriends entirely, or to give up trying to save them, he devised the following way to offer guidance that was voluntary.

2. I shall explain what he did by making up a story in the style of the Phrygian's[5] fables. A shepherd and a butcher were walking together down a road. When they saw a well-fed lamb separated from its fellow grazers and straying from the flock, both rushed after it. Since that was a time when humans and animals spoke a common language, the lamb asked who each of them was and why he wished to seize him and lead him away. Once he learned the truth about each man's occupation, he went and turned himself over to the shepherd, saying to the butcher, "You are an executioner and murderer of flocks of lambs, whereas this man will be quite content to see us thrive." Apply, if you will, the lesson of the fable by comparing those wicked lovers to a mob of butchers, Socrates to a single shepherd, and the Athenian boys to stray animals who really can talk, unlike what is allowed in fables.

What then would this shepherd of ours do, when he sees these executioners longing for the boys' youthful beauty and rushing at full speed after it? Will he allow this to happen and stand idly by? If so, he would be more

[4] *neaniskoi* are young adults.

[5] That is, Aesop's.

τῶν δημίων. οὐκοῦν θεύσεται καὶ κοινωνήσει τοῦ δρόμου καὶ διώξεται σὺν αὐτοῖς, οὐκ ἐπὶ τῇ ἴσῃ. καί τις ἰδὼν τῶν ἀπείρων τῆς τέχνης καὶ τῆς αἰτίας τοῦ δρόμου, αὐτὸ ἐκεῖνο οἰήσεται ἐπ' ὀλέθρῳ καὶ τοῦτον θεῖν· ἐὰν δὲ ἀναμείνῃ τὸ τέλος, ἐπαινέσεται τὸν δρόμον καὶ μιμήσεται τὴν σπουδὴν καὶ θαυμάσει τὸν θηρευτὴν καὶ μακαρίσει τὴν ἄγραν. διὰ τοῦτο καὶ ὁ Σωκράτης ἐρᾶν ἔλεγεν καὶ πάντων ἐρᾶν· καὶ ἐκοινώνει τοῦ δρόμου καὶ ἐδίωκεν τοὺς καλοὺς καὶ τοὺς συνεραστὰς ἔφθανεν καὶ τοὺς δημίους ὑπετέμνετο. καὶ γὰρ ἦν αὐτῶν καὶ πονεῖν ἱκανώτερος καὶ ἐρᾶν δεινότερος καὶ λαμβάνειν εὐστοχώτερος.

Καὶ πάνυ εἰκότως· τοῖς μὲν γὰρ ἄλλοις ὁ ἔρως ἦν ὄνομα ἐπιθυμίας ἐν ἡδοναῖς πλανώμενον. ἀρχὴ δὲ αὐτοῦ ἄνθος σώματος ἐρχόμενον εἰς ὀφθαλμοὺς καὶ δι' αὐτῶν ἐπὶ τὴν ψυχὴν ῥέον· ὁδοὶ γὰρ κάλλους οἱ ὀφθαλμοί· τῷ δὲ Σωκράτει ὁ ἔρως ἦν κατὰ μὲν τὴν σπουδὴν τοῖς ἄλλοις ὅμοιος, κατὰ δὲ τὴν ἐπιθυμίαν διαφέρων, κατὰ δὲ τὴν ἡδονὴν σωφρονέστερος, κατὰ δὲ τὴν ἀρετὴν εὐστοχώτερος· ἀρχὴ δὲ αὐτοῦ ψυχῆς ἄνθος ἐν σώματι διαφαινόμενον· οἷον εἰ ξυνείης καὶ ποταμοῦ κάλλος λειμῶνι ἐπιρρέον, καλὰ μὲν τὰ ἐπ' αὐτῷ ἄνθη, λαμπρυνόμενα δὲ ὑπὸ ὕδατος πρὸς τὴν ὄψιν· τοῦτο δύναται καὶ ψυχῆς ἄνθος ἐμπεφυτευμένον σώματι καλῷ, ἐκλαμπρύνεται ὑπ' αὐτοῦ καὶ ἐκλάμπει καὶ διαφαίνεται. καὶ ἔστιν σωμάτων ὥρα οὐδὲν ἄλλο

murderous than those very executioners. Consequently, he will take off running, enter the race, and join them in pursuit—but not with the same intention. Any onlooker who was unfamiliar with his art of love and the reason for his pursuit would accordingly conclude that he too was running to destroy them. But if the onlooker just waits until the end, he will praise his speed, imitate his zeal, admire the hunter, and consider his quarry fortunate. This is why Socrates professed to being in love and to loving them all, and why he joined in the chase, pursued beautiful boys, outstripped his rival lovers, and forestalled the executioners. For he was more fit for hard work than they were, more skilled in love, and had a surer aim for the capture.

And this was perfectly reasonable, because for the others love was nothing more than a name for desire roaming in the midst of pleasures, and the impulse for it was the youthful bloom[6] of a body entering the eyes and flowing on through them to the soul, for the eyes are the pathways of beauty. But although Socrates' love was like theirs in its fervor, it was different in its desire, more chaste in its pleasure, and aimed more accurately at virtue. The impulse for his love was the youthful bloom of a soul shining out from within its body. Think of this in terms of a beautiful river flowing over a meadow. The flowers in the meadow are indeed beautiful, but the water makes them lustrous to the eye. This is the effect of the youthful bloom of a soul implanted in a beautiful body: it is made lustrous by its body and shines out through it. Thus the beauty of bodies

[6] Maximus plays on ἄνθος as "youthful bloom" and, literally, as "flower." The trope recurs in §5 below.

ἢ μελλούσης ἀρετῆς ἄνθος καὶ οἱονεὶ προοίμιον κάλλους ὡραιοτέρου. ὥσπερ γὰρ τοῦ ἡλίου προανίσχει τις αὐγὴ ὑπὲρ ἄκρων ὀρῶν, ἀγαπητὸν ὀφθαλμοῖς θέαμα διὰ τὴν προσδοκίαν τοῦ μέλλοντος, οὕτως καὶ τῆς λαμπρᾶς ψυχῆς προανίσχει τις ὥρα ὑπὲρ ἄκρων τῶν σωμάτων, ἀγαπητὸν φιλοσόφοις θέαμα διὰ τὴν προσδοκίαν τοῦ μέλλοντος.

3. Ἀλλὰ Θετταλὸς μὲν ἀγαπήσει πωλίον καὶ Αἰγύπτιος πόρτιν καὶ Σπαρτιάτης σκύλακα, φιλάνθρωπος δ' ἀνὴρ καὶ φιλοθρέμμων τοῦ ζῴου τούτου, οὐ κατὰ γεωργὸν Αἰγύπτιον, οὐδὲ κατὰ ἱππικὸν Θετταλόν, οὐδὲ κατὰ κυνηγέτην Λακωνικόν· τούτοις μὲν γὰρ ἡ θεραπεία προμνᾶται τοῖς ζῴοις πόνους·[2] ὁ δὲ ἐραστὴς ὁ φιλάνθρωπος θεραπεύει τὰ παιδικὰ ἐπὶ κοινωνίᾳ τῆς ἀρετῆς, θεραπεύει δὲ ἐπιλεξάμενος τὰ ἐπιτηδειότατα, ἐπιτήδεια δὲ εἰς προσδοκίαν ἀρετῆς τὰ κάλλιστα.

Τὸ δὲ κάλλος, τὸ αὐτὸ ὄν, ἀλλοιότερον μὲν φαίνεται μοχθηροῖς ὀφθαλμοῖς, ἀλλοιότερον δὲ ἐρασταῖς νομίμοις· καὶ γὰρ τὸ ξίφος, τὸ αὐτὸ ὄν, ἀλλοιότερον μὲν φαίνεται τῷ ἀριστεῖ, ἀλλοιότερον δὲ τῷ δημίῳ· καὶ τὴν μὲν Πενελόπην ἀλλοίως μὲν Ὀδυσσεὺς ὁρᾷ, ἀλλοίως δὲ ὁ Εὐρύμαχος· καὶ τὸν ἥλιον ἄλλως μὲν ὁρᾷ Πυθαγόρας, ἄλλως δὲ Ἀναξαγόρας, Πυθαγόρας μὲν ὡς θεόν, Ἀναξαγόρας δὲ ὡς λίθον· καὶ τὴν ἀρετὴν

[2] πόνους Davies², Trapp, Koniaris: πονοῦσα R: lacunam post θεραπεία stat. Hobein, Trapp

is nothing other than the flower of virtue yet to come—the prelude, as it were, to a beauty that is even more lovely. For just as a certain glimmer above the peaks of mountains precedes the coming of the sun, and is a welcome sight for the eyes because of the expectation of what is yet to come, so a certain beauty above the surface of bodies precedes the coming of a splendid soul, and is a welcome sight to philosophers because of their expectation of what is yet to come.[7]

3. Now, a Thessalian will shower affection on a colt, an Egyptian on a calf, and a Spartan on a puppy. A philanthropist, however, who is fond of rearing this human creature, shows his affection differently from the Egyptian farmer, the Thessalian horseman, or the Spartan hunter. For their affectionate care results in physical toil for their animals, whereas the philanthropic lover cares for his boyfriend with a view to their sharing in virtue, and for this care he selects the most suitable candidates, these being the most beautiful and best suited to fulfill his expectation of virtue.

Beauty, however, although being one and the same, appears quite differently to the eyes of wicked men than it does to law-abiding lovers. Likewise, a sword, although being one and the same, appears quite differently to a war hero than it does to an executioner. Then too, Odysseus sees Penelope one way, and Eurymachus another. Pythagoras sees the sun one way, and Anaxagoras another: Pythagoras sees it as a god,[8] and Anaxagoras as a stone.[9]

[7] That is, virtue.

[8] Diog. Laert. 8.27 (Pythagoras): "The sun, moon, and the other stars are gods."

[9] Cf. Pl. *Ap.* 26d.

ἄλλως μὲν διώκει Σωκράτης, ἄλλως δὲ Ἐπίκουρος, Σωκράτης μὲν ὡς εὐδαιμονίας ἐραστής, Ἐπίκουρος δὲ ὡς ἡδονῆς. οὕτω καὶ καλὸν σῶμα ἄλλως μὲν διώκει Σωκράτης, ἄλλως δὲ Κλεισθένης, Σωκράτης μὲν ὡς ἀρετῆς ἐραστής, Κλεισθένης δὲ ὡς ἡδονῆς.

4. Ὁπόταν τοίνυν ἀκούσῃς ἐρῶντα μὲν τὸν φιλόσοφον, ἐρῶντα δὲ καὶ τὸν μοχθηρὸν ἄνδρα, μὴ προσείπῃς τὸ γιγνόμενον ὀνόματι ἑνί. ὁ μὲν ἐφ' ἡδονὴν οἰστρεῖ, ὁ δὲ κάλλους ἐρᾷ· ὁ μὲν ἄκων νοσεῖ, ὁ δὲ ἑκὼν ἐρᾷ· ὁ μὲν ἐπ' ἀγαθῷ ἐρᾷ τοῦ ἐρωμένου, ὁ δὲ ἐπ' ὀλέθρῳ ἀμφοῖν. ἐκείνου τοῦ ἔρωτος ἀρετὴ ἔργον, τοῦδε τοῦ ἔρωτος ἔργον ὕβρις· ἐκείνου τοῦ ἔρωτος φιλία τέλος, τούτου τοῦ ἔρωτος ἔχθρα τέλος· ἄμισθος ὁ ἔρως ἐκεῖνος, μισθοφόρος ὁ ἔρως οὗτος· ἐκεῖνος ὁ ἔρως ἐπαινετός, ἐπονείδιστος οὗτος· ἐκεῖνος Ἑλληνικός, βαρβαρικὸς οὗτος· ἐκεῖνος ἄρρην, ἁπαλὸς οὗτος· ἐκεῖνος ἑστώς, πτηνὸς οὗτος· [ἀβέβαιος][3] ἐκεῖνον τὸν ἔρωτα ἐρῶν ἀνὴρ φίλος θεῷ, φίλος νόμῳ, μεστὸς αἰδοῦς, μεστὸς παρρησίας· ἐκεῖνος καὶ μεθ' ἡμέραν τὸν ἐρώμενον περιέπει καὶ ἀγάλλεται τῷ ἔρωτι, καὶ ἐν γυμνασίῳ συμπλέκεται καὶ ἐν δρόμῳ συνθεῖ καὶ ἐν θήρᾳ συγκυνηγετεῖ, καὶ ἐν πολέμῳ συναριστεύει καὶ ἐν εὐτυχίαις συνευτυχεῖ καὶ ἀποθανόντος συναποθνήσκει· καὶ οὐδὲν αὐτῷ δεῖ πρὸς τὴν συνουσίαν οὐ νυκτός, οὐκ ἐρημίας. ὁ δὲ ἕτερος ἐραστὴς θεοῖς μὲν ἐχθρός, πλημμελὴς γάρ· ἐχθρὸς δὲ καὶ νόμῳ, παρά-

[3] del. Trapp

Socrates pursues virtue in one way, Epicurus in another: Socrates does so as a lover of happiness, Epicurus as a lover of pleasure. And in just the same way, Socrates pursues a beautiful body in one way, Cleisthenes[10] in another: Socrates does so as a lover of virtue, Cleisthenes as a lover of pleasure.

4. Therefore, when you hear that both the philosopher and the wicked man are in love, do not describe what they experience with a single word. The one is goaded to pursue pleasure; the other is in love with beauty; the one is sick in spite of himself; the other loves willingly; the one loves for the good of his boyfriend; the other for the ruination of them both. The one love produces virtue; the other produces abuse. The one love ends in friendship; the other in hatred. The one love is given for free; the other exacts its price. The one love is praiseworthy; the other is disgraceful. The one is Greek; the other is barbarian. The one is masculine; the other is effeminate. The one is stable; the other is fickle. The one lover is dear to god and dear to the law, full of respect and openness. He tends his beloved during the day and proudly displays his love, wrestling with him in the gymnasium, running beside him on the racetrack, joining him when he hunts, fighting bravely alongside him in battle, sharing in his good fortune, and dying with him when he dies. He has no need whatsoever of nighttime or solitude in order to be with him. The other lover is hated by the gods because he is sinful; he is hated by the law because he is a lawbreaker.

10 An Athenian lampooned by Aristophanes (*Nub*. 355–56) for being effeminate.

νομος γάρ· ἀθαρσής, δύσελπις, αἰδοῦς ἄπορος, ἐρημίᾳ φίλος καὶ νυκτὶ καὶ φωλεοῖς, μηδαμοῦ ἂν ἐθέλων ὀφθῆναι συνδιημερεύων τοῖς παιδικοῖς, φεύγων ἥλιον, διώκων νύκτα καὶ

ὀμίχλην
ποιμέσιν οὔ τι φίλην, κλέπτῃ δὲ

ἀγαθήν. ὁ μὲν ποιμένι ἔοικεν, ὁ δὲ κλέπτῃ ἔοικεν καὶ λανθάνειν εὔχεται· οἶδεν γὰρ τὸ κακὸν ὃ δρᾷ, ἀλλὰ εἰδὼς ὑφ᾽ ἡδονῆς ἕλκεται. καὶ γὰρ ἐν τοῖς εὐκάρποις φυτοῖς ὁ μὲν γεωργὸς τημελῶς πρόσεισιν, ὁ δὲ κλέπτης ἐμπεσὼν δρέπει καὶ λυμαίνεται καὶ σπαράττει.

5. Καλὸν σῶμα ὁρᾷς ἀνθοῦν καὶ ἔγκαρπον· μὴ χράνῃς, μὴ μιάνῃς, μὴ προσάψῃ τοῦ ἄνθους· ἐπαίνεσον, ὡς ὁδοιπόρος φυτόν ποτε·

τοῖον Ἀπόλλωνος παρὰ βωμῷ
φοίνικος νέον ἔρνος ἀνερχόμενον ἐνόησα.

φεῖσαι τοῦ φυτοῦ τοῦ Ἀπόλλωνος καὶ τοῦ Διός, ἀνάμεινον τοὺς καρπούς, καὶ ἐρασθήσῃ δικαιότερον. οὐ χαλεπὸν τὸ ἔργον· οὐ γὰρ Σωκράτους μόνον, οὐδὲ φιλοσόφου μόνον. ἤδη καὶ Σπαρτιάτης ἀνὴρ οὐκ ἐν Λυκείῳ τραφεὶς οὐδὲ ἐν Ἀκαδημίᾳ γυμνασάμενος οὐδὲ ἐν φιλοσοφίᾳ πεπαιδευμένος, ἐντυχὼν μειρακίῳ βαρβαρικῷ μέν, ἀλλ᾽ ἄκρως καλῷ καὶ ἀνθοῦντι ἄρτι,

He is craven, despondent, devoid of respect, fond of solitude, night, and hiding places, unwilling to be seen anywhere with his boyfriend during the day, as he flees the light of the sun, seeking night and

> the misty darkness
> that shepherds hate, but a thief finds[11]

advantageous. The one lover is like a shepherd; the other is like a thief who prays to remain hidden, for he knows that what he is doing is evil, but in spite of that knowledge, is dragged along by pleasure. And unlike the farmer who approaches his flourishing crops to care for them, the thief attacks them, plucks their fruit, damages them, and rips them up.

5. When you see a beautiful body that is flowering and soon to bear fruit, do not defile or stain it, or lay your hands on its flower. Instead, praise it, as a traveler once praised a tree:

> like the young shoot sprouting from a palm tree
> that I once saw by the altar of Apollo.[12]

Spare the sapling of Apollo and of Zeus. Wait for its fruits to develop and your love will be more just. This is not a difficult task, requiring only a Socrates or only a philosopher. In fact, a Spartiate[13] who was not educated in the Lyceum, or trained in the Academy, or educated in philosophy, happened to meet a barbarian boy, yet one who was supremely beautiful and just coming into the flower

[11] *Il.* 3.10–11. [12] *Od.* 6.162–63, Odysseus complimenting Nausicaa. [13] Agesilaus (ca. 445–359 BC), named below. His refusal to kiss Megabates is told at Xen. *Ages.* 5.4–6.

ἠράσθη μὲν αὐτοῦ (πῶς δ' οὐκ ἔμελλεν;), ἀλλ' οὐ περαιτέρω τῶν ὀφθαλμῶν. ἐπαινῶ τῆς ἀριστείας τὸν Ἀγησίλαον μᾶλλον ἢ τὸν Λεωνίδην [μαχίμων·][4] ἀμαχώτερος γὰρ ὁ ἔρως ἦν τοῦ βαρβάρου, καὶ τὰ τοῦ ἔρωτος βλήματα τιτρώσκει μᾶλλον ἢ τὰ Καδούσια ἢ τὰ Μηδικά.

Τοιγαροῦν ὁ Ξέρξης μὲν ἐπέβη Λεωνίδου κειμένου καὶ παρῆλθεν ἔσω Πυλῶν· Ἀγησιλάῳ δὲ μέχρι τῶν ὀφθαλμῶν προελθὼν ὁ ἔρως ἐνταῦθα ἔστη ἐπὶ θύραις τῆς ψυχῆς. μεῖζον τὸ ἔργον· δίδωμι τὰ ἀριστεῖα. ταῦτα δρῶντα ἐπαινῶ τὸν Ἀγησίλαον μᾶλλον ἢ Τισσαφέρνην διώκοντα ἢ Θηβαίων κρατοῦντα ἢ τὰς μάστιγας καρτεροῦντα· ἐκεῖνα μὲν γὰρ ἦν τῆς τῶν σωμάτων τροφῆς καὶ παιδαγωγίας, ταῦτα δὲ ἔργα ψυχῆς τῷ ὄντι ἠσκημένης καὶ μεμαστιγωμένης.

[4] secl. Meiser: obel. Trapp

of age. He fell in love with the boy (how could he not?), but his love advanced no further than his eyes. I praise Agesilaus more highly for his bravery than I do Leonidas for his,[14] because love proves to be a more irresistible opponent than the barbarian,[15] and the arrows of love wound more gravely than those of any Cadusian or Mede.[16]

And so, Xerxes trampled on Leonidas when he lay dead and passed through the Gates,[17] whereas love advanced only as far as Agesilaus' eyes and halted there at the gateway of his soul. His is the greater achievement; I award it the prize for valor. I praise Agesilaus more highly for accomplishing this than for pursuing Tissaphernes, or defeating the Thebans, or enduring whipping,[18] because these latter deeds resulted from his physical training and upbringing, whereas the former was the work of a soul truly disciplined and whipped into shape.

14 The Spartiate Leonidas died defending the pass at Thermopylae in 480 BC.

15 That is, Xerxes.

16 Two peoples in Persia.

17 That is, Thermopylae (Hot Gates).

18 Agesilaus' campaigns against Tissaphernes and the Thebans are recounted in Xen. *Ages.* 1.10–34 and 2.5–12. Spartan boys were whipped to toughen them up; cf. *Orr.* 23.2, 32.10, and 34.9.

# *ORATION* 20

## INTRODUCTION

This third installment on love does not concern Socrates, but is a general discussion that seeks to differentiate vicious from virtuous love. As elsewhere in the *Orations*, it equates sexual abuse (*hybris*) with tyrannical power and the license (*exousia*) it enjoys in pursuit of pleasure.[1] Here, however, it argues that proper pederastic love should consist only of admiration and be free of sex. It concludes with a general condemnation of intercourse between males.

The oration opens with the youth Smerdies being courted by the tyrant Polycrates and the poet Anacreon. The tyrant employs bribes and coercion; the poet offers poems of praise (§1). Genuine love, however, does not exist in any unequal relationship based on compulsion and fear, for true love is fearless and free (§2). The problem remains of distinguishing this genuine love from its counterfeit (§3). There are two kinds of love: the virtuous one controlled by reason that is healthy, and the vicious one controlled by emotion alone that is diseased (§4). Love is a desire (*orexis*) of the soul, and if left unchecked, it runs rampant like the horse in the Homeric simile, burning to couple with another body, and spurred on by mere report

[1] See especially the discussion at *Or.* 18.1.

of beauty in that body (§5). The opposing kind of love is that required by nature between a male and a female for the propagation of the species, whether spontaneously or under the supervision of a breeder. The human species needs reason to restrain sexual desire with its persuasion. (§6). Examples of unrestrained love in pursuit of pleasure are provided by Paris and Xerxes (§7). The speaker lauds the love of Cretan and Spartan men for boys, with its chaste admiration rather than physical contact (§8).[2] The example of a Locrian boy shows that men can be driven to suicide by the frenzy of physical love. Darius the Persian was so in love with gold that he broke into a tomb where gold was reputed to be buried, but he found only an inscription chastising him for touching a corpse because of his love of gold. The same warning applies to any Greek man who "touches" flesh, thinking to find beauty buried in it. It is sterile intercourse (§9).

[2] A similar argument is at Pl. *Leg*. 8.837c.

# *ORATION* 20

Ἔτι περὶ τῆς Σωκράτους ἐρωτικῆς. γʹ

1. Σμερδίης Θρᾷξ ὑπὸ Ἑλλήνων ἁλούς, μειράκιον βασιλικὸν ὀφθῆναι γαῦρον, ἐκομίσθη δῶρον τυράννῳ Ἴωνι, Πολυκράτει τῷ Σαμίῳ. ὁ δὲ ἥσθη τῷ δώρῳ, καὶ ἐρᾷ Πολυκράτης Σμερδίου, καὶ αὐτῷ συνερᾷ ὁ Τήϊος ποιητὴς Ἀνακρέων. καὶ Σμερδίης παρὰ μὲν Πολυκράτους ἔλαβεν χρυσὸν καὶ ἄργυρον καὶ ὅσα εἰκὸς ἦν μειράκιον καλὸν παρὰ τυράννου ἐρῶντος· παρὰ δὲ Ἀνακρέοντος ᾠδὰς καὶ ἐπαίνους καὶ ὅσα εἰκὸς ἦν παρὰ ποιητοῦ ἐραστοῦ. εἰ δή τις παραβάλοι ἔρωτα ἔρωτι, τυραννικὸν ποιητικῷ, πότερος ἂν αὐτοῖν φανείη ἐνθεώτερος καὶ οὐράνιος καὶ ἄξιος Ἀφροδίτης ἐπονομάζεσθαι καὶ ἔργον εἶναι θεοῦ; ἐγὼ μὲν οἶμαι κρατεῖν ἂν τὸν Μούσαις καὶ Χάρισιν ἀνακεκραμένον μᾶλλον ἢ τὸν ἀνάγκῃ καὶ δέει· ὁ μὲν γὰρ αἰχμαλώτῳ ἔοικεν ἢ μισθοφόρῳ οὐ πάνυ τι εὐτυχεῖ, ὁ δὲ ἐλευθέρῳ καὶ Ἕλληνι.

2. Διόπερ μοι δοκεῖ οὐδὲ ἐν τοῖς βαρβάροις πάνυ τι ἐπιχωριάσαι τὰ τοῦ ἔρωτος. ὅπου γὰρ τὸ μὲν

# *ORATION* 20

## More on Socrates' art of love. Part III

1. A Thracian named Smerdies, a royal youth with a proud demeanor, was captured by some Greeks and taken as a gift to the Ionian tyrant, Polycrates of Samos. Polycrates was delighted with the gift and was in love with Smerdies, but so too was his rival, the poet Anacreon of Teos. From Polycrates Smerdies received gold and silver and everything else a beautiful boy was likely to receive from a tyrant in love with him, whereas from Anacreon he received poems and encomia and everything else likely to come from a lover who was a poet. If one were to compare the one love with the other, the tyrant's with the poet's, which one would seem more divinely inspired and heavenly[1] and worthy to bear Aphrodite's name, and to be the work of a god? I believe that the love imbued with the Muses and Graces would prevail over the one steeped in compulsion and fear, for the one befits a prisoner of war or some unfortunate mercenary, the other a free Greek.

2. It is for this reason, I believe, that genuine love simply has no place among barbarians, for wherever the

[1] Heavenly (*ouranios*) alludes to "Heavenly Aphrodite" in Pausanias' speech at Pl. *Symp.* 180d–85c.

πλῆθος δουλεύει, τὸ δὲ ἄρχον δεσπόζει, τὸ διὰ μέσου ἐνθένδε ἐξῄρηται, τὸ ἰσήγορόν τε καὶ ἰσότιμον καὶ ξύννομον. ὁ δὲ ἔρως οὐδενὶ οὕτως πολεμεῖ ὡς ἀνάγκῃ καὶ δέει, καὶ ἔστιν χρῆμα γαῦρον καὶ δεινῶς ἐλεύθερον καὶ τῆς Σπάρτης αὐτῆς ἐλευθερώτερον.

Μόνον γάρ τοι τῶν ἐν ἀνθρώποις ἔρως, ἐπειδάν τῳ καθαρῶς ξυγγένηται, οὐ πλοῦτον τέθηπεν, οὐ τύραννον δέδιεν, οὐ βασίλεια ἐκπλήττεται, οὐ δικαστήριον φυλάττεται, οὐ φεύγει θάνατον· οὐ θηρίον αὐτῷ δεινόν, οὐ πῦρ, οὐ κρημνός, οὐ θάλαττα, οὐ ξίφος, οὐ βρόχος, ἀλλὰ καὶ τὰ ἄπορα αὐτῷ εὐπορώτατα καὶ τὰ δεινὰ εὐμαχώτατα καὶ τὰ φοβερὰ εὐπετέστατα καὶ τὰ χαλεπὰ εὐκολώτατα· ποταμοὶ πάντες περάσιμοι, χειμῶνες πλοϊμώτατοι, ὄρη εὐδρομώτατα· πανταχοῦ θαρσεῖ, πάντων ὑπερορᾷ, πάντων κρατεῖ. πολλοῦ γε ἄξιον τὸ ἐρᾶν, τοιοῦτον ὄν. ἐγὼ μὲν οἶμαι κἂν εὔξασθαί τινα νοῦν ἔχοντα μηδαμοῦ ἀπαλλαγῆναι αὐτοῦ, εἰ μέλλοι ὁμοῦ ἐρῶν ἐλεύθερός τ' εἶναι καὶ ἀδεὴς καὶ ἄπταιστος.

3. Δέδια δὲ μὴ οὐ τοιοῦτον ᾖ πᾶσιν ἑξῆς, ἀλλά τις ὁμοιότης ἐπιτηδεύματος αἰσχροῦ, ὑποδῦσα ἔργον καλόν, τῇ πρὸς αὐτὸ εἰκασίᾳ καλλωπιζομένη τυγχάνει μὲν τῆς φαντασίας ὁμοίας, τοῦ δὲ τέλους ἀστοχεῖ. μιμεῖταί που καὶ φαρμακοπώλης ἰατρὸν καὶ συκοφάντης ῥήτορα καὶ σοφιστὴς φιλόσοφον. καὶ πανταχοῦ εὕροις ἂν ξυμφυὲς ἀγαθῷ κακόν, πολλῷ τῷ ὁμοίῳ ἀνακεκραμένον, ἢ προαιρέσει χωριζόμενον, ὡς ὁ ῥήτωρ τοῦ συκοφάντου, ἢ τέλει, ὡς ὁ ἰατρὸς τοῦ φαρ-

populace is enslaved and the rule is despotic, there the middle ground has been eliminated, along with equality of speech, equality of status, and equal partnership. Love, however, has no worse enemy than compulsion and fear, for it is a proud thing and ferociously free, even more free than Sparta itself.

Love is unique among human experiences, and once it bonds with someone in its pure form, it is not dazzled by wealth, afraid of tyrants, or in awe of palaces; it does not avoid a court of law or flee from death. No wild beast can frighten it, no fire, no cliff, no sea, no sword, no noose, but even impossible tasks are very easily accomplished, fearsome foes easily defeated, terrors easily faced, and difficulties easily handled. All rivers can be crossed, stormy seas easily navigated, and mountains easily scaled. In every situation love is confident: it scorns every foe and defeats them all. Love like that is worth a fortune, and in my opinion any sensible person would hope and pray never to be deprived of it, if being in love means that he will at the same time be free and fearless and never go wrong.

3. I fear, however, that love is not like that for each and every person, for there is a shameful practice that bears a certain similarity to it. By assuming the guise of noble conduct, and by making a show of the resemblance, it achieves a similar outward appearance, but fails to achieve the same objective. To a certain degree a druggist imitates a doctor, a prosecutor imitates an orator, and a sophist imitates a philosopher. In every sphere you can find good and evil intermingled and sharing much that is similar, but differing either in intention (as the orator differs from the prosecutor), or in objective (as the doctor differs from the

μακέως, ἢ ἀρετῇ, ὡς ὁ φιλόσοφος τοῦ σοφιστοῦ· προαίρεσις δὲ καὶ ἀρετὴ καὶ τέλος ὀλίγοις γνώριμα. ὅταν οὖν ἐν ἐπιτηδεύμασιν διπλοῖς καὶ ἀμφιβόλοις τὰ μὲν ὅμοια <ἐμφανῆ, τὰ δὲ ἀνόμοια>[1] ἀφανῆ,[2] ἀνάγκη κατὰ τὸ ἀγνοούμενον οὐ δυναμένοις χωρίζειν τὰς τέχνας κατὰ τὸ εἰκαζόμενον αὐτὰς συνάπτειν.

4. Μήποτ᾽ οὖν καὶ περὶ ἔρωτος ταύτῃ κριτέον, καὶ ἡγητέον αὐτὸν εἶναι ὄνομα κοινὸν ἐν μεταιχμίῳ ἀρετῆς καὶ κακίας τεταγμένον, ὑπ᾽ ἀμφοῖν δημαγωγούμενον· σχηματιζόμενον δὲ πρὸς ἑκατέραν, ὁποτέρᾳ ξυγγένοιτο, τῷ τῆς ἐπαγομένης πάθει προσονομάζεσθαι. καὶ μὴν τῆς ψυχῆς δίχα νενεμημένης, ὡς ὁ Πλάτωνός φησιν λόγος, ἧς τῷ μὲν τῶν μερῶν ὄνομα λόγος, τῷ δὲ πάθος, ἀνάγκη τὸν ἔρωτα, εἰ μὲν κακία εἴη, πάθος τι εἶναι ἔρημον λόγου· εἰ δέ τι τῶν καλῶν, δυοῖν θάτερον, ἢ κατὰ τὸν λόγον τετάχθαι πάθους ἀπηλλαγμένον, ἢ κατὰ τὸ πάθος λόγῳ συμπεπλεγμένον.

Καὶ εἰ μὲν ὁ ἔρως φιλίας ἐστὶν ὁρμὴ καὶ ὄρεξις τοῦ ὁμοίου πρὸς τὸ ὅμοιον ᾄττοντος φύσει καὶ ἀνακραθῆναι αὐτῷ ὀρεγομένου—πάθος ἂν εἴη τοῦτο, οὐ λόγος—δεῖ προστεθῆναι τῷ πάθει τούτῳ ἐπιστάτην λόγον ἵνα ἀρετὴ γένηται καὶ μὴ νόσος. καθάπερ γὰρ

1 suppl. Schenkl
2 ἀφανῆ Schenkl: ἂν ἀπῇ R: obel. Trapp, Koniaris

---

2 That is, it becomes virtuous love or vicious love.

druggist), or in virtue (as the philosopher differs from the sophist). But intentions, virtue, and objectives are things few people can discern. So, whenever ambiguous activities with two different forms share similar aspects (that are apparent) and dissimilar ones (that lie hidden), it is inevitable that people whose lack of knowledge renders them unable to distinguish between these professions will confuse them because of their similarities.

4. So, should we not judge love in a similar way, and consider it to be a shared name that is located in between virtue and vice and is courted by both sides, that it takes on the character of whichever side it joins, and that it takes its name from the quality of the one that wins it over?[2] Furthermore, if the soul is divided into two parts, as Plato's argument states,[3] with one part called reason, the other emotion, and if love is a vice, then it must be a kind of emotion devoid of reason. If, however, it is something noble, then it must be assigned to one of two categories: either that of reason separate from emotion, or that of emotion entangled with reason.

Now, if love is an impulse toward friendship and a desire of one thing speeding naturally to meet its like and desiring to be joined with it,[4] then this would constitute emotion, not reason, and therefore the supervision of reason would need to be added to this emotion for it to become a virtue rather than a sickness. For just as in the

[3] This twofold division of the soul derives principally from the allegory of the charioteer of the soul at Pl. *Phdr.* 246aff. It is also attributed to Plato at *Or.* 27.5. For three (political) divisions of the soul, see *Or.* 16.4–5.

[4] Cf. Aristophanes' speech at Pl. *Symp.* 189c–93d.

ἐπὶ τῆς τῶν σωμάτων κράσεως καὶ ἡ ὑγεία πάθος τί ἐστιν ὑγρῶν καὶ ξηρῶν καὶ ψυχρῶν καὶ θερμῶν δυνάμεων, ἢ ὑπὸ τέχνης συγκραθεισῶν καλῶς ἢ ὑπὸ φύσεως ἁρμοσθεισῶν τεχνικῶς, ἂν δὲ ἀφέλῃς τῆς φύσεως ἢ τῆς τέχνης, τὸ μὲν πάθος συνετάραξας, τὴν δὲ ὑγείαν ἐξήλασας· οὕτως ἀμέλει καὶ ἐπὶ τοῦ ἔρωτος, {τὸ}[3] πάθος μὲν ὁμοίως ἐστὶν κἂν ἔχῃ λόγον, ἐὰν δὲ ἀφέλῃς τὸν λόγον, ἐπετάραξας αὐτοῦ τὴν συμμετρίαν καὶ νόσον ἐποίησας τὸ πᾶν.

5. Ἔστω δὴ ὁ ἔρως ὄρεξίς τις ψυχῆς, ἀλλὰ τῇ ὀρέξει ταύτῃ χαλινοῦ δεῖ, καθάπερ ἵππου θυμῷ· ἐὰν δὲ ἐπιτρέψῃς τῇ ψυχῇ φέρεσθαι, αὐτὸ ἐκεῖνο κατὰ τὴν Ὁμηρικὴν εἰκόνα, ἵππον ἀνῆκας ἀδηφάγον διὰ πεδίου κροαίνειν καὶ ὑβρίζειν, οὐκ ἐπὶ λουτρὰ νόμιμα οὐδὲ ἐπὶ δρόμους τεχνικοὺς θέοντα, ἀχάλινον, ἀδέσποτον. ἀλλὰ αἰσχρὸν μὲν θέαμα ἵππος ἄφετος, αἰσχρὸν δὲ ἄκουσμα ὑβριστὴς ἔρως.

Οὗτός ἐστιν ὁ ἔρως ὁ τοὺς κρημνοὺς πηδῶν, οὗτος ὁ ποταμοὺς περῶν, ὁ ξίφος λαμβάνων, ὁ ἅπτων βρόχον, ὁ μητρυιᾷ ἐπιτιθέμενος, ὁ προγόνοις ἐπιβουλεύων, ὁ παράνομος, ὁ ἔμπληκτος, ὁ †ἄδωρος†·[4] οὗτος ὁ ἐν σκηναῖς τραγῳδούμενος, ὁ ἐν μύθοις μισούμενος, μεστὸς ἐρινυῶν, μεστὸς δακρύων, οἴμοι βοῶν καὶ στένων, ὀλίγα μὲν εὐτυχῶν, ἐπαιρόμενος δὲ παρὰ τὴν ἀξίαν, καὶ τρεπόμενος παντοδαπὰς τροπὰς καὶ αἰφνι-

[3] del. Markland, edd.

[4] obel. Trapp: ἄωρος Heinsius: ἄλογος Meiser: alia alii

constitution of our bodies, health is a certain condition of the properties of wet, dry, cold, and warm, either properly combined by medical art or artfully harmonized by nature, and if you remove the role played by nature or by art, you will disturb the condition and drive health away; in just the same way, when it comes to love, the emotional aspect nonetheless remains, even if reason controls it, but if you take reason away, you will upset its balance and make all of it sick.

5. Let love, then, be a desire of the soul, but this desire needs a bridle, as does the exuberance of a horse. If you give free rein to the soul, just as in the Homeric simile[5] you will set loose a gluttonous horse to gallop over the plain and behave wantonly, not headed for its customary bathing place or for a man-made racetrack, but running without a bridle or master. A horse on the loose is a shameful thing to see, just as wanton love is a shameful thing to hear about.

This is the kind of love that jumps off cliffs, crosses rivers, seizes a sword, hangs up a noose, assaults a stepmother, plots against stepchildren, and is lawless, impulsive, and. . . .[6] It is the kind portrayed on the tragic stage and vilified in myths; it is full of avenging spirits, tears, cries of anguish, and groans; it seldom achieves its end, is exalted beyond its true worth, and makes all sorts of sud-

[5] *Il.* 6.506–11 (and 15.263–68), comparing Paris (and Hector) going forth to battle to a stallion galloping over the plain to join the mares.

[6] No satisfactory emendation has been proposed for the manuscripts' ἄδωρος (without gifts); Trapp rightly obelizes it.

δίους· ἐπὶ σαρκῶν ἡδονὰς συντεταμένος καὶ φλεγμαίνων σῶμα σώματι ἀναμιγνύει, καὶ προσφυόμενος οὔτε τινὰ εὐσχήμονα οὔτε νόμιμον οὔτε ἐρωτικὴν τῷ ὄντι ξυνυφήν·[5] ἐπισπᾶται δὲ αὐτὸν κάλλους φήμη οἰστρούμενον, ὑπὸ δὲ τῆς ἀγνοίας πλανώμενον.

6. Ὁ δὲ τούτῳ ἐναντίος, μόνῳ τῷ τίκτοντι εἰς γένεσιν τοῦ ὁμοίου ἀπὸ ὀρέξεως ἐμφύτου μετὰ δικαιοσύνης ξυνὼν καὶ διορίζων τὸ θῆλυ, οὗτος θεῶν Γαμηλίων τε καὶ Ὁμογνίων καὶ Γενεθλίων θεσμός, ἐπὶ πάσῃ ζῴων φύσει τεταγμένος, τῶν μὲν αὐτομάτων εἰς τὴν κοινωνίαν ὑπὸ οἰκείου ἔρωτος ἐν ὥρᾳ τοῦ γεννᾶν ἰόντων, τῶν δὲ καὶ διὰ τέχνης ἐπιστάτου, ποιμενικῆς τε καὶ αἰπολικῆς καὶ βουφορβοῦ καὶ ἱπποκόμου, ζευγνύντων ἑκάστων κατὰ φύσιν τὰ αὑτῶν θρέμματα καὶ διακρινόντων αὖθις δέει ὕβρεως·

> χωρὶς μὲν πρόγονοι, χωρὶς δὲ μέτασσαι,
> χωρὶς δ' αὖθ' ἕρσαι.

Ἡ δὲ τῶν ἀνθρώπων ἀγελαιοτρόφος ἐπιστάτις, βασιλικὴ καὶ ποιμενικὴ τέχνη, οὐδεμίαν ἐξεύροι ἂν ἄλλην ὕβρεως ἀρωγὸν μηχανήν, πρὶν ἄν τις ἑκὼν εἴξῃ τῷ λόγῳ καὶ τὴν ψυχὴν παραδῷ ποιμαίνειν αἰδοῖ καὶ σωφροσύνῃ. ὥσπερ γὰρ ἄλλο ἄλλῳ ζῴῳ ἀλέξημα ἥκει παρὰ τῆς φύσεως εἰς τὸν αὑτοῦ βίον, ὑφ' οὗ

[5] ξυνυφήν R: ξυμφυήν Reiske, Trapp

den twists and turns, wholly intent on pleasures of the flesh and burning to couple one body with another, clinging in an embrace that is neither seemly, nor lawful, nor loving in any true sense. A mere report of beauty draws it on in a frenzy, and it roams about in ignorance.

6. But its opposite kind of love distinguishes between male and female and has intercourse solely with a fertile partner for the propagation of its own kind, being driven by an innate desire according to nature's laws. This is the institution of the gods of Marriage, Kinship, and Birth, which presides over all creatures in nature.[7] Some, driven by their inherent love, spontaneously enter into partnerships at the season of breeding; others do so through the supervisory art of shepherds, goatherds, cowherds, and horsemen, as each of them breeds his animals according to nature and separates them again for fear of abusive behavior:

> the firstlings in one place, the older lambs in another,
> and the newly born apart from them.[8]

But that which supervises the human flock, namely the art of king and shepherd, will find no other means to prevent abusive behavior, until each individual willingly yields to reason and entrusts his soul to the shepherding care of shame and self-restraint. For just as nature furnishes different animals with different forms of protection

[7] The privileging of procreative love here and the condemnation of abusive pederastic love in §9 owe much to Pl. *Leg*. 8.836b–37d. [8] *Od*. 9.221–22, describing Polyphemus' separation of his sheep.

σώζεται, λέουσιν ἀλκή, ἐλάφοις δρόμοι, θῆραι κυσίν, καὶ τῷ μὲν διερῷ γένει αἱ νήξεις, τῷ δὲ μεταρσίῳ αἱ πτήσεις, τῷ δὲ εἰλυσπωμένῳ οἱ φωλεοί, ὧδε καὶ τοῖς ἀνθρώποις, τὰ ἄλλα ἐλαττουμένοις τῶν ἁπάντων· καὶ γὰρ ἀλκὴν ἀσθενέστατοι καὶ θεῖν βράδιστοι καὶ ἀνίπτασθαι ἀδύνατοι καὶ νήχειν ἀσθενεῖς καὶ φωλεύειν ἀμήχανοι· λόγον δὲ αὐτοῖς θεὸς ἔδωκεν πρὸς τὰς ἁπάντων εὐπορίας ἀντίρροπον, ὑποβάλλων αὐτῷ τὴν ἐρωτικὴν ὄρεξιν, ὡς χαλινῷ ἵππον, ὡς τοξότῃ τόξον, ὡς οἴακι ναῦν καὶ τεχνίτῃ ὄργανον.

Ὅ τε οὖν λόγος αὐτὸς αὑτοῦ ἀμβλύτατος, ἀνέραστος ὤν· ὅ τε ἔρως αὐτὸς αὑτοῦ ἐμπληκτότατος, ἀπειθέστατος ὢν τῷ λόγῳ. ἔστιν δὲ ἡ πειθὼ συζυγία ἔρωτος καὶ λόγου πρὸς τὸ καλὸν ὁρμωμένων καὶ λαμπρυνομένων ἐπ᾿ αὐτὸ πολλῷ δρόμῳ. ὁ δὲ οἰόμενος ἐν τῇ σαρκῶν φύσει κατορωρύχθαι τὸ καλόν, ἡδονὴν κάλλους ἀλλάττεται καὶ ἐξαπατᾶται ὑπ᾿ αὐτῆς· πιθανὸν γὰρ κακὸν ἡδονὴ καὶ κολακείας ἀνάπλεων.

7. Τοῦτο καὶ μειράκιον Τρωϊκὸν βουκολοῦν τέως καὶ περὶ τὴν Ἴδην πλανώμενον, οὐκ ἀνασχόμενον τὰς οἴκοι ἡδονάς, ἐπὶ θάλατταν ἐκ τῶν ὀρῶν καταβιβασάμενον, εἰς ναῦν ἐνθέμενον, ἐπὶ Πελοποννήσου ἐπεραίωσεν λῃστὴν ἐραστήν. οὐ γὰρ ἦν περὶ τὴν Ἀσίαν σῶμα ἄλλο καλόν, οὐ Τρωϊκόν, οὐ Δαρδανικόν, οὐχ Ἑλλησπόντιον, οὐ Λύδιον, ὁμόφωνον τῷ ἐραστῇ, ἐν τοῖς αὐτοῖς ἤθεσίν τε καὶ νομίμοις τεθραμμένον· ἀλλ᾿

to preserve their lives (strength to lions, speed to deer, hunting ability to dogs, swimming to aquatic creatures, flight to birds, lairs for reptiles), so too in the case of humans, who in other respects are inferior to all other creatures (for they are weakest in strength, slowest in speed, unable to fly, poor at swimming, and incapable of living in lairs), god gave them reason to compensate for all the other creatures' advantages and subjected sexual desire to its control, like a horse to its bridle, a bow to its archer, a ship to its rudder, and a tool to its craftsman.

Now, reason itself is at its dullest in the absence of love, and love itself is at its most crazed when it least heeds the persuasion of reason. For persuasion is what yokes love and reason, as the two of them strive for the Beautiful and become illustrious[9] in their speedy rush to it. But anyone who thinks that the Beautiful is buried in fleshly nature[10] chooses pleasure over beauty and is deceived by it, for pleasure is a persuasive evil, rife with seductive flattery.

7. It was pleasure that sent a Trojan youth[11]—who until then had roamed around Ida tending his cattle, but subsequently became discontented with local pleasures—down from the mountains to the sea, set him aboard a ship, and ferried him across to the Peloponnesus—a lover bent on plunder. For apparently in all Asia there was no sufficiently beautiful body, not Trojan or Dardanian, not from the Hellespont or from Lydia, that spoke the same language as this lover and was raised with the same habits and customs. So this reveler from across the sea, this lover

[9] The verb is in doubt, and no satisfactory emendation has been proposed. [10] The notion of beauty buried in flesh is exploited in §9 below. [11] Paris/Alexander.

*ἐπὶ τὴν Σπάρτην καὶ τὸν Εὐρώταν ἔρχεται κωμαστὴς διαπόντιος, ἐξ ὀνείρων ἐραστής, καὶ ἀδικεῖ τὸν ὑποδεξάμενον καὶ ἀνίστησιν καὶ διαλύει γάμον Ἑλληνικόν. ὢ λίχνου ἔρωτος καὶ ἀδίκων ἐνυπνίων καὶ ὀφθαλμῶν πονηρῶν καὶ ἡδονῆς ἡγεμόνος πολλῶν κακῶν.*

*Οὕτω καὶ Ξέρξην τὸν μέγαν ἐκεῖνον, τὸν ἐν Σαλαμῖνι καὶ Πλαταιαῖς τοῖς Ἕλλησι παραταξάμενον, τοσούτων σωμάτων θεατὴν καὶ δεσπότην γενόμενον, οὐκ ἐπηγάγετο εἰς ἔρωτα οὐκ Ἰνδικὴ κόρη ὑψηλὴ οὐδὲ Μηδικὴ τιαραφόρος οὐδὲ Μυγδονικὴ μιτρηφόρος οὐδὲ Καρικὴ ὡπλισμένη, οὐδὲ Λυδία ᾄδουσα, οὐκ Ἰωνική, οὐχ Ἑλλησποντία· ἀλλ' ἐπὶ Ἄμηστριν ᾖξεν τὴν τοῦ παιδὸς γαμετήν. ὢ κακίστου ἔρωτος, ὃς παραλιπὼν τὰ ἐδώδιμα ἐπὶ τὰ πικρὰ ἦλθεν καὶ ἄβρωτα, ὑπ' ἀκολάστου ἐξουσίας εἰς τὴν τοῦ φιλεῖν δύναμιν ὑβριζούσης. ὅταν γὰρ ψυχῆς ἀφέλῃς μὲν τὸ εἰδέναι, παράσχῃς δὲ τὸ δύνασθαι, δίδως τοῖς ἁμαρτήμασιν ἐπιρροὴν καὶ ἐξουσίαν καὶ δρόμον. ἄφελε Ἀλεξάνδρου μὲν τὴν Πριάμου δύναμιν καὶ τὸ ἐκεῖ θάρσος, καὶ μένει βουκολῶν καὶ τὴν Ἑλένην οὐκ ὀνειρώττει· ἄφελε Ξέρξου τὴν ἐξουσίαν, καὶ Ἄμηστρις οὐκ αἰσχρά;*[6]

8. *Ἔστι καὶ ἐν ἰδιώταις τυραννὶς ἀκόλαστος, ὅταν ἀπῇ μὲν ὁ λόγος, οἱ δὲ ὀφθαλμοὶ λιχνεύωσιν· ὧν ἐὰν ἀφέλῃς τὴν ἐξουσίαν, οὔτε Κριτόβουλος Εὐθυδήμῳ*

[6] *ἔστι καὶ ἐν ἰδιώταις* supra post *αἰσχρά* infra ante *τυραννὶς* locavit Trapp

inspired by dreams, came to Sparta and the Eurotas, where he wronged his host, and corrupted and broke up a Greek marriage. O greedy love, immoral dreams, wicked eyes, and pleasure that leads to so many evils!

So too Xerxes, that great king who engaged the Greeks at Salamis and Plataea, and who ruled over and gazed upon so many of his subjects' bodies, could not be induced to love a tall girl from India, a Median with a tiara, a Mygdonian with a headdress, a Carian with a helmet,[12] a Lydian singer, or a woman from Ionia or from the Hellespont. No, he lusted after Amestris, his own son's wife![13] O most wicked love that passes up wholesome food and makes for what is bitter and inedible, driven by an unbridled license that commits an outrage against the power of affection.[14] For whenever you deprive the soul of knowledge while granting it power, you give license to sinfulness and a pathway for it to flow in. Only take away Priam's power from Alexander and the boldness that goes with it, and he will remain a cowherd, and not even dream of Helen. Take away Xerxes' license, and won't Amestris then become unattractive?[15]

8. An unbridled tyranny also exists among ordinary citizens, when reason is absent and the eyes fall prey to greed. But if you deprive the eyes of their license, Critobu-

[12] An allusion to Artemisia of Halicarnassus; cf. Hdt. 8.87.

[13] A version of this story involving Artaynte (not Amestris, who was in fact Xerxes' wife) is told at Hdt. 9.108–13.

[14] That is, affection for his son.

[15] I am following Trapp's excellent suggestion of moving the last part of this sentence ("and among ordinary citizens") to the beginning of the following paragraph.

*προσκυνήσασθαι ἐρᾷ οὔτε* Αὐτολύκῳ Καλλίας *οὔτε* Ἀγάθωνι Παυσανίας, *οὔτε ἄλλος ἄλλῳ. διὰ τοῦτο ἐγὼ ἐπαινῶ τὸν* Κρητῶν *νόμον καὶ τὸν* Ἠλείων *μέμφομαι· τὸν μὲν* Κρητικὸν *ἐπαινῶ τῆς ἀνάγκης, τὸν δὲ* Ἠλείων *μέμφομαι τῆς ἐξουσίας.* Κρητικῷ *μειρακίῳ αἰσχρὸν ἀνέραστον εἶναι,* Κρητικῷ *νεανίσκῳ αἰσχρὸν προσάψασθαι παιδικῶν. ὦ νόμου κεκραμένου καλῶς σωφροσύνῃ καὶ ἔρωτι. τὰ δὲ* Ἠλείων *οὐ λέγω, τὰ δὲ* Λακεδαιμονίων *λέγω· ἐρᾷ* Σπαρτιάτης *ἀνὴρ μειρακίου* Λακωνικοῦ, *ἀλλ' ἐρᾷ μόνον ὡς ἀγάλματος καλοῦ, καὶ ἑνὸς πολλοί, καὶ εἷς πολλῶν. ἡ μὲν γὰρ ἐξ ὕβρεως ἡδονὴ ἀκοινώνητος πρὸς ἄλλους, ὁ δὲ ἐξ ὀφθαλμῶν ἔρως κοινωνικός, μόνον οὐκ ἐπὶ πάσας ἐξικνούμενος φύσεις ἐρωτικάς. τί γὰρ ἂν εἴη ὡραιότερον τοῦ ἡλίου καὶ ἐρασταῖς πολυαρκέστερον; ἀλλ' ὅμως ἐρῶσιν ἡλίου οἱ πάντων ὀφθαλμοί.*

9. Ἐν Λοκροῖς *τοῖς* Ἰταλιώταις *ἔφηβος ἦν καλὸς καὶ νόμος καλὸς καὶ ἐρασταὶ πονηροί· ἐρᾶν μὲν ἠναγκάζοντο ὑπὸ τοῦ κάλλους, εἴργοντο δὲ ὑπὸ τοῦ νόμου κακῶς ἐρᾶν· οἰστρούμενοι δὲ ὑπὸ τοῦ πάθους πρὸς τὴν ὕβριν, τὸν μὲν ἔφηβον οὐκ ἔπεισαν, νόμιμος γὰρ*

---

[16] Cf. Xen., *Mem.* 1.2.30–31, although said of Critias, not Critobulus. [17] Cf. Xen. *Symp.* 1.2.

[18] Cf. Pl. *Symp.* 193b.

[19] For the Cretan customs, cf. Pl. *Leg.* 8.836b and Strabo 10.4.21; for the complete permissiveness of the Eleans, cf. Pl. *Symp.* 182b.

lus will not desire to rub himself against Euthydemus,[16] Callias against Autolycus,[17] Pausanias against Agathon,[18] or anyone against anyone else. That is why I praise the customs of the Cretans and censure those of the Eleans.[19] I praise the Cretan customs for the restraint they impose, and blame the Elean ones for the license they permit. It is a disgrace for a Cretan boy not to have a lover, but at the same time it is a disgrace for a Cretan youth to lay hands on his boyfriend. That is a custom with a beautiful combination of self-restraint and love! I have nothing to say about the practices in Elis, but I do about those in Lacedaemon.[20] A Spartiate may well love a Laconian boy, but he only loves him as he would love a beautiful statue. As a result, many can love a single boy, and one person can love many boys. That is because the pleasure derived from sexual abuse cannot be shared with others, whereas the love derived from sight can be shared, and it extends to well nigh all natures capable of feeling love. What could be lovelier or more capable of satisfying many lovers than the sun? And yet, everyone's eyes love the sun none the less.

9. In Italian Locri there was once a beautiful ephebe,[21] a noble law, and some wicked lovers. They were compelled by his beauty to love him, but were prevented from engaging in wicked love because of the law. When they, goaded by their passion to abuse him, failed to persuade the boy because he stood by the law, every single one of those

[20] For Spartan customs, cf. Xen. *Lac.* 2.13 and *Symp.* 8.35.

[21] An adolescent aged eighteen to twenty undergoing military training. Italian (Western) Locri was famous for the strict laws of its seventh-century BC lawgiver Zaleucis.

ἦν, ἦξαν δὲ οἱ δυστυχεῖς ἐπὶ βρόχον πάντες ἑξῆς. ἄξιοι μὲν θανάτου· τί γὰρ δεῖ ζῆν ἄνδρα μηδὲ ὀφθαλμῶν ἀνεχόμενον; ἄγαλμα μέν τις ἰδὼν καὶ ἐπαινέσας τὸ κάλλος οὐκ ἐδεήθη βρόχου· ἀλλὰ κἂν ἵππον ἴδῃ ἱππικὸς ἀνὴρ καὶ τοῦ κάλλους ἐπαινέσῃ καὶ κτήσασθαι μὴ δυνηθῇ, οὐ δεῖται βρόχου· ἐξαρκεῖ δὲ καὶ τῷ γεωργῷ, κἂν ἐν γειτόνων ἴδῃ φυτὸν καλόν, ἡ ὄψις αὐτή· ἐξαρκεῖ καὶ τῷ θηρευτῇ, κἂν παρ' ἄλλῳ ἴδῃ σκύλακα ὡραῖον, ἡ ὄψις αὐτή· καὶ οὐδεὶς τούτων θανατᾷ δι' ἀπορίαν τῶν κτημάτων.

Ἐρῶσιν καὶ οἱ φιλοχρήματοι χρυσοῦ μᾶλλον ἢ οἱ ἐρασταὶ σωμάτων, καὶ συγκατορύττεσθαι ἐθέλουσιν τῷ χρυσῷ μᾶλλον ἢ τοῖς σώμασιν οἱ ἐρασταί· ἀλλ' οὐδεὶς θανατᾷ τούτων, ἐὰν μὴ τύχῃ χρυσοῦ. οὐδὲ γὰρ ὁ Πέρσης βασιλεὺς ἧψεν βρόχον ἀτυχήσας χρυσίου, ὁ πάντων χρηματιστῶν ἀκορεστότατος καὶ ἐπιμανέστατος, ὃς ἄρχων τοσαύτης γῆς καὶ ἐν τοσαύταις ἡδοναῖς φυρόμενος, ὅσαι πληροῦσιν βασιλέως ἀκολάστου ὀρέξεις, ἐπεβούλευσεν νεκροῦ τάφῳ. φήμη δὲ αὐτὸν ἐπεσπάσατο χρυσοῦ κατορωρυγμένου σὺν τῷ νεκρῷ καὶ ἐτυμβωρύχει ὁ μέγας βασιλεὺς τὴν τιάραν ἔχων, καὶ τὸν μὲν χρυσὸν οὐχ εὗρεν, ἐπίγραμμα δὲ ἔνδοθεν ἐπὶ τῷ τάφῳ, ὃ {νεκρὸς}[7] λέγει· "ὦ πάντων ἀνθρώπων ἀπληστότατε, ὃς ἔτλης καὶ νεκροῦ θιγεῖν δι' ἔρωτα χρυσοῦ."

[7] del. Trapp

miserable men rushed to hang himself. And indeed they deserved death, for what man ought to go on living who cannot even restrain his eyes? If someone sees a statue and praises its beauty, he does not need a noose. If a horseman sees a horse and praises its beauty, but cannot possess it, he does not need a noose. If a farmer sees a beautiful plant in his neighbors' fields, he is satisfied just to look at it. And if a hunter sees a fine puppy belonging to someone else, he is satisfied just to look at it. But none of them chooses to die simply because he does not possess these things.

Misers love gold more than lovers love bodies, and they wish to be buried with their gold more than lovers wish to be buried with the bodies of their beloved. But none of these misers chooses to die, if he fails to get gold. Not even the king of Persia,[22] the most insatiable and obsessive money-grubber of them all, strung up a noose when he once failed to get gold. For although he ruled over so much territory, and indulged in all the pleasures that can satisfy the desires of an intemperate king, he nonetheless plotted to rob a corpse's tomb. Enticed by a report that gold had been buried with the corpse, the great king, with his tiara on his head, set about robbing the tomb. Although he did not find the gold, he did find an inscription inside the tomb that said: "O most insatiable of all men, you have dared to touch even a corpse for love of gold."[23]

[22] Darius (r. 522–486 BC). A version of the story is told at Hdt. 1.187. The tomb was that of Nitocris, a Babylonian queen.

[23] I follow Trapp in deleting *νεκρός*, which awkwardly implies that the corpse is speaking.

Τοῦτο εἴποι ἂν καὶ Ἕλλην λόγος πρὸς Ἕλληνα ἄνδρα ἐπὶ ὕβριν σαρκῶν ὑπὸ ἀκορέστου ἐπιθυμίας ὁρμηθέντα, ὅταν αὐτὸν ἐπισπάσηται φήμη κάλλους κατορωρυγμένου ἐν σώματι· "ὦ πάντων ἀνθρώπων ἀνοητότατε, νεκρὸν ἀνορύττεις· οὐ γὰρ ἂν ἔτλης θίγειν σαρκὸς ἄρρενος, ἀθίκτου χρήματος σαρκὶ ἄρρενι. ἄδικος ἡ μῖξις, ἄγονος ἡ συνουσία· ἐπὶ πετρῶν σπείρεις, ψάμμους ἀροῖς· μετένεγκε τὰς εὐφροσύνας ἐπὶ τὴν φύσιν, τρέψον ἐπὶ τὴν γεωργίαν τοὺς ὀφθαλμούς, ἐγκάρποις ἥσθητι ἡδοναῖς,

ὥς κε μὴ ἄσπερμος γενεὴ μετόπισθεν ὄληται."

This too is what a Greek story might well say to any Greek man, who, driven by insatiable desire, rushes to abuse flesh, when lured by a report that beauty is buried in some body: "O most foolish of all men, you are digging up a corpse, for if you knew better, you would not dare to touch male flesh, something forbidden for male flesh to touch. Such sex is illegal; such intercourse is sterile. You are sowing seed on rocks; you are plowing sand.[24] Change your joys to natural ones; look to the art of farming and enjoy pleasures that bear fruit,

> that hereafter the race may not perish for want of seed."[25]

[24] A close echo of Pl. *Leg.* 8.838e–39a.

[25] *Il.* 20.303 (slightly altered). Poseidon is speaking of the end of the Trojan lineage if Aeneas is killed.

# *ORATION* 21

## INTRODUCTION

Plato's *Phaedrus* lies behind the oration, from its opening reference in §1 to Stesichorus' palinode (242e–43b) to the soul's vision of Beauty itself in §7 (247c–51e).[1] Just as Stesichorus had offended Helen with a false account, the speaker claims to have sinned against Love and, like Stesichorus, needs to replace a falsehood with the truth (§1). The power of Love to punish offenders is illustrated by the story of Anacreon having to appease Cleobulus with many poems of praise because he had cursed at him as a baby (§2). The offense, it turns out, is confusing true love (that is, the love of Beauty) with desire for pleasure. Love cannot inspire people to commit evil acts, and so when anyone says that someone is in love with money (Darius), war (Clearchus), tyranny (Critias), or Sicily (Alcibiades), he offends truth itself (§3). True love is a yearning (*orexis*) for beauty, whereas desire (*epithymia*) aims for pleasure; beauty must truly *be* beautiful, whereas pleasure needs only *to seem* to be pleasant (§4). For example, in the case of cuisine, the food's nourishment is its essential nature, whereas the pleasure it provides is relative to accustomed

[1] Also relevant is the vision of true Beauty at *Symp.* 210e–11c and the soul's impaired vision on earth at *Phd.* 109a–10b.

tastes of those consuming it (§5). The same is true of drink, as illustrated by the great variety of drinking habits (§6). Beauty, therefore, is like the essential nourishment of food and drink, which must actually *be*, whereas pleasure is produced artificially to suit the consumer and must merely *seem* to be. If love, then, is the love of Beauty, then love must consist of reason to discern what is true, virtue to have the proper disposition, and expertise to ensure a correct aim, whereas desire for pleasure is irrational and seeks irrational pleasures. According to Socrates, the human soul in the distant past beheld Beauty itself but is now separated from it by its murky existence on earth (§7). Beauty emanates from on high and weakens as it descends, just as a river flowing into the sea loses its original freshness as it mixes with the salty waters. Likewise, a portion of true Beauty may be glimpsed in physical nature, but the love it inspires is not for the object itself, but for the truer Beauty inherent in it. Thus it was to recollect true Beauty that Socrates was on the hunt for beautiful bodies (§8).

# *ORATION* 21

Ἔτι περὶ ἔρωτος. δʹ

1. Οὐκ ἔστ' ἔτυμος λόγος,

λέγει που τῶν αὑτοῦ ᾀσμάτων ὁ Ἱμεραῖος ποιητής, ἐξομνύμενος τὴν ἔμπροσθεν ᾠδήν, ἐν ᾗ περὶ τῆς Ἑλένης εἰπεῖν φησιν οὐκ ἀληθεῖς λόγους· ἀναμάχεται οὖν ἐπαίνῳ τὸν ἔμπροσθεν ψόγον. δοκῶ δή μοι, κατὰ τὸν ποιητὴν ἐκεῖνον, δεήσεσθαι καὶ αὐτὸς παλινῳδίας ἐν τοῖς περὶ τοῦ ἔρωτος λόγοις· θεὸς γὰρ καὶ οὗτος, καὶ οὐχ ἧττον τῆς Ἑλένης ἐπιτιθέναι δίκην τοῖς πλημμελοῦσιν ἐς αὐτὸν ἐρρωμενέστατος. τί δὴ οὖν ἐστιν τὸ πλημμέλημα, ὅπερ καὶ ἀναμαχέσασθαι δεῖν φημι ἡμᾶς; δεινὸν καὶ μέγα καὶ δεόμενον γενναίου ποιητοῦ καὶ τελεστοῦ, εἰ μέλλοι τις ἱκανῶς ἐξευμενιεῖσθαι ἀδέκαστον δαίμονα, οὐ τρίποδας ἑπτὰ δοὺς οὐδὲ χρυσοῦ τάλαντα δέκα οὐδὲ γυναῖκας Λεσβιάδας οὐδὲ ἵππους Τρωϊκούς, ἀλλὰ λόγον λόγῳ, πονηρὸν χρηστῷ, καὶ ψευδῆ ἀληθεῖ ἐξαλείψας.

---

1 Stesichorus, fr. 192.1 (Campbell). Helen punished his speaking ill of her by blinding him, until he recanted with a true account. Plato employs this trope at *Phdr*. 243a–b.

# *ORATION* 21

## More on love. Part IV

1. The story is not true,

says the poet from Himera[1] in one of his lyrics, thus renouncing the previous ode in which he admits to having spoken false words about Helen. And so he makes amends for his previous censure by offering praise. For my part, I believe that I too, like that poet, shall need to offer a palinode in this discussion of Love. For he too is a god, and a very powerful one, no less capable than Helen of punishing those who sin against him. So what exactly is the sin for which I say we need to make amends? It is a great and grave one that requires a noble poet and initiatory priest, if one is to provide sufficient appeasement to an unbribable divinity,[2] not by offering seven tripods, ten talents of gold, women from Lesbos,[3] or Trojan horses, but by wiping out one account with another, a bad one with a good one, and a false one with one that is true.

[2] Above, Love was called a god (*theos*), here, a divinity (*daimōn*), indicating his ambiguous status.

[3] A selection from the gifts that Agamemnon promises Achilles, in the hope of appeasing him, at *Il.* 9.121–30.

2. Τοιαύτην φασὶ καὶ τὸν Ἀνακρέοντα ἐκεῖνον τὸν Τήϊον ποιητὴν δοῦναι δίκην τῷ ἔρωτι. ἐν τῇ τῶν Ἰώνων ἀγορᾷ, ἐν Πανιωνίῳ, ἐκόμιζεν τιτθὴ βρέφος. ὁ δὲ Ἀνακρέων βαδίζων, μεθύων, ᾄδων, ἐστεφανωμένος, σφαλλόμενος, ὠθεῖ τὴν τιτθὴν σὺν τῷ βρέφει καί τι καὶ εἰς τὸ παιδίον ἀπέρριψεν βλάσφημον ἔπος. ἡ δὲ γυνὴ ἄλλο μὲν οὐδὲν ἐχαλέπηνεν τῷ Ἀνακρέοντι, ἐπεύξατο δὲ τὸν αὐτὸν τοῦτον ὑβριστὴν ἄνθρωπον τοσαῦτα καὶ ἔτι πλείω ἐπαινέσαι ποτὲ τὸ παιδίον, ὅσα νῦν ἐπηράσατο. τελεῖ ταῦτα ὁ θεός· τὸ γὰρ παιδίον ἐκεῖνο δὴ αὐξηθὲν γίγνεται Κλεόβουλος ὁ ὡραιότατος, καὶ ἀντὶ μιᾶς ἀρᾶς ἔδωκεν ὁ Ἀνακρέων Κλεοβούλῳ δίκην δι᾽ ἐπαίνων πολλῶν.

3. Τί κωλύει δὴ καὶ ἡμᾶς ἀναμαχέσασθαι τήμερον ‹καὶ›[1] κατὰ τὸν Ἀνακρέοντα ἐκεῖνον δοῦναι δίκην τῷ ἔρωτι αὐτοὺς ἑκόντας γλώττης ἀδίκου; τὸ φάναι ὅτι ὁ ἔρως ἐπὶ μοιχείαν ἀνάπτει ὥσπερ τὸν Ἀλέξανδρον, ἢ ἐπὶ παρανομίαν ὡς τὸν Ξέρξην, ἢ ἐπὶ ὕβριν ὡς Κριτόβουλον, καὶ ἀνατιθέναι θεῷ πρᾶγμα ἄθεον, πῶς οὐ πλημμελές; οὑτωσὶ δὲ αὐτὸ θεασώμεθα. ὁ ἔρως ἄλλου του ἔρως ἢ κάλλους ἐστίν; οὐδαμῶς· σχολῇ γὰρ ἂν εἴη ἔρως εἰ μὴ κάλλους εἴη. ὁπόταν λέγωμεν ἐρᾶν χρημάτων Δαρεῖον ἢ Ξέρξην τῆς Ἑλλήνων γῆς ἢ Κλέαρχον πολέμου ἢ Ἀγησίλαον τιμῆς ἢ Κριτίαν τυ-

[1] suppl. Reiske, Trapp, Koniaris

2. Anacreon, the famous poet from Teos, is said to have paid a similar penalty to Love. At the gathering of the Ionians in the Panionium,[4] was a nurse carrying a baby. As Anacreon was walking along, drunk, singing, wearing garlands, and staggering, he bumped into the nurse with her baby and went so far as to hurl a curse at the little boy. The nurse said no angry word to Anacreon, but instead prayed that this same insolent man would one day praise the boy as much as he had just now cursed him, or even more so. The god fulfilled her prayer, for that very boy grew up to be the stunningly beautiful Cleobulus, and for a single curse Anacreon repaid Cleobulus with many praises.[5]

3. What then prevents us too from making amends today, and, like that Anacreon, be willing to pay the penalty to Love for our unjust tongue? For how can it not be sinful to say that Love inflames anyone to commit adultery like Alexander,[6] or to break the law like Xerxes, or to abuse others like Critobulus,[7] and to ascribe any impious act to a god? Let us look at the matter this way. Is love the love of anything other than beauty? Certainly not! It could scarcely be love, if it were not the love of beauty. Whenever we say that Darius is in love with money, or Xerxes with the land of Greece, or Clearchus with war,[8] or Agesi-

[4] A place where all the Ionians gathered to engage in politics or attend festivals.

[5] Cf. Anac. fr. 357 and esp. 359: "I love Cleobulus, I am mad about Cleobulus, I gaze at Cleobulus" (trans. Campbell).

[6] That is, Paris.

[7] For his abusive behavior, see *Or*. 20.8.

[8] Spartan general who died in 401 BC, leading the ten thousand Greek mercenaries against Artoxerxes II (variant of Artaxerxes).

ραννίδος ἢ Ἀλκιβιάδην Σικελίας ἢ Γύλιππον χρυσίου, ἆρα κάλλος τι ὁρῶντες ἐμφαινόμενον, τὴν πρὸς αὐτὸ ἐπαγωγὴν ἔρωτα ἐπονομάζοντες, ἕκαστον τούτων ἐρᾶν φαμέν, τὸν μὲν τοῦδε, τὸν δὲ τοῦδε, ἄλλον ἄλλου; πολλοῦ γε καὶ δεῖ. ἦ γὰρ ἂν τὰ αἴσχιστα τῶν ἐν ἀνθρώποις πραγμάτων τῷ μὴ προσήκοντι ὀνόματι ἐπικοσμοῦντες πλημμελοῖμεν ἂν εἰς τὸ ἀληθὲς αὐτό.

Ποῦ γὰρ ἢ ἐν χρήμασιν κάλλος, τῷ πάντων πραγμάτων κακίστῳ; ἢ ἐν πολέμῳ, τῷ πάντων ἀβεβαιοτάτῳ; ἢ ἐν τυραννίδι, τῷ πάντων ἀγριωτάτῳ; ἢ ἐν χρυσῷ τῷ πάντων γαυροτάτῳ; Σικελίαν δὲ εἴ μοι λέγοις ἢ τὴν Ἑλλήνων γῆν, ἐλπίδας λέγεις ἡδονῶν, κάλλος δὲ οὐδαμοῦ· οὐδ' εἴ μοι νὴ Δία τὴν Αἰγυπτίων γῆν λέγοις τὴν τὰς πυραμίδας ἔχουσαν τὰς μεγάλας καὶ τὸν πολὺν ποταμόν, οὐδὲ Βαβυλῶνα αὖ τὴν εὐτειχοτάτην, οὐδὲ Μηδίαν τὴν εὐιπποτάτην, οὐδὲ τὴν Φρυγῶν γῆν τὴν εὐβοτωτάτην, οὐδὲ Σάρδεις τὰς εὐχρυσοτάτας. ἕκαστον γὰρ τούτων τοσούτου δεῖ εἶναι καλόν, ὅσουπερ καὶ ἡδύ· μᾶλλον μὲν ἡδὺ τῷ δυναμένῳ πορίσασθαι ἐξ αὐτοῦ ἡδονήν, ἢ καλὸν τῷ μὴ δυναμένῳ ἐξ αὐτοῦ ὄνασθαι· οὐδὲν γὰρ καλὸν ἐπιβλαβὲς οὐδὲ σφαλερὸν οὐδὲ εἰς μοχθηρίαν συντελοῦν οὐδὲ εἰς δυστυχίαν ἄγον οὐδὲ εἰς συμφορὰν χειραγωγοῦν οὐδὲ εἰς μετάγνωσιν τελευτῶν.

9 Agesilaus (ca. 445–359 BC). Cf. *Or.* 19.5 and Plut. *Ages.* 7.3.

laus with honor,[9] or Critias with tyranny,[10] or Alcibiades with Sicily,[11] or Gylippus with gold,[12] is it because we can see some kind of apparent beauty and call the attraction to it love, and then say that each of those men is in love, one with one thing, another with another, and so on? Far from it! For truly we would be sinning against truth itself, if we adorned the ugliest human actions with an inappropriate name.

For where is there beauty in money, the basest of all things; or in war, the most unstable; or in tyranny, the most cruel; or in gold, the most conceited? If you should cite Sicily or the land of Greece to me, you are speaking about expectations of pleasure, but by no means about beauty. Nor, by Zeus, would it matter if you should cite the land of Egypt with its great pyramids and mighty river, or Babylon with its great walls, or Media with its excellent horses, or the land of Phrygia with its outstanding pastures, or Sardis, richest in gold. For each of these is as far from being beautiful as it is from being pleasant. In fact, they come closer to being pleasant to someone who can derive pleasure from them, than they are beautiful to someone who cannot benefit from them. For nothing can be beautiful that is harmful or precarious, or contributes to depravity, conduces to unhappiness, leads to disaster, or ends in regret.

[10] Critias was the leader of the "Thirty Tyrants" in Athens, killed in 403 BC.

[11] Alcibiades championed the disastrous invasion of Sicily in 415 BC.

[12] A Spartan commander accused of stealing gold entrusted to him in 401 BC; cf. Plut. *Lys*. 16–17.

4. Εἶεν· ὁ ἔρως ἡμῖν κάλλους ἦν ἔρως· ὁ δὲ ἐρῶν ἄλλου του καὶ μὴ κάλλους, ἡδονῆς ἐρᾷ. ἀφαιρῶμεν δέ, εἰ βούλει, τοὔνομα καὶ ἐπιθυμεῖν λέγωμεν τοῦτον ἀλλ' οὐκ ἐρᾶν, ἵνα μὴ τῇ περὶ τὴν φωνὴν παρανομίᾳ πρᾶγμα ὑπαλλάξαντες λάθωμεν, ἀλλ' οὐ τοὔνομα μόνον. ἔστω τοίνυν ἔρως μὲν κάλλους, ἐπιθυμία δὲ ἡδονῆς. ὁ τοίνυν κάλλους ἐρῶν ἆρα οὐκ ἐπιθυμεῖ αὐτοῦ; καὶ μάλα· σχολῇ γὰρ ἂν εἴη τι ἄλλο ὁ ἔρως, εἰ μὴ ὄρεξίς τις. παραιτοῦμαι δὲ τοὺς σοφοὺς τῆς τῶν ὀνομάτων θήρας, εἰ τὸ αὐτὸ νῦν μὲν ὄρεξιν, νῦν δὲ ἐπιθυμίαν καλῶ· ἐγὼ γάρ τοι τά τε ἄλλα καὶ ἐν τῇ τῶν ὀνομάτων ἐλευθερίᾳ πείθομαι Πλάτωνι. ἔστω δέ, εἰ βούλονται, ὄρεξις καὶ μὴ ἐπιθυμία ὁ ἔρως.

Διῃρήσθω δὲ τῇδε· ἐὰν μὲν ἐπὶ τὸ καλὸν φαινόμενον ἡ ψυχὴ ᾄξῃ,[2] ἔρως καλείσθω τοῦτο, οὐκ ἐπιθυμία· ἐὰν δὲ μή, ἐπιθυμία καλείσθω τοῦτο, οὐκ ἔρως. τί οὖν εἰ ἀκόλαστός τις σοφιστής, τῇ τοῦ φαινομένου προσθήκῃ χρώμενος, τὸ ἡδὺ τοῦτο φῇ φαντάζεσθαι αὐτῷ καλόν; ἐρᾶν καὶ τούτῳ συγχωρήσομεν; καὶ πάλιν αὖ, εἴ τις ἀποβλέψας εἰς τοὺς τῷ ὄντι ἐραστὰς τοὺς πρὸς τὸ καλὸν ὡρμημένους, καὶ θεασάμενος τὸ ἐν τῇ ὀρέξει τοῦ κάλλους ἡδύ, διὰ τὴν ἐπιμιξίαν τῆς ἡδονῆς ἐπιθυμεῖν καὶ τούτους φῇ, ἀλλ' οὐκ ἐρᾶν, πῇ ἂν ταῦτα

[2] ᾄξῃ Davies[2], Trapp: ἄξῃ R

4. Fair enough. We have shown that love is the love of beauty, and that anyone who loves something other than beauty is in love with pleasure. So, if you are willing, let us withdraw the name "love" in the latter case, and say that such a person "desires," rather than "loves," to ensure that by our misuse of language we do not inadvertently change the thing itself, and not just its name.[13] Therefore, let love be what one feels for beauty, and desire what one feels for pleasure. So, if someone is in love with beauty, does he not desire it? Of course he does, for love could scarcely be anything other than a certain yearning. I ask indulgence from those experts who pursue precise terminology,[14] if I call the same phenomenon "yearning" at one time and "desire" at another. For just as I agree with Plato in other matters, I do so as well in his free use of terms. So, if the experts are willing, let love be a matter of yearning, not desire.

Let us then adopt the following distinction. If the soul is rushing toward apparent beauty, let us call it love, not desire; but if not, then let us call it desire, not love. But what if some overzealous sophist latches on to our qualification of "apparent" and says that some pleasant thing *appears* beautiful to *him*? Shall we concede that he too loves it? Then again, what if someone observes true lovers hastening toward the beautiful, and sees the pleasure in their yearning for that beauty, and uses this admixture of pleasure to claim that they too feel desire rather than love? How then are we to distinguish between the two? For if

[13] The following discussion draws distinctions between desire (*epithymia*), yearning (*orexis*), and love (*erōs*). [14] Cf. Pl. *Prt.* 358a: "I ask to be exempt from Prodicus' verbal distinctions."

ἡμῖν διακριθείη; εἰ γὰρ τά τε ἡδέα φαντάζεται καλά, τά τε καλὰ ἀνακέκραται ἡδοναῖς, κίνδυνος οὕτω καὶ τὴν ἐπιθυμίαν τῷ ἔρωτι ἐπιμιχθῆναι.

Βούλει τοίνυν τοῦ μὲν καλοῦ ἀφαιροῦμεν τὸ φαινόμενον, ἵνα μήποτε λάθῃ σχηματισαμένη πρὸς αὐτὸ ἡ ἡδονή, τῆς δὲ ἡδονῆς οὐκ ἔτι; τὸ μὲν γὰρ καλόν, τίμιον ὂν κατὰ τὴν αὑτοῦ φύσιν, εἶναι δεῖ καλὸν ἵνα καὶ ἐράσμιον ᾖ· τῇ δὲ ἡδονῇ ἀπόχρη φαίνεσθαι, καὶ μὴ οὔσῃ· τῇ γὰρ τοῦ πεπονθότος εὐφροσύνῃ λαμβάνουσα τὴν σύστασιν, οὐ τῇ αὑτῆς φύσει, ἱκανῶς ἕξει ἐὰν τὸ δοκεῖν ὑπάρχῃ αὐτῇ, καὶ μὴ οὔσῃ.

5. Οἷον τὸ τοιόνδε λέγω· αἰσθάνομαι γάρ τοι ἐμαυτοῦ γλίσχρως τὸ πρᾶγμα διελομένου καὶ δεομένου εἰκόνος· σῶμά που τραφῆναι ἀδύνατον, ὅτι μὴ σιτίων προσφορᾷ καὶ ἐργασίᾳ ὀδόντων καὶ σπλάγχνων ὑποδοχῇ καὶ τῇ ἔνδον οἰκονομίᾳ, προσγινομένης αὐτῷ τῆς ὑποτροφῆς. ἦσαν δέ που κατὰ τὸν ἐπὶ Κρόνου, φασίν, βίον αἱ τροφαὶ τοῖς ἀνθρώποις φηγοὶ καὶ ὄγχναι· καὶ διὰ τοῦτο ἐπεφημίσθη φέρειν ἡ γῆ τοὺς καρποὺς αὐτομάτους, ὅτι αὐτοῖς οὐδὲν ἔδει γεωπονίας ἐξ αὐτοφυοῦς τροφῆς βιοτεύουσιν.

Ἐὰν τοίνυν προσθῇς ὀψοποιὸν καὶ ἡδύσματα καὶ τροφὴν ποικίλην, ἄλλῳ ἄλλην, καρυκείαν Σικελικὴν καὶ Συβαριτικὴν χλιδὴν καὶ Περσικὴν τρυφήν, πάντα ταῦτα ἐρεῖς ἡδονῆς ὀνόματα· καὶ κοινὸν μὲν πᾶσι τὴν τροφὴν ἐρεῖς, ἴδιον δὲ ἑκάστῳ τὴν ἡδονήν, καὶ κατὰ φύσιν μὲν τὴν τροφήν, κατὰ τέχνην δὲ τὴν ἡδονήν. κἂν μεταθῇς τραπέζας, τὴν Σικελικὴν τοῖς Πέρσαις

things that are pleasant can appear to be beautiful, and if beautiful things are imbued with pleasure, then there is a risk of conflating desire and love.

Then do you wish us to remove the qualification of "apparent" from beauty, so that pleasure never surreptitiously takes on the guise of beauty, but still not remove it from pleasure? For beauty, which is precious in its very nature, must itself be beautiful in order to attract love, whereas it is sufficient for pleasure to *seem* to be pleasant, without actually *being* so. Therefore, since pleasure has its basis in the enjoyment felt by the person experiencing it and not in its own nature, it will be enough for it to *seem*, without actually *being* so.

5. I mean something like this, for I sense that I am drawing a subtle distinction in this matter and need to offer an illustration. Now a body cannot be nourished unless food is supplied, the teeth do their work, the intestines receive it, the digestive system processes it, and the nourishment is supplied to the body. They say that when men lived during the reign of Cronus, their nourishment consisted of acorns and pears, and for this reason the earth was reputed to produce crops of its own accord, because with this naturally produced food they had no need to work the land in order to live.

But then, if you add chefs, sauces, and various foods that suit different populations, such as Sicilian sauces, Sybaritic luxuries, and Persian delicacies, you will apply the term pleasure to all of them, and will say that while nourishment is common to all of them, the pleasure is specific to each group, and that the nourishment comes about naturally, but the pleasure is produced artificially. And if you switch these dishes, and serve the Sicilian cui-

καὶ τὴν Περσικὴν Σικελιώταις, τροφὴ μὲν ὁμοίως ἑκατέροις ἑκατέρα, τὸ δὲ τῆς ἡδονῆς ὑπαλλαχθὲν δι' ἀήθειαν εἰς λύπην μετέβαλεν. γίγνεται τοίνυν ἡ μὲν τροφὴ κατὰ τὴν οὐσίαν τοῦ τρέφειν δυναμένου, ἡ δὲ ἡδονὴ κατὰ τὸ πάθος τοῦ ἥδεσθαι εἰθισμένου.

6. Τὸ δὲ ἔθος ἄλλο ἄλλῳ. αὐτίκα Ἕλληνες μὲν καὶ Πέρσαι καὶ Λυδοὶ καὶ Φοίνικες καὶ εἴ τι δὴ ἄλλο γένος, φυτευσάμενοι ἀμπέλους, πονηθέντες περὶ αὐτάς, ἐξελόμενοι τὸν βότρυν, εὐτρεπίσαντες τὸν οἶνον, παρεσκευάσαντο ποτόν, κατὰ μὲν τὴν χρείαν οὐκ ἀναγκαῖον, κατὰ δὲ τὴν ἡδονὴν ἀκμαιότατον. Σκυθῶν δὲ οἱ μὲν πολλοὶ γάλακτι βιοτεύουσιν, ὅσα οἱ ἄλλοι ἐπὶ οἴνῳ· τοῖς δὲ αἱ μέλιτται καθηδύνουσι τὸ πόμα, ἐπὶ πετρῶν καὶ δρυῶν διαπλάττουσαι τοὺς σίμβλους· εἰσὶν δὲ οἳ τῇ παρὰ τῶν νυμφῶν ὀχετείᾳ καὶ ἐπιρροῇ οὐδὲν λυμαίνονται, ἀλλ' αὐτοφυεῖ προσχρῶνται ποτῷ ὕδατι. ἓν δέ τι, οἶμαι, Σκυθῶν γένος πίνουσιν μὲν ὕδωρ, ἐπειδὰν δὲ αὐτοῖς δέῃ τῆς κατὰ μέθην ἡδονῆς, νήσαντες πυράν, θυμιῶντες εὐώδεις βοτάνας, περικαθίσαντες ἐν κύκλῳ τῇ πυρᾷ ὥσπερ κρατῆρι, εὐωχοῦνται τῆς ὀδμῆς καθάπερ οἱ ἄλλοι τοῦ ποτοῦ, καὶ μεθύσκονταί γε ὑπ' αὐτῆς καὶ ἀναπηδῶσιν καὶ ᾄδουσιν καὶ ὀρχοῦνται.

7. Τί δή μοι βούλεται ἡ περίοδος τοῦ λόγου; ἐνδείξασθαι ὑμῖν διάκρισιν καλοῦ καὶ ἡδονῆς. τίθει γάρ μοι, κατὰ μὲν τὸ ἀναγκαῖον καὶ τὸ αὐτοφυὲς τῆς τροφῆς καὶ τοῦ ποτοῦ, τὸ καλὸν αὐτό, ὅπερ εἶναι δεῖ καὶ

sine to the Persians or the Persian cuisine to the Sicilians, each cuisine will nourish each group all the same, but the exchange will convert the pleasure to displeasure because they are unused to it. Therefore, nourishment results from the essence of that which is able to provide nourishment, whereas pleasure results from the reaction of someone accustomed to enjoy it.

6. Furthermore, different peoples are accustomed to different things. For instance, the Greeks, Persians, Lydians, Phoenicians, and other similar nations plant grape vines, laboriously care for them, harvest their clusters, make the wine, and produce a drink that is not essential for use, but supremely pleasurable. Most Scythians live on milk, just as those others do on wine, but the drink for some of them is sweetened by the bees that build their hives in rocks and oaks. And there are also others who do not contaminate the flow from channels of the Nymphs, but have natural water as their drink. There is even a tribe of Scythians, I believe, who drink water, but when they want the pleasure of intoxication, they build a fire and burn sweet-smelling herbs on it. They sit in a circle around the fire as if around a wine krater, and take delight in the smell just as those others do in drink, and they even get drunk on it and leap up, sing, and dance.[15]

7. What is the point of my lengthy account? It is to demonstrate to all of you[16] the difference between beauty and pleasure. Compare, if you will, Beauty itself to that indispensable and natural food and drink, which must ac-

[15] Cf. Hdt. 1.202.2, where the custom is ascribed to the Massagetae.

[16] A rare address to the audience in the plural. He switches immediately to the singular "compare" (τίθει).

μὴ δοκεῖν μόνον, κατὰ δὲ τὸ ποικίλον καὶ ἐπίκτητον τῶν ἄλλων ἄλλους ἄλλως εὐφραινόντων, τὴν ἡδονήν· δοκεῖν γὰρ {εἶναι}[3] δεῖ ταύτην μόνον. οὕτω δὴ τούτων ἐχόντων, γίγνεται ὁ μὲν ἔρως λόγος καὶ ἀρετὴ καὶ τέχνη· λόγος μὲν κατὰ τὴν ἀλήθειαν, ἀρετὴ δὲ κατὰ τὴν διάθεσιν, τέχνη δὲ κατὰ τὴν εὐστοχίαν τοῦ καλοῦ· ἐπιθυμίαι δὲ ἡδονῶν, ἄλογοι ἀλόγων.

Ἐπεὶ τοίνυν τὸ καλὸν εἶναι δεῖ καλόν, ἵν' ἔρωτα ποιῇ, ποῖόν τι εἶναι αὐτὸ φῶμεν καὶ πῶς ποιοῦν; βούλει σοι λέγω κατὰ τὴν Σωκράτους μαντείαν; ὡς τὸ καλὸν αὐτὸ ἄρρητον ὂν καὶ ὀφθαλμῶν κρεῖττον ἡ ψυχὴ τεθεαμένη πάλαι καὶ ὀνειρώττουσα αὐτοῦ τὴν μνήμην, ἐν τῇ δεῦρο συνουσίᾳ οὐ πάντῃ ἐναργῶς ὁρᾷ, ἅτε ἀπολελειμμένη αὐτοῦ καὶ τῷ χωρίῳ καὶ τῇ τύχῃ, καὶ ἀπεξενωμένη ἐκείνων τῶν θεαμάτων εἰς τὸν ἐν γῇ τόπον καὶ περιβεβλημένη πολλὴν καὶ παντοδαπὴν ἰλύν,[4] ὑφ' ἧς ταράττεται, συνδεδεμένη ἀσαφεῖ βίῳ καὶ συγκεχυμένῳ καὶ μεστῷ ταράχου καὶ πλημμελείας πολλῆς· ἡ δέ γε τοῦ καλοῦ φύσις ἀρξαμένη ἐκεῖθεν κάτεισιν δεῦρο πρόσω ἰοῦσα ἠρέμα καὶ ἀμβλυνομένη μᾶλλον καὶ ἀπολείπουσα τὴν ἀρχαίαν ἀκμήν.

8. Καθάπερ τῶν ποταμῶν οἱ γενναιότατοι ἐξιόντες

[3] del. Markland, Trapp
[4] ἰλύν R: ὕλην Heinsius

tually *be* and not merely *seem* to be, and pleasure to the variety and artificiality of those other things that give enjoyment to different people in different ways, but which must merely *seem* to be. If such is the case, then love emerges as a matter of reason, virtue, and expertise: reason with regard to the truth, virtue with regard to one's proper disposition, and expertise with regard to a sure aim for the beautiful. In contrast, desires for pleasures are themselves irrational and aim for irrational pleasures.

So, since the beautiful must truly be beautiful in order to inspire love, what sort of thing should we say that it is, and how should we say that it functions? Do you want me to tell you how Socrates divined it to be?[17] According to him, our soul long ago beheld Beauty itself, something ineffable and beyond the power of human sight, which it recollects as in a dream, but in its existence here on earth the soul cannot see it altogether clearly, being separated from it by its location and circumstance, and banished from those sights it saw to this earthly place, where it is enveloped in thick mud of all sorts,[18] confounded by it and imprisoned in a life of darkness and confusion that is full of turbulence and great discord. For its part, Beauty in its natural state originates from on high and descends here to earth, proceeding gradually and becoming duller and duller as it loses its original intensity.

8. And just as when the mightiest rivers flow into the

[17] The following is based on the soul's vision of Beauty in Plato's *Phaedrus*, esp. 247c–51e.

[18] For the image of mud (there, πηλός) impeding our view of reality, see Pl. *Phd.* 110a. For the soul's impaired vision on earth, see also *Orr.* 9.6, 10.9, and 11.7.

ἐπὶ τὴν θάλατταν, κατὰ μὲν τὴν πρώτην ἐκβολὴν σώζουσιν τὸ ῥεῦμα ἀμιγὲς ἄλλῃ φύσει πικροτέρᾳ καὶ τοῖς ναύταις θαλαττίοις προσπλεύσασιν ἀκραιφνὲς ποτόν, προελθόντες δὲ οἱ ποταμοὶ πόρρω καὶ εἰσπεσόντες εἰς πέλαγος πλατὺ καὶ παραδόντες τὸ ῥεῦμα ἀνέμοις καὶ κύμασιν καὶ ζάλῃ καὶ κλύδωνι, ἠφάνισαν δι' ἐπιμιξίαν τὴν ἀρχαίαν φύσιν· οὕτω καὶ τὸ κάλλος τὸ ἄρρητον καὶ ἀθάνατον ἔρχεται μὲν πρῶτον δι' οὐρανοῦ καὶ τῶν ἐν αὐτῷ σωμάτων, καὶ εἰσπεσὸν ἐκεῖ ἀκραιφνὲς μένει καὶ ἀμιγὲς καὶ ὁλόκληρον· ἐπειδὰν δὲ ὑπερκύψῃ τοῦ οὐρανοῦ εἰς τὸν δεῦρο τόπον, ἀμβλύνεται καὶ ἀμαυροῦται, καὶ μόλις ἂν αὐτοῦ γνωρίσαι τὴν ἐπιρροὴν ναύτης θαλάττιος, συνήθης τῷ ποταμῷ, διὰ μνήμης ἔχων τὴν ἐκείνου φύσιν, ὁρῶν αὐτὴν ἀμυδρὰν ἐν γῇ πλανωμένην καὶ ἀνακεκραμένην ἀλλοτρίᾳ φύσει· ὁ δέ, ἐπειδὰν ἐντύχῃ καὶ γνωρίσῃ καὶ ἴχνος αὐτῷ φανέν, ὥσπερ ὁ Ὀδυσσεὺς ἀποθρώσκοντα καπνόν, σκιρτᾷ καὶ φλογοῦται καὶ φαιδρύνεται καὶ ἐρᾷ.

Τοῦ δὲ κάλλους τούτου ἔλθοι μὲν ἄν τις μοῖρα καὶ ἐπὶ ποταμὸν εὐροώτατον καὶ ἐπὶ φυτὸν εὐβλαστότατον καὶ ἐπὶ ἵππον γενναιότατον, ἀλλ' ὅτιπερ κάλλους ἀργότατον καὶ ἀμβλύτατον· εἰ δέ τίς ἐστιν <αὐγὴ καθαρὰ>[5] αὐτοῦ ἐπιφοιτῶσα τὴν γῆν, ἴδοις ἂν ταύτην οὐκ ἄλλοθι ἢ ἐν ἀνθρώπῳ, τῷ καλλίστῳ καὶ νοερωτάτῳ γηΐνων σωμάτων καὶ τῷ ψυχῆς μεμοιραμένῳ

[5] suppl. Meiser e *Phdr.* 250c: ἀμιγὴς (sc. μοῖρα) suppl. Markland, Dübner: alia alii

sea, and in their initial discharge keep their stream uncontaminated with the waters of a brinier nature, and provide pure drinking water to mariners sailing in from the sea, but as these rivers flow further out and enter the open sea, they expose their current to winds, waves, gales, and swells, and lose their original nature in the mixture; in just the same way, that ineffable and immortal Beauty first passes through heaven and the heavenly bodies. Upon entering there it remains pure, uncontaminated, and whole, but once it emerges from heaven and comes to this earthly place, it is dulled and weakened, and scarcely could our mariner, who is acquainted with the river and retains a recollection of its nature, recognize its stream, when he sees it wandering on earth, faint and contaminated with material of a foreign nature. And yet, when he does encounter it and recognizes even a trace that is visible to him, then like Odysseus seeing the smoke rising up,[19] he leaps for joy, burns with passion, beams with joy, and falls in love.

Some portion of that Beauty may find its way into a river with the fairest streams, a plant with the most splendid growth, or a horse with the finest pedigree, but only in its most sluggish and dullest form of beauty. But if there is any pure ray of it roaming the earth, you could see it nowhere else than in man, who possesses the most beautiful and intelligent of earthly bodies and is endowed with

[19] That is, the smoke rising from his homeland at *Od.* 1.58–59.

συγγενοῦς αὐτῷ τῷ καλῷ. καὶ διὰ τοῦτο <ὁ>[6] νοῦν ἔχων, ἄγαλμα μὲν ἰδών, ἐπαινεῖ τῆς τέχνης, ἀλλ' οὐκ ἐρᾷ τοῦ ἀγάλματος· καὶ φυτὸν ἰδών, ἐπαινεῖ τοῦ καρποῦ, ἀλλ' οὐκ ἐρᾷ τοῦ φυτοῦ· καὶ ποταμὸν ἐπαινεῖ τῆς πραότητος, ἀλλ' οὐκ ἐρᾷ τοῦ ποταμοῦ· ἐν δὲ ἀνθρώπῳ ἐπειδὰν ἴδῃ κάλλος ἔμπνουν καὶ νοερὸν καὶ ἀρετὴν προοιμιαζόμενον, καὶ τὴν μνήμην ἐγείρει καὶ ἐρᾷ, πρόφασιν μὲν τοῦ ὁρωμένου, τὸ δὲ ἀληθὲς ἐρᾷ κάλλους ἀληθεστέρου.

Διὰ ταῦτα καὶ Σωκράτης ἐθήρα τὰ καλὰ τῶν σωμάτων, καὶ ταχέως ἔβλεπεν καὶ πάντα ἔβλεπεν· οὐκ ἐλάνθανεν δὲ αὐτὸν κάλλος, οὐκ ἐν παλαίστρᾳ καταδεδυκός, οὐκ ἐν Ἀκαδημίᾳ πλανώμενον, οὐκ ἐν συμποσίοις εὐωχούμενον, ἀλλ' οἷα θηρευτὴς δεινὸς διὰ σωμάτων ἀνθρωπίνων διετέλει μεμνημένος κάλλους ἀληθινοῦ.

[6] suppl. Markland, Trapp

a soul akin to Beauty itself. And for that reason, when any sane man sees a statue, he praises it for its craftsmanship, but is not in love with the statue. When he sees a plant, he praises it for its fruit, but is not in love with the plant. He praises a river for its gentle flow, but is not in love with the river. But when, in a human being he sees beauty that is alive, intelligent, and portending virtue,[20] it awakens his recollection and he falls in love—ostensibly in love with what he sees, but actually in love with a truer Beauty.

That is why Socrates was always on the hunt for bodies that were beautiful: he quickly surveyed them and surveyed them all. And beauty could not elude him, whether he went into a palaestra, roamed about the Academy, or enjoyed himself at symposia, but like "a skilled hunter,"[21] he was always recollecting true Beauty through the medium of human bodies.

20 For the expectation of virtue arising from a beautiful body, see *Or.* 19.2–3.

21 Pl. *Symp.* 203d, said by Diotima of Love; see also *Orr.* 18.4 and 19.2 for Socrates as a hunter.